Pelican Books

Fascism: A Reader's Guide

Fascism:

A Reader's Guide

ANALYSES, INTERPRETATIONS,
BIBLIOGRAPHY

Edited by Walter Laqueur

Penguin Books

Penguin Books Ltd, Harmondsworth,
Middlesex, England
Penguin Books, 625 Madison Avenue,
New York, New York 10022, U.S.A.
Penguin Books Australia Ltd, Ringwood,
Victoria, Australia
Penguin Books Canada Ltd, 2801 John Street,
Markham, Ontario, Canada L3R 1B4
Penguin Books (N.Z.) Ltd, 182–190 Wairau Road,
Auckland 10, New Zealand

First published by Wildwood House Ltd 1976
Published in Pelican Books 1979
Copyright © Walter Laqueur, 1976
All rights reserved
Made and printed in Great Britain by
Hazell Watson & Viney Ltd, Aylesbury, Bucks
Set in Monotype Times

Contents

Part IV

Part V

Part VI   Interpretations

Preface

Despite the three decades that have passed since the end of the Second World War, fascism remains a subject of much heated argument. In daily usage it is hurled as an invective against political enemies. It is frequently invoked in the media; in the universities it attracts more students of history and political science than almost any other subject; and on the loftiest level, it has become the topic of metaphysical speculation. It also continues to be a subject of controversy, partly because it collides with so many preconceived ideological notions, partly because generalizations are made difficult by the fact that there was not one fascism but several fascisms. While these fascisms have certain features in common, the differences between them are not negligible. It would be surprising if there were unanimity on such issues as the relevance of ideology to the understanding of fascism, its social character, the importance of the leader, to name but a few aspects; many issues more distant in history remain unresolved to this day.

If much remains to be explored and agreed upon, much has been achieved and the present volume aims at presenting an interim balance sheet of fifty years of the study of fascism. One book cannot replace libraries, but it can at the very least distil some of the accumulated wisdom and point to areas of particular importance. The contributors to this volume discuss the work that has been done in the field, thus providing a guide to further study and reflection. The essays point to the main issues that have emerged, the arguments and counter-arguments that have been voiced, and they try, whenever possible, to take the interpretation of various aspects of fascism a few steps further. It provides a synopsis of the work in the field done hitherto, discusses the important studies published since the 1920s, including the most up-to-date work, and at the same time identifies the main problems that have arisen and have led to discussion among students of twentieth-century history. Thus it provides on the one hand a reference work summarizing previous research in the field and at the same time it is an original work of synthesis and new interpretation. Lastly, it indicates lines of future research. It is one of the first works on fascism to look at many aspects of the phenomenon. Among the contributors are historians, political scientists, sociologists, economists, and a psychoanalyst. The contributors are recognized as leading authorities in their field.

This project was organized and supported by the *Institute of Contemporary History and Wiener Library*. Our thanks are also due to *Stiftung Volkswagenwerk* for its generous financial assistance.

W.L.

Notes on Contributors

KARL DIETRICH BRACHER is Professor of Political Science and Contemporary History at the University of Bonn. His publications include *Die Auflösung der Weimarer Republik* (1971), *Die nationalsozialistische Machtergreifung* (1962), *Deutschland zwischen Demokratie und Diktatur* (1964), *The German Dictatorship* (1970), *The German Dilemma* (1975) and *The Crisis of Europe* (forthcoming).

WILLIAM CARR is a Fellow of the Royal Historical Society and Reader in Modern History at the University of Sheffield. He is the author of *A History of Germany 1815–1945* (1969) and other studies.

FRANCIS L. CARSTEN is Masaryk Professor of Central European History at the University of London. He is the author of *Reichswehr und Politik 1918–1933* (1964), *The Rise of Fascism* (1967) and *Revolution in Central Europe 1918–1919* (1972).

ALISTAIR HENNESSY is Professor of History and Chairman of the Joint School of Comparative American Studies at the University of Warwick. His publications include *The Federal Republic of Spain, 1868–74* and *Modern Spain.*

JUAN J. LINZ is Professor of Sociology and Political Science at Yale University. He is Chairman of the Committee on Political Sociology, Research Committee of the International Sociological Association and the International Political Science Association.

ADRIAN LYTTELTON is Senior Research Fellow at St Antony's College, Oxford. His publications include *The Seizure of Power: Fascism in Italy 1919–1929* (1973).

ALAN S. MILWARD is Professor of European Studies at the University of Manchester Institute of Science and Technology and is the author of *The German Economy at War* and other books.

HANS MOMMSEN is Professor of Modern History at the Ruhr-Universitaet Bochum. His publications include *Die Sozialdemokratie und die*

Nationalitaetenfragen im Habsburgischen Vielvoelkerstaat (1963) and *Beamtentum im Dritten Reich* (1966).

STANLEY G. PAYNE is Professor of History at the University of Wisconsin and the author of *Falange: A History of Spanish Fascism* (1961), *Politics and the Military in Modern Spain* (1967) and other studies.

ZEEV STERNHELL is Senior Lecturer in Political Theory at the Hebrew University, Jerusalem and the author of *Maurice Barrès et le Nationalisme français* (1972).

BELA VAGO is Professor of General History at the University of Haifa and is the author of several books on the political and social problems of Central and East European countries.

EUGEN WEBER is Professor of History at UCLA and is the author of *Action Française, Varieties of Fascism*, with Hans Rogger, *The European Right*, and *Peasants into Frenchmen. The Modernization of Rural France 1870–1914*.

Part I

JUAN B. LINZ

1 Some Notes Toward a Comparative Study of Fascism in Sociological Historical Perspective*

When Lipset and Rokkan published their *Party Systems and Voter Alignments*, they made little effort to place the fascist movement in their comprehensive model of social cleavages and the emergence of the European party system.[1] It could be argued that there was no need to do so since fascist parties have not survived with any significant strength in post-Second World War Europe, and they were unable to conquer permanently any distinctive social base comparable to those of socialist, communist, Christian Democratic, conservative and north European farmer parties. They rightly emphasize that at some point in the twenties there was a freezing of the major party alternatives in the wake of the extension of suffrage and the mobilization of major reservoirs of new potential supporters. Even further, the party systems of the 1960s reflect with few but significant exceptions the cleavage structures of the 1920s. 'A crucial characteristic of Western competitive politics in the age "of high mass consumption" [is that] the party alternatives, and in remarkably many cases the party organizations, are older than the majorities of the national electorates. To most of the citizens of the west the currently active parties have been part of the political landscape since their childhood or at least since they were first faced with the choice between alternative "packages" on election day.'[2] Certainly, there have been important shifts between the old socialist bases and the strengthened communist parties after the Second World War, and from many conservative and liberal bourgeois parties to the strengthened Christian Democratic parties. However, between 1918 and 1945, the party system that had started to crystallize in

* This is the first part of an empirical study of Fascism, and for the complete work people can refer to the hardback edition published by Wildwood House, 1976.

the first elections after the First World War, if not earlier, was confronted by the more or less successful competition of fascist movements. Many of their supporters had been voters and even members of other parties and after the defeat of fascism would again turn to other banners. Does this mean that fascism did not have, in contrast to other parties, a distinctive social base? Was it only a conjunctural phenomenon, perhaps attracting supporters from a heterogeneous social base largely on the basis of generational cleavages rather than on account of structural characteristics? This might be the clue why a strictly sociological analysis of fascism fails when compared to other political movements. Obviously, it could also be argued that fascism was displaced from the political scene, not only by its failure to satisfy the expectations of many of its supporters but by the monstrosity of its rule, particularly in the case of nazism, and ultimately by its involvement in the war and its defeat in 1945. Certainly, fascism did not experience a slow and continuous growth in opposition and power, in competition with other political forces but, by its own nature, aimed at gaining power revolutionarily or by coup d'état and thereby losing its character of 'a party among other parties', attempting instead to be a representation of the whole national community rather than of particular social strata. As an official party, either ruling in a totalitarian manner or as part of an authoritarian régime and, in many cases, linked with a foreign occupier, such parties could not build up a distinctive social base.

Fascism, a latecomer on the political scene

For an understanding of fascist movements it is essential to note that they were latecomers on the political scene, at a time when, in most countries, the party system had already crystallized. The different sectors of society had identified with particular political options and with the organizations of different parties, trade unions, and associated interest groups had penetrated the social structure. This meant that irrespective of the intentions of their leadership, their ideological and programmatic appeals, and their ambition to represent particular social strata, their success was largely pre-empted. Contemporary political sociology has shown how strong party loyalty is despite changes in the political outlook of parties, changes in the social structure, and even policy reversals and failures. In our view, it is essential to remember that fascist parties, more often than not, could not gain the support of the social groups to which they directed their appeal and that, therefore, they were often forced to appeal, integrate, and represent social forces with which, in terms of the initial ideological commitments, we might not have expected them to become strongly identified.[3] It also meant that in many countries they remained minority movements with little or no electoral appeal. In many cases only the strength of the commitment of their minority following, the new forms of political organization and tactics that gave them an advantage in the struggle for power by violent means rather than ballots, made them successful contenders for power. Moreover, in several cases only the vagaries of war and foreign help gave their leaders an opportunity to play their tragic role on the political scene.

The fact that fascism is a latecomer helps to explain, in part, the essential anti-character of its ideology and appeal. Undoubtedly, fascism was much more than an anti-this or anti-that movement (a point to which we shall turn later). Its distinctiveness lies in its style and in its confused vision of the future which it in many respects incorporated, transforming elements present in other ideologies and movements. The various 'antis' of fascism served to define its identity in contrast to other parties and to appeal to the supporters of one or another on the basis of being more militantly against others. It is paradoxical that for each rejection there was also an incorporation of elements of what they rejected. This largely accounts for the heterogeneous following in the initial group of fascists, and the fact that many of its initial cadres were recruited among men who had been active in other parties and even gained pre-eminence in their leadership (the Nazis were an exception in this). It also meant that those men, when they failed in their efforts to carry along support from the constituencies in which they had risen, turned to other social strata and became bitterly hostile not only to their former comrades but also to the social forces that continued following them. In this perspective, the turn toward middle and upper classes, the willingness to enter into collusion or coalition with conservative, bourgeois, and capitalist interests is not so much a reflection of the ideological initial commitment and goals of the leaders but of their failure to gain working class and sometimes any support. So it becomes understandable that leaders with a relatively similar ideology and style should have found echoes in terms of party membership and electoral support in quite different social strata in the various countries. As a latecomer with a large number of 'anti' appeals and an ideological hope to integrate the whole nation, overcoming the cleavages created in modern society and expressed through modern parties, their social bases and relative success would depend more than any other type of political movement on the particular historical constellation of social and political forces in each country. This would be particularly true when we go beyond the initial founding nucleus, when they became mass organizations, in their electoral bases and the kind of alliances they were able to make in the effort to take power. This accounts for the often quite different social compositions of the initial founding nucleus, the activists particularly in the paramilitary organizations, the electorate, and finally the support for the parties in power or the coalition in which they participated under authoritarian rule.

Fascist movements, in their ideological and pragmatic eclecticism and their effort to appeal to all strata, were a prefiguration of the post-Second World War catch-all party described by Otto Kirchheimer.[4] Perhaps the greater rigidity of the social structure inherited from the nineteenth century, the greater faith in ideology in the twenties, and the fixation on the urban proletariat as the class of the future among most Marxists made such an attempt appear unprincipled and unviable and only possible in an authoritarian framework. With different points of gravity in institutional bases, Christian democracy and social democratic parties have now become such parties of broad integration – *Volksparteien* – electorally, if not in their membership. Even communists have learned from the fascist experience the importance of appealing to various lower-middle-class sectors, including even the old middle class which had no future in the nineteenth-century Marxian view of social evolution. A more fluid social structure, the exhaustion of ideological passion, the needs of national reconstruction in post-fascist Europe made programmatically eclectic heterogeneous parties possible and successful.

Any comparative study of fascist movements has to focus on the unique historical constellation of forces in each country at the time of the founding of the party and in the course of its struggle for support and power. This is true for any party but more so for fascism, due to its nationalistic character and to its being a latecomer. Other parties emerged from the cleavages and tensions basically common with varying intensities to all western societies or particular groups of western societies. There is no question that in most countries the basic parties emerged to some extent independently but in close succession, even when the ideological formulations that acquired particular clarity and success in some of them rapidly diffused in others. Liberalism had appeared in the wake of the French Revolution with the emergence and strengthening of the bourgeoisie in many countries, linking more or less explicitly with the traditions of the Enlightenment, Jacobinism, and English constitutionalism. In response to it with varying strength, conservative ideologies and parties, even reactionary movements made their appearance, often linking with feudal agrarian and pre-capitalist social structures.

Undoubtedly there were important national variations in the degree to which the religious and secularizing sentiments became identified with conservatism and liberalism, and contributed to the factional splits within those parties. There were also differences in the degree to which the national identity, the nation-building forces, became identified with conservatives or liberals and in some cases with the bourgeois left. Industrialization in all countries led to the organization of trade unions or workingmen's associations, which in some cases could link with the left wings of the liberal bourgeoisie but in most countries soon led to the emergence of proletarian parties with one or another socialist ideology. Only in a few cases was the working-class protest led into anarchist and later anarcho-syndicalist movements. The threat of a more or less secularizing liberalism and an anti-clerical and even anti-religious working-class revolutionary movement, Marxist or anarchist, in Catholic countries, soon produced a reaction in the form of Catholic conservative or Christian Democratic parties. They very often emerged without the blessing of the hierarchy of the Church which was still linked to the state and the monarchical establishment. But the response of the Papacy to those two threats in the encyclicals, particularly of Leo XIII's *Rerum Novarum*, and the creation of a Catholic lay movement gave to those parties a common orientation. The peasant and farmers' parties in the less industrialized countries (in which, in addition a state church did not mobilize the peasant masses as did the Catholic church) responded to a greater extent to unique national constellations of forces. Even so, soon an international of peasant parties appeared in eastern and south-eastern Europe. Only the regional nationalist parties on the peripheries of unintegrated states rather than nations, empires rather than modern nation-states, did not have a distinct and comparable social base nor in many cases an ideology shared across the borders, and this accounts for the fact that they could be conservative, clerical, republican Jacobin, peasantist, and even incipiently socialist. It is no accident that some of the peripheral nationalisms would develop considerable affinity with fascism; that in Eastern Europe integral nationalism would often be fascist or quasi-fascist.[5] The party system on the eve of or in the first election after the First World War responded to common structural characteristics of European societies and based its appeal on ideologies diffused across borders from a few centres of ideological creativity.

Fascism was the novel response to the crisis – profound or temporary – of the pre-war social structure and party system and to the emergence of new institutional arrangements as a result of war and post-war dislocations. It would be particularly acute in defeated nations, in those which were divided about entry into the war and disappointed with the fruits of victory, such as Italy, and those countries where the crisis led to unsuccessful revolutionary attempts. Fascism would be a counter-revolutionary response led by a revolutionary élite. To paraphrase Borkenau's characterization of the Communist party[6] as a party of revolutionaries linked with the proletariat, we could define fascism as a party of revolutionaries linked with the middle classes of city and/or countryside.

When fascism appeared on the scene first in Italy, it had to attempt to find its place within this already largely pre-empted political space. It was a unique response to the particular Italian situation and for some time fascists themselves and scholars studying the movement attempted to understand it from that distinctive Italian perspective.[7] However, similar strains existed in other European societies and led to the emergence in the early twenties of similar movements which in their nationalism attempted to emphasize their links with the historical past of their country and with the unique problems faced by their states and societies in a post-Versailles world. Soon, however, like other parties before them, they turned to the most successful of them, Italian fascism, and later to the even more successful National Socialists for inspiration and guidance. In this way, paradoxically, fascism that was ultra-nationalist turned also into an international movement, like those whose internationalism the fascists rejected.[8] However, in contrast to those other parties, which reflected some of the common social structure characteristics of European societies, fascists in their goal of representing the whole national community, integrating all classes, overcoming class conflict, and appealing to former supporters of old parties on account of common national interests in conflict with other societies or with groups defined as alien such as the Jews, would be ultimately less comparable in their social support. Their success would range widely from a mass electorate in Germany to almost insignificant groups in many countries.

The Christian Democrats, another relative latecomer, did not emerge in some countries and achieved very different degrees of mobilization of the potential Catholic electorate. They also encountered difficulty in gaining the support of the working class and the peasantry to which ideologically much of their effort was directed, depending on the earlier success of the socialist labour movement and of different conservative, liberal, and left liberal parties. In the case of Christian Democracy, too, the mass electoral support did not depend exclusively on the ideological appeal or the social composition of the initial leadership nucleus. Both were often very similar in societies where the parties had quite different electoral social bases.

The same is true for the communists, another latecomer of the twenties, whose success depended on their capacity to split the socialist parties and to appeal to the followers of the socialist labour movement. Even when the strength of communism in the inter-war years and after the Second World War varies very much from country to country, from mass parties like the Italian or the French and small minorities in Scandinavia and the Low Countries, the distance between the successful and the least successful never was as great as between insignificant and mass fascist parties. The opportunity to build on the pre-war and particularly wartime tensions within the socialist party gave the communists in most countries an initially organized basis of support to start with.

Unity and heterogeneity of fascism

Different national conditions account for the different opportunities to emerge, the very different space still to be occupied in the political arena, and the very different and contradictory social basis available to the initially comparable leadership nucleus. While fascism more than any other western political movement did not appeal to a particular constituency defined in terms of socio-economic interest, religious institutional loyalty, or ethnic national identity except in irredenta border areas or nations that had not gained statehood, fascist ideologies responded to distinct political historical and social situations and their relative success can therefore be understood by a comparative sociological historical analysis. Undoubtedly, personal characteristics of the leadership group, demagogic and organizational skills account for some of the national differences, but the fact that some of the parties never got off the ground cannot be attributed to the quality of leadership.[9]

We need to keep quite distinct the conditions for the emergence of the fascist movement in each national context and not just by diffusion and imitation, and those leading to varying degrees of success.

To answer those questions, we have to start with a definition of fascism, or at least a description of an ideal type which with some deviations would fit the variety of movements around the world.

To do so is far from easy since the success of Italian fascism and National Socialism in Germany led many movements and parties, particularly single parties created from above by royal and military bureaucratic dictatorships, to incorporate fascist elements in their ideology, their style, and their organization, attempting to capitalize on the appeal of fascism.[10] In our view, it is necessary to use a narrow definition of fascism, even when the analysis of semi-fascist, pseudo-fascist, and proto-fascist movements and ideologies can contribute to our better understanding of the phenomenon. Such a narrow definition excludes proto-fascist movements like nineteenth-century Bonapartism, Boulangism, and even Action Française.[11] It also excludes the typical official single dominant or privileged parties of the royal military-bureaucratic-oligarchic dictatorships in Hungary, Romania, Yugoslavia, the Unión Patriótica of Primo de Rivera, the União Nacional of Portugal, the Vaterländische Front created by Dollfuss, the Camp of National Unity (OZON) in Poland, the Imperial Rule Assistance Association in Japan, and even the Movimiento Nacional in the later years of the Franco régime despite their incorporation of fascist elements. They were parties created from above rather than parties that conquered power for their leaders and supporters. We would exclude them not only for their ideological syncretism and flexibility but above all for their recruitment of leaders and members through cooption of leaders of pre-existing parties, of higher civil servants, officers, successful professionals, and many opportunists who otherwise might have remained apolitical; men sociologically and psychologically very different from the activists of the fascist movements before taking power. All imitations of fascism and its style could not hide the essentially different spirit. Our narrow definition also excludes the authoritarian, nationalist monarchical parties like the Deutschnationale Volkspartei (DNVP) and Renovación Española despite their extreme right and anti-democratic authoritarianism. Neither would it include those Catholic parties that turned toward authoritarian corporativist positions in the thirties.

It is, however, not as narrow as it would be if we were to accept the distinction between fascism and National Socialism suggested by Eugen Weber and Stanley Payne.[12] It would cover those distinguished by Wolfgang Sauer as western, central, and east European types of movements and those that Henry Turner is inclined to distinguish as more anti-modernist and modernizing.

The movements and their appeal cannot be understood from the perspective of an analysis of fascist parties in power, as it would be difficult to understand the attraction of communism to workers and peasants in many countries in terms of the policies of parties in power in the Soviet Union or Eastern Europe, even when the successes of parties in power in both cases contributed to their attraction in other countries, particularly to certain types of intellectuals. Undoubtedly, fascism in power in Italy and Hitler in Germany and their successors contributed to the emergence of other fascist movements and their appeal but, like Stalinism in the Soviet Union, also to the strong rejection by many who otherwise might have found fascist ideas and national fascist parties attractive. Our focus, therefore, will be on the emergence of the parties and their appeal before coming to power, since take-over of the state or participation as coalition partners in authoritarian régimes without being obliged to compete with other parties for social support creates quite different conditions for the building of a distinct social constituency.[13]

The question we have to raise is, to what extent did different fascist parties not in power attract to the initial nucleus, to their cadres, and to their electorate similar or different social groups, and what kind of explanation can we offer for those differences? Our basic hypothesis is that while ideological differences between those movements account for some of the variations, the most important ones are due to the particular historical national situation in which they were born, the political space already occupied before the arrival of those latecomers, and some distinctive social structural problems of the different societies.

We obviously start from the assumption that there is such a phenomenon as fascism, making its appearance in many countries, not only in Europe,[14] with sufficiently common characteristics to be studied as a distinctive socio-political-historical phenomenon. While there are pre-fascist ideological currents and small movements that can be considered as antecedents, fascism only makes its appearance after the First World War. After the

Second World War it is merely a survival of the past even when many political tendencies in the world today incorporate consciously or unconsciously elements which we would call fascist. The Movimento Sociale Italiano (MSI), the small German neo-Nazi groups, the Nationaldemokratische Partei Deutschlands (NPD), and other such parties[15] are only historical survivals, as Spanish Carlism is a reminder of the struggle between counter-revolution and liberalism in the first half of the nineteenth century, of protest parties with characteristics recalling fascism. Only Peronism occupies a special position as a movement emerging at the end of the fascist era with some links with the fascist past but without many of its distinctive characteristics. It is highly debatable but it can be argued that it is the last successful survivor of that era. The same is true to a limited extent for the Spanish Movimiento in which the fascist components have been mixed and transformed in thirty years of Franco rule, but not of the small radical neo-fascist groups appearing in Spain today. In fact their emergence is an indicator that they do not feel at home in what was supposed to be their party. Fascism like anarchism has had its great historical moment and, like it, has left a heritage that in very different ways will resurface in other movements, often undetected except by observers very familiar with it. It could be argued that only a few of the fascist movements were original in their ideology and that the leadership of many of them was more oriented toward Rome or Berlin than to the problems and traditions of their own country. But we guess that the same could be said about some of the least successful and more derivative communist parties, particularly in the Stalinist era.

Once we have denied that fascism was a uniquely Italian phenomenon not for export, we still have to face the question, was German National Socialism a fascist movement or something different? Certainly, Hitler and his followers did not perceive their movement as derivative from the Italian but, with some exceptions, even before taking power and the creation of the Axis alliance, even when their interests were in conflict with Italy, felt the affinity and recognized the early achievement of Mussolini.[16] Despite many criticisms of their German comrades and the distaste of Mussolini and many fascists – before the later thirties – for Nazi racism, Italian fascists saw nazism as a kindred movement even when distrusting German power. Conflicts between fascist powers, different emphases in their ideology and policies are not an argument against the use of a broader category of fascism as the divergences between the Russian leadership, Mao, and even Tito do not prevent us from speaking of communism. However, many of the distinctive features of National Socialism, mostly derived from the cultural ideological heritage of Germany and Austria in the nineteenth century, the elements that might be described by the term *völkisch* and biological racism, make nazism a distinctive branch grafted on the fascist tree. The success and power of Hitler's Germany gave the Nazi ideology a particular strength which exercised its attraction even on a few Italian fascists and contributed to the introduction of alien elements into its ideology – such as racism[17] – and should the war not have destroyed both, might have led some of its leaders even to challenge the authority of the Duce. Certainly National Socialism was in the thirties already a different pole of ideological attraction and influence for fascist parties that might be distinguished as being in the Italian or the German sphere of ideological influence. National Socialism under the leadership of Hitler carried some of the implications of the fascist conception of politics to a monstrous extreme. But it would be a mistake to interpret the fascist phenomenon from the perspective provided by Hitler's rule, as it would be to analyse communism only in the light of Stalinism.

How can we define fascism? Any definition of this latecomer movement has to emphasize the things against which it stood; we noted earlier its anti-dimension but we should also consider its new appeal and its conception of man and society. In addition to those ideological elements, no definition can ignore the importance of its distinctive style, its rhetoric and its symbolism, its chants, ceremonies, and shirts that attracted so many young people in the years between the two wars. But neither ideology nor style, given its electoral weakness, except in Germany, would have made it a decisive factor in the political life of many societies without the new forms of organization and political action. The discovery of the paramilitary political organization ready to use violence against its opponents, rather than electioneering or conspiring, was a tragic innovation that made even minor fascist parties a significant factor in the crisis of many European democracies. The appeal of fascism was not only its ideology but its style and the new forms of political action it developed. Other movements would imitate one or another of those aspects but they would not synthesize them and link them so perfectly. In addition, the combination of electoral politics with the politics of violence in the streets, of legalism, and the readiness to enter coalitions with the use of violence, assured its road to power in a way previously unknown. Obviously, after its success in Italy and Germany, the formula became more difficult to apply; both democratic and authoritarian régimes denied fascist movements the opportunity and the freedom to build up their strength,[18] and fewer of the old parties were ready to enter into coalition with the fascists in the hope of coopting them or would act disunitedly in the face of the fascist threat. This has to be taken into account in attempting to understand the relative strength of early and late fascist parties.

We shall use a multi-dimensional typological definition of fascism in our analysis, a definition which in our view covers all the movements discussed here even when some dimensions might be more central to one or another of them. We define fascism as a hypernationalist, often pan-nationalist, anti-parliamentary, anti-liberal, anti-communist, populist and therefore anti-proletarian, partly anti-capitalist and anti-bourgeois, anti-clerical, or at least, non-clerical movement, with the aim of national social integration through a single party and corporate representation not always equally emphasized; with a distinctive style and rhetoric, it relied on activist cadres ready for violent action combined with electoral participation to gain power with totalitarian goals by a combination of legal and violent tactics. The ideology and above all the rhetoric appeals for the incorporation of a national cultural tradition selectively in the new synthesis in response to new social classes, new social and economic problems, and with new organizational conceptions of mobilization and participation, differentiate them from conservative parties. The appeal based on emotion, myth, idealism, and action on the basis of a vitalistic philosophy is initially directed at those least integrated into the class structure – youth, students, demobilized officers – to constitute a self-appointed élite and later to all those disadvantageously affected by social change and political and economic crisis against the political system. In a plebiscitarian mobilization of the masses, the fascist appeal is based on an inflation of national solidarity and the rejection of the institutionalization of conflict and cleavages in modern societies and therefore a destruction and/or demobilization of the parties that organize those cleavages, particularly working-class but also clerical parties. Hypernationalism is reflected in a deep-seated hostility to all organizations and movements that can be conceived as international in character – that is communism, even socialism, international finance capitalism, the Catholic church or at least the Vatican, Freemasonry, the League of Nations, pacifism, and the Jews, even in those movements that are not initially anti-Semitic and even less racist.

A proof that this definition is not far from the self-image of the fascists can be found in the following definition of the fascist attitude by the founder of the Spanish Juntas de Ofensiva Nacional Sindicalista (JONS), Ramiro Ledesma Ramos. 'Deep national idea. Opposition to demi-bourgeois institutions, to the liberal parliamentary state. Unmasking of the true feudalistic powers of present society. National economy and people's economy against the great financial and monopolistic capitalism. Sense of authority, discipline and violence. Hostility to the anti-national and anti-human solution that proletarian classism offers to solve the obvious problems and injustices of the capitalist system.'[19]

Contrary to those who would argue that fascist ideology is of little interest in understanding its appeal, success and, particularly, policies when in power, on account of the opportunism of the leaders on the road to power, and the betrayal of their ideology and their followers with their policies, we shall argue that the ideology accounts for much of the success or failure in any particular country of the movement. Certainly, the initial nucleus of followers that provided fascism with the cadres in its struggle for power and much of the élite once in the saddle was attracted by that ideology. Without a sufficient number of people susceptible to it, fascist movements would not have got going even when their later success in becoming a mass movement depended on the capacity of that initial nucleus to seize opportunities created by social crises, to appeal on more pragmatic grounds to particular social strata and to make compromises with the Establishment, to gain access to power. The inconsistency between policies of fascists in power, particularly in a period of consolidation of their control and later in war time, does not make the ideology irrelevant. The fact that the life of fascist régimes, particularly National Socialism, was cut short by defeat should not be forgotten in the analysis of those compromises. Let us imagine that Lenin had disappeared from the political scene after the NEP period in order to suggest how dangerous it would be to ignore the potentialities for practical implementation of even the most out-of-the-way ideas of fascist leaders. The readiness to enter into coalitions, compromises with the Establishment and vested interests, and institutions of the pre-fascist society has to be seen in the light of the fact that none of the societies in which they attempted to come to power was fully disorganized by war, defeat, civil war, or foreign dependency. Despite the crises in the states in which the fascists aspired to gain power, the Establishment forces retained considerable strength, and fascists were intelligent enough to realize that a revolutionary take-over was impossible. That is why they turned to 'legal revolution', as they called it, and the tactic of neutralizing by ideological deflection and often by real concessions, potential opponents like the churches, the army, the monarchy, and big business, as well as appealing to their fears of an apparently revolutionary working class. Only keeping in mind that these latecomers on the political scene appeared in societies not fully disorganized can we understand that, despite their ideological and often personally deep-seated hostility against the Establishment, they would use other elements in their ideological conception and particularly the fear of communism and the class-conscious working class to gain access to power. The ambiguities and contradictions in the ideology and even more in the policies leading to power can also be better understood when we consider the failure of the initial leadership nucleus in making any inroads among the well-organized working-class parties, trade unions, and cooperatives. The negative integration achieved by the social-democratic, and in some cases, communist working-class sub-culture, isolated the fascist activists from a constituency which, ideologically, they were often strongly committed to gain. Their goal of integrating the working class into a national community of producers, a national socialism or national syndicalism on the basis of a common struggle of all classes against one form or another of foreign dependence or for a larger share of the so-called proletarian nations in the wealth of the world was largely unsuccessful. In fact it could be argued that hostility toward the proletariat is in many cases the result of an unrequited love. As we shall see in a few cases in Hungary and to some extent in Romania, semi-authoritarian rule had prevented the integration of popular strata into Marxist movements, and their availability allowed the Arrow Cross[20] and Iron Guard[21] to gain the support of the masses – workers in one case and peasants in another – against the Establishment which turned against them, brutally suppressing them as in the case of Romania. In analysing ideology we have to keep in mind that not all movements can get the support of the social groups to which they direct their appeal and that all movements gain support among unlikely classes, often with the consequence of adding to their ideology apparently incongruous elements, or redefining it (the position of the Italian Communist Party toward the so-called *ceti medi produttivi* is a good example).

Fascism is above all a nationalist movement and therefore wherever the nation and the state are strongly identified it also exalts the authority of the state, and its supremacy over all social groups and conflicting interests. In those countries where the nation is not yet a state, it sometimes becomes difficult to say if the movement is just an extremist nationalist one or a fascist movement. In some cases, as in Slovakia, a movement that is not originally fascist becomes increasingly fascist in the struggle for national independence. For complex historical reasons, nationalism occupied a very different place in the minds of people in different societies and this probably accounts for the relative strength of fascism more than any other variable. It is no accident that Nolte should consider the integral nationalism of the Action Française as an immediate predecessor of fascism. The Action Française, after all, was born in the climate created in the France of the turn of the century in the aftermath of the defeat of 1870. The defeated nations or those like Italy which considered themselves cheated by the victorious powers were those where fascism made its greatest gains and emerged earliest: Italy, Germany, Hungary, Austria. Nationalism in less extreme forms was shared by many political movements, particularly by conservatives and liberals including Jacobin liberalism. Fascism in addition to exacerbating nationalist sentiments combined them with its distinctive anti-positions which all had an implicit or latent anti-international component. Many fascist movements were also characterized by pan-nationalist ideas which represented a challenge to the existing states and account for much of their aggressive expansionist foreign policy.

The 'anti' character of fascism

Fascism is an anti-movement; it defines itself by the things against which it stands but this antithesis in the minds of the ideologists should lead to a new synthesis integrating elements from the political creeds they so violently attack. This is one of the roots of the basic ambivalence and ambiguity of the fascist appeal and is not only a pragmatic opportunism in the struggle for power but also is understandable in terms of its being a latecomer that could not ignore the interests and sentiments appealed to by its competitors. The basic anti-dimensions of fascism can be summarized as follows: it is anti-Marxist, anti-communist, anti-proletarian, but also anti-liberal, anti-parliamentarian and, in a very special sense, anti-conservative and anti-bourgeois. Anti-clericalism, perhaps with the exception of the Iron Guard, the Ustacha, and Brazilian Integralismo, is a more or less central component which in some cases drifts into hostility to established religion. Anti-individualism and anti-democratic authoritarianism and élitism are combined with a strong populist appeal. Anti-Semitism is not originally characteristic of all fascist movements but central to many of them. Anti-urbanism, or at least anti-metropolitanism, is not found in all fascist movements but is often an important element.[22] A distinctive type of anti-capitalism is originally present in many fascist movements. Sometimes anti-feminism appears. Those anti-positions have been summarized as anti-modernism, but that interpretation seems dubious in many cases.

A number of these anti-positions can be best understood by considering them anti-international and anti-cosmopolitan positions. Thus anti-Marxism, anti-communism and hostility to the socialist party is originally directed to their ideological internationalism. Let us not forget that Mussolini's break with his old party was due to his turn toward interventionism in 1919 and the rejection of the neutralist position of the Italian socialists. The conception of the proletarian nation substitutes for the conflict between proletariat and bourgeoisie *within* each society a class conflict *between* societies, rich and poor. This formulation served both to reject the Marxist view of modern industrial society and to build bridges across class cleavages within each society. It is no accident that fascists should look with sympathy upon national communism and that the boundaries between left fascism and national communism were sometimes grey.[23] It also accounts for an understanding by some fascists of Stalinism as another national revolution of the same type as they were pursuing, in an attempt to make a distinction between Russian national communism and international communism.[24]

Anti-Marxism is a common characteristic but responds in different countries to a variety of roots. In all of them it serves to challenge the dominance of the social-democratic and communist parties among the working-class electorate, and to rally the support of all those classes who feel threatened by those parties. In some cases it is linked explicitly with the Jewish leadership of many socialist movements and the Jewishness of Marx. In others it is more closely tied to the rejection of the militant secularism, if not atheism, of Marxist movements. Elsewhere, the internationalism, anti-militarism, anti-imperialism of the Marxists serves as a rallying cry that appeals to army officers, civil servants, veterans, and what Salvatorelli has called 'the humanistic bourgeoisie'[25] inspired by a sense of national mission, including overseas expansion of the fatherland. On a deeper level fascist ideologists reject the economic and determinist view of the social process, substituting for it a basically political and voluntaristic view of social change and nation building. The fixation of Marxist conceptions on the role of the proletariat, the industrial working class and its theoretical identification of the dependent white-collar middle classes with the proletariat, ignoring the status and cultural differences between them and the blue-collar workers, offers fascists a new opportunity with the growth, through downward and upward mobility, of those classes in modernizing societies, particularly Germany. The lack of understanding of traditional Marxist theory and especially Central European social democracy for the plight of the peasant and pre-industrial strata, like the artisans and small independent businessmen,[26] allows fascists to oppose their populism to the idealization of the proletariat. The broader category of 'producer', of 'workers of brow and fist' (*Stirn und Faust*) allows left fascists to combine anti-capitalism with the rejection of proletarian Marxism.[27] It is significant that the Italian communists after the experience of fascism have been very careful to include in their post-Second World War appeal those strata that in a strictly Marxist view would be inevitably reactionary and condemned to disappear in the process of social economic change. Let us note that the anti-proletarian affect was not incompatible with socialist and welfare state programmatic commitments. The failure in most countries to draw any widespread support among the working class already deeply integrated into a class community – a socialist sub-culture – was compensated by success among a peasantry with strong anti-urban working-class interests and effects, and among a variety of middle-class groups. The bitter hatred against the working-class parties, from which fascist leaders had often broken away, led them to fight the working-class organization and, in countries where the capitalist entrepreneurial classes had been threatened, led that group to look upon the fascist squads as a defence of their interests. However, this was the case only in certain countries where the state-bureaucratic-military apparat did not provide them with an adequate defence, and where they had experienced a serious revolutionary threat from the anarchist, communist, or maximalist-socialist working class.

As Theodor Geiger's[28] analysis of the social basis of the NSDAP has shown and the electoral map of Germany makes clearly apparent, the Nazis found support among Protestants in the same strata in which the Catholic Zentrum was able to hold on to most of its electorate. The same has been shown for Austria by Walter Simon.[29] Catholic parties and the organizational network of Catholic sub-culture in many countries, particularly Germany, Belgium, the Netherlands, Austria, and the Czech territories of the Republic, had integrated many of the social groups to which fascists wanted to appeal and succeeded in gaining in other societies. This competition accounts for the strong hostilities between them and the clerical and Christian Democratic parties. The fact that in Italy the *Partito Populare Italiano* (PPI) of Sturzo and in Spain the CEDA of Gil Robles appeared on the political scene almost at the same time as the fascist movements made their competition particularly bitter, especially in the northern Italian countryside. In the case of Germany, the Nazis exploited much of the latent distrust against the Catholics of the northern German Protestant bourgeoisie identified with the Bismarckian Reich that had not forgotten the *Kulturkampf*, something that might account for their success among some segments of the Protestant clergy, school teachers, and students. Certainly, fascist anti-communism, anti-Marxism, and in some cases, anti-liberalism and even anti-Semitism could be linked with the defence of the Christian tradition using ambiguous phrases like 'positive Christianity' and identifying the national cultural tradition with the Christian heritage. That combination was obviously particularly feasible in the case of Romania where a traditional national Greek Orthodox Church rooted in the peasantry was challenged by cosmopolitan influences coming from Bucharest, a secularized bourgeoisie and an important Jewish community. It is no accident that the only religiously oriented fascist movement with considerable appeal to the local clergy and the sons of clergymen should have been the Iron Guard that called itself symbolically the Legion of the Archangel Saint Michael. The nationalism of the fascists, however, excluded any identification with the churches and religions, since they were strongly aware that large segments of their societies were already secularized and that an effort of national integration, particularly of the working class, on a religious basis was already impossible.[30] The authoritarian emphasis on the role of the state also made them advocate separation of church and state. Fascist anti-clericalism often underlines the international character of the Church and the interference of Vatican politics in national political life. Even anti-Semitism is often formulated as anti-Zionism in the countries in which there is no large non-integrated Jewish population. Zionism is then defined as a competing loyalty with that of the nation for the Jewry of their country. Cosmopolitan cultural styles are another argument against the Jewish intelligentsia, the leftist cultural bohemians, and have an important impact on the cultural policies of fascist régimes.

Paradoxically, the more or less explicit anti-clericalism was combined in many cases with an historicist identification with the religious national heritage. The positivist use of the Catholic tradition for political purposes by Maurras, in this as in other respects, set an example for many fascists. Only in those countries like Germany, where it was possible to link with the mythical pre-Christian tradition along the lines of völkisch Germanic thought, an explicit anti-Christian component entered into the ideology.[31] The anti-Marxism, and in some cases anti-liberalism, the hatred of Freemasonry, and the pseudo-conservative return to a national tradition endeared fascism to some churchmen unaware of the neo-pagan component of fascism. On the other hand, the success of fascist movements among youth, the appeal of their style, the exaltation of pre-industrial social groups, the use of corporatism to overcome class cleavages also found a certain echo in Catholic parties which felt that they could that way better compete with the fascists. This phenomenon found expression in movements and régimes that have been labelled 'clerico-fascist' which were looked upon with special scorn by the true fascists. Those later movements therefore encountered many more difficulties in penetrating the social strata under the influence of the Church, something that accounts for the failure of Belgian and particularly Spanish fascism.

These ambiguities in the position of fascist parties towards religion and the churches obviously initially limited their appeal to traditional conservative sectors of the society; but at a later stage also allowed them adroitly to neutralize some of the hostility they encountered in the established church, and to appeal at the same time to those segments of the intelligentsia that rejected clericalism in politics and the church monopoly of the national cultural heritage.

The bourgeois and capitalist revolution had succeeded very unevenly in different European countries. In many of them its achievements had been limited and many sectors of society were critical of those representing it. The individualism, the moral justification of selfishness, the high evaluation of economic compared to other activities had not been accepted by many sectors of society. Those same sectors, however, were hostile to the political ambitions of the organized working class and felt their status to be threatened. Fascist ideologies and propagandists could combine an ambiguous anti-bourgeois and anti-capitalist appeal with the commitment to respect for private property and the middle-class status order. Certainly, the peasantry – often squeezed between rising industrial prices and lower agricultural prices and the demands of the urban population for cheaper food, affected by overseas imports of foodstuffs, sometimes favoured by urban oriented governments, resentful of the credit givers and tax collectors – offered a sympathetic ear to such appeals. The same was true in some cases for a self-conscious artisan stratum, the German *Handwerk*. Sometimes the public sector with fixed incomes which compared unfavourably with the profits of business, hurt by inflation and disturbed by the demands and actions of a militant working class, could identify with the critique of a plutocratic bourgeoisie, particularly war profiteers and sometimes Jewish and foreign businessmen. The stereotype of the self-contented, selfish, and hedonistic bourgeoisie could become a negative symbol for those returning from the front lines of the First World War, for the youth not yet integrated into bourgeois society, for certain intellectuals, and for the students. A romantic youth protest against bourgeois society was captured by the fascists, often recruiting the sons of the bourgeoisie themselves, who resented the style of life and values of their parents. The distinction made between financial, banking, international capitalism, and the individual entrepreneur appears in many fascist movements, particularly those of the fascist left, and among their intellectual spokesmen. Once the movements failed to gain an important working-class basis and access to power required economic resources, those ideological elements were tuned down to reappear later when economic interests challenged the policies of some of the fascist régimes. The emphasis on style, on symbolic expression, allowed fascism to challenge the bourgeois style of life and bourgeois conventions, without threatening its immediate economic interests.

The bourgeoisie is often perceived as uprooted compared to the peasants, the artisans, 'the people'. Frequently anti-capitalism is centred on finance capitalism, the banks and the stock exchange, whose international links make them suspicious. The strong anti-bourgeois character of some fascist movements is, particularly in Eastern Europe, linked with the cosmopolitan orientation of the national bourgeoisie, its cultural dependency on foreign centres setting their life style.

In some cases, the economic backwardness of their countries is interpreted by fascists as a result of their dependency. Much of the hostility towards the great democratic powers of the time, England and France, is linked with their internationally dominant position after the First World War. They are described as the plutocratic democracies that are behind the League of Nations, another preferred target not only in the countries which were negatively affected by the Versailles settlement but even in places as far off from Geneva politics as Spain.[32] Democracy is often hated because it provides a political arena in which these various anational influences and the movements linked with them can express themselves freely. In some cases, particularly Germany, democracy is also perceived as a political form influenced by foreign models whose installation was made possible and fostered by foreign defeat. To understand better the appeal of these various internally oriented anti-international responses, we have only to look at many third-world countries today. Let us not forget that fascism was particularly successful in a number of new states in central and eastern Europe.

The hostility against the existing parties, against parliamentarism, and against the professional politicians and notables in political life was obviously appealing to those young people with political ambitions but without the social status, the economic position, the local influence, the professional standing to be successful in the old parties of notables. They also found it difficult to accept the discipline and the atmosphere of working-class parties, and were too secularized to make their political career in religious parties where access was largely through religious organizations of laymen under the indirect leadership of the clergy. There were in the lower middle and middle class many men in that situation, particularly in some countries where there was considerable professional unemployment of semi-intellectuals. The more acute consciousness of national problems of politics created by the First World War and its aftermath of semi-revolutionary situations plus the interrupted careers due to the economic crises created a pool of men eager to enter politics through a different and faster channel than the old parties. They could despise parliamentary politics, notables, and party bureaucrats, and demand power on account of their share in the war effort, of their commitment to the ideals of a better national community rather than the representation of specific narrow interests. They would be a new political élite, justified by their devotion to the cause and the leadership that would leave the more prosaic aspects of interest politics to corporative representation.

While fascists would have accepted our emphasis on the various anti-positions we have described, they would not necessarily have accepted the label of 'anti-democratic'. In fact, many of them argued that they were fighting for a purer and more genuine democracy in which the participation of the individual in politics would not be mediated by professional politicians, clerical influences, the availability of the mass media, but through personal, almost full-time involvement in a political movement and through identification with the leader who would represent the feelings and sentiments of the whole people. Elections for them corrupted the opportunity for the expression of the genuine interest of all the people. Democracy reduced to voting occasionally and secretly represented a low level of political involvement in the fate of the nation. The anti-democratic position of fascism was certainly not that of the old-fashioned conservative. The élite was not based on adscriptive characteristics or on high social educational or economic status but on those dedicated to the cause, open to all those, irrespective of social origin, willing to devote their energies to the movement. The authoritarianly-led fascist parties were to be genuinely democratic in their recruitment and the opportunities of access to power they were to offer. The new movements, representing the whole society rather than a particular class, occupational group, religious community (and not recruiting their leadership from organized groups like trade unions, religious associations of laymen, masonic orders, economic interest groups, or rural notables) would be more democratic. To them the old parties in which very often the highest positions were only accessible after a slow *cursus honorum* appeared as oligarchical, and the new movement open to the young and those without adscribed status or even achieved status appeared as more democratic. The élitism and the authoritarianism of the parties appeared to the initial nucleus of activists compatible with a claim to be democratic on account of their populism. Their success would later establish the most oligarchic rule of a small revolutionary group. The leadership principle – *Führerprinzip* – was not always there initially, but soon became characteristic and a source of many difficulties in the growth and development of the movement. It was congruent with many elements in the ideology, organization, and initial social basis, but we would argue that it was not essential.

Movements with this type of programme and ideology in societies that had not experienced a serious social dislocation by war and failed revolutions, depression and inflation could find an important nucleus of activitists, but generally failed in creating a mass membership and even more in gaining the support of a mass electorate. The frantic and single-minded effort to gain power by the use of violence and the readiness to enter coalitions with the Establishment, the putschist mentality, the *hic et nunc* activist voluntaristic time perspective, are very congruent, both with the ideology and the difficulties encountered within the framework of democratic mass politics of these latecomers.

One of the great paradoxes of fascism is that, from its inception, being a nationalistic movement, responding to the particular problems of each society, it would become one of the most international European political movements with strong affinities between the leaders in different countries, mutual support in the struggle for power, extreme dependency of the minor parties on the stronger ones, and often a betrayal of national self-interests for the solidarity of the movement. In a sense, fascism underwent the opposite development from communism, which started with a strong international orientation, and recognizing the leadership of the first socialist country, moved towards a polycentric and sometimes quite nationally oriented group of parties. Some of the fascists were aware of this contradiction and refused to attend meetings like that of Montreux. Obviously, the Germans often betrayed kindred political movements for the sake of their power interests. In addition to ideological affinities, certainly the fact of having common enemies contributed much to the sense of solidarity between fascist movements in the same way as anti-fascism was temporarily able to unite quite different political forces.[33] This internal contradiction, however, was another important obstacle, particularly in view of the national egoism of the German Nazis and even the Italians for the success of particular fascist movements.

Even if fascism had not been radical and extremist in its tactics, in its violence, and in its demagogy, this accumulation of anti-positions and its lack of overt links with established structures of society, as well as the comparative youthfulness of its leadership, made its radical character unavoidable. Fascism in many countries was unable to make a revolution but, as one ex-fascist put it very well, the fascists, even when they were only making punitive expeditions against working-class organizations, serving the stability of the old order, behaved emotionally and subjectively as if they were living through a real revolution.[34]

The anti-positions of fascism on their own are not sufficient to define the phenomenon. They certainly were decisive in its capacity to attract a following but they probably would have been almost as much an obstacle as an advantage if they had not been combined with other characteristics to which we shall turn later. It is important to stress that many other movements would have emphasized one or another of the anti-characteristics but that would not allow us to define them as fascist. Anti-parliamentarism and the dream of a corporative system of representation as a substitute for parliaments was widely shared by Catholics, conservatives, and even some liberals.[35] Conservatives criticized democracy, liberalism, and party politics as much as the fascists but they would not have shared their populism, their anti-capitalism, and probably would have been reluctant to take the same position towards the Church. We could go on noting how elements of the fascist creed could be found in other movements, more in some than in others, who because of that would be more likely to be initial allies but also often deeply resented as competitors by the fascists. The fact that these programmatic positions were, so to speak, in the air at the time is an obvious sign that they could be appealing. The question in each country would be to what extent the particular combination of these elements offered with varying emphasis by the fascist movement could attract a large enough following and to what extent the defence of those different positions could attract from existing parties and movements a sufficient number of followers for the new combination. The greater or lesser success in attracting followers from competing movements with common political goals would depend on the particular historical, social, and political constellation in each country and on the leadership and organizational capabilities of the fascists.

Pre-conditions for the success of fascist anti-appeals

Only a few countries provided the conditions which made the emergence of a fascist party possible, and in even fewer were there the necessary conditions for achieving mass support for these movements. In the following pages the different 'anti-appeals' of fascism are analysed and the extent to which different European societies were susceptible to such an appeal are explored.

The basis of anti-parliamentarism and anti-'democracy'

The opposition to parliamentarism and political parties, directed against oligarchical landed interests and professional politicians controlling them, by the educated classes and intellectuals did not exist in all countries. In the well-established democracies that had emerged slowly out of an estate society by a progressive democratization of suffrage in which the protective élites retained considerable prestige and in which a relatively democratic and autonomous local government linked the élites with the people, the negative image of parliamentarism that we find in other countries did not develop. Nor could opposition to parliament have the same strength in societies in which parties and their élites were strongly integrated with a complex network of secondary groups like trade unions, cooperatives, farmers' organizations, local chambers of commerce, and religious associations, particularly when those religious associations were also linked with functional groups. When those interest groups were not identified with particular parties, but wanted to be above party strife, they were particularly susceptible to fascist infiltration. Such criticism would acquire a special strength in those countries in which a relatively widespread suffrage was introduced before the art of association of which Tocqueville wrote had developed – countries with large rural populations, economically dependent on noble and particularly bourgeois landowners, societies with a large illiterate rural population, and in which, in addition, the centralized bureaucratic Napoleonic type of state made local government dependent on the decisions of the central administration and the prefects. In such societies, a corrupt form of semi-liberal, semi-democratic politics with manipulated elections producing deputies heavily dependent on the government that had made possible their election, could easily be criticized. The post-Risorgimento Italy particularly in the south, the Italy of the *transformismo*, the Spain of the Restoration with its *caciquismo*, the even more politically backward Portugal, and the independent states of eastern Europe, like Hungary and Romania, could certainly not arouse enthusiasm for parliamentary liberal democracy. It is no accident that some of the critics of that type of system, Pareto, Mosca, and many other Italian writers,[36] Joaquín Costa[37] and others in Spain, would contribute to a critical climate of opinion that would later be linked with fascism. Certainly such criticism was not absent in France, even when the links between parliamentary representation and local and departmental government probably made French deputies more genuinely representative of their communities than was usual. It seems doubtful that the same kind of criticism of parliamentary representation would be valid for northern Europe, Belgium, and the Netherlands, and even less so for the United Kingdom. In the latter country the respect for the Constitution that Bagehot emphasized and the traditional legitimacy of aristocratic élites and the élite produced by the educational system, combined with the success of the state in the world, prevented any such bitter criticism. The hostility towards parliamentarism in the case of Germany is, however, more difficult to explain, except in terms of the fragmentation of political parties, their relative lack of responsibility due to their dependency on interest groups, and the contrast of the political instability of the Weimar Republic with an idealized image of the Imperial past. Certainly scandals and corruption contributed in critical moments to the success of the extreme right groups in France in the thirties and the initial appeal of Rex in Belgium.

Sources of hostility to socialism and the proletariat, and the appeal of fascism

Unfortunately, we do not have an accurate account of the reaction of different groups in European societies to the labour movement. To a greater or lesser degree, certainly those most directly affected, employers in city and countryside, were hostile to the emerging trade union movement and to political parties representing the working class. Undoubtedly in countries without an agricultural proletariat and particularly a large unemployed or under-employed rural working class, the class conflict did not extend to the countryside to the same extent as, for example, in Italy, and in the thirties in Spain, and potentially in Eastern Europe. It should not be forgotten that the most violent activist fascist *squadrismo* developed in the agricultural regions of the Po

Valley where the peasants had only recently acquired their land and were forced to submit to the pressures of poorer farm labourers and peasants.[38] What is more difficult to explain is the response to the socialist labour movement of those segments of society not directly involved in the economic class struggle. Here certainly there is a difference between those countries which are involved in international political conflicts in which the internal social conflicts appear as a threat to the national goals, particularly in the case of latecomers to the overseas colonial expansion where they could not rely on foreign auxiliaries in that expansion. Certainly, the conflict between the nationalists and the labour movement in Italy was exacerbated by the African wars of colonial expansion.[39] The same is true when foreign policy goals, such as the recovery of the irredenta on the Austrian and Dalmatian border, encounter the lack of support for intervention on the part of the Italian socialist party. In France, nationalism also created tensions between those not directly involved in the economic conflicts and the labour movement but the nationalist turn of the latter assisted by the Jacobin tradition, the historical hostility to Germany, and the identification of imperial Germany with reaction, facilitated the integration of labour in a way that was not possible in other major powers. In Germany, had it not been for defeat and the yearning for peace that coincided with tensions created by delayed democratization, the patriotic behaviour of the social-democratic leadership, with some notable exceptions at the beginning of the war, would have facilitated a similar process of integration.[40] These problems were not present in the case of the smaller European democracies except for Finland and the Baltic countries, where there were ambivalences created by the Russian Revolution and the combination of struggle for national independence and conservative political reaction. It is obviously difficult to prove, but it seems as if the hostility of a large part of the establishment of army officers, civil servants, professionals, and intellectuals to the labour movement cannot be explained in terms of the economic class conflict but rather in their dislike of the position of social democracy – at least on the ideological level – and later the Communist parties in relation to the national political aims particularly strongly held by those groups.[41] Another major difference between countries is obviously the degree to which the working classes, or segments of them, were ready to respond to the revolutionary opportunities provided by social and economic crisis at the end of the First World War and the response to the Russian Revolution in different countries. While it is historically false that communist revolutions were defeated by fascism, it is true that fascism was more successful in those societies in which the bourgeoisie had been deeply scared by revolutionary attempts, however unsuccessful, and where the labour movement held on to a maximalist revolutionary rhetoric, even when it was unable to mobilize for revolution. The Räterepublik and the Spartakist attempts in Germany, the occupation of factories and the Red domination of the countryside in the Po Valley in Italy, the Bela Kun régime in Hungary, the revolutionary attempts of the working class in Finland, certainly left such a heritage. The same would be true in Spain with the 1934 October Revolution and the endemic anarcho-syndicalist violence. In some of these cases international links with the Russian Revolution, real or imaginary, contributed to the desire to strengthen the state against such threats or to overthrow a state whose weakness had led it to make compromises with demands perceived as revolutionary. Unsuccessful revolutions, as the Linz programme of the Austro-Marxists emphasized, contributed much to the authoritarian responses, both conservative and fascist. In those cases where Jews played prominent roles among the leadership of the labour movement, this became an additional stimulus for the fascist response, rationalizing their anti-Semitism.

Secularization, religion and fascism

It has been noted already how the Christian democratic parties and, before them, the Catholic conservative parties developed as a response to the strains of modern society in the process of liberal democratization and the secularizing policies of liberals and socialists. Wherever that response incorporated a large part of the population, particularly pre-industrial sectors such as peasants, artisans, independent middle classes, civil servants, and even white-collar employees, and in a few cases large segments of the working class, fascist hostility to liberalism and Marxist socialism encountered a serious competitor that had pre-empted much of its political space. This certainly was true in the Netherlands where the verzuilingen both by Catholic and Calvinist parties never allowed its National Socialist party to make much progress. Thus in Belgium a semi-fascist movement like Rex and Flemish nationalist groups, when faced with the overt hostility of the Church hierarchy and the Catholic sub-culture, found it difficult to make progress, even when not overtly attacking the Church. In spite of the many factors favouring a fascist response in Austria, neither the native semi-fascist Heimwehr movement nor the Nazis gained a strength comparable to their comrades in non-Catholic Germany. Despite the rapid success of the Partito Populare Italiano in the first post-war elections in Italy, the delayed entry of the Catholics into public life (due to the Roman question that had imposed on Catholics for so many years the 'non-expedit', and limited the development of their lay organizations) together with the strong element of anti-clericalism remaining from the unification struggles, left significant sectors of Italian society open to competition from the fascists. It is no accident that the most secularized parts of Italy, formerly part of the Papal States, would become a stronghold of fascism in the countryside and small towns. In Spain in the thirties the success of a Catholic defensive movement against the laicist left-bourgeois policies mobilized behind Gil Robles and the CEDA a large part of peasant and provincial middle-class Spain, which on other grounds would have been a potential basis for the Falange. In fact, the disintegration of the CEDA probably allowed many of its supporters to turn to the Falangist banners during the Civil War. The availability of secularized or at least anti-clerical middle classes with strong nationalistic sentiments, hostile to a revolutionary or maximalist labour movement, represented a limit to Catholic and Christian democratic parties which they would overcome successfully only after the Second World War with the defeat of fascism and disillusionment with nationalism. It is our impression that the latent hostility of much of the Protestant bourgeoisie and educated classes against the *Kaplanokratie* of the Zentrum and the memories of the *Kulturkampf* of the Bismarckian empire with the Church contributed to the hostility to the Weimar coalition. After all the new régime had brought together in the government the Zentrum and the Social Democrats, the two main opponents of Bismarck. The regional strength of the Nazis in areas like Franconia, the Protestant enclave in Bavaria, might be linked to this historical heritage. The same is true for the areas traditionally supporting 'liberal Germanism' rather than the Catholic party in Austria. In Spain the recent disestablishment of the Church with the coming of the Republic, the illusion still tying the secularized middle classes to the leadership of the left Republicans like Azaña, and in the case of Catalonia the left-bourgeois nationalist radicalism of Esquerra, deprived Spanish fascists of another potential social base. It is perhaps no accident that some of the founding nucleus of the first Spanish fascist group, *La Conquista del Estado*, should have moved towards Azaña, and that an early admirer of Italian fascism like Giménez Caballero should also have been an admirer of the left-bourgeois leader for whom José Antonio had more respect than for Gil Robles. Unfortunately we do not know how much of the support of the Belgian Rex came from ex-liberals, but there is evidence that the Dutch fascists encountered more difficulty in making gains among voters of the religious parties than among voters of the secular bourgeois parties. We should not forget that Germany was one of the few countries in which there was a tradition of conservative bourgeois in addition to working-class criticism of religion in politics, and a sufficiently important minority of religiously confused fringe groups in the völkisch milieu. The traditions of the Lutheran state church in a militaristic nationalist country provided another fertile ground for the strange combination that Hitler would offer under the confused label of positive Christianity, anti-Marxism, and nationalistic reconstruction of the national community.

We have obviously ignored in this discussion the eastern European cases, partly because we know too little about the religious base of movements like the Arrow Cross in Hungary and because the Romanian situation is radically different. In Croatia and Slovakia the integral nationalism, given the links between nationality and religion, also creates a unique situation, even when in Slovakia the different degrees of integration into the Church might have distinguished the more fascist nationalists from those closer to a Catholic nationalist party. It should be stressed, to avoid any misunderstanding, that to some extent the successful competition of Catholic parties with the fascists, particularly in Spain in the thirties for the youth of the universities, and in Austria, was made possible by the incorporation of some semi-fascist positions like anti-liberalism, anti-parliamentarism, corporativism, and in some cases the assimilation of a pseudo-fascist style. There is in this a certain parallelism to the success of the Austro-Marxists compared to the German social democrats in their competition with the communists.

Rural-urban conflict and fascism

We have noted how certain ideological positions and the constellation of political social forces favoured the success of fascism among the independent peasantry in a number of countries, particularly so in Germany and Romania. In this context it is especially important to stress that in countries in which agrarian and peasant parties had built a strong organizational base, reinforced in some cases by successful agrarian reforms as in Finland and the Baltic countries, the fascists encountered an insurmountable obstacle. This was not the case in Germany where the independent peasantry of northern and western Protestant regions had been slowly abandoning the liberal urban-based parties or the great agrarian-oriented conservative party dominated by East Elbian landlords whose interests did not coincide with theirs. The peasantry of those areas moved through a variety of political changes from local or small agrarian interest-group-based parties, and finally, in the 1928 election and afterwards, massively towards the National Socialists. Something similar started to occur in Austria. In eastern Europe the peasant parties also offered an obstacle, but their lack of success, given the constraints of the oligarchic authoritarian régimes and the difficulties caused by the relationship of dependent agricultural nations with industrial central European countries, and the disintegration of peasant parties offered new opportunities to the populist fascists. Sten Nilson,[42] in an analysis of the success of nazism compared with Scandinavian fascism, has emphasized the very different response of the social democrats in both areas to the plight of the peasantry during the depression, and particularly the possibility and the willingness to make a social democratic–farmer party alliance. The studies of German Protestant rural communities show clearly the isolation in which the few social democrats found themselves in those areas.[43] Given the traditional position of the social democratic party after the failure of David's revisionism to make an effort to penetrate the countryside and the late formulation of an agrarian programme at the Kiel Congress, the Nazi strength in the countryside is not surprising. In France, despite the attempts by demagogues like Agricola in Brittany to capitalize on rural discontent and the later success of Poujade, parties of the left had sufficient roots in provincial rural France, including the socialists and even the communists, to leave little room for the later emerging fascist groups.

Conditions for extreme nationalism and fascism

Nationalism was the central appeal of fascist movements and certainly countries where the national boundaries had been historically fixed long ago such as Spain, Portugal, the United Kingdom, Netherlands, Scandinavia (with the exception of Denmark), and Switzerland offered little opportunity for appeals based on irredentism and the struggle of ethnic communities in mixed border areas. In this context it should never be forgotten that the initial style of fascist movements, many of their symbols, shouts, parades, banners and even programmatic positions were invented by D'Annunzio in the struggle for Fiume, and that the areas that most disproportionately gave their support in terms of membership to the PNF were the areas bordering on the old Austro-Hungarian Empire.[44] Even today neo-fascism has some of its strongholds in this part of Italy. The historical antecedents of National Socialism also were born in the ethnic border struggle in the Sudeten and in the context of the struggle between a German and Czech working class for occupational opportunities. Border conflicts contributed decisively to the emergence of the irregular armed forces of Heimwehren and Freikorps. In Germany they would contribute many of the initial cadres of the National Socialist movement and the same is true for Carinthia in Austria. Balkan fascisms would also draw much of their strength from border area ethnic cultural conflicts. Finnish right-wing nationalism, particularly of the Karelia Society students and some of the support of the *Lapua* movement, would be linked with the existence of an irredenta of great symbolic value across the border with the Soviet Union and the existence of a communist Finnish régime on the other side of the border that justified the view of the communist movement as not only a socio-economic threat but a national threat. In the western nations only Belgium with its unsettled identity of Flemish and Walloons, with the possibility of a Flemish nationalism or a Dietsch larger unit with the Netherlands offered opportunities for a radical nationalism of a semi-fascist or fascist character.[45] Interestingly enough, Spanish fascism made much of the problem of the identity of the Spanish state and its historical mission when confronted with the threat of regional peripheral linguistic cultural nationalism. It is perhaps no accident that Valladolid, a city identified with a liberal party hostile to Catalan regionalism under the Monarchy, should also be one of the initial nuclei of Spanish fascism. It is often forgotten that in Catalonia Dr Dencàs created a semi-fascist movement of Catalan separatists, *Estat Català*, that apparently also had Italian support and combined extreme nationalism with some of the external trappings of fascism.[46] Sociologically, the Basque Country would have been fertile ground for the kind of nationalistic fascism that we find in the eastern European periphery with its peasant small entrepreneur and skilled working class, resentful both of a capitalist oligarchy oriented towards Spain and a Marxist socialist labour movement. In this case, however, the dominant role of the Church in the regional community oriented the Basque Nationalist Party, the PNV, in a Christian Democratic direction.

Democratic and authoritarian régimes and the growth of fascism

This analysis of the space available in the social and political map of Europe for fascist movements indicates the limits in which their appeal would find a response and helps to explain the early or late appearance of such movements. However, the reader might ask why fascism had so little success in some of the eastern European and Balkan countries, where even an impressionistic view would suggest there was such fertile ground for it. Here an additional variable needs to be introduced. Fascism, to become a mass movement and even to organize successfully its nucleus of militant activists, required a minimum degree of political freedom, and a number of countries in this part of the world were under royal bureaucratic military dictatorships which in their more liberal phases allowed relatively tamed parties to compete unequally with the official government sponsored or created authoritarian national party, ready to coopt them or corrupt them, if not suppress them. Under these circumstances, fascist movements could not gain sufficient strength. In a number of those countries, particularly in the Baltic area, when fascist movements or semi-fascist parties made their appearance, leaders of the established parties moved towards authoritarian rule to prevent their growth. In addition, a number of eastern European countries had not reached the level of economic, social, cultural, and political development that would have made the more complex ideological response to the historical social situation possible and necessary. The oligarchies of those countries were ready to turn to other, simpler solutions. In addition, the urban classes that could have provided the ideological leadership for fascist-type movements were as state bourgeoisies too closely tied to the bureaucratic military professional and commercial establishment exploiting the countryside. In other cases, such as Macedonia, the nationalist movement facing suppression from different states covering the area had no choice but to turn to conspiratorial terrorist revolutionary politics rather than to the creation of a mass movement of the fascist type. In addition, too little is known about the minor fascist movements and parties emerging in this area and their chequered history, moving between suppression and cooption by pragmatic authoritarian rulers. Even so, in Romania we find one of the most interesting fascist movements of the inter-war years: the Iron Guard whose leaders felt an affinity with their comrades in other countries and whose history belies the typical Marxist interpretation of the fascist phenomenon. The same is largely true for the Arrow Cross in Hungary. Unfortunately, except for the excellent study by Eugen Weber of the Iron Guard and the work of Lackó on the Arrow Cross, we have little sociological analysis of the basis of support or leadership of the Balkan and East European fascist movements.

The different historical fate of various nationalities contributes to account for the success or failure of fascism in that part of the world. Certainly the dominant Serbian state-building nationality had little interest in the fascist extremists since their military bureaucratic bourgeois élites were ruling the country. The same is largely true for the Polish supporters of the authoritarian régime of Pilsudski who could identify with a nationalistic army guaranteeing the newly-won statehood. In the Czech territory of Czechoslovakia, the veterans of the legions that had struggled for the independence of the country could identify with the new democratic régime of Benes and Masaryk that had founded the state and could also identify with them in their anti-fascism. In those three countries only fringe groups seem to have supported minor fascist-type parties or organizations.[47]

The case of Slovakia exemplifies the interaction of the different variables accounting for the emergence and strength of fascism. The marginal national society, mostly composed of peasants and small-town dwellers, a magyarized upper class, a Jewish community occupying a dominant position in the business life, with a left largely dominated by the Communist Party, hostile to the Czechs dominant in the new state, would lead one to expect a strong fascist movement.[48] In addition, the identification of Prague with cosmopolitanism, free thinking, and Freemasonry would reinforce such a predisposition. However, until the thirties the nationalist movement, which included pseudo-fascist elements, was led by the priests, Hlinka and later Tiso, who in moderate terms, stood for regional autonomy. Later, the younger generation in the movement emerged from the paramilitary organization, the Hlinka Guard, under the leadership of new men like Tuka, Mach, and Durčansky who, advocating separatism, an authoritarian state, and violent anti-Semitism, were ready to follow the lead of Germany and the National Socialists. As Nolte formulates it, Catholicism was the 'father of fascism'. It led initially only to a pseudo-fascist Catholic populist movement, but the second generation turned to real fascism. The common commitment to nationalism, however, led Tiso and the older generation to protect the younger competitors against outside opponents. Moreover, one of the barriers to the success of these movements was the strength of the peasant party in the area.

Crises situations as an opportunity, stabilization as an obstacle

It has been stressed how fascism as a latecomer, with its 'anti-positions' and its ambiguous reformulation of the things it stood against, in a form that it thought was a new synthesis dominated by nationalism, inevitably found it difficult to build mass support, particularly in relatively stable societies that had not experienced defeat, failed or pseudo-revolutions, and had weathered the depression relatively well. Certainly in some countries nationalism, which was advocated by other parties too, against a non-national state, provided them with a unique opportunity, but one which pushed their distinctively fascist aims into the background. The compromises and alliances that Italian fascism and later Hitler had to make, or appear to make, with conservative and Establishment interests gave anti-fascists an excellent opportunity to reject the ideology as insincere and to isolate the masses from its appeal. In this respect, as in many others, the Spanish Civil War was decisive in defining fascism as socially conservative. Moreover, in most countries, after an initial revolutionary shock in the immediate post-world war period, it was realized that there were safer ways of protecting the established socio-economic order and that the threat of revolution was not as immediate as had been feared. For the sake of democracy and their own freedom, the social democratic parties gave up some of their revolutionary rhetoric and were able to cooperate with other parties in the defence of democracy. All this seriously limited the success of the fascist parties founded in the thirties. Even the successes of the Axis powers could not serve for a mass attraction to those parties, as similarly the success of the Soviet Union after the Second World War was not able to boost the appeal of communist parties that had not achieved a mass basis before the war. The contradiction between a nationalistic programme and appeal and the internationalism of the fascist movement, that is, the leadership of Italy and particularly Germany, in fact lowered their chances even among their potential constituencies in a number of societies. One of the great paradoxes in the history of fascism is that in the last years of the Second World War, with the struggle against the Soviet Union and communism and the emergence of the United States as a major power in the war and an ally of the Soviet Union, many fascist leaders also shifted, with more or less sincerity, to a new theme: the defence of Europe. At that point the international solidarity of fascist European nations in a new order became one of their slogans, which paradoxically is reflected in the fact that post-war fascism has as one of its organs of expression a magazine and a movement labelled 'Young Europe'. In this new form, it attempted to appeal to a new young generation but defeat and the ability of other political forces, particularly the post-war Christian democrats, to integrate into their appeal the European idea plus the terrible legacy of Nazi terror meant the end of fascism as it was known in the inter-war years.

Fascism: a generational revolt

While the social structure, the historical and political situation of different countries, and the inherent ambiguities of the fascist appeal that became particularly explicit in the case of those movements founded late account for their failure to gain a mass base, and even more, a mass electorate, it still has to be explained why in so many countries they could recruit a small but devoted following of activists, and how men who had achieved positions of influence in other parties in the thirties broke with them and felt moved to create new fascist movements. To understand this success of fascism we have to look less to structural variables than to the analysis of their success or failure in building a mass base. In that context we have to pay infinitely more attention to the positive appeal rather than the 'anti-themes' of fascism, the ideological, intellectual, and emotional needs it satisfied. Here the poetry, the symbolism, the rhetoric, the new forms of participation offered by fascism became central. Here, too, the worst aspects of the fascist phenomenon, its opportunity for activists' violence and the sublimated expression of criminal impulses also became relevant. Social scientists have devoted much attention to the psychological interpretations of extremist movements, particularly fascism, and even more, nazism, as in the literature on the authoritarian personality and some analysis of national character. In our view, those efforts are not particularly fruitful in explaining mass electoral support or even mass membership, but may help our understanding of individual activists. Similarly, a study of communist supporters using psychological variables seems to be fruitful in understanding the appeal of communism in the United Kingdom and the United States, but off the mark for French or Italian communism. A psychological approach might be important to understand why some people joined the British Union of Fascists or the variety of fascist parties under the occupation in France but the same would not be true for the PNF after 1921, the NSDAP in the early thirties, or the Iron Guard. This does not mean that the activists, even of those parties, would not have distinctive psychological characteristics, but the fact that men of those characteristics would join those parties rather than other movements is more easily explained by social, structural and historical factors. Without denying the importance of psychological factors, the positive appeals of fascism can also be used to explain the success of the movements among particular social groups, like students, veterans, officers, certain segments of the old élites, even some types of intellectuals, and for the different attractions of fascism to those groups in different societies. To do so, however, we have to describe something that is far from easy, the image that fascism created, the appeals it offered, that were significant for such groups. It is difficult to describe them because they were more a matter of style, of rhetoric, of action than of ideas, and today it is difficult to convey the emotional tone created at the time without extensive quotes and, ideally, unavailable audiovisual documentation. Autobiographical material from fascists is perhaps our best source for grasping the emotional appeal of fascism.[49] However, from this distance in time and with an unsympathetic attitude inevitable after the fact, it is difficult to understand today that experience of conversion to fascism of a significant segment of the inter-war generations.

Fascist movements in their style and organization offered those generations a particular appeal that cannot be understood simply in terms of their ideology or their programmatic positions, and even less in terms of the policies pursued by their leaders when about to take power and after the takeover. It is those appeals that explain the composition of the initial nucleus of many fascist parties, rather than their mass membership and even less their mass electorates, wherever they succeeded in gaining them. Those elements of style combine in a contradictory and paradoxical way the best and the worst of fascism. Ignoring national variants, fascism offered from its beginnings, inspired by D'Annunzio and his Fiume adventure, a new style in politics; new symbols, new rhetoric, new forms of action, new patterns of social relations that satisfied certain basic yearnings of young people and that were particularly congruent with a sector of post-war generations.[50] Fascism had a strong romantic component – an appeal to emotion and sentiment, to the love of adventure and heroism, the belief in action rather than words, the exultation of violence and even death – elements that had not been alien to the romantic nationalist movement of the nineteenth century and anarchism, and that in the past had attracted students and the bohemian intelligentsia. However, those elements were combined in a new way with the search for community and discipline. The desire for community rather than individualism was symbolically expressed in the love for uniforms. The discovery of shirts of different colours as a way of rejecting the individualized bourgeois business suit, at the same time symbolized the rejection of the grey everyday life, the deviance from conventionality and the vicarious identification with the lower classes against the bourgeoisie.[51] The uniform was also a link with the recent military experience of the generation and offered the younger ones the vicarious experience of being in uniform that their age had not allowed them to satisfy during the First World War. The new style of political activity, the marches, the rallies, the songs, the burials of dead comrades, the salute, represented something essentially different from the style of political activity of their parents: the occasional electioneering, the clubhouses, the formal banquets of the notables, the hypocrisy imposed by parliamentary procedures at party meetings, the deals of city-hall politics, etc. This new style found particularly fertile ground in Germany, where the youth movement had for similar reasons emotionally rejected the style of politics and public life of the rising bourgeoisie of the *Gründerjahre* and the stiff status structures of the aristocracy.[52] It allowed people to be close to each other, cutting across status barriers, breaking away from traditional bourgeois and aristocratic conventions, sharing an adventurous and sometimes dangerous experience. In the autobiographies of Nazis collected by Abel and analysed by Merkl, the war experience and that of the Free Corps[53] in breaking the rigid conventions of German status-ridden society appears over and over, and is empirical evidence that the *Volksgemeinschaft*, breaking class and status barriers, overcoming the class conflict that divided the nation, was again possible, as it had been in the trenches in the face of the common enemy. Fascism in its actions satisfied both the desire for the heroic deed of romantic individualism and the desire to submerge in a collective enterprise, in a group, for a bourgeois youth that had been socialized in a culture based on conventionality and whose mentors proposed to them goals of individual, private success. Obviously, those motives became mixed with those we know from the gang of adolescents beating up those of another gang, the cravings for self-aggrandizement and abuse of authority, and sometimes the basest motives of aggression, brutality, and sadism. Those impulses, sometimes unleashed by the experience of war, could find an ideologically legitimized channel in the punitive expeditions of the fascist squads in the brawls with opponents for the sake of a higher cause. The resentments against a militant working class which, with its increase of consciousness, with its access to political power, and its organization, had crossed the boundaries of subordination to its betters, could also find expression in the new style of radical violent politics. The new movement also contrasted with the traditional style of religious organizations, the meetings of Catholic youth under the leadership of priests with their devotions, their formalism, their repression of sexuality and violence that made those participating in them look effeminate. Fascism appealed to a confused sense of manliness. The new style equated frankness, spontaneity, lack of manners, public use of insult and ridicule with honesty, sincerity, and a break with bourgeois hypocrisy and conventionality. Passion was to be a substitute for reason, readiness to fight a substitute for useless sophistic arguments. Let us not forget that fascist movements directed their appeal mostly to young men and that apparently even the electorate remained disproportionately male, a point on which they were distinct from the Christian Democratic parties which competed for the same social strata but had a distinctive success among the women.[54] It is hard to judge to what extent the war experience – in which young men spent years together in close comradeship, the years of university studies again in a male community, in societies in which the interaction between the sexes was still controlled, among the bourgeoisie particularly, by conventionality, and ultimately the risk of committing oneself to marriage, at that time economically difficult for this generation – might have made this male political community attractive. The romanticization of the male community with its homosexual undertones in the German youth movement has not escaped attention, and it might not have been an accident that in the SA such tendencies were not absent. The idealization of leadership, of loyalty to leaders, also satisfied certain needs in an atomized society and was particularly congruent with the generation that had before it the worship of military leadership and heroism.

Veterans and officers

The new style politics obviously was particularly attractive to certain social groups that were salient among the founding nucleus of fascist parties. Prominent among them we find the war veterans, those who had volunteered and often succeeded on account probably of their better education and personal qualities of heroism in becoming reserve officers, but who would find it difficult either to return seriously to their studies or to a relatively grey existence in unexciting jobs. It is perhaps no accident that among the initial fascist leadership we should find a disproportionate number of war pilots, and the pilot was a romantic figure at the time.[55] Young army officers who after demobilization would find their careers interrupted or reduced to dull garrison duty, would certainly find fascist activism attractive. University students unwilling to commit themselves fully to the goals of a successful professional career sometimes with uncertain prospects for the future, undecided vocations, would constitute another group. In societies where border conflicts or semi-revolutionary situations after the war had mobilized otherwise stable segments of the society into civic guards, volunteer services, to maintain order and fight external or internal enemies, would in the process have discovered a new 'camaraderie' and a new style of politics. Returning veterans and young students were obviously less integrated into the existing class and status structures of society and therefore more prone to accept the fascist view of the national community, of politics as a collective endeavour rather than a conflict of interests. Nationalism could have for them a special appeal beyond class and religion – the two main bases of politics in Europe. Academic unemployment, the impact of the economic crisis of inflation and depression, the number of those who pursued studies in view of the difficulties of entering the labour market, the initial easing of education requirements for those returning from the war, for example in Italy, must all have contributed to increase the size of this group. The frustrations of downward and upward mobility, the tensions created by a change from a society of individual entrepreneurship and professionalism to a more bureaucratic society must have made escapism into political activism, even if only at weekends, highly attractive. The new camaraderie would also offer to those who had come from rural or small-town backgrounds an opportunity for social integration in the new metropolis. Demographic changes must have contributed to this emergence of the generational politics of youth, including the demand for positions of authority for those under thirty-five and the caricature of the Establishment and élites as fat old men. Certainly, a longer life in societies with a relatively stagnant economy must in contrast with the period after the Second World War have limited the career horizons and the choices of occupational mobility for those generations. The evident failures of the older generation to solve the problems of their societies inevitably justified the demands for power of the new movements and the new men leading them. Soon their elders, who would disagree with the methods, the violence and the strife, but who shared many of the same nationalistic values, the same resentment against international structures they did not understand, the same anti-clericalism, in some countries the same anti-Semitism, the same resentment against a disrespectful if not unruly working class, would ambivalently sympathize with their youngsters. They would give them economic support, join the party but not the squad, and increasingly become important as experts and respectable leaders, particularly when the new movements came closer to power. Certainly, fascism initially was a generational movement, but if the age composition of the initial nucleus and of the later joiners is studied, a slow and continuous change becomes apparent. The core of fascism generally came from a generational revolt, but the beneficiaries and the later leadership would be found in a wider age spectrum. The generational experience of the First World War seems to have been unique and not repeated in the Second World War and therefore hard for us to understand. Reading the biographies of leaders and rank-and-file members, not only German, the *Fronterlebnis* and even the vicarious participation of those too young to fight, it is clear that the war experience strongly marked a segment of that generation. Certainly other segments would draw other political conclusions and those different ways of experiencing an historical event would contribute to the bitterness of other, particularly social economic, conflicts.[56] Let us not forget that the basic stimulus for Italian fascism noted by Salvemini and many other observers and well documented for the Nazis in the Abel data and Merkl's analysis was the culture shock after returning home and particularly the real or pseudo-revolutionary situations, the lack of deference to uniforms, medals, and wounds by an anti-militarist, pacifist working class, and in some cases the complacent living of the rearguard bourgeois. That deep sense of crisis based on the contrast between discipline and class solidarity in the trenches was heightened by politically organized class conflict in the defeated countries. This crisis was made more acute in Germany, Austria, and Hungary by threats on their borders of irredentist nationalist uprisings, and further exacerbated by military occupation, particularly the occupation of the Ruhr by the French,[57] and for Hungarians the loss of a large part of their territory. These external events coinciding with attempted revolutions at home provided the necessary ingredients for the growth of fascism. The immediate post-independence struggle on the Finnish and Baltic borders had a similar impact.

It would seem useful to speculate briefly why the participants in the Second World War do not seem to have felt the same way about their war service, particularly after fascism had in the interwar years given ideological expression to such ultra-nationalistic heroic values. The difference between the two wars might have been that the first one followed more than forty years of peace, decades in which the educational systems from primary school to university built up the feeling of national identity and romanticized the struggles that had contributed to nation building. Most participants perceived the war as either defensive, or as necessary for the achievement of national goals. Life in the trenches and life at home were two different worlds – so unlike the Second World War where bombing, total mobilization, rationing, and war service reduced the inequities so visible in 1918. The rigid status structures of pre-First World War society in which the aristocracy still occupied a distinct position particularly among the professional officers, in which educational differences defined social position, could be contrasted with the reality of social equality in front of the enemy, the opportunities for promotion for valour to non-commissioned and even officer status, that represented a new experience of solidarity. The return to civilian life with its lower-class hostility and upper-class snobbism and a basically unchanged status structure of society shocked many veterans. Against these experiences, how welcome then was the appeal of a national community free of class conflict that the fascists offered as an alternative to the heightened self-confidence of the proletariat. To this we have to add the lack of planning for the demobilization and incorporation into civilian life of those returning from the front, compared to the end of the second war. This time the assumption of full authority by the victors prevented revolutionary or pseudo-revolutionary bids for power. Nor did it allow the emergence of the complex world of *Heimatwehren*, civic and white guards, free corps, legionaires of Fiume, volunteers fighting the Russian revolution in the east, and so forth, that allowed so many of the war generation and the youth of the early twenties to enter a heroic life of violence and romanticism rather than grey everyday jobs in civilian society, to which many never returned. Obviously, the economic and social impact of unemployment caused by demobilization,[58] loss of positions in the bureaucracy in Vienna or Budapest with the emergence of new independent nations, economic insecurity caused by inflation and depression, growth of the intellectual proletariat with expansion of education without a change in expectations and the structure of occupations, heightened the frustrations of these generations, the hostility to the present social political order, the longing for many aspects of the pre-war society without, however, ignoring the impossibility of returning to the status and class structure of the past. The First World War not only produced an unexpected and deep dislocation of the bourgeois-aristocratic class and status order and the identity of political units but also, reacting to these crises, an emergent group that perceived the war and these changes in an unique way. Unfortunately, it is not possible to trace the impact of that generational experience systematically in the available data, except perhaps for the Nazi activists, and if the research were to be done probably for the core of the fascist leadership in Italy. There can be no question, however, that the size and commitment of the initial nucleus of fascists in the different countries of Europe is clearly related to the importance and the character of those generational experiences in each country.

In this context it is no accident that the fascist leaders, militants, and members would be disproportionately war veterans and that the number of those with a distinguished war record, those with wartime promotions, and with a favourable memory of those days, would be over-represented among them. The exaltation of military virtues, the anti-pacifism, in addition to the nationalism, made those parties attractive to professional officers, particularly junior officers. Obviously the restraint on political activity of officers in many cases limited or prevented public adherence, and in countries with bureaucratic military authoritarian régimes the attraction of the revolutionary fascist movements might have been weaker than in liberal democracies. The attraction was probably higher for retired rather than active officers. It is likely that quite similar personality types among officers would be attracted to fascists and the left, for example in the milieu of the *tenentes* in Brazil and even in Spain in the thirties, while the bulk of the officer corps remained attached to the army as a national institution above parties and régimes, ready to play the role of the moderating power and to fill the vacuum left by civilian authority in crisis-ridden societies. Officers might have looked with sympathy upon some of the goals of the fascists, the mentality and ideology of the armed forces might have assimilated fascist conceptions, but other themes of the new movements must have cooled their enthusiasm. In the Abel sample, for example, we find only six career officers among 581 respondents. In Italy, the proportion might have been higher, and the highest we know from the limited data we have seems to be found among the Brazilian Integralists.[59]

Intellectuals and fascism

It is beyond the scope of our analysis to explore the role of intellectuals, academics, writers, and artists in fascist movements. The anti-intellectualism, or more specifically, the anti-rationalism of fascism and particularly the petit-bourgeois tastes imposed by Hitler should not obscure the attraction of fascist movements and ideas for many intellectuals. However, few among them would commit themselves to the organized parties and accept the party discipline, and many would only pass through the movement or flirt with it. In a number of cases like early Italian fascism, some of the French fascist groupuscules, the initial support of Mosley, Falange, the Brazilian Integralists, the movement had a particular attraction for some intellectuals. They probably never played a role in fascist parties as politically important as in liberal-democratic parties and socialist parties, and the fascist leadership never would find equally successful ways of linking them with the movement, as the communists did through their various front organizations in the era of anti-fascism of the late thirties. Even though it is perhaps a risky generalization, it seems that western, rather than central and northern European, and eastern Balkan fascism found an answering echo among the intellectuals. A reading of Alastair Hamilton's *The Appeal of Fascism*[60] suggests that it was more an aesthetic, literary type of intellectual rather than members of the academic establishment, the social scientists, and above all, the natural scientists who were attracted, often passingly, by the new politics: poets, playwrights, and critics rather than professors, who when they were on the right supported more conservative authoritarian alternatives, like the Nationalists in Italy, Renovación Española in Spain, conservative Catholicism in Austria, and authoritarian bureaucratic régimes in eastern Europe.

The mass basis and social crisis

It cannot be emphasized enough how difficult it is to generalize about the membership of parties ranging from small sectarian groups to a mass membership party like the NSDAP. We probably will never have the data to trace the changing social composition of parties expanding rapidly in a crisis situation and on the road to power, and therefore, will be unable to account in terms of changes in social composition for the shift in ideological and policy emphasis over time. Similarly for the comparison between small sectarian communist parties in, let us say, the United Kingdom and the United States, and mass electoral parties as in France, Italy, and Finland, different explanations will be more fruitful for one or another type.[61] The smaller parties are likely to be understood more in terms of a particular generational experience of personal crisis preventing the integration into the existing party system, or leading to a break with other parties, as well as in psychological variables. Mass parties are more susceptible to a sociological explanation in terms of interests not finding adequate representation through other parties, like northern central Protestant German farmers shifting from one party to another after finding the representation of their interests through the conservatives dominated by eastern agrarian interest groups inadequate, and finally finding a home in the national-socialist mass movement. Given the short period of participation of fascist parties in democratic political competition and their growth coinciding with national, political, and economic crises like the depression, it is hard to say if they would without gaining full power have retained over decades the support of the strata to which they appealed. It cannot be excluded that through a network of organized interests identified with the movement representing in the opposition and in coalition governments interests neglected by other parties, they could have become a permanent component of democratic multi-party systems. In that case, they would have retained a much smaller proportion of the support they mobilized as the result of a particularly deep crisis, with an appeal based on a total critique of the system which allowed them not to offer specific solutions that would alienate one group or another. The appeal on the basis of a principled critique and charismatic leadership would have had to be replaced by specific programmatic policies. In this respect the persistent re-emergence of neo-Nazi parties in certain rural and provincial areas of Germany in recent decades without direct continuity with the symbols and the leadership of the past indicate that they could serve as a vehicle for certain structural strains of European societies. This however might have meant splits in the movement between a more national socialist and a more petit-bourgeois party. In the case of Germany the latter probably would have been more anti-Semitic and the National Socialists would have had, probably, to disavow the emerging charismatic leadership of Hitler. In the process they would have become parties of negative integration of groups marginal to the major integrative cleavages of class and religion that had appeared before the First World War. However, the destiny of fascism and the inherent dynamics of its activist core pushed in another direction and the particular historical crisis of liberal democracy in Italy, compounded in Germany with the economic crisis, gave it a unique chance to gain power. In understanding that process, clues should not be searched for in the social composition but in the organizational capacity, the impact of activism, the combination of violence with the capacity to penetrate a complex network of interest groups loosely linked with existing party structures whose members were ideologically predisposed to some but not all the themes of the movement, and which exercised enormous influence over the members and the community networks of rural and small-town Germany. The works of Heberle, Stoltenberg, Wulf, Noakes, Allen, Mierendorff, Winkler, and the theoretical analysis of Lepsius suggest that the sociological explanation should not focus on the individual joining or voting for the party, but on the process by which the intermediary structure was taken over by the Nazis.[62] Contrary to the theorists of mass society,[63] their success was not due to the attraction of isolated mass men, but to the gaining of control by devoted activists of a complex pre-existing set of networks. It was the absence of such networks, their resistance to being infiltrated, their close ties with the Church and in some countries with interest-oriented parties, like the farmers' parties in northern Europe, that constituted the most serious obstacle to the growth of fascism, even in countries undergoing serious crisis. In this context it would be particularly important to study the process of take-over of northern Italian and Po Valley society by the fascists before the March on Rome, the link established between the activists and the agrarian interest groups and even some labour organizations, rather than to focus, as much of the historiographic material does, on the process of destruction of the socialist networks of organization and power at the local level. It is probably no accident that the fascists would succeed in the most developed and commercially viable agricultural region and make almost no progress in the socially much more disintegrated atomistic or clientelistic south. Rural and provincial Spain, except those regions where the Church or nationalistic anti-centralist movements had created social networks, was more similar to southern Italy and this must have, until almost before taking power or even after, limited the success of Falangism. In this context it should be emphasized that the failure of the neofascist movement, particularly in Germany but also in Italy, after the Second World War has been largely due to their incapacity to penetrate into interest groups and to coopt their leadership, even when their appeals and programmatic positions would seem congruent with the dissatisfactions of their members. The fact that pragmatic catch-all parties like the Christian Democrats, once they had abandoned a dominant religious and clerical orientation and even the parties of the left, once they had abandoned ideological *ouvririsme*, were able to retain the loyalty of such organizations, placed an insuperable limit to the expansion of neo-fascism.

Notes

The research for this paper was made possible by my stay at the Institute for Advanced Study, Princeton, supported by a grant from the National Science Foundation number CS-31730X2 to the Institute. The collection of data, particularly those on the leadership of different parties, has been supported by the Concilium on International and Area Studies of Yale University.

I want to thank my wife, Rocío de Terán, for her collaboration and analysis of data used in the paper. Rainer M. Lepsius offered useful criticism of an early version.

1. Seymour M. Lipset and Stein Rokkan, *Party Systems and Voter Alignments Cross-National Perspectives* (New York, 1967). Introduction pp. 1–64.

2. ibid.

3. The problem of availability of support rather than search for support is well stated by Ramiro Ledesma Ramos, *Fascismo en España? Discurso a-las juventudes de España* (Barcelona, 1968), p. 294, when accounting for the limited social change accomplished by Italian fascism, the persistence of the 'old anti-historical powers representing the great bourgeoisie and the reactionary spirit' among possible explanations, who writes: 'One of them is that every regime needs as broad a basis of support as possible, and if fascism arriving at victory after a struggle with a marxist oriented working class found itself deprived of the due support and collaboration of large proletarian nuclei, it had to lean more than is convenient on a different constellation.'

4. Otto Kirchheimer, 'Germany: The Vanishing Opposition,' in Robert A. Dahl, ed., *Political Oppositions in Western Democracies* (New Haven, 1966), pp. 237–59.

5. John Armstrong, 'Collaborationism in World War II: The Integral Nationalist variant in Eastern Europe', in *Journal of Modern History*, vol. 40, no. 3 (September, 1968), pp. 396–410.

6. Franz Borkenau, *The Communist International* (London, 1938), p. 374.

7. Let us emphasize that an explanation of fascism on the basis of the distinctive Italian historical, social, intellectual context is not incompatible with interpretations of fascism based on some common characteristics of certain European societies present to a heightened degree in Italy. Perhaps without

the additional distinctively Italian factors, the first fascist movement would not have become so powerful, would not have developed some of its more appealing features, its unique style, and without success in a west European society, there would not have been a paradigmatic model to serve as a source of legitimation and ideas for weaker tendencies of similar character and for extremist nationalists in less advanced and 'central' societies. Methodologically the problem has some similarity with that of the origins of capitalism in the Weberian tradition. Without an unique constellation of circumstances, the first capitalism might not have emerged when and as it did; but once it did, it was easier in other societies with functionally equivalent or alternative conditions, to grow.

We cannot summarize here the interesting early Italian contributions to an interpretation of fascism as an Italian phenomenon. See Ernst Nolte, *Theorien über den Faschismus* (Cologne, 1967), pp. 18–34, for a review of the writings of Zibordi, Nanni, Labriola, Gobetti, Salvatorelli, Croce, and among the Germans Hermann Heller, to which we would add the Italo-German Robert Michels. Three Italian works, Renzo de Felice, *Il Fascismo. Le interpretazioni dei contemporanei e degli storici* (Bari, 1970); and Renzo de Felice, ed., *Il Fascismo e i partiti politici italiani. Testimonianze del 1921–1923* (Rocca San Casciano, 1966), reprint essays by contemporary figures and analysts ranging over the whole political spectrum, but all written before 1923; and Constanzo Casucci, ed., *Il Fascismo. Antologia di scritti critici* (Bologna, 1961) are indispensable.

Robert Michels, *Socialismus und Faschismus als politische Strömungen in Italien. Historische Studien* (Munich, 1925), particularly vol. 2, *Sozialismus und Faschismus in Italien*, provides an excellent background with particular emphasis on the early fusion of the socialists and nationalists and the revolutionary romantic heritage, and the social structure facilitating those developments. Let us not forget, to give one example, that the Garibaldi redshirts were the first shirts that became a political symbol. His analysis of the links between the demographic pressures and the birth of imperialism represented by Nationalism and the thought of Corradini is particularly interesting.

The early Italian interpretations emphasizing the economic under-development, the weakness of the capitalist bourgeoisie, the dual economy, the lack of social integration of the recently unified state, the peculiar position of sectors of the intelligentsia and the educated, the weakness of the state, the problems of resistance of a new working class to industrial discipline, etc., are obviously relevant to understand an authoritarian, partly fascist response to their problems in semi-developed countries in the so-called third world today.

The analysis of Arthur Rosenberg, a Marxist scholar, in 'Der Faschismus als Massenbewegung, Sein Aufstieg und seine Zersetzung', reprinted in Wolfgang Abendroth, ed., *Faschismus und Kapitalismus* (Frankfurt a. M., 1968), pp. 93–114, in his specific analysis but not in his general theoretical position, summarizes well that Italian development.

8. Michael Arthur Ledeen, *Universal Fascism. The Theory and Practice of the Fascist International, 1928–1936* (New York, 1972).

9. To give some examples: while it would be possible to attribute the failure of the British Union of Fascists, despite the personality of its leader Mosley, to the blatantly imitative character of the movement, the same would not be true for the Spanish fascists who despite a capable leadership could not rally even an effective nucleus of party cadres and sympathizers and, even less, an electoral support.

10. Andrew C. Janos, 'The One-Party State and Social Mobilization: East Europe between the Wars', pp. 204–36, and Juan J. Linz, 'From Falange to Movimiento-Organización: The Spanish Single Party and the Franco Regime, 1936–1968', in Samuel P. Huntington and Clement H. Moore, eds., *Authoritarian Politics in Modern Society* (New York, 1970), pp. 128–203. Let us note that this distinction between fascism and authoritarian régimes and military dictatorships was made by early Marxist analysts, like Clara Zetkin (1923) and Ignazio Silone (1934). See E. Nolte, *Theorien über den Faschismus*, pp. 23, 55, and 88–9.

11. Action Française poses a special problem. It is certainly not a typical fascist movement, but it also has affinities with fascism rightly stressed by Ernst Nolte in *Three Faces of Fascism. Action Française, Italian Fascism, National Socialism* (New York 1969, first published in German, Munich, 1964). It is, however, distinct, by the central place given initially to royalism, while other fascist movements were in principle republican, even when they, like Mussolini, ended accepting the monarchy. This combined with the anti-democratic social élitism, the original identification with Catholicism, the support among traditional sectors of society, particularly the nobility, distinguishes it from the basically more plebeian and generally more secular fascist movements. However, the activism of the Camelots du Roi, the anti-capitalist national socialist ideas inherited from Barrès, the willingness to risk a conflict with the Church, even its anti-Semitism, its romantic appeal to intellectuals, its relatively limited support for big business, the efforts of a Georges Valois to woo the workers, bring it closer to fascism than other conservative or reactionary parties, like the Deutschnationale Volkspartei (DNVP) or Renovación Española, that ideologically were strongly influenced by Action Française. In our view, it occupies even in time an intermediary position like the Italian Nationalism of Enrico Corradini that fused with fascism. We would consider Action Française, the Italian Nationalists and, perhaps, the German Alldeutscher Verband as proto-fascist movements. Their organization and in many respects their style, and above all their social bases were, however, quite distinct from fascist parties.

It is natural that Nolte, emphasizing rightly but perhaps excessively the ideological dimension of fascism, should include the Action Française in his purview. Since the movement led by Charles Maurras was an ideological movement that did not succeed to the same extent, let us say, as the DNVP or even Renovación Española to link with organized interest groups, it was closer to the primacy of politics, the 'politique d'abord' of fascism that so often conceived politics 'like a religion'. The same is largely true for the Italian Nationalists. In addition, in terms of ideology, Drumont and Barrès were in many respects closer to the fascists than the more intellectual Maurras.

12. Stanley G. Payne, 'Spanish Fascism in Comparative Perspective', in *Iberian Studies*, vol. II, no. 1 (Spring 1973), pp. 3–12.

13. We certainly would not compare the social composition of the Communist Party of the USSR with that of the Italian or French Communist Party. In the same way it makes little sense to compare the social basis of the NSDAP or the PNF in power with fascist parties before taking power. On the contrary, it would make a lot of sense to compare those parties while in power and before the *Machtergreifung* and perhaps also with Communist Parties in power, since in both cases the fact that the party is the government party with major tasks assigned to it in the state is likely to attract significant membership from similar groups: civil servants, teachers, officers, the younger generation emerging out of the Komsomol or Hitler-Jugend, etc.

14. It should be noted that this essay does not attempt to review the ideological, sociological, and socio-psychological interpretations of fascism – latu sensu – a task already performed. See Ernst Nolte, *Theorien über den Faschismus*, in his introductory essay, pp. 12–75; Renzo de Felice, *Le Interpretazioni del Fascismo* (Bari, 1969), with particular emphasis on the Italian analyses. See also A. James Gregor, *Interpretations of Fascism* (Morristown, N.J., 1974). The work of Nolte, *Three Faces of Fascism*, has provoked a lively discussion which he reviews in: *Die Krise des liberalen Systems und die faschistischen Bewegungen* (Munich, 1968), pp. 432–58. A recent contribution to the debate is the collection 'Faschismus Theorien' first published in *Das Argument*, and translated in *International Journal of Politics* (Winter 1972–73). The collection of papers by Otto Bauer, Herbert Marcuse, Arthur Rosenberg, August Thalheimer, and Angelo Tasca, edited by Wolfgang Abendroth, *Faschismus und Kapitalismus*, is useful for the more sophisticated Marxist interpretations. A good analysis with reference to empirical data from this perspective is Eike Henning, *Thesen zur deutschen Sozial- und Wirtschaftsgeschichte 1933 bis 1938* (Frankfurt a.M., 1973).

15. The German neo-Nazis have attracted considerable attention. See John David Nagle, *The National Democratic Party. Right Radicalism in the Federal Republic of Germany* (Berkeley and Los Angeles, 1970); E. K. Scheuch and H. D. Klingemann have written a number of detailed reports on the sociology of the NPD vote published in mimeograph form by the Köln Institut für Vergleichende Sozialforschung, Zentralarchiv für empirische Sozialforschung, 1967, 1969, and later the Forschungsinstitut der Konrad-Adenauer Stiftung. For detailed references *see* Erwin K. Scheuch, *Politischer Extremismus in der Bundesrepublik*, forthcoming; Reinhard Kühnl, Rainer Rilling, Christine Sager, *Die NPD Struktur, Ideologie und Funktion einer neofaschistischen Partei* (Frankfurt a.M., 1969); Peter von Oertzen, *Soziologische und Psychologische Struktur der Wähler und Mitgliedschaft der NPD* (Hanover, 1967). For an earlier neo-Nazi party see Otto

Busch and Peter Furth, *Rechtsradikalismus im Nachkriegsdeutschland* (Berlin, 1957). In contrast, the much more politically important Movimento Sociale Italiano has been neglected by scholarship. Frank L. Casale, University of Kentucky, is preparing a monograph on the MSI.

16. Ernst Nolte 'Nationalsozialismus im Urteil Mussolinis und Hitlers' in *Faschismus-Nationalsozialismus. Ergebnisse und Referate der sechsten italienisch-deutschen Historiker Tagung in Trier, 1963* (Braunschweig, 1964), pp. 60–72. Klaus-Peter Hoepke, *Die deutsche Rechte und der italienische Faschismus* (Düsseldorf, 1968), pp. 125–240. See also on fascism and Nazi racism Renzo de Felice, *Storia degli ebrei italiani sotto il fascismo* (Turin, 1961); Joseph Goebbels, *Der Faschismus und seine praktischen Ergebnisse* (Schriften der Deutschen Hochschule für Politik, Heft 1) (Berlin, 1934). George Mosse, *The Crisis of German Ideology. Intellectual Origins of the Third Reich* (New York, 1964), pp. 312–17, offers important insights into the profound differences between National Socialism and other fascisms, and the criticism by other fascists of the German variant. In that context the confused work by Otto Strasser, *Der Faschismus, Geschichte und Gefahr* (Munich, 1965), pp. 71–82, on 'Faschismus und Nationalsozialismus' which interprets Hitlerism as fascism but attempts to save a distinct national-socialist tradition he links with Masaryk, emphasizing the socially progressive versus the conversative tendencies, should also be mentioned.

17. Renzo de Felice, *Storia degli ebrei italiani*, the major study on the problem.

18. Let us not forget that the Romanian Iron Guard, the Hungarian Arrow Cross, the Estonian Vabadussõ jalaste Liit, the Latvian *Ugunkrust* (which changed its name to *Perkondrust*), the Ação Integralista Brasileira, and other minor parties, were persecuted or outlawed by authoritarian régimes. Democracies also imposed restrictions on fascist parties, for example: several of the top leaders of the Falange, including José Antonio Primo de Rivera and Onésimo Redondo, were in jail in March 1936 and party headquarters were closed.

19. Ramiro Ledesma Ramos, *Fascismo en España? Discurso a las juventudes de España*, pp. 53, 55.

20. Lackó Miklós, *Nyilasok Nemzetiszicialisták 1935–1944* (Budapest, 1966), and *Arrow-Cross Men. National Socialists 1935–1944* (Budapest, 1969).

21. Nicholas M. Nagy-Talavera, *The Green Shirts and the Others. A History of Fascism in Hungary and Rumania* (Stanford, 1970); Eugen Weber, 'The Men of the Archangel', in Walter Laqueur and George L. Mosse, eds., *International Fascism, 1920–1945* (New York, 1966), pp. 101–26.

22. The question of anti-modernism and fascism is a moot one and deserves more research. There can be no doubt that a number of fascist movements romanticized pre-industrial social structures, the peasant, the artisan, the soldier, and rejected urban, industrial, commercial values and styles of life. In their rejection of cosmopolitanism, commercialism, consumerism, and their appeal for a return to nature, they coincided with the peasantist

ideologists, with certain brands of populism and powerful intellectual currents at the turn of the century. They were particularly articulate in Germany, as Klaus Bergmann has shown in his *Agrarromantik und Grossstadtfeindlichkeit* (Meisenheim am Glan, 1970). See particularly pp. 277–366. It would seem that, with some exceptions like Onésimo Redondo in the provincial Castilian city of Valladolid, that this ruralist outlook was more characteristic of German, Nordic, and east European fascism than of its western manifestations. It certainly would not be true for British fascism, Ramiro Ledesma Ramos, Rex, and particularly Mussolini. Let us not forget that Franz Borkenau linked fascism with the requirements for industrialization of less developed countries, an interpretation that led him to reject the possibility of Hitler coming to power in an article that appeared days after the *Machtergreifung*. In this context the work by Juan Velarde Fuertes, *El Nacionalsindicalismo cuarenta años después* (*análisis crítico*) (Madrid, 1972), deserves to be mentioned as an analysis of the economic thought of Spanish fascism. We should not forget that the nationalism, the concern with dependency from the plutocratic capitalist democracies, the expansionism and the commitment to military preparedness, the concern for planning for collective purposes, inevitably pushed fascists towards industrialization policy. It is no accident that Mihail Manoilescu, an engineer-economist, sympathizer with the Iron Guard, author of one of the most interesting books on the single parties of the thirties, should also have been one of the first formulators of a theory about the unequal relationship between agrarian societies and the advanced industrial countries. Finally, we cannot ignore the futurist passion for technology, shared by Mussolini, and following him by other fascist leaders. In view of all this, we would not include 'anti-modernism' in our definition of fascism. On this question see Henry Ashby Turner, Jr, 'Fascism and Modernization', *World Politics*, no. 24 (4 July 1972), pp. 547–64, the critique by A. James Gregor, 'Fascism and Modernization: Some Addenda', *World Politics*, vol. 26, no. 3 (April 1974), pp. 370–84, and Turner's response 'Fascism and Modernization: A Few Corrections', in the same journal (forthcoming).

23. For a better understanding of the ideological commitments of fascism and the impossibility of overcoming sociological obstacles that it faced, it is particularly interesting to study the numerous groupuscules attempting to combine nationalism against Versailles and the western plutocratic democracies with genuine social revolutionary aspirations, and the left dissidents from Hitler-dominated national socialism. On these groups, see Otto Ernst Schüddekopf, *Linke Leute von rechts. Die nationalrevolutionären Minderheiten und der Kommunismus in der Weimarer Republik* (Stuttgart, 1969), and Karl O. Paetel, *Versuchung oder Chance? Zur Geschichte des deutschen Nationalbolschewismus 1918/1932* (Göttingen, 1965). Unfortunately, due to the small size of those groups, their lack of electoral presence, and their later fate, the information on their efforts to gain a social base and the social composition of their following in contrast to their ideological disputes have been little studied. The fact that they were late-latecomers to a scene domin-

ated by the KPD and the NSDAP in addition to the democratic parties made their efforts quite futile, but tells us much about the failure of left fascism, and national communism, in advanced societies with electoral and organizational mass politics.

There is a parallelism in the sympathy of some other dissident national socialists with the national Bolshevists, in the comments of Ramiro Ledesma Ramos in *Fascismo en España*, pp. 66–67, about Joaquín Maurin, a leader of dissident communism in Catalonia and later of the POUM (Partido Obrero de Unificación Marxista), under the heading 'Un nacionalismo obrero español?'. Tragically for those men, fascism as a party of national integration confronted with an already organized working class and with a more articulate Marxist ideological heritage, could be nothing but a radicalism of the centre often condemned to be coopted by the right. It is important to note how the fascist left in Germany, for example, Otto Strasser and Ledesma Ramos, increasingly reject the label fascist to avoid being confused with Italian fascism whose conservative social character they perceived and criticized.

24. See for example Ramiro Ledesma Ramos, *Fascismo en España*, p. 62: 'In our epoch, in our own days, national revolutions develop with unbelievable success. See these names that represent them: Mussolini, Kemal, Hitler, and – why not – Stalin,' and pp. 288–91 on 'Bolshevism, Russian Nationalist Revolution'. Similar statements can be found among the left of nazism which favoured an eastern orientation in German foreign policy and a Bund of the oppressed nations, including the USSR; see Reinhard Kühnl, *Die nationalsozialistische Linke, 1925–1930* (Meisenheim am Glan, 1966), pp. 38, 118–26. In Italy, James Gregor, 'On understanding Fascism: A Review of Some Contemporary Literature', *American Political Science Review*, vol. 67, no. 4 (1973), pp. 1332–47, n. 36, quotes the following articles: Agostino Nasti, 'L'Italia, il bolcevismo, la Russia', *Critica Fascista* (15 March 1937), pp. 162–3; Tomaso Napolitano, 'Il fascismo di Satlin ovvero l'URSS e noi', *Critica Fascista* (15 October 1937), pp. 396–8; Berto Ricci, 'Il fascismo di Stalin', *Critica Fascista* (15 July 1937), pp. 317–19.

25. Luigi Salvatorelli, *Nazionalfascismo* (Turin, 1923), selection reprinted in de Felice, *Il Fascismo. Le interpretazioni . . .*, pp. 54–63, see also pp. 59–61.

26. Theodor Geiger, 'Die Mittelschichten und die Sozialdemokratie', *Die Arbeit*, 8 (1931), pp. 617–35.

27. Max H. Kele, *Nazis and Workers. National Socialist Appeals to German Labor, 1919–1933* (Chapel Hill, N.C., 1972); Joseph Nyomarkay, *Charisma and Factionalism in the Nazi Party* (Minneapolis, 1967), pp. 74–135, provides evidence on the orientation toward the working class of the 'Working Association of the North and West' and the later shift toward other constituencies; Dietrich Orlow, *The History of the Nazi Party: 1919–1933*, 2 vols. (Pittsburgh, 1969 and 1973), vol. I, 1917–1933, chap. 4, 1926–1928, 'The Failure of the Urban Plan', pp. 76–127, and chap. 5, 1928–1930, 'Socialism: That is really an unfortunate word', pp. 128–85, is a good history of the internal evolution of the party and its changing orientation. The fail-

ure to gain the support of the working class is well reflected in the membership figures for the NSBO despite their growth from approximately 3,000 in
January 1931 to 294,042 in December 1932 when we compare them with the
membership of the trade unions (p. 167 vs. pp. 163–6) and the lack of success
in work council elections even after being in power (pp. 126–9), in Hans-
Gerd Schumann, *Nationalsozialismus und Gewerkschaftsbewegung* (Han-
nover, 1958). On 1935 industrial elections, see also Theodor Eschenburg,
'Streiflichter zur Geschichte der Wahlen im Dritten Reich', *Vierteljahreshefte für Zeitgeschichte* (3 July 1955), pp. 311–16.

28. Theodor Geiger, *Die soziale Schichtung des deutschen Volkes. Sozio-
graphischer Versuch auf statisticher Grundlage* (Stuttgart, 1932). On Geiger's
work see Paolo Farneti, *Theodor Geiger e la coscienza della società industriale* (Turin, 1966).

29. Walter B. Simon, 'The Political Parties of Austria', (Ph.D. diss.,
Columbia University, 1957).

30. Ramiro Ledesma Ramos, *Fascismo en España*, pp. 238–40, 260–63.

31. Not only many Nazis played with pseudo-religious or non-Christian
conceptions as the cases of Szálasi in Hungary, Celmiņš in Latvia and Quisling in Norway show.

32. Ramiro Ledesma Ramos, *Fascismo en España*, pp. 283–7: 'Geneva reactionary trench, Geneva metropolitan capital of French Imperialism'.

33. It would be important to analyse how the anti-fascism of liberals, the
socialist left, manipulated and simplified by the communists and, after the
rise to power of Hitler, by Jewish groups, particularly at the time of the
Spanish Civil War, contributed to create a greater sense of common identity
and affinity of fascist movements, to overcome serious conflicts of national
interest and differences in ideology, particularly on the issue of racial anti-
Semitism and to bring Mussolini closer to Hitler. In this there is some similarity with the identification of communists with Stalinist communism rather
than a polycentrism in the years of cold-war anti-communism.

In addition the readiness of the left to prevent fascist propaganda by all
means contributed to reinforce the proclivity for violence of fascists, even
where the leaders did not particularly glory in it.

34. Dionisio Ridruejo, *Escrito en España* (Buenos Aires, 1962), p. 79,
quoted in Juan J. Linz, 'From Falange to Movimiento Organización . . . ',
p. 136.

35. See the excellent analysis of the variety of *corporativisms* in Philippe
Schmitter, 'Still the Century of Corporatism?', *Review of Politics* (January
1974), pp. 85–131.

36. William Salomone, *Italian Democracy in the Making. The Political
Scene in the Giolittian Era 1900–1914* (Philadelphia, 1945), and the extensive
literature on Mosca, Pareto, Sorel, Michels, and their influence.

37. Enrique Tierno Galván, 'Costa y el regeneracionismo', *Escritos 1950–
1960* (Madrid, 1971), pp. 369–539. A comparative historico-sociological
study of intellectual critiques of liberal-democracy-parliamentarism at the

turn of the century in different countries would be an important contribution to intellectual and political history.

38. The history of how the urban-intellectual-youthful-interventionist and in many aspects still radical fascism linked with the agrarian reaction to socialist trade union and party dominance in the Po Valley remains to be written. Mario Missiroli, 'Il Fascismo e la crisi italiana' (1921), pp. 293–357, in Renzo de Felice, ed., *Il Fascismo e i partiti politici italiani*, provides many insights into that socio-economic-political context. The many local histories of fascism and its heroes, and the recent works on the popular struggle of the left against fascism, provide a wealth of information that could be linked with data on property, tenancy, wages, changes in economic relations, overtime, elections, etc., in those areas. See Albert Szymanski, 'Fascism, Industrialism and Socialism: The Case of Italy', *Comparative Studies in Society and History*, vol. XV, no. 4 (October 1973), pp. 395–404, for an excellent ecological analysis of fascist violence in relation to rural socialist strength. Manfredo de Simone, ed., *PNF. Pagine Eroiche della Rivoluzione Fascista* (Milano, 1925) for accounts of incidents and biographical sketches of dead fascists. Friedrich Vochting, *Die Romagna. Eine Studie über Halbpacht und Landarbeiterwesen in Italien* (Karlsruhe, 1927), an excellent study of social relations in the area, the historical background, the political alignments, etc. Frank M. Snowden, 'On the Social Origins of Agrarian Fascism in Italy', *European Journal of Sociology*, vol. 13, no. 2 (1972), pp. 268–95, is an excellent study of rural social conflicts and their political consequences with references to numerous recent Italian monographic and local studies. See also Luigi Preti, *Lotte Agrarie nella Valle Padana* (Torino, 1955), pp. 371–477; Walter Zanotti, 'Lotte Agrarie nel Primo Dopoguerra nella Provincia di Forli e le Origini del Fascismo', Ilva Vaccari, 'Il Sorgere del Fascismo nel Modenese', and Bruno Casonato, 'Agli Inizi del Fascismo Parmense', all three in Luciano Casali, ed., *Movimento Operaio e Fascismo nell'Emilia Romagna* (Roma, 1973); Alessandro Roveri, *Dal Sindacalismo Rivoluzionario al Fascismo. Capitalismo Agrario e Socialismo nel Ferrarese. (1870–1920)*, p. 297 ff.; A. Roveri, 'Il Fascismo Ferrarese nel 1919–1920', *Annali* (Milano, 1972), pp. 106–54; Mario Vaini, *Le Origini del Fascismo a Mantova* (Roma, 1961), pp. 54–154; Renato Zangheri, ed., *Le Campagne Emiliane nell'Epoca Moderna* (Milano, 1957), p. 273 ff. Dora Marucco, 'Note sulla Mezzadria all'Avvento del Fascismo', *Rivista di Storia Contemporanea*, 3 (1974), pp. 377–88; Emilio Sereni, 'L'Agricultura Toscana e la messadrina nel Regime Fascista e l'Opera di Arrigo Serpieri', in the collective volume, *La Toscana nel Regime Fascista*, 2 vols. (Firenze, 1971), vol. II, p. 316 ff.; Rodolfo Cavandoli, *Le Origini del Fascismo a Reggio Emilia* (Roma, 1972), passim; Simona Colarizi, *Dopoguerra e Fascismo in Puglia (1919–1926)* (Bari, 1971), passim.

39. The link between nationalism, imperialism, and the discovery by Corradini of the idea of the proletarian nation, with the problems of emigration of a country without colonies, was first emphasized by Robert Michels,

L'Imperialismo italiano, Studi politico demografici (Milan, 1914; first published in German, 1912). The importance of protest against the African adventures in the radicalization of Italian and Spanish labour, and perhaps in France too, has never been studied. William Sheridan Allen, 'The Appeal of Fascism and the Problem of National Disintegration', in Henry A. Turner, Jr., ed., *Reappraisals of Fascism* (New York, 1975), has emphasized the role of incomplete national integration, becoming visible with the First World War and the conflict over interventionism in Italy and the war goals in Germany, in the emergence of fascism.

40. This point is highly debated among historians; see Guenther Roth, *The Social Democrats in Imperial Germany* (Totowa, N.J., 1963).

41. Heinrich August Winkler, *Mittelstand, Demokratie und Nationalsozialismus, Die Politische Entwicklung von Handwerk und Kleinhandel in der Weimarer Republik* (Cologne, 1972), chap. 8, 'Mittelstand und Nationalsozialismus', pp. 157–82 has noted how the Marxist interpretation linking capitalism and fascism is insufficient, how the radicalization of certain middle-class property owners requires additional explanation. In that context he writes:

the lack of a successful bourgeois revolution that would have overcome the institutional and ideological elements of pre-industrial society would be one. Formulated positively, fascist movements had special opportunities for success where pre-industrial power holders, mainly the nobility, the military, the bureaucracy, the Church, could save their privileges beyond the industrial revolution and gain a determining influence on other social groups. Schumpeter, who seriously failed to understand imperialism as a general phenomenon when he defined it as the objective predisposition of a state to forceful expansion without definable limits, with that analysis hit on fascism, *malgré lui*, much better. He called attention to the decisive role of pre-industrial feudal elements in the attempts of quasi-objectless expansion. (p. 162).

Winkler's interpretation differs from ours, but is in part complementary.

42. Sten S. Nilson, 'Wahlsoziologische Probleme des Nationalsozialismus', *Zeitschrift für die gesamten Staatswissenschaften*, 110, Bd. 2 (1954), pp. 297–311.

43. Juan J. Linz, 'The Social Bases of West German Politics' (Ph.D. diss., Columbia University, 1959), p. 772, shows how farmers supporting the SPD in 1953 were more socially isolated in terms of their number of acquaintances. Chap. 24, pp. 753–90 on post-Second World War German farmers' politics analyses some of the social and political attitudes of farmers that must have facilitated their susceptibility to the Nazi appeal or the persistence of attitudes acquired in the thirties.

44. For an example of border nationalism-fascism, see Elio Apih, *Italia, Fascismo e Anti-fascismo nella Venezia Giulia (1918–1943), Ricerche Storiche* (Bari, 1966), passim. For example in Trieste the list including the fascists received 45.3 per cent of the votes, with 8.8 per cent going to Slavic candidates, 20.0 per cent communists, 25.9 per cent for other Italian parties. In Istria the proportions were respectively 56.9 per cent, 19.4 per cent, 7.3 per

cent, 16.3 per cent (see p. 162). This pattern has a continuity in the electoral strength of the MSI in the 1944 municipal elections in Trieste with 10,170 votes, 9.4 per cent among 106,872 votes for Italian parties. See François Duprat, *L'Ascension du M.S.I.* (Paris, 1972), p. 43. Another example of nationalistic-border area fascism was the Styrian Heimatschutz; see Bruce Frederick Pauley, 'Hahnenschwanz and Swastika: The Styrian Heimatschutz and Austrian National Socialism 1918–1934' (Ph.D. diss., University of Rochester, 1967). The Styrian Heimatschutz was the largest single segment of the entire Austrian Heimwehr – the native non-Nazi fascist organization – whose leaders and members later would fuse with the Austrian NSDAP. It was also the area of greatest Hitler-Jugend strength. In Carinthia, Styria and Salzburg – three border regions – the Korneuburg declaration, with its fascist ideology, was received most favourably, in contrast to the response of the Upper Austrian leadership. For an ecological analysis of Carinthian and Styrian border area support for nazism, see Walter B. Simon, 'Political Parties of Austria'. The appeal of Doriot's PPF to the colons in Algeria shows the success of the combination of nationalism with social reform to those self-made upward mobile immigrants in a cultural border position, particularly in Oran where many of the colons were assimilated Spanish immigrants. In addition the colons felt threatened by communist anti-colonialism (see Dieter Wolf, *Die Doriot-Bewegung* [Stuttgart, 1967], pp. 135–6). The Mussert-led Nazi party also found considerable support among Dutch residents in Indonesia (2,000 of 29,000 members, 1940), and one of the most important leaders, van Tonningens, was born there as son of an officer; see Konrad Kwiet, 'Zur Geschichte der Mussert Bewegung', *Vierteljahreshefte für Zeitgeschichte*, no. 18 (1970), pp. 164–95.

45. Jean Stengers, 'Belgium', in Hans Rogger and Eugen Weber, eds., *The European Right. A Historical Profile* (Berkeley and Los Angeles, 1966), pp. 128–67. R. Baes, *Joris van Severen. Une Ame* (Zulte, 1965), for a sympathetic biography of the leader of Verdinaso. Jean-Michel Etienne, *Le Mouvement Rexiste jusqu'en 1940* (Paris, 1968).

46. Ricardo de la Cierva, *Historia de la Guerra Civil española, Antecedentes, Monarquía y República, 1898–1936* (Madrid, 1969), pp. 284–91.

47. Jan Havránek, 'Fascism in Czechoslovakia', pp. 47–55 and Joseph F. Zacek, 'Czechoslovak Fascisms', pp. 52–62, in Peter F. Sugar, ed., *Native Fascism in the Successor States 1918–1945* (Santa Barbara, Calif., 1971). The same dominant position of the Serbs and Poles in their victor states account for their resistance to the appeal of fascism or fascisticized nationalism.

48. The literature on Slovak nationalism and the politics of independent Slovakia is highly partisan and provides practically no information on the social bases of parties and the fascist wing emerging in the nationalist movement. Yeshayahu Andrew Jelinek, 'Hlinka's Slovak People's Party, 1939–1945' (Ph.D. diss., Indiana University, 1966), is a competent review of the history and the factional fights.

49. Theodor Abel, *The Nazi Movement* (New York, 1965) (first published

1938 as *Why Hitler came to power*). For a unique socio-psychological analysis see Peter H. Merkl, *Political Violence under the Swastika: 581 Early Nazis* (Princeton, 1975).

50. The appeal to youth is central to Ledesma Ramos, *Discurso a las juventudes de España*, pp. 269–77. Let us not forget that the Italian Fascist anthem was Giovinezza (youth).

51. The symbolic significance of uniforms is discussed by ibid., pp. 332–4. A systematic and comparative study of fascist symbolism still remains to be written.

52. On the German youth movement, its ideology and style as well as the partial affinity with fascism, see Walter Z. Laqueur, *Young Germany. A History of the German Youth Movement* (London, 1962); George L. Mosse, *The Crisis of German Ideology*, chap. 9, pp. 171–89; Peter H. Merkl on the youth movement background of Nazis in the Abel collection of biographies (forthcoming); Peter Loewenberg, 'The Psycho-Historical Origins of the Nazi Youth Cohort', *American Historical Review*, 76 (1971), pp. 1457–1502, is an interesting, even when sometimes highly speculative, attempt to link the historico-socio-economic experiences of different German age cohorts with their political expressions introducing psychological intervening variables.

The average age of the NSDAP members in 1923, studied by Michael H. Kater, 'Zur Soziographie der frühen NSDAP', *Vierteljahreshefte für Zeitgeschichte*, no. 19 (1971), p. 159, ranged for different occupational groups around the mean of 28 years, from 25 for the white-collar employees (*Angestellte*), 26–27 for workers and *Handwerker,* to 33 for businessmen, 35 for army officers, 39 for the higher civil servants and *leitende Angestellte* (upper white collar), a good indication of the youthfulness even of those in slower career lines. Only the welfare recipients were an older group, with an average of 44 years. Apparently, they were somewhat younger than the founding nucleus studied by Franz-Willing for 1920 whose age was 30 to 32, indicating that new members were younger and shaped by the *Fronterlebnis*. The 48 per cent male members 23 years or younger certainly could not have been integrated in the parties of pre-war. The north German members, particularly the rural supporters, were even younger, while the Munich contingent was older (67 per cent over 23) which might contribute to explain its 'old-fashioned' anti-Semitic character and the more anti-class Gemeinschaft radicalism of the northern wing. Between 1930 and 1933 the youthful component seems to have increased.

53. Ernst Posse, *Die politischen Kampfbünde Deutschlands* (Berlin, 1931), and Robert G. L. Waite, *Vanguard of Nazism. The Free Corps Movement in Postwar Germany 1918–1923* (Cambridge, Mass., 1952).

54. On the differential appeal of National Socialists and the Zentrum to women, see Herbert Tingsten, *Political Behavior*, *Studies in Election Statistics* (London, 1937), pp. 41–71.

55. The names of D'Annunzio, Balbo, Bono, Goering, Mosley, Ruiz de Alda, come to mind.

56. The biographies of the founders of communist parties also suggest a generational basis for the split of the socialist movement and that the war experience, opposition to war, participation in soldiers' protests and councils, must have contributed to the radicalization of the left. See the data on age composition of the KPD leadership and biographies in Hermann Weber, *Die Wandlung des deutschen Kommunismus. Die Stalinisierung der KPD in der Weimarer Republik*, 2 vols. (Frankfurt a.M., 1969).

57. The impact of the Ruhr occupation is well documented in the Merkl monograph. It was that experience that led Karl Radek to his famous Schlageter speech and, incidentally, to his more sophisticated analysis of the fascist phenomenon.

58. On the demobilization process with all its economic and indirectly political implications, see Giorgio Rochat, *L'Esercito Italiano da Vittorio Veneto a Mussolini (1919–1925)* (Bari, 1967), pp. 26–7, 170–83. In June 1919 there were 85,891 reserve officers – *officiali di complemento* – of whom 59,732 were discharged by March 1920, leaving some 26,000, many garrisoned in cities, to be able to engage in private activities or with two to four months' leave to take university examinations. By summer 1922 they would be some 4,000. The border tensions particularly with Yugoslavia retained many men under arms, in an area where they could be politicized. In addition the number of professional officers fluctuated from 14,509 in 1910 to 21,926 in December 1918 to 1,500 foreseen in the *ordinamento* of 1920 (see chap. VII, 'I rapporti tra Fascismo e Esercito', in p. 185, in ibid.).

59. Hélgio Henrique Casses Trindade, *Integralismo (O fascismo brasileiro na década de 30)* (São Paulo, 1974). Available in French as *L'Action Intégraliste Brésilienne. Un Mouvement de type fasciste des années 30*, Thèse pour le Doctorat de Recherches, Fondation Nationale des Sciences Politiques, Cycle Supérieur d'Etudes Politiques (Paris, 1971).

60. Alastair Hamilton, *The Appeal of Fascism. A Study of Intellectuals and Fascism 1919–1945* (New York, 1971).

61. Gabriel Almond, *The Appeals of Communism* (Princeton, 1954).

62. Rudolf Heberle, *Landbevölkerung und Nationalsozialismus. Eine soziologische Untersuchung der politischen Willensbildung in Schleswig-Holstein 1918–1932* (Stuttgart, 1963). Horst Gies, 'NSDAP und landwirtschaftliche Organisationen in der Endphase der Weimarer Republik', *Vierteljahreshefte für Zeitgeschichte*, XV (October 1967), pp. 341–76; Jeremy Noakes, *The Nazi Party in Lower Saxony 1921–1933* (Oxford, 1971); Peter Wulf, *Die politische Haltung des schleswigholsteinischen Handwerks 1928–1932* (Cologne, 1969), pp. 56–7, 96–9.

For a theoretical analysis, see Rainer Lepsius, 'The Collapse of an Intermediary Power Structure: Germany 1933–1934', *International Journal of Comparative Sociology*, vol. IX, no. 3–4 (September–December 1968), pp. 289–301. For an excellent account of events in a north German town, William Sheridan Allan, *The Nazi Seizure of Power. The Experience of a Single German Town 1930–1935* (Chicago, 1965). Heinrich August Winkler, *Mittelstand, Demokratie und Nationalsozialismus. Die politische Entwicklung von*

Handwerk und Kleinhandel in der Weimarer Republik (Cologne, 1972), chap. 8, pp. 156–82, provides an analysis of the pre-*Machtergreifung Gleich-schaltung* through local and regional grassroots pressure of national interest groups.

63. The classic formulation is William Kornhauser, *The Politics of Mass Society* (Glencoe, Ill., 1959), who reviews the theoretical literature and empirical evidence relevant to it.

Part II
Italy and Germany

ADRIAN LYTTELTON

2   Italian Fascism

A guide to the literature on Italian fascism must start with the works of two men, Gaetano Salvemini and Angelo Tasca. Both had been deeply involved in politics before fascism forced them into exile. Both had previously been militants; Salvemini had left the socialist party to become an independent democrat, while Tasca had seceded from the communist party. They were each possessed of an unusual degree of intellectual independence and courage. Here the resemblance ends. Salvemini was a polemicist and moralist of passionate temperament; Tasca had a more prosaic and analytical mind. This contrast should not, however, be overdrawn. It is always necessary when reading Salvemini's works on fascism to remember their purpose. He saw himself as a front-line combatant in the war against the lies of fascist propagandists and the half-truths of their apologists. In his anxiety to prove that fascism was irrational and absurd, he perhaps comes close at times to making it incomprehensible in historical terms. For instance, his anxiety to prove that fascism did not save Italy from revolution arguably led him to underrate the gravity of the post-war crisis. He was prescient in his warnings that Mussolini's rhetoric about expansion and war must be taken seriously, because in the end he would be forced by the momentum of his own creation to try to translate words into action. But in Salvemini's work on Mussolini's foreign policy his determination to show Mussolini's irresponsibility and ignorance on every occasion is excessive.[1] In saying this, however, one is dealing with only one side of Salvemini. He was no mere polemicist, but a historian by vocation, with an enormous appetite for facts and great intellectual energy. The overriding lesson to be learnt from both Salvemini and Tasca is that it is the historian's duty to be concrete. They both insisted that there were no short-cuts to the understanding of fascism, in Italy or in general. Tasca warned his readers against the temptation of simple and abstract formulae: there were already, he wrote, too many conflicting 'definitions' of fascism, and he had no intention of adding to their number – 'For us, to define fascism is above all to write its history.'[2] Fascism was not static, but continually changing; and it was not an entity in itself but 'the resultant of a whole situation from which it cannot be separated.' Tasca's warning against the mania for definitions, which had particularly afflicted Marxists, should not however be read as an unqualified commitment to pure narrative history, or as a condemnation of the general concept of 'fascism'. Tasca recognizes clearly that, if we speak of fascism in general, and not just Italian fascism, we must use the comparative method 'to indicate a certain number of common characteristics susceptible of being incorporated into a general definition of fascism'.[3]

Salvemini's knowledge of Britain and America made him conscious of a different kind of danger. In the older and wealthier democracies there was a tendency, even among intellectuals, to regard fascism simply as a manifestation of 'racial instinct' or 'national character'. This, Salvemini said, was a mark of the 'lazy mind'; instead, 'if one wants to understand why democratic institutions collapsed in Italy or in France and are in jeopardy everywhere, one has to set aside a priori schemes and empty slogans and must ascertain why and how the fascist movement arose in a given country, what social groups contributed to it, why and how the struggle between fascists and anti-fascists developed, and why and how the fascists overcame their foes'.[4]

Fascism and liberalism: the problem of continuity

One of the problems most often debated has been that of the continuity between the liberal and the fascist régime. Did fascism represent a break with the past, or did it merely accentuate trends already evident? Was it a 'parenthesis', or a 'revelation' of the national past? The clarity of these alternatives is deceptive. They originate in slogans which their own authors did not perhaps believe wholeheartedly. Thus Piero Gobetti, the young theorist of the 'liberal revolution', who described fascism as the 'auto-biography of the nation', seems also to have been the first to describe fascism as a 'parenthesis'.[5] The problem of fascism is still a live one in Italy, and so the problem of continuity has two aspects, that of the continuity between liberal Italy and fascism, and that of the continuity between fascism and the Republic of today. The attitude of historians to the past is inevitably coloured by the present, and there is a tendency to identify these two different aspects of the question; but they are to some degree distinct.

How did the fascists themselves see this problem of continuity? The two most distinguished intellectuals of the régime, the philosopher Gentile and the historian Volpe, gave distinct but similar answers. Neither Gentile nor Volpe, it should be noted, had been fascists before Mussolini came to power in October 1922. As representatives of a broader tradition of conservative nationalism, they were particularly concerned with the problem of how to relate fascism to the Italian past. For Gentile, fascism represented the return to the heroic ideals of the Risorgimento.[6] It was the continuation of a struggle between the 'two souls' of Italy, the idealist spirit of Mazzini and the materialist scepticism of the liberal statesman Giovanni Giolitti, who had ruled Italy for most of the decade before the war. Both Gentile and Volpe saw 1915, when Italy intervened in the war, as a first decisive break, in which the forces of 'idealism', 'action', or 'will', had successfully revolted against the spirit of compromise. This element in the fascist interpretation of fascism does, I think, offer one valuable clue. The 'break' in Italian history took place as much in 1915, with the intervention crisis, as in 1922 with the March on Rome. The second common feature in the interpretations of Gentile and Volpe was the attempt to present fascism as the successor to socialism. They recognized, that is to say, that socialism and the rise of the masses had undermined the old liberal oligarchy. The fascist régime was a new synthesis, in which the new force of the masses would be finally identified with the patriotic ideal, which in the Risorgimento had been the belief only of minorities.

No anti-fascist could agree with Gentile or Volpe that Italian fascism fulfilled the kind of aspirations aroused by socialism.

Words like justice and equality were not part of the basic fascist vocabulary. But nonetheless Italian fascism did aspire to incorporate the masses in a new political structure. The communist leader Togliatti described fascism as a reactionary régime with mass support.[7] Insofar as this description is correct, it can be argued that such a régime did represent a break with the past. If one had to provide an equally synthetic definition of the régime which governed Italy until 1913–14 one could suggest that it was a 'progressive oligarchy'. But at this point the reader will probably already have remembered the warning of Tasca which I quoted at the beginning of this essay. Simple definitions do violence to the reality of history.

The problem of continuity needs to be seen in a comparative perspective. The deficiencies of the Italian political system before 1914, though real enough, sometimes look less remarkable when compared with the experience of other countries. The existence of a limited electorate until 1912 is one example. The obvious comparisons are with Germany on the one hand and with England and France on the other. Why did Italy and Germany go fascist while England and France remained democratic? A whole line of Marxist interpretations of Italian history has followed Lenin's hypothesis that one can distinguish a 'Prussian way' to capitalism, marked by the persistence of feudal residues and the alliance between aristocracy and bourgeoisie in a single power bloc, from an 'English way', in which the capitalist bourgeoisie at a decisive stage of its development attacks the aristocracy, destroys its feudal character, and eventually forces it into a subordinate position. Gramsci applied Lenin's theory to Italy, and his interpretation has served as the basis for more recent works by Marxist scholars. Particularly worthy of note are E. Sereni's works on agrarian history, and an article by G. Procacci.[8] More recently a young Marxist historian N. Tranfaglia has re-examined the question, arguing that the Italian way to capitalism essentially resembled the German and differed from the French and English. One may not feel entirely convinced by the traditional arguments put forward to prove this point. One might argue equally well that Italy was like France in that the bourgeoisie and middle classes really had replaced the aristocracy as the ruling class, whereas in England as in Germany there was a condominium. In fact, Tranfaglia notes that 'the Giolittian experiment in the first ten years of the century appears as the reflection of the greater relative force of the Italian bourgeoisie compared to the German'.[9] However, the case can perhaps be made out in a modified form. It is rather striking that the three Axis nations – Germany, Italy and Japan – were all faced with similar problems in the second half of the nineteenth century. They were latecomers both in industrial and in national development; that is to say that they had to achieve industrialization and full national independence simultaneously. Each of these achievements was a condition of the other: for in an industrial age non-industrial states were client states, while industry could not develop without a large and protected market. The specifically economic reasons for the accentuated role of the state in the economic development of the 'latecomers' have been explained in a classic work by Gerschenkron (*Economic Backwardness in Historical Perspective*) – which makes full proviso for individual variations from the pattern. But in addition, when dealing with the political consequences of industrialization, one ought to emphasize the importance of the association between these two processes of institutional unification and industrialization. One can see this most clearly if one compares the Italian nationalist movement with the Action Française. The Italian nationalists were convinced that national self-assertion and industrial power were part of the same package; for the French the connection was less obvious, and therefore the thought of the Action Française remained traditionalist. The resemblance between Italy and Germany in this respect was latent until the war; it only became striking when in both countries the reaction to industrialization, in the shape of a powerful working-class movement, seemed to pose a decisive challenge to the ideals and structures of the unitary national state. Hence the rigidity of the ruling classes and the violence of the 'patriots' when faced with this dual threat.[10]

I am not sure how far the recognition of this similarity in Italian and German development implies, as some authors seem to think, an acceptance of the continuity thesis. Tranfaglia, for example, treats the Giolittian period, rather than fascism, as a 'parenthesis'. The intervention crisis marked a break with the Giolittian 'experiment', but this, he argues, merely signified a reversion to the dominance of the old power bloc. But was this really the case? The success of the interventionist movement was vitally dependent on the participation of new social forces, still overtly democratic or revolutionary in ideology. When the prime minister Salandra, the representative of the old power bloc par excellence, tried to ignore this reality, he fell from power. For Procacci, on the other hand, in the essay cited, the state of the wartime period 'marks a profound break with the liberal state'.[11] The concentration of industry, the increasingly close co-ordination between industry and the state, and the emancipation of the government and bureaucracy from all effective control by parliament – all foreshadowed the structures of the fascist régime. Of course the wartime régime was intended to be temporary; but the return to peacetime conditions was prevented by what R. Vivarelli has called 'the psychological reality of the war',[12] as well as by the weight of the new vested interests that it constituted.

The class struggle

The success of fascism in Italy was the consequence of a period of acute class struggle. This raises a number of problems. Why did the class struggle become so acute at this particular time? Why did various forms of mediation not succeed? And why were the fascists rather than their opponents victorious? Beyond these questions there is the problem of the weakness of the Italian state.

The origins of the accentuated class tension in Italy go back to the period between the Libyan and the Great War. Although there are a number of useful histories of Italian socialism,[13] there has as yet been no real study of the social base of the *massimalisti*, as the revolutionary wing of the Italian socialists were known. The only studies which really succeed in showing the relationship between the politics of the working-class movement and its social base are those of Procacci, but these only deal with the first years of the century. However, a good history of the trade union movement has appeared recently.[14] L. Lotti's book on the 'Red Week' of June 1914 (*La settimana rossa*) shows the success of Mussolini's new tactics and style of oratory in mobilizing the disorganized, and the doubts which other socialists had about this process. The classic judgements of Tasca and Nenni on the failings of the socialist leadership in the postwar period have not been, and perhaps cannot be, refuted; but there have been a number of attempts to rehabilitate the leader of the socialist party, Serrati, and Gramsci's ultra-left antagonist in the Communist Party, Bordiga.[15] The best argument that can be made out for the leaders of Italian socialism is that they faithfully reflected the moods and attitudes of their followers. Popular discontent expressed itself spontaneously and the leaders were often powerless to restrain it; while the democratic traditions of the party precluded the acceptance without question of any unitary strategy imposed from above. Moreover, though the *massimalisti* had conquered the majority in the party, the reformists were still strong in the parliamentary group, in the communes, and above all in the unions. The expulsion of the reformists, as demanded by the Third International, would inevitably have led to a temporary weakening of the party. Nevertheless, to accept Lenin's revolutionary aims while rejecting his strategy of separation from the reformists was a logical contradiction, which was bound to condemn the socialist party to impotence.[16] One of the most important weaknesses of the working-class movement was its provincialism. It was a provincialism of structure rather than attitude; the Italian workers and peasants often showed themselves willing to give generous support to national and international causes. However, the most characteristic and effective organizations of Italian socialism were the provincial *Camere del Lavoro*[17] and the *fasci* were in many respects their mirror-image. The *Camere del Lavoro* were broad, local alliances of the working classes; the fasci were broad, local alliances of the middle classes. Both, with the aid of a certain initial imprecision of aim, succeeded in forming a united bloc out of somewhat disparate interests. However, while the members of the *Camere del Lavoro* shared at least a large degree of common socialist and democratic aims, the fasci were much more heterogeneous still.

It is at least arguable that the class struggle in industry could have been contained by the structures of the liberal state. The decline of working-class militancy was in part the result of the

1921–2 recession and some industrialists seem to have thought that the assistance of the fascists had not been truly decisive and was, in any case, of only temporary utility. Where the mediating function of the state really broke down completely was in the countryside. The fascist movement 'took off' in the regions of capitalist agriculture of the Po Valley, as well as in the share-cropping regions of Tuscany and Umbria. It is interesting to note that there is some apparent discordance between this fact and the well-known theses of Barrington Moore,[18] who has suggested that capitalist commercial agriculture based on wage labour has been favourable to democratic development. However, whereas in England the rise of industry absorbed surplus population, this did not take place in Italy. Consequently rural capitalism in Italy did not drive the workers off the land, or even lead to the dis-appearance of peasant family farms. An alternative explanation stresses the incomplete nature of this capitalist development and the persistence of 'feudal residues'. Certainly, in some areas, the landowners, alarmed by the growth of rural socialism, deliber-ately tried to reverse the trend towards wage labour in favour of sharecropping or tenancy. An interesting general approach to the problem of fascism and the agrarian structure of Italy has been formulated by Frank Snowden, along lines suggested by Barring-ton Moore.[19]

The post-war crisis and the rise of fascism

For an understanding of the post-war crisis, the classic work of Tasca remains indispensable. Until 1956, no work appeared which had much to add in the way of serious research. In the last eight-een years, however, there have been a wealth of serious and well-documented studies. One of the most important conditions for the progress of research has been the opening of the state archives to scholars. The most notable contributions to the interpretation of the rise of fascism have been those of Valeri, de Felice, and Vivarelli.[20] Valeri's study is highly selective and concentrates on two problems: the significance of d'Annunzio's new style of poli-tics, and the relationship between fascism and liberalism. The literary elegance and psychological insight of Valeri's work are in a class by themselves. No one else has explained with such brilliance the extraordinary change in cultural climate which d'Annunzio helped to bring about. Valeri's archive researches enabled him to shed much new light on Mussolini's strategy in the period of the March on Rome, and particularly on his complicated intrigues with the liberal statesmen. One may have some reservations about his thesis that the prime minister Facta betrayed his political mentor, Giolitti. A. Repaci has defended Facta against this charge with perhaps excessive zeal in his work on the March on Rome.[21] Repaci in his two volumes has assembled an impressive amount of information gathered from newspapers, personal interviews, and private archives. Repaci's work is of great assistance in reconstructing the narrative of events: his revelations on the obscure but crucial subject of the attitude of the king, Victor Emmanuel III, are of particular interest. He is less successful in his depiction of the general context of the March, and I do not find his analysis of the role of the army or of Mussolini's strategy ultimately convincing. The mobilization of the fascist para-military forces, though not a true 'revolution' as the fascists claimed, was nonetheless a necessary element in the process which brought Mussolini to power. I have argued in my own book, *The Seizure of Power*, that 'the military and political planes of action were not separate but complementary'.[22]

De Felice's massive biography of Mussolini touches on every aspect of Italian history between 1911 and 1929. It is perhaps to be read with more profit as a general history of the period than as a study of Mussolini's personality, although of course the two cannot be separated. It is the first volume of de Felice's work, *Mussolini il rivoluzionario*, which has created the greatest controversy. His interpretation of the nature of Mussolini's early socialism and of his conversion from internationalism to patriotism in 1914 has been questioned by Valiani and others.[23] Even more serious doubts have been expressed about de Felice's interpretation of the next phase in Mussolini's career (1915–19). According to Vivarelli, de Felice has in the first place failed to distinguish between the 'revolutionary interventionism' of Mussolini and his friends, whose inherently contradictory nature explains its convergence with imperialist nationalism, and the 'democratic interventionism' of men like Bissolati and Salvemini, who were fighting for a new 'Europe of the peoples' based on self-determination.[24] Italy's annexationist ambitions in the Adriatic were the crucial issue which divided nationalists from democrats in 1918–19, and Mussolini sided without hesitation with the latter. De Felice shows that Mussolini was receiving large subsidies from armament firms from 1918 on, and that he had many contacts with military and nationalist circles; yet he still describes him as a 'revolutionary' in 1919. Even if one accepts that any movement whether of right or left which is directed to the overthrow of the existing political structure is 'revolutionary', there is still reason to question this description of Mussolini in 1919, on the evidence which de Felice himself adduces. For in fact Mussolini was so concerned with the threat of a thorough-going Bolshevist revolution, that he gave only hesitant and partial support to the efforts of d'Annunzio to launch a 'national revolution' after his seizure of Fiume in September 1919. If this kind of 'revolution' is meant, then Mussolini was more of a revolutionary in 1921–2 than in 1919.

Perhaps the clearest explanation of Mussolini's stance in 1919 remains that of Tasca. He describes Mussolini not as a 'revolutionary' but as an 'adventurer'.[25] He agrees that in 1919 Mussolini made overtures to the unions and other left-wing groups, and that he still gave support to strikes and punitive taxation of profits; but this did not in any way mean that he had returned to socialism. He was simply trying to gain time, to acquire a following, and to divide the opposition. It is highly significant that other groups of apparently similar aims such as the republicans came to show a marked distrust of the fasci after even their first few months of life. Vivarelli shows that from the outset the fasci were above all anti-socialist in character, and that there was much in common between them and other anti-Bolshevik associations. This does not mean that one should go to the other extreme and ignore the differences between the fasci and the old right, even including the nationalists. The fascist movement was novel in its violent activism and its demagogic use of propaganda motifs derived from the revolutionary left. The origins of the new phenomenon of 'national syndicalism' or 'subversive nationalism' have been well investigated by E. Santarelli,[26] although more work needs to be done, especially on the various patriotic organizations of the 'home front' from 1915 through 1918.

During 1921 fascism became a mass movement. It ceased to be an organization exclusively of displaced or 'marginal' men and professional adventurers, and attracted a huge influx of recruits. The study of this process of expansion has been until recently comparatively neglected. The reader who wants a broad, impressionistic picture of the sources of fascist support will still find it worthwhile to consult the series of essays edited by R. Mondolfo between 1921 and 1923 under the title, *Il Fascismo e i partiti politici*; Mondolfo invited representatives of all the major political parties to contribute. The series has recently been republished in a single volume edited by de Felice.[27] The contributors revealed a fair measure of agreement on the nature and origins of the new movement. They agreed that fascism was a movement of the middle classes, the petty bourgeoisie, and the *déclassés*, in which particular importance attached to the role of the young demobilized ex-officers and the students. They also agreed, though with considerable differences of emphasis, that the movement had become a tool in the hands of agrarians and industrialists who had used it to destroy the power of working-class organizations in the countryside and the factories. Both middle-class participation and the employers' support could be explained by the heightened level of class conflict which resulted from the war, and by the fear of a 'bolshevist' revolution. However, several writers noted that the fascist attack on the working class only really got under way when the danger of revolution had already passed. The anarchist Luigi Fabbri termed fascism a *preventive counter-revolution*; but in his essay he makes the important point that the employers, particularly in agriculture, were not so much moved by fear of a general revolution as by the erosion of their own authority and property rights which had already taken place locally: 'The bosses felt they were no longer bosses'.[28] An article by Gramsci in 1921 already distinguished between 'two fascisms', urban and agrarian.[29] At this time, it looked as if the fascist movement might split into two parts over the question of the 'pact of pacification' with the socialists. Very approximately, the division over this question coincided with the social divide between middle-class urban fascists, who supported Mussolini and pacification, and the agrarians, who refused to relax the terror. The recent analyses of the movement by de Felice and by myself have tended to confirm the validity of this interpretation.

The chief way in which knowledge of the fascist movement has advanced recently is through local studies. There have been several good studies of agrarian fascism, notably that of M. Vaini on Mantua and S. Colarizi on Apulia.[30] Vaini's study gives valuable details about the protests of urban fascists against the reactionary policy of the agrarians. This theme is also stressed by P. Corner in his excellent study of Ferrara.[31] Corner also provides very important evidence on the success of fascist propaganda in winning over sectors of the peasantry by grants to individual cultivators, in contrast to the Socialist policy of collectivization. Emilia, the region of the first fascist breakthrough, has naturally been the object of the most research. The success of agrarian fascism in other regions of Italy, such as the Veneto, Piedmont, and Tuscany, has not as yet been examined in sufficient detail.

The peculiarities of fascism in southern Italy have received more attention. Aside from the work of Colarizi, already mentioned, there is an excellent study of Sardinia by S. Sechi, and the rise of fascism in Naples has been described by R. Colapietra.[32] In the south, the fascist movement was soon caught up in the factional struggles between local political cliques. Many of the latter joined the nationalist association to provide a counterweight to the fascists. Another important theme which emerges from these studies is that of the relationship between fascism and the official ex-servicemen's organization. During 1919–20 the majority of the ex-combatant organizations favoured a democratic policy and were suspicious of the extreme nationalism of the fasci. This was particularly true in the south where the combatant movement achieved its greatest successes. In both Apulia and Sardinia in 1919, the movement succeeded in organizing large masses of peasant ex-combatants under the leadership of their former officers. But there the resemblance ends. In Sardinia, peculiar factors gave the ex-combatant movement a cohesion which it did not have elsewhere, and it served as the basis for the foundation of a regionalist party, the Partito Sardo d'Azione. This was at first a barrier to the progress of fascism in the island; the story of how it was overcome during 1922–3 is a particularly intriguing example of Mussolini's tactical flexibility. Whereas elsewhere he favoured an agreement with the old liberal clientèles, in Sardinia he gave credit to the illusion of a 'pure' and revolutionary fascism in order to divide the leadership of the Sardinian combatants and to absorb their following.

The growth of fascism in urban and industrial areas is still a neglected field of research. The case of Trieste is an exception. Trieste, annexed by Italy in 1918, presented a particularly favourable atmosphere for the growth of fascism, thanks to the national tension between the Italians and the Slavs. The movement took hold there even before its expansion in Emilia. There is a good general study of the area by E. Apih which pays particular attention to economic factors and more recently C. Silvestri has published a most illuminating study of the origins of the movement.[33] Silvestri shows how the superficial radicalism of the fascists and their successful exploitation of syndicalist slogans enabled them to acquire a mass following, which comprised not only the middle classes but large numbers of workers. This success enabled the fascist movement to assert its leadership over the old bourgeois parties who had tried to control it. However, if fascism triumphed over the bourgeois politicians, it soon proved subservient to the interests of the industrialists and ship owners. The radical elements in fascism, indispensable during the period of growth, were rapidly purged or reduced to insignificance once success had been achieved. Trieste, though important, was certainly not a typical city. To understand more about urban fascism and the mood of the middle classes, we need studies of fascism in the big cities such as Milan, Turin, or Genoa.

However, the most serious deficiencies in the study of the growth of fascism are not geographical in nature. What we really need above all to increase our understanding of the problems is to know more about Italian society. The middle classes, it is commonly agreed, were the backbone of fascism. Until we have studied their structure, their income levels and the effect of inflation, and their previous political allegiances, the analysis of fascism will lack an important dimension. The study of particular occupational groups and their professional organizations (artisans, shopkeepers, bank clerks, urban landowners) might also be revealing.

Another, more surprising, gap is that there is no good history of the fascist party. The relationship between the party and the state during the period 1922–6 has been examined in considerable detail by de Felice and by myself; but the internal organization of the party, the effect of the various purges on membership, and so forth, still require further study. The failure of the party to create an efficient, centralized machine, specialized according to functions, was part and parcel of its eventual decline as an effective political force. A study of this failure cannot be separated from a study of the shortcomings of fascism as an operative ideology. An attempt was made to create a kind of parallel bureaucracy within the fascist movement in the shape of the so-called groups of competence. Their inglorious history is examined in an article by Aquarone.[34]

Fascism and the Italian state

The problem of continuity is inextricably involved with the problem of the relationship between fascism and the administrative and judicial apparatus of the state. Recent studies have shown that fascism did not make a clean break with the previous legal order, at least in formal terms. It is certainly important to draw attention to the width of discretion allowed to the police under Italian law, and to the corresponding insecurity of the rights of the citizen, to the lack of independence of the magistracy from the executive, and to the all-important political function of the prefects, who were members of the bureaucracy strictly dependent on the minister of the interior. A study by G. Neppi Modona has shown the limitations imposed on the right to strike throughout the liberal period, and also the constant response by the magistracy to the directions of the government of the day.[35] All these features of the Italian state made the transition to fascism smoother. However, even these continuities may be seen as not truly decisive compared with the change represented by the effective suppression of almost all possibility of protest against administrative injustice, and the creation of parallel organizations (the fascist party and the unions) which brought the formerly free associative life of society under the control of the state. Finally, one should note here the importance of the problem of the persistence of fascist legislation in post-war Italy.

The best general study of the fascist state is Aquarone's *L'organizzazione dello stato totalitario*.[36] This study deals with institutions and laws rather than decisions and policies, although it is often revealing even in the latter sphere. The title is a little misleading, as Aquarone does not in fact conclude that fascism was a true totalitarian state. Several independent centres of power survived, which did not depend on the will of the dictator or on the fascist movement, notably the king and the army, the Church and big business. The slogan of the 'totalitarian state' itself was interpreted to mean that the fascist party must be subordinate to the organs of government. In general, it seems well established that Mussolini from 1926 onwards consolidated his dictatorship by strengthening the old administrative apparatus, rather than by destroying it and creating something new. The studies of Neppi Modona on the magistracy, already mentioned, suggests that the fascist régime for the most part needed only to intensify the traditional methods of pressure which the government had always exerted in order to bring the magistrates into line with its policies. G. Rochat's studies on the army[37] have shown how the fascist government bought the army's support by abandoning plans for reform and allowing the generals to run things as they wanted, under Mussolini's nominal control. The surrender of fascism to the military was to have fatal consequences for the régime; the fascist state exalted preparation for war as the highest priority, and yet Mussolini's coordination of the armed forces was only nominal.

In what, then, did the novelty of the fascist state consist? I would suggest that the beginning of a solution to the contradictions both in the thesis of 'continuity' and in the thesis of the 'break' is to be found in the observation that the structures of the Italian state evolved more slowly than those of Italian society. An important qualification must at once be added: the evolution of Italian society was highly uneven, indeed dualistic, so that most of the south, together with some other rural areas, shared and supported the state's slow tempo. Nonetheless, the general trend between 1870 and 1920 was towards the growth of parties, unions, associations, and a free press; the administrative state remained, and the mechanism of parliamentary control over its operations was imperfect in the extreme. But against and in spite of it, this autonomous growth of social institutions did take place. The war accentuated this contradiction: (1) it greatly reinforced the power of the administrative state; (2) it produced a serious schism inside the ruling class (between interventionists and neutralists), which affected even the institutions of the state; and (3) in the reaction to the war the authority of the state was radically challenged. Fascism continued the trend described in (1) but reversed both (2) and (3): the ruling class, reinforced by new elements, was unified by a system of hierarchical controls, and new *social* institutions were devised (party, corporations, etc.) to take the place of the old free associations. These new institutions, however, were both authoritarian in their internal structure and formally subordinated to the administrative state.

Even this fairly complicated scheme expresses the theory rather than the reality of the fascist state. It is a description of the fascist state as envisaged by the nationalist legislator Alfredo Rocco, rather than of the actual practice of the régime as guided by Mussolini. Mussolini deliberately fostered untidiness and illogicality in the structure of government. Like other dictators, he saw in instability and the conflict between different authorities with overlapping fields of authority a guarantee for his personal power.

Historians have only recently begun to turn their attention to the 1930s, and there is still much that we do not know about the working of the régime in those years. Of the earlier works on fascism, the book by H. Finer, *Mussolini's Italy*, is still useful, in spite of a rather uncritical view of the Duce's genius.[38] His description of the fascist party as 'a species of civil service for the manufacture of obedience' is apt. Finer's work is also interesting because it was written during the period 1933–5, at a time when the prestige of the régime was at its maximum, both abroad and at home. Both Aquarone and Deakin[39] have examined the problem of the decline of fascism with much insight. The principal reasons for the fall of fascism were, of course, military and foreign policy failures; but it is still necessary to explain why Mussolini was overthrown with such ease in 1943. What were the flaws in the apparently imposing structure of the so-called totalitarian state? Both Aquarone and Deakin have pointed to the vital importance of the problem of the succession. By leaving the question of his successor open, and by deliberately encouraging the fragmentation of the fascist governing class, Mussolini weakened his own régime. Many leading fascists were convinced that if Mussolini should die the monarchy and the army would be the decisive force, and therefore developed a dual loyalty, to the king as well as the Duce. This was the foundation for the later anti-German and monarchist 'fronde' which brought about Mussolini's fall from power in July 1943.

The contrast between the appearance and the reality of fascist institutions was striking. The most remarkable example is that of the corporations. Held up as fascism's most imposing creation, they in fact performed no serious function, except, during the period of autarchy, that of serving as a front for the control of raw material allocations and investment decisions by groups of leading industrialists. In the case of the fascist party itself the façade of strength was deceptive. Admittedly, we do not yet have a satisfactory study of the party during this period. Germino's book takes fascist claims to totalitarian control at their face value.[40] The studies of Aquarone and Deakin show, however, the degeneration of the party's capacity for real leadership, and the consequent decline in its morale. The secretariat of Giuriati (1930–1) was a critical period in this process. His fall marked the decisive defeat of the attempt to make the party into an active and functional élite, and to free it from corruption. The failure of Giuriati was determined by Mussolini's own attitude. Under the secretariat of Starace, the huge growth in numbers of the party was not a sign of strength but the effect of new criteria, which made membership in the party obligatory for those seeking office in the state or local administration. In these circumstances membership in the party ceased to be truly voluntary and became a simple badge of good conduct. However, in a recent essay E. Ragionieri has suggested that the change in the nature of the party under Starace did not signify the end of its functions. 'If, it is true, the type of fascist party that had tried to dispute the direction of Italian life with the traditional organs of the State came to an end, a type of party which organized the Italian population in its various components and social strata in support of the fascist state was fully realised.'[41] The activity of the fascist party needs to be studied both locally, especially in the major cities, and nationally. How did the party (and the Militia) respond (a) to the great slump of 1929–33? (b) to the Ethiopian and Spanish wars, or (c) to the world war itself? We do not know the answer to these questions and until we do our knowledge of the régime's political evolution will be imperfect.

Another field which needs more detailed study is that of the relationship between fascism and the Church. There has been a relative neglect of this theme after a promising beginning. With the exception of a brief but interesting anthology of texts edited by P. Scoppola, the most authoritative works are still those of Jemolo, Binchy, and Webster.[42] Jemolo's insight, which derives from a passionate commitment to the lost cause of liberal Catholicism, makes his work a classic. It is one of the books which will always be worth reading, even if some of his conclusions are disputed. Webster gives a valuable analysis of the activities of various Catholic groups, both pro- and anti-fascist, under the régime. Binchy's book, written from a more orthodox standpoint, gives a subtle if somewhat apologetic picture of the relationship between Pius XI and Mussolini. One crucial episode in the history of the relationship between Church and fascism is the conflict over Catholic Action in 1931. We can expect that the next volume of de Felice's biography will throw new light on this question. There is a stimulating essay by Mario G. Rossi in the volume *La Toscana nel regime fascista*; he points out that the Church and Catholic Action saw the alliance with fascism not merely as a means of maintaining their position, but as a way of restoring their power in society. 'The crucifix in the schools, religious teaching, the recognition of the Catholic university, the banning of freemasonry were immediately seen not as final concessions but as the first steps towards the return of the Catholics in society, towards a reconquest that would annul the effects of a sixty years' absence.'[43] How successful was this restoration of the power of the Church? The question needs more investigation, and given the diversity of traditions, further regional studies will make an important contribution.

Fascism and capitalism

Was fascism characteristic of a particular phase of the development of capitalism? If so, why did it appear in Italy before it did elsewhere? Such questions have clearly been of central importance to Marxist writers. Recently the a priori solutions to these problems imposed during the Stalinist period have been questioned, and the relationship between the régime and economic forces, particularly industry, has become the object of empirical research.

Fascism claimed to have reconciled capital and labour within the framework of the so-called corporate state. In the 1930s these claims were subjected to meticulous examination by a French scholar, L. Rosenstock-Franck. He demonstrated the fraudulent nature of the 'representation' allowed to labour, and the subjection of the whole system to government directives.[44] Salvemini came to the same conclusions in his work, *Under the Axe of Fascism!* Salvemini stresses throughout that the state usually acted in the interests of the great capitalist enterprises; but in his conclusion he nonetheless rejected the idea that fascism was a 'capitalist dictatorship'. Instead, Mussolini's personal dictatorship rested on a process of mediation between several powerful interest groups; the influence of the capitalists was contested by the officials of the party, the civil administration, and the army. The fascist party with its satellite organizations no longer depended on the subsidies of big business and was therefore 'no longer an organization of mercenaries in the service of capitalism . . . but an independent force'.[45] Tasca, in his epilogue, came to conclusions very similar to Salvemini's. The policy of autarchy adopted after 1936 was certainly leading to an even greater concentration of capital and to the ruin of the small producers, both urban and rural; but not all the middle classes had been sacrificed to capital. On the contrary, the fascist petty and middle bourgeoisie had penetrated the régime en masse, 'contributing to the formation of the immense fascist bureaucracy which is today the political ruling class of the nation'. Moreover, Tasca argues, to claim that fascism is the dictatorship of capital involves an even more fundamental misunderstanding. 'The sphere of fascism is that of *power* and not that of *profit*.'[46] The fascist economy was planned for war, and in this sense the political objectives of fascism determined the limits even of the 'sphere of profit'. Vice versa, the capitalists could not determine the political objectives of fascism; they could influence them, not as an independent class but only through their participation in the political and administrative apparatus of the new state.

The first studies after the war which were specifically devoted to the theme of capitalism and the fascist state rejected the reservations of Salvemini and Tasca. The Marxist P. Grifone and the Salveminian radical Ernesto Rossi were much more unilateral in their view of the dominance of big business. Rossi stated bluntly that 'the will of the great industrialists has been a determining factor in the political and legal order . . . because the great industrialists had a lot of cash at their disposal.' Politicians, in his view, were merely puppets who declaimed on the stage, while the industrialists pulled the strings.[47] Rossi's book belongs to the tradition of the Italian free-trade propagandists, who ever since the introduction of tariff protection in 1887 had denounced the collusion of the state with industry at the expense of the consumer. Rossi's assumption that the great industrialists controlled the fortunes of the early fascist movement has been attacked by P. Melograni and by de Felice. De Felice discovered that the administrative secretary of the fascist movement, Marinelli, had kept detailed records of donations; on the basis of these records he argued that the role of ordinary members and above all of the agrarians in financing fascism had been more significant than that of industry.[48] Another article by de Felice on the revaluation of the lira in 1926–7 showed that Mussolini's decision to fix the exchange rate at 'quota 90' (to the £) was criticized by the dominant groups in finance and industry, on the grounds that it would damage exports and produce a recession. From this, de Felice drew the conclusion that the main motives of Mussolini's decision had been a desire for prestige and the deliberate intention to show his independence from the capitalists.[49] In favour of this last thesis one can also cite the fact of the industrialists' opposition to the establishment of obligatory arbitration in labour relations in the preceding period. Mussolini during 1925–6 had achieved a *modus vivendi* with industry and finance; but he wished to make clear that the responsibility for major decisions rested with him. Subsequent articles, especially those by R. Sarti and G. G. Migone, have shed more light on the problem of 'quota 90'.[50] They have tended rather to play down the importance of the disagreement between Mussolini and the industrialists, and to emphasize that a moderate revaluation was actively desired by industry, as well as by the inflation-haunted middle classes. Sarti shows how the industrialists rapidly recovered from 'quota 90' and in fact used it to aid their efforts towards rationalization. Migone's research, in a field hitherto unexplored, that of the economic relations between Italy and the United States, has shown the importance of the international context for an understanding of Mussolini's economic policy. His most striking discovery is that the unification of the banks of issue, hitherto attributed to the fascist drive towards centralization, was in fact suggested by the great house of J. P. Morgan. He argues also that de Felice does not sufficiently stress the social objectives of Mussolini's revaluation policy designed to placate the discontent of the petty bourgeoisie and middle classes, who formed the mass base of the fascist party.

Was the fascist movement manipulated from the beginning by the interests of industry, or was it instead a relatively autonomous reaction of the agrarians and the middle classes, which only later received the support, more grudging than wholehearted, of industry? The works of P. Melograni and M. Abrate have argued in favour of this latter thesis. Melograni showed that the Italian Confederation of Industry had not supported the idea of the March on Rome, and would have preferred a conservative government under Salandra or Giolitti (though with fascist participation) to one headed by Mussolini.[51] Abrate, in a long and closely documented book based on the records of the *Lega industriale* of Turin, paid particular attention to the attitude and policies of the secretary of the confederation, Gino Olivetti.[52] Even after 1922 Olivetti continued to distrust fascism, above all because he feared that the party and the government might intervene in industry in support of the fascist trade unions. In general, recent studies have shown that, although industry often turned even the new forms of state intervention to good account, the traditional free-enterprise ideology retained its hold over most industrialists. The extension of state power over industry was seen as a potential if not always an actual threat.

The revisionist interpretations of de Felice, Melograni, and Abrate have not gone unchallenged. Sarti strikes a judicious balance between the de Felice–Melograni line and the older interpretation.[53] He is perhaps nearer the former, insofar as he regards the dominant process as being that of the expansion of private power. The so-called corporative state in essence merely gave legal sanction and confirmation to the power of the Confederation of Industry, which in real terms retained a very large degree of autonomy in the economic sphere. On the other hand, Sarti stresses that the industrialists' influence operated within strict limits. They recognized that 'politics', which meant above all foreign policy, was exclusively Mussolini's responsibility. But this neat division between the political and the economic sphere became increasingly impracticable during the 1930s, when the growth of state intervention was inextricably linked to the demands made by an aggressive foreign policy. The 1930s were marked, in fact, by a growing confusion between the roles of private enterprise and the state. The result was a mixed economy, whose direction was not in the main determined either by central planning or by market forces, but by agreement between powerful oligopolistic groups, some of them under public control. Sarti's book has the great merit of clarity. Its chief (though deliberate) limitation seems to me to be the author's refusal to examine the objectives of the leading industrial sectors, or of great 'captains of industry', like Agnelli or Pirelli. This robs his analysis of a necessary dimension. The Confederation of Industry, though powerful, was not dictatorial, and had to mediate between the desires of different industrial groups.

The huge biography of the founder of Fiat, Agnelli, by V. Castronovo helps us to see further into this question.[54] In particular, he shows the conflict in 1932 between the Keynesian views of Agnelli and the deflationary policy favoured by the Edison and Montecatini combines and the later, even more significant, clash of 1936–7 between the 'German' strategy of Volpi and the 'American' strategy of Agnelli. Castronovo is in some respects close to the traditional interpretation. Although he agrees that the agrarians may have been more wholehearted in their support of fascism, the alliance of the latter with the industrialists was nonetheless, he argues, decisive. He has amply documented the growing control exerted by the large industrialists over the Italian press, both before and under fascism. However, the picture that emerges both of Agnelli and of the other industrialists in relationship to fascism is still notably different from that of Rossi or Grifone. In substance he agrees with Sarti and even Abrate in substituting for the image of an united group of industrial magnates pursuing a single-minded strategy that of a divided class which adapted to the changing political situation, and which in general allowed short-term and partial gains to obscure the long-term economic and social issues posed by fascist policy.

The only recent book which deals with fascist economic policy as a whole is that of S. La Francesca.[55] The older book by R. Romeo, *Breve storia della grande industria*[56] is still extremely useful for the period in question. However, a number of recent articles show that an active attempt is also being made here to question traditional interpretations. An attack has been mounted, this time from the left, on the assumption made by the first generation of anti-fascist historians that the régime had pursued an archaic and irrational economic policy, resulting in stagnation. The observation that the Italian economy grew more slowly under fascism than during comparable periods either before 1914 or after 1945, though true, is certainly not in itself conclusive, since this fact primarily reflects the general slow-down of the European economy due to the great recession of 1929–33. A recent article by D. Preti points out, moreover, the crucial importance of the American restrictions on emigration for the Italian balance of payments.[57] In this light, the fascist policy of 'ruralism', which in real terms signified the restraint of internal emigration from the countryside to the city, appears less as an arbitrary ideological decision, and more as a response to changed economic conditions. However, the ideological and political explanation of 'ruralism' cannot be altogether discarded, since the associated decision to launch a 'demographic campaign' to check the decline in the birth rate must be regarded as quite irrational from an economic point of view. It remains true, I believe, that the policy of 'ruralism' was directed primarily towards ensuring the régime a stable social base and to appeasing agrarian interests.

There is an urgent need for a new study of the period of autarchy (1936–40). E. Fano Damascelli, in a recent article, argues that the high degree of industrial concentration during the 1930s marked a qualitative leap forward of the industrial economy.[58] As in the case of the dispute between the theses of 'continuity' and 'break', the issue of whether the fascist period was one of 'stagnation' or 'development' cannot easily be resolved in absolute terms. It is not a question of black or white, but of less or more; and in the economic field the answers can and should be quantified. It is necessary, I believe, to question the assumption that concentration necessarily implies rationalization from a productive point of view. This is almost as doubtful in the Italian case as the old belief in the virtues of free enterprise and the small firm. G. Mori, for instance, has recalled that the period 1936–8 was marked by a growth in industrial concentration, but also by a fall in productivity.[59] It would seem justified to conclude that the compression of wages and of internal consumption under fascism served to maintain rather than accelerate industrial development. The essential contradiction of fascist economic policy was that between the tendency towards a closed economy (which was only in part deliberate, but in large measure, particularly after 1929, the result of a general international trend), and the impoverishment of the home market produced by the régime's inegalitarian social policies. This contradiction could only be overcome by a return to a policy of heavy state expenditure on armaments and war. From an economic point of view, Keynesian policies would have been an alternative; but, like the land reclamation programme, they ran up against obstacles of a social nature. There is a constant risk of underestimating the autonomy of foreign policy. Few capitalists showed much enthusiasm for imperialist expansion during the 1920s, and in 1938–9 leading circles in industry were markedly unenthusiastic about German alliance. But given the nature of the régime, empire and rearmament were the only way out of the impasse in which the fascist economy found itself after the slump, and once this policy had been chosen, it became increasingly hard both in political and economic terms to reverse it.

Fascism and culture

The study of culture under fascism has still a long way to go. It is understandable, but hardly helpful, that a number of historians have taken the line that there can, a priori, be no connection between fascism and culture. The reduction of all manifestations of support for the régime to 'opportunism' is not valid. It does not make sense either to assume that the intellectuals who supported fascism were all deluded about its nature and aims. It is true that a number of intellectuals, especially among the younger generation in the 1930s, were inspired by the illusion that fascism was a revolutionary and anti-capitalist force. Their state of mind has been described in a well-known book by R. Zagrandi, the most valuable part of which is autobiographical.[60] The ideology of the 'fascist left' in literature and its precedents has been studied with great acumen, if sometimes questionable conclusions, by A. Asor Rosa.[61] The ideology of Ugo Spirito and the idea of the 'proprietary corporation', have been critically examined in a recent article.[62] The propaganda in favour of the universality of fascism is the subject of a book by M. Ledeen.[63] This centres on the activities of a curious organization, the CAUR (Comitati d'Azione per l'universalità di Roma). There is a certain danger in taking too seriously the importance of the activities of such groups, who operated on the margins of official policy. To form a serious estimate of the directives and effect of fascist propaganda abroad, it would be necessary to make a serious study of the organization of the *Fasci all'estero*, as well as the consular service and such bodies as the Dante Alighieri Society. Some interesting information about this is to be found in the important work of J. P. Diggins on American reactions to fascism.[64]

The archives of the Ministry of Popular Culture have now been made available to scholars. They contain an abundance of material on all aspects of fascist propaganda and also on the relationship of intellectuals to the régime. An American scholar, P. V. Cannistraro, is expected to publish a general study based on his research in these archives. Cannistraro has already published several articles from which interesting conclusions emerge. In the first place, his studies seem to confirm the impression that the inconsistency and uncertainty of aim of fascist propaganda were a serious hindrance to its effectiveness, in spite of the great expansion of the propaganda *apparat* from 1934 onwards. However, this expansion was nonetheless, as Cannistraro points out, the symptom of a new phase in the development of the 'totalitarian ambitions' of fascism, in great part stimulated by the example of Nazi Germany.[65] The hesitant beginnings of fascist cultural policy during the 1920s have also received some attention. In these years intellectuals were still drawn to fascism either out of spontaneous conviction or in the hope of securing patronage. Overt censorship was comparatively rare, and in the artistic and literary fields both modernists and traditionalists could claim in good faith to be in harmony with the spirit of fascism. Gentile was prepared to overlook the anti-fascist political attitudes of contributors to the Italian encyclopaedia, in spite of opposition from the party.[66] The main threat to the intellectual independence of the enterprise came from the Church. Other institutions, such as the Italian Academy (created by Mussolini), the universities, and the Venice Biennale, would repay study. The policy of fascism towards education and the organization of youth is another important field in which much remains to be done. There is a useful book by T. Tomasi on education, while the general problem of fascist attempts to indoctrinate youth has been posed with lucidity in an article by G. Germani.[67] In general, one might say that so far the higher forms of culture have received disproportionate attention compared with those which were addressed to a wider audience. Both the postcard and the comic strip have been the subject of recent works. But we still do not have a comprehensive study of school textbooks or of the régime's leisure-time organization, the *Dopolavoro*, whose importance was rightly emphasized by Togliatti in his lectures on fascism.[68]

Fascism and foreign policy

The study of fascist foreign policy has been influenced by the progress of studies in other fields. Several historians have shown their discontent with the methods of traditional diplomatic history and have attempted to relate internal to external policy. They have before them a magnificent example: the work of F. Chabod on the 'premises' of Italian foreign policy after unification.[69] Chabod wished to demonstrate the difference between the moral atmosphere of the Risorgimento and that of fascism. His analyses of the cult of Rome, of hero-worship, and of the modifications in the idea of the nation, are all obligatory reading for anyone who wants to understand the success of Mussolini's appeal.

It has been suggested that Mussolini conceived of foreign policy as an adjunct of propaganda. This assertion does not however by itself tell us much. It raises important further questions: how far did Mussolini sacrifice long-term objectives for short-term popularity? And what was really new about his methods? Recent studies, particularly of the 1920s, have tended to show a greater constancy in Mussolini's policy than Salvemini was willing to concede. At the same time, they have not confirmed the conservative and apologetic view of Mussolini's 'decade of good conduct' before the rise of Hitler and the Ethiopian adventure. The studies of Rumi, Di Nolfo, and Carocci[70] all show the early origin and continuing importance of Mussolini's 'revisionism', or desire to change the Versailles settlement. Alan Cassels has drawn particular attention to Mussolini's contacts with the German right, and to the importance of anti-fascist exiles and public opinion as factors influencing his policy.[71] At the same time, Carocci's study, the most thorough yet to have appeared, though limited to the years 1925–8, shows that friendship with England was still a cornerstone of Mussolini's policy. One factor which Carocci's otherwise comprehensive approach overlooks is that of financial relations with the United States. The dependence of Italian industry on American capital was arguably an important restraining influence on Mussolini's adventurism. After 1929 this influence was removed, at the same time as the rise of Hitler shifted the balance of forces in Mussolini's favour. A lucid analysis by a young German historian suggests that Mussolini was aware that the success of Hitler gave him an advantage, which would be, however, only temporary.[72] The fear of German revival and rearmament would keep France occupied and make her anxious for an agreement with Italy; but if and when Germany really recovered freedom of action, then Italy herself would be menaced and her bargaining power would thus be reduced. It was determination to exploit the uniquely favourable circumstances of the transition period which, Peterson argues, determined the timing of the Ethiopian adventure. The alternative explanation, favoured by G. Rochat and G. W. Baer,[73] puts more emphasis on the régime's internal difficulties. If it is true that by 1935 the Italian economy was well on the way to recovery, it must be remembered that planning for the attack had begun as early as November 1932, when the economic crisis was at its most grave.

There would seem to be a particular need to integrate the study of home and foreign policy in the years 1936–40. The policy of autarchy, and the attempts of Mussolini to achieve a new 'totalitarian break-through' in internal affairs (which signified among other things, reducing if not abolishing the residual power of the monarchy), interacted powerfully with the course of foreign policy. Economic weakness seriously handicapped Mussolini's attempts to preserve a degree of independence from Hitler and to retain a sphere of influence in the Balkans. On the other hand, it was an important and for a time decisive argument in favour of neutrality. For the moment, the best guides to the policy of these years are still old works such as E. Wiskemann's *Axis*, and, of course, Ciano's *Diaries*.[74] In general, anyone who wants to understand the decline and fall of fascism should begin by reading the *Diaries*. They throw as much light on the men and institutions of fascism as they do on the conduct of fascist diplomacy. Their fascination – all the greater because of Ciano's superficiality – has of course always been recognized.

Conclusion: fascism and Mussolini

Fascism cannot be reduced to an expression of Mussolini's personality, nor can Mussolini's personality be identified entirely with fascism. But certainly one cannot conceive of the fascist régime in Italy without Mussolini, and the relationship of personality to history is a theme which his career imposes upon our attention. How can we explain his success, his policies, the acceptance of the myth of his infallibility? D. Cantimori, in his introduction to de Felice's biography, lays emphasis upon the representative character of Mussolini's career, and de Felice himself speaks of Mussolini as a 'symbol of crisis'.[75] His complex and contradictory personality, and his instability of aim allowed a variety of different groups to project their hopes upon him. On the other hand, de Felice, like Deakin and others, sees Mussolini as far less of a 'leader' than might appear from his myth. He had little capacity for long-range planning, and for all his brilliance as a political tactician in the really serious crises of his political career, he often proved himself hesitant and vacillating. At the outset, he possessed at least a keen perception of political realities; but as de Felice points out in his third volume, from 1927 to 1928 onwards his natural tendency to suspicion and scepticism aggravated the isolation which tends to afflict dictators. Here de Felice shows very well the interaction between personality and situation.[76]

The more weaknesses we find in Mussolini, the more inexplicable at first sight does his myth become. Of course, one can argue that any dictator can achieve a reputation for infallibility with the aid of such a massive deployment of propaganda as Mussolini put into action during the 1930s. But is this true? Mussolini did to some extent make his own myth, and we can perhaps still find out more about how he did it. It is through a study of his technique and particularly of his language that we may be able to go beyond the obvious, and identify, at least in part, the source of the fascination which he exerted over the Italians, and not only Italians. Secondly, it may be profitable to trace the emergence in Mussolini's thought and actions of a more universal characteristic of modern dictators. This is the need to claim that they have a special understanding of history, whether derived from doctrine or intuition; it is the secular equivalent of the special relationship with the divine which formerly constituted charisma. The need to appear as a 'historic' figure was all the greater in Mussolini's case because of the compromises on which his rule in fact rested; he could not claim to represent tradition in the face of the Church and the crown. He needed a new principle; and that only fascism could provide. There was a certain necessity about Mussolini's megalomania.

Notes

1. See G. Salvemini, *Prelude to World War II* (London, 1953), passim.

2. A. Tasca, *Nascita e avvento del fascismo* (Bari, 1965), vol. 2, p. 553.

3. ibid., vol. 2, no. 554. N.B. the *Epilogue* from which these quotations are taken is not included in the English edition which Tasca published under the pseudonym of A. Rossi – *The Rise of Italian Fascism* (London, 1938).

4. G. Salvemini, *The Origins of Fascism in Italy*, trans. with introd. by R. Vivarelli (New York and London, 1973). This is the text of the lectures which Salvemini gave at Harvard in 1942. The volume contains a good short bibliography.

5. P. Gobetti, *Scritti politici*, ed. P. Spriano (Turin, 1960), p. 1065. See also the comments of C. Pavone, 'Italy: trends and problems', *Journal of Contemporary History*, vol. II, no. 1 (January 1967), p. 65.

6. G. Gentile, *Origini e dottrina del fascismo*, in *Il fascismo, antologia di scritti critici*, ed. C. Casucci (Bologna, 1961), pp. 15–50.

7. P. Togliatti, *Lezioni sul fascismo*, pp. 9–10. Togliatti had, of course, formally to subscribe to the empty definition laid down by the Comintern. (ibid., p. 3.)

8. E. Sereni, *La questione agraria nella rinascita nazionale italiana* (Rome, 1946). *Il capitalismo nelle campagne 1860–1900*, 2nd ed. (Turin, 1971); idem, *Capitalismo e mercato nazionale in Italia* (Rome, 1966); G. Procacci, 'Crisi dello stato liberale e origini del fascismo', *Studi storici*, 1965, pp. 221–37. For the analysis of fascism by Gramsci and Togliatti, the so-called Lyons theses, prepared for the 3rd congress of the Italian Communist party, are the fundamental document. They can now be consulted in A. Gramsci, *La costruzione del partito comunista 1923-1926* (Turin, 1971), pp. 488–513.

9. N. Tranfaglia, *Dallo stato liberale al regime fascista* (Milan, 1973), p. 27.

10. Several attempts at a systematic comparison between the origins and nature of German national socialism and Italian fascism have been made by Marxists outside Italy; see D. Guerin, *Fascisme et grand capital* (Paris, 1945); N. Poulantzas, *Fascisme et dictature: à la IIIème internationale face*

au fascisme (Paris, 1970); R. Kühnl (Ital. trans.) *Due forme di dominio borghese: liberalismo e fascismo* (Milan, 1973).

11. Procacci, 'Crisi dello stato liberale', op. cit., p. 233.

12. R. Vivarelli, *Il dopoguerra in Italia e l'avvento del fascismo (1918–1922)*, I, *Dalla fine della guerra all'impresa di Fiume* (Naples, 1967), p. 100.

13. G. Arfe, *Storia del socialismo italiano 1892–1926* (Turin, 1965); L. Cortesi, *Il Socialismo italiano tra riforme e rivoluzione* (Bari, 1969) represent respectively the reformist and the revolutionary viewpoint.

14. G. Procacci, *La lotta di classe in Italia agli inizi del secolo XX* (Rome, 1972); I. Barbadoro, *Storia del sindacalismo italiano*, 2 vols (Florence, 1973).

15. See R. de Felice, *Serrati, Bordiga, Gramsci e il problema della rivoluzione in Italia 1919–1920* (Bari, 1971); A. de Clementi, *Amadeo Bordiga* (Turin, 1971).

16. Vivarelli, *Il dopoguerra in Italia*, op. cit., p. 72.

17. Procacci, *Lotta di classe*, op. cit., pp. 62–3.

18. Barrington Moore Jr, *The Social Origins of Dictatorship and Democracy: Lord and Peasant in the Modern World* (London, 1967). For the employment problem in the countryside and the rise of fascism, see Barbadoro, *Storia del sindacalismo italiano*, op. cit., vol. I, pp. 236–53.

19. F. M. Snowden, *European Journal of Sociology*, vol. XIII, no. 2 (1972), pp. 268–95.

20. N. Valeri, *Da Giolitti a Mussolini: momenti della crisi del liberalismo* (Florence, 1956); R. de Felice, *Mussolini il rivoluzionario (1883–1920)* (Turin, 1965); idem, *Mussolini il fascista*; vol. 1, *La conquista del potere (1921–25)* (Turin, 1966); vol. 2, *L'organizzazione dello stato fascista (1925–29)* (Turin, 1968); Vivarelli, *Il dopoguerra in Italia*, op. cit. N.B. also the important work by G. De Rosa, *Storia del movimento cattolico*, vol. 2, *Il partito popolare* (Bari, 1966).

21. A. Repaci, *La marcia su Roma*, 2 vols (Rome, 1963).

22. A. Lyttelton, *The Seizure of Power* (London, 1973), p. 90.

23. See L. Valiani, 'Le origini della guerra del 1914 e dell'intervento italiano nelle ricerche e nelle pubblicazioni dell'ultimo ventennio', *Rivista storica italiana* (1966), no. 3, p. 609.

24. R. Vivarelli, 'Benito Mussolini dal socialismo al fascismo', *Rivista storica italiana* (1967), no. 2, pp. 428–58.

25. A. Tasca, *Nascita e avvento del fascismo*, op. cit., pp. 549–53.

26. E. Santarelli, *Origini del fascismo* (Urbino, 1963).

27. R. de Felice, ed., *Il Fascismo e i partiti politici italiani* (Bologna, 1966).

28. L. Fabbri, 'La controrivoluzione preventiva', ibid., p. 178 ff.

29. A. Gramsci, *Socialismo e fascismo, L'Ordine Nuovo 1921–1922* (Turin, 1966), pp. 297–302.

30. M. Vaini, *Le origini del fascismo a Mantova* (Rome, 1961); S. Colarizi, *Dopoguerra e fascismo in Puglia (1919–1926)* (Bari, 1971).

31. P. Corner, *Fascism in Ferrara 1915–1925* (Oxford, 1974).

32. S. Sechi, *Dopoguerra e fascismo in Sardegna* (Turin, 1971); R. Colapietra, *Napoli tra dopoguerra e fascismo* (Milan, 1962).

33. E. Apih, *Italia, fascismo e antifascismo nella Venezia Giulia, 1918–1943* (Bari, 1966); C. Silvestri, 'Storia del fascio di Trieste dalle origini alla conquista del potere (1919–1922)', in *Fascismo, guerra, resistenza; lotte politiche e sociali nel Friuli-Venezia Giulia 1918–1943* (Trieste, 1969).

34. A. Aquarone 'Aspirazioni tecnocratiche del primo fascismo', *Nord e Sud*, vol. XI, n.s., no. 52 (April, 1964), pp. 109–28.

35. G. Neppi Modona, *Sciopero, potere politico e magistratura, 1870–1920* (Bari, 1969). See also idem 'La magistratura e il fascismo', in *Fascismo e società italiana*, ed. G. Quazza (Turin, 1965), pp. 127–81.

36. A. Aquarone, *L'organizzazione dello stato totalitario* (Turin, 1965).

37. G. Rochat, *L'esercito italiano da Vittorio Veneto a Mussolini* (Bari, 1967); ibid., *Militari e politici nella preparazione della campagna d'Etiopia (1932–1936)* (Milan, 1971); idem., 'L'esercito e il fascismo', in *Fascismo e società*, op. cit. pp. 125–81.

38. H. Finer, *Mussolini's Italy*, 2nd ed. (London, 1964).

39. F. W. Deakin, *The Brutal Friendship: Mussolini, Hitler and the Fall of Italian Fascism* (London, 1962).

40. D. Germino, *The Italian Fascist Party in Power: a study in totalitarian rule* (Minneapolis, 1959).

41. E. Ragionieri, 'Il partito fascista', in *La Toscana nel regime fascista (1922–1939)*, p. 80.

42. P. Scoppola, *La chiesa e il fascismo: documenti e interpretazioni* (Bari, 1971); A. C. Jemolo, *Chiesa e stato in Italia negli ultimi cento anni* (Turin, 1948), transl. [incomplete] D. Moore, *Church and State in Italy 1850–1960* (Oxford, 1960); D. A. Binchy, *Church and State in Fascist Italy*, 2nd ed. (Oxford, 1970); R. A. Webster, *Christian Democracy in Italy 1860–1960* (London, 1961).

43. Mario G. Rossi, 'La chiesa e le organizzazioni religiose', in *La Toscana*, op. cit. p. 360.

44. L. Rosenstock-Franck, *L'économie corporative fasciste en doctrine et en fait* (Paris, 1934).

45. G. Salvemini, *Under the Axe of Fascism* (London, 1936), p. 420.

46. A. Tasca, *Nascita e avvento*, no. 2, p. 568.

47. E. Rossi, *Padroni del vapore e fascismo*, 2nd ed. (Bari, 1966), p. 9; P. Grifone, *Il capitale finanziario in Italia*, 2nd ed. with introd. by V. Foa (Turin, 1971). Grifone had worked for a time as an official of the Confindustria; his book was written during his confinement as a political prisoner on the island of Ventotene.

48. R. de Felice, 'Primi elementi sul finanziamento del fascismo dalle origini al 1924', *Revista Storica del Socialismo*, vol. 22 (August 1964), p. 224 ff.; P. Melograni, 'Confindustria e fascismo tra il 1919 e il 1925', *Il Nuovo Osservatore*, vol. VI (November 1965), pp. 834–73.

49. R. de Felice, 'I lineamenti politici della "quota 90" attraverso i documenti di Mussolini e di Volpi', *Il Nuovo Osservatore*, vol. VII (May, 1966), pp. 270–95.

50. R. Sarti, 'Mussolini and the industrial leadership in the battle of the

lira 1925–1927', *Past and Present* (May 1970), pp. 97–112; G. G. Migone, 'La stabilizzazione della lira: la finanza americana e Mussolini', *Rivista di storia contemporanea* (1973), p. 2. See also ibid., *Problemi di storia nei rapporti tra Italia e Stati Uniti* (Turin, n.d.), pp. 64–5.

51. Melograni, 'Confindustria e fascismo', op. cit., pp. 842–4.

52. M. Abrate, *La lotta sindacale nella industrializzazione in Italia 1906–26* (Turin, 1967).

53. R. Sarti, *Fascism and the Industrial Leadership in Italy, 1919–1940* (Berkeley, Los Angeles, London, 1971).

54. V. Castronovo, *Giovanni Agnelli* (Turin, 1971).

55. S. La Francesca, *La politica economica del fascismo* (Bari, 1972).

56. R. Romeo, *Breve storia della grande industria*, 2nd ed. (Bologna, 1961).

57. D. Preti, 'La politica agraria del fascismo: note introduttive', *Studi storici*, vol. XIV, no. 4 (1973), pp. 802–69.

58. E. Fano Damascelli, 'La "restaurazione antifascista liberista"; ristagno e sviluppo economico durante il fascismo', *Movimento di liberazione in Italia*, vol. XXIII (1971), p. 104.

59. G. Mori, 'Per una storia dell'industria italiana durante il fascismo' *Studi storici*, vol. XIII (1971), pp. 13–14.

60. R. Zagrandi, *Il lungo viaggio attraverso il fascismo* (Milan, 1962).

61. A. Asor Rosa, *Scrittori e popolo: il populismo nella letteratura italiana contemporanea*, 2 vols, 2nd ed. (Rome, 1966).

62. G. Santomassimo, 'U. Spirito e il corporativismo', *Studi storici*, vol. XIV, no. 1 (1973), pp. 61–113.

63. M. Ledeen, *Universal Fascism: the theory and practice of the Fascist International, 1928–1936* (New York, 1972).

64. J. P. Diggins, *Mussolini and Fascism: the view from America* (Princeton, 1972).

65. P. V. Cannistraro, 'Burocrazia e politica culturale nello stato fascista: il ministero della cultura popolare', *Storia contemporanea*, vol. I, no. 2 (1970), pp. 273–98. See now, ibid., *La fabbrica del consenso. Fascismo e mass media* (Bari, 1975).

66. See G. Turi, 'Il progetto dell'Enciclopedia Italiana: l'organizzazione del consenso fra gli intellettuali', pp. 93–152.

67. T. Tomasi, *Idealismo e fascismo nella scuola italiana* (Florence, 1969); G. Germani, 'Political socialization of youth in Fascist regimes: Italy and Spain', in *Authoritarian Politics in Modern Society*, ed. S. P. Huntington and C. H. Moore (New York, 1970).

68. P. Togliatti, *Lezioni sul fascismo*, pp. 97–116; C. Carabba, *Il fascismo a fumetti* (Florence, 1973).

69. F. Chabod, *Storia della politica estera italiana dal 1870 al 1896: le premesse*, 2nd ed. (Bari, 1962).

70. G. Rumi, *Alle origini della politica estera fascista (1918–1923)* (Bari, 1968); E. Di Nolfo, *Mussolini e la politica estera italiana (1919–1933)* (Padua, 1960); G. Carocci, *La politica estera dell'Italia fascista 1925–1928* (Bari, 1969).

71. A. Cassels, *Mussolini's early diplomacy* (Princeton, 1970), pp. 146–74, 354–5, 365–76.

72. J. Petersen, 'La politica estera del fascismo come problema storiografico', in R. de Felice, ed., *L'Italia tra tedeschi e alleati: la politica estera fascista e la seconda guerra mondiale* (Bologna, 1973), pp. 11–55.

73. Rochat, *Militari e politici*, op. cit.; G. W. Baer, *The Coming of the Italian-Ethiopian War* (Cambridge, Mass., 1967).

74. E. Wiskemann, *The Rome–Berlin Axis* (New York, 1949); A. Mayer, ed., *The Ciano Diaries 1937–1938* (London, 1952); H. Gibson, ed., *The Ciano Diaries 1939–1943* (New York, 1946). See also M. Muggeridge, ed., *Ciano's Diplomatic Papers* (London, 1948).

75. de Felice, *Mussolini il rivoluzionario*, op. cit. vols IX–X; de Felice, *Mussolini il fascista*, vol. 1, pp. 460 ff.

76. de Felice, *Mussolini il fascista*, vol. 2, p. 357; see also ibid., vol. 1, pp. 464–5.

Note: The last volume of Professor de Felice's biography, *Mussolini il duce: I. Gli anni del consenso, 1929–1936* (Turin, 1974) appeared after the completion of this survey.

WILLIAM CARR

3 National Socialism: Foreign Policy and Wehrmacht

In the years immediately following the collapse of Hitler's Reich, as the full horror of Nazi brutality was revealed in all its grisly detail in concentration camps overrun by allied armies, and later in testimony given at the Nuremberg Trials, objective writing on Nazi Germany was virtually impossible. The all-embracing nature of modern war, in particular the mobilization of popular passion and prejudice which is an essential ingredient of it, does not leave historians unmoved. Nowhere is this more poignantly recorded for posterity than in A. J. P. Taylor's *The Course of German History* (London, 1945), a period piece bristling with anti-German sentiment which reflected fairly accurately the prevailing mood of public opinion in Britain when it appeared in 1945. At a more sophisticated level Sir Lewis Namier, turning from the minutiae of politics in the reign of George III to the study of international politics in the 1930s, was not one whit less vehement in his denunciation of Nazi leaders and appeasement-minded politicians alike in a series of highly readable works: *Diplomatic Prelude 1938–1939* (London, 1948), *Europe in Decay: a study of disintegration 1936–1940* (London, 1950), and *In the Nazi Era* (London, 1952). A robust and avowed Germanophobe, Namier never doubted for one moment that Hitler was an unspeakably evil man who established his barbaric empire by force of arms in accordance with a premeditated plan of aggression precisely formulated in November 1937; the annexation of Austria, the seizure of Czechoslovakia, and the attack on Poland were not disconnected episodes but calculated steps on the road to eastern expansion. Writing with great panache, a bitterly sardonic wit, and an unrivalled command of the available source material, Namier expressed a point of view held by a whole generation of historians. Sir John Wheeler-Bennett, the first historian of the German army; Alan

Bullock, author of a still unsurpassed biography of Hitler; Professor Hugh Trevor-Roper, whose *The Last Days of Hitler* (London, 1947) remains the classic account of Hitler's miserable end in the Berlin bunker; and the Swiss historian Walter Hofer, whose study of the last days of peace *Die Entfesselung des zweiten Weltkrieges* (Stuttgart, 1954) was quickly translated into English under the significant title of *War Premeditated* – all were in complete agreement with Namier. In *The Gathering Storm* (London, 1948), the first volume of his history of the war, Sir Winston Churchill set his imprimatur on this interpretation of the origins of the war. And as late as 1960 the gospel according to Sir Lewis was being preached as confidently as ever by the American journalist William L. Shirer in *The Rise and Fall of the Third Reich* (London, 1960), a massive anti-German compilation which enjoyed immense success in Britain and in the United States.

Much of the archival material used by these historians was published as a direct result of the decision of the allied governments to place the political and military leaders of Nazi Germany on trial for crimes against peace and humanity. Immediately after the German surrender, investigating teams ransacked the captured German archives and assembled a formidable mass of documentation on various aspects of the Third Reich. *The Trial of the Major War Criminals before the Nuremberg Military Tribunal*, 42 vols (Nuremberg, 1946–9) and additional documentation in *Nazi Conspiracy and Aggression*, 8 vols (Washington, 1951–3) supplied historians with valuable material on German foreign policy drawn principally from foreign office and military archives. Though the authenticity of this documentation has not, by and large, been called into question, it was assembled very hurriedly and in a highly selective manner by prosecution lawyers whose brief was to prove the guilt of the accused, not to place the events of the 1930s in any kind of historical perspective. The contributory blunders and miscalculations of the victorious powers were passed over in silence for only the fact not the circumstances of German aggression mattered to the tribunal. And as the defence counsels were allowed only extremely limited access to the captured archives, the balance of the documentation is weighted very heavily on the side of the prosecution. If a better case could have been made out for the defendants in answer to the charge of planning wars of aggression, it was certainly not possible to make it in these emotionally charged circumstances.

To remove any lingering doubt that war had been forced on the reluctant and blameless democracies by the calculated wickedness of Hitler, the allied governments decided to publish with all speed a selection of documents from the captured German foreign office archives. The nineteen volumes of *Documents on German Foreign Policy 1919–1945* covering the period 1933 to 1941 offer as comprehensive a picture as is possible on the basis of foreign office material (an important qualification) thanks to the enlightened editorial policy of including some military directives from the OKW and minutes from the ministry of economics and the Führer's chancellery as well as official dispatches to and from the Wilhelmstrasse. Because of the sheer volume of material it was decided not to proceed beyond 1941 nor to publish material before 1933. The German archives were, however, extensively microfilmed to facilitate the task of the editors, and these records – which include material from the naval high command and from party offices – are available for research in the National Archives Washington and in the Public Records Office in London.[1] A Quadripartite Commission established in 1960 has started to publish documents from 1918 to 1932 and from 1941 to 1945.[2]

The inevitable spate of memoirs appeared in the immediate post-war years from diplomats, statesmen, and soldiers. On the German side they were mostly written to defend the actions of individuals and made little attempt to see the Nazi era in any kind of historical perspective. There is little of value in the reminiscences of Ribbentrop, Papen, Weizsäcker (the permanent head of the foreign office), or Meissner (the secretary of state). Exceptions are B. Dahlerus, whose *The Last Attempt* (London, 1947) is an important source on the unofficial contacts between British and German officials on the eve of war; P. Schmidt, *Statist auf diplomatischer Bühne 1923–1945* (Bonn, 1949), Hitler's chief interpreter who attended many important conferences; and *Inside the Third Reich* (London, 1970), the long-awaited memoirs of Albert Speer full of fascinating material on Hitler and Nazi Germany though thin on foreign policy where he was clearly an outsider.

Towards the close of the 1950s an Irish historian had already expressed serious reservations about Namier's tidy and uncomplicated explanation of the outbreak of the war.[3] Shortly afterwards in 1961, a major attack was launched on it by A. J. P. Taylor in *The Origins of the Second World War*, a lively and provocative book which precipitated a fierce controversy about the nature of German policy still smouldering a decade later.

Claiming to be doing no more than looking afresh at the documents, Taylor arrived at characteristically iconoclastic conclusions. For the thesis of premeditated war he could find no shred of evidence. He brushed aside Hitler's much publicized 'declaration of intent' in *Mein Kampf* as idle chatter, having no long-term significance. Taylor saw Hitler not as a man of ideas or a planner but as a feckless coffee-house dreamer, a vaguely Chaplinesque figure who wanted, like all German leaders before him, to make Germany master of Europe but had no clear idea how to achieve this. By bluff and intrigue he had clawed his way to power and by the same means he hoped to win success abroad. Micawber-like, he hung around for something to turn up and his enemies obliged him. It was Schuschnigg who forced him to seize Austria when he threatened to allow the Austrian people to decide their own destiny by plebiscite; and it was Chamberlain who took the initiative over the Sudetenland and created a crisis where none had existed. With such accommodating opponents on his side, Hitler bluffed his way with impunity from the Rhineland to Czechoslovakia. Is it altogether surprising that he attempted similar tactics over Poland and by error stumbled over the precipice? 'He became involved in war through launching on 29 August a diplomatic manoeuvre which he ought to have launched on 28 August,' says Taylor.[4] Thus he concludes that 'the war of 1939, far from being premeditated, was a mistake, the result on both sides of diplomatic blunders,' and that Hitler 'was no more wicked and unscrupulous than many other contemporary statesmen' even if 'in wickedness he outdid them all.'[5] Not surprisingly, neo-Nazi circles in West Germany hailed the book with glee, seeing in it a complete vindication of Hitler's policy which was certainly not Taylor's intention. In the other corner some critics, greatly incensed that a professional historian could bring himself to transform the ogre of Berchtesgaden into a rational statesman and equate him with his democratic opponents, vehemently denounced the book as a mischievous, irresponsible, and deliberately perverse exercise by the Puck of the historical fraternity.

Admittedly the book suffers from several defects. It is not free from ambiguities and contradictions about Hitler's objectives; in several instances Taylor ignores evidence in conflict with his thesis; and, most serious of all, he has allowed his love of paradox to cloud his historical sense. To suggest that Schuschnigg, Chamberlain, and Hacha made the running while Hitler stumbled after them willy-nilly is to stand the truth on its head as those who lived through the period – including Taylor, as staunch an opponent of Hitler as any – were well aware. Finally, the book illustrates the weakness of diplomatic history too narrowly conceived. Taylor relies almost exclusively on diplomatic records and memoirs. In fact, these tell us relatively little about Hitler (who preferred to operate independently) but much about the Wilhelmstrasse personnel, who, like Taylor, regarded international affairs as a perpetual quadrille conducted by the Great Powers in defence of their national interests. Far too little attention is paid by Taylor to socio-economic pressures inside Germany and to the dynamic ideology of the Nazi movement, both factors of some importance in any analysis of Nazi policy, as T. W. Mason pointed out in a perceptive review.[6]

For these reasons Taylor's book has not transformed the study of the origins of the Second World War in the way Fritz Fischer's *Griff nach der Weltmacht* (Düsseldorf, 1961) altered quite fundamentally historical interpretation of the First World War. Nevertheless, by challenging accepted wisdom in forthright and provocative terms Taylor did historians a great service; he has liberated them at long last from Namier's seductive literary spell and has encouraged a more objective and less emotive approach to the subject. If most historians – especially German – still believe that Hitler had far-reaching aims which he pursued with some degree of consistency to the point of war, no one would now subscribe to the belief that there was a detailed blueprint for aggression, or deny that in evaluating Hitler's intentions we are dealing with a balance of probability not with verifiable certainties; this change of attitude is due in no small measure to Taylor's perceptive book.

Curiously enough, Namier's generation, though ready to believe that Hitler was fanatically bent on having his own way to the point of war, paid scant attention to the nature of these fanatical beliefs. For practically thirty years it was fashionable to regard him as an unscrupulous opportunist and committed power-seeker, completely without firm ideological convictions, though able, chameleon-like, to assume the correct colouration to suit the immediate occasion. Lack of principle seemed the obvious explanation of a man who protested his love of peace one minute and practised blatant aggression the next, and who, after preaching hatred of communism all his political life, sent Ribbentrop posthaste to negotiate with Stalin in 1939. This picture of Hitler as 'the supreme opportunist' we owe very largely to Hermann Rauschning, a former associate of Hitler's and one-time Gauleiter of Danzig, who eventually broke with nazism and published in 1939 *Hitler speaks*, an account of conversations with Hitler in the mid-1930s which, despite all the doubts expressed by several historians about its reliability, still remains an important source for that period.[6a] Hugh Trevor-Roper questioned the validity of Rauschning's opportunistic thesis in the preface to *The Table Talk of Adolf Hitler 1941–1944* (London, 1953), where he argued forcefully that however repulsive, shallow and unoriginal Hitler's ideas seem to civilized people, they were the expression of a powerful intellect and as such merited more serious consideration than they had hitherto received.

Surprisingly enough, despite further signs of dissatisfaction with Rauschning in the course of the 1960s, no systematic analysis of Hitler's ideology appeared until Eberhard Jäckel's important study *Hitlers Weltanschauung. Entwurf einer Herrschaft* in 1969.[7] Jäckel probably overstates the degree of rationality and consistency in Hitler, but he succeeded in demonstrating that Hitler had a coherent philosophy of life. The evolution of his ideas was much more complex than Hitler pretended in *Mein Kampf*, and was not complete until the late 1920s by which time he had forged a coherent programme of action for the Nazi party out of three major concepts: anti-Semitism, the Social Darwinian belief that struggle was the basis of all human existence, and a new-found conviction that Germany's destiny lay in the east. Destruction of Jewry at home coupled with the conquest of 'Jewish-Bolshevik' Russia became the dominant theme of the Nazi programme. Despite all the tactical twists and turns along the road, a fanatical sense of mission and a dedication to first principles kept Hitler on course to the bitter end, or so Jäckel argues. It is, therefore, no accident that what Hitler did coincided more or less with what he promised to do in *Mein Kampf*. The exact relationship between tactical necessity and ideological commitment must remain a matter for conjecture but it is fair to say that historians now agree that Hitler's ideology has been seriously undervalued, and that his opportunistic policy must be seen within the framework of a firmly held *Weltanschauung*.[8]

One important consequence has been to enhance the significance of Hitler's writings and sayings. If what he believed did matter after all, then *Mein Kampf*, the bible of the movement published in 1925–6 in Munich, and the so-called *Secret Book*, a treatise on foreign affairs written in 1928 but only published in 1961 in New York, become important sources on Hitler's foreign policy. By the same token his speeches cannot be neglected either (especially the ones delivered at intimate gatherings); the most comprehensive and useful collections are N. H. Baynes, *The Speeches of Adolf Hitler 1922–39*, 2 vols (London, 1942) and M. Domarus, *Hitler: Reden und Proklamationen*, 2 vols (Würzburg, 1962–3).[9] References to foreign policy appear in *Hitlers Tischgespräche im Führerhauptquartier 1941–42* (Stuttgart, 1951; new edition 1963), Hitler's rambling disquisitions in the Wolfsschanze,[10] and in A. Hillgruber, editor, *Staatsmänner und Diplomaten bei Hitler. Vertrauliche Aufzeichnungen über Unterredungen mit Vertretern des Auslandes*, 2 vols (Frankfurt a.M., 1967–70), a most valuable source on Hitler's wartime meetings with foreign statesmen and diplomats. Finally, *The Testament of Adolf Hitler: the Hitler–Bormann Documents February–April 1945* (London, 1961) contains interesting retrospective comment but must be used with caution as long as the owner of the letters will not permit their examination by scholars.

As long as historians believed in the monolithic unity of Nazi

Germany where all power was concentrated in the hands of the dictator, it was a natural corollary to credit Hitler with sole responsibility for foreign policy. After the war ex-Nazis were swift to pounce upon this inviting alibi and absolve themselves from all blame for what had gone wrong. However, recent research has shown that behind a façade of unity the Third Reich was in reality a battleground for powerful quasi-feudal interest groups all struggling for dominant influence while Hitler deftly played off one against the other to maintain his own authority. Inevitably, this raises the question whether one can continue to equate German policy with Hitler. Even if we accept – as we must in the present state of research – that he played a major role in the formulation and direction of foreign policy, one must not overlook the part played by institutions and organizations – the armed forces, party organizations, and economic pressure groups as well as the foreign office – and also by individuals such as Goebbels and Himmler who were often blamed in post-war memoirs for the radicalization of foreign policy after 1937.[11]

About the role of the foreign office much is already known thanks to the documentary publications referred to above. P. Seabury examined the role of the foreign office in *Die Wilhelmstrasse. A study of German diplomats under the Nazi régime* (Berkeley and Los Angeles, 1954). There are two useful essays in *The Diplomats 1919–1939* (Princeton, 1953) edited by G. Craig and F. Gilbert; Gordon Craig describes the German foreign office from Neurath to Ribbentrop, that is, to 1938, and Carl E. Schorske discusses the diplomats Dirksen and Schulenburg.

By far the most important study on the structure of foreign policy to appear in recent years is H. A. Jacobsen's massive *Nationalsozialistische Aussenpolitik 1933–1938* (Frankfurt a.M., 1968). Jacobsen emphasizes the basic duality at the heart of German foreign policy after 1933. Nominally the conduct of foreign affairs remained in the hands of the Wilhelmstrasse for, despite Hitler's contempt for foreign office officials and diplomats, whom he consulted less and less with the passage of time, he recognized that peaceful revision of the Versailles Treaty – a policy in which the foreign office genuinely believed – was a convenient smokescreen until such time as the army was ready for a more adventurous policy. Simultaneously and behind the scenes Hitler's real revolutionary aims, in particular the dream of establishing a new racial order in Europe, were being assiduously promoted by a number of party organizations, all fighting tooth and claw for the Führer's favour. Rosenberg's *Aussenpolitisches Amt* was busily working out the implications of Hitler's anti-communism and planning the break-up of Soviet Russia, while the *Volksdeutsche Mittelstelle* had the more practical task of turning the German minorities in central and eastern Europe into obedient instruments for the disruption of neighbouring states, a device of which Hitler made full use in 1938–9. Possibly most influential of all was the *Dienststelle Ribbentrop*; when Ribbentrop became foreign minister in 1938 the last vestiges of independence were snuffed out and the foreign office was brought completely under Nazi control. It is clear from Jacobsen's pioneer study (regrettably it does not go beyond 1938) that while Hitler made the vital decisions on foreign policy, party agencies were still able to exert some influence, though probably not quite as much as Jacobsen imagines. One thing is certain; we need further studies of this calibre before we can disentangle the web of internecine rivalry and personal feuding round the person of Hitler and are able to assess objectively the influence of pressure groups and of individuals on foreign policy.[12]

Subversion and armed might were not the only weapons Hitler used to achieve his objectives. In the initial stages, at least, he attached very great importance to the adoption of what he considered to be the 'correct' diplomatic strategy. This, like the 'grand design' itself, only crystallized in the mid-1920s as Günther Schubert demonstrated in a well-documented analysis of the origins of Hitler's policy: *Anfänge einer nationalsozialistischen Aussenpolitik* (Köln, 1963). When Hitler entered politics in 1919 he was indistinguishable from any run-of-the-mill nationalist agitator; his enemies were Britain and France, his aim the destruction of the Versailles '*Diktat*', the recovery of the lost colonies (to solve the over-population problem), and the general restoration of Germany's greatness, possibly with Italy as an ally. Towards Russia, the traditional ally of conservatives, he remained ambivalent. Though staunchly anti-communist, he showed a shrewd awareness of her potential value as an ally against the west always provided that she could shake off bolshevism. By 1924 his ideas had undergone a profound metamorphosis. France remained the arch enemy; but Russia now joined her as a major foe – at whose expense Germany would expand – while Britain was bracketed with Italy as a potential ally. To win Italian friendship Hitler abandoned the Germans in the South Tyrol (much to the discomfiture of his nationalist friends), and to secure British support he wrote off the former colonies. Once assured of British and Italian support, he calculated that Germany would be able to defeat France and then turn eastwards to smash Russia.

There is no doubt about Hitler's change of direction but the reasons for it remain a matter for conjecture. In a recent contribution to the argument, *Hitlers aussenpolitisches Programm* (Stuttgart, 1970), Axel Kuhn seeks to demonstrate, somewhat unconvincingly, that neither Pan-German nor geopolitical considerations turned Hitler against Russia but a simple realization in 1923 during the Ruhr crisis that Britain had become a potential ally against France; and that the logical alternative to the abandonment of colonial claims against Britain was a commitment to expand eastwards in order to solve the over-population problem. The influence of individuals such as Ludecke, Rosenberg, and Scheubner-Richter on Hitler in this seminal period is still obscure. It is touched upon most fully in W. Laqueur, *Russia and Germany. A century of conflict* (London, 1965). On Rosenberg there is much interesting material in R. Cecil's biography *The Myth of the Master Race. Rosenberg and Nazi ideology* (London, 1972).

Turning to the sequence of events in the 1930s, the most reliable general account is G. Weinberg, *The foreign policy of Hitler's Germany. Diplomatic Revolution in Europe 1933–1936* (Chicago, 1970). This, the first of a two-volume study of the pre-war years, is a model of meticulous scholarship based on an exceptionally wide knowledge of the sources. Though primarily diplomatic history, Weinberg pays some attention to domestic developments, though without establishing very positive connections between internal and external affairs.

In the first two years of power Hitler went out of his way to reassure the world of his pacific intentions, being well aware that a forward policy was excluded until the armed forces were ready for action (whether to fight or intimidate opponents is another question). Only when the risks were minimal did he take unilateral action, withdrawing from the Disarmament Conference and the League of Nations in 1933 and re-introducing conscription in 1935. A clear account of the early years, especially good on the Great Powers' initial reactions to the Hitler régime, is C. Bloch, *Hitler und die europäischen Mächte 1933/4 Kontinuität oder Bruch?* (Frankfurt a.M., 1966) which suggests it was a mixture of both. So on the whole does the most recent work by Günter Wollstein, *Vom Weimarer Revisionismus zu Hitler* (Bonn, 1973). Another valuable analysis of the first two years is K. D. Bracher, 'Das Anfangsstadium der Hitlerschen Aussenpolitik', *Vierteljahrshefte für Zeitgeschichte* (Stuttgart, 1957) which argued – before the 'primacy of internal policy' was a fashionable doctrine – that the key to Hitler's policy was the internal consolidation of the régime.

Germany remained isolated at the beginning of 1935 (the Polish Pact apart). Hitler's conciliatory gestures had not allayed suspicion aroused by his clumsy interference in Austria nor diminished the revulsion Nazi treatment of the Jews had aroused abroad. Then in midsummer Germany's diplomatic position suddenly improved with the signing of the Anglo-German naval treaty, an agreement which a delighted Hitler confidently expected would lead to a formal alliance.[13]

The whole issue of Anglo-German relations is of central importance between 1933 and 1941 because the failure to obtain the British alliance obviously upset Hitler's strategy for the conquest of Europe and possibly of the world as well – a point to be taken up later. The story of the deteriorating relationship has been traced most recently and with great clarity by Axel Kuhn in the second part of *Hitlers aussenpolitisches Programm*. At first Hitler tried to pressurize Britain into active cooperation with Germany, Italy, and Japan in a new Holy Alliance, the so-called Anti-Comintern Pact. By the end of 1937 an increasingly impatient Führer had virtually abandoned hope of securing the alliance and simply hoped that the solidarity of the Anti-Comintern powers would frighten Britain into a neutral posture whilst Germany expanded in Europe. Finally, British intervention over Czechoslovakia and the guarantee to Poland appear to have convinced him that the anti-British Ribbentrop was right to anticipate war with Britain at some point before Germany completed her conquest of Europe. It might well be argued that the *Mein Kampf* strategy now lay in ruins; for by attacking Poland without British acquiescence, he plunged into a general war which it had not been his intention to wage or certainly not in 1939. On British policy towards Germany the standard work is likely to be O. Hauser, *England und das dritte Reich*, the first volume (Stuttgart, 1972) covering the years 1933 to 1936. Using cabinet papers, committee proceedings, and foreign office records, Hauser confirms the utter unreality of Hitler's hopes of a British alliance. Also important for the economic background to appeasement is B.-J. Wendt, *Economic appeasement. Handel und Finanz in der britischen Deutschlandpolitik 1933–1939* (Düsseldorf, 1971).[14]

Attempts to establish cordial relations with Italy fared much better after a temporary setback in 1934 when Mussolini, alarmed by events in Austria, dispatched troops to the Brenner frontier. On the partnership with the Italian dictator there are two general works of quality: Elizabeth Wiskemann, *The Rome–Berlin Axis* (London, 1949 and 1966) and F. W. Deakin, *The brutal friendship. Hitler, Mussolini and the decline of Italian fascism* (London, 1962). The dictators were brought together more by the dynamics of power politics than by any affinity of ideology as M. Funke demonstrates convincingly in a careful analysis of the diplomacy of the mid-1930s: *Sanktionen und Kanonen. Hitler, Mussolini und der nationale Abessinienkonflikt 1934–1936* (Düsseldorf, 1970). The Italian attack on Abyssinia and the imposition of sanctions by the League of Nations helped pave the way for an eventual understanding, though it certainly did not lead to an immediate *rapprochement*. Both dictators played unashamed power politics. Despite Hitler's benevolent neutrality towards Italy, he simultaneously supplied arms to the Negus hoping that prolonged Italian involvement in Ethiopia would give the Germans the free hand they wanted in Central Europe. With Britain, France, and Italy at loggerheads, Hitler seized his chance in March 1936 and re-occupied the Rhineland, a real turning-point in the inter-war years which marked the beginning of a shift in the balance of power away from Paris and back to Berlin. The most reliable account of this event is M. Braubach, *Der Einmarsch deutscher Truppen in die entmilitarisierte Zone am Rhein im März 1936* (Köln, 1956). Incidentally, it used to be thought that had the French called Hitler's bluff, he would have withdrawn his three battalions at once and suffered a humiliating defeat. D. C. Watt suggested recently that it would have been a fighting withdrawal, which, if true, is a significant comment on the growing confidence of the régime.[15]

What really brought Germany and Italy together was Spain. The outbreak of the Spanish Civil War repeated the Abyssinian syndrome; the Italians were tied down this time in the Iberian peninsula and increasingly dependent on the Germans. In the autumn the Axis came into being, dividing Europe into armed camps once more, though the dictators were very far from a complete meeting of minds on all subjects. Hitler's own motives in agreeing to send limited assistance to Spanish fascists are still obscure; ideology, *Machtpolitik*, and economic considerations (the pressing need for raw materials) probably all played a part.[16]

The few fragmentary records we possess of Hitler's secret conferences in the 1930s are a valuable source for the evolution of his policy. One of the most controversial of these gatherings took place in November 1937 in the Reichs chancellery when Hitler addressed a group of top Nazi leaders on the future pattern of German foreign policy. In a long monologue – his 'political testament' as he called it (though Goering denied that the phrase was ever used) – Hitler insisted that Germany's economic problems had to be solved at the latest by 1943–5 and by force if necessary. He discussed the possibility of seizing Austria and Czechoslovakia even before that date if favourable circumstances arose. In 1945 a copy of a summary of the speech drawn up by Colonel Hossbach, one of Hitler's adjutants, came into American hands. The Nuremberg Tribunal accepted the prosecution submission that this, the so-called Hossbach Protocol, was proof positive of Nazi intent to wage wars of aggression. Doubts have been cast on the authenticity of the document, but there seems no reason to believe that it is not a fair summary of what Hitler said.[17]

It is not, in fact, the authenticity of the Hossbach Protocol which is in question so much as the interpretation placed on it. Alan Taylor was the first to argue in *The Origins of the Second World War* that the importance of the meeting had been grossly exaggerated. Basically, Taylor maintains that Hitler frequently rambled on alarmingly for effect and that close associates, well aware of the Führer's weakness, discounted most of his private diatribes. A more likely explanation of the speech was Hitler's desire to isolate Schacht and pressurize Fritsch into further re-armament; and had it not been for Nuremberg no one would have given a second thought to the speech. A good deal can be said for this re-interpretation. All the same, even if one accepts that this was no blueprint for aggression, the consensus of opinion still favours the view that Hitler was serving notice on Blomberg and Fritsch that a more adventurous (and dangerous) phase in foreign policy was imminent. Set against the background of Hit-ler's other pronouncements in the autumn of 1937, the Hossbach speech assumes its real significance; at Augsburg on 21 November he referred to Germany's shortage of *Lebensraum* and empha-sized the need to accomplish 'the tasks set before us'; and three days later he repeated these arguments to political cadets at Sont-hofen. This points to a hardening of attitude and to a determina-tion to run greater risks whatever the reasons. Another relevant factor, rather neglected in the past, was Hitler's conviction that he was mortally ill and had to act while there was still time.[18] But the most compelling evidence for taking the speech of 5 November seriously is the fact that in December Hitler's threat to attack Aus-tria and Czechoslovakia in the near future was incorporated in the annual army directive. Hitler may have refused to read Hoss-bach's protocol (which Taylor regards as proof that it signified little) but he did not hesitate to sign the amended directive, surely proof that he meant what he said in broad terms at least.

Military strategy in the 1930s has been examined in three im-portant books. G. Meinck in *Hitler und die deutsche Aufrüstung 1933–1937* (1959) relates the progress of rearmament to foreign policy with some reference to economic affairs. He shows that military planning was at first purely defensive, being based on the not unreasonable assumption that Germany might be attacked by a combination of France, Russia and Czechoslovakia. It seems likely, though Meinck is not of this opinion, that aggressive intent was implicit in the 1937 army directive in the passage where Blomberg (probably in consultation with Hitler) declared that the army must exploit favourable political situations as and when they arose. The transition to open aggression clearly dates from December 1937 when the amended directive gave the highest priority to a preventive strike at Czechoslovakia in time of peace.

The second work, *Hitler's pre-war policy and military plans 1933–1939* (1963) by E. M. Robertson, also examines the connection between foreign policy and military planning. This book has, in fact, been quoted with approval by revisionists and Namierites alike in defence of their respective positions. Robertson is clearly a traditionalist insofar as he believes that Hitler's objective was the conquest of *Lebensraum*; that he fully intended to seize the Sudetenland by force; and that he was not bluffing over Poland. On the other hand, Robertson implies that Hitler, whom he thinks seldom saw more than one step ahead, had been blown off course by 1937. Mounting hostility to Britain superseded the traditional anti-Russian policy, a change of direction for which Mussolini was more responsible than previously supposed, in Robertson's opinion. Military planning took the form of improvisations to meet a rapidly changing situation; thus Hitler talked in May 1938 of seizing Czechoslovakia, not as a step on the road to eastward expansion, but rather as an essential precaution to secure Germany's rear during war with the west. Robertson concludes that Hitler was swept along by events outside his control and ended up fighting a general war against the west which had not been expected for another three or four years (if then, and for which Germany was militarily unprepared). Finally, W. Bernhardt in a most illuminating study *Die deutsche Aufrüstung 1934–39. Militärische und politische Konzeptionen und ihre Einschätzung durch die Allierten* (1969) examines the politico-military assumptions behind German strategy and draws attention to the considerable element of bluff in Hitler's programme which the western powers failed to understand.

Whatever the reasons, there is no doubt that German policy accelerated in pace in 1938. The first quarter of the year was dominated by the Austrian problem. The best general account of this is Jürgen Gehl, *Austria, Germany and the Anschluss 1931–1939* (London, 1963). The first crisis in Austrian affairs, when Austrian Nazis staged an abortive putsch in Vienna and murdered Dollfuss, is examined in detail by Dieter Ross in *Hitler und Dollfuss. Die deutsche Österreichpolitik 1933–1934* (Hamburg, 1966) and by G. Brook-Shepherd in *Dollfuss* (London, 1961). What still remains uncertain is Hitler's role in the putsch. It is generally thought that he had no prior knowledge of it, though Weinberg feels this is scarcely credible given Hitler's dominant position in Germany by 1934. On the other hand, there is no conclusive proof of his involvement. One thing is certain. German policy changed abruptly; the bullying tactics of open subversion were abandoned in favour of the restrained, but equally subversive tactics of von Papen, the newly appointed special envoy in Vienna.

The second crisis occurred in the spring of 1938. At a meeting with Schuschnigg in February, Hitler succeeded in tightening his grip over Austria to such an extent that peaceful absorption seemed only a matter of time. No doubt Hitler was taken aback early in March when Schuschnigg announced the holding of a plebiscite. In that sense the crisis was of Schuschnigg's making as Alan Taylor argues. What this overlooks, of course, is the elementary fact that the threat of a plebiscite forced Hitler to invade and annex Austria only because he had designs on that country and dared not allow its people to decide their own future if the decision was likely to go against union with the Reich.

Hardly was the Austrian crisis over before Czechoslovakia erupted on the international scene. In the events of the next six months leading to the controversial decision to surrender the Sudetenland at the Munich Conference, Britain played a leading role. After the war – which seemed to many critics the inevitable consequence of the Chamberlain appeasement policy – British historians made determined efforts to lay the ghost of Munich. The first account of the origins of the Czech crisis *Munich: Prologue to Tragedy* (London, 1948; unrevised edition, 1962) by John Wheeler-Bennett depicted Chamberlain as the culpable dupe of a Hitler bent on having his way with Czechoslovakia by war if necessary and only headed off at the last moment by a combination of fortuitous circumstances. The same line is taken in the *Survey of International Affairs for 1938*, vol. II: *The crisis over Czechoslovakia* (London, 1951) and vol. III (London, 1952) by R. G. D. Laffan. On the German side there is B. Celovsky, *Das Münchener Abkommen von 1938* (Stuttgart, 1958), a diplomatic history written by a Sudeten German also hostile to Chamberlain and loyal to Benes. To date the most detailed and reliable study is Helmuth K. G. Rönnefarth, *Die Sudetenkrise in der internationalen Politik. Entstehung-Verlauf-Auswirkung* (Wiesbaden, 1961).

Without guidance and support from Hitler's Germany, the Sudeten Germans could not have disrupted the Czech state in 1938. That is not to say that the form the crisis took was entirely predetermined. Both E. M. Robertson and G. K. Robbins in *Munich 1938* (London, 1968) feel that Konrad Henlein's Sudeten German party was not the completely passive and subservient instrument of Berlin it is usually depicted as being. For example, when Hitler revealed his aggressive intentions towards Czechoslovakia on 5 November 1937 could it not have been because the serious disturbances at Teplitz Schönau in October had drawn Nazi attention forcibly to the smouldering fire on the frontiers of the Reich? Is it inconceivable that on meeting Henlein in March 1938 Hitler, far from encouraging the impatient Sudeten German leader as is usually supposed, was really anxious not 'to drive things to the limit?' Even the September crisis may have taken Hitler by surprise; the Sudeten Germans broke off negotiations with the Czechs on their own initiative and staged an uprising which Hitler certainly approved but had not planned and which occurred before his military preparations were complete. This is an interesting interpretation which calls for further examination in depth. At the same time, it must not be carried too far, for we know that since November 1937 Henlein was totally committed to the incorporation of Bohemia in the Reich and not to dominion status inside Czechoslovakia for which most of his followers would probably have settled.

Did Hitler seriously intend to go to war in the autumn of 1938? Or was he, as Taylor and Robbins maintain, bluffing from start to finish, rattling the sabre because he believed Britain and France had written off Czechoslovakia and felt instinctively that sustained pressure would break up the Czech state? No one can know what went on in Hitler's mind. All one can say is that the evidence we possess suggests very strongly that the threat to Czechoslovakia was a very real one. It is scarcely credible that elaborate military preparations for a Blitzkrieg would have been made – with Hitler's eager participation – had armed intervention not been seriously contemplated. And if it was deception, then Hitler was so accomplished an actor that he took in his closest associates as well. Probably Alan Bullock comes nearest to solving the riddle when he suggests that Hitler kept the options of war or peace open to the very last moment. War was the preferred solution for putting the upstart Czechs in their place *ceteris paribus*. But should the western powers threaten, unexpectedly, to intervene, then a negotiated settlement was never excluded from his calculations. And by late September this 'partial solution' became virtually unavoidable because of the embarrassing eagerness of Britain and France to accommodate him. Either way he stood to gain, evading a peaceful solution when it suited him as at Bad Godesberg, only to agree to it at Munich.[19]

Characteristically, Hitler was quickly disgruntled at the peaceful outcome and almost at once set about the complete destruction of Czechoslovakia. Taylor's view that the occupation of Prague in March 1939 was 'without design' is quite untenable. As J. K. Hoensch demonstrates in an indispensable study *Die Slowakei und Hitlers Ostpolitik* (Köln, 1965), the Nazis undermined Czechoslovakia assiduously in the winter of 1938–9, having discovered in the Slovaks a willing Trojan horse, tailor-made to their requirements. Only the exact timing of the final operation is still obscure. Hoensch thinks that Hitler decided as early as December 1938 to occupy Prague in the spring while other writers favour the end of January or the end of February 1939.[20] It seems likely that Hacha's last despairing effort to preserve the Czech state from complete disruption in March preceded German action by only a few days.

The six months between the Munich Agreement and the British guarantee to Poland are probably the most decisive in the history of the 1930s and deserve much closer attention than they have hitherto received. For it seems likely that Hitler lost his bearings temporarily and was genuinely uncertain where to turn next. With Poland delicate negotiations were under way to take her into a junior partnership. Had Hitler succeeded in this operation – as well he might – he would then have had a clear choice: either to thrust eastwards into the Ukraine with active Polish support or to turn westwards against Britain and France, a not impossible course of action in view of his endorsement of Ribbentrop's argument that war with Britain was probably inevitable even before Germany was master of Europe. So much hung in the balance that winter, when history might easily have taken a dramatically different turn, that an investigation in depth of the various possibilities facing Hitler and of his reactions to them would be a valuable exercise if only to dispel the lingering illusion that he moved with the 'assurance of a sleepwalker' from Czechoslovakia to Poland.[21]

The breakdown of the negotiations with Poland and the British guarantee to that country ended Hitler's indecision. The course was set to the east. The diplomacy of the next six months has been thoroughly examined by Namier and Hofer in the works mentioned earlier, and also by Hans Roos, *Polen und Europa. Studien zur polnischen Aussenpolitik 1931–1939* (Tübingen, 1957). As over Czechoslovakia, it is impossible to divine Hitler's intentions with mathematical precision. Did he hope for a Polish 'Munich' as Taylor believes? That is always possible but on balance hardly credible in view of the elaborate military preparations. Furthermore, as Bullock remarks in his British Academy lecture, Hitler knew that his room for manoeuvre was diminishing rapidly and that the temporary balance of military advantage in Germany's favour would decline as her opponents grew in strength. It is even more difficult to decide whether he was reconciled to the inevitability of (possibly token) intervention by the west. Certainly, the Russo-German Non-Aggression Pact was designed to scare off the western powers, an effect which, much to Hitler's surprise, it failed to have. On the origins of the pact and on Russo-German relations generally G. Weinberg, *Germany and the Soviet Union 1939–1941* (Leiden, 1954) is now somewhat outdated. A more recent but unexciting account is J. E. McSherry, *Stalin, Hitler and Europe 1939–1941*, 2 vols (Cleveland, Ohio, 1970).

In recent years work has begun in earnest on the economic history of the Third Reich. Recent research in this field has, indirectly, thrown a good deal of light on German foreign policy. Even before Taylor delivered his broadside at the Namierites, Burton Klein had paved the way for a revision of orthodoxy with his *Germany's economic preparations for war* (Cambridge, Mass., 1959). Using the voluminous reports of the United States Strategic Bombing Survey, Klein came to the conclusion that, contrary to popular belief, Germany was not armed to the teeth and fully prepared for war in 1939. Though Klein went too far in the opposite direction, seriously underestimating the extent to which Germany was actually geared to war by 1939, he did succeed in demonstrating that she lacked the resources for waging major wars; at most, she could afford a series of small wars executed with lightning speed to ensure success. It is no accident that Taylor relied heavily on Klein's work, interpreting his findings, however, as proof that Hitler never intended war at all.

In the 1960s two important books appeared. First, and quite outstanding was Alan Milward's *The German economy at war* (London, 1965) which analyses in depth the work of Todt and Speer in the total war situation after 1942. In a brilliant first chapter Milward pinpoints the political and economic realities underlying the Blitzkrieg strategy and Germany's preference for rearmament in breadth not in depth. Hitler's instinctive fears that a concentration of economic power in a few hands and a depression of living standards (both likely consequences of total war preparations) would undermine the régime emerge as the decisive factors; whatever the irrepressible Goering said, the Germans had guns *and* butter up to 1942. Bernice Carroll confirms Milward's thesis in her lucidly written *Design for Total War, Arms and Economics in the Third Reich* (The Hague, 1968). She shows that one may speak of a 'war economy' only after 1938 when 17 per cent of the GNP was spent on rearmament (compared with 8 per cent in Britain), and not until 1942 was the economy totally geared to war. To some extent the findings of economic historians strengthen the revisionist case. It clearly made sound economic, as well as political sense, for Hitler to try and obtain as much as possible by bluff – though this is not necessarily conclusive proof that he was averse to war as 'the supreme arbiter'.

By way of contrast the work of historians in the German Democratic Republic points back towards the Namierite interpretation, if for very different reasons. Rigidly committed to an inflexible Marxism-Leninism, East German historians maintain that an unholy alliance of landowners and monopoly capitalists put Hitler in power with the express intention of breaking the power of the organized working class and of launching Germany on an imperialist war of aggression. Their summary dismissal of Hitler as a shadowy puppet of capitalism is so much at variance with all that we know of his very real influence on policy that there is a danger of underestimating the importance of their investigations into the role of powerful pressure groups, in particular of the autarky lobby led by I. G. Farben. D. Eichholtz in *Geschichte der deutschen Kriegswirtschaft 1939–1945*, vol. I (East Berlin, 1969) and in *Anatomie des Krieges. Neue Dokumente über die Rolle des deutschen Monopolkapitals bei der Vorbereitung und Durchführung des zweiten Weltkrieges*, vol. I (East Berlin, 1969) with W. Schumann – especially important for the war years – shows that I. G. Farben directors such as Carl Krauch were in the corridors of power from the beginning. Thus the Four Year Plan of 1936 'the weapon of monopoly capitalism for expansion' was based on a Krauch memorandum; in the shadow of the Czech crisis Krauch urged that the production of gunpowder, explosives, and vital chemicals be accelerated to reach a maximum – significantly enough – in the autumn of 1939; and in his report to the Four Year Plan Council in April 1939 he referred openly to the imminence of war and to the need for a great economic empire capable of exploiting the wealth of the Ukraine.

What is much more difficult to sustain is the thesis that monopoly capitalism was the driving force behind Hitler's foreign policy. On the evidence we possess, a more likely explanation is that monopoly capitalists, like other pressure groups, followed in Hitler's wake seizing opportunities to secure positions of power and profit without necessarily determining the course of policy.[22] A modest attempt to examine the relationships between economic pressures, rearmament, and foreign policy is made by W. Carr in *Arms, Autarky and Aggression. A study in German foreign policy 1933–1939* (London, 1972). Carr does not deny the importance of socio-economic factors – he believes that Hitler imposed priorities on the economy which in turn created tensions confirming him in his expansionist diagnosis – but he thinks military considerations were probably of paramount importance in 1939. There is a need for much solid work on the mass of archival material still largely untouched before definitive conclusions can be arrived at – if then. For, very probably, as in the parallel case of the origins of the First World War on which Fritz Fischer assembled much impressive material relating to the socio-economic structure of pre-war Germany, documentary proof of a direct causal relationship between the economic substructure and the foreign policy super-structure will continue to elude historians. This raises the more fundamental question of whether one should expect such an exacting degree of proof in this area of investigation. On the face of it, it does seem highly probable that the existence of a common cultural heritage and of a broad identity of interest between the Nazis and their supporters on social and economic matters would have exerted some influence on foreign policy. The problem facing the historian is that influences of this kind are not ordinarily expressed in documentary form but in those subtle nuances, unspoken assumptions, and delicate undertones which the tools presently at the disposal of political historians are too insensitive to detect.

Since the appearance of Fischer's seminal work, West German historians have also begun to re-interpret the nineteenth and twentieth centuries in less rigidly political terms. At times it almost seems as if Ranke's 'primacy of foreign policy' has been superseded by a no less dogmatically held belief in the 'primacy of domestic policy'. H. Böhme, U. Wehler, and M. Stürmer have already shown how intimately foreign and domestic policy were interwoven in the days of Bismarck and William II. More recently, Klaus Hildebrand, in a stimulating essay now translated as *The foreign policy of the Third Reich* (London, 1972), has performed a similar function for the Nazi era, placing it squarely in the mainstream of German history since 1871. He argues that the essential social function of foreign policy was to divert the attention of the masses from the inequitable distribution of wealth and power at home. In William II's Germany a jingoistic *Weltpolitik* had sufficed to rally the masses round the throne but by 1930 the increasing polarization of propertied classes on the one hand, and the proletariat on the other, necessitated much more radical expedients – anti-bolshevism, anti-Semitism, and a stronger dose of Bonapartism in the shape of Hitler – to preserve the status quo. Far from being unique, Hitler's programme merely integrated 'all the political demands, economic requirements and sociopolitical expectations prevailing in German society since the days of Bismarck'.[23] That it finally failed is attributed to the predominance in the equation of racial fanaticism which plunged Germany into war and eventually destroyed the very social order the dictatorship was designed to preserve.

Re-interpretations which depend on the validity of parallels between autocratic empire and popular dictatorship obviously raise the related question of continuity in German history. In their day the Nazis, for propaganda purposes, emphasized the element of continuity between their Reich and previous political forms. On the other side Anglo-Saxon hack-writers during the war cheerfully traced Hitler's pedigree back to Luther, Frederick the Great, and Bismarck with a complete disregard for historical accuracy. After the war German historians not unnaturally reacted strongly against accusations of 'collective guilt' and treated the Nazi era as an aberration, qualitatively different from all that had preceded it, a view advanced as late as 1969 in H.-A. Jacobsen's *Nationalsozialistische Aussenpolitik*.

However, Fischer's contention that Germany was as responsible for the outbreak of the First World War as she was universally held to be for the Second – two acts in a single drama – sparked off anew the old controversy. The case for continuity has been developed most vigorously by A. Hillgruber in *Deutschlands Rolle in der Vorgeschichte der beiden Weltkriege* (Göttingen, 1967) and *Kontinuität und Diskontinuität in der deutschen Aussenpolitik von Bismarck bis Hitler* (Düsseldorf, 1969). There is much to be said on both sides. The appalling brutality of the Nazis taken in conjunction with Hitler's plans for a biologically pure master race to rule Europe are still weighty arguments for regarding 1933 as a caesura. Yet at least as powerful a case can be made on the other side. Eastward expansion and Weltpolitik were both well-established themes deeply embedded in the socio-economic structure of Germany between 1871 and 1945; as Hillgruber has shown, Hitler's *Lebensraum* plans bear a striking resemblance to Ludendorff's annexationist wartime plans; and from Bismarck to Hitler it is notorious that Germans have used the same bullying tactics to intimidate opponents and have never hesitated, on occasion, to go to war in order to impose their will on the rest of Europe.

The arguments in favour of continuity have been further strengthened by current research into Hitler's alleged plans for world domination. For long it was assumed by historians that Hitler's ambitions were exclusively continental in nature; he understood Czechs and Poles but, unlike William II, had no interest whatsoever in the wider world outside Europe. Doubts were first expressed by G. Moltmann who inferred from an analysis of what Hitler said in *Mein Kampf* and in the *Second Book* that world domination was indeed the logical consequence of the Nazi belief in Aryan racial superiority, as well as forming a counterblast to the 'Jewish plan for world mastery'.[24] Andreas Hillgruber in *Hitlers Strategie. Kriegführung und Politik 1940–1941* (Frankfurt a.M., 1965) was the first to argue, in broad terms, that Hitler thought, in fact, in terms of a two-phase strategy, that is, he envisaged a second phase – long after his day – when Europe, dominated by Germany from the Atlantic to the Urals, would have to fight the United States (and possibly Britain) for world supremacy. Thus Hillgruber regards Hitler's revival of Germany's colonial demands in 1936 not as a tactical manoeuvre to force Britain's hand, but as a serious preparation for the second phase of expansion. Obviously Hillgruber's thesis implies that the British alliance, far from being the sheet-anchor of Hitler's policy, was a temporary agreement likely to be dissolved once Germany was master of Europe.

Klaus Hildebrand has elaborated on this theme in a major study of the somewhat neglected colonial question *Vom Reich zum Weltreich. Hitler, NSDAP und koloniale Frage 1919–1945* (München, 1969). He shows that Britain's refusal to consider a

German alliance seriously upset the timing of the two-phase strategy. By 1937 Hitler began to suspect that the struggle for world mastery would not be delayed until some distant future but would, in all probability, occur in the late 1940s; that explains the new emphasis after 1937 on naval rearmament, particularly the adoption of the Z Plan in 1939. Though the swift victory in the west in 1940 temporarily reawakened hopes that Britain might still come to terms, it is significant that Hitler now toyed with the idea of acquiring colonial bases in preparation for the second round against the United States. But with the attack on Russia all prospect of moving on to the second phase quickly receded into the distant future once again.

Hillgruber and Hildebrand have fathered a flourishing school of research into various aspects of Hitler's *Weltpolitik*. Several important studies have already appeared. On naval policy M. Salewski, *Die deutsche Seekriegsleitung 1935–1945*, vol. I, *1935–1939* (1970) and J. Dülfer, *Weimar, Hitler und die Marine. Reichspolitik und Flottenbau* (Düsseldorf, 1971); and on Anglo-German relations J. Henke *England in Hitlers politischem Kalkul 1935–1939* (Boppard am Rhein, 1972). At this stage it would be premature to attempt any final evaluation of the Hillgruber-Hildebrand thesis. But it is already becoming apparent that we will have to modify considerably the old view of Hitler as interested exclusively in Europe and indifferent to the rest of the world.

Prussian militarism has always been an emotive phrase in the Anglo-Saxon world where Mirabeau's celebrated comment: 'La Prusse n'est pas un pays qui a une armée: c'est une armée qui a un pays' has never been quite forgotten. During the Second World War 'Prussian generals' were blamed as much as Ruhr industrialists and East Prussian landowners for putting Hitler in power in the first place and giving him unflagging support since 1933.

The anti-militaristic mood of 1945 is faithfully mirrored in what is still one of the most widely read (and informative) studies of the German army, J. W. Wheeler-Bennett, *The nemesis of power. The German army in politics 1918–1945* (London, 1953). Germany's military leaders emerge from the book as shabby and sinister figures who contributed substantially to the rise of Hitler (if only because they failed to act against him), and who dishonoured the army through shameful complicity in the purge of 1934 when they could have overthrown the régime 'with a nod'. Wheeler-Bennett is equally scathing about the German opposition to Hitler; it was not primarily moral revulsion at Nazi excesses which turned many officers into active opponents of Hitler by 1943 but fear of a humiliating military defeat if they remained inactive. Furthermore, while conceding that the 1944 conspirators were honourable men, he argues that even if the conspiracy had succeeded, negotiation with a government of reactionaries would have constituted a betrayal of all the allied powers were fighting for; far better unconditional surrender and the complete destruction of militarism. The arrangements for a German contribution to the defence of Europe being worked out in the early 1950s prompted Wheeler-Bennett to wonder whether this was '. . . "where we came in" in the repetitive history of the German army in politics'.[25] An equally unsympathetic view was taken by the American historian Gordon Craig in *The Politics of the Prussian Army 1640–1945* (Oxford, 1955). As the Federal Republic began to recover some of its old power at the close of the 1950s, there were signs of dissatisfaction with this blanket condemnation of the German military. For example, in 1957 Gerhard Ritter, the doyen of the German historical fraternity, then engaged on his monumental work on German militarism, attempted to exonerate the German generals from at least some of the blame by drawing attention to the fact that massive popular support rather than the machinations of the military put Hitler in power in 1933.[26]

In more recent years, with West Germany re-established as a powerful – and peaceful – member of the European Community, the old fears of militarism have largely subsided. A less emotive and more objective treatment of the Wehrmacht is at last possible as, for example, in R. O'Neill's important study: *The German army and the Nazi Party 1933–1939* (London, 1966). Whilst not attempting to exculpate the army from all responsibility for the German catastrophe, the author, who is a soldier by profession, shows considerable sympathy for the predicament of the German officer class. Though a few influential officers, notably von Blomberg and von Reichenau, played a conscious political game, the vast majority were 'rudderless ships amidst swift currents',[27] quite out of their depth in a complex situation, slow to appreciate the criminal nature of the régime, and ultimately trapped into acquiescence by their instinctive habit of obedience.

New studies on the army by German historians also emphasize the complexity of the relationship with the Nazis. In the most detailed and recent account *Das Heer und Hitler. Armee und nationalsozialistisches Regime 1933–1940* (Stuttgart, 1969), K. J. Müller reminds us that the attitude of individual officers ranged from unrestrained enthusiasm through lukewarm approval to outright rejection. On the other hand, both Müller and K. D. Bracher in *The German Dictatorship* (London, 1970) – a good general account of the Nazi era – are much less inclined than O'Neill to give the army leaders the benefit of the doubt. Great blame rightly attaches, in their view, to men who were generally well disposed to the Third Reich because it approximated more closely to their authoritarian ideas than the Weimar Republic had done. Rapid expansion, Hitler's repeated assurances that army and party were 'the twin pillars of the state', as well as the general euphoria generated by the 'national revolution' symbolized by the continued presence of Hindenburg at the head of affairs – all encouraged the military leaders to believe that they could exert great influence on the régime and even restore the old intimacy between officer corps and state which had characterized William II's Germany, another example, *en passant*, of continuity in modern German history from Bismarck to Hitler. Disagreements among the leading generals were, so Müller argues, purely tactical in nature. Whereas enthusiastic Nazis such as von Blomberg, the minister of war, and von Reichenau, his cool, calculating assistant, were convinced that the army must embrace the Nazi movement if it was to exert effective influence, other officers such as von Fritsch, the commander-in-chief of the army, and Beck, his chief of staff, hoped to achieve exactly the same end by keeping the party at arm's length.

That the 'alliance' with the Nazis failed to preserve the army's independence is a matter of history. Recent writing strongly suggests that the explanation is not to be found in Wheeler-Bennett's sinister 'nemesis of power' but in sheer political ineptitude. Blomberg and Fritsch failed completely to appreciate that totalitarianism in the state was incompatible with genuine independence in the army. Only politically naive men could have congratulated themselves in 1934 on the removal of a dangerous rival in the SA without appreciating the ugly implications of Hitler's ruthless methods. And only men who had woefully misread Hitler's character could have supposed that an oath of personal allegiance would bind the Führer more closely to the army, turn it into the main pillar of the régime, and put the party in its place. Because Hitler refrained from interference in military matters before 1938, army leaders were encouraged in their fond belief that he respected them. In fact, Hitler resented their social exclusiveness, despised their caution, and tolerated them only because he desperately required their expertise to create a powerful army.

The illusions were rudely shattered in 1938 with the controversial dismissal of Blomberg and Fritsch.[28] It has been argued that Hitler had planned their removal ever since their criticism of his schemes at the Hossbach meeting. This seems unlikely in Blomberg's case as Hitler owed much to the minister of war's smooth handling of the army. On the other hand, the *mésalliance* with Erna Gruhn forced his hand and may well have genuinely shocked him. The distasteful prospect of having the cautious Fritsch as his next minister of war fully explains Hitler's ready acceptance of the trumped-up Gestapo charges against the commander-in-chief. What is not in dispute are the epoch-making consequences of the structural changes in the high command. With Hitler as commander-in-chief of the Wehrmacht, the OKW reduced to a personal planning staff under the subservient Keitel, and with the pliable Brauchitsch as commander-in-chief of the army, the conservative-aristocratic dream of an autonomous army was destroyed forever. On Keitel, Jodl, and Brauchitsch, Hitler could rely absolutely; these were technocrats of a new breed, dazzled by the Führer, ready to subordinate professional scruples to his intuition and content to follow him slavishly to the bitter end.

Resentment at this dramatic shift of power probably played some part in the emergence of opposition to Hitler during the Czech crisis. Opinions differ about the motives which prompted this small group of officers and civilians, led by Beck and Goerdeler, to plan the removal of Hitler.[29] Some historians, for example Harold Deutsch, emphasize the moral revulsion older officers and civil servants felt towards the inhuman (and vulgar) Nazis; others, such as K. J. Müller, tend to see the major causes in the conspirators' realization that Germany was too weak to face a major war, and in their chagrin at Hitler's contemptuous dismissal of their weighty objections to his plans. Revealing on the political and social objectives of the conspirators are essays by H. Graml and H. Mommsen in *The German Resistance to Hitler* (London, 1970). The chances of the conspiracy succeeding were, in fact, extremely slight, and after Hitler's triumph at Munich resistance melted away overnight. During the Polish crisis there was virtually no opposition to Hitler, partly because he had removed many unreliable officers after Munich and abolished the long-established right of chiefs of staff to share in strategic decisions, but also because this was a popular war against a hated foe.

With the outbreak of war, Hitler, unlike William II in 1914, quickly emerged as the dominant figure in the Wehrmacht. Until fairly recently it was customary to dismiss Hitler as a bungling amateur in military matters, the opinionated corporal of the First World War, who brought ruin on Germany through his insane conduct of the war. This interpretation owed much to the memoirs of generals, particularly Halder, Guderian, and Manstein, who were quick to blame Hitler for the defeats while claiming the credit for operations that went well.[30]

Some re-appraisal of Hitler as a military leader has been long overdue and is possible now that so much important archival material has been returned to Germany. Especially important publications based on this material are the official war diary of the high command: *Kriegstagebuch des Oberkommandos der Wehrmacht 1940–1945*, 7 vols (1961–5) edited by P. Schramm; the private diary of F. Halder, *Kriegstagebuch 1939–1942*, 3 vols (Stuttgart, 1962–4); W. Hubatsch, ed. *Hitlers Weisungen für die Kriegsführung 1939–1945 Dokumente des OKW* (Frankfurt a.M., 1962); and H. Heiber, ed. *Hitlers Lagebesprechungen. Die Protokollfragmente seiner militärischen Konferenzen 1942–1945* (Stuttgart, 1962), 900 pages of the stenographic reports of the Führer's daily war conferences. This material has not, as yet, been properly assimilated in an authoritative study of the war leader. There is a useful preliminary essay 'The Military Leader' by Percy Schramm in *Hitler the man and the military leader* (London, 1972). Werner Maser, one of the many Hitler biographers, pays particular attention to this somewhat neglected aspect in his *Hitler* (trans., München, 1973) though the attempt to correlate the progression of Hitler's illness with Germany's decline after 1941 is unconvincing. It is already quite clear that we can no longer accept the folk myth of a carpet-biting maniac utterly immune to all rational argument. The truth is that he did possess at least some of the qualities expected of a military leader: a flair for strategy; an understanding of tactics, and a knowledge of weaponry which astonished general staff officers and enabled him to hold his own with experts; and a quite amazing will power and determination to achieve his objectives.

Early in the war Hitler served notice on the army that he intended to take charge personally of strategic planning. After the Polish campaign, Hitler's generals were perfectly content to remain on the defensive in the west and even inclined to a negotiated peace, when to their utter consternation Hitler ordered an attack before the winter. The story of their opposition and the abortive plot in November to remove Hitler is told in minute detail by Harold Deutsch in *The conspiracy against Hitler in the twilight war* (Minneapolis, 1968). For the controversial origins of the strategic plan of 1940, H. A. Jacobsen, *Fall Gelb: Der Kampf um den deutschen Operationsplan zur Westoffensive* (Wiesbaden 1957) is indispensable. It would appear that several factors conspired together to produce *Sichelschnitt*: army dissatisfaction with Halder's Schlieffen-style plan; unavoidable delays which allowed time for second thoughts; Manstein's genius; and, not least, Hitler's instinct for the unconventional. Characteristically, he claimed full credit for the victory in the west though it is clear from the campaign that the Germans enjoyed much good fortune in what a leading military expert described as 'a lucky series of long-odds chances'.[31] After the fall of France few generals went as far as the sycophantic Keitel who triumphantly proclaimed Hitler 'the greatest strategist of all time'. Yet, with Germany virtually master of all Europe, grudging admiration for the Führer's 'genius' overcame much of the real apprehension aroused by his personal intervention in the Norwegian and Western campaigns. In this context it should also be remembered that lack of coordination between the three services greatly assisted Hitler in assuming overall direction of the war.

In the light of recent research, the six months which elapsed after the fall of France while an increasingly perplexed Hitler waited in vain for Britain to capitulate, emerge as a period of central importance for the subsequent course of the war. From June to December 1940 Hitler wrestled with the problem of how to end the unwelcome war with Britain. Invasion – to which he turned reluctantly in July – was abandoned for sound military reasons in September. For a time he toyed with a 'peripheral' strategy of attacking British bases in the Mediterranean and Atlantic.[32] He also looked with apparent favour on Ribbentrop's scheme for a huge continental block stretching from Madrid to Tokyo which might pressurize Britain into surrender and secure a Central African empire for Germany into the bargain. This should not be interpreted as a sign that Hitler was seriously committed to the traditional anti-British strategy of foreign office and naval command. More likely it was stop-gap improvisation on the road to war in the east, as Andreas Hillgruber argues in an authoritative study of the complex period, *Hitlers Strategie. Kriegführung und Politik 1940–1941* (Frankfurt a.M., 1965). However, when Hitler finally opted in December 1940 for war in the east he contrived to combine the anti-British and anti-Russian strategies in a 'world Blitzkrieg' strategy designed to solve his problems 'at a stroke'. The attack on Russia not only represented a life's ambition but would have far-reaching strategic consequences: Japan would be encouraged to expand in Asia; this, in turn, would prevent American intervention in Europe – and Hitler was acutely aware of deepening bonds between Britain and America throughout 1940 – so that, finally, Britain, without allies, would have to capitulate. Germany would then be master of Europe and in a position to make a bid for world power. That Hitler was seriously contemplating this is suggested by the order in July 1940 for the resumption of work on the Z Plan suspended at the outbreak of war; and while the Russian campaign was going well in July 1941

Hitler discussed with the Japanese ambassador a joint operation against the United States.

When the Blitzkrieg came to a halt before the gates of Moscow in December 1941, Hitler's gamble had failed and final defeat was inescapable, as he was one of the first to realize. Good comprehensive accounts of the Russian campaign are A. Clark, *Barbarossa* (London, 1965) and A. Seaton, *The Russo-German War 1941–1945* (London, 1971). Barry A. Leach throws light on the origins of the plan of attack in *German strategy against Russia 1939–1941* (Oxford, 1973). Until recently it was fashionable to lay the blame for the German failure on Hitler's reckless disregard of the lessons of history. Leach rightly points out that army command was as committed to the attack as Hitler; it was every bit as optimistic about the outcome and underestimated the Russians as grossly as he did. Indeed, it might well be argued that during the first six months of the campaign Hitler often showed more perception than his military advisers; and in the critical month of December it was only Hitler's determination to stand fast which prevented a disastrous German retreat.

On the other hand, as the tide turned against Germany after 1942, Hitler, now his own commander-in-chief, revealed very serious defects of character: a frightful obstinacy about matters of detail; a paranoid mistrust of many staff officers; a growing belief, as dream and reality ceased to coincide, that fanatical determination and will power were the real keys to victory; stubbornness in withdrawing units until it was often too late to save more than a remnant; and a habit of interfering in operations which cramped initiative by subordinates. The inability to appreciate the proper relationship between operational goals and available resources, which lay at the root of his troubles, may have been accentuated by illness, for example, during the Kursk offensive of July 1943, but in the main it was attributable to a deep-seated repugnance for the harsh realities of failure coupled with the conviction that he had no alternative but to resist until the bitter end.

After the Stalingrad débâcle – for which Hitler must bear major responsibility – the army's faith in the Führer began to falter, and opposition to the régime grew rapidly both in military and civilian circles. The attempts to remove Hitler by assassination culminating in the abortive Bomb Plot of July 1944 are described in E. Zeller, *The flame of freedom* (London, 1968) and R. Manvell and H. Fraenkel, *The July Plot* (London, 1964). This was the end of the road for the army. Hitler's pent-up resentment of the officer corps burst forth in a savage repression of the July plotters; hundreds of officers were arrested and many executed; the Nazi salute was at last made compulsory in the army; and for the last few months of the Third Reich the SS was in the ascendancy with Himmler as commander-in-chief of the replacement army.

By this time the allied invasion of Europe, the liberation of France and Belgium, and the mounting devastation caused by allied bombardment of German cities had brought Germany near to the point of collapse. Indeed, had it not been for disagreements in the allied camp, Germany would have been overrun in the autumn. As it was, the allied advance came to a halt, enabling the Reich to hold out through the winter of 1944–5. Hitler made use of this unexpected breathing space to launch one last offensive in the Ardennes where the great victory of 1940 was forged. The standard work on this campaign will probably be *Die Ardennenoffensive 1944/5. Ein Beispiel für die Kriegsführung Hitlers* (Göttingen, 1971) by H. Jung who treats it as a classic example of the strengths and weakness of Hitler's military leadership. Whether he genuinely thought there was still hope for Germany remains uncertain. Some evidence suggests he expected disagreements with Russia to disrupt the grand alliance, and hoped that the Ardennes offensive would surprise the allies and make them amenable to a compromise peace, in itself an indication of the unreal atmosphere he lived in, oscillating between wild hope and deep despair. Ends and means were hopelessly out of joint; there was no hope of seizing Liège (the army's objective) let alone Antwerp (Hitler's aim).

The Ardennes offensive was decisive in one sense. The eastern front was so weakened by this last effort that when the Russians launched their last great offensive in the spring of 1945 and the Anglo-Americans crossed the Rhine, Germany was utterly without resources and forced to surrender unconditionally. In the midst of the great catastrophe which now engulfed Germany and destroyed the old Europe forever, the suicide of the Führer in the chancellery bunker on 30 April was an almost irrelevant comment on the margin of events which left the Wehrmacht and the German people largely unmoved.

Notes

1. G. O. Kent, ed., *A catalogue of files and microfilms of the German Foreign Ministry archives 1920–45*, 3 vols (Stanford, 1962–6).

2. Other major collections containing material on German foreign policy are: *Documents on British Foreign Policy 1919–1939: Documents diplomatiques français 1932–1939* (see especially the perceptive reports of François-Poncet, French ambassador in Berlin 1931–8); *I documenti diplomatici italiani* (so far only material from March 1939 to July 1940); *Foreign Relations of the United States* for 1931–41; and *Documents and Materials relating to the eve of the Second World War*, 2 vols, the second volume being the papers of Dirksen, German ambassador in London 1938–9.

3. T. Desmond Williams, 'The historiography of World War II', in E. M. Robertson, ed., *The Origins of the Second World War. Historical Interpretations* (London, 1971).

4. A. J. P. Taylor, *The Origins of the Second World War* (London, 1961), p. 278.

5. ibid., p. 79.

6. T. W. Mason, 'Some Origins of the Second World War', *Past and Present* (Oxford, 1964).

6a. For a careful evaluation, see T. Schieder, *Hermann Rauschnings Gespräche mit Hitler* (Opladen, 1972).

7. Eberhard Jäckel, *Hitlers Weltanschauung. Entwurf einer Herrschaft* (Tübingen, 1969); recently translated as *Hitler's Weltanschauung: A Blueprint for Power* (Middletown, Conn., 1972).

8. N. Rich in *Hitler's War Aims. Ideology, the Nazi State, and the Course of Expansion* (London, 1973), the first of a two-volume study tracing the development of Hitler's policy to 1941 against the background of his ideas, favours a much higher degree of consistency than most historians would now be inclined to accept.

9. A comprehensive collection of Hitler speeches, memoranda, and letters to 1925 is being published by the Institut für Zeitgeschichte and the Historisches Institut, University of Stuttgart.

10. The English version: *The Table Talk of Adolf Hitler 1941–1944*, ed. Hugh Trevor-Roper (London, 1953) is based on Bormann's notes. It has been treated with reserve by many historians because Bormann undoubtedly formulated Hitler's views more sharply for party ends. For a dissenting opinion see N. Rich, *Hitler's War Aims*, pp. 269–70.

11. A study of the role of Ribbentrop and Goering in foreign affairs would

be particularly useful; we do not know how far Hitler's disillusionment with Britain was due to Ribbentrop nor why Goering, a powerful figure in the hierarchy in 1939, was unable to do more to restrain Hitler from war.

12. In *Vom Reich zum Weltreich* (München, 1969) K. Hildebrand shows that the colonial movement exerted some influence on Hitler without changing the direction of his policy.

13. The best treatment of the agreement is D. C. Watt, 'The Anglo-German naval agreement of 1935; an interim judgment', *Journal of Modern History* (Chicago, 1956) written, however, before the publication of the German documents. On the German side W. Malonowski, 'Das deutsch-englische Flottenabkommen vom 18 Juni 1935 als Ausgangspunkt für Hitlers doktrinäre Bundnispolitik', *Wehrwissenschaftliche Rundschau* (1958).

14. See also C. A. MacDonald, 'Economic appeasement and the German "moderates" 1937–1939. An introductory essay', *Past and Present* (Oxford, 1972).

15. D. C. Watt, 'German plans for the reoccupation of the Rhineland: a note', *Journal of Contemporary History* (London, 1966).

16. On economic aspects see G. T. Harper, *German economic policy in Spain during the Spanish Civil War* (The Hague, 1967) and M. Einhorn, *Die ökonomischen Hintergründe der faschistischen deutschen Intervention in Spanien 1936–1939* (Berlin, 1962).

17. H. W. Koch, 'Hitler and the origins of the Second World War: second thoughts on the status of some of the documents', *Historical Journal* (London, 1968) expresses reservations. The essay is reprinted in E. M. Robertson, ed., *The Origins of the Second World War. Historical Interpretations.* See W. Bussmann, 'Zur Entstehung und Überlieferung der Hossbach Niederschrift', *Vierteljahrshefte für Zeitgeschichte* (München, 1968) for a convincing defence.

18. The salient facts about Hitler's health are in W. Maser, *Hitler* (1973), though the interpretation placed on them is questionable.

19. Alan Bullock, 'Hitler and the Origins of the Second World War', *Proceedings of the British Academy*, vol. L, no. III (1967).

20. L. Hill, 'Three crises 1938–39', *Journal of Contemporary History* (London, 1968); W. H. C. Frend, 'Hitler and his foreign ministry 1937–1939', *History* (London, 1957).

21. D. C. Watt's forthcoming study of the year war came may cast some light on Hitler's options in the early months of 1939.

22. This is substantially the thesis of A. Schweitzer, *Big Business in the Third Reich* (London, 1964) who argues that industry, army, and party worked together harmoniously from 1933 to 1936, each deriving benefit from the general expansion of the economy. After 1936, when the economy switched to war preparations, industry and army found themselves subordinate partners in a party-dominated state. Schweitzer's thesis is strongly criticized by the East German historian D. Eichholtz in *Jahrbuch für Wirtschaftsgeschichte*, vol. III (Berlin, 1971).

23. K. Hildebrand, *The foreign policy of the Third Reich*, p. 146.

24. G. Moltmann, 'Weltherrschaftsideen Hitlers', in *Europa und Übersee: Festschrift für E. Zechlin* (Hamburg, 1961).

25. J. M. Wheeler-Bennett, *The nemesis of power*, p. 702.

26. Gerhard Ritter, 'The military and politics in Germany', *Journal of Central European Affairs* (Boulder, Colo., 1957).

27. R. O'Neill, *The German army and the Nazi party 1933–1939*, p. 172.

28. The latest study is Harold Deutsch, *Hitler and his generals. January–June 1938* (1974).

29. On Beck see W. Foerster, *Ein General kämpft gegen den Krieg: aus nachgelassenen Papieren des Generalstabschefs Ludwig Beck* (München, 1949). N. E. Reynolds of Trinity College, Oxford, is preparing a study of him based on new material. On Goerdeler the standard work by G. Ritter is *Carl Goerdeler und die deutsche Widerstandsbewegung* (Stuttgart, 1954; trans., London, 1958).

30. F. Halder, *Hitler as Warlord* (London, 1950); H. Guderian, *Panzer Leader* (London, 1952); Erich von Manstein, *Lost Victories* (London, 1958).

31. B. H. Liddell-Hart, *History of the Second World War* (London, 1970), p. 66.

32. M. van Creveld, *Hitler's Strategy 1940–1941. The Balkan Clue* (London, 1973), argues that Hitler attached greater importance to the peripheral strategy than is usually believed.

HANS MOMMSEN

4 National Socialism: Continuity and Change

1

Explanations of the national socialist variety of fascism have so far fallen into two categories; one starting from a consideration of the fascist mass movement, the other interpreting the specific features of the National Socialist governmental system. Particularly during the immediate aftermath of the Second World War, stress was laid on the ideological forbears of National Socialism[1] and on attempts, starting in the late thirties, to provide a sociological explanation, which paid especial attention to the radicalization of the lower middle classes during the Weimar Republic.[2] This line of research belongs to the first type of interpretation and usually assumes that the mobilization of people to the fascist cause during the pre-1933 campaign decisively shaped the policies of the National Socialist régime. As against this, almost all Marxist and neo-Marxist theories of fascism start from the realities of fascist dictatorship, conceived, with variations, as the reign of 'finance capitalism'.[3] To a greater or lesser degree, these theories fail, like the original Comintern theory of fascism, in that they take insufficient account of the social causes and the specific manifestations of fascist mass parties.[4] This is also true of the totalitarian dictatorship theory[5] that evolved as early as the war years and was disseminated mainly by German refugees, deriving some indirect support from attempted interpretations by conservative teachers of constitutional law within the Third Reich.[6] Its various forms[7] are pre-eminently based on the National Socialist régime, stressing its monolithic and terrorist aspects.[8] Elsewhere a mirror-image reverse of the Comintern theory of fascism, it shares with it the presupposition of a rationally structured government apparatus and of an effective centre of political decision.

Initially, the concept of totalitarian dictatorship served a useful purpose. By replacing the earlier, mainly ideological derivation of National Socialism, it provided a starting point for a comparative study of fascist movements[9] and systems, despite the drawback that parallels drawn (more markedly under the influence of the Cold War) between fascist and bolshevist régimes tended to obscure the specific elements of fascist policies and government. Historical researchers have in consequence largely abandoned this concept as a hindrance to the understanding of the National Socialist régime's antagonistic power structure.[10] Quite apart from this aspect, however, the weakness of such a theoretical starting point was that it gave a somewhat inadequate answer to the question as to which factors were instrumental in the NSDAP's success as a mass movement. The concept of totalitarianism as a definite rational government by a single party was reduced to an ideological syndrome, by which it was assumed that the chief attraction of National Socialist propaganda was essentially to be found in the authoritarian and totalitarian disposition of the population groups to whom it was addressed.[11]

Special emphasis was, however, laid on the plebiscitary and charismatic elements of Hitler's leadership; the 'leadership principle' and the part played by the centralized party structure were made to appear as the trademarks of National Socialist policy. This theory does, it is true, overcome the difficulty that National Socialist *Weltanschauung* was neither consistent nor particularly original: rather it was an eclectic conglomeration of völkisch concepts indistinguishable from the programmes of out-and-out nationalist organizations and parties of the imperialist period, or from the ideas of right-wing bourgeois parties during the Weimar era. The interpretation of National Socialism as a Machiavellian technique, tailored to Hitler's personality, for seizing and exercising power may have lent credibility to conservative apologists who have presented National Socialism essentially as 'Hitlerism', characterized partly by its ruthlessness in the choice and application of political methods and partly by Hitler's own destructive fanaticism.[12]

The totalitarian dictatorship theory may indirectly have taken over a function similar to that of the Comintern analysis of fascism, which started from the premise that the National Socialist régime relied on the effective suppression of the greatest possible number of the people and should therefore be regarded as a specific manifestation of domination by a capitalist élite. Such a view also served to strengthen the hypothesis of a growing resistance among the mass of the people under the leadership of the Communist Party.[13] The KPD's obstinate attachment to the slogan of 'social fascism' and its continued struggle against the SPD as the main enemy, even after Hitler's seizure of power, was thereby quietly relegated to the background.[14] At the same time, the totalitarianism theory, with its emphasis on the Machiavellian and demagogic nature of the Hitler régime, favoured the conspiracy of silence about the conservatives' share of responsibility in the eventual victory of National Socialism.[15]

Moreover, the totalitarian theory, by equating bolshevism and National Socialism, has stood in the way of a proper understanding of the structural features peculiar to fascist parties. It is undoubtedly true that both Mussolini and Hitler, in developing their own movements, took socialist party movements for their model; the Austrian Christlich-Soziale Partei, too, served Hitler as a pattern. Attempts were also made by the National Socialists to take over some structural elements of the Communist party, such as the system of blocks and cells. The main difference between the NSDAP and the existing parliamentary parties consisted in the substitution of the Leadership Principle for the principle of democratic procedure within the party. At the same time, however, its organizational structure differed widely from the communist principle of democratic centralism which, by preventing the formation of splinter groups among the lower echelons and insisting on their commitment to party decisions, ensured strict obedience to the central leadership. In Communist parties, elections and internal discussions about central issues nevertheless continued to exist at all party levels, including, despite the cult of Stalin, collective decisions as to leadership.

The form of the NSDAP, which evolved in the later twenties under the influence of the central Munich leadership, presented a completely new type of party, fundamentally different both from the Communist and from the traditional democratic parliamentary parties. Simulating, with increasing success, the pattern of nineteenth-century socialist party movements, it deliberately moulded itself into a 'negative' people's party. It neither saw itself as a traditional parliamentary party which would give its followers some kind of share in directing the party's own ideological development, nor did it see its function as the fighting of electoral campaigns, despite its ever-increasing success in this field after 1926. The NSDAP was in essence a political propaganda organization. Party officials and members limited their efforts to making propaganda, to obtaining the means for propaganda, and to representing the party in public, if only by sporting its badge. Since the party's policies were in all essentials established by the central office and the party press, and since any discussion of party matters was regarded as obsolete and a lapse into the despised 'parliamentarianism', the NSDAP was, as it were, held together from outside, by its own propaganda and, more and more, by a systematically built up Führer cult.[16] Similarly, the aestheticization of politics, a characteristic of fascist movements, served the purpose of externalizing the party; as by the cult of uniforms, the adoption of the völkisch salute, the observance of rituals such as consecration of banners and standards, the hoisting of flags at party rallies and meetings, the development of a peculiar and intentionally spectacular ceremonial, and the predilection for paramilitary demonstrations.[17]

A significant feature of the organizational structure of the NSDAP is the virtual absence of any internal mechanism of integration. Hitler's first accession to power in 1920, with the fusion of the DAP and the NSDAP, was accomplished by means of propaganda meetings rather than by the intervention of the official party leadership; the executive committee was faced with his ultimatum, sanctioned by the acclaim of party audiences at public meetings, as a fait accompli. The leadership principle which replaced the statutory executive was not exclusive to the NSDAP; it took its model from the Alldeutscher Verband and völkisch groups such as the Deutschvölkischer Schutz- und Trutzbund. In the NSDAP, however, it reached an acme of refinement, dispensing with all responsible, even merely advisory, bodies. More and more, NSDAP party rallies lost any other function than to cheer the leader. Whereas at first, some motion or another might have been introduced at local or regional level or sporadic political discussion might have taken place, the party rally eventually became no more than a propaganda platform, a medium for the acclamation of the Führer: even in internal party committees, exchange of political views dwindled. Leadership conferences, which had still retained some importance in the latter half of the twenties, either vanished altogether or were transformed into demonstrations or gatherings whose sole purpose was to receive orders from above. When, in 1928, Hermann Dinter demanded an advisory council for Hitler, party headquarters in Munich saw to it that the motion was unanimously rejected. The Senate Hall in the Brown House was never put to its proper use. Despite honest endeavours by the Reichs Chancellery,[18] Hitler's often-repeated promise to institute a senate or some similar body to elect a leader was never kept.

The intensification of the leadership principle resulted in the absence of any institutional means available to the NSDAP for dealing with conflicts of interest within the party. Such conflicts were, however, inherent in the principle of imposing on party officials a duplicated control – as to their function and by means of discipline – and were further aggravated by the fact that, apart from occasional interference by instructors from headquarters, there was no effective supervision of section leaders, who were usually appointed from above. Obviously, such a mass organization, bolstered up by an ever-growing bureaucracy and engaged almost exclusively in propaganda activities,[19] was totally unable to cope with the exercise of control and guidance urgently needed after the National Socialist seizure of power.

It follows that the NSDAP, as a political mass organization within the National Socialist régime, became almost devoid of political function and restricted to welfare and training activities; the party as a whole never achieved the role of a central control agency, effectively overseeing both administration and social institutions and directing their policies. Such a theoretical presupposition of totalitarian dictatorship was in line with the Third Reich's self-image rather than with its reality. On the other hand, the political style evolved in the Movement phase and the specific organizational pattern of a dynamic party exclusively devoted to propaganda activities decisively influenced both the process of political decision-making and the internal structure of the National Socialist régime. To this extent, the tension between the elements surviving from the Movement phase and the political requirements of the System phase of National Socialism is of basic importance to any adequate description of the political process within the Third Reich. In consequence, modern comparative fascism theory has introduced an essential criterion in differentiating between the Movement phase and the System phase.[20]

In the main, the model of totalitarian dictatorship evolved from the attempt to explain the relative stability and effectiveness of fascist governments. In the case of the Third Reich, as opposed, say, to the Spanish Falange, successfully subdued by authoritarian groups led by General Franco, the question why the Nazi régime could not curb its plethora of objectives and so achieve lasting stability of the system is at least of equal importance. Surely, Hitler's personal charisma and the role of Nazi ideology can hardly suffice as the sole explanation. The process of cumulative radicalization, hampering any creative reform by the régime, exposing it to early disintegration and eventually to inevitable dissolution from within, cannot simply be ascribed to the effect of ideological factors. The latter may rather be correlated with the régime's specific inability to adjust itself to interim priorities and to find constructive solutions for existing social and political conflicts of interest.[21]

The explanation of the National Socialist régime's relative stability is that, during the Seizure of Power phase, Hitler had been obliged to make far-reaching concessions to the conservative élite controlling the army, economy, and administration, thereby frustrating those elements in the Nazi movement who pressed for total seizure of all social and political institutions. Although indirectly annulled as time went by, these concessions acted as a brake, enabling the régime to consolidate itself with remarkable success before the movement's destructive forces, geared to disintegrate the system of government, could bring about a final overstretching and overtaxing of available resources and the economic bases of power. The root of these forces lay in the movement's own apolitical and millennial dynamics and also in the antagonistic interests among the various groups in the National Socialist leadership. Nevertheless, it was this structure which allowed an unprecedented short-term mobilization of all available political energies to achieve particular political ends, especially in foreign and military policy areas, although the price paid was an epidemic of split political responsibility, an unbounded and increasing antagonism between all power groups and institutions having any say in the political process, and a growing irrationality in political decision-making, which was completely subordinated to the rivalries among the National Socialist leadership élite.[22] In this respect the régime failed to overcome the shortcomings of the Movement phase; the relative stabilization, achieved in 1933–4 with the dismantling of the National Socialist 'revolution', was in fact nullified by the customary quarrels and conflicts which, exacerbated by the Second World War, again broke out within the National Socialist movement. The leadership rivalries during the last weeks of the Third Reich were a characteristic expression of this development, arising from the inner logic of fascist policies.[23]

2

Central to contemporary historical research is the elucidation of the social and political causes of the NSDAP's breakthrough as a mass movement. Marxist interpretations tend to underrate the fact that substantial big business support for the NSDAP, if indeed there was any, occurred only after the September 1930 elections,[24] when it had managed to become the second largest parliamentary party with 18.3 per cent of the vote. Consequently, tentative 'agent' theories miss the point of the problem. Contrary to current belief, the NSDAP's rise was by no means uninterrupted. Anton Drexler's Deutsche Arbeiterpartei, set up with the support of the völkisch organizations and the Bavarian Reichswehr, had at first been an insignificant splinter group; it achieved regional importance after the early twenties as the NSDAP under Hitler's leadership. The rise of the party was linked with the nationalist restoration counter-movement following the defeat of the Munich Soviet Republic, within the counterrevolutionary climate of the Bavarian capital, marked by the illegal activities of the subsequently disbanded Freikorps and Heimwehr organizations.[25]

In the crisis year of 1923 the NSDAP, absorbing the nationalist völkisch groups in Munich and some parts of Bavaria, was able to enlist 55,000 more members and to extend its organizational activities to Württemberg, Baden, and northern Germany. As it became involved in plots to overthrow the government, engineered by authoritarian Bavarian groups associated with Captain Ehrhardt and Erich Ludendorff, Hitler attempted to enforce his leadership by staging the Beer Hall Putsch. Following the failure of the march on the Feldherrenhalle, Hitler's arrest and sentence, and the proscription of the party, NSDAP membership suffered a sharp decline.[26] The North German NSDAP and surrogate organizations, such as Alfred Rosenberg's Grossdeutsche Volksgemeinschaft and Julius Streicher's Franconian Deutsche Arbeiterpartei, ensured continuity of the organization, although competition arose from von Graege's Deutschvölkische Freiheitspartei, which was for a time joined by part of the successor organizations to form the Nationalsozialistische Freiheitspartei.[27] Hitler's adroit move in re-establishing the NSDAP and driving Ludendorff into political isolation by supporting his hopeless candidature for the Reich presidency in 1925, enabled him to assume unquestioned leadership of the party. In this he was assisted by the Führer mythology, built up to a peak of elaboration, particularly by Hermann Essler, during Hitler's imprisonment in Landsberg Fortress. To obtain control, Hitler had to grant independence for a time to a federation of Gauleiters in northwest Germany who, however, never managed to dislodge the power monopoly of the Munich branch and, although they deprecated the opportunism of the Munich leadership, lacked the ideological consistency to prevail against it.[28]

Despite continued legal harassment, the NSDAP made remarkable strides during the 1925 through 1928 phase, membership rising from 27,000 to 108,000. Electoral success, however, did not keep pace: during the May 1928 Reichstag elections, the

NSDAP suffered a crushing defeat, obtaining only 2.6 per cent of the vote. For a time the party was proscribed and, in Prussia, Hitler was forbidden to speak until 1928; that these prohibitions were lifted must be taken in conjunction with the general opinion that the party had lost all parliamentary influence. The contradiction between a flourishing of the organization and a lack of electoral success during the decisive phase of consolidation is explicable by the absorption into the party at that time of the potential adherents of their former competitors, the völkisch associations and especially the Deutsch-Völkische Freiheitspartei.[29] Extreme racial anti-Semitism, with its implied resentment of capitalism, and the uncompromising anti-parliamentarianism of National Socialist propaganda ensured a monopoly for the NSDAP within the völkisch movement. No genuine mass basis, however, could be gained in this way; what was needed was the penetration of large sectors of the bourgeois-conservative electorate.[30]

From the end of 1928 onward, however, that is, even before the devastating effects of the world economic crisis had been felt in Germany, the NSDAP enjoyed rapid growth, culminating in considerable success in the local elections of 1929 and thereafter in the break-through of September 1930. Evidently this turning-point was not preceded by any basic change in National Socialist propaganda, as Dietrich Orlow has suggested, but thereafter National Socialist propaganda was intensified in rural areas and middle-sized towns. This does not mean a deliberate break with an alleged 'urban plan'.[31] NSDAP invasion of the bourgeois centre and right-wing parties – the Zentrum alone was almost totally immune to fascist infiltration – presupposes the beginnings of doubt among bourgeois middle-of-the-road voters as to the efficiency of their political representation, particularly in relation to the protection of middle-class and agrarian interests. One indication of this process is the growing importance of parties, such as the Wirtschaftspartei, standing for bourgeois middle-class interests; this led to splinter groups, particularly among the conservative organizations, and to a multiplication of parties in general. The political undermining of the centre and right-wing parties must be seen in the light of increasing anti-parliamentarian tendencies during the phase of bourgeois party coalition governments.

Recent publications, including Jeremy Noakes's excellent study,[32] point out that during this phase, the NSDAP, here and there allied to the DNVP and DVP, succeeded in invading the political infrastructure of the bourgeois parties at the local level (the Zentrum again excepted), at the same time obtaining a decisive influence over bourgeois and agrarian pressure groups. This applied to every kind of middle-class organization, as well as to the Reichslandbund. With the memory of November 1918 in mind, Walther Darré's 'agrarian political apparatus' had originally been set up to forestall a possible agricultural boycott and the ensuing collapse of food supplies in the event of a revolutionary take-over by the NSDAP. By this strategic move, coupled with preliminary 'packing' of local groups followed by propaganda pressure on their central leadership, the agrarian organizations were successfully subverted.[33]

Through their growing influence in bourgeois and agrarian bodies and local tie-ups with the DNVP, the National Socialists were assured not only of increasingly favourable treatment by the right-wing nationalist press but also of a measure of respect from bourgeois groups, previously repelled by the political rowdiness of the party and particularly the SA. Hitler's about-turn after Landsberg towards strict legality, in the formal sense, and his far-reaching concessions to capitalist notions, did not mean that party propaganda ceased at the same time to use pseudo-socialist slogans to win over marginal groups from the SPD. Under the pretext that a united front was needed to combat the 'Marxist' parties, strenuous efforts were later made to secure all vital key positions for NSDAP officials. The consequent mobilization of voters, especially of agrarian groups, ensured the NSDAP's tactical error in giving it a share in the agitation for a plebiscite against the Young Plan.

The conquest of the bourgeois infrastructure, at the end of the National Socialist phase of consolidation, simultaneously linked with the perfecting of both the National Socialist propaganda machine and the vast local and regional bureaucratic organization of the party, was one of the most important social preconditions for its seemingly irresistible momentum up to mid-1932.

Moreover, the NSDAP's undoubted attraction for younger people was an important socio-psychological factor.[34] At that time, Ludwig Kaas was appointed leader of the Zentrum, the DNVP's chairmanship passed from Westarp to Hugenberg, opposition to Stresemann's policies was increasing on the DVP right wing, and later on the DDP was transformed into the Deutsche Staatspartei. In this way, all the bourgeois parties were displaying a tendency towards the strengthening of traditional ideological alignments, whereas attempts at revision in the intermediate parties – Volkskonservative, Jungdeutscher Orden, and Christlich-Sozialer Volksdienst – met with no success. The rift between the generations was thereby widened: the high-level political leadership of the Weimar Republic, including the Social Democrats, were striving to regain their respective pre-war political positions; while the younger generation in all political camps, to whom the Kaiser's era and the world war meant only post-war privations and inflation, endeavoured to create new political styles and structures. Young people were thirsting for a new political perspective, offering something more than a return to 1913: the desire for a new German future was, however, systematically and with growing success exploited by the NSDAP to recruit young members and voters. The unfavourable age structure of the SPD and the bourgeois parties (except the Zentrum, which drew its support from the broad spectrum of Catholic organizations) clearly showed their lack of political attraction for the younger generation,[35] whereas the age structure of the NSDAP, and to some extent that of the KPD, showed a decided tendency towards a decreasing age level. Whilst the traditional bourgeois youth movement had already become outdated,[36] the NSDAP profited from the need of large sectors of bourgeois youth for political integration and commitment to forward-looking policies.

Up to the summer of 1932, the NSDAP drew roughly a third of its gains in voting strength from former DNVP and DVP voters, another third from young voters, and the remainder from those who had previously abstained.[37] Nevertheless, its influence on working-class youth was limited; possibly it was only effective on young trainees, unable to begin their working life because of mass unemployment, and therefore never having been exposed to trade union influence, whether independent or Christian. Although the NSDAP had succeeded in transforming itself into a mass movement, it could not achieve an overall landslide; both Catholic areas and urban centres displayed a marked immunity to National Socialist propaganda.[38] The consequences of the world economic crisis exacerbated the situation. Not only mass unemployment but also the social disorientation of middle-class groups, aggravated by the crisis and the lowering of wages and incomes, particularly affected employees, minor officials, and small traders. The comparatively passive acceptance by Social Democrats and the Zentrum of Brüning's deflationary policies reinforced these socio-psychological effects and the desire for a fundamental change of direction in German politics. At the same time, the anti-Marxist propaganda by right-wing parties, clearly shown by William Sheridan Allen,[39] coupled with the growing polarization among the parties and the increase in communist voting strength, acted in favour of the NSDAP, which, for instance, now attacked the von Papen government's capitalism and the SPD's passive, and therefore pro-capitalist, attitude during the crisis. By this means it was to a large extent able to mobilize in its own favour the resentment among non-socialists against capitalism, revived by the economic crisis, and at the same time gain the sympathies of part of the army and a number of industrial magnates. These men, fearing a serious threat to the capitalist structure from recently intensified left-wing demands for nationalization, intended to use the NSDAP as auxiliaries on this particular front, even though in other respects they had strong reservations about it and fully supported von Papen's idea of a 'new state'.

Impressed by its extraordinarily rapid growth after 1928, the public viewed the NSDAP as an irresistible force. Propaganda manoeuvres deliberately stressed this aspect; incessant skirmishing kept all party members constantly on the move and the NSDAP seemed to be everywhere at once.[40] By innumerable individual actions, meetings, rallies, and also by systematic provocation of terrorist incidents, the party leadership achieved an approximate imitation of traditional Socialist party movements. Even during the Régime phase, mass rallies, processions, and well-rehearsed public appearances by the Führer were used to give an impression of a party based on mass support, an impression confirmed by the plebiscites of 12 November 1933 and 19 August 1934.[41] As a consequence, the mass-movement nature of the NSDAP and the plebiscitary foundation of Hitler's rule have been greatly overestimated, even up to the present day.

Closer analysis of the membership and voting patterns, however, puts a different complexion on the matter. Prior to 30 January 1933, sharp fluctuations in membership occurred; this to a lesser extent was also true of the KPD. Out of 239,000 members joining before 14 September 1930, only 44 per cent were still in the party by early 1935; at that time, the membership was 2,494,000, but another 1,506,000 had already left the party.[42] Even though the statistical data available permit no absolutely precise deductions to be made, it is virtually certain that the NSDAP could not permanently assimilate its mass following to any significant extent, apart from a small, predominately middle-class hard core. From this it is reasonable to conclude that the mass-movement aspect of the NSDAP was a transient phenomenon, for the millionfold membership of the Régime phase can scarcely be ascribed to actual political mobilization, but rather to the need to conform. What is known of the violent fluctuations within the corps of political leaders,[43] too, suggests that the organization's mass character was preserved only by the petrifaction of the largely depoliticized party apparatus and by massive political pressure.

Researches so far carried out, especially Heberle's and Stoltenberg's studies of Schleswig-Holstein,[44] throw some doubt upon Seymour Martin Lipset's argument that in the main National Socialism represented a revolt by formerly liberal sectors of the middle class.[45] Rather, the NSDAP succeeded in penetrating various fields of voting potential, without, however, effecting more than a temporary capture. Agrarian voters, the mainstay of the party's electoral success in September 1930, had for the greater part already defected by the November 1932 elections. The false impression of a popular movement was given by the fact that various social and professional groups – not industrial workers nor the stalwarts among the Zentrum voters – joined the NSDAP for a time, only to fall off again fairly rapidly. Confirmation for this may be seen in the NSDAP's internal crisis at the end of 1932, especially in the decreasing commitment among members.[46] Under the influence of the economic crisis, a simultaneous band-wagon effect masked this tendency, and is sufficient, quite apart from exploitation of anti-Communist tendencies and political pressure, to explain, if not diminish, the electoral success of 5 March 1933.

In view of the NSDAP's internal inconsistency and its inability to mobilize much more than a third of the electorate, Hitler's appointment (as a result of von Papen's intrigues against Schlei-cher) as Chancellor of a Cabinet of National Concentration, assumed major importance. Whereas Gregor Strasser had urged the adoption of a constructive policy, Hitler's obstinacy in de-manding vital key positions in a presidential government now reaped its political reward. Whether Hitler sensed that, in view of the cracks within the National Socialist movement, a partial suc-cess would be tantamount to defeat is a matter which might repay closer investigation. In any event, it should be emphasized that the National Socialist share in the governments of Brunswick and Thuringia had led to disillusion among the electors and a fall in voting strength.[47] To that extent, Brüning's tactics of allowing the NSDAP to fritter away its strength in various *Länder* coali-tions are shown to have been correct in principle, however prob-lematical a Zentrum-NSDAP coalition might have been.[48] Apart from this, however, the NSDAP – as has been repeatedly stressed – would have suffered considerable losses in any further electoral campaign. Goebbels was quite aware that the party's success depended on the maintenance of its propaganda dynamic; his sceptical feeling that the NSDAP would, in electoral terms, 'kill itself with winning',[49] since no outward success in the form of any responsible share of government was forthcoming, throws some light on the critical situation before the turning point en-gineered by von Papen came at the end of December 1932.

3

Seldom has any party been so unprepared for political power as was the NSDAP on 30 January 1933.[50] Basically, their objectives did not go beyond a political power monopoly. Some sporadic groundwork, it is true, had been carried out at central and Gau headquarters as a preliminary to a possible achievement of power. It had not progressed very far and was primarily concerned with measures to safeguard power once it had been obtained. Draft legislation for a prospective National Socialist government, such as there was, had been produced by outsiders.[51] In addition, the Nazi leadership had envisaged the setting up of a comprehensive indoctrination machinery, which was to be realized only imperfectly in the Ministry for Public Enlightenment and Propaganda.[52] No model for the construction of a state was contained in the Boxheim documents; they merely sketched extensive measures for eliminating political adversaries and dealt with a transition period before National Socialist rule should have become stable. The institutional form of such rule was visualized in contradictory terms. Opinions were united on the necessity of removing the parliamentary system; middle-class tradesmen and skilled workers in particular welcomed endeavours at that time to replace parliamentarianism by corporate order. Nowhere, however, not even in the leadership circles closest to Hitler, were there any clear ideas as to the nature of a National Socialist state. Hitler had referred in *Mein Kampf* to the transfer of the National Socialist party organization to the state, but without going into details.[53] How this could be put into practice remained to be seen. The party, almost exclusively bent on propaganda, had adopted a political style in which all options remained open and decisions were dealt with ad hoc.

Moreover, the quasi-legal seizure of power, achieved on 30 January 1933, had come as a complete surprise. The party as a whole had always believed that its accession to power would in some way be linked with the suppression of a communist rising and would therefore be revolutionary. Presidential government politics had offered the alternative of a pseudo-legal seizure of power through the existing constitution and by strategic use of the parliamentary system for the party's own purposes. A majority within the party regarded the formation of a Cabinet of National Concentration and the elimination of the Reichstag by means of the Enabling Act as preliminaries to the achievement of total power. They expected complete revolutionary change, analogous to the November Revolution of 1918, without, however, any clear idea of its eventual form and aims. When Goebbels called the formation of the government on 30 January 1933 a 'national' and later a 'National Socialist' *revolution*, it was not simply a stroke of propaganda to justify the NSDAP's immediate usurpation of power positions supposedly under constitutional safeguard; its aim was also to appease the mass following of the movement. Goebbels remarked that it was extremely difficult to lead the movement out of its previous frenzy into the legality of the National Socialist state.[54] He interpreted the process of *Gleichschaltung*, accelerated after March 1933, as a revolutionary act and maintained that 'the German revolution had been carried out from below and not from above'.[55] To the same end, Hitler and Frick repeatedly vowed in the summer of 1933 that the National Socialist revolution had been completed, adding the assurance that complete Gleichschaltung of state and society would be introduced by legal means.

Party supporters, however, regarded the seizure of power and the marriage with the apparatus of state – Goebbels spoke of it as the 'last stage of a revolutionary act'[56] – as a further stage in the progress of a revolutionary act and not at all as its termination. Hitler's alliance with the traditional army, civil service, and economic élites seemed to them a tactically motivated transition state, beyond which lay the party's undivided mastery. Corroboration for this view was provided by the agreement made prior to the seizure of power that National Socialist holders of government appointments should also retain their party appointments.[57] Party veterans (*Alte Kämpfer*) and active members of the SA, in particular, still clung to their expectations of revolution and readiness to fight in its cause; they dreamt of the day when the NSDAP and the SA would comprise virtually the whole of the population and replace the existing social order.[58] In fact, the evolving National Socialist system of government was necessarily rather tentative and temporary in nature, characterized as it was by the tension between the old institutions and the superimposed areas of government by party élites. In some National Socialist cadres, there still survived the utopian idea of a future more radical new order, although without any definite programme for this; the conviction that a truly National Socialist state would yet be built was once again revived during the Second World War. At first, local party organizations imagined that they were carrying out the wishes of the leadership by arbitrary action on their own account: they needed no sophisticated combination of revolutionary measures from below and sanctioning legislation from above, even though, during the process of seizing power, such tactics might have proved highly effective.[59] Except for the SA under Ernst Roehm, the party acquiesced in national disciplinary measures, though sometimes with reluctance.

Only against the background of the myth of the National Socialist movement's final victory can the reality of the Third Reich be interpreted. The party, as an organization of the whole people, became more and more politically expendable, to the same degree as its membership rose to several million, before the May 1933 clampdown on new enrolments. It was, as it were, fixed in its Movement phase structure; in consequence, clashes intensified between the divergent regional, social, and economic interests represented in the NSDAP and its affiliated organizations, nor was there any apparent possibility of reconciling these interests. Conflicts first appeared in the field of social Gleichschaltung, although this was a continuation of party policy prior to 30 January. Predictably, party officials at all levels sought compensation for the party's dwindling influence on central decisions and were at pains to build up subsidiary power positions.

In Spring 1933 the need for a renewed electoral campaign, mounted with vast expenditure of effort, masked the party's atrophy of function. In Prussia, Gleichschaltung had been well prepared and anticipated the total seizure of power elsewhere. This sparked off Gleichschaltung within the Länder, even before the March 1933 elections, and to the party it predominantly appeared as a tactical manoeuvre to facilitate the intended suppression of left-wing parties by means of controlling the police. More-over, the Reichstag fire gave the National Socialists a chance to anticipate the Enabling Act by declaring a state of civil emerg-ency; the emergency decrees of 28 February, despite the qualifica-tions of Goering's[60] implementing ordinance, amounted in effect to such a declaration.[61] While the original strategy had foreseen the act as the starting point for the acquisition of total power and the elimination of conservative competition, it would now set the seal of legality on National Socialist rule. In fact, the aura of legitimacy conferred by the election results had already been used by the government to initiate a mounting stream of ever harsher elimination measures.

Yet again, and for the last time, were the energies of the move-ment committed to the actions by which first the SPD and the trade unions, and then the bourgeois parties and associations (in-cluding the Stahlhelm) were eliminated, and which must be con-sidered as a continuation of an electoral campaign rife with repression and propaganda.[62] For the radical elements of the NSDAP, this heightened activity carried with it the vague hope of a 'second revolution'. Disappointment at the absence of a decis-ive change and at the waning of NSDAP influence in local and regional sectors was expressed in a growing irritation with govern-mental bureaucracy. An outlet was, however, provided by the exercise of patronage in official appointments, particularly in local government posts. For the SA, with its growing numbers and insufficient funds, there was on the whole no such outlet, since Roehm, for tactical reasons, strongly objected to simulta-neous tenure of party and government positions. Small wonder then that the SA, although its social composition differed little from that of the NSDAP, was the focus of discontent manifesting itself in the call for a 'second revolution'. Under pressure from Goering and Frick, it had been obliged to surrender its function as an auxiliary police force and to a large extent abandon the Commissar system.[63] Apart from the rancorous Bavarians,[64] the SA had no place in the evolving power structure of the régime; Hitler, believing an alliance with the Reichswehr leaders to be essential, was determined to curb Roehm's military ambitions, whose aim was to make the Reichswehr equal or subordinate to the projected SA People's Army. Once Gleichschaltung was complete, the SA lost all function in power politics. On 30 June 1934, as a result of intrigues by Himmler and Goering and from fear of a counter-coup by the conservatives, the final blow was delivered, precipitately and at grave risk to the prestige of the régime.[65] In the eyes of the public, the SA's fall opened the way for a stable form of government.

Measures to supplant Länder autonomy and to institute structural reform of the Reich were introduced by the Ministry of the Interior, at first in emulation of Prussia. Though initially ambiguous,[66] their purpose was to end or at least control the overlaps in areas of competence, particularly the usurpation of official positions, which stemmed from the ideology of the Movement phase. At local government level, this was achieved by the introduction of the *Deutsche Gemeindeordnung* (German Local Government Order) of 1935, with its far-reaching concessions, counterbalanced however by a tightening of the state's supervisory powers. It is common knowledge that no such success was forthcoming at the level of the controversial 'intermediate government' because of opposition among the Gauleiters, who either favoured particularism or were anxious to protect their personal authority. This is not the place for an account of the often-quoted defeat – foreseeable at an early stage and finally brought about in 1942 – of the Ministry of the Interior's attempts to build up some kind of rational state structure.[67] Frick's endeavours are known to have foundered not least because of Hitler himself and his characteristic rejection, partly influenced by legal considerations, of the suggestion that a Reichs Constitution should replace the Enabling Act. Further, Hitler prevented any attempt to assist him by introducing a legislative senate, or even a senate whose sole function would be to elect the Führer, although this would have been a source of political unification, after the cabinet as an integrating influence had lost all power and fallen into desuetude.[68] The question here is rather how far a perpetuation of specific elements of the Movement phase was responsible for the National Socialist régime's metamorphosis, so often described, into an antagonistic and chaotic rivalry of individual power blocs, which it would be an over-simplification to call a dualism of party and state.

For a true internal stabilization of the régime, fundamental re-organization of the NSDAP was a prerequisite, and Hitler was neither ready nor in a position to carry this out. He saw the NSDAP as a driving force on which to rely should the state apparatus fail or oppose him. At one time, the Ministry of the Interior debated whether the party should again become an élite body entrusted with the selection of political leaders. The position of the Gauleiters, answerable only to the Führer, made this impossible. The Law to Safeguard Unity of State and Party (December 1933) granted wide autonomy to the party but deprived it of all real political function. Even before this, Hitler as Chancellor had largely neglected the duties of the party leader; the appointment of Rudolf Hess as Deputy Führer intensified the incessant rivalry among the NSDAP's top rank. Hess proved quite inadequate as de facto head of the party, which promptly split into a myriad widely-separated power blocs and competing organizations.[69]

While the SS managed to take over a number of functions within the state and so gradually to acquire an all-important position of power in the régime, ultimately monopolizing political control,[70] the NSDAP itself was confined more and more to non-political social work. Significantly, its highest ambition was to supplant the local priest. Consequently, leading party members idealized the institution of the Catholic Church.[71] Propaganda duties, hitherto the main task of the party, were now taken over by the Reichs Propaganda Ministry which, in a typical fusion of state and party machinery, assumed direct control over the NSDAP propaganda sections. Political indoctrination work was still left to the party, but even here it was faced with competition from Alfred Rosenberg and the Deutsche Arbeitsfront.[72] As a result, the party organization per se became more and more de-politicized and incapable of integrating divergent community interests. Languishing behind the lines, it might well regret the gradual loss of its vaunted 'common touch' and its growing inability to bridge the gaps – Hess deplored the 'vacuum' between leadership and grass roots.[73]

To curb the prevalent opportunism and increasing bureaucratic inflexibility, the NSDAP would have needed to absorb the independently administered positions of political power as they stood. Instead, the principle of simultaneous tenure of state and party office led to an ever-tightening grip on the party by officialdom, the loss of many party functionaries who preferred state to party employment, and indirectly to progressive depoliticization. Many foreign observers, impressed by well-organized mass rallies and plebiscitary support for the system, took it for granted that the NSDAP as a political mass organization exerted an authoritative radicalizing influence on decision-making; yet, in fact, it was increasingly condemned to political sterility.[74]

Political importance resided not in the party but rather in high-ranking party officials who used their position as a stepping-stone to the usurpation of public office and functions of state. Only the personal drive of the men concerned determined how far they were able to interfere in local or regional affairs; significantly, party influence at local level varied to a remarkable degree with the political forces involved.[75] Even in the Third Reich, effective political ascendancy depended on holding public office. Party officials, unless they took on some additional state assignment, remained more or less impotent. Notably, Martin Bormann's growing pre-eminence was due far less to his immensely strong personal position within the party than to his success, through the office of Deputy Führer and later through the Party Chancellery, in ensuring for himself a monopoly of control over the legislation, although total mastery of the Gauleiter group eluded him. The function of the Party Chancellery as a co-ordinating ministry in competition with the Reichs Chancellery gave him a further chance to dominate subsidiary party apparatus – often over the heads of the Gauleiters; despite this, he never quite managed to turn the party into a true channel of executive power.[76]

Similarly, Himmler's power stemmed from the fusion of the offices of Reichsführer SS and Chief of German Police, although in the latter position he was nominally subordinate to Frick. As

Reichs Commissar for the consolidation of the German *Volkstum*, he was able to neutralize the authority of the Ministry of the Interior in the annexed and occupied territories up to 1943, when he himself became head of the ministry and could further erode its jurisdiction for the benefit of the Reichssicherheitshauptamt.[77] Again, Robert Ley's influence as head of the NSDAP Reichs Organization was reinforced by his simultaneous leadership of the Deutsche Arbeitsfront, numerically and financially far and away the strongest mass organization in the Third Reich.

The much-discussed enmity between different offices in the Third Reich arose largely because the party organization, while not troubling itself to integrate them politically, lent a veneer of legality to the usurpation of public office by National Socialist party officials, a practice which Frick had only temporarily been able to hold in check. Moreover, the party itself exemplified the progressive fragmentation of political competence and responsibility which finally led to the loss of political rationality and the disintegration of the régime. Whilst the NSDAP as a mass organization declined into political sterility, party officials, first and foremost the Gauleiters, persistently created spheres of influence for themselves, so establishing a system of patronage and cliques. The strictly personal concept of politics, absence of respect for institutions, pretensions to the guardianship of the movement's true interests, the party's susceptibility to corruption – these were the contributory causes for the transformation of the national socialist government system into a tangle of personal interdependence, clashing governmental machinery, disputed claims to fields of competence and the unbridled rule of each man for himself among the Nazi élite.

4

Leadership rivalries, internal power struggles, and the eventual self-disintegration of the régime have been ascribed to Hitler's basic Social Darwinist ideas, coupled with his multiplication of areas of competence in order to consolidate his own position as supreme arbiter and at the same time to bring his own ends nearer to achievement. Hitler was undeniably motivated by Social Darwinism; nevertheless, the question remains how far he himself felt obliged to make his position, by that time incontestable, even more secure by putting this mechanism into action. Tim Mason has pointed out Hitler's continual uncertainty as to popular reactions, particularly those of the workers, and Alan Milward has shown that fear of unpopularity induced him to relegate measures for the prosecution of total war to the background.[78] Nevertheless, he certainly did not see his position threatened by any organization, however powerful. Hitler never impeded the ascendancy of the SS; on the contrary, he emphatically supported it, evidenced by his appointment of Thierack as Reichs Minister of Justice.[79] Furthermore, apart from interference with the judiciary, Hitler usually intervened only if potentates of the régime had put pressure on him. Peterson makes the down-to-earth comment that Hitler's disinclination to determine priorities often arose more from a sense of inadequacy and a truly characteristic hesitancy, than from simple lack of interest.[80] Accordingly, his escape into Social Darwinism when faced with the need to resolve conflicts can hardly be called a rational pattern of decision on the lines of *divide et impera*.

Throughout his reign, Hitler was fearful of institution-backed power; he certainly never displayed the slightest understanding of any attempts towards setting it up. His aversion from any institutional restriction may indeed be explained by the circumstances of his life; in some respects an element of personal insecurity seems to be involved. His call for assent by plebiscite to his union of the Chancellorship and Presidency may have been due in part to some similar over-caution in domestic politics; in the main, however, the plebiscite was held for reasons of foreign policy and therefore of propaganda, in order to strengthen the government. In this it was undoubtedly successful. Hitler resigned as party leader but transferred his accustomed style of political leadership to the affairs of state. This meant concentration on matters of current priority, combined with utter neglect not only of routine business but also of all long-term problems. In February 1933 he told Sefton Delmer that there was nothing at all to the business of governing.[81]

Instead of acting as a balancing element in the government,

Hitler disrupted the conduct of affairs, partly by continually acting on sudden impulses, each one different, and partly by delaying decisions on current matters. His totally unbureaucratic type of leadership, nothing being dealt with in writing, his frequent absences from Berlin, his utter lack of contact with departmental ministers, his dependence on advice from outsiders (often given by chance-comers and usually incompetent), and his dismissal of officialdom as too unwieldy to carry out political necessities – all this gave his government an aura of instability and sometimes of self-contradiction. As party leader, he had always avoided early intervention in quarrels within the party, not wishing to put the loyalties of lower-rank leaders at risk. By deliberately remaining impartial in the policy dispute between the party leaders in Munich and the Gauleiters of north-west Germany, and restricting himself to tactical measures, he preserved the many facets of the party programme, opening the way for the bandwagon of the early thirties. Not only that, he also stabilized his position of leadership as a unifying force and the symbolic representative of the whole movement.

And all this was not merely the outcome of Machiavellian deliberation, but rather of Hitler's experience as a propagandist. As Chancellor and President of the Reich – significantly, he refrained from using the latter title – he had no real need to consolidate his power by such means. He avoided all measures which might have been considered inconsistent or an admission of earlier mistakes. He baulked at breaking with men who had held leading positions in the movement or the state; he appointed Baron von Neurath President of the Privy Council, he delayed dealing with Frick's resignation. To part from Gauleiters cost him a severe inner struggle; and it was only after a virtual ultimatum from Goering and Himmler that he assented to Roehm being shot. Creation of double and triple competencies was the inevitable consequence. 'The principle of letting things take their course until the stronger man has won the day',[82] which the Gauleiter of Weser-Ems called the 'secret of the movement's astounding development and achievement', in short that Social Darwinism so often attributed to Hitler, hardly ever brought about the absolute elimination of the loser. The alleged logic of the Social Darwinist style of leadership, therefore, failed to achieve its full effect, since victor and vanquished might still change places. Karl Dietrich Bracher sees this aspect of the Third Reich as intentional: 'The antagonism between rival agencies was resolved only in the omnipotent key position of the Führer. But precisely herein and not in the functioning of the state as such lay the profound purpose of an "integration" that was by no means complete. For the key position of the dictator derived precisely from the complex coexistence and opposition of the power groups and from conflicting ties.'[83] Unquestionably, this was the case. Increasingly relieved from the actual duties of leadership, particularly during the last months of the Third Reich, Hitler remained throughout the point of reference for all the rival power blocs. The question is, however, whether a personalized interpretation, hinging on Hitler's attempts to consolidate his absolute leadership, can suffice; a Machiavellian enjoyment of power would seem to imply rough handling of subordinate leaders, but, on the contrary, Hitler exerted himself to win them over by forceful oratory and personal appeals, with marked success. The ruthless action demanded from his subordinates, which he himself practised by arbitrary interference in jurisdiction and elsewhere, contrasts somewhat with his extremely careful manipulations whenever he felt his personal prestige to be at risk. The common denominator of these two attitudes was his reliance on propaganda. No quarter towards political adversaries had long been one of Hitler's propaganda maxims, qualified by the characteristic proviso never to get involved with a superior enemy: on matters of prestige, however, he advocated the greatest flexibility.

As Chancellor, therefore, Hitler personified the specific political style which had ensured the movement's success. One aspect of this was the postponement of decisions on political priorities, for the sake of tactical flexibility: even after 1933, Hitler did his utmost to avoid hard-and-fast political rulings wherever possible. A side effect of this tendency was to obscure the real intentions of the National Socialist leadership, however often they might be displayed in all their ambiguity. As dictator, Hitler still obeyed the maxims of the successful publicity man: to concentrate on the aims of the moment, to profess unshakable determination to achieve them, and to use parallel strategies, heedless of the political consequences resulting from the inevitable inter-institutional friction entailed. When he spoke, time and again, of the need to inspire the masses with a close-knit ideology and a fanatical will to fight, it was from a genuine belief in the superiority of a publicity campaign to a totalitarian, and hence necessarily pragmatic, organization. His insuperable dislike for any form of bureaucracy must be seen in this context, as must his emphasis on a principle of 'leadership of men', which caused him to despise all administrative activity, and which led to the fiction of a 'government without administration'.[84] Playing off rival power blocs against one another was not so much a matter of securing his own omnipotence, but rather for the satisfaction of an instinctive need to reward all and any fanatical pursuit of an end, no matter whether institutionally fixed competencies were ignored or whether, an advantage having been gained, its bureaucratic safeguards were sacrificed to overt dynamics.

Such an attitude had, in the days of campaigning, allowed total mobilization of the movement; once a full-scale dictatorship had been established, however, it engendered substantial losses as a result of friction, as well as a lack of objective efficiency. Overall meddling and unbureaucratic 'leadership of men', coupled with a chronic underrating of professional skill, led to an uncontrolled hegemony of personal patronage at all levels, to the spread of corruption and denunciations, and to total fragmentation of political decision-making. The cabinet soon lost all importance and did not meet after 1938; party leader meetings were sporadic and little more than a claque; the nominal Reichs leadership of the NSDAP was an uncoordinated bureaucratic apparatus devoid of real power. In short, no formal mechanism leading to integration was in existence. In its absence, clashes of interest within the party were of necessity settled by intrigue and horse-trading, so that all conflicts inevitably sank to the personal level. Significantly, the National Socialist leadership evolved the naive premise that, by picking the right men, the ubiquitous petty frictions could be obviated, although in fact the clashes were structurally inherent. For the system to function, the Führer would have had to fix the political guidelines and give his casting vote on matters of principle; this, however, was the exception rather than the rule and when it did occur, it was always too late. An atmosphere of personal distrust among the leaders of the Third Reich was unavoidable.

Researchers into this period frequently assert that, in the last instance, Hitler was the invariable driving force pushing the régime into a progressive radicalization of its aims and thereby overtaxing its strength.[85] The point is repeatedly made that, despite some tactical flexibility now and then, he pursued and achieved the fixed objectives already set out in *Mein Kampf*.[86] Such an interpretation, based solely on ideology, is necessarily open to considerable objections. Schoenbaum has demonstrated that, precisely in the field of domestic policies, National Socialist achievements were, in many cases, the exact opposite of the original intentions.[87] It is questionable, too, whether National Socialist foreign policy can be considered as an unchanging pursuit of established priorities. Hitler's foreign policy aims, purely dynamic in nature, knew no bounds; Joseph Schumpeter's reference to 'expansion without object' is entirely justified.[88] For this very reason, to interpret their implementation as in any way consistent or logical is highly problematic.

One question above all others remains open: how was it possible that remote and fantastic aims should suddenly be brought within easy reach? In reality, the régime's foreign policy ambitions were many and varied, without any clear aims and only linked by the ultimate goal: hindsight alone gives them some air of consistency.[89] In domestic politics, the question is more easily answered. The specific style of leadership, largely based on postponement of decisions and delay in defining fundamental priorities, necessarily led to a diminishing sense of reality. The leadership's one-sided attitude was reflected in highly coloured reports and hand-picked information; but impressionistic reportages could never replace hard news as an ingredient in the formation of public opinion.[90] Increasing blindness to reality was the result. Political decision-making was more and more influenced by personal ambitions and official corruption, and took on the irrationals guise of non-institutional power struggles between the clients of state and party patronage. In place of the civil service, there was an overt system of competitive ruling cliques which, while using existing institutions to bolster up their own power, were at the same time parasitically eroding them. The merry-go-round of changing potentials for influence revolved about the dictator, who in his turn followed a policy of balance between divergent political interests, not so much by pragmatic compromise as by reference either to objectives in the far distant future or to those which were immediate and short-term. In this way, any vestige of political stability was dissipated as soon as it was achieved. In this context, Martin Broszat has referred to the 'negative selection of some elements of *Weltanschauung*' activated by this system.[91]

Wherever massive interests of the various power blocs conflicted, no viable solution was to be found. Any initial attempts towards positive reorganization were sacrificed to an unbridled clash of social interests, clearly to be seen in rival party mechanisms no less than in society at large. Political motive forces, such as the desire on the part of the power blocs to prove themselves politically and so to extend and secure their position, had to take the line of least resistance. This state of affairs was evident in, for example, the treatment of the 'Jewish question'. In each individual case, the common denominator of the competing power blocs was not a mid-stream compromise, but whatever in any given circumstances was the most radical solution, previously considered as beyond the realms of possibility. To avoid surrendering its overall authority on the Jewish question, the Ministry of the Interior consented to drastic discriminatory measures which once and for all showed that the 'rule of law' had been nothing but a painstakingly maintained façade. To prevent Jewish property falling into the hands of the Gau organizations as a result of wild-cat 'aryanization', Goering, following the November Pogrom (of which he, like Heydrich, disapproved), gave orders for aryanization by the state; the departments involved hastily busied themselves with supporting legislation, even if only to retain their share of responsibility. The impossible situation created by the material and social dispossession of the Jews caused individual Gauleiters to resort to deportations, regardless of consequences, a move bitterly resisted by the departments concerned. However, the result was not the replacement of deportation by a politically 'acceptable' solution but, on the contrary, the systematic mass murder of the Jews, which no one had previously imagined possible – the most radical solution, and incidentally one which coincided with Hitler's own wishes.[92]

Typical of fascist politics and also of the Movement phase is the use of propaganda slogans, such as *Volksgemeinschaft* (community of the people), to cover up actual social conflicts and to replace political compromise and choice of priorities. While the Movement as such was steadily declining in importance within the régime and no longer initiated any policies, its principle of 'solutions without conflict' was carried over into the sphere of government, now divested of much of its authority. This tendency led to a cumulative radicalization, so that extravagant objectives, far away at first, came nearer to immediate realization. In this way, it provided the possibility of anticipating some of the millennial aims of the Third Reich, such as annihilation of the Jews, eradication of Eastern European élites, Himmler's chimerical plans for resettlement, and the breeding of a Greater German élite. These efforts were choked by a torrent of crime, blood, and mediocrity, and stood revealed in all their inadequacy; nevertheless, they were still impelled by the inhuman consistency of machinery running on, without the slightest relevance to actual political interests and realities. Ample evidence shows that Hitler drew back whenever he met public resistance, such as on euthanasia[93] and the Church question.[94] Early in his reign, too, he tended to listen more to the representations of Schacht and civil servants at the Ministry of the Interior than to the radical promptings of his party colleagues. It is not enough, therefore, to cast Hitler as the fanatical instigator. Even the 'Final Solution of the Jewish Question' came to pass only in the uncertain light of the dictator's fanatical propaganda utterances, eagerly seized upon as orders for action by men wishing to prove their diligence, the efficiency of their machinery, and their political indispensability. Characteristically, Goering took it upon himself to give the word of command for the Final Solution, although, as in other cases, he gladly left it to others (in this case Himmler) to put it into practice.

In this regard, the search for the elements of continuity and change after the Movement phase must be taken up anew. National Socialist dictatorship was based, not on the movement's popular plebiscitary victory but on an alliance of interests between the conservative élites and the fascist party. This equilibrium rapidly gave way to the total exercise of fascist power, but was still propped up by the more or less undisturbed apparatus of government, including the overwhelmingly conservative nationalist civil service, staffed in the main by the same men as before.[95] Initially, too, the autonomy and weapon monopoly of the armed forces was maintained, and the capitalist structure of the economy was kept in being, though politically subordinated. At the same time, the economic sector was rewarded for political good behaviour, by such means as elimination of organized labour and by an armaments boom, enthusiastically welcomed, at least in its beginnings.[96] Fusion of the party and its associated groups (the SA excluded) with the government apparatus seemed at first to ensure internal and external stabilization of the régime. Material assistance in this respect was contributed by the restraining power of the ministerial civil service which was initially able to prevent calamitous errors of judgement in foreign and domestic affairs: but this presented a bitter paradox. The civil service largely succeeded in curbing the plebiscitary role of the mass party and in giving the dictatorship an independent standing as the Führer State[97] by means of subsidiary methods of legitimization. However, its ability to control Hitler and moderate his actions diminished with time. His tendency to pile office on office continually reduced his involvement in individual decisions; proportionately, however, the unbridled forces of the Movement phase, now transformed into uncontrollable and uninhibited power conflicts between independent factions, established a type of cumulative radicalization which annulled the temporary stabilization. The result was an erosion of the apparatus of government and the independence of the army, and increasing inroads into the monopoly of capitalist economy, so that the conservative social foundations of the system itself were threatened even though they had undergone no marked change. A similar process occurred in the field of foreign policy, where excessive and overtaxing demands drove the Reich into a hopeless military situation.

5

By delaying the revelation of the insoluble contradictions within the régime, the war provided it with some stability, at the same time, however, presenting a threat for the not too distant future. The régime's internal ambiguity, the restlessness caused by constant innovation, and the impossibility of pinpointing responsibility prevented consolidation of oppositional forces, both within and outside the party. The people's grievances concerning the régime's many abuses were never moulded into a nationwide criticism of the whole system. As a mythical figure inspiring unity, Hitler could be loyally accepted even by those who utterly despised the rule of party bosses. The confusing coexistence and antagonisms of rival mechanisms and power blocs nurtured the fiction of one rational entity high above the turmoil – the dictator, that is, in the role of Providence – whilst abuses were laid at the door of subordinate leaders. In such a diffuse atmosphere of conflicting power structures, the resistance movement of 20 July could develop without coming to the Gestapo's notice at an early stage. Nevertheless, it too was fatally hampered by the feverishness and instability of the National Socialist leadership.[98] The failure of Operation Walküre meant the senseless prolongation of the war in just those last few months of terrible losses. Hitler's order to apply the 'scorched earth' policy to Germany, effectively countermanded by Albert Speer, his curse on the German nation as unworthy of survival, and his injunction on posterity to continue the annihilation of the Jews – all this throws light on the falsehood at the core of a gangster régime which had destroyed traditional social and political structures only to proliferate corruption, petty-bourgeois mediocrity, and a band of criminals of historical proportions, regarded as heroes by shallow moralists. How far the National Socialist state had disintegrated from within is reflected in the internecine struggles during the last weeks of the régime: the deposing of Himmler and Goering, the awarding of the Reichs Presidency to the politically colourless Grand Admiral Doenitz, and the turning over of the Chancellorship to Goebbels, who evaded the absurd prospect by suicide, while somewhere in Schleswig-Holstein, Doenitz was forming an impotent rump government.[99]

In fascist Italy, the conservative élites had maintained some measure of independence from the fascist government and were able to protect Italy from total destruction and political paralysis by a successful rebellion. Hitler, on the other hand, managed to wield his fatal influence to the last: the National Socialist leadership cliques, burdened with guilt, could not free themselves from their traumatic dependence on the dictator, now verging on physical and mental collapse and encapsulated from the outside world within the Führer bunker.[100] Was this the result of the integrating force of the Führer myth, or was that myth only the lie at the heart of a régime now reeling towards total bankruptcy? The Führer myth and the leadership rivalries were interdependent. In combination, they formed an atavistic principle of political rule, entirely consonant with propaganda objectives and allowing maximum tactical flexibility, yet condemned to failure under the conditions of a great modern industrialized state, even when allied to up-to-date forms of bureaucratic rule within the emergent patterns of power competing with the traditional apparatus of government. The destructive dynamics of atavistic leadership rivalries gained extraordinary strength by the total exploitation of the technical and bureaucratic efficiency of rapidly established commissions and organizations. Initially held in check by foreign policy considerations and by the restraining power of a hidebound civil service, the emergent National Socialist leadership groups lost all sense of reality and proportion in the chase after loosely connected aims.

Ever more embroiled in the feverish and confused process of decision-making, the traditional leading élites in the apparatus of government, in the army and the economy, were forced either to join in the cumulative radicalization of the régime or to decline into political oblivion. What ensued was that political decision-making was altogether lowered to the personal level and became progressively more irrational; the unified administrative system was destroyed; communication between divergent leadership factions, and from them to their subordinates, was lost; and feed-back mechanism, which might have allowed effective supervision of the increasingly independent power groups, was non-existent. From this stemmed a sense of insecurity as to the success of the régime's domestic policies.

Political energy was, by the same token, dissipated in endless and increasingly obdurate personal squabbles, as well as in actions of dubious value in terms of practical politics, squandering the régime's strength. Such actions included the fateful destruction of European Jewry and of a large proportion of the élite of Eastern Europe, Himmler's fanciful resettlement plans, and his concept of a 'Greater German Empire of the German Nation', whose end result was envisaged as overlordship by a Germanic élite at some future time. In the same category, too, were Speer's misconceived plans for armaments, with their laborious, but belated, amendments, and the systematic theft of art treasures throughout Europe by Goering and Rosenberg – a mixture of hubris and dilettantism.

The Nazi régime could unleash gigantic energies for short-term priorities. Total mobilization of available resources occurred only at a late stage, and even then only in the face of Hitler's delaying manoeuvres, resulting from his anxiety to avoid an internal political situation like that of late autumn 1918.[101] As in the Movement phase, the existence of the régime depended on the people never being allowed to settle. Certainly this was not consciously intended. The dynamic force of precipitate and overlapping actions, cutting across all previous planning, was quite in keeping with the fascist leaders' way of life and with Hitler's mentality; the irrationality of political decision-making also bore an equal part in the general restlessness. Undoubtedly Hitler welcomed the flurry of activity brought about by leadership rivalries. It exactly reproduced the pre-1933 NSDAP style of politics and propaganda, and glossed over the lack of internal political integration and thoughtful future planning. Paradoxically, this confused political opponents to the same extent that it kept the people in suspense and neutralized political resistance.

The régime knew well how to perpetuate the crisis atmosphere which had given it birth and how to transmute policies into a series of emergency measures before which internal political differences had to give way. It was incapable of stabilization or of any progress beyond a parasitic erosion of traditional political structures. Hence the chameleon character of the National Socialist system; hope of a return to normality persisted, and side by side with the 'prerogative state', the 'normative state', however insignificantly, continued to exist.[102] The inner contradictions of the system – a magnified reflection of the contradictions in the National Socialist programme – necessarily led to its internal and external disintegration, while preventing early destruction from within.

Glossing over social tensions, unchanged if not intensified, was a well-tried NSDAP propaganda technique. Terrorist pressure exerted by an ever more bureaucratic police force for an outward show of compliance with the crumbling letter of the law gave the lie to the tenet, stoutly maintained by the inner circle of National Socialist leaders, that planned indoctrination would achieve their desired aim: ideological unity and the 'fanatical closing of the ranks', called for by Hitler again and again. Significantly, Hitler's subordinate leaders increasingly began to dream of the *Kampfzeit*, when 'genuine idealism' still existed and positive tasks had been assigned to them. Bormann hoped to revive the party, at least after the war, as a self-contained political fighting unit. But the movement was dead; only its elements remained – corruption, rivalry, and the supplanting of policy by propaganda. The myth of the 'thousand-year Reich' faded among the ruins of German cities and defeated German armies; political power lay almost entirely in the hands of Himmler and his henchmen, and the Gauleiters as Reichs Defence Commissaries. The goal of total domination over state and society had been attained; the NSDAP had transferred its 'revolutionary legality' to the state; but as the relics of traditional government structures disappeared, so vanished the basis of National Socialist dictatorship. In all its ghastly inhumanity, it was now revealed as a gigantic farce upon the stage of world history.

Notes

1. For the study of German self-assessment after 1945, Friedrich Meinecke, *The German Catastrophe* (Cambridge, Mass., 1950) is of fundamental importance. For the conventional interpretation, see William L. Shirer, *The Rise and Fall of the Third Reich* (New York, 1960) and A. J. P. Taylor, *The Course of German History* (London, 1945). Ideological critical analyses are: Martin Broszat, *German National Socialism 1919–1945* (Santa Barbara, Calif., 1966), George L. Mosse, *The Crisis of German Ideology* (New York, 1964), Fritz Stern, *The Politics of Cultural Despair* (New York, 1961), Kurt Sontheimer, *Antidemokratisches Denken in der Weimarer Republik* (Munich, 1962). A good summary is to be found in Karl Dietrich Bracher, *The German Dictatorship*, 4th ed. (New York, 1973).

2. Seymour Martin Lipset, 'Der "Faschismus", die Linke, die Rechte und die Mitte', in *Kölner Zeitschrift für Soziologie und Sozialpsychologie*, vol. XI (1959); Talcott Parsons, 'Some Sociological Aspects of the Fascist Movements 1942', in *Essays in Sociological Theory* (Glencoe, Ill., 1964); Theodor Geiger, *Die soziale Schichtung des deutschen Volkes* (Stuttgart, 1932; new ed. Darmstadt, 1967); Ernst Nolte, *Die faschistische Bewegung* (Munich, 1966); Michael Kater, 'Zur Soziographie der frühen NSDAP', in *Vierteljahrshefte für Zeitgeschichte*, no. XIX (Munich, 1971) (hereafter cited as *VifZ*); also Heinrich-August Winkler, *Mittelstand, Demokratie und Nationalsozialismus* (Cologne, 1972).

3. Cf. Iring Fetscher, 'Faschismus und Nationalsozialismus: Zur Kritik des sowjet-marxistischen Faschismusbegriffs', in *Politische Vierteljahresschrift*, vol. III (Cologne, 1962) (hereafter cited as *PVS*); Theodore Pirker, ed. *Komintern und Faschismus 1920–1940* (Stuttgart, 1965); also my 'Antifascism', article in *Marxism, Communism and Western Society*, vol. I (New York, 1972), pp. 134–41 (hereafter cited as *MCWS*); Wolfgang Abendroth, ed., *Faschismus und Kapitalismus* (Frankfurt, 1967); E. Nolte, ed., *Theorien über den Faschismus*, 2nd ed. (Cologne, 1970).

4. Cf. my article on 'National Socialism', in *MCWS*, vol. VI (New York, 1973); D. Eichholtz, 'Probleme einer Wirtschaftsgeschichte des Faschismus in Deutschland', in *Jahrbuch für Wirtschaftsgeschichte 1963*, pt 3.

5. From the now enormous literature on the subject, the following are the most important: Hans Kohn, 'Communist and Fascist Dictatorship: A Comparative Study', in *Dictatorship in the Modern World* (Minneapolis, 1935); Franz L. Neumann, *Behemoth: The Structure and Practice of National Socialism 1933–1944*, 2nd ed. (New York, 1944); Franz L. Neumann, *The Democratic and the Authoritarian State*, ed. H. Marcuse (Glencoe, Ill., 1957); Sigmund Neumann, *Permanent Revolution*, ed. Hans Kohn, 2nd ed. (New York, 1965); C. J. Friedrich and Z. K. Brzezinski, *Totalitarian Dictatorship and Autocracy*, 2nd ed. (Cambridge, Mass.). A survey by Bruno Seidel and Siegfried Jenkner, 'Wege der Totalitarismus-Forschung', in *Wege der Forschung*, vol. CXL (Darmstadt, 1968); M. Grieffenhagen et al., *Totalitarismus: Zur Problematik eines politischen Begriffs* (Munich, 1972).

6. Above all, Carl Schmitt, 'Die Wendung zum totalen Staat 1931', in *Positionen und Begriffe* (Hamburg, 1940); Ernst Forsthoff, *Der totale Staat* (Hamburg, 1933); Ulrich Scheuner, 'Die nationale Revolution: Eine staatsrechtliche Untersuchung', in *Archiv des öffentlichen Rechts*, new series XXIV (1933–4); and cf. Gerhard Schulz, 'Der Begriff des Totalitarismus und des Nationalsozialismus', in Seidel and Jenkner, op. cit., p. 438 ff.

7. It should be remembered here that Hannah Arendt, *Origins of Totalitarianism* (New York, 1951) starts from a different premise in dealing with the ideological and social origins of National Socialism, and therefore refers only to a 'so-called totalitarian state'. For more recent discussion, see K. Hildebrand, 'Stufen der Totalitarismus-Forschung', in *PVS*, vol. IX (1968); M. Greiffenhagen, 'Der Totalitarismus-Begriff in der Regimenlehre', op. cit.; Howard D. Mehlinger, *The Study of Totalitarianism: An Inductive Approach* (Washington, D.C., 1965); Tim Mason, 'Das Unwesen der Totalitarismustheorien', in *Der Politologe*, vol. VII, 1966).

8. Apart from Franz Neumann's *Behemoth*, which is still relevant, Ernst Fraenkel's analysis, *The Dual State* (New York, 1941) is of basic importance and, with Sigmund Neumann, influenced the earlier writings of K. D. Bracher, particularly in Bracher et al., *Die nationalsozialistische Machtergreifung*, 2nd ed. (Cologne, 1962).

9. The initiative for the comparative study of fascism arose from E. Nolte's fundamental study, *Der Faschismus in seiner Epoche* (Munich, 1963), English title, *The Three Faces of Fascism* (New York, 1966). For the present state of the discussion, see Wolfgang Schieder 'Faschismus und kein Ende?' in *Neue Politische Literatur*, vol. XV (1970), Heft 2.

10. David Schoenbaum, *Hitler's Social Revolution*, 2nd ed. (Garden City, N.Y., 1967), p. xiii. A survey of recent tendencies and research problems is to be found in Hans Mommsen et al., 'Faschistische Diktatur in Deutschland', in *Politische Bildung*, vol. V (Stuttgart, 1972), Heft 1, and in Wolfgang Sauer, 'National Socialism: Totalitarianism or Fascism?', in *American Historical Review*, no. LXXIII (1967).

11. For socio-political analyses of 'totalitarian' mass movements, see first and foremost Theodor W. Adorno et al., *The Authoritarian Personality* (New York, 1950); Eric Fromm, *Escape from Freedom* (New York, 1941). The wealth of differing versions precludes a summary survey of the psychological and sociological attempts to explain the 'totalitarian' susceptibility of the German middle classes. Besides the linking of socialist and liberal attitudes stemming from the atomization and depoliticization of German society under the influence of a capitalist national state (H. Arendt), there is the widely held conviction that totalitarianism was a pathological extension of radical democracy (J. L. Talmon, *The Origins of Totalitarian Democracy* [New York, 1961]). However, the theory of F. Neumann and S. Neumann, postulating that National Socialism destroyed the existing social structure and intentionally kept the mass of the people in a state of constant tension and permanent revolution has had an even more lasting influence on subsequent research, by stressing that these were the specific totalitarian intentions

of Hitler's policies. But National Socialism, notwithstanding its dynamic social power, did not effectively level out social differences and structures (except in the anti-aristocrat campaign following 20 July 1944). Instead, it camouflaged them by its community ideologies (see Schoenbaum, op. cit., p. 275 ff.).

12. Cf. Hans Buchheim, *Das Dritte Reich* (Munich, 1958) and *Totalitäre Herrschaft* (Munich, 1962). See also Robert C. Tucker, 'Towards a Comparative Politics of Movement-Régimes', in *The American Political Science Review*, no. LV (1961), who points out that the party's tendency to abandon sociological and plebiscitary fundamentals in favour of the psychopathological character of the Führer was a characteristic of fascist mass movement rule; he considers 'Hitlerism' to be the appropriate term for this development.

13. See Günther Plum's article, 'Resistance Movements', in *MCWS*, vol. VII (New York, 1973).

14. On KPD policy see Siegfried Bahne, in Erich Matthias and Rudolf Morsey, eds, *Das Ende der Parteien 1933* (Düsseldorf, 1960).

15. One of K. D. Bracher's great merits is that, in *Die Auflösung der Weimarer Republik*, 4th ed. (Villingen, 1964), he brings out the continuity between the presidential cabinets and the Third Reich, and contradicts the widely held belief that January 1933 represented a major break with the past.

16. See in particular Wolfgang Horn, *Führerideologie und Parteiorganisation in der NSDAP 1919–1933* (Düsseldorf, 1972), and also J. Nyomarkay, *Charisma and Factionalism in the Nazi Party* (Minneapolis, 1967). Central to the latter's research is the connection between the Führer cult and the party's forming itself into sub-groups.

17. Deliberate fostering of aestheticizing elements as a means of integration distinguishes fascist from imperialist movements; see S. J. Woolf, ed., *European Fascism* (New York, 1969) and W. Laqueur and G. Mosse, eds., *International Fascism 1920–1945* (London, 1969).

18. Cf. the Reichs Chancellery draft for the establishment of a senate to elect the leader, June 1941 (Bundesarchiv Coblenz, R. 43 II, p. 1213a); and M. Broszat, *Der Staat Hitlers: Grundlegung und Entwicklung seiner inneren Verfassung* (Munich, 1969), p. 360 f.

19. See in particular Jeremy Noakes, *The Nazi Party in Lower Saxony 1921–1933* (Oxford, 1971), p. 156 ff., p. 164 f. Cf. also Geoffrey Pridham, *Hitler's Rise to Power, The Nazi Movement in Bavaria* (New York, London, 1974).

20. Wolfgang Schieder, 'Fascism', in *MCWS*, vol. III (New York, 1972), p. 282 ff.

21. See the authoritative essay by M. Broszat, 'Soziale Motivation und Führerbindung des Nationalsozialismus', in *VjfZ*, no. XVII (1970), as distinct from the over-emphasis on biographical elements in interpretative models relating to Hitler, found in Eberhard Jäckel, *Hitler's Weltanschauung: A Blueprint for Power* (Middletown, Conn., 1972; German ed. Tübingen, 1969), and the earlier tendency, reintroduced recently by Joachim C.

Fest, *Adolf Hitler* (Berlin, 1973), to exaggerate Hitler's role in political decision-making. For criticism of this method, see Edward N. Peterson, *The Limits of Hitler's Power* (Princeton, 1969), p. 11 ff.

22. This is the unanimous conclusion of many recent monographs: A. S. Milward, *The German Economy at War* (London, 1965); Reinhard Bollmus, *Das Amt Rosenberg und seine Gegner* (Stuttgart, 1970); Heinz Höhne, *The Order of the Death's Head: The Story of Hitler's SS* (London, 1969); see also my study, *Beamtentum im Dritten Reich* (Stuttgart, 1969); and the earlier comments by Robert Koehl, 'Feudal Aspects of National Socialism', in *American Political Science Review*, no. LIV (1960).

23. Hugh Trevor-Roper, *The Last Days of Hitler* (London, 1949); Reimer Hansen, *Das Ende des Dritten Reiches* (Stuttgart, 1966).

24. See Henry A. Turner, 'Big Business and the Rise of Hitler', in *American Historical Review*, no. LXXV (1969), and *Faschismus und Kapitalismus in Deutschland* (Göttingen, 1972); on the role of industry see also H. Mommsen et al., eds, *Industrielle Entwicklung und politisches System in der Weimarer Republik* (Düsseldorf, 1964).

25. Werner Maser, *Die Frühgeschichte der NSDAP* (Frankfurt, 1965); Georg Franz-Willing, *Die Hitlerbewegung* (Hamburg, 1962).

26. Henry J. Gordon, *Hitler and the Beer Hall Putsch*, 2nd ed. (Oxford, 1973); Ernst Deuerlein, *Der Hitler-Putsch* (Stuttgart, 1962).

27. See in particular W. Horn, op. cit., and Dietrich Orlow, *The History of the Nazi Party 1919–1933* (Pittsburgh, 1969).

28. For the National Socialist left, see W. Horn, op. cit., as well as an earlier study by Reinhard Kühnl, *Die nationalsozialistische Linke 1925–1930* (Meisenheim, 1966) and Noakes, op. cit., p. 72 ff. Max H. Kele's theory, in *Nazis and Workers* (Pittsburgh, 1973) that Goebbels remained true to his socialist beliefs whereas Gregor Strasser conformed to Hitler's ideas, is without precedent.

29. See Uwe Lohalm, *Völkischer Radikalismus: Die Geschichte des Deutschvölkischen Schutz- und Trutzbundes 1919–1933* (Hamburg, 1970).

30. For the part played by anti-Semitism in the political power struggle during the last stages of the Weimar Republic, see the detailed analyses in Werner E. Mosse, ed., *Entscheidungsjahr 1932* (Tübingen, 1965).

31. Orlow, op. cit., pp. 89 ff., 95 ff., 140 ff.; cf. Noakes, op. cit., p. 106.

32. Noakes, op. cit., p. 121 ff.

33. ibid., p. 129 ff., Horst Gies, 'NSDAP and landwirtschaftliche Organisationen in der Endphase der Weimarer Republik', in *VjfZ*, no. XV (1967).

34. See Niethammer in Mommsen et al., *Politische Bildung*, op. cit.

35. See Richard N. Hunt, *German Social Democracy 1918–1933* (New York, 1964); and my essay 'Sozialdemokratie in der Defensive', in H. Mommsen, ed., *Sozialdemokratie zwischen Klassenbewegung und Volkspartei* (Frankfurt, 1974).

36. Walter Z. Laqueur, *Young Germany* (New York, 1962).

37. See Attila Chanady, 'The Disintegration of the German People's Party 1924–1930', in *Journal of Modern History*, no. XXXIX (1967), p. 65

ff.; Karl O'Lessker, 'Who Voted for Hitler?', in *American Journal of Sociology*, no. LXXIV (1968–9), pp. 63–9.

38. See voting analyses in Alfred Milatz, *Wähler und Wahlen in der Weimarer Republik* (Bonn, 1965), p. 141 ff.

39. William Sheridan Allen, *The Nazi Seizure of Power* (Chicago, 1965).

40. See Z. A. B. Zeman, *Nazi Propaganda*, 2nd ed. (London, 1973).

41. Cf. Bracher et al., *Die nationalsozialistische Machtergreifung*, op. cit., p. 95 ff., p. 350 ff., and also Bracher, *The German Dictatorship*, op. cit. p. 29.

42. Reichsorganisationsleiter der NSDAP, ed., *Parteistatistik (Als Manuskript gedruckt*: Munich, 1935), p. 26; Reichsführer SS, ed., *Der Weg der NSDAP* (Berlin, 1934), p. 91; cf. Niethammer, op. cit., p. 29.

43. On this, see above all Wolfgang Schaefer, *NSDAP* (Frankfurt, 1956) and Hans Gerth, 'The Nazi Party: Its Leadership and Social Composition', in *American Journal of Sociology*, no. XLV (1940), p. 517 ff.

44. Rudolf Heberle, *Landbevölkerung und Nationalsozialismus* (Stuttgart, 1963); Gerhard Stoltenberg, *Politische Strömungen im schleswig-holsteinische Landvolk* (Düsseldorf, 1962).

45. Cf. also Heinrich-August Winkler, op. cit.

46. Cf. particularly Noakes, op. cit., p. 233 f.

47. ibid., p. 230 f.

48. See Josef Becker, 'Brüning, Prälat Kaas und das Problem einer Regierungsbeteiligung der NSDAP 1930–1932', in *Historische Zeitschrift*, no. CXCVI (1963), p. 74 ff., and also Detlef Junker, *Die Deutsche Zentrumpartei und Hitler 1932/33* (Stuttgart, 1969), p. 86 ff.

49. Joseph Goebbels, *Vom Kaiserhof zur Reichskanzlei* (Berlin, 1934), pp. 87, 143.

50. See Peter Diehl-Thiele, *Partei und Staat im Dritten Reich* (Munich, 1969), p. 33.

51. Above all Helmut Nicolai, Ernst von Heydebrand und der Lasa, as well as Hans Pfundtner: cf. H. Mommsen, *Beamtentum im Dritten Reich*, op. cit., p. 28 ff.; Diehl-Thiele, op. cit., pp. 32 n., 90.

52. Joseph Goebbels, op. cit., pp. 140, 158; cf. Helmut Heiber, *Joseph Goebbels* (New York, 1972).

53. Adolf Hitler, *Mein Kampf*, 67th ed. (Munich, 1933), p. 503.

54. Goebbels, op. cit., p. 294.

55. Joseph Goebbels, *Idee und Gestalt des Nationalsozialismus* (Berlin, 1935).

56. ibid.

57. Joseph Goebbels, *Vom Kaiserhof zur Reichskanzlei*, op. cit., p. 261.

58. Cf. Heinrich Bennecke, *Hitler und die SA* (Munich, 1962), and also W. Sauer in Bracher et al., *Die nationalsozialistische Machtergriefung*, op. cit., pp. 880 ff., 927 ff.

59. Cf. K. D. Bracher, 'Stages of Totalitarian "Integration"', in Hajo Holborn, ed., *Republic to Reich: The Making of the Nazi Revolution* (New York, 1972), p. 115; and K. D. Bracher, *The German Dictatorship*, op. cit., p. 206.

60. See M. Broszat, *Der Staat Hitlers*, op. cit., p. 103 f.

61. See my 'The Political Effects of the Reichstag Fire', in H. A. Turner, ed., *Nazism and the Third Reich* (New York, 1972), p. 134 f.

62. K. D. Bracher's strongly intentionalistic interpretation, in *Stages of Totalitarian 'Integration'*, in my view overrates the degree of central direction involved in spontaneous actions by the SA and party groups.

63. Bracher et al., *Die nationalsozialistische Machtergreifung*, p. 460 ff.

64. See Diehl-Thiele, op. cit., p. 86 ff., and Broszat, *Der Staat Hitlers*, p. 137 ff.; Peterson, op. cit., p. 166 ff.

65. See mainly Heinrich Bennecke, *Die Reichswehr und der 'Roehmputsch'* (Munich, 1964). The number of victims is usually overestimated in the relevant literature; there were eighty-eight.

66. The *Reichsstatthaltergesetz* (7 April 1933), the *Neuaufbaugesetz* (30 January 1934), and the measures preceding them were quite inadequately co-ordinated. Cf. Broszat, *Der Staat Hitlers*, p. 151 ff.; Diehl-Thiele, op. cit., p. 40 ff. and 61; also Walter Baum, 'Reichsreform im Dritten Reich', in *VjfZ*, no. III (1955).

67. Cf. Diehl-Thiele, op. cit., p. 195 ff.; Mommsen, *Beamtentum*, p. 117 ff.

68. See n. 18 above.

69. See Dietrich Orlow, *History of the Nazi Party 1933–1945* (Pittsburgh, 1973), pp. 102 ff., 139 ff.; Diehl-Thiele, op. cit., p. 34.

70. See above all H. Höhne, op. cit.; Hans Buchheim et al., *Anatomy of the SS-State* (London, 1970).

71. See memorandum of the Gauleiter Weser-Ems (1942) National Archives Microcopy No. T-81, Roll No. R-71, *NSDAP-Parteikanzlei*, p. 14591 f.; Orlow, op. cit., p. 352 f , proves that the memorandum cannot have originated with Röver, but was probably written by his successor, Paul Wegener, and hence reflects the opinions of the Party Chancellery

72. Orlow, op cit., p. 84 ff.; Orlow, 'Die Adolf Hitler Schulen', in *VjfZ*, no. XIII (1965); R. Bollmus, op. cit.

73. Speech by Rudolf Hess to the Leader Corps of the NSDAP at the Reichsparteitag in Nuremberg, 16 September 1935 (Bundesarchiv Coblenz NS 25/vorl. 1183; abstracted in *Faschistische Diktatur in Deutschland*, op. cit., M 20 ff.).

74. Cf. Sigmund Neumann, op. cit., p. 115 ff.; Franz L. Neumann, *The Democratic and the Authoritarian State*, p. 249.

75. Apart from W. S. Allen and E. N. Peterson (chaps. 4–8), see H.-P. Görgen's study, *Düsseldorf und der Nationalsozialismus* (Cologne, 1968). Horst Matzerath, *Nationalsozialismus und kommunale Selbstverwaltung* (Stuttgart, 1970) has great merits but limits itself to headquarters level. That regional studies are necessary and fruitful is shown by Jeremy Noakes' book, already mentioned on several occasions.

76. Cf. Orlow, *History of the Nazi Party 1933–1945*, pp. 77 ff., 139 ff., 339 ff., and Diehl-Thiele, op. cit., p. 216 ff.; see also the informative research by Peter Hüttenberger, *Die Gauleiter* (Stuttgart, 1969).

77. Diehl-Thiele, op. cit., p. 197 ff.

78. A. S. Milward, op. cit., p. 11 f.; Tim Mason, 'The Legacy of 1918 for National Socialism', in Anthony Nicholls and Erich Matthias, eds, *German Democracy and the Triumph of Hitler* (London, 1971), pp. 220 ff., 238 f.

79. Cf. Broszat, *Der Staat Hitlers*, p. 421.

80. Peterson, op. cit., pp. 4 ff., 15 f.

81. Sefton Delmer, *Trail Sinister* (London, 1961), vol. I, p. 181.

82. Memorandum of the Gauleiter Weser-Ems (cf. n. 18 above), p. 14517.

83. Bracher, *Stages of Totalitarian 'Synchronisation'*, p. 127 f.

84. Jane Caplan, *The Civil Service in the Third Reich* (Ph.D. diss., Oxford, 1973).

85. Cf. H.-J. Fest, op. cit., p. 1028; Bracher, *German Dictatorship*, p. 348; Broszat, *Der Staat Hitlers*, p. 436 ff.

86. Cf. E. Jäckel, op. cit.; Hans-Adolf Jacobsen, *Nationalsozialistische Aussenpolitik* (Frankfurt, 1968), p. 16 f.

87. D. Schoenbaum, op. cit., above all p. 285 f.

88. Cf. Joseph Schumpeter, 'Zur Soziologie der Imperialismen', in *Archiv für Sozialwissenschaft und Sozialpolitik*, vol. XLVI (1918–19).

89. Cf. Klaus Hildebrand, *The Foreign Policy of the Third Reich* (English ed.; Berkeley, 1973); Andreas Hillgruber, *Kontinuität und Diskontinuität in der deutschen Aussenpolitik von Bismarck bis Hitler*, 3rd ed. (Düsseldorf, 1971).

90. On the problem of the 'mood' in the Third Reich, see, apart from Heinz Boberach, *Meldungen aus dem Reich: Auswahl aus den geheimen Lageberichten des Sicherheitsdienstes der SS 1939–1944* (Neuwied, 1965), the investigation by Marlies G. Steinert, *Hitlers Krieg und die Deutschen: Stimmung und Haltung der deutschen Bevölkerung im 2. Weltkrieg* (Düsseldorf, 1970).

91. M. Broszat, *Soziale Motivation und Führer-Bindung des Nationalsozialismus*, p. 405.

92. On National Socialist persecution of the Jews, see, as well as the description of the Final Solution policy by Raul Hilberg, *The Destruction of the European Jews* (Chicago, 1961), the researches by Uwe D. Adam, *Judenpolitik im Dritten Reich* (Düsseldorf, 1972), and Karl A. Schleunes, *The Twisted Road to Auschwitz: Nazi Policy toward German Jews 1933–1939* (Urbana, Ill., 1970).

93. On euthanasia, see Klaus Dörner, 'Nationalsozialismus und Lebensvernichtung', in *VjfZ*, no. XV (1967), pp. 121–52.

94. See, above all, John S. Conway, *The Nazi Persecution of the Churches* (New York, 1968); Günther Lewy, *The Catholic Church and Nazi Germany* (London, 1954).

95. On the role of the civil service, as well as the works by J. Caplan, E. N. Peterson, and H. Mommsen already quoted above, see D. Schoenbaum, op. cit., p. 193 ff.

96. Tim W. Mason, 'Labour in the Third Reich 1933–1939', in *Past and Present*, no. XXXIII (1966), pp. 112–41; Hans-Gerd Schumann, *National-*

sozialismus und Gewerkschaftsbewegung (Frankfurt, 1958); A. Schweitzer *Big Business in the Third Reich* (London, 1964).

97. Typical of this is the commentary by Ernst Rudolf Huber, *Verfassungsrecht des Grossdeutschen Reiches* (Hamburg, 1939); cf. Diehl-Thiele, op. cit., p. 29, and also Helmut Krausnick et al., *Anatomy of the SS-State* (New York, 1968), pp. 129, 133.

98. On the Resistance movement, see above all Hermann Graml et al., *German Resistance to Hitler* (London, 1970).

99. Cf. R. Hansen, op. cit.

100. See the impressive and still valid report by H. Trevor-Roper, *The Last Days of Hitler*, 1st ed. (London, 1947).

101. Cf. T. Mason, *The Legacy of 1918 for National Socialism*, p. 227.

102. Cf. Fraenkel, op. cit., and Buchheim, op. cit., p. 133 f.

KARL DIETRICH BRACHER

5　The Role of Hitler: Perspectives of Interpretation

1

For more than half a century National Socialism and its leader have been the object of countless reports and polemics, and of extensive research and interpretation. Since the days when fifty years ago the frustrated ex-soldier and self-styled demagogue Adolf Hitler made his attempted putsch in Munich, which was intended to instigate a march on Berlin following the model of Mussolini's legendary march on Rome, the literature on both Hitler and National Socialism has been growing abundantly, with no evidence of a foreseeable slowdown.[1] On the contrary, looking back at the dramatic post-war developments – the cold war and Stalinism, Hungary and Suez, the crisis of colonialism and the Near East, Czechoslovakia and Vietnam, with all their shocking consequences – we realize that they have all contributed to a continuing interest in the phenomenon of nazism. Personified by Hitler, the Nazi period somehow seems to be in the background of most of these contemporary and revolutionary events. The Second World War, which was foremost Hitler's war, has indeed changed the world, or at least has made it ripe for change, perhaps more profoundly than in any preceding period of history.

This cannot, however, be the only reason for the recurring waves of interest and for what has been called the Hitler-boom during the past few years, with the resultant mass of publications – books, pamphlets, films, cartoons, and so forth, appearing on both sides of the Atlantic. It seems strange that this should happen in face of the much more real and pressing issues of the day, when important political changes are taking place and the long process of stabilization of the European and German status quo in the aftermath of Hitler has been achieved, marking the definitive end of the post-Second World War period. We now acknowledge that the world-wide best-seller written by one of Hitler's closest collaborators, Albert Speer, in 1969–70 is the symbolic counterpart to the equally successful *Rise and Fall of the Third Reich*, written ten years earlier in 1960 by William Shirer and expressing opposite points of view. The appearance of extensive studies such as that of Werner Maser in 1971[2] and the largest and most recent biography of Hitler by Joachim Fest are also notable.

All this points to a set of motives which extends far beyond the historico-political interest. Of course, there is the inevitable and continuing sensational aspect caused by the excessive features of Hitlerism, which can be taken as a kind of modern Ghengis Khanism or an example of that combination of cruel efficiency and superhuman will-power which frequently is identified as typically German, to be horrified at or admired, or both simultaneously. It is indeed the function of a prototype beyond the historical phenomenon that makes for the lasting importance of Hitler and National Socialism.

This seems equally true with respect to very diverse types and groups of interests from the scholarly and academic and the political and literary 'user' of the Hitler topic, to the masses of spectators observing the monumental horrors and catastrophes of history, who primarily expect it to be translated into stories and pictures of human interest.

Yet at the same time we are confronted with the fact that this preoccupation concentrates on a man who seems to be much less than a great individual, even the evil Renaissance-Borgia type. He does not appear as one of the great personalities of history. There is little to arouse one's interest in the man himself, indeed he is almost totally submerged in the history of his political movement and the Third Reich. Aside from the relatively few incidents we know of his childhood and youth in Linz and Vienna, and of his experiences in the First World War and afterwards, there is very little to constitute a personal biography – his life being identical to, and often disappearing behind, the life of National Socialism. It is only at the end of his life, in the Führerbunker in Berlin in 1945, that it becomes more visible again. How difficult is it then to understand and explain the rise of a man from so narrow and parochial an existence to a formidable figure on whom depended a development of such universally historical dimensions and consequences.

But this is the precise core of the Hitler phenomenon, marking the basic features of its appearance and effect, and hinting at the most important problem of nazism: its fundamental underestimation by (1) political groupings and parties of both the right and left within Germany, thus enabling Hitler to come to power, and (2) externally on the international scene, facilitating his march to war and quest for European domination.

The problem of adequate estimation and interpretation has become even more complicated today, as the immediate experience of both nazism and Stalinism disappears into distant history. As a consequence, it has again become fashionable among intellectuals to deny any possible comparison between right- and left-wing extremism, fascism, and communist dictatorship, or between Hitler and Stalin – in short to attack and abolish the notion of totalitarianism as it was used in post-war discussion and research.[3]

At the same time, the names of Hitler or fascism are used to denounce anti-communist politics in general and in the present, with comparisons (e.g., of Vietnam to Nazi crimes) that amount to a gigantic misinterpretation of both, thus minimizing nazism.

One important argument for such misleading comparisons and distinctions is the apparent difference in ideological substance and direction between communism and fascism. This leads to the assumption that fascist or Nazi movements, by their very nature and by their lesser emphasis on, and the poorer intellectual quality of their ideology, if compared to socialist or communist Marxism, are not to be taken seriously as independent political movements in their own right, but only as a part or instrument of reactionary and capitalistic power agencies. This so-called agent theory seems to be proved not only by the poor and trivial intellectual substance of fascist movements, but also by the mediocre human and ideological stature of most of their leaders and followers.

But it is exactly at this point that illusions and fictions occurred that led to the fatal underestimation of Hitler and his movement. They were never taken seriously intellectually because its proclaimed 'national socialism' lacked the sort of coherent doctrine which was evident in Marxist socialism, although it was in fact the eclectic nature of fascist and Nazi ideology that proved to be a source of strength and paved the way for the formation of mass movements and for the politics of fanaticism.

In view of this problem of achieving a realistic assessment of nazism, it is noticeable even today that the large number of publications on the subject contrasts sharply with the small quantity of substantial contributions they make. Most publications are dedicated to the collection and display of details that satisfy private curiosity, whilst only very few have something to say on the question of Hitler's historical role and weight with respect to the great currents of our time.

This applies also to the fundamental problem of any discussion about Hitler: how is the place of the individual within the historico-political process to be defined under modern conditions? What are the possibilities and the limits of a rational explanation of a movement like National Socialism? And to what degree do we have to perceive its shape and success in terms of the demonic force of a specific individual? Here the problem of Hitler's personality remains crucial indeed. It is, of course, true that we have to be made fully aware of the dangers of a demonological interpretation of National Socialism (as well as of communism). This danger was felt acutely in Germany immediately after 1945 when many commentators tried to hide German responsibility behind the back of the superhuman and all-responsible demon Hitler. Such views represented a reversion to the leader cult, suitable to and often used for the purpose of conservative and nationalistic apologies or mystifications. They even influenced respected older historians like Gerhard Ritter in for example his contribution to the UNESCO volume of 1955, *The Third Reich*.

In view of these problems, we are still faced as before with two basic questions which are central to all serious books on Hitler from the pioneer work of Konrad Heiden in 1936 to the classic by Alan Bullock in 1952: to what degree *does* a biography of the 'Leader' disclose the nature and essence of National Socialism, or could and should we simply speak of Hitlerism? Or conversely, is it possible at all to get a true personal biography of the man whose life appears almost as nothing apart from the complete identification with the history of National Socialism? Is it not true that he lacks the stature of other great personalities of world history? And yet his career manifested a power to move men and events almost unequalled in history.

Indeed, the categories of historical greatness as discussed by Jacob Burckhard and other 'classical' historians and philosophers are not to apply to him, and it becomes clear that in our age of mass society, of totalitarian movements in democratic disguise, of pseudo-religious ideologies, the concept of historical greatness is no longer valid nor are the measures of eighteenth- and nine-teenth-century humanism, culture, and statecraft that may have been applied to figures like Napoleon, Bismarck, Lincoln, and maybe even Lenin. Hitler and, in his way, Stalin represent a new type of the great movement and party leader combining the quali-ties of fanatical ideological fixation and virtuoso mass demagogy, and replacing the traditional statesman and warrior as the great type of historical figure.

It may be better not to use the renaissance and romantic idea of the great man and political greatness any longer when basic con-ditions of political leadership have changed so drastically. But this does not mean that the role of the individual has become less important. The fashionable tendency to dissolve all historical de-velopments into structural and collective processes represents an understandable reaction to the crude concept of *Männer machen Geschichte* – history is made by great men. It is true that this con-cept of history as the history of great men was propagated not only by fascism and nazism, corresponding as it did to their very nature as dictatorships with a sole leader, but also by communist régimes where, although quite contrary to their dogma of collec-tivism, it was in keeping with the psychology of mass mobilization by charismatic leadership. The great examples of this cult of leadership and pseudo-religious veneration and adoration are Lenin, Stalin and Mao and, at present, the North Korean demi-god Kim Il Sung.

But if we critically analyse the ideological character of the cult of leadership, we have to recognize the impact it makes on the structure of the régime and at the same time what part the leader plays in the totalitarian systems of the twentieth century. Leonard Shapiro and Robert Tucker have also stressed this point with respect to Russian and Chinese totalitarianism.[4] The integral role of the great man, often denied in communist theory, was, of course, always underlined in fascism and National Socialism. But while in the case of Mussolini the totalitarian role of the Duce was never wholly realized, and fascism may therefore be defined beyond and apart from a Mussolinism, in the case of Hitler there was never any question of a *fronde* against the leader, and one of the significant features of both National Socialism and the Third Reich is the fact that from the beginning to the very end it stood and fell with this man, with his decisions, his ideological fixations, his purely political way of life, and his need for the grandiose alternative of victory or catastrophe. This indicates a passion for extreme solutions and for ultimate consequences that have been seen as the transplantation, onto the stage of history, of the theatrical pathos of Richard Wagner's operas, in which Hitler had been immersed since his youth in Linz and Vienna. It influenced not only the ideological goals of the movement but even more the organization of mass meetings displaying overwhelming power and leader-worship. For these reasons, National Socialism can indeed be called Hitlerism. This man and his intentions and actions will always be in the very centre of nazi history. But at the same time, Hitler himself is to be understood and analysed in terms of the German and European traditions which formed the framework and feeding ground of a National Socialist movement that existed well before Hitler.

The question of the role of the individual may thus be answered simultaneously in two ways. First, Hitler was the most radical expressor and the most effective propagator of a set of ideas and emotions forming the nucleus of extreme German nationalism, that is, anti-democratism, imperialism, racism. Without his activity and success, German and European history including the Second World War would have followed a totally different course. Second, the real and long-term consequences of Hitler's politics have produced results almost diametrically opposite to those he intended. But if seen as an actor or agent of world history in the terms of Hegel's *List der Vernunft*, Hitler has brought about or left behind him revolutionary changes that cannot be grasped within the clichés of the counter-revolutionary role of fascism. One may have reservations against the thesis of Ralf Dahrendorf,[5] that Hitler and National Socialism have decisively influenced (or even brought about) modernization in Germany. At any rate, the experience of the Hitler régime has deeply changed the German élite, German attitudes and behaviour, and facilitated the more stable experiment of the second German democracy.

2

If one goes beyond the general discussion of the role of the individual in history and tries to define Hitler's place in his epoch and after, one can then concentrate on a set of questions which seems central to any discussion of the problem:

1. What is the nature and the relevance of the changes, short and long term, brought about by Hitler's politics? Did they not only profoundly alter history but amount to a revolution (as proclaimed in another sense also by Nazi propaganda)? Or is the verdict of most contemporary critics that they were basically a reactionary counter-revolution still correct?

2. What is the consequence of such definitions with regard to the important problems posed by a generalization of the Hitler phenomenon, that is, Hitler as a type or symbol, and the quest for a general theory of fascism? Is Hitler, with his movement and régime, primarily a form (if most extreme) of *the* fascist in general, as for example the studies of Ernst Nolte have stated and many new general books on fascism maintain?[6] And, moreover, is fascism, in the Marxist definition, nothing but the form, the system, and the instrument of monopoly capitalism exposing its most aggressive nature and potential in all bourgeois democracies, which, of course, means that there is no clear cut borderline between western democracies and fascism?

All these formulas imply that nazism and the Hitler phenomenon should no longer be studied and explained as a specifically German problem, but rather in terms of its European and twentieth-century reference.

Against this background, there is a tendency among younger historians and social scientists to question seriously the main findings and conclusions of research during the fifties and the sixties. Although this of course seems quite natural, there has in the meantime been more research into detail so that interest is shifting from a strongly German to a more general focus of explanation and interpretation. Moreover, the moral and liberal set of values which originally determined the interpretation of Nazism, is being questioned by a sceptical relativism; the standards of western democracy seem no longer to be a reliable yardstick against which to measure the man and the system. Nothing less than a so-called normalizing of the debate on Nazi history is demanded.

Such criticism was expressed for instance in a series of reviews by Geoffrey Barraclough in the *New York Review of Books* (October/November 1972). This rather unqualified attack made more noise than was justified by its conclusions and neglects or misrepresents our research positions. It is, of course, true that the interpretation of history depends on the political age and problems of the historians themselves, and these have altered since the days of clear-cut fronts against totalitarianism in the era of Hitler and Stalin.

Seen in the light of current interpretations, what then is the nature and relevance of the Hitler phenomenon – reaction or revolution? There can first of all be no doubt that, quite contrary to both the Nazi and the Marxist interpretation, Hitler's road to power was never inevitable, since rarely in history has there been such a close inter-dependence of general and personal factors and the indispensable role of the individual as in the crucial period between 1919 and 1945, from Hitler's entry into politics to his exit.

This applies, in particular, to the decisive period of the seizure of power around 1933. The key role played by a small camarilla around President Hindenburg is as obvious as the impact of Hitler's tactics of legal revolution, which represents the key concept of the Nazi take-over. Neither the German parties, from centre to communist, nor the social groups and organizations had any determining influence in the decisions which were made, so that in the final analysis the process of definitive power seizure, *Machtergreifung*, between February and March 1933, corresponds almost exactly to the legality concept which Hitler developed from his experience of the abortive putsch of 1923.[7]

From such analysis it becomes clear that the nature of the Nazi revolution cannot be defined in terms of a capitalist manoeuvre nor of Hitler being the servant and slave of reactionary forces. It was exactly this misunderstanding of Hitler's 'legal revolution' that kept conservatives as well as socialists and communists from a realistic judgement. They were all paralysed and reacted ineffectively not least because they failed to recognize the revolutionary character of the process: the conservatives when they believed they would be able to tame Hitler, and the left when they expected (and even feared) the reactionary right around Hindenburg, Papen, and Hugenberg to be the real masters of the situation and the real enemies of the left. But instead of the anticipated counter-revolution, be it in the form of the restoration of monarchy or a military dictatorship, Hitler's total take-over on his own became complete within a few months, being much faster and more radical than that of Mussolini ten years before. Furthermore the Duce had to respect the condominium of powerful rivals like the monarchy, the aristocracy, the church, and the army.

Here again, a basic difference between fascism and National Socialism becomes apparent. But it is even more evident with respect to the political aims and the ideological fixations lurking behind them. It was indeed Hitler's *Weltanschauung* and nothing else that mattered in the end, as is seen from the terrible consequences of his racist anti-Semitism in the planned murder of the Jews.

A general theory of fascism will always remain questionable when confronted with this problem. It is, of course, possible to find and define similarities in the realm of ideas between nationalist dictatorships in various countries. But not only was Hitler's background deeply different from that of Mussolini, the same applied also to the leading ideology. While fascism centred around the quest for the strong state, *stato totalitario* as the basis of a renewed *impero Romano*, Hitler's basic notion was the primary role of the race, the racist foundation of a future empire, to which the organization of a strong state was no more than instrumental – never an end in itself. The modish use of the general catchword *fascist* explains little and produces many clichés. What is more, it means minimizing the insane ideas and terrible reality of Hitlerism if we throw it into one and the same category with fascism. Surely, it is wrong for this term to be used as indiscriminately as it is today not only in political polemics but also in the writings of many historians and social scientists. Should they not primarily be interested in coming to grips with reality by *distinguishing* the phenomena instead of lumping them together under the slogan of fascism, not to speak of the current pseudo-Marxist practice of calling all non-'socialist' systems (and even social-democrats) potentially fascist, as was done in the early thirties with the fatal consequence that the communists were fighting against the Weimar Republic and even entered into an unholy alliance with the National Socialists at times.

This problem also belongs to the crucial chapter of underestimation. Quoting Hitler and the Nazi example today, with application to contemporary tendencies and events, and referring to them as fascist lends itself to manifold manipulations, both in revitalizing the Nazi atrocities and in defaming present political enemies. Comparisons can be justified only on the grounds of a sober analysis of the matter in question, and it should be understood primarily in the sense of actualizing the terrible experience of the past in its full dimensions. One should be wary of introducing, for daily use, terms emanating from and applied to the Nazi extermination policy. As Peter Gay rightly criticizes people to whom Hitler's dictatorship is mere history, 'in their indiscriminate indictment of modern society, [they] tend to treat the Nazi crimes as no less reprehensible, certainly, but also as no more reprehensible than the bombing of Dresden or the war in Vietnam'.[8]

In this context we also have to look critically at the revisionism of historians like Geoffrey Barraclough (in his article in the *New York Review of Books* already mentioned), who think that we have now arrived at a period of complete detachment where the historian should no longer, as we supposedly did, magnify the

Nazi experience. Against such criticism of the liberal historiography of the past thirty years, which goes so far as to deny the fact that 1945 was a chasm in German history (and in European and world history, for that matter), I should like to stress the moral and intellectual obligation of the responsible historian who upholds the Nazi experience, 'terrible and oppressive as it was, as the tragic but indispensable counterpoint of a saner, humane view of the world and even of our time' (P. Gay).

3

Coming back to the historical case one has to stress the degree to which Mussolini and Hitler acted from basically diverging points, and this can also be found quite distinctly in each of the other later so-called fascist systems, from the Balkans through Austria to Spain, Portugal, and Peronism: indeed it makes little sense to insist on *the* idea or *the* theory of fascism. Indeed, the formation and translation of Hitler's ideology remains the central problem of any analysis, and the question of the revolutionary role of Hitler and his politics can be answered only in this context.

The most important lesson to be learnt with respect to a theory of revolution is that of the successful technique of legal revolution as demonstrated by both Mussolini and Hitler to represent the twentieth-century type of take-over. We have to adapt the term of revolution to such phenomena instead of trying to keep to the romantic nineteenth-century idea of the 'good' revolution as against evil counter-revolutions.

The myth of the good revolution is, of course, still part of our political reality insofar as it is used for manipulating public opinion in favour of take-overs by leftist minorities while similar manoeuvres by the right are disqualified: the misjudgement of Hitler's revolution in being incomparable to a socialist revolution (and no revolution at all) continues in the allegation that revolution is possible only from the left.

It seems necessary also for this politico-practical reason that a re-evaluation of the revolutionary aspect of Hitlerism takes place with respect to its specific features of take-over and power structure as well as to its general perspectives. *Revolution from the*

Right (1931) was the title of a widely read book by the German sociologist and Nazi sympathizer, Hans Freyer. The slogan should be taken more seriously than it was and is by the ideologists of the so-called true revolution. The reality of our times is, of course, communist dictatorship. But equally important remains the possibility of revolutionary régimes led by nationalists with socialist claims and with the broad consent of the masses, driven and mobilized by way of articulation and mystification by the great fear of socio-economic technological and political threats, and manipulated by plebiscites, anti-capitalist slogans, the old *panem et circenses*, and a charismatic leader.

It is true that the degree of social and economic change accompanying Hitler's political revolution is still a topic of controversy both among contemporaries of Hitler and historians. And it is of course also true that in the end Hitler failed utterly in all his aims. But not only were the human costs and the political consequences of this failure immensely high and far reaching, they amounted to a truly revolutionary acceleration of processes of historical dimensions: in Germany, division and modernization; in Western Europe, close cooperation; and in the world, decolonization, shifting of power, and the rise of the Soviet Union.

It was a paradoxical revolution – paradoxical in the way in 1933 it posed simultaneously as legal and revolutionary. But it may also be called a 'blind' revolution, with a course and with results far from, and even opposed to, the intended goals of Hitler and nazism. Think, for instance, of the Hitler-Stalin Pact of 1939, gravely contrary to the whole of Hitler's deeply fixed ideology, with the equally momentous consequence of opening Central Europe to Stalin. But, of course, there are many more examples of this, including the communist revolutions that diverge so deeply from the prognosis and expectations of Marx and Engels, and, in part, even Lenin. This interpretation of the paradoxical and even self-contradictory character of revolution is also plausible because the very nature of Hitler's thought and action is clearly ambivalent: romantic-irrationalist *whilst* technocratic-modernizing, backward and future oriented elements are closely combined and even intertwined in the Weltanschauung as in the political practice of National Socialism.

I would, however, be reluctant to positively identify it with modernization, even if unintentional. Such a thesis is expounded by Ralf Dahrendorf and also by scholars like David Schoenbaum, who in his *Hitler's Social Revolution*, speaks of a 'double revolution . . . at the same time a revolution of means and ends'.[9] The modernization thesis tends to move too far away from the concrete phenomenon of National Socialism and particularly Hitler to be of much real help in the interpretation of such a movement and system, and such political figures. It is true that in his way Hitler was modern and an admirer of modern techniques and a rationally organized industrial state, which he needed for a realization of his war and his goals of domination. The same is true of some of his closest cooperators like Goebbels, the virtuoso promoter of mass communications, and Albert Speer and other technicians of power.

But I would prefer more cautious interpretations like that of Henry Ashby Turner who tries to do full justice to the ambivalence and intentional structure of nazism (in its connections with capitalism).[10] It remains essential that the very manner of the Nazi revolution is characterized by this ambiguity and by the fact that it was brought about and performed largely and emphatically in the name of a glorified past, of a pre- and post-industrial age, and with a set of anti-modernistic values (e.g., agrarian society against urbanization, corporative state against parliamentary democracy). It was exactly this revolt against modernism that found a strong backing and echo within the middle-class population which formed the main following of Hitler. And we have to be aware of the fact that among the elements and motives for neo-fascist and related movements in our time anti-modernist arguments and emotions still rank high.

If there remain doubts about the revolutionary 'quality' of National Socialism, surely Hitler the ideologist and the politician, the sovereign manipulator of the means and ends of this movement was a revolutionary man. When he came to power as a pseudo-democratically legalized dictator, many contemporaries were deceived by his disguise. Today we know that not for one moment in his career did he waver in his unbending intention of encompassing and realizing the visions of forceful change and domination. He not only represented the essential tendencies of his time; he was, in the words of Hugh Trevor-Roper, 'the Rousseau, the Mirabeau, the Robespierre, and the Napoleon of his revolution, he was its Marx, its Lenin, its Trotsky, and its Stalin. By his character and nature he may have been inferior to most of them, yet he succeeded, as none before him, in controlling his revolution in each phase, even in the moment of defeat. This speaks for a considerable understanding of the forces he has brought about.'[11]

And we may add that he effected cataclysms like few before – for example, Lenin, Napoleon, the French revolutionaries. His concept of a racist world empire, his conviction of a Social Darwinism determining all life, his cult of force and power, and his ideal of the artist of genius as the true master of the world – all this points to strong contemporary currents of thought and behaviour. But he outdid all other exponents of such ideas in his mental rigidity and in the practical consequences that followed. He was indeed that extremely rare exception – an intellectual with a practical sense of power. If a revolutionary is defined by his ability to combine a radical concept of change with the capacity to mobilize the necessary forces, then Hitler can even be called the prototype of a revolutionary; and some of the actual interest in Hitler, despite his failure, may be caused by the incredible interplay of ideological fixation and ability to introduce it into the realm of politics.

4

Many attempts have been made to trace not only the historical framework and the intellectual and socio-economic conditions that made National Socialism possible but to explain also the psychological roots and meaning of the Hitler phenomenon. Most recently this gave rise to the new school of psychohistory, whose efforts have been widely publicized especially in the American discussion. In 1973 this event led to the founding of a new periodical, *The History of Childhood Quarterly*, covering 'cases' as different as Bismarck, Hitler and, most recently, Henry Kissinger.[12] To date the new method has not been particularly rewarding; there are more hypothetical guesses than established facts. We shall have to wait for the announced Hitler books by the declared psychohistorians Rudolph Binion and Robert G. L. Waite, among others. There is a danger of even more speculations around the Hitler phenomenon, mystifying rather than enlightening the real connections, as it has already been the case for many years with the discussion about alleged Jewish ancestors of Hitler, which I think was and is pointless.[13]

There are of course arguments pro and contra psychohistory. On the positive side, a new emphasis on the dimension of persons and their complicated role in history is to be welcomed, as against a mainly structural view of history stressing the collective and predetermined elements. On the other hand, the question of reliable sources with respect to a verification of the various psychological theories seems in most cases quite insoluble, and especially in the case of Hitler. The lack of reliable sources on his childhood furthers the tendency of psychohistorical reconstructions derived from theories supplanting evidence. Indeed, psychohistory must be founded 'on hard factual evidence to support psychological interpretations', and not the other way round.[14] As to the psychoanalytical approach in particular, it would be quite misleading to concentrate the research for causes and motives almost exclusively on childhood: in the case of Hitler, the age from 20 to 35, that is, the years 1909–24, contain the real crucial process of personal and political formation. After all, he was a political man, and his way into politics is what really matters. There may be thousands of people with similar childhood history, including close relationship to the mother and a mother trauma (as stressed by Binion) or sexual perversion (as maintained by Waite), yet with quite different or no political consequences at all, at least as far as our scarce knowledge of Hitler's childhood allows any comparisons.

And thus the real historical problems remain – with or without a hypothetical childhood analysis – namely, how the formative coincidence of personal and political conditions came about. It is foremost the process of political transformation that has to be studied from the manner and the utterances of the man before and after November 1918, when Hitler had his much-stressed hysterical shock at the end of the war. And such a comprehensive analysis is certainly to be continued up to 1933, when he attained the final crucial experience of gaining absolute power by means of a pseudo-legal revolution: an experience he repeated during the following years in expanding his foreign policy, by means of peace talk and threats simultaneously.

For all these reasons it is certainly not enough to call Hitler a criminal of super-dimensions and to stamp his accomplices as mere caricatures of butchers and murderers, as the cartoons like to do – another underestimation of the Nazi phenomenon. Hitler's strength of will and his fascination for a fanatical following was based on a perverted moral energy, to which the most terrible acts of suppression and extermination were special proof of his highest values: unfeeling rigour against himself as justification for the rigour practised against others; and the readiness to kill for the régime and its superhuman Weltanschauung was praised by Hitler and his chief executioner, Himmler, as heroic moral virtue comprising and sublimating all the inner values of National Socialism, such as the respectable values of faith, sincerity, loyalty, rigidity, decency, and courage, but now reversed in a truly revolutionary fashion to serve the ideological terror system.

The real danger of this perverted political and moral justification of the crime can be seen from the easy functioning of the extermination apparatus of the SS, constantly driven and justified by such a mechanism of ideological moralism. It was based on the possible combination of primitive instincts and lust for cruelty with a fanatical conviction of the higher legitimacy of such crimes – a combination well known in all totalitarian systems. The contempt for bourgeois morality, *bürgerliche Moral*, expresses this ideological perversion which can be found on the extreme left as well as the right.

Hitler himself, with his ideological fixation and his sense of mission as saviour of a world doomed by racist decline, was the prototype of such a transvaluation, taking literally Nietzsche's vision of *Umwertung aller Werte* and transcending *bürgerliche Moral*.

This had been an obsession since his early days, when Hitler, the would-be artist of genius, declined to have the same concept of life and pleasure as the rest of the world, and when he got into the habit of posing as the man of special purity, of idealistic frugality, of readiness for sacrifice. He was always very careful to uphold this image and to hide his private life and emotions. In the end, he saw himself as the last person faithful to the idea and dying for its preservation, while the German people and even most of his closest collaborators received his final verdict of not having been strict enough with themselves, and, therefore, neither fit nor entitled to survive. He even reproached himself for not having been radical enough in his revolution and therefore failing to realize his idea fully. This was his only reaction to a war and a totalitarian régime that cost the lives of more than fifty million people.

The excesses accompanying the eclipse and decline of the Third Reich indeed illustrated the true character of a system which, contrary to the seductive theory of dictatorship, did not give its citizens political order and effective government or greater security and opportunities, but rather rested solely on organized despotism and pseudo-legal, ill-concealed crimes. Hitler had only one, egomaniacal answer: if the German people failed their historic test they thereby forfeited their national existence. He was obsessed with one idea to the end: that he would never capitulate, that what happened in November 1918 would never recur in German history. In his political testament written one day before his death he repeated the fixed ideas which had governed the rise and rule of National Socialism beginning with the ferocious hatred of 'international Jewry and its helpers', who in Hitler's world were responsible for everything that was happening.

Ideas have to be taken seriously, even when they seem utterly abstruse and far from any possible realization. As the philosopher Hegel, himself a powerful generator of ideologies both of conservative étatism and of socialist Marxism, put it, 'the idea is not as powerless as to become only the idea!' It will always be a complex problem to recognize and explain the origin of ideas and their development into political strength and consequence. In the case of the man Adolf Hitler, the ideas of racist superiority, of living space, and of the uniqueness of a greater German nation found a carrier who was not a simple fascist agitator or dreamer, but a man with the radically fixed will to put his thoughts against reality. He aimed not simply at a traditional empire like Mussolini or the like, but in his very own way he oriented his politics totally, and with all the consequences of force and war and mass murder, on the theoretical construction of a racist empire in which finally reality was to match the idea completely.

In this respect, with his principles, rigorism, and perfectionism in following a deadly 'general' idea, he has been called very German and he indeed personified one among many different German traditions.[15] Thus he fulfilled the anxious prophecy of a German-Jewish poet writing one hundred years before Hitler's revolution. Heinrich Heine viewed with deep concern the sharp discrepancy between idea and reality, between intellectual radicalism and political backwardness in nineteenth-century Germany. This was the hotbed of Hitler's political thought, while corresponding political action became possible only under the conditions of the twentieth century, and in particular the First World War and its aftermath. In 1834 Heine wrote, as if to enlarge on Hegel's dictum of the idea always becoming more than an idea, 'The thought precedes the action like the lightning and the thunder. The German thunder though (to be sure) is also a German and not very flexible, and comes rolling somewhat slower; but it will come, and when you hear it roar one day as it has never roared in world history, you should know: the German thunder has finally reached its destination.'

Indeed, despite the world-wide repercussions, Hitler and National Socialism remain foremost a German – and Austrian – phenomenon. But it should be kept in mind and understood by all nations and politicians as transcending the national and historical conditionality and symbolizing a warning lesson never to be forgotten and never to be easily mistaken and misused. It is the lesson that extreme political concepts propagated as final solutions of all problems never serve humane ends but degrade people and their values into mere instruments of a destructive power mania and the régime of barbarism. That such extreme concepts would be doomed to ultimate failure is the hope to be drawn from the fall of Hitler.

Notes

1. Among the most recent interpretations of Hitler are two balanced articles by Klaus Hildebrand, 'Hitlers Ort in der Geschichte des preussisch-deutschen Nationalstaats', in *Historische Zeitschrift*, no. 217 (1973), pp. 584–632; 'Zwischen Mythos und Moderne: Hitler in seiner Zeit', in *Das Historisch-politische Buch*, no. 22 (1974), pp. 33–7. The comprehensive biography by Joachim Fest, *Hitler* (Frankfurt a.M., 1973), the best treatment since – and besides – Alan Bullock's classic work, has brought forth new discussions; cf. also K. D. Bracher, 'Hitler – die deutsche Revolution', in *Die Zeit*, no. 42 (1973), p. 25.

2. See my critical remarks on Speer, in *Die deutsche Diktatur*, p. 545 ff; and on Maser, in *Encounter*, no. 39/3 (September 1972), p. 75 ff.

3. For the arguments in favour of a modified but comprehensive concept of totalitarianism, cf. especially Leonard Shapiro, *Totalitarianism* (London, 1972); also K. D. Bracher, 'Totalitarianism', in *Dictionary of the History of Ideas*, vol. 4 (New York, 1973).

4. Leonard Shapiro, 'The Role of the Monolithic Party under the Totalitarian Leader', in J. W. Lewis, ed., *Party Leadership and Revolutionary Power in China* (Cambridge, 1970); Robert C. Tucker, 'The Dictator and Totalitarianism', in *World Politics*, no. 17 (1965), p. 555 ff.

5. Ralf Dahrendorf, *Society and Democracy in Germany* (New York, 1967) with considerable influence on the international reinterpretation of Nazi Germany in the sense of a modernization process against the will.

6. Ernst Nolte's well-known books *Three Faces of Fascism* (London, 1965), *Theorien uber den Faschismus* (Cologne, 1967), and *Die faschistischen Bewegungen* (Munich, 1966) have been followed by a renaissance of 'general fascism', from the traditional communist and the more elaborated Marxist versions to the liberal (English-American) use of the term.

7. Cf. Hajo Holborn, ed., *Republic to Reich, the Making of the Nazi Revolution* (New York, 1972); also *The Path to Dictatorship 1918–1933* (New York, 1966); K. D. Bracher, *Stufen der Machtergreifung* (Frankfurt, 1974). On the other hand there is the very competent book by Adrian Lyttelton, *The Seizure of Power, Fascism in Italy 1919–1929* (London, 1973), and Renzo de Felice's fundamental *Mussolini il rivoluzionario* (Turin, 1965), and *Mussolini il fascista* (Turin, 1966), p. 196 ff.

8. Peter Gay's introduction to *The German Dictatorship* (New York, 1970), p. vii.

9. David Schoenbaum, *Hitler's Social Revolution* (New York, 1966), p. xxii f. Since then a growing number of contemporary historians have followed those theses, which by no means are a specialty of conservative or rightist interpretation. From a more substantial point of view, the most recent interpretation by George Mosse is fundamental, *The Nationalization of the Masses* (New York, 1975); on the problem of a 'fascist revolution', see his introduction to *International Fascism, 1920–1945* (London, 1965), p. 14 ff.

10. Henry A. Turner, *Faschismus und Kapitalismus in Deutschland* (Göttingen, 1972).

11. Hugh Trevor-Roper, *Le testament politique de Hitler* (Paris, 1959), p. 13.

12. Cf. especially Rudolph Binion, 'Hitler's Concept of Lebensraum: The Psychological Basis', in *History of Childhood Quarterly* 1 (1973), pp. 187–258, with the important comments by George H. Stein, Bradley F. Smith, George L. Mosse, Andreas Dorpalen, and Dietrich Orlow, among others.

13. I have been criticized for this by psychohistorians; e.g., Peter Loewenberg, in *Central European History*, no. 7 (1974), p. 262 ff. – a review in praise of Walter C. Langer, *The Mind of Adolf Hitler*, the wartime psychoanalysis (1943) whose reprint of 1972 served as exit point for the psychohistorical part of the Hitler wave. For a critical assessment, see especially the review article by Hans W. Gatzke, in *American Historical Review*, no. 78 (1973), pp. 394 ff. and 1155 ff. (discussion); cf. also L. Papeleux, 'Psychanalyse d'Adolf Hitler', in *Revue d'histoire de la deuxieme guerre mondiale* vol. 24, no. 96 (October 1974), pp. 105–8.

14. The quotation is from G. H. Stein, op. cit., p. 216 ff. A typical example of the deductive, unhistorical treatment of disputable sources may be found in Langer, op. cit., p. 17 (also quoted by Gatzke). He starts with a diagnosis (which fluctuates from hysteric psychopath to neurotic psychopath) and continues 'With this diagnosis as a point of orientation, we are able to evaluate the data in terms of probability. Those fragments that could most easily be fitted [!] into this general clinical category were tentatively regarded as possessing a higher degree of probability – as far as reliability and relevance was concerned – than those which seemed alien to the clinical picture.' The sources have to fit the picture – shouldn't it be the contrary?

15. Cf. J. Fest, op. cit., pp. 513, 517 (German ed.).

Part III
Local Fascisms

6 Fascism in Eastern Europe

Almost from the moment of its birth Italian fascism had its historians, some of whom were outstanding. Bonomi, Nitti, Sturzo, and Ferrero, Villari or Salvemini[1] published their works in the early twenties, some of them at a time when Mussolini had not yet seized complete control over Italy. Similarly, valuable documentary and analytical works on National Socialism had already appeared in Germany and elsewhere, before Hitler came to power.[2] By the end of the thirties the historical literature on nazism could already have filled entire libraries. East European fascism, however, unlike the Western fascist movements, received only secondary treatment. Not one single scholarly work about the East European fascist movements was published either in the countries involved or in the West until the first post-war years. Though their own 'court' historians or their paid chroniclers did publish some writings about their movements during the Second World War, these were no more than official eulogies.[3] In the West too, during the war years, nothing important on this subject was published, as, understandably, Western historiography paid scant attention to East European fascism.

Naturally, immediately after the war National Socialism, and secondarily Italian fascism 'stole the show'. The lack of interest in East European fascism could also be attributed to the marked tendency to ascribe all that occurred on the extreme right in Eastern Europe to Hitler's and Mussolini's impact – a view that was not entirely in accord with reality. The external factor, that is, the German and Italian role in the fascist transformation of the area was given priority over the local struggles for power. Paradoxically enough, instead of stimulating scientific research into fascism, communist rule and Soviet control over Eastern Europe exerted a doubly discouraging influence upon such scholarly activities both in the East and in the West. The new régimes of the East European People's democracies in their early years were more interested in their struggle against social democracy and against bourgeois democratic and pro-Western forces on the ideological level, than in the struggle against fascism. At the same time the West was rather more concerned about the process of communization and contemporary Sovietization than about the recent fascist past. Decades had to elapse before the first noteworthy results of research into East European fascism appeared either in the West or the East.

At the outset it is necessary to indicate which movements are highlighted in the present survey of East European fascism. To this end, without attempting to delimit the controversial and arbitrary borders between Central and Eastern Europe, or for that matter without going into the complex problem of defining the notions of East-Central Europe or South Eastern Europe, it is taken for granted that Eastern Europe covers the area east of Germany and Austria, overlooking the inner regional divisions.

Significant fascist movements did not spring up in all parts of Eastern Europe in the inter-war period and during the Second World War, and in only four countries (Romania, Hungary, and the two by-products of the liquidation of Czechoslovakia and of Yugoslavia, Slovakia and Croatia) did they actually seize power, and this only towards the end of the period and for a short span. Only two fascist movements played an important part for a relatively longer time, enjoying mass support: the Romanian Iron Guard and the Hungarian Arrow Cross. The bulk of this survey will be devoted to the historiography of these two movements. A rather more restricted scope will be allotted to the Slovakian Hlinka party, which can only be listed as a 'classical' fascist movement after the setting up of the Slovakian puppet state in 1939. Similarly, the Croatian Ustasha movement, which hardly had any history before April 1941 and whose programme and ideological foundation were little known among the Croatian masses, will only be given a brief treatment. Finally, some of the relatively few articles written about the insignificant Polish fascist organizations are noted. The scarce, fragmentary literature about Serbian, Bulgarian, or Baltic fascism, mostly published in their respective languages, does not merit inclusion in a short survey. The literature on East European fascism falls into three groups: (1) Post-Second World War local (communist) literature: (2) fascist emigré literature; and (3) works written in the west by non-involved historians. This survey will distinguish between the few general, synthesizing works about East European fascism, published mainly in the West, and the great number of monographs about the main fascist movements, most of them published in Eastern Europe, or by fascist emigrés in the West. Because of the varieties of East European fascism and the chronological differences in the history of their appearance and disappearance, the relevant literature is treated on a regional basis.

As early as 1919 and in the twenties numerous fascist-type organizations, movements, and parties had sprung up in Romania, but only two of them had come to the forefront by the mid-thirties: Professor A. C. Cuza's and Octavian Goga's National Christian Party and Corneliu Zelea Codreanu's Iron Guard.

In 1923 Cuza founded the League of Christian National Defence, an extreme nationalistic and, par excellence, anti-Semitic organization, which gained only marginal votes in the parliamentary elections during the twenties and in the early thirties. The young student leader, Codreanu, left Cuza's League in 1927, founded the Legion of Archangel Michael, set up the Iron Guard in 1930, as a complementary mass organization of the Legion, and after the Iron Guard was disbanded several times, he renamed the movement Totul pentru Tară (All for the Fatherland) party in 1934. The movement, known as the Iroñ Guard, and its followers, Legionaries or guardists, irrespective of their official designation, achieved a spectacular success in the 1937 elections, polling almost 16 per cent of the votes. However, it was again dissolved in February 1938 when all political parties were banned by King Carol's dictatorial régime, and its leaders were decimated during 1938 and 1939. It emerged anew in Autumn 1940 led by Horia Sima, in the wake of the dismemberment of Greater Romania, and acceded to power in a peculiar alliance with General Ion Antonescu's military clique. The so-called National Legionary State lasted barely five months. The armed rebellion of the Legionaries against Antonescu at the end of January 1941 and their crushing defeat put a violent end to their rule and to their activity in the country. Antonescu continued to rule without the Legionaries in the framework of a fascist-type military dictatorship until the coup d'état of August 1944, when Romania joined the Allies against Nazi Germany. However, a strong legionary emigration, supplemented by minor groups of emigrés of former Cuza, Goga, and Antonescu followers, continued to be active after the war in Western Europe and in the Americas, mainly engaged in polemics against communist Romania and amongst themselves.

The second important factor on the Romanian extreme right was the National Christian party, founded in 1935 after the merger of Cuza's League and Goga's rightist, ultra-nationalist agrarian party. This new party, which polled less than 10 per cent of the votes in the 1937 elections, came to power at the end of 1937 as a transitional solution to the internal crisis and actually served for 44 days until the inauguration of King Carol's dictatorship in February 1938. Although this survey concentrates on the Iron Guard, attention is also paid to the Goga-Cuza party, to the royalist dictatorship, and to the Antonescu régime.

In Hungary the emergence of fascist-type organizations and movements coincided with the counter-revolutionary organizing activity against Béla Kun's communist régime in 1919. A great many extreme right, extreme nationalist, racist, and later national socialist groupings emerged in the twenties and in the early thirties. The only movement which paralleled the role of the Iron Guard, and which actually came to power in October 1944 in the wake of the military débâcle on the German-Hungarian front, and after Horthy's unsuccessful attempt to break with Nazi Germany, was Ferenc Szálasi's Arrow Cross. Although the arrow cross was the symbol of a number of national socialist parties and groups, it is only used here to refer to Szálasi's movement. Beside the Arrow Cross, Béla Imrédy's Party of Hungarian Revival will also be mentioned, as the second most important extreme right party which played any role during the Second World War on the Hungarian fascist scene.

*

The three periods can roughly be distinguished in the historiography of fascism in Romania and Hungary in the course of the three decades that have elapsed since the Second World War.

The works that appeared soon after the war in both countries – more in Hungary, less in Romania – were mainly of a journalistic nature, with no scientific pretensions. Around 1948–9, when the consolidation of the communist régimes had become an accomplished fact, and even later, in the early fifties, fascism as a topic of research was kept under wraps. In neither country did any noteworthy work appear on fascism in that period. The cold war imposed anti-imperialist, anti-Western, and anti-cosmopolitan slogans upon the satellite countries; the unmasking of local fascism was not considered of topical interest. The defeated enemy was not dangerous any longer and Moscow did not attribute any practical significance to research into East European fascism. Another reason that may have accounted for the lack of interest in this subject was probably the circumstance that in both countries the new régimes were doing their utmost to 're-educate' and win over the rank and file of the former fascist movements. The Romanian communist leaders, including Ana Pauker, opened the gates of the Communist party to the masses of 'petty' legionaries who had been 'led astray', and Rákosi followed a similar policy towards the Hungarian *kisnyilasok* (the little men of the Arrow Cross). It should also be noted that in the first post-war years the documentary sources relating to local fascism counted as classified security material. In this period discussion of fascism appeared only in party literature and in the propaganda media. It was a term of abuse and was used to describe most of the inter-war political parties and régimes. It was only in the early sixties that the first works of a scientific character appeared about the main fascist movements, yet even more years were to elapse before the publication of any significant works dealing with the subject – earlier in Hungary and later in Romania.

All in all, there are rather few works about the origins and the nature of East European fascism. The literature explaining the role of ideas in the life of the fascist movements is particularly poor, and few if any bibliographical reports of these movements have come out so far (none for the Arrow Cross for instance).

The ideological literature of the various movements is relatively scarce compared with Italian fascism or with German National Socialism, while the published, or re-published, basic material appeared mostly in the local languages and even this source material is hardly available.

There is a further difficulty. With the possible exception of a few non-involved Western scholars, historians engaged in the research work are extremely prejudiced, personally, politically, and in other ways. Even in basic matters which seem to be beyond any controversy, precisely because they are based on facts (such as the resort to violence, terror, or anti-Semitic excesses), views are widely divergent, making it most difficult to present an impartial, unequivocal synthesis. Nor is there any consensus among historians of differing political backgrounds and attitudes in such *imponderabilia*, as for example the mass enthusiasm in the case of the Iron Guard or of the Arrow Cross.

Returning to the first stage of the historiography of East European fascism, the survey of the literature of the first post-war years begins with an exception. At the end of 1944, a few months after the anti-Nazi coup d'état in Romania, a book appeared in Bucharest by Lucretiu Pătrășcanu, *Sub trei dictaturi*[4] (*Under Three Dictatorships*), which analyses with amazing clarity the basic problems of Romanian fascism. Pătrășcanu's early analysis is roughly valid to this day. The law graduate communist leader (the first communist minister of justice of post-war Romania and one of the first victims of Gheorghiu-Dej's purges) had elaborated his work as early as 1941. His book disappeared from the market in 1949 and only under Ceaușescu's nationalist rehabilitation campaign did a new edition appear in 1970. Pătrășcanu's work essentially comprises those theses to which Romanian historiography has returned in recent years after a long and tortuous path, and which are partly shared by non-involved Western researchers as well. He emphasized the strong mass basis of Cuza's League and of the Iron Guard and believed that the reason for the relative successes achieved by these movements should be sought less in 'imports from abroad' than in the ability of Cuza and Codreanu to adapt fascism to the 'autochthonous' medium.[5] In the case of both movements Pătrășcanu makes a point of stressing the incorporation of Christian Orthodoxy into political agitation both as to content and form.[6] To this day Pătrăşcanu's book is one of the very few attempts to analyse the social composition of the Iron Guard rank and file and of its élite. Naturally, he could only avail himself of very scarce documentary source material and he lacked the advantage of historical perspective; nevertheless, his analysis has hardly been surpassed to this day.

Pătrăşcanu does not deny the fact that the Iron Guard was essentially made up of the peasant and working-class elements, but he attempts to lay special stress on the *Lumpen* elements in the midst of the Legionary masses, thus exonerating the conscious working class and the enlightened peasants from the charge of fascism. He even ventures into psychological interpretations by pointing out the significantly high rate of neurotics with inferiority complexes and even physically disabled people in the ranks of the Legion. Nevertheless, Pătrăşcanu does not minimize the decisive role of the young intellectuals in the Iron Guard, nor of the Orthodox clergy, for that matter. At the same time, however, he cannot help resorting to the Dimitrovian official Muscovite formulae, and he himself seems to believe that the Romanian fascist movements essentially constituted 'a political mass manoeuvre at the disposal of the ruling forces' against the democratic parties and the workers' movements.[7]

For the official stand towards the problem of fascism in the early years of the communist régime, there is the authoritative standard *History of the Romanian People's Republic*, edited in 1948 by Mihail Roller, the founder of the post-war Romanian communist historical school.[8] The work attributes the impetus of the fascist movements to the manoeuvrings of the bourgeois and land-owner strata, while designating as fascist, without discrimination, the royalist dictatorship, the Legionary rule, as well as Antonescu's military dictatorship. There is no mention whatsoever of the social structure of Romanian fascism and no attempt made towards an analysis of its ideology.

Even in the spate of works on fascism in the early sixties, the researchers dealt less with the character of Romanian fascism than with blown-up descriptions of the anti-fascist struggle. A number of studies appeared in the mid-sixties about the characteristics of the régimes between 1940 and 1944[9] and about the penetration of Nazi ideology,[10] but a bibliographical essay published as late as 1965 did not yet mention any book on fascism. Only in the late sixties and the first years of this decade was there a turning point. The central event in this respect was the organization in Bucharest of a symposium concerning the critical analysis and the unmasking of fascism in Romania – in the words of the organizers – followed by the publication of the proceedings.[11] In the same year the first book to be published in communist Romania about the Iron Guard appeared, written by Mihail Fătu and Ion Spălăţelu.[12] Characteristically, the main title of the symposium book is *Against Fascism*, denoting the militant tone and the principal aim of the symposium: less analysis and more unmasking, bringing the anti-fascist struggle to the fore. Nevertheless, most of the twenty-two papers published in this volume represent the first scholarly contribution to a Marxist analysis of fascism in Romania. A non-orthodox and non-dogmatic line pervades a number of essays (about the socio-economic foundation of fascism in Romania, the Iron Guard ideology, the 'Legionarism' and literature, as well as the characterization of the Antonescu Legionary régime in 1940–41.[13]) However, the symposium volume did not even try to tackle such thorny problems as, for example, the mass support enjoyed by the Iron Guard and even by Goga and Cuza in the ranks of the peasantry and the working class, or the contradiction between the allegation on the one hand of the support given by the National Liberal Party and by King Carol to Codreanu, and on the other, the deadly blows administered by the same two forces to the Iron Guard. In my opinion, regarding the symposium and its book, it is essential, first and foremost, to keep in mind the words of Valter Roman, who, surveying the blank areas of Romanian historiography, pointed to the lack of works dealing with the theoretical origins and the ideological aspects of Romanian fascism, and stated that there were still no basic works in Romanian about fascism in general and about Romanian fascism in particular. 'The history of Romanian fascism is only about to be written,' concluded Valter Roman in March 1971.[14]

Fătu's and Spălăţelu's book about the Iron Guard has the great merit of using, for the first time, a rich archival material – that of the State Archives, of the Communist party and other collections usually hermetically closed to researchers. But the selection of the archival material is obviously biased and the work suffers from some grave shortcomings. One of the main aims of the authors seems to have been the emphasis on the alleged collusion between the ruling circles (the Camarilla, the National Liberal, and the National Peasant leaders) and the Iron Guard. The authors fail to convince the reader that such collusion existed, precisely because they overplayed this aspect. The polemical tone of the work and the outspoken aim of appealing to the widest possible public detracts considerably from the scholarly value of the book.

One major work dealing with the extreme right is Al. Gh. Savu's book about the royalist dictatorship (1938–40).[15] Although the work deals mainly with the political history of King Carol's dictatorship, laying stress upon its relations with Nazi Germany, the author devotes sufficient space to the analysis of the Goga-Cuza government (30 December 1937–10 February 1938), scrutinizes the political character of the royalist régime and examines it as the 'antechamber' of the fascist dictatorship inaugurated in September 1940. Unlike some Romanian historians Savu deems Cuza's movement to be fascist. In common with quite a few other historians he calls attention to the anti-Semitic agitation in the inter-war period, which – in his opinion too – proved itself a useful means of winning over a certain section of the population to fascism.[16] One of his assertions is particularly noteworthy, namely, that Romanian fascism was born in the guise of anti-Semitism.[17] Like other authors in contemporary Romania, Savu, too, contents himself with this assertion and does not devote much space to the problem of anti-Semitism. It is characteristic that the study of this most important component of Romanian nationalism and fascism should be completely absent from the works of Marxist authors. It seems that no study has yet been devoted in post-war Romanian historiography to the Jewish question or to the problem of anti-Semitism, not even in the context of research on fascism.

Among the essays published in Romania (in English, French, and also Russian), those that attempt to cast light upon the theoretical and ideological facets of the Iron Guard, and secondarily, of the Cuza movement should be singled out. Regarding the Iron Guard each work made a point of emphasizing its mysticism, irrationalism, cult of death and the dead, and its fanaticism. There is but one point which gives rise to diverging and even contradictory views: the racism of the Iron Guard. While it has generally been taken for granted that racism was not a characteristic feature of the Iron Guard, some contemporary authors assert the contrary.[18] There are some contradictions in the more recent literature about the relative independence, originality, and autochthonous character of the two main fascist movements. While more attention has lately been turned to the local origins of Romanian fascism, the rigid view prevailing a quarter of a century ago still persists, according to which Romanian fascism and primarily the Iron Guard were strengthened by foreign influence and foreign support. The view still dominates contemporary works that the Iron Guard essentially fulfilled the role of Nazi Germany's Fifth Column.[19] However, there are still numerous studies that, in accordance with the original communist conception, consider the oligarchical and reactionary upper circles as the main motive power behind the Iron Guard, the League of National Christian Defence and other fascist formations.[20] On the other hand, quite a number of recent studies draw a clear distinction between the different extreme-right parties and régimes. While in the first postwar years the Goga-Cuza government was equated with the Legionary period and with Antonescu's régime, and even with King Carol's dictatorship – all of them being qualified as fascist – some works published in recent years draw a clear distinction between the royalist dictatorship and Antonescu's rule, for example, denying the previous assertions about the fascist character of King Carol's dictatorial régime.[21] Despite this positive symptom, Romanian historiography has still a long way to go in defining the nature of the different inter-war régimes and in renouncing the automatic use of fascism when characterizing rightist anti-Marxist parties and régimes. It seems probable that the lacunae found at the 1971 Bucharest symposium will serve as stimulants for researchers to bring out some non-dogmatic synthesizing works on Romanian fascism.

In the early post-war years the fascist Romanian emigrés, first of all the Legionaries, and also some extreme right non-fascist emigrés (for example among Antonescu's followers) produced a considerable number of works in two categories. They re-edited and commented on the basic writings and documents of the Iron Guard, and some former Legionaries and leading figures of different dictatorial régimes embarked upon elaborating or re-writing the history of the inter-war period.[22] The publications which had come out in wartime Germany and in Italy before 1943 were invariably crude propaganda, hardly acceptable as historical works.

The first post-war work which deserves attention is the volu-minous history of the Iron Guard published by Ştefan Pălăghiţă in 1951.[23] The author, an Orthodox priest belonging to the second-rank leadership of the Iron Guard, wields his detailed des-cription of the Legionary movement as a polemical weapon in the factional struggle waged in the ranks of the Iron Guard emigra-tion. As a spokesman for the anti-Sima group, Pălăghiţă accuses Horia Sima of terrorism and of common crimes, and of betraying the Iron Guard as an agent of King Carol and his Camarilla.[24] On the other hand, Pălăghiţă tried to embellish Codreanu's image in a most peculiar manner – by extolling his alleged non-violence and humanism. In the same year (1951) a senior official of the Antonescu administration, G. Barbul, published a eulogistic work in the defence of Ion Antonescu, the military dictator from January 1941 after the break with the Iron Guard, with which he had shared power from September 1940, acquitting him of the charges made by the Legionaries, communists, and democrats.[25] An authoritative book on Ion Antonescu appeared at about the same time (1952) written by General Ion Gheorghe, Antonescu's last minister in Berlin.[26] The general, a non-Legionary and a typical representative of the extreme-rightist and extreme-nation-alist officer group which supported Antonescu's dictatorship, acquits the 'Conducator' of the crimes committed by the Iron Guard during the months of the common rule (September 1940–January 1941) and of the charge of having served as a Nazi tool. He denies the fascist character of the Antonescu régime and asserts that after the abortive Legionary rebellion in January

1941, fascist ideas were extirpated from the political life of his country.

All these works mainly deal with the political development of Romania in the pre-war years and during the war, focusing attention on German-Romanian relations, but lacking any scientific analysis of the origins and ideas of local fascism.

In their writings published in the early post-war years, Pălăghiță, Barbul, Gheorghe, and others in the forefront of the Legionary and Antonescu emigration, most conspicuously concealed or minimized the anti-Semitism of both the Iron Guard and of the Antonescu administration, although Gheorghe, for example, does not fail to emphasize the element of violence resorted to by the Iron Guard in the 'solution' of the Jewish question. Remarkably, however, at a later stage authors like Horia Sima became more outspoken about the extreme anti-Semitism of the Romanian nationalist camp.

Two major works on the Iron Guard have recently appeared by two senior survivors of the Legionary leadership: the memoirs of Prince Michel Sturdza,[27] Foreign Minister of the short-lived National-Legionary régime (September 1940–January 1941), and Horia Sima's history of the Legionary movement.[28]

Sturdza's non-scholarly work, largely devoted to foreign affairs, is a bitter attack not only against the anti-fascist opponents of the Iron Guard, but against Marshal Ion Antonescu too. In Sturdza's view Antonescu, whom he considers 'insane', betrayed not only the Iron Guard but had earlier betrayed even Goga, and was one of those who brought about the collapse of the Goga-Cuza government. In the final analysis he shares Horia Sima's conviction that Antonescu 'caused Rumania as much evil as did Carol.'[29] The same Sturdza, who was wont to mention the 'Anonymous Forces', having in mind the 'Occult Forces', an expression scattered throughout Sima's writings, namely the 'Judeo-Marxist-Capitalist-Freemason' forces embodied in the Camarilla, is anxious to 'humanize' Codreanu's anti-Semitism. In his view, and contrary to reality, Codreanu had always proclaimed that 'violence against Jews was a stupid mistake. He [Codreanu] would have immediately expelled from the Movement any fool who had so much as broken a window in a Jewish-owned shop.'[30]

Sima's history of the Legionary Movement (he has only published the first part of the history of the Iron Guard, up to the December 1937 electoral success of Codreanu) is a very biased and passionate plea on behalf of the Iron Guard, and a vehement attack against practically each and every political force in interwar Romania. Sima, unlike Pălăghiţă, Sturdza, and others, devotes whole chapters to the doctrine and the ideology of the Iron Guard. However, his pattern of the individual, the Nation, and God as the three components of the axis round which the Legionary movement turns, is not much of a contribution to the elucidation of the Legionary dogma. According to the less analytical Pălăghiţă, the three main components of the Legionary doctrine were Jesus Christ (i.e., religion), the Nation, and the King, while Ion Gheorghe designated religious mysticism, anti-Semitism, and National Socialism as the three basic principles of the Iron Guard.

As already pointed out, on the subject of the anti-Semitism of the Iron Guard, Sima is more sincere and less cautious than his fellow chroniclers. His work contains elaborate and strongly worded indictments against Romanian Jewry, defending and justifying the extreme anti-Semitism of the Legionaries. It seems likely that Sima's book ranks first among the most vulgar anti-Semitic writings that saw the light after the submergence of National Socialism, although he never fails to point out that the motivation of the Legionary anti-Semitism was neither racial nor religious but social and economic. His history of the Legionary movement is a regression compared to his *Destinée du nationalisme*,[31] a work about the fate of post-war European nationalism, published in 1951, when he seemed to be more reasonable and more restrained. After all, Sima's book, a passionate plea for religious mysticism, irrationalism, fanaticism, and a glorification of the 'Legionary spiritual revolution' is an eloquent example of the distortion of facts, which by no means contributes to the elucidation of the controversies around the Iron Guard. Even worse is Carlo Sburlati's history of the Iron Guard,[32] centred on Codreanu's biography. It is no more than a thoroughly erroneous and naive eulogy of the Legionary movement.

Cuza and Goga are very scantily represented in the emigré literature. Apart from short chapters and fleeting references in most of the emigré publications, the only works devoted to Cuza and Goga appear to be a few pamphlets written by Pamfil Șeicaru.[33] These short writings of the former leading rightist publicist fall far below anything that deserves to be considered as serious history.

Western historiography, including works by non-fascist Romanian scholars writing in the West, has so far produced only a few studies about Romanian fascism, and these came rather late, in the mid-sixties. As with the previous two groups these historians also concentrate almost exclusively on the Iron Guard. Apart from some essays, not a single book has been published about the Legionary movement, excepting Nicholas Nagy-Talavera's comparative work about the Arrow Cross and the Iron Guard.[34] However, the few collections of studies about European fascism, which also include Eastern Europe, and those published about Eastern Europe show keen interest both in the Iron Guard and, as a matter of course, in the Arrow Cross. Western historians, more or less free from the prejudices and passions of the involved researchers and of the communist opponents of fascism, produced some valuable essays. It is not surprising that Western scholars should be interested primarily in those problems which, for some reason, rank second or even altogether elude the fascist and the Marxist researchers: the origins of Romanian fascism, its autochthonous characteristics, its degree of indebtedness to the Italian and German 'big brothers', its links with orthodoxy, the real components of its doctrine, its anti-Semitism and, finally, the social composition of its mass following and its leadership.

First mention should be made of Eugen Weber, a pioneer researcher into the Legionary movement, for his three basic essays,[35] Zevedei Barbu, who published an excellent study from a philosophical and sociological point of view,[36] and Stephen Fischer-Galati, author of a number of interesting essays about nationalism and fascism in Romania.[37] Short chapters are devoted to East European fascism, including the Iron Guard and the Arrow Cross, in Ernst Nolte's *Die Faschistischen Bewegungen*[38] and in the *Rise of Fascism*[39] by F. L. Carsten. The Iron Guard is the subject of a number of essays published in recent years in Western specialized journals,[40] and is also dealt with in a number of general studies on East European fascism, as for example H. Seton-Watson's 'Fascism, Right and Left', published in the *Journal of Contemporary History*.[41] The international symposium on Fascism and Europe, held in Prague in 1969, deserves mention as an attempt at reviewing the main characteristics of East European fascism in the framework of a synthesis. The paper presented by Miklós Lackó (from Hungary) about the characteristic features of South-East European fascism is noteworthy.[42] However, Romanian historians did not participate in this first event and among the twenty-five studies published in two volumes not a single one is devoted to Romania. I have mentioned the Prague symposium in this connection in order to point out the paucity of literature on Romanian fascism in the 'repertoire' of Western scholars and the reluctance of Romanian scholars to cope with this complex of problems at an international level.

The handful of Western historians who have published works on Romanian fascism stress *populism* as a characteristic feature of the Legionaries, and almost all of them treat Codreanu's Legion as a *radical* movement. H. Seton-Watson writes about 'Romanian Fascist populism', and about the young Romanian *narodniki*, who were fascists.[43] Eugen Weber, who tends somewhat to idealize Codreanu, emphasizes more than others the populist character of the Iron Guard. In his view 'Far from being a bourgeois or petty-bourgeois movement . . . the Legion was a popular and populist movement, with a programme which the masses (in the Romanian context of peasants and workers) recognized as radical enough for them . . .'[44] He considers the Legion as a distinctly radical social force,[45] and mentions, even in the case of Cuza's League, the peasant support in the poorest counties, thus crediting Cuza with a kind of social radicalism, albeit only in the guise of anti-Semitism ('anti-Semitism could easily be preached as a solution to economic and political problems in the midst of the poor peasantry.')[46] Fischer-Galati also advocates the thesis of 'populist fascism'. He attributes this characteristic not only to the Iron Guard but, like Weber, even to Cuza's League (at least until 1927 when Codreanu broke with Cuza – according to the author – precisely because of the latter's non-radicalism in agrarian problems).[47] As to the social composition of the Iron Guard, the merit of trying to tackle this little-documented question belongs to Weber and to Barbu.

Nagy-Talavera, in his uneven work about the Arrow Cross and the Iron Guard, differs from some previously mentioned Western historians in his faith in the 'sincere devotion' of Codreanu (and of Szálasi) to social justice.[48] He writes about the 'Archangelic Socialism of the Legion' and about the class struggle waged by the radical fascist movements against their own ruling classes.[49] He does not consider Cuza and Goga fascists but on the contrary shares Codreanu's views about Cuza and Goga as 'the other face of the Government',[50] thus belonging to the non-fascist establishment.

Naturally, Western historians pay much more attention to the anti-Semitism of Romanian fascism than historians publishing in Romania, or even emigré writers, excepting perhaps Sima. But in none of their works is a single chapter, let alone a separate study, allotted to fascist anti-Semitism and to the Jewish policy of the fascist régimes.[51] In spite of the fact that Codreanu himself, and later Sima, in common with most of the Legionaries saw their movement as an anti-communist (and of course anti-Semitic) movement par excellence from its very inception, most Western historians deny that communism played any significant part in the emergence of Romanian fascism (Z. Barbu for example),[52] and Weber points to the circumstance that in under-developed and under-industrialized Romania no working-class parties could have threatened the vested interests of the ruling classes.[53] Most Western scholars emphasize the independent development of Romanian fascism ('Ideological and financial contacts between the Romanian fascists and their counterparts elsewhere were surprisingly limited in the early thirties'),[54] and all dwell upon the uniqueness of the Iron Guard on the European fascist map, even if they differ in the degree of emphasis. In his chapter about Romania in *Die Faschistischen Bewegungen* (a chapter unfortunately not without misunderstandings and minor inaccuracies), Nolte sees the Iron Guard as one of the most original political formations in inter-war Europe, and considers it the most interesting and most complex fascist movement in Europe.[55] Finally, there is a consensus among Western scholars that 'as far as primary sources are concerned . . . most of the studies published so far, in Rumanian or other languages, are on the whole under-documented'[56] (Z. Barbu). Therefore it is not surprising that most of the Western studies should end with unanswered questions[57] and the demand for more source material.

The numerous similarities, at least superficial, between the Iron Guard and the Arrow Cross, the two main fascist movements of Eastern Europe, tempt researchers to do comparative studies. Yet there are striking differences too, ideological, structural, and political, and the history of the two movements shows diverging lines. The dissimilarities between the history of the two countries and the fate of the two movements in the last years of the war could not but affect the historiography of local fascism, bringing about significant differences between the character and the quantity of the relevant historical literature in the two countries.

Hungary suffered a traumatic shock in the last phase of the Second World War. While Romania managed to get rid of the Iron Guard as early as January 1941 and in August 1944 was brought over to the Allied camp in the wake of a successful coup d'état, Horthy's belated and amateurish attempt to break with Hitler in October 1944 failed, and the country fell prey to Arrow Cross terror. Szálasi seized power at a time when a fascist *Machtergreifung* had become a mere anachronism. A devastating war and a bloody reign of savage, enraged *Lumpen*-elements marked the last months of Hungary, before its complete liberation in April 1945. While the Iron Guard emigration started in January 1941, and its former leaders could re-emerge in the West after the war (among them Sima, the last head of the movement, and a number of former Legionary ministers), the Arrow Cross leadership did not survive the war. Szálasi and his friends were captured, killed, or executed during the two post-war years. Not one front rank Hungarist Arrow Cross leader has survived who could have written an authoritative work about his movement. All those former Hungarian fascists who turned up in the West after the war with pretensions of writing history were in fact ob-

scure publicists or politicians lacking any prestige – like Ferenc
Fiala, Lajos Marschalkó, and Pál Vágó – and their writings
amount to journalistic polemics.

In Hungary proper the shocking experience of Arrow Cross
rule gave impetus to a rich anti-fascist literature, which was also
outside the sphere of historical literature. As in Romania, historical research into fascism as such was not encouraged officially.
Miklós Lackó, the best known Hungarian historian of local fascism, bluntly pointed to the lack of interest and will to tackle the
fascist past. He found that the first post-war decades failed to
produce a well-documented struggle against fascist ideologies,
and he discerned a kind of 'pudency' towards fascist tradition,
which in his view was hampering their complete extirpation. He
also complains of the lack of sincere anti-fascist indignation
among the large masses in post-war Hungary.[58] If tactical factors
which influenced the officially guided research in the People's
Democracies are added to all these circumstances, the scarcity of
historical literature about local fascism in post-war Hungary is
easily accounted for. The first thoroughly documented and
scholarly works about Hungarian fascism came out in Hungary
and abroad at about the same time as the first major scientific
works about Romanian fascism, that is, as late as the mid-sixties.
As mentioned earlier, only two fascist movements captured the
attention of researchers: Szálasi's Arrow-Cross-Hungarist movement and Imrédy's Party of Hungarian Revival, though a few
works also dealt with other groups and parties, such as the
Scythe-Cross movements of Zoltán Böszörményi in the early
thirties.

The first post-war book about Hungarian fascism was Jenö
Lévai's *Horogkereszt, kaszáskereszt, nyilaskereszt*[59] (*Swastika,
Scythe-Cross, Arrow-Cross*) published in 1945. The writer, a very
prolific journalist, is the author of a number of useful works about
the catastrophe of Hungarian Jewry. His book is essentially
journalism rather than history. A similar book about fascism was
published by Endre Sós,[60] also a publicist and belletrist. It contains only scanty data about Hungarian fascism.

The fifties produced the first seriously researched essays, mainly
about the pre-fascist period, but they still suffer from party jargon

and from cold-war militancy imposed on the researchers of that period. A pertinent example is a study by György Magos, 'The Role of the British and American Imperialists in the Stabilization of Horthy Fascism',[61] published in the prestigious *Acta Historica*. The labelling of the Horthy régime as fascist should be noted here as a characteristic feature of the earlier interpretation when no demarcation line was drawn between the nature of the authoritarian but parliamentarian Horthy régime and the Szálasi dictatorship. Later, by the end of the fifties, a few studies came out about the Szálasi period, indicating that systematic research was in progress and that the time was ripe for the appearance of major scholarly writings about fascism in Hungary. And indeed, in the early sixties a few monographs were published about the Arrow Cross coup d'état and Szálasi's rule, as well as about the Scythe-Cross movement.[62]

A book deserving special mention in this context, although it does not fit into this group of works, is pertinent here because of its impact on Hungarian historiography. In 1957 C. A. Macartney published his monumental *October Fifteenth*.[63] In spite of the fact that the author prepared his work outside Hungary and did not use Hungarian archives, he draws on primary source material that was not available to researchers in Hungary itself. Macartney's work, which analyses Hungarian history between 1929 and 1945, is excellently documented about Szálasi's movement, and has been extensively used by Hungarian researchers, even when not quoted (as in the case of Agnes Rozsnyai). Macartney was obviously influenced by his numerous conservative-minded informants who stood close to the Horthy régime, and his not entirely negative views about Ferenc Szálasi are also controversial; nevertheless, his work remains to this day the most informative and most detailed history of wartime Hungary, the Arrow Cross included.

The aforementioned work of Miklós Lackó on the Arrow Cross and Hungarian National Socialists was published in 1966, marking the beginning of a more liberal and outspoken era in Hungarian historiography. Despite all the limitations imposed on the historian in an East European country, Lackó's work goes beyond political history and offers a scholarly insight into the social and ideological roots of Hungarian fascism, also tackling such delicate topics in a communist country as, for example, the social basis and the mass support of the Arrow Cross (although he overplays the role and the number of criminal and *Lumpen*-elements in the Arrow Cross following).[64] Lackó is cautious in using the term *fascist* and does not consider Horthy a fascist nor any government preceding the German occupation of Hungary as such. His book stresses the autochthonous character of most of the Hungarian fascist movements without overestimating, for example, Szálasi's independence of Nazi Germany. The author's sphere of interest embraces the ideological-political components of fascism, which lend a *couleur locale* to Hungarian fascism, such as its specific nationalism, the agrarian and Christian idea, and Szálasi's peculiar peasant and worker policy. However, in the last analysis, Lackó tends to minimize the appeal of fascism among the peasantry and the working class, thus somehow losing in scientific objectivity.[65]

Lackó's book is complemented by a scholarly work about Béla Imrédy and his Party of Hungarian Revival, written by Péter Sipos.[66] While Lackó deals with the 'popular' or 'plebeian' movements, Sipos concentrates on the 'gentleman' or upper class in the wide spectrum of Hungarian fascism. He juxtaposes Szálasi, who built his movement on the support of the petty bourgeoisie and the *Lumpenproletariat*, and Imrédy, a first-class financial expert, a former governor of the National Bank, and a former prime minister at the head of the rightist ruling party, who had gathered around him, from 1940, the extreme-right and fascist-minded elements of the mostly urban middle and upper classes. Sipos's work is an interesting research into the special problems of the fascist radicalization of different bourgeois, landowner, officer, clerical, and intellectual circles. However, his use and interpretation of 'total Fascism' in Imrédy's movement is somewhat vague and confusing. But even so, it is a valuable work which places in opposition radical fascism, that of the 'have-nots', to the gentleman-type fascism of the 'haves', in the early forties. This work, like Lackó's book, is more outspoken about anti-Semitism than most works on local fascism in Romania, for example. It should be emphasized that Hungarian historians

largely agreed as to the strong racial basis of Hungarian anti-
Semitism, a characteristic almost absent from the anti-Semitism
of Romanian fascism.

A contribution by the Budapest historian, György Ránki, to
Native Fascism, is worth mentioning. The author of 'The Problem of Fascism in Hungary'[67] exemplifies the embarrassment of
Marxist scholars working in Eastern Europe when they appear
in western forums dealing with ideological problems deemed delicate in their own countries. His writing, on one hand, is an odd
mixture of dogmatic remnants and of lip-service towards the
communist authorities, and on the other hand, of tendencies to
emancipation from the official dogmatic patterns. Ránki believes
that the fascists did not attempt to approach the working class,
which was considered to be Marxist and social-democratic; he
also asserts that the fascist movement was not able to free itself
from the ideology of the Hungarian gentry.[68] Such doubtful
assertions prove once more that in Eastern Europe there still
exist limitations of a dogmatic nature that hinder historians in
reaching independent conclusions in certain fields of research.
Ránki, an influential figure in Hungarian intellectual life, took a
courageous step forward in the direction of re-formulating the
outdated Dimitrovian conception of fascism. While urging intensified research in order to elucidate the differences between
'classical' fascism (German and Italian) and special versions of
fascism (including the Hungarian one), Ránki sounds a note of
warning, hinting probably to his old-fashioned Marxist colleagues, or perhaps to the official ideologists of the régime, that
considering fascism as simply a regressive mass movement, or a
reactionary manifestation of big capital is a dangerous over-
simplification.[69]

Western historians, excepting C. A. Macartney, did not enrich
our factual knowledge about Hungarian fascism. Yet they asked
questions which their colleagues in Hungary today would find
difficult to raise, and they tried to provide answers to problems
that were not clarified in the past. One of these questions concerns the fluctuation of some worker elements between the extreme left and the extreme right. János Erös is among those researchers who discern such a fluctuation. ('In 1939 thousands of

communist sympathisers must have voted for the Arrow Cross; in 1944 they showed their true colours.')[70] There seems to be general agreement over the issue of the preponderance of workers among Szálasi's henchmen. Erös asserts that the workers were indeed over-represented, but this following was recruited from among the unemployed, unskilled, or unorganized workers, whilst the workers in the big industries were as a rule anti-fascist.[71] István Deák asserts that 'for unskilled or unemployed workers, and for small artisans and their journeymen – the Arrow Cross was their first friend . . . The Arrow Cross performed a function that the socialists were unable to fulfil.'[72] In George Mosse's view a further reason could account for the influx of worker elements into the ranks of the Arrow Cross: the chance offered by Szálasi (as by Codreanu in Romania) for the lower strata of the working classes to participate actively in the country's life as organic parts of the national community.[73] Though George Bárány attributes Szálasi's appeal to the masses to his social demagoguery and the ruthless methods advocated by the Arrow Cross,[74] neither he nor any other Western researcher fails to stress the important role played by proletarian, or semi-proletarian, elements in the Hungarian fascist movements. (It should be noted that some Western historians seem to exaggerate the worker participation in the Iron Guard, probably under the impact of the Arrow Cross analogy, just as they exaggerated the populist character of the Arrow Cross under the influence of the Iron Guard analogy.) Great interest is attached to the character of the Horthy régime itself. While for example Nagy-Talavera writes about the 'Szeged-Fascists',[75] Erös makes a point of bringing out the dual character of the Horthy régime (divided between a fascist and a conservative wing, complemented by groups floating around the centre),[76] and Deák emphasizes the tolerant, non-fascist nature of the régime.[77] For his part, although Bárány rejects the slogans about Horthy's 'counter-revolutionary fascist dictatorship', he nevertheless holds to the view that 'the social premises for the fascisation [sic] of Hungarian life were taking shape well before the full impact of fascism could be felt,'[78] a suggestion which implies a gradual process of political life turning fascist long in advance of Szálasi's take-over.

Views about the Arrow Cross differ considerably among Western historians and one may ask what facts are there that can make such divergent interpretations and conclusions possible among non-involved and non-biased researchers. For some of them the Arrow Cross had been 'the only right-wing movement [in Hungary] seriously to bother with (and about) the workers' (Eugen Weber), and Ferenc Szálasi was 'the prophet of the new Hungary, able to impress many humble people' (F. L. Carsten). For others Hungarian fascism was backward and semi-feudal (J. Erös), while Szálasi was nothing but an insane demagogue. One can read about the most brutal anti-Semitism of the Arrow Cross, which ended up in the atrocities and massacres among Budapest Jewry in the autumn and end of 1944, but then at a symposium held in Jerusalem in 1969, Jenö Lévai, the Budapest Jewish researcher of the Jewish Holocaust, denied Szálasi's involvement in the anti-Jewish crimes and considerably diminished his responsibility. The way leading out of the labyrinth of contradictory assertions can only be via the publication of the relevant source material and a better knowledge of the multifarious aspects of modern Hungarian history.

As in Romanian and Hungarian fascism, Slovak fascism has its writers among the post-war Marxist historians in Czechoslovakia, among fascist or rightist emigrés in the West, and it also captured the interest of a handful of 'non-involved' Western scholars. Little was written about inter-war Slovakia during the first two decades after the liberation of Czechoslovakia, and particularly little about the Hlinka party.[79] An essay about Slovak historiography by Ludovit Holotik[80] published in 1967 greatly contributes to the survey of local research into fascism. It is remarkably outspoken about the reasons for the apparent lack of interest in Slovak issues. Holotik accuses the leadership in the Stalinist era in Czechoslovakia of hindering any critical research into the national problems of Czechoslovakia, a situation that persisted up to the mid-sixties. It becomes evident from his review that the few historians who treated the subject were more concerned with the relations of the Slovak state with Nazi Germany, than with the analysis of internal issues, local fascism included. This void has not been filled in Cezchoslovakia up to this day – at least not to my knowledge – and though quite a number of essays in Slovakian do deal with some aspects of fascism in Slovakia, there are no works available in other languages. As with Romania, for example, attention has been centred mainly on the anti-fascist struggle rather than on the history and nature of Fascism itself.

In Western literature the interpretations of Slovak fascism are quite controversial. Although the separatist and fascist- (or Nazi-) oriented wing of Hlinka's People's Party gathered strength in the mid-thirties, there seems to be no justification for labelling the party fascist prior to 1938. As to its nature after 1938 and the characteristics of 'independent' Slovakia ruled by the party leadership, there is no consensus as to the term *Clerical-Fascism* (or *Clerico-Fascism*).[81] A vast Slovak rightist emigré literature denies the fascist character of the Hlinka movement and even of the Tiso régime.[82] A few Western historians also indulge in white-washing the Tiso régime, and especially Tiso himself.[83] Some impartial scholars tend to see the People's Party as conservative-nationalist or reactionary-nationalist rather than Clerico-Fascist.[84] (Nolte does not consider either Hlinka or Tiso as Fascists.)[85]

On the contrary, Slovak researchers, former opponents of the Hlinka-Tiso party, or Marxist historians of the pre-Dubček era, regard the People's party and Tiso's state as typically fascist and totalitarian.[86] Most historians studying Slovak fascism – Marxists in Czechoslovakia, as well as Western researchers – emphasize the extreme nationalism (mostly anti-Czech and anti-Magyar, though some Slovak fascist leaders did not hesitate to join hands with Horthy's Hungary), anti-communism, anti-Semitism, and the clerical (Catholic) nature of the movement and of the régime. But then, there are controversies about the originality of Slovak fascism and of the Tiso régime. Slovak fascism was a 'ludicrous imitation of the Reich model'[87] wrote one of the researchers recently, while others see an interwoven pattern of conservatism, clericalism, and fascism, typical only of Slovakia. One would suppose that the 1969 Prague Symposium about fascism was a good opportunity to elucidate some open questions concerning Slovak fascism. But among the twenty-five papers presented at this forum not a single one dealt with Slovakia (six were devoted to

Czech subjects and one to the problem of fascism in the Sudeten-land).

Among the types of fascism in the Danubian countries and the four fascist régimes in the area, the scantiest literature available is that on the Ustasha movement and the Croatian state of the Ustashi (1941–5). There is no controversy about the fact that the Ustasha take-over in April 1941 was solely a German and Italian act and was not the outcome of a mass uprising in the wake of the military defeat and the dismemberment of Yugoslavia. However, the torrential influx of nationalistic masses to the Ustashi once Ante Pavelič had been installed in Zagreb, cannot be denied. In the typology of fascism the Ustasha movement belongs with the East European movements in spite of its long-standing links with Italian fascism. The main characteristics of the Ustashi are to be sought elsewhere than in its diffuse, nebulous ideology. They are rooted in the fanatical anti-Serbian ultra-nationalism, supple-mented by anti-communist, anti-Semitic, and anti-democratic ideas, and by a *sui generis völkisch*-Christian (Catholic) anti-modernism. All the researchers make a point of stressing the savage terrorist nature of the Ustashi.

Anyone looking for sources and scholarly works about the Ustashi will be disappointed. Apart from the pamphlets published in Croatia after 1941 by Pavelič and his entourage (in both Italian and in German), and a few works published mainly in Italy and in Vienna during the thirties, no comprehensive or analytical work about the movement has yet appeared. Nor is the literature about the so-called independent Croatia much more informative. An exhaustive work on Yugoslav historiography[88] published in 1965 in Belgrade is ample evidence of the reluctance of historians in post-war Yugoslavia to tackle the Ustasha movement; there is little to be found about the subject in contemporary Yugoslav writings, except for a number of essays about the relationships of the movement with Nazi Germany and fascist Italy.

The relevant literature substantiates the assumption that the social make-up of the Ustashi was by no means similar to that of the Arrow Cross, or of the Iron Guard, for example. Workers and peasants were conspicuously under-represented, while the rela-tively high number of Catholic priests and of persons active in the secular organs and organizations of the Catholic Church, as well as the high percentage of officers, intellectuals, professionals, and mainly students, endowed the movement with a specific character, different from other fascist movements in the area. All these peculiarities leave some doubt about the justification of its being treated as a 'purely' fascist movement. The authors of a detailed scholarly work about the Croatian State – Andreas Hory and Martin Broszat – suggest the term *pre-fascist* or *semi-fascist* for the movement.[89] And in Nolte's view there is no certainty whatsoever that the Ustasha movement actually qualifies as fascist at all. Precisely the opposite thesis is expressed by Ivan Abakumovic who considers that the student of fascism in Yugoslavia 'is struck by the fact that the native fascists displayed repeatedly the same characteristics as fascists elsewhere in Europe.'[90] He also points out that the 'fascists had some working-class support, a fact that the communists will be the first to admit'[91] (contrary to Seton-Watson's view, who asserts that the working-class element was almost completely lacking in Croatia and in Slovakia).[92] Yugoslav Marxist historians (Dimitrije Djordjević, for example) ascribe the growth of the Ustashi mainly to external factors – while not overlooking certain internal factors, among them some termed as 'unsettled national problems'.[93] Djordjević concludes that fascism in Yugoslavia (Croatia included) was confined to extremist separatists – and it seems that he is representative of the 'official view' in Yugoslavia today – and its ideas 'never grew deep roots among the small, insignificant minority of youths and middle and upper middle class people.'[94]

For Poland it is sufficient to cite Janusz Żarnowski, a leading figure among contemporary Polish historians. There was no fascist mass party in Poland, nor was there a fascist and totalitarian régime, so that according to Żarnowski there are difficulties in discussing the characteristics of a Polish fascism.[95] There were merely fascist tendencies discernible in interwar Poland including a few extreme-right and extreme-nationalist *fascisant* groups, and even genuinely fascist organizations as the ONR-Falanga. But all these groups remained on the periphery, without gaining a mass following, and lacked any peasant or worker support. On the other hand, Pilsudski's or the colonels' rightist, ultra-nationalist and authoritarian régime could only be treated as fascist by communist party propagandists of the old school. Polish fascism 'operating on the margins of Poland's political life, was in many instances an artificial and imported product', wrote a Western authority on Polish history.[96] One need not necessarily agree with these views (rejected, incidentally, by some Polish researchers). But all those who are not specifically engaged in researching this subject will have to wait for some convincing scholarly works in favour of another interpretation.

Miklós Lackó's paper about the characteristics of South-East European Fascism, presented in 1969, has already been noted. Now attention should be drawn to his essay about East-Central European Fascism, published in 1973 in Munich.[97] The point in mentioning the two studies is to stress the necessity felt by the author to delimit different areas of Eastern and Central Europe when tracing the development of fascist movements in this part of Europe. The few comparative studies and attempts at syntheses come up against obstacles inherent in the subject. The terminology 'East European Fascism' is used as opposed to the 'classic' Italian and German type of fascism. It would better fit reality if the term fascism *in* Eastern Europe were used or perhaps fascisms in Eastern Europe. Dissimilarities seem to prevail and when trying to outline the main common characteristics of the fascist movements one should first try to elucidate the specific local features and varieties, and join forces with those who are researching, for example, the problem of modern nationalism and anti-Semitism in the area, the inter-relationship between the great powers and the small countries, and the specific socio-economic problems of under-developed, or belatedly and partially industrialized societies.

This short survey testifies to the fact that the available literature is by no means sufficient to provide satisfactory answers to the basic problems of the fascist movements in Eastern Europe.[98] The blank spots are particularly large on the map of problems with an ideological and social character. As to the doctrine and ideology of these movements, not a single monograph has seen the light of day in the west nor is there any satisfactory publication of sources of an ideological character. The social composition of most of the movements and of their élite is not sufficiently known nor can we reconstruct, even roughly, the make-up of those social forces that supported the fascist movements in the parliamentary elections. Similarly no work has yet appeared which sets itself the task of studying pre-fascist thought, or the belletristic literature that fostered the Iron Guard and the Arrow Cross ideas. Analyses of the relationship between these movements and religion and Church are also missing. Quite peculiarly, the rich literature of anti-Semitism lacks a systematic description and analysis of the anti-Jewish policy of the Arrow Cross or of the Iron Guard, for example.

Subjective reasons alone cannot account for these shortcomings. Apart from the scarcity of researchers who could have explored these problems, research has been considerably hampered to this day by a number of objective circumstances: for example, the availability of source material and other documentation. It is true, though, that there exists plenty of material in the West, which, unaccountably, has not been made use of by researchers. The periodical material lying about in Western libraries has remained unexploited for the most part. However, the source material freely available is insufficient to fill the gaps in our knowledge. A *sine qua non* for attaining the level of research equivalent to that into Italian fascism for example, would be the opening of the East European archives to Western scholars. It is only natural that the bulk of source material should be found in the respective countries. The record offices and the archives of the main ministries concerned (interior, education, etc.) must necessarily have in their possession a considerable amount of source-material which would be helpful in answering quite a number of puzzling questions. Yet these archives are practically closed to Western scholars and are accessible even to the local researchers in rare cases only, and then to a limited degree. Pending a radical change in this respect, scholars should consider the publication of the available source material and of monographs on the most neglected areas and about the most controversial problems.

Notes

1. G. Ferrero, *Four Years of Fascism* (New York, 1924); Luigi Villari, *The Fascist Experiment* (New York, 1925); Luigi Sturzo, *Italien und der Faschismus* (Cologne, 1926), Francesco Nitti, *Bolschewismus, Faschismus und Demokratie* (Munich, 1926).

2. e.g., Ernst Niekisch, *Hitler – ein deutsches Verhängnis* (Berlin, 1931); Otto Strasser, *Ministersessel oder Revolution?* (Berlin, 1930); Gregor Strasser, *Kampf um Deutschland* (Munich, 1932); Konrad Heiden, *Geschichte des Nationalsozialismus* (Berlin, 1932); Otto Dietrich, *With Hitler on the Road to Power* (London, 1934); F. L. Schuman, *The Nazi Dictatorship. A Study in Social Pathology and the Politics of Fascism* (New York, 1936); R. A. Brady, *The Spirit and Structure of German Fascism* (New York, 1937); Vilmos Böhm, *A nagy tragédia* (*The Great Tragedy*) (Vienna, Leipzig, 1933).

3. e.g., Klaus Charlé, *Die Eiserne Garde* (Berlin, 1939); Alfonso Panini-Finotti, *La Guardia di Ferro* (Florence, 1938); idem, *Da Codreanu a Antonescu. Romania di ieri e di oggi* (Verona, 1941); Harald Laeuen, *Marschall Antonescu* (Essen, 1943).

4. Lucrețiu Pătrășcănu, *Sub Trei Dictaturi* (*Under Three Dictatorships*) (Bucharest, 1944). (The 1970 edition of Pătrășcănu's work will be quoted.)

5. ibid., p. 46.

6. ibid., p. 52.

7. ibid., p. 61.

8. *Istoria R.P.R.* (*The History of the Romanian Peoples' Republic*), ed. Mihail Roller (Bucharest, 1952).

9. Ion Popescu-Puțuri, 'Les principales caractéristiques du régime politique de Roumanie pendant la dictature militaire-fasciste et l'agression hitlérienne', in *La Roumanie pendant la Deuxième Guerre Mondiale* (Bucharest, 1964), pp. 9–36.

10. N. Copoiu, 'Sur la pénétration de l'idéologie nazie en Roumanie et l'attitude protestaire des intellectuels du pays (1940–1944)', in *La Roumanie pendant la Deuxième Guerre Mondiale*.

11. *Impotriva fascismului* (*Against Fascism*). Scientific session concerning the critical analysis and the unmasking of fascism in Romania, Bucharest, 4–5 March 1971 (Bucharest, 1971).

12. Mihai Fătu and Ion Spălățelu, *Garda de Fier. Organizație teroristă de tip fascist* (*The Iron Guard. A Fascist-type terrorist organization*) (Bucharest, 1971).

13. e.g., Constanța Bogdan about the social-economic foundation of fascism in Romania (pp. 29–43), Șerban Cioculescu about Legionarism and literature (pp. 118–23), and Gheorghe Zaharia about the nature of the régime set up in September 1940 (pp. 183–93).

14. Valter Roman, 'Condițiile apariției fascismului pe plan mondial si lupta poporului român impotriva fascismului international' ('The Conditions under which Fascism appeared on a world scale and the fight of the

Romanian people against international Fascism'), in *Impotriva fascismului*, p. 11.

15. Al. Gh. Savu, *Dictatura regală (1938–1940)* (*The Royalist Dictatorship*) (Bucharest, 1970).

16. ibid., p. 21.

17. ibid., p. 16.

18. See for example Copoiu, op. cit., pp. 131, 138.

19. Characteristic for this view is the title of an article by Titu Georgescu, 'Sur la cinquième colonne hitlérienne en Roumanie', *Revue d'Histoire de la Deuxième Guerre Mondiale*, no. 18 (1968), pp. 19–38. See also Ştefan Muşat, 'Coloana a V-a hitlerista in România' ('The Hitlerist Fifth Column in Romania'), in *Anale de Istorie*, no. 6 (1970), and Florea Nedelcu, 'Etude concernant le role de l'Allemagne hitlérienne dans l'évolution des organisations fascistes de Roumanie dans la période 1933–1937', in *Revue roumaine d'histoire*, no. 6 (1971), pp. 991–1011.

20. e.g., Gh. I. Ioniţă, 'Sur l'histoire de la lutte antifasciste du peuple roumain', in *Etudes d'histoire contemporaine de la Roumanie* (Bucharest, 1971), vol. II, pp. 47–98. Popescu-Puţuri, op. cit., pp. 12–14; and Florea Nedelcu, 'Carol al II-lea şi Garda de Fier – de la relaţii amicale la criză (1930–1937)', ('Carol II and the Iron Guard – From Friendly Relations to Crisis'), in *Studii*, no. 5 (1971), pp. 1009–28.

21. e.g., Savu, op. cit., pp. 455–6.

22. See my two bibliographical notes: *Rumania During the War. A Survey of Literature*, in 'The Wiener Library Bulletin' (April 1963), and *Rumanian Fascist Emigrés. A Survey of Their Literature*, in 'The Wiener Library Bulletin' (July 1964).

23. Ştefan Pălăghiţă, *Garda de Fer. Spre Reinvierea României* (*The Iron Guard. Towards Romania's Revival*) (Buenos Aires, 1951).

24. Pălăghiţă considers Sima demented, as he does King Carol and Ion Antonescu. ibid., p. 173.

25. G. Barbul, *Memorial Antonescu: Le III-e Homme de l'Axe*, vol. I (Paris, 1951).

26. Ion Gheorghe, *Rumäniens Weg zum Satellitenstaat* (Heidelberg, 1952).

27. Michel Sturdza, *The Suicide of Europe* (Belmont, Mass., 1968).

28. Horia Sima, *Histoire du mouvement légionnaire* (Rio de Janeiro, 1972). Like almost every former Legionary, Sima too uses extensively the *Mein Kampf* of the Iron Guard, Corneliu Zelea Codreanu's *Către Legionari* (*To the Legionaires*) (Sibiu, 1936). Published in German as *Eiserne Garde* (Berlin, 1939).

29. Sturdza quotes Sima's writing *Cazul Iorga-Madgearu* (*The Iorga-Madgearu Affair*), op. cit., p. 165; see also pp. 107, 165.

30. ibid., p. 233.

31. Horia Sima, *Destinée du Nationalisme* (Paris, 1951).

32. Carlo Sburlati, *Codreanu il capitano* (Roma, 1970).

33. Pamfil Şeicaru, *Octavian Goga* and *A. C. Cuza* ('Carpaţii' Collection, Madrid).

34. Nicholas M. Nagy-Talavera, *The Green Shirts and the Others. A History of Fascism in Hungary and Rumania* (Stanford, 1970).

35. Eugen Weber, 'Romania', in his *Varieties of Fascism* (Princeton, N.J., 1964), pp. 96–105; 'Romania', in *The European Right. A Historical Profile*, ed., Hans Rogger and Eugen Weber (London, 1965), pp. 501–74; and 'The Men of the Archangel' in *Journal of Contemporary History*, no. 1 (1966), pp. 101–26.

36. Z. Barbu, 'Rumania' in *European Fascism*, ed. S. J. Woolf (London, 1968), pp. 146–66.

37. Stephen Fischer-Galati, 'Fascism in Romania', in *Native Fascism in the Successor States, 1918–1945*, ed. Peter F. Sugar (Santa Barbara, Calif., 1971), pp. 112–22. His contribution 'Romanian Nationalism', in *Nationalism in Eastern Europe*, ed., Peter F. Sugar and Ivo J. Lederer (Seattle and London, 1969), pp. 373–95, contains some valuable references to Romanian fascism too. Emanuel Turczynski published in *Native Fascism* a useful article titled 'The Background of Romanian Fascism', pp. 101–11.

38. Ernst Nolte, *Die Faschistischen Bewegungen* (Berlin, 1966). (I used the French edition of this work, *Les mouvements fascistes* [Paris, 1969]).

39. F. L. Carsten, *The Rise of Fascism* (Berkley and Los Angeles; 2nd printing 1969); the chapter about Romania: 'Anti-Semitism and Anti-Communism: the Iron Guard', pp. 181–93.

40. E.g., Theodor I. Armon, 'Fascismo Italiano e Guardia di Ferro' in *Storia contemporanea*, no. 3 (1972), pp. 505–48.

41. H. Seton-Watson, 'Fascism, Right and Left', in *Journal of Contemporary History*, no. 1 (1966), pp. 183–97.

42. Miklós Lackó, 'Zur Frage der Besonderheiten des südosteuropäischen Faschismus', in *Fascism and Europe* (Prague, 1970), vol. II, pp. 2–22, Mimeo.

43. Seton-Watson, op. cit., p. 193.

44. Weber, 'The Men of the Archangel', op. cit., pp. 117–18.

45. ibid., p. 122.

46. ibid., pp. 107, 114.

47. Fischer-Galati, op. cit., pp. 114, 116.

48. Nagy-Talavera, op. cit., p. 363.

49. ibid., pp. 357, 360–61, 374.

50. ibid., p. 353.

51. My article about the Jewish policy of King Carol's dictatorship, published in Hebrew, is not available to a wide circle of readers, and anyhow is not relevant to the main Fascist movements. *Zion*, nos 1–2 (Jerusalem, 1964), pp. 133–51.

52. Barbu, op. cit., p. 153.

53. Weber, 'The Men of the Archangel', op. cit., p. 103.

54. Fischer-Galati, op. cit., p. 116. Cf. Weber, 'While Codreanu lived, the Legion was no conscious agent of Nazism'. (Weber, *The European Right*, op. cit., p. 554).

55. Nolte, op. cit., pp. 243, 251.

56. Barbu, op. cit., p. 150.

57. For example Turczynski, op. cit., p. 111.

58. Miklós Lackó, *Nyilasok, Nemzetiszocialisták, 1935–1944* (*Men of the Arrow Cross, National Socialists*) (Budapest, 1966), pp. 331–2. (An abridged version of this work was published in English under the same title in Budapest, 1969.)

59. Jenö Lévai, *Horogkereszt, kaszáskereszt, nyilaskereszt* (*Swastika, Scythe-Cross, Arrow-Cross*) (Budapest, 1945).

60. Endre Sós, *Európai fasizmus és antiszemitizmus* (*European Fascism and anti-Semitism*) (Budapest [s.a.]).

61. György Magos, 'The Role of the British and American Imperialists in the Stabilization of Horthy Fascism' in *Acta Historica* (1954), vol. II, pp. 161–217.

62. At the end of the fifties and the beginning of the sixties, quite a number of studies about Hungarian fascism was published by Mihály Korom, Kálmán Szakács, Ágnes Rozsnyai, and Miklós Lackó. The first books appeared in the early sixties: Ágnes Rozsnyai, *A Szálasi puccs* (*The Szálasi Putsch*) (Budapest, 1962); Mihály Korom, *A fasizmus bukása Magyarországon. A népi demokratikus átalakulás feltételeinke létrejötte, 1943–1945* (*The Downfall of Fascism in Hungary. The Ripening of the People's Democratic Revolution* [*sic*]) (Budapest, 1961); Kálmán Szakács, *Kaszáskeresztesek* (*The Scythe-Cross-Men*) (Budapest, 1963).

63. C. A. Macartney, *October Fifteenth. A History of Modern Hungary, 1929–1945* (Edinburgh, 1957; 2nd ed., Edinburgh, 1961).

64. See n. 58.

65. Lackó, op. cit., pp. 74–5, 117–36, 166–83.

66. Péter Sipos, *Imrédy Béla és a Magyar Megujulás Pártja* (*Béla Imrédy and the Party of Hungarian Revival*) (Budapest, 1970).

67. György Ránki, 'The Problem of Fascism in Hungary', in *Native Fascism*, pp. 65–72.

68. ibid., p. 70.

69. ibid., pp. 71–2.

70. J. Erös, 'Hungary', in *European Fascism*, p. 137.

71. ibid.

72. István Deák, 'Hungary', in *The European Right*, p. 397.

73. George Mosse, Introduction: 'The Genesis of Fascism', *Journal of Contemporary History*, no. 1 (1966), p. 21.

74. George Bárány, 'The Dragons' Teeth: The Roots of Hungarian Fascism', in *Native Fascism*, p. 78.

75. See his *Green Shirts and the Others*, p. 75.

76. Erös, op. cit., pp. 111–12.

77. Deák, op. cit., pp. 364–5.

78. Bárány, op. cit., p. 75.

79. For the relevant Slovak research see R. E. Lamberg, 'Father Hlinka's Separatists. New Slovak Publications', in *The Wiener Library Bulletin*, no. 2 (April 1963).

80. Ludovit Holotik, 'Slowakische Geschichtschreibung der Gegenwart', in *Historica Slovaca* (Bratislava, 1967), vol. V, pp. 255–86.

81. For the use of the expression *Clerical Fascism* see Yeshayahu Jelinek, 'Bohemia-Moravia, Slovakia and the Third Reich During the Second World War', in *East European Quarterly*, no. 2 (1969), p. 236. About the character of the Hlinka Guard and of the Tiso régime see ibid., 'Slovakia's Internal Policy and the Third Reich, August 1940–February 1941', in *Central European History* (September 1971), pp. 242–70, and 'Storm-troopers in Slovakia: the Rodobrana and the Hlinka-Guard', in *Journal of Contemporary History*, no. 3 (1971), pp. 97–120.

82. e.g., Joseph A. Mikus, *Slovakia. A Political History: 1918–1950* (Milwaukee, 1963); Milan Stanislao Durica, *La Slovacchia e le sue relazioni politiche con la Germania, 1938–1945, I–II* (Padova, 1964); and ibid., *Die slowakische Politik im Lichte der Staatslehre Tisos* (Bonn, 1967).

83. e.g., Gilbert L. Oddo, *Slovakia and Its People* (New York, 1960).

84. Joseph F. Zacek, 'Czechoslovak Fascisms', in *Native Fascism*, p. 59.

85. Nolte, op. cit., p. 277.

86. A view held by among others Jozef Lettrich, *History of Modern Slovakia* (New York, 1955).

87. Zacek, op. cit., p. 62.

88. *Historiographie Yougoslave 1955–1965*, ed. Jorjo Tadić (Beograd, 1965).

89. Andreas Hory and Martin Broszat, *Der kroatische Ustascha-Staat, 1941–1945* (Stuttgart, 1964), p. 177.

90. Ivan Abakumovic, 'Yugoslavia's Fascist Movements', in *Native Fascism*, p. 140.

91. ibid., p. 141.

92. Seton-Watson, op. cit., p. 193.

93. Dimitrije Djordjevič, 'Fascism in Yugoslavia: 1918–1941', in *Native Fascism*, p. 132.

94. ibid., p. 133.

95. Janusz Żarnowski, 'Courants et tendences fascistes dans la Pologne des années 1918–1939', in *Fascism and Europe*, vol. I, p. 158.

96. Piotr S. Wandycz, 'Fascism in Poland: 1918–1939', in *Native Fascism*, p. 96.

97. Miklós Lackó, 'Ostmitteleuropäischer Faschismus', in *Vierteljahrshefte für Zeitgeschichte*, no. 1 (1973), pp. 39–51.

98. The proceedings of a Conference on Comparative European Nazism and Fascism held in Bergen in 1974 have not yet appeared in print; the typed material does not enable us to assess the contribution of these papers to the study of fascism in Eastern Europe.

7 Fascism and Populism in Latin America

At first sight it is surprising that in spite of Latin America's turbulent history of dictatorship and authoritarianism, fascist movements did not take root there and that even régimes which have the trappings of fascism such as Vargas's Brazil and Perón's Argentina cannot easily be fitted into the fascist mould. In Europe fascism was a major expression of mass politics in the inter-war years and of the response to social and economic crisis: in Latin America the equivalent response is to be found in a wide range of mass nationalist movements which cannot easily be categorized in European terms and to which scholars have given the generic name 'populism'. Unsatisfactory though this term may be, as the Latin American usage differs broadly from usage elsewhere, it has now entered the political vocabulary and refers to a variety of reformist movements, such as Aprismo in Peru and its derivatives in Venezuela, Cuba, and Costa Rica, the MNR (Movimiento Nacionalista Revolucionario) in Bolivia, Getulismo in Brazil, Peronismo in Argentina, which are opposed to traditional parties narrowly based on conservative landowning élites. The heyday of these movements coincided with the period of import-substitute industrialization which lasted from the early 1930s and petered out in the mid-1960s.

There were also, in the 1930s, self-styled fascist movements but only the Brazilian Integralistas achieved a mass following sufficiently large to cause alarm; others such as the Mexican Dorados, the Chilean and Teuto-Brazilian Nazis and numerous Argentinian groups were limited in size if vocal in expression, but in no case did any fascist movement come to power and in every case where a fascist movement confronted a populist movement it suffered defeat and eclipse or was co-opted and absorbed. It might be argued that the conflict between Vargas and the Integralistas in Brazil was a struggle between rival fascisms or even that populism is a Latin American variant of European fascism, but to argue this is to transfer a European concept over which there is still a wide measure of disagreement in its application to Europe itself to a political, social, economic, and cultural situation where the use of the concept can only obfuscate although, as we will see later, there is a certain logic in the 'colonial fascist' thesis if one accepts Marxist premises.

Intellectuals flirted with fascist ideas in the 1930s as they did with every *nouvelle vague* emanating from Europe, but these ideas could not be easily reconciled with the imperatives of an aroused popular nationalism and were soon dropped. German and Italian diplomacy exerted great efforts to encourage and subsidize Nazi and fascist groups among the ill-assimilated sections of German and Italian minorities in Argentina and Brazil but their success was limited, as were the efforts of the Spanish government to strengthen ties with Spanish America by propagating the doctrine of *Hispanidad*.[1] The Spanish Civil War (the influence of which in Spanish America still awaits its historian) divided opinion, as Franco's propaganda convinced churchmen (many of whom were Spaniards) and the conservative élite that the Nationalists were fighting a religious crusade against atheistic communism which since the influential writings of Donoso Cortés in the mid-nineteenth century had been regarded by the Spanish church as a logical and inevitable consequence of liberty of conscience. The propaganda was aimed at those Latin Americans who avidly seize on anything which confirms their anti-United States, anti-Protestant, and anti-democratic prejudices. But even this influence was largely tempered by the Spaniards' assumption that they were the natural leaders of the Hispanic world and was limited to traditionalist elements among the clergy, landowners, and peasants. Hispanidad did not provide an inspiration for movements of the radical right. Hispanidad, in any case, had little appeal to immigrants of non-Spanish stock whilst German nazism with its assumptions of racial supremacy could have little influence in societies with a high proportion of mixed-bloods and where nativism was becoming an integral part of nationalist ideology. Thus one can largely discount the direct influence of European fascism. If there was to be a Latin American fascism it had to be of the home-grown variety.

Nevertheless, immediately after the Second World War there was a widespread fear among the Allies (and this perhaps reflects their lack of knowledge of Latin American affairs) that fascism, defeated in Europe, would be rejuvenated in Latin America. This fear was encouraged by Perón's admiration for the Axis powers and his support for Franco's régime, by the fascist sympathies of Bolivia's revolutionary officers, by the corporatist trappings of Vargas's Estado Novo with its expressed admiration for Salazar's Portugal, and by the refuge given to fascist exiles. These exiles from Hitler's New Order eked out a precarious existence, haunted by the fear of retribution, but their influence seems to have been minimal, except possibly as a source for some virulent strains in Argentinian anti-Semitism, and as a stimulus to fiction writers. Fears of a phoenix-like revival of fascism were misplaced. Fascism, like other political movements inspired by the European example – liberalism, conservatism, socialism, and communism – failed to take root and was modified, under Latin American conditions, until the connections appeared tenuous and the similarities superficial. Part of the explanation for this must lie in the absence in Latin America of those conditioning factors which gave fascist movements in Europe their distinctive style. Six points are worth briefly considering:

1. Foremost is that in the twentieth century, Latin American countries have not experienced total war.[2] War has been a major factor in impelling social change: its absence deprives countries of the consequences of mass mobilization and of great collective effort; it removes an important impetus to the acceleration of social mobility and to the improvement of the position of women, minorities, and labour organizations, and it reduces the urgency for rationalizing productive processes and for strengthening state power. Most importantly, in the context of fascist movements, Latin America was spared the psychological legacies of war in such phenomena as veterans attempting to recapture the camaraderie of the trenches, and the psycho-social consequences of generational and sex imbalances caused by massive losses of men in their prime of life. Unlike the history of Europe, that of Latin

America has not been conditioned by endemic warfare, and although the major impetus to change has occurred as a result of the economic impact of the two world wars together with that of the Great Depression, this was scarcely comparable to those factors described above. Nor have Latin American intellectuals been receptive to ideologies growing out of intra-national conflict. The Social Darwinist assumptions of much fascist theorizing were confined in Latin America to explaining, in racial terms, the gap in social development between predominantly European and predominantly mestizo nations rather than to providing justification for inevitable conflict between them.

The most important political consequence stemming from absence of war in Latin America is that soldiers lack a military function, from which emerges a distinctive pattern of civil-military relations. In Europe, conservative officer corps had an ambivalent attitude towards fascist parties, distrusting upstart leaders with their stridency and radical aims but tolerating the rise of paramilitary militias which could counter-balance left-wing organizations, thus relieving the army of internal policing and releasing it for its proper function of national defence.[3] In Latin America, where there has been a tradition of military involvement in politics since the wars of independence of the early nineteenth century, and where there was little threat from the left and only an attenuated frontier defence function, the military have always looked askance at alternative sources of firepower which might compete with their own political ambitions. Even the habitual weakness and divisions of Latin American police forces reflect military distrust as well as indicate a willingness on the part of the military to undertake internal security tasks themselves. Thus the only road to success for fascist groups is to infiltrate the military as the Integralists tried to do with indifferent success in Brazil. Alternatively, the military itself might come under fascist influence independently of civilian parties, as happened in Bolivia after the Chaco war or in Argentina, but this is a very different matter from having to coexist and compete with an independently organized fascist movement drawing its strength from a mobilized and politicized mass.

Militarism, whether as old-fashioned *caudillismo*, or under its institutionalized, bureaucratic form, reduces the area within which a fascist movement can operate. The culture of violence has permeated Latin American politics since the early nineteenth century. Where the use of violence has become a recognized means of changing power, that peculiar élan offered by fascist movements has a lower resonance than in societies where the use of violence for political ends invites moral opprobrium. Fascist movements become irrelevant as their appeal to alienated, marginalized elements is offset by the clientilist and patronage techniques of the populist politician. Nor can fascists claim to have the monopoly of the ruthless use of violence, for if ruthlessness is necessary to purge the body politic there is a tradition, sanctified by its longevity, of military intervention. The military, too, are able to exploit the symbols of nationality more effectively than civilian politicians. Indeed, it is precisely at this point that the military are able to fulfil the role ostensibly claimed by fascist parties of clearing out the stables of an unheroic, stock-jobbing, materialist, parliamentary liberalism.

In Europe a restraint is placed on military intervention by professional ethics. In Latin America, in contrast, the military's role as defender of constitutional government may be widely, if sometimes reluctantly, accepted. Nor can the fascist cult of the superman have much to offer Latin Americans with the *macho* ways of generations of caudillos behind them. Finally, one might point to the devaluation of the vocabulary of revolt in Latin America habituated to an imagery of blood which might tend to reduce the shock effect of fascism's appeal.[4] Given these pre-conditions, fascist movements find it difficult to gain a mass response, and they end up as a refuge for alienated intellectuals and those excluded from patronage handouts.

2. An area where pre-conditions for fascism were unfavourable rises from the ubiquity of Catholic culture. Catholicism's predominance throughout society is shown both in the strength of the institutionalized Church and in the pervasiveness of folk-Catholicism. Nor did the Church feel itself threatened by alternative religious traditions or by a strong atheistic left, so thus did not need alliance with, or the protection of, fascist groups. The Church in Latin America might give whole-hearted support to conservative,

traditional movements but adopted more caution towards fascist groups, which, in Europe – even in Spain – were anti-clerical.

Where anti-clericalism took a militant form, as in Mexico in the 1920s, the Church became a rallying point for a counter-revolutionary peasantry akin, in some respects, to Spanish Carlism,[5] sharing a similar nativist outlook, reacting against the creeping influence of foreign and urban values.

Although a number of groups appeared in the 1930s calling themselves Falange these did not necessarily bear much relationship to the Spanish Falange. In the Colombian and Bolivian cases there were some parallels but in the case of Chile the Falange emerged as a liberal wing of the conservatives, and influenced by liberal Catholics like Maritain developed into the Christian Democrat party.

3. The absence of a strongly organized left removed an important incentive to the growth of fascist movements. The slow rate of industrialization was a brake on the growth of an urban proletariat and the predominance in some countries of a mining economy meant that the most militant workers were often far removed geographically from the centres of power. Where, as in the case of Buenos Aires, there was a large urban proletariat, much of the initiative for labour organization came from immigrants who brought with them conflicting socialist and anarchist traditions which fragmented the left. The foreign provenance of left-wing movements was a positive disadvantage in a period of rising nationalist feeling. Labour organizations were further weakened by cheap labour resulting from an ever-increasing flow of rural migrants driven off the land by an unreformed agrarian sector.

Urbanization without accompanying industrialization created a marginalized urban population susceptible to the appeal of the populist politician. In the absence of a strong left, Latin America might seem to approximate more closely to Eastern than Western Europe, but what is distinctive about Latin America was the skill with which populist politicians worked within a familiar patronage network which perpetuated, in an urban environment, the patron-dependent relationship of the countryside. Considerable attention has been focused on 'clientilism' which many observers see as the key to explaining why, even under the twin pro-

cesses of modernization and political mobilization, the consciousness of workers nevertheless remained frozen in a traditional
mould of thought. The survival and strengthening of institutions
like *compadrazgo* or the Brazilian *panelinha* are adduced as evidence of the ready acceptance of the mores of personalist politics
in preference to impersonal bureaucratic norms. What weight
should be given to these cultural factors has become a matter of
dispute and we need many more studies of marginalism and of
interest articulation before generalizations can be validated, but
patriarchalism dies hard and the emphasis placed by radicals on
'raising the level of consciousness' and thereby breaking the
crust of habitual deference and the expectation that benefits come
from above, is indicative of the persistence of traditional behaviour patterns.[6]

4. The cultural crisis growing out of the First World War and
the Great Depression, which drove many European intellectuals
to adopt positions on the extreme left or extreme right, took a distinctive form in Latin America where the intelligentsia's reaction
was anti-liberal, anti-European, and anti-United States. This reaction took two forms: on one side a nativism, influenced by the
Mexican revolution's vindication of Indians and which had a mass
popular base, especially in Peru and Bolivia where large Indian
populations underlined the relevance of the Mexican experience;
on the other, there was a reappraisal of Hispanic traditions which
had been largely repudiated after independence in favour of British and French models of constitutional liberalism. Here the
social base was narrower and took the form of an assertion of
traditional 'creole' values against radical immigrant influences,
emphasizing the spiritual traditions of Hispanic Catholicism.
This current was strengthened by ontological quests into 'national character' (paralleling a similar quest in Spain itself).[7] One
consequence was to stimulate a revival of interest in Catholic
social thought, with its corporatist assumptions, which, it was believed, was more 'natural' to peoples rooted in an Iberian and
Mediterranean cultural ethos than the borrowed postulates of
Lockean individualism. This became one inspiration of the Christian Democrat parties with their emphasis on communitarian
democracy which began to appear in the 1930s. Fascist ideas were

acceptable only insofar as these could be assimilated within this tradition, but running through most of the writings of the Latin American right is a repudiation of fascist *étatisme*.[8]

5. Another limitation on the adoption of the fascist model was its stress on economic autarchy. This originally was an attraction to nationalist groups, especially the Argentine military, but the pre-conditions of a fascist economy did not exist. No Latin American country was able to free itself from dependence on foreign trade. Sufficient capital could not be generated internally to finance heavy industry and there was a continuing need to maintain exports in order to purchase capital equipment from abroad. The fundamental weakness, however, lay in a restricted domestic market, which was insufficient to maintain a self-sustaining industrialization programme.

6. Fascist movements in Europe sustained much of their momentum from the support of student/youth movements. In Latin America, where students have a tradition of political involvement, their loyalties were already pre-empted by the University Reform movement dating from 1918 with its nationalist, Pan-Latin American, and radical ideology. In general, Latin American student movements are traditionally left of centre and the development of militant right-wing students is a comparatively recent growth dating from the late 1960s.

Given these pre-conditions the 1930s and 1940s saw the growth of populist parties – cross-class coalitions, a complex amalgam of nationalism, popular participation, social reform, and authoritarian centralism – rather than fascist parties. One of the first books to discuss the Janus-faced nature of these parties, which were reformist at the same time as they increased structural blockages, was C. Veliz, ed., *Obstacles to change in Latin America* (Oxford, 1965). These essays by prominent Latin American academics, many of whom had practical experience in government, showed that the obstacles to reform were far more deep-seated than the optimistic planners of the Alliance for Progress in the early 1960s had assumed. They also showed the irrelevance of the historical experience of the advanced industrial countries for Latin America, and nowhere more clearly than in the role played by the middle classes. Unlike the European middle classes which had achieved economic power and then political power, those in Latin America had acquired political power first. They were essentially professional, bureaucratic sectors aspiring to land-owner status, or to the security of government employment, rather than a national bourgeoisie generating its own scale of values, confident in its own economic power. Thus patronage and state paternalism became the fulcrum of the political system. Lacking autonomous power and lacking entrepreneurial drive, the state became the main promoter of industrialization at times hostile to and at others acting in concert with foreign capital.

These essays raised the question of whether mass populist par-ties could overcome these deficiencies and fulfil a reforming role. The one by Torcuato di Tella on 'Populism and reform in Latin America' was the first, and is still the most sophisticated analysis of the populist phenomenon and, with its five-fold typology, is the starting point for any serious analysis. His conclusion, guardedly optimistic, was that 'populism was the only force on the side of reform in Latin America.' Di Tella's trail-blazing essay has been followed up by few people. In his chapter in E. Gellner and G. Ionescu, *Populism: its meaning and national characteristics* (London, 1969), A. Hennessy is more pessimistic about popu-lism's reform potential but he is more concerned with placing populism in a wider context and to draw the distinction between predominantly urban populist movements and movements which have a rural emphasis, such as Mexican *zapatismo* and *sinar-quismo*, Acción Popular in Peru and even Castroism – those move-ments which seek national redemption through an uncorrupted peasantry and which are more akin to the Russian *narodnik* con-cept and to some (though not many) aspects of agrarian populism in the United States. H. Neira in 'Populismes ou césarismes popu-listes', in the *Revue française de science politique*, vol. 19, no. 3 (1969) is a very useful overview and he rightly questions the use of the word and wonders whether 'caesarism' might not be more appropriate, although this is also open to objections.

General books on Latin American politics have brief analyses of populism such as Jacques Lambert in *Amérique Latine: struc-tures sociales et institutions politiques* (Paris, 1963; English trans-lation, Berkeley and Los Angeles, 1967). One full-length book is

Von Niekerk, *Populism and political development in Latin America* (Rotterdam, 1974). The concept remains diffuse, and for an adequate detailed general treatment it would have to be based on a comprehensive theory of Latin American politics. An enormous literature is accumulating on this but until more empirical work has been done, a more fruitful approach would seem to be the analysis of specific examples of national populist parties. A key reference work for Latin American political parties generally is J. P. Bernard et al., *Guide to the political parties of Latin America* (London, 1973). One of the most controversial aspects of populism is the role played in it by the military. The crucial relationship between the middle classes and the military is explored by J. Nun in 'The middle class military coup' the most important essay in C. Veliz, ed., *The politics of conformity in Latin America* (Oxford, 1967).

If there have been few attempts to cover populism on a continental scale there have been none for fascism. It would be useful to have a descriptive book detailing the various self-styled fascist groups which have existed and, in some cases, still exist. The two countries, Brazil and Argentina, which have produced the most complex populist régimes as well as the greatest variety of fascist-style movements must now be examined in detail.

Brazil: the 1930 Revolution was a watershed in Brazilian history, overthrowing the Old Republic, ushering in the fifteen-year domination of Getulio Vargas, as well as the era of mass politics and the polarization of political forces between right and left on a scale which had no parallel in Latin America at that time. The most remarkable feature of the early 1930s in Brazil was the scale and speed of political mobilization – a reflection of urbanization and the growth of the middle classes. Politics became nationalized; there was a swing against the decentralization of the Old Republic, enshrined in the 1891 Constitution, when politics consisted of conflicts between local state factions and between the most powerful states, São Paulo, Minas Gerais, and the capital Rio de Janeiro – the *politica dos governadores*. The death knell of the ephemeral state parties was sounded with the growth of national based parties, the most important of which were the Integralistas founded in 1932 and the Aliança Libertadora Nacional, the popular front party formed in 1935.

The Integralists, a fascist-style party, sprouted, flowered, and withered within the space of six years, crushed in 1938 after Vargas established his Estado Novo.[9] How were they able to expand so rapidly and why did they collapse so suddenly? The answer to the first question lies primarily in their originality in the context of Brazilian politics. They were sharply differentiated in both style and organization from preceding parties. The main thrust of their appeal lay originally in their anti-liberalism (this was to be replaced by anti-communism as the left grew in strength) and in their repudiation of the attendant *coronelismo* system and their desire to replace manipulative politics and narrow state loyalties by loyalty to a regenerated national state. Their visibility, their marches, salutes, rituals, songs, their press propaganda, educational and social organizations, and the deliberate externalization of their activities marked a total rejection of the hermetic style of traditional politics. Their leader Plinio Salgado's obsessional appeals to sentiment; his emotional and mystical rhetoric aimed at implanting in his readers and listeners a consciousness of *brasilidade*, made a direct appeal, as no other party had done, at a time of social and economic crisis when newly roused groups were seeking identity and reassurance. Those who joined the party entered a self-contained sub-culture. The Integralists had their own organizations for almost every aspect of social life.

They also benefited from the groundswell of nationalist sentiment which had been growing since the early 1920s and which is covered in a short general survey of nationalism by E. B. Burns, *Nationalism in Brazil: an historical survey* (New York, 1968). The pessimistic self-questioning of the early years of the Old Republic had been giving way to a more positive evaluation of Brazilian potentialities. T. Skidmore analyses some of these intellectual currents in 'Brazil's search for identity in the Old Republic', in R. S. Sayers, ed., *Portugal and Brazil in transition* (Minneapolis, 1968). Among the most important influences on nationalist thought in 1930 were the élitist, anti-democratic writings of Alberto Torres, especially *O problema nacional brasileiro*, published in 1914 and reprinted in 1933. His work is analysed in a useful article by

W. D. McLain Jr., 'Alberto Torres ad hoc nationalist', in *The Luso-Brazilian Review*, vol. IV, no. 2 (December, 1967) and in a fuller study by Barbosa Lima Sobrinho. Torres's influence was particularly strong among the *tenentes* although his Jeffersonian agrarianism was not taken up as a prescription for Brazil's ills: the lure of industrialization was too strong. *Tenentismo* was the most significant expression of radical dissent during the 1920s and an early example of younger officers acting as a radical reforming force. Although their risings in 1922 and 1924 were crushed and they broke up as a coherent political force, after 1930 a considerable number became active in the communist and Integralist parties and during the Estado Novo. Their definitive history has yet to be written. In English a useful introduction is R. J. Alexander, 'Brazilian *Tenentismo*', in the *Hispanic American Historical Review*, vol. 36 (1956). Their role in 1930 is discussed in J. D. Wirth, '*Tenentismo* in the Brazilian Revolution of 1930', *Hispanic American Historical Review*, vol. 44, no. 2 (May 1964). A further article by Alexander, 'The Brazilian *tenentes* after the Revolution of 1930', in *Journal of Inter-American Studies*, vol. 15, no. 2 (May 1973) traces their subsequent career and influence up to and beyond 1964.

We still lack a comprehensive treatment of the 1930 revolution. J. Young, *The 1930 Revolution and its aftermath* (New Brunswick, N.J., 1967) provides one introduction. The Revolution is treated in the general histories of modern Brazil, the best of which in English is T. Skidmore, *Politics in Brazil, 1930–1964: an experiment in democracy* (New York, 1969). P. Flynn has a detailed examination of the proto-fascist groups between 1930 and 1932 in 'The Revolutionary Legions and the Brazilian Revolution of 1930', in R. Carr, ed., *Latin American Affairs: St. Antony's Papers*, no. 2 (Oxford, 1970). This is an important article for understanding later developments. Based on Aranha's archives, it discusses the revolutionary programmes, some hitherto unpublished, of the various 'legions' which sprang up in a number of states during and after 1930. Flynn shows how the failure to create a national revolutionary party in the midst of an intensely personalist and localized political system created a vacuum which neither integralists nor communists were able to fill, leaving the army as the only vehicle for national political mobilization. Be that as it may, the programmes of the legions provide an interesting insight into the moralistic strain which was to be one of integralism's distinguishing features. Salgado himself held aloof from Vargas's revolution sensing, one suspects, that Vargas was changing the rules of the game rather than the game itself.

The standard work dealing with the middle thirties, the years of integralism's flowering, is R. Levine, *The Vargas régime: the critical years, 1934–1938* (New York, 1970), which has a comprehensive bibliography. The best short account of integralism is S. Hilton, '*Acção Integralista Brasileira:* fascism in Brazil, 1932–1938', in *Luso-Brazilian Review*, vol. IX, no. 2 (December 1972). An early book which gives a German view, reflecting the interest shown in integralism by the Teuto-Brazilian communities in Rio Grande do Sul is K. Hunsche, *Der brasilianische Integralismus* (Stuttgart, 1938). The most ambitious analysis of integralism is H. H. Trindade, *Integralismo: o fascismo brasileiro na decada de 30* (São Paulo, 1974). A full scale study of Plinio Salgado and integralism in English is E. R. Broxson, 'Plinio Salgado and Brazilian Integralism' (Ph.D. diss., Catholic University, 1973), available from University Microfilms. Researched from Salgado's own writings and the integralists' press, it is very useful for his early life and party organization, but has little on the party's social composition. Salgado may be studied from his writings, many of which have been reprinted, such as *O integralismo perante a nação* (Rio de Janeiro, 1955); *Discursos*, 2 vols. (São Paulo, 1948); *O integralismo na vida brasileira* (Rio de Janeiro, 1967); and two articles 'A marcha de integralismo', in *Jornal do Brasil* (25 and 26 October 1970).

To trace Salgado's intellectual and spiritual odyssey it is necessary to study the influence of Catholic thinkers like Jackson Figueiredo and Cardinal Leme. There is a brief discussion of Jackson, as also of Farias Brito, another key influence, in J. Cruz Costa, *A History of ideas in Brazil*, trans. S. Macedo (Berkeley and Los Angeles, 1964). The relationship of the Catholic church to integralism is briefly discussed in T. C. Bruneau, *The Political transformation of the Brazilian Catholic Church* (Cambridge, 1973) and in M. T. Williams, 'Integralism and the Brazilian

Catholic Church', *Hispanic American Historical Review*, vol. 53, no. 4 (August 1974). Salgado's ideas as well as the pre-1930 intellectual ambience is discussed in H. H. Trindade, 'Plinio Salgado e a revolução de 30: antecedentes da AIB', in *Revista Brasileira Estudos Politicos*, no. 38 (January 1974).

The anti-Semitic strain in integralism is touched on in R. Levine, 'Brazil's Jews during the Vargas régime and after', *Luso-Brazilian Review*, vol. V, no. 1 (June 1968). Although the integralists had a branch of their intelligence service devoted to monitoring Jewish activities, the small number of Brazilian Jewry – some 42,000 and internally divided – did not seem to pose a threat comparable to the much larger Jewish community in Argentina, numbering nearer half a million, where anti-Semitism took a more virulent form. Gustavo Barroso, the integralists' Jewbaiter, who wrote a number of anti-Semitic books, is an interesting example (like Salgado himself) of the type of marginal, autodidact, provincial intellectual who is often attracted to fascist-style movements, but he has not received the attentions of a biographer.[10]

The reason why integralism collapsed so easily lies partly in Salgado's tactical mistakes and in an overestimate of the party's strength. Hilton, in the article cited above, attributes their ultimate failure to lack of support in the army. The only hope for a fascist movement to succeed in Latin America, as mentioned earlier, lies in its ability to infiltrate the military. The integralists tried to do this (as the communists had tried to do before their disastrous coup in 1935), but although they gained some support among senior officers and NCOs, as well as acquiring a considerable following in the navy, for reasons which have not been satisfactorily explained, they were unable to wean influential officers away from Vargas. In a further article by Hilton, 'Military influence on Brazilian economic policy, 1930–1945: a different view', *Hispanic American Historical Review*, vol. 53, no. 1 (February 1973) (in which he is primarily concerned to challenge J. Wirth's view of military influence on economic planning in *The Politics of Brazilian Development* [Stanford, 1970]) it is suggested that throughout the 1930s the military were obsessed by their weakness and lack of equipment – both in relation to the power of state militias (that of São Paulo had taken two months to subdue in 1932) and to Argentina's expanding military power, and hence were more interested in influencing Vargas's trade policies, by which arms purchases could be made from Germany, than in ambitious industrialization schemes to which they gave a lower priority. By playing off the United States against Germany, which is analysed by S. Hilton, *Brazil and the Great Powers 1930–39: the politics of trade rivalry* (Austin, 1974), Vargas was able to acquire German arms and so satisfy the generals. What tied the military to Vargas rather than to the integralists was true also of civilians, as in the ultimate instance Vargas's success lay in his powers of patronage, which control of an expanded federal bureaucracy put at his disposal. With the federalization of taxes and the expansion of national enterprises, the individual state governments could no longer offer patronage plums, and although the integralists might retain the support of the quixotic and of certain sections of the professional classes (medical doctors, for example), they could offer few financial inducements to a job-hungry middle class. The integralists demanded financial self-sacrifices from their followers and although it has never been established how much money was contributed by big business interests there seems to have been no Brazilian Hugenberg. As the decade progressed and the economy picked up, Vargas was prepared to support coffee planters and industrialists so these possible sources of finance were not available, whilst during the early years of the Estado Novo, as Warren Dean shows in *The Industrialization of São Paulo, 1880–1945* (Austin, 1969), support for domestic industry and labour legislation, favouring employers, rallied them to Vargas. The much-publicized subventions which the integralists were supposed to have received from foreign embassies seem to have added up to very little. An Italian subsidy paid for headquarters expenses, but the more considerable local expenses were met by subscription and dues.

The ways in which Vargas outmanoeuvred the integralists and crushed them, just at the moment they thought they would come into their own, is recounted in Levine and Broxson and in an article by F. D. McCann, 'Vargas and the destruction of the Brazilian *Integralista* and Nazi parties', in *The Americas* (July 1969).

The details of Vargas's conflicts with the German ambassador over Nazi infiltration among the Teuto-Brazilians are spelt out in McCann, *Brazilian-American Alliance, 1937–1945* (Princeton, 1973). Some unusual information and illustrations of Nazi activities in southern Brazil are provided by the regional police chief A. da Silva Py in *A 5a Coluna no Brasil* (Porto Alegre, 1942).

Vargas himself is not an immediately attractive figure for a biographer who is not prepared to become wholly immersed in the machinations of a political genius, exquisitely sensitive to changing political forces. It is still impossible to assess the magnitude and variety of his achievement, being a precursor of post-1964 authoritarianism and of the populist democracy of the 1945 to 1964 period and the creator, by his suicide in 1955, of a potent nationalist myth. Two biographies in English have been attempted. J. W. F. Dulles, *Vargas of Brazil: a political biography* (Austin, 1967) is strong on political narrative, weak on analysis. R. Bourne, *Getulio Vargas of Brazil, 1883–1955* (London, 1974) is the latest biography of possibly the most skilful politician Latin America has produced. There is an intimate portrait by his daughter, Alzira Vargas, in Amaral Peixoto's *Getulio Vargas, meu pai* (Rio de Janeiro, 1960). Vargas's own pronouncements have been collected in *A nova politica do Brasil*, 11 vols (Rio de Janeiro, 1933–47). An informative but uncompleted history of the Vargas era is H. Silva, *O ciclo de Vargas* (Rio de Janeiro, 1964). J. Love's, *Rio Grande do Sul and Brazilian regionalism 1882–1930* (Stanford, 1970) provides a masterly account of Vargas's home state and the political background of his early career. An old book, recently reprinted and still worth reading is K. Loewenstein, *Brazil under Vargas* (New York, 1942; reprinted 1973). His contemporary summing up of Vargas's régime was that it was:

neither democratic nor a disciplined democracy: it is neither totalitarian nor fascist; it is an authoritarian dictatorship for which French constitutional theory has coined the apt term of *régime personnel*. It is one which exercises its theoretically unlimited power with the moderation demanded by the liberal democratic habitat of the Brazilian nation ... If ever Brazil were to be converted into a genuinely fascist state ... not a jot would have to be changed of the existing legislation, nor anything added to the statute book . . . but fascist laws of the statute book alone do not make a state fascist in its entirety. [pp. 372–3].

The reasons why Vargas established the Estado Novo can be explained by the support he gained from the middle classes which had failed to form viable national parties after 1930. A convincing hypothesis to explain Brazilian political development has been Helio Jaguaribe's Cartorial State model which he elaborated in *O nacionalismo na atualidade brasileira* (Rio de Janeiro, 1958), shorter accounts of which in English are his 'Dynamics of Brazilian nationalism', in C. Veliz, ed., *Obstacles to change*, and in 'Political strategies of national development in Brazil', in I. L. Horowitz, J. Gerassi, J. de Castro, eds, *Latin American radicalism: a documentary report on left and nationalist movements* (New York, 1969).

The Cartorial State is a polity in which superfluous jobs are exchanged for votes. The recipients are the middle classes, professional and bureaucratic groups, the product of urbanization without industrialization. Towards the end of the 1920s as urbanization increased, the middle classes had expanded beyond the capacity of the ruling coffee plantocracy to satisfy them. The final blow came when the collapse of the coffee economy in the Great Depression removed the source of funding the bureaucracy, creating a revolutionary situation in which the middle classes played a leading role. After the 1930 revolution, government by planters and export merchants was replaced by government by the middle classes, but the failure to organize a national reformist party created a stalemate which extremists of the left and right tried but failed to exploit. Fear that the broader suffrage of the 1934 constitution would enable the Old Republic élite to make a comeback, using their control of rural dependents to outvote the urban middle classes, gave Vargas the support of the latter when he abolished constitutional government and established the Estado Novo in 1937. An expanded civil and military bureaucracy was prepared to forego its liberal principles in return for the security which Vargas could offer. Vargas was not prepared to press the conflict with the plantocracy and São Paulo industrialists; thus landowners were left undisturbed in control of their rural dependents at the same time as industrialists were given state support. In this manner the Estado Novo established a balance between conflicting forces.

With the left crushed, the middle classes bought off by posts in the expanded federal bureaucracy, and the landowners left with a free hand in the rural areas, there was no need for a fascist-style party and the integralists were expendable. Both left and right were now proscribed: Prestes, the communist leader was imprisoned and Salgado exiled. Jaguaribe writes:

Vargas's Estado Novo was much nearer to Franco's Spanish Falangism or to Salazar's Portuguese Corporativism than to the German or even the Italian models ... The middle class was assured of its continued co-optation by the New State bureaucracy. It no longer had to barter jobs for votes. For the landowners the Estado Novo offered the advantage of not interfering in the agrarian economy of the country and of accepting them as official spokesmen for the countryside, thus keeping them in political control of their rural strongholds ... In terms of the interests of the urban bourgeoisie the Estado Novo repressed the socialist tendencies that were beginning to menace private appropriation of the means of production. It also offered the benefit of favouring the expansion of the internal market and protecting it with its right wing nationalism from foreign competition ... For the working class the Estado Novo, although repressing any attempt to create an independent political organization, adopted a strongly paternalist posture, introducing important new social legislation and assuring the protection of the workers' rights. [p. 398].

Interpretations of the Estado Novo (1937–45) distinguish between the early years and the period 1942–5 when Vargas began to shift the basis of his support away from the bureaucratic middle class and rural notables to the new industrial bourgeoisie and urban working class created by the expansion of industry during the war. *Trabalhismo*, based on paternalist and corporatist labour organizations, made Vargas the spokesman for the mobilized urban masses. The revolutionary implications of this new alliance was one reason why the military deposed Vargas in 1945. The return of constitutional government now enabled the rural notables to reassert their political power but with the difference that now the newly formed parties had to incorporate a bigger electorate which had risen from 2.7 millions in 1934 to 7.4 millions in 1945.

A useful article discussing the ways in which the Brazilian electorate has expanded and comparing coronelismo with similar forms of vote manipulation elsewhere is J. Love, 'Political participation in Brazil, 1881–1969', in *The Luso-Brazilian Review*, vol. 7, no. 2 (December 1970). The expectations of this new electorate went far beyond the limited patronage capacity of either the cartorial state or the Estado Novo. In this fluid situation the populist politician came into his own.

Populism presupposes the existence of a free vote and depends on the ability of the populist leader to satisfy the material and psychological needs of his followers.[11] It was the response to an open political system as distinct from the closed systems of either the Estado Novo or the predictable results of the coronelismo system of the Old Republic when landowners were able to manipulate the votes of their rural dependents. The mechanics of this new populism have been examined by F. Weffort, 'State and Mass in Brazil', in I. L. Horowitz, ed., *Masses in Latin America* (New York, 1970); in 'Le populisme', *Les Temps modernes* (October 1967); and in the *Revista civilazação brasileira*, vol. I, no. 2 (May 1965). There is a full neo-Marxist study by O. Ianni, *Crisis in Brazil* (New York, 1970).

Andrew Pearse describes the setting within which populism operated in Rio de Janeiro in his chapter in P. Hauser, ed., *Urbanisation in Latin America* (Paris, 1961):

... populism is concerned with political power at the level of the municipality, the state and the Union, which is exercised directly and indirectly through the body of functionaries. It is supported by structures based on clientage in which benefits are handed down in return for votes and personal loyalties in manoeuvres. Most of these structures are informal and non-institutionalized and do not coincide with the formal structures of administration. Whilst the intermediary ranks receive benefits through the allocation of posts in the system of functionaries, jobs, contracts, grants-in-aid of charitable, cultural and sports enterprises, etc., the masses receive them through defensive labour legislation and access to the services of medical assistance posts, sports clubs, religious and cult groups, etc., subsidized through the intervention of populist leaders at various levels, whose names are given due prominence. Populism does not favour the organization of common interest groups or co-operative groups, and power is usually delegated downwards rather than upwards. Representatives are appointed, but they are seldom elected from below. In its appeal to the masses populism uses symbols stressing the protective role of the great charismatic leaders, and the small scale operators use to the full the confidence of the populace in the great leaders: and even if confidence in the small-scale operator was lost, that in the great leader is apparently durable. [p. 202].

It can be readily seen from this that Brazilian populism is a variant of Boss Tweed's New York city politics and not of agrarian populism.

Vargas's response to these changing pressures was to organize urban workers in the PTB, the Brazilian Labour party, which provided him with mass support enabling him to be returned for the first time as a democratically elected president in 1950. The populist period continued for another nine years after Vargas's suicide in 1955 under a series of populist presidents, but the contradictions within the populist alliances became so acute that the cross-class coalitions began to break up into their constituent components. This polarization together with attempts to radicalize the rural areas alarmed conservatives and forced the military to intervene in 1964 as they had in 1889, 1930, and 1945. This time, however, they did not hand over to a civilian government but established an authoritarian military régime which has attracted considerable attention from foreign scholars, especially political scientists. Historians have fewer contributions to make. Skidmore's general study is crucial for the pre-1964 period whilst his contribution in Stepan's volume (see below) is a useful comparison of the Estado Novo with post-1964 authoritarianism. J. W. F. Dulles, *Unrest in Brazil: Civil military conflict, 1955–1964* (Austin, 1970), is a political chronicle rather than analysis whilst I. L. Horowitz, *Revolution in Brazil* (New York, 1964), collects a variety of viewpoints.

Ambitious attempts to explain Brazilian politics have been made in terms of systems analysis: prominent among these is R. M. Schneider, *The political system of Brazil: the emergence of a modernizing authoritarian régime* (New York, 1971). The second volume, in preparation, is to analyse the military's role since the end of the nineteenth century. This will supplement Alfred Stepan's fundamental *The military in politics: changing patterns in Brazil* (Princeton, 1971) which questions a number of long-held assumptions. Phillipe Schmitter's *Interest conflict and political change in Brazil* (Stanford, 1971) focuses on civilian interest groups and is one of the most significant contributions to the understanding of Brazilian politics to have appeared in any language. He has opened up an area of study which has equal relevance for Spanish American countries. Schmitter is one of a group of scholars in the United States to be discussed below, who are deriving new insights from comparisons with Iberian experience as may be seen from his essay, 'The Portugalization of Brazil', in the important collection of essays edited by Stepan, *Authoritarian Brazil* (New Haven, 1973). Stepan's own essay attempts a comparison between the present Peruvian and Brazilian military régimes. Juan Linz's essay, 'The future of an authoritarian situation or the institutionalization of an authoritarian régime: the case of Brazil', applies the model originally formulated in his 'An authoritarian régime: Spain', in E. Allardt and V. Littunen, eds, *Cleavages, ideologies and party systems* (Helsinki, 1964) designed to explain why Franco Spain was difficult to fit into the fascist model. This article is indispensable for its insights into the nature of post-fascist authoritarianism.

An important essay in the Stepan collection is that by Fernando Henrique Cardoso, 'Associated-dependent development: theoretical and practical implications', which introduces English readers to his analysis of the changing nature of dependency rising out of changes in the international economy. Cardoso criticizes models by other Brazilian theorists such as Celso Furtado, Candido Mendes, and Helio Jaguaribe's 'colonial fascist' hypothesis. This latter started from the assumption that 'fascism is a model for promoting economic development without changing the existing social order and that the adjustment of this model to dependence on foreign metropolitan centres transforms it into colonial fascism.' In this model the state is strengthened in order to preserve stability, the political and economic system is integrated into the Western system (the geo-political thinking of the military, their violent anti-communism and self-appointed role as defenders of the West in the South Atlantic has encouraged the United States to regard Brazil as the guardian of the West's interests in Latin America), and the economy remains, as far as possible, in private hands. Although Jaguaribe sees a trend to 'colonial fascism' after 1964, he does not believe it to be viable in the long run. Unlike Germany and Italy where the bourgeoisie allowed the middle class to take over political leadership in exchange for preserving the ownership of industry, in Brazil structural obstacles rising from dependence on foreign capital and markets would make such an arrangement unlikely and the polarization of political forces as a result of economic stagnation would eventually bring about the system's downfall. Jaguaribe argued that the metropolitan-colonial relationship was essentially undynamic, whereas in Cardoso's opinion, on the contrary, the relationship has become dynamic because of the changing role of the multinational company.

He argues that the 1964 coup was not a simple restoration of authoritarian rule but a new departure coming as a response to changes in the international division of labour. Multinational companies were now interested in establishing industries in peripheral states and thus had an interest in 'development', but this development breaks up old alliances between the traditional, bureaucratic middle classes and backward agrarian sectors, replacing it by a new alliance between technocratic military and civilian bureaucracies together with the new industrialists and their workers in the new industries associated with multinational companies. The growing class conflict of the declining populist system has now been replaced by clashes between those sectors of the middle classes who benefit from the new system and those who do not, as well as between a new labour aristocracy and workers in the purely national sector. The economy may be dynamic but the beneficiaries are limited, as the gap between the developing urban centres and underdeveloped rural areas – the 'internal colonies' the function of which is to provide cheap labour for the cities – grows wider. Meanwhile, foreign indebtedness grows as does social marginality: first, because the multinational companies are more concerned with producing consumer durables for the growing urban middle-class market than with producing basic necessities for the urban and rural poor, and second, because capital-intensive industrialization cannot provide employment for a rapidly increasing population. In this situation, authoritarian control becomes necessary to smother the opposition of the disadvantaged sectors of the middle classes, to dismantle dissident labour unions which had provided populist politicians with one of their power bases, and to ensure that the marginal sectors remain depoliticized. As to the future, Cardoso's conclusions, in common with Schmitter and Linz, are not optimistic. Although the régime may not be totalitarian, lacking both an ideology and an official party, there is no guarantee that it is simply a transitional phase in an inevitable progression towards a more broadly based participatory system.

Argentina: The origins of Peronism, the most baffling and least understood of all Latin American populisms, must be sought historically in the weaknesses of the political system as well as in the distortions caused by a semi-colonial economy. Analyses of these factors by contemporaries produced a counter-tradition of anti-liberal political thought and historiography which was to be an important pre-condition of Perón's rise to power.

Crucial to an understanding of Perón's success in the 1940s was the failure of Radicalism to bring about any substantial social changes and the blunting of their reforming drive when they were in power under Irigoyen between 1916 and 1930. Resulting from the introduction of universal male suffrage in 1912, Irigoyen's Radicals provide an early example of a populist movement based on the urban masses of Buenos Aires. D. Rock's article, which is amplified in his *Politics in Argentina 1890–1930: The rise and fall of Radicalism* (Cambridge, 1975), 'Machine politics in Buenos Aires and the Argentine Radical Party, 1912–1930' in the *Journal of Latin American Studies*, no. 4 (1972) is an important analysis of politics at the grass-roots level and of the mechanics of patronage which provides a model for much needed studies of other populist movements as well as for Peronism itself. Irigoyen is one of the most controversial figures in modern Argentinian history and biographies tend to be hagiography or defamation. He is an archetypical figure of the civilian caudillo; capable of inspiring fanatical devotion and incorruptible, he was nevertheless incapable of curbing the corruption of many of his followers. Radicalism's failure virtually closed the way to a reformist solution to Argentina's social and economic problems in the 1930s, as well as anticipating and foreshadowing many of the features of later populist movements.

The Perón period was preceded by a decade or more of ideological turbulence during which the cosmopolitanism of the Argentinian literary establishment and the economic and political assumptions of the ruling élite were called into question. This was a reflection of the general nationalist revival shared by all Latin American countries in the years following the First World War when peace brought the return of foreign economic interests, the re-establishment of pre-war patterns of economic activity, and the incursion of United States economic power. A major expression of the nationalism was the University Reform movement with its founding manifesto in the Argentinian city of Córdoba in 1918 which had repercussions throughout Latin America. Anti-European, anti-imperialist, and influenced by nativism and the Mexican Revolution, the Reform did not share the illiberalism of the right-wing nationalists which developed during the late 1920s.

A useful analysis of this new nationalism, tracing the ideological roots of Peronism is J. Hernández Arreguí, *La formación de la conciencia nacional* (Buenos Aires, 1960). The best and most lucid detailed analysis of the myriad right-wing groups is M. H. Gerassi, *Los nacionalistas* (Buenos Aires, 1968) which has a comprehensive bibliography. A. Ciria, *Partidos y poder en la Argentina moderna* (Buenos Aires, 1964) has a useful chapter on the right. The repudiation by right-wing intellectuals in the 1930s and 1940s of the established values of Argentinian culture and society had their roots in the growth of a cultural nationalism formulated in the writings of Ricardo Rojas earlier in the century, but although he was critical of the cosmopolitanism of Argentinian culture, he remained within the liberal tradition. Earl T. Glauert has written a useful introductory article, 'Ricardo Rojas and the emergence of Argentine cultural nationalism', in *Hispanic American Historical Review*, vol. 43, no. 3 (August 1963). Rojas's writings elaborate on an Argentinian Volksgeist and must be seen against the threat posed by the flood of immigrants in the years preceding the First World War. His career shows how difficult it was for a nationalist intellectual to remain a liberal. When he realized the use to which his ideas were being put by the right in the 1930s, he joined the Radicals, only to withdraw disillusioned. Other nationalist writers such as Manuel Galvez in his *El espíritu de la aristocracia* published in 1924 were unashamedly élitist.

The gap between Rojas's liberal nationalism and the increasingly strident nationalism of the right is best reflected in a new revisionist school of historiography which sought to rehabilitate the dictator Juan Manuel de Rosas who had dominated Argentina between 1829 and 1852. In liberal historiography, enshrined in school texts, the overthrow of Rosas ushered in the era of liberal enlightenment. The first salvo in the rehabilitation of Rosas was the publication of a biography by Carlos Ibarguren, the 'maestro de la juventud nacionalista' who had been a founder member of the nationalist La Nueva República in 1928 and who was the first person to try and organize an extreme right-wing party from among conservatives.[12] In 1938 the new approach was institutionalized by the foundation of the Instituto Histórico Juan Manuel de Rosas. The literature of rehabilitation is summarized in C. B. Kroeber 'Rosas and the revision of Argentine history, 1880–1955', in *Revista Interamericana de Bibliografía*, vol. 11, no. 1 (1960). By the 1940s Rosas was ready for adoption by Peronist ideologues as a counter-hero to the heroes of liberal historiography.

Historical controversy also raged round the figure of General San Martín, the country's liberator during the Wars of Independence, who was now adopted as the symbol of the self-abnegation of the military patriot. Rojas felt compelled to write San Martín's biography to repudiate the militarist interpretation of his career. But this interpretation was symptomatic of a thread within both military and civilian nationalist thinking going back to the violent strike and street demonstrations of the Tragic Week in Buenos Aires in 1919. For Leopoldo Lugones, an erstwhile anarchist poet, on whom there is a useful study by N. Kitrik, *Leopoldo Lugones: mito nacional* (Buenos Aires, 1960), only the military could now save Argentina from anarchy. From the mid-1920s he argued that the *hora de espada* had come. Lugones was perhaps the most important single influence on the Argentinian right in the early 1930s. Federico Ibarguren, son of Carlos, in his *Orígines del nacionalismo argentina* (Buenos Aires, 1969) (a hotch-potch but useful source book) writes: 'We were all *lugonianos* which is very different from fascist. "Fascism" as a theory was engendered in a laboratory of intellectuals, the socialist sperm – law and totalitarian – of the nineteenth century; in contrast Argentinian nationalism is nourished on the old Spanish cult of personality where the Catholic tradition germinates like a seed well ploughed in the earth.' (p. 14). Under Lugones eight pro-fascist groups were united in ADUNA (Afirmación de una Nueva Argentina) in 1933 but his own personal troubles and the fragmentation of these groups led to his suicide in 1938. Lugones, who exalted a life of action as compensation for a humdrum life as a school inspector, is well described by Gerassi as 'the Argentinian d'Annunzio who never knew his Fiume'. The military on whom Lugones set such store was slow to reciprocate his interest in it. The Germanophile General Uriburu, with a following among young officers, made his coup in 1930 with only minimal civilian support, breaking a seventy-year tradition of military non-involvement in politics and intending to establish a fascist-corporate style state. Most older officers, however, failed to respond, preferring to support General Justo in his understanding with liberals and conservatives in the *Concordancia* which lasted from 1932 to 1943. Thus the first attempt to establish a fascist-style régime failed, repudiated by the civilian oligarchy and the majority of the officer corps.

The romantic euphoria of civilian intellectuals was no substitute for the lack of a mass following, and they were not taken too seriously by the military nationalists. Strong German influence in the officer corps as shown in G. P. Atkins and L. V. Thompson, 'German military influence in Argentina, 1921–40', *Journal of*

Latin American Studies, vol. IV, no. 2 (1972), had bred a spirit of exclusiveness but General Bautista Molina was attracted as well by Hitler's political techniques and from 1937 to 1943 he was president of the para-military Alianza de la Juventud Nacionalista. Facilities for weekend training were available in army barracks which enabled the army to retain some control.

The role of radical nationalism in the officers' lodges which is crucial to understanding the military origins of Peronism can be studied in R. Potash's path-breaking book, *The army and politics in Argentina, 1928–45* (Stanford, 1969). Potash was the first to use German Foreign Office files and he has also made wide use of interviews. His book is the most detailed study to date on any Latin American officer corps. He is at present engaged on a second volume to cover post-1945. Military politics are ably analysed in less detail by M. Goldwert, *Democracy, militarism and nationalism in Argentina, 1930–66* (Austin, 1972) and in D. Canton, *La política de los militares argentinos, 1900–1971* (Buenos Aires, 1971). The problem of political control of the military once in power under Perón is discussed by H. Rouquie, 'Adhesión militar y control del ejército en el régimen peronista (1946–1955)', *Aportes*, no. 19 (January 1971).

The dilemma of civilian nationalists was how to find a mass base. Rebuffed by the left, hostile to the Radicals, they were ignored by the landowning élite, but the various strands of nationalist thought created a pool of ideas from which could be fabricated a Peronist ideology, although Peronism was a very different type of régime from that envisaged by civilian nationalists. Like the integralists, the nationalists thought their hour had struck when Perón came to power, but Perón was not exclusive in his loyalties. For example, Raul Scalabrini Ortiz, the leading intellectual of FORJA, the left wing of the Radicals, whose life and ideas are discussed in M. Falcoff, 'Raul Scalabrini Ortiz, the making of an Argentinian nationalist', *Hispanic American Historical Review*, vol. 52, no. 1 (February 1972), became one of Perón's confidants. It was the practical hard-headed nationalism of men like Scalabrini with his critical analysis of the British-owned railways which could aid Perón's plans for autarchy and not the windy rhetoric of Lugones's admirers.

The nationalist right either came to terms with Peronism because they shared its anti-liberal, anti-imperialist stance or they degenerated into terrorist groups like the Tacuara, recruited from the psychopathic detritus of big-city life and from right-wing Catholic students, many of whose fathers were veterans of the Legión Cívica and other nationalist groups of the thirties. The Tacuara learnt its anti-Semitism from Mgr Julio Meinvielle, their spiritual assessor, who was the doyen of right-wing Catholics and whose writings echoed the worst excesses of Hispanidad. The development of Catholic thought is traced from independence by J. J. Kennedy, in *Catholicism, nationalism and democracy* (Notre Dame, 1958) but he tends to ignore the lunatic fringe of extremist Catholicism which became an integral component of right-wing nationalism.

In the same way as historians and political scientists have been drawn to study the past in order to explain post-1964 authoritarian Brazil, so also with Peronism, but with the difference that Peronism, unlike *getulismo*, is still *the* crucial issue in Argentinian politics. During the seventeen years of Perón's exile it was almost impossible for serious work to be done on Peronism because of its political overtones with the Peronists themselves proscribed from political activity. Two bibliographical articles which survey the early literature on the Perón period are F. Hoffman, 'Perón and After', *Hispanic American Historical Review*, vol. 36, no. 4 (November 1956), and vol. 39, no. 2 (May 1959). Little scholarly work has been done in the immediate Perón period. One useful study which analyses conflicts within the meat industry and clarifies some of the labour union background is P. H. Smith, *Politics and Beef in Argentina: Patterns of Conflict and Change* (New York, 1969) to which may be added his article 'Social Mobilization, Political Participation and the Rise of Juan Perón', in *Political Science Quarterly*, no. LXXXIV (March 1969). He has also written an important analysis of intra-élite conflict. A general study of the labour background is S. L. Baily, *Labor, Nationalism and Politics in Argentina* (New Brunswick, N. J., 1967). A broad study of United States–Argentinian relations which deals with the controversy over the 'Blue Book' is H. F. Peterson, *Argentina and the United States, 1810–1960* (New York, 1964).

The fallow period of Peronist studies is past and now we are being engulfed by a flood of exegetical literature. Most of this is by Argentinians and is characterized by strong disagreements over the nature of Peronism, swinging from those who regard it as an indigenous revolutionary movement, Castroism before Castro, aiming at making Argentina the leader of a 'justicialist' third force, neither capitalist nor communist, to those who condemn it as basically a conservative movement masquerading behind demogogic revolutionary slogans. Much of the analysis is committed and reflects not only deep differences within the Peronist movement but between Peronists and the non-Peronist left.

An interesting and provocative example of the new analysis is the review essay by E. Laclau, 'Argentina: Perón and the Revolution', in *Latin America Review of Books* (London, 1973). Laclau divides the interpretations, most of which have appeared since 1969, under four headings: the liberal view, the 'third world' view, the national left, and the ultra-left. The liberal view, which is also that of the Argentine Communist party, saw Peronism as a peculiar form of Argentinian fascism. Few take this seriously now although most of the older books in English subscribe to this view, such as R. J. Alexander, *The Perón Era* (New York, 1951); G. I. Blanksten, *Perón's Argentina* (New York, 1953; reprint, 1967); and A. P. Whitaker, *Argentina* (New York, 1964) whilst S. M. Lipset in *Political Man* (New York, 1969) characterized it as a 'fascism of the left'. Laclau rejects the description of fascism on the grounds that fascism's strategy is based on smashing the unions whereas Perón's power derived from the unions and that, so far from having the support of financial groups which is essential to fascism, Peronism's most determined enemies were landowners, traditional industrialists, and the commercial bourgeoisie. He is also rightly critical of the over-schematization and lack of historical awareness in the political science approach of J. Kirkpatrick, *Leader and vanguard in mass society: a study of Peronist Argentina* (Cambridge, Mass., 1971). Nor has he much time for work written under the influence of the 'sociology of modernization' and the 'politics of mass society' approaches, represented most notably by Gino Germani, in *Política y sociedad en una época de transición: de la sociedad tradicional a la sociedad de masas* (Buenos Aires, 1962) and also in a comparison with Italian fascism in S. J. Woolf, ed., *The nature of fascism* (London, 1968) where he analyses the four attempts to establish fascism in Argentina in 1930–3, 1943–5, 1955, and after 1966, in terms of primary and secondary mobilization. Germani explains Peronism in terms of the 'disposable mass' hypothesis whereby Perón's mass base was provided by uprooted rural migrants (of which an estimated one million moved into Buenos Aires in the course of ten years) who composed a lumpenproletariat – the *descamisados* – who could not be integrated into a stable democratic society and so were available for manipulation by a dictator. There is some substance in Laclau's criticism as electoral studies and more detailed studies of the mechanics of Peronist politics are made. Electoral analyses can throw light on Peronism because of the four national elections held in 1946, 1948, 1951, and 1954 during Perón's régime. Important electoral studies are P. H. Smith, 'The social base of Peronism', *Hispanic American Historical Review*, vol. 52, no. 1 (February 1972) and W. Little, 'Electoral aspects of Peronism, 1945–55', *Journal of Inter-American Studies*, no. 53 (August 1973).

For Laclau the 'third world' interpretation consists of Marxists and non-Marxists, pro-Peronist communists and Peronists. Here Peronism is seen as the anti-oligarchic and anti-imperialist movement of a semi-colonial country. There is a prescriptive element in these groups in that they both argue that the fundamental contradiction in dependent countries is between imperialism and nationalism and not between bourgeoisie and proletariat.

The national left interpretation argues that although Peronism was initially the democratic-bourgeois stage of a semi-colonial country, the bourgeoisie is not strong enough to carry on the revolution, so that the working class must build its own organization independent of Peronism.

The final interpretation is the ultra-left view of Peronism as simply an inter-bourgeois struggle in which the working class has no motive for intervention. This view Laclau easily refutes by pointing out that it fails to distinguish between the agrarian and industrial bourgeoisie.

These interpretations tell us more about the prescriptions of their authors than about the historical origins and development of Peronism. In a different category are the essays in M. Murmis and J. C. Portantiero, *Estudios sobre los orígines del peronismo* (Buenos Aires, 1972). This sets out to explain the clash between cattle owners and industrialists in the 1930s and within the cattle interests themselves, as well as the internal conflict that developed among industrialists which caused an important sector to support Perón in 1943. The essays in this volume point the way to future research by exploring the complexities of inter-sectoral clashes rather than by talking in terms of undifferentiated classes.

Laclau's own general conclusion is that Peronism's originality lay in its policy of income redistribution in favour of wage earners rather than in its industrialization strategy: 'the working class always carried greater weight than the national bourgeoisie in the determination of the policies of the movement' (p. 125); and 'it would be completely false to see in Peronism a kind of national bourgeois régime that made use of the working class as a tactical manoeuvre in its confrontation in the agrarian sector, but restricted the trade union movement to a secondary role within the alliance' (p. 126). He argues that what enabled Peronism to survive the fall of Perón, and what made it unique among populist movements, was that the working class constituted its social base in contrast with the more disparate alliances of other populist movements which fragmented under the influence of monopoly capitalism.

There is also a prescriptive element in Laclau's argument and his account of Peronism leaves many questions unposed. How is one to account for the bureaucratization of the labour unions and for those divisions between unions which the subsequent history of intra-Peronist conflict would suggest were as deep as those between sectors of the middle and upper classes? What form did participation take and how were labour leaders elected and once elected how responsive were they to their members? We need more studies like W. Little's 'La tendencia peronista en el sindicalismo argentino: el caso de los obreros de la carne', in *Aportes*, no. 19 (January 1971) who also studies how the unions took the place of an official party in 'Party and State in Peronist Argentina', *Hispanic American Historical Review*, vol. 53, no. 4 (November 1973). How did the mechanism of Peronist control work at the grass-roots level? How revolutionary can a labour movement be which receives most of its benefits as handouts from the state? As with the Mexican labour movement, so in Perón's Argentina workers gained benefits by decree, and although it is true that unions acquired autonomy after Perón's fall (unlike those in Mexico which have never succeeded or wanted to escape from close state control), how autonomous were they during the Peronist period?

A cardinal feature of the Peronist régime which would seem to differentiate it from other populist movements in Latin America, as well as from fascist movements in Europe, was that it coincided in its initial phase with a period of unprecedented economic prosperity when huge financial reserves accumulated during the war could be redistributed in the form of higher wages and social benefits, thus enabling Perón to avoid a direct confrontation with the agrarian interests on which the wealth of the country continued to rest. If the influence of the workers in the Peronist alliance was as strong as Laclau stresses, and if they were as wedded to revolution as he suggests, why was the social structure virtually unaltered when Perón fell from power? As Little puts it, 'it is ironic that its [Peronism's] conservative tendencies were lost upon the conservative critics of the régime who saw only the illiberalism which accompanied it.'

Some light is thrown on this by an unpublished doctoral thesis by J. Taylor, 'Myth and Reality: the Case of Eva Perón', (D. Phil. diss., Oxford University, 1973) where she uses a social anthropological approach to analyse the pervasive myths in Argentine culture showing how the attitudes of the landowning élite towards the populace have remained virtually unchanged since the days of Rosas through Irigoyen up to Perón. The rigidity of these attitudes has made it impossible for the élite to reach any objective evaluation of movements which involve participation by the Buenos Aires populace.

Two points connected with Peronism's loss of revolutionary impetus need elucidating. To what extent did the movement suffer from an influx of ex-Radicals whose job hunger dulled the edge of revolutionary fervour much as the Spanish Falange was swamped by office seekers during and after the civil war? And second, how crucial was Eva Perón to the sustaining of revolutionary purpose? Peronism was the first Latin American political movement to mobilize women and this was reflected in electoral support for Perón but how effective were they in contributing to the processes of mobilization? A scholarly assessment of the role of Eva is overdue. The current growth of 'Evitism' – the tendency to emphasize the figure of Eva more than Perón himself – takes us to the core of the tensions within the movement. The Peronist left, represented by its youth movement, disillusioned by Perón's conservatism on his return from exile, look back to Eva as the repository of revolutionary virtue as a counter to what they believe to have been the manipulative, opportunist, and demagogic characteristics of Perón. In this view Eva is seen as the spokeswoman of the *descamisados* and the intercessor with Perón on behalf of their interests. We know very little about the complex relationship between Perón and Eva, between Perón and the populace, and between Eva and the populace.

With the revival of Peronism as an active force in Argentinian politics, it is likely that the movement's history will become a battleground between rival factions as each group tries to appropriate the master's or the mistress's mantle. Out of these conflicts some light may be thrown on what promises to remain for many years a paradoxical and elusive phenomenon. Two useful British contributions are W. Little, 'The popular origins of Peronism', and D. Rock, 'The survival and restoration of Peronism', in Rock's *Argentina in the Twentieth Century* (London, 1975).

Mexico: Considering the volume of material which has been published on the Mexican political system, it is surprising that so little attention has been paid to the Mexican right. The resources and talents of the prestigious research centre at the Colegio de México have been concentrated on pre-revolutionary history or on the early years of the Revolution, although a new cooperative history of the post-1910 period is in process of being written. Research may have been deflected from more recent periods by the pervasiveness of an official revolutionary historiography and the ruling party's dislike of heterodox interpretations. For this reason most research on opposition movements has been done by foreigners who encounter difficulties in gaining access to private archival sources without the study of which (even supposing these exist) many questions must remain unanswered. Some progress has been made with oral history projects such as the pioneer work by J. W. Wilkie and E. Monzón de Wilkie, *México visto en el siglo XX* (Mexico, 1969).

A triumph over considerable difficulties is J. Meyer's superb study of the *cristeros*, *La Cristiada*, 3 vols. (Mexico, 1973), which reveals for the first time in a scholarly manner the massive scale of peasant mobilization in counter-revolutionary opposition to the Revolution's anti-clerical policies in the 1920s. An English version is to be published by Cambridge University Press. J. W. Wilkie, 'The meaning of the *cristero* religious war against the Mexican Revolution', in *The Journal of Church and State*, vol. VIII, no. 2 (1966), is concerned primarily with the political conflict.

Unfortunately, we lack any academic study of the *sinarquista* movement founded in 1936 and which claimed over half a million supporters at the height of its power in the early 1940s (although Meyer is at present studying this). Much of the movement's history is shrouded in mystery, as in the question of its precise relationship to the Base, a secret Catholic organization, aimed at penetrating all aspects of secular life somewhat in the manner of Opus Dei. M. Gill's *El sinarquismo: su origen, su esencia, su misión*, 3rd ed. (Mexico, 1962) is undocumented and tells little about organization, source of funds, or social composition. A. Michaels's 'Fascism and *Sinarquismo*: popular nationalisms against the Mexican Revolution', in *The Journal of Church and State*, vol. VIII, no. 2 (1966) is a useful introduction, relying as do most writers on the sinarquista's press. Broader in scope is his article 'El nacionalismo conservador mexicano desde la revolución hasta 1940', *Historia Mexicana*, no. XVI (October-December 1966). There is also H. G. Campbell, *The Radical Right in Mexico, 1929–49* (Ph.D. diss., University of California, Los Angeles, 1968). We need to know much more about the relationship between cristeros and sinarquistas: to what extent was there continuity and overlap? The cristero movement invites comparison with Spanish Carlism whereas sinarquismo is a more complex phenomenon, representing an attempt by Catholic intellectuals to canalize peasant discontent into counter-revolutionary channels in areas where the agrarian reform had little success and where administrative corruption seems to have been rife. It had strong ruralist, moralistic anti-foreign, and apolitical overtones. Like the cristero movement it was mainly a regional phenomenon and did not have much influence outside the western states and the Bajío. It had some of the characteristics of rural populism with middle-class students proselytizing among the villages for a spiritual uprising against the godless communism of the Revolution but, unlike the cristeros, the sinarquistas lived more by a non-violent ethic which, in the context of Mexican politics and combined with their lack of grasp and even perhaps of interest in the realities of power and their absence of any economic programme, accounts for the gradual decline of their influence. The expansion of their numbers in the early 1940s may be explained by the widespread disillusionment with the latter years of the Cárdenas régime. This has been studied by A. Michaels in 'The crisis of Cardenismo', in *Journal of Latin American Studies*, no. 2 (1970) whilst the inner contradictions of Cárdenas's régime have been analysed by David Raby in 'La contribución del cardenismo en el desarrollo de México', in *Aportes*, no. 26 (October 1972), questioning some of the long-accepted assumptions about the nature of *cardenismo*.

Sinarquismo grew out of the *Centro anti-comunista* which had been founded in Guanajuato by a German professor at the university. But when the next year this group adopted the name Sinarquista (the antithesis to the anarchism which they felt was sweeping the country) the influence of foreign ideas, apart from Hispanidad, was minimal. The sinarquista equated nationalism with Catholicism in the tradition of nineteenth-century Mexican conservatives. Catholicism was regarded as the best bulwark against the insidious influence of the United States to which Mexico's backwardness was attributed. The anti-American current in sinarquista ideology was one reason why it enjoyed some following among Mexican-Americans, especially in the Los

Angeles area where friction was acute after the 'zoot-suit' riots. Sinarquismo provided one way, albeit a minor one, by which chicanos expressed their resentment at their inferior position in United States society.

Part of the reason for the sinarquistas' decline in influence may be explained by the defection of middle-class supporters to the Acción Nacional, the Catholic professional, business-oriented party which was founded in 1939 and which was to become the major opposition party to the PRI and which has been studied by Donald J. Mabry in *Mexico's Acción Nacional: a Catholic alternative to revolution* (Syracuse, 1973) (with an extensive bibliographical essay). However, this does not explain the falling off in rural support: no one has shown, for example, that the social conditions which gave rise to sinarquismo had been substantially improved. It may be that rural support fell away as the manipulative tendencies of the movement became apparent.

Specifically fascist groups had far less influence in Mexico although the apparent increase in communist influence during Cárdenas's presidency led to an increase in their number. The Acción Revolucionaria Mexicana founded in 1933 as an anti-Semitic, anti-communist para-military organization, under an ex-villista general Nicolás Rodríguez and known as the Dorados after their gold shirts and Villa's élite troops, conducted rowdy meetings and held military parades until they were routed by the communists in street battles and proscribed by Cárdenas. They have not been seriously studied and merit consideration in conjunction with other fascist inspired groups such as the *Falange Español Tradicionalista*, formed by Spanish merchants resident in Mexico to offset the consistent support given by Cárdenas to the Republicans in the Spanish Civil War. Although the Mexican Jewish community only numbered some 18,000 both the left and the right shared anti-Semitic prejudices.

The Mexican revolution had a particular resonance in the Andean countries where the Mexicans' revindication of Indians influenced *indigenista* theorizing. Large Indian populations, together with evidence of a great historical past, gave nationalist theorists an alternative basis for a nationalist ideology to Hispanic Catholicism.

*

Peru: Peruvians took the lead in formulating an indigenista-based ideology with Haya de la Torre's concept of Indo-America and Mariátegui's attempts to adapt Marxism to Peruvian conditions. Haya's ideology was an amalgam of eclectic borrowings from Marxism, the British Labour party, earlier Peruvian writers, and nazism and, although ostensibly indianist, the practical expression of the party's indianism was minimal. In its hey-day it influenced other reformist parties like Acción Democrática in Venezuela, Figueres's Social Democratic party in Costa Rica and the Auténticos in Cuba, but unlike them Apra has never been in power, mainly because of the army's hostility. Partly because of this, the party changed its anti-imperialist and anti-capitalist stance and came to understandings with conservative politicians. With the subsequent erosion of its student support much of the party's dynamism evaporated. Surprisingly, there have been few studies of this, the most successful unsuccessful party in Latin American politics, founded in 1926 and still under the same leader. The key to the party's longevity does not seem to me to lie in its political aspirations so much as in the security which its sub-culture, touching all aspects of social life, offers to established as well as to socially mobile mestizos. Apra's opponents have always questioned its democratic pretensions, emphasizing the caudillo nature of Haya's domination of the party and what they sense to be its totalitarian tendencies. The *búfalos*, Apra strong-arm squads, lend some credence to this view as did Haya's admiration for the Nazis' organizational efficiency. Ultimately, it is not ideology (which has been the most studied aspect of the party) but organization which has held it together. H. Kantor's *The ideology and programme of the Aprista movement* (Berkeley, 1964) and R. J. Alexander's *Aprismo* (Kent, Ohio, 1973) which makes a wide selection of Haya's writings available in English for the first time, stress ideology. G. Hilliker, *The politics of reform in Peru: the aprista and other mass parties of Latin America* (Baltimore, 1971) concentrates on organization but he does not seem aware of the literature on populism. Apra is perceptively treated in F. Bourricaud, *Pouvoir et société dans le Pérou contemporain* (Paris, 1967; trans. London, 1971) and in F. B. Pike, *The modern history of Peru* (London, 1967). J. L. Payne *Labor and Politics in Peru*

(New Haven, 1965) is an important contribution to the wider problem of 'structured violence' as well as throwing light on Apra which he regards with a critical eye.

Apra's failure to mobilize the Indian masses and its faded radicalism left the way open for the emergence of Fernando Belaúnde's Acción Popular party in 1956. This was a multi-class populist party with a strong narodnik-style ideology of regeneration via ancient Indian folkways matched with an emphasis on technocratic élitism. No serious study of Acción Popular has been attempted, although many of its ideas were taken up by the military reformists after 1968. Unlike Apra, Acción Popular succeeded in incorporating the military into the populist alliance, but because of divisions and corruption within the wide spectrum of its civilian support, the military overthrew Belaúnde in 1968 and introduced their own brand of technocratic nationalistic military reformism. Useful articles on 'military populism' are J. Cotler, 'Crisis popular y populismo militar en el Perú', in *Estudios Internacionales*, no. 12 (January–March 1970) and on the corporative aspects of the present military régime J. Malloy's 'Authoritarianism, corporatism and mobilization in Peru', in *The Review of Politics* (January 1974).

Peru is perhaps the most interesting country in Latin America for studying populist movements as, in addition to Apra and Acción Popular, General Odría's National Union had a strong populist appeal among the shanty-towns of Lima.

Bolivia: It is a unique case in Latin America, insofar as war provided the main impetus to the development of mass politics. Unexpected defeat in the Chaco war with Paraguay led to a period of national self-questioning in the course of which younger military officers, partly influenced by Nazi ideas, established a series of proto-revolutionary régimes which prepared the way for the revolution of 1952. The MNR was a multi-class coalition of militant miners and an aroused peasantry under mainly middle-class leadership, which faced more acutely than any other populist movement the dilemma of how to satisfy roused expectations at the same time as increasing productivity. An early standard account of the revolution is R. J. Alexander, *The Bolivian National*

Revolution (New Brunswick, N.J., 1948) now partly superseded by J. M. Malloy, *Bolivia: the uncompleted Revolution* (Pittsburgh, 1970). The historical origins of the revolution have attracted few researchers except for the excellent study by H. Klein, *Parties and political change in Bolivia, 1880–1952* (Cambridge, 1969) whilst he discusses the military's reforming role in 'David Toro and the establishment of "Military Socialism" in Bolivia', *Hispanic American Historical Review* vol. 45, no. 1 (February 1965) and 'German Busch and the era of "Military Socialism" in Bolivia', *Hispanic American Historical Review* vol. 47, no. 2 (May 1967). Interesting light is thrown on United States attitudes to the early MNR and its allegedly Nazi sympathies by Cole Blaiser in 'The United States, Germany and the Bolivian revolutionaries, 1941–46', *Hispanic American Historical Review* vol. 52, no. 1 (February 1972). A more general discussion of the military's role is W. H. Brill, *Military Intervention in Bolivia; the overthrow of Paz Estenssoro and the MNR* (Washington, 1967).

There is no study of the Falange Socialista Boliviano which was founded by exiles in Chile in the late 1930s and became the main opposition to the MNR. It was recruited from dispossessed landowners and from the MNR's lower-middle- and middle-class supporters hit by the high inflation after 1952. It also has regional support in Santa Cruz. The Falange was inspired by the Spanish Falange and had fascist overtones, with its leader Unzaga de la Vega aspiring to become a führer-style leader until his assassination in 1959. It has never succeeded in building up a mass following nor in acquiring political respectability by developing into a Christian Democrat style party in the manner of the Chilean Falange.

There is a larger literature on the post-1952 period than for any other Latin American country of comparable size. All that can be mentioned here is an important article by M. Burke and J. M. Malloy, 'Del populismo nacional al corporativismo nacional: el caso de Bolivia, 1952–1970', *Aportes*, no. 26 (October 1972). Although the revolution of 1952 was regarded by Peronists as the first success of a Peronist-style revolution outside Argentina, no serious analysis of the links between the two has yet been attempted.

*

Chile: True to the Chileans' self-image of their Europeanism, the fascist versus popular front confrontation was acted out in the 1930s but with curious consequences. A small Nazi-style party, the MNS (Movimiento Nacional Socialista de Chile) was founded in 1932 by Jorge González von Marées in the same year as the Partido Socialista, founded to fill the gap left by the internecine rivalry between Stalinists and Trotskyites. It was not limited, as its leader's name might imply, to Chile's sizable German community but appealed, as did its rival the Partido Socialista, to students and young workers. The MNS has been described as the one recognizably European-style Nazi group in Latin America, but F. B. Pike in *Chile and the United States, 1880–1962* (Notre Dame, 1963) (which is far wider in scope than the title indicates), denies it was simply imitative and stresses the perceptiveness of its criticisms of Chilean society but suggests that it failed to attract a larger membership because of the aristocracy's dislike of its upstart leader and the party's stridency, and the threat which a potential mass party posed to the delicate balance on which Chilean politics rested, as well as to the hitherto successful policy of cooption by which the landed élite had managed to assimilate a rising middle class. Significantly, too, it was distrusted by the army for its para-military pretensions.

In 1938 young *nacistas* captured in an unsuccessful coup against Alessandri were assassinated in cold blood by the police. Ironically, this event led ex-dictator Carlos Ibáñez with whom the nacistas had an understanding, to throw the weight of his support behind the Popular Front candidate which thus came in partly with fascist support. Although the MNS itself withered away, an extreme right tradition was revived when the foundation of the MNCh. (Movimiento Nacionalista de Chile) in 1940 united ex-nacistas and *ibañistas* on a corporatist programme. This group may be traced through to the FNPL (Frente Nacionalista Patria y Libertad) founded in 1970 to provide ᵗhe shock troops of the anti-Allende opposition. An excellent analysis of the right is contained in H. E. Bicheno, 'Anti-parliamentary themes in Chilean history, 1920–1970', *Government and Opposition*, no. 3 (1972). Bicheno is at present working on a Ph.D. dissertation at Cambridge on the nacistas.

The Chilean army has not received the attention its behaviour warrants. F. Nunn, *Chilean Politics, 1920–1931: the Honorable Mission of the Armed Forces* (Albuquerque, 1970) is an introduction. The populist origins of the Socialist party are examined in P. Drake, 'The Chilean Socialist party and coalition politics, 1936–46', *Hispanic American Historical Review*, vol. 47, no. 1 (February 1973) where he concludes that 'by channelling the populist drive of the lower sectors into a Marxist framework but also into the existing system, the Chilean socialists may have given "mass politics" the potential to be a more heady agent of change, however gradual and limited, than in any Latin American country.' The influence of Perón's justicialist doctrines in Chile have been studied by W. Bray, 'Peronism in Chile', *Hispanic American Historical Review*, vol. 47, no. 1 (February 1967). We need more analyses of the impact of Peronism on other countries as well.

The Chilean Falange had been founded in 1938 by a breakaway group of young members of the Conservative party. Despite the name, they bore little relation to the Spanish Falange and were mostly influenced by the writings of liberal Catholics. In 1957 the group absorbed the bulk of another small Christian group and was reconstituted as the Christian Democrat party with populist and corporatist strains, emphasizing communitarianism. Their views are discussed, within the general context of Chilean politics, in J. Petras, *Politics and social forces in Chilean development* (Berkeley and Los Angeles, 1969). By populism, the Christian Democrats understood the active participation in decision-making by the poor, especially the marginal groups who had been largely overlooked by the secular left as an unreliable lumpenproletariat. The Christian Democrats were the first to recognize their electoral potential – especially the support they could get from women. Populism, in the Christian Democrats' sense, had a different emphasis, at least in theory, from the manipulative tendencies of Brazilian populism, although in practice the differences may not have been all that great. Some of the paradoxical features of Christian Democrat populism are discussed by E. de Kadt in 'Paternalists and populists: views on

Catholicism in Latin America', *Journal of Contemporary History*, no. 2 (November 1967).

Other Latin American countries have had their fringe fascist groups and their populist style movements, but they have not exercised much influence. In Ecuador, ARNE (Alianza Revolucionaria Nacionalista Ecuatoriana) was founded as a fascist-style group in 1948, but although it was prepared to support Velasco Ibarra it could not hope to compete against his old-style personalist, not to say populist, appeal. In Colombia, where politics have traditionally revolved around the two historical parties, the Liberals and Conservatives, with their clientilist followings, there are no disposable masses for a fascist party to mobilize. Falangist ideas and Hispanidad exercised some influence on Laureano Gómez in the late 1930s and there was a Falangist group active in the early 1940s. Colombia produced in Jorge Eliecer Gaitán one of the most striking populist leaders of any Latin American country, but his assassination in 1948 cut short the development of any populist movement. Since then no one has been able to break the monopoly exercised by the two traditional parties although General Rojas Pinilla, influenced to some extent by Perón, tried to do so. A. Angell discusses populism in 'Populism and political change: the Colombian case', in *Sociological Review Monograph*, no. 11 (February 1967). The military have still to receive full-length treatment although there is a brief analysis of its role in J. L. Payne's general book on Colombian politics, *Patterns of Conflict in Colombia* (New Haven, 1968), in R. H. Dix, *Colombia: the political dimensions of change* (New Haven, 1967), who also discusses populistic authoritarianism, and in V. L. Fluharty, *Dance of the Millions: military rule and social revolution in Colombia, 1930–56* (Pittsburgh, 1957). Venezuelan political parties have not been analysed from the criterion of populism, although J. D. Martz, *Acción Democrática* (Princeton, 1966) is one of the fullest analyses of a Latin American political party we have. Venezuela produced in Valenilla Lanz's *Cesarismo democrático*, published in 1929, one of the only theoretical expositions of a military leader with a mass popular appeal, but mainly as an apologia for the rule of the dictator Juan Vicente Gómez, although it has also been taken as a prescription for successful government under prevailing Latin American conditions. It is an open question whether Batista in the 1930s or Castro in the early 1960s can be subsumed under the populist umbrella, although both their régimes had populist characteristics.

The serious study of Latin America's contemporary history and politics which has now become a major academic growth industry is of comparatively recent origin but, in spite of (or perhaps because of) the sophisticated techniques employed, many problems remain unsolved. During the key formative years of the 1930s and 1940s Latin American politics were virtually unstudied both abroad and in Latin America itself. Abroad, they were widely regarded as a corrupted strain of the liberal constitutionalism Latin America so avidly imitated, and the apparent inability to operate parliamentary government was adduced as evidence of congenital deficiencies and rarely attributed to structural problems. Latin Americans themselves contributed little to off-set widespread foreign misconceptions. Most political studies were cast in an arid juridico-legal mould and by taking the premises of their own political behaviour for granted they denied to foreigners insights which a native tradition of academic self-analysis might otherwise have provided.

It needed the jolt of the Cuban revolution to change attitudes and to give an impetus to serious academic study both within and outside Latin America, releasing a flood of money and endowing prestige to a field which had previously lacked serious recognition. Inevitably, much of the social science research done by United States scholars, who dominate the field, has tended to be of a predictive nature and policy-oriented. In the opening phase of this newly awakened interest, research was still culture-bound: few scholars were attuned to underlying cultural nuances and there was a tendency to apply uncritically techniques which had originally been devised for advanced industrial societies. However, there was a well-established tradition of social anthropological research which helped to provide the basis for a more realistic assessment once the advantages of an inter-disciplinary approach were recognized.

Attention was directed primarily towards development problems and the process of modernization. Financial aid to Latin American countries was intended to serve a prophylactic function and neutralize the effects of the Cuban revolution. It was implicitly assumed that this aid would help the process of nation-building, establish social justice, increase the standard of living, bolster democracy, support agrarian reform, and stimulate industrialization. These aims were regarded as being both desirable and inevitable. All that was needed for their achievement was the injection of the much needed capital and technical assistance which Latin Americans lacked. In the early 1960s both official and academic circles in the United States were optimistic about the contribution which the Alliance for Progress would make towards modernization and democracy, which were regarded as being inseparable and mutually reinforcing. Latin America was not like Africa with its tribal complexities, or Asia with its impermeable culture and religious taboos: it was recognizably Western, a largely immigrant continent like the United States, an extension of Europe and hence obeying the laws of European social and historical development. Of all the areas of the Third World, Latin America seemed to be the furthest advanced along the traditional–modern continuum.

By the end of the 1960s, this reformist euphoria had evaporated, as the assumptions on which it had been based were shown to be false. It was true that the failure of countless guerrilla campaigns, climaxed in Guevara's failure in Bolivia in 1967, had revealed that Latin America was not ripe for revolution in the Cuban fashion but neither, it seemed, was it ripe for Western-style democracy. Instead a series of military coups initiated a new cycle of authoritarian government until by 1976 only a handful of Latin American states were under civilian rule. Even Uruguay, long regarded as a model of parliamentary probity, succumbed, and Chile which had prided itself on its European-style political stability showed that when it came to violence it could emulate its exemplars in that respect as well. Events in Brazil since the 'revolution' of 1964, and more particularly, events during and after the Allende régime in Chile, have re-introduced fascism into the vocabulary of Latin American political analysis as something more than a term of abuse. To the liberal democrat's question of what has gone wrong, Marxists might reply 'nothing', as given the preconditions of a capitalist system in crisis the trend to authoritarianism and 'colonial fascism' is inevitable and, from the standpoint of United States interests and those of multinational companies, desirable as well, a view which is concisely expressed in books like Dick Parker's *La nueva cara del fascismo* (Santiago, 1972). In this view, fascism is seen as the form of government arising in capitalist societies when contradictions develop between a technologically advanced industrial sector and a low productivity traditional sector. In the face of working-class demands the fascist state attempts to defend the interests of proprietors in both sectors, supported by insecure elements of the lower-middle and middle classes. The private interests in the modern sector can be national or foreign. If the former, fascism takes the classic autarchic form. If the latter, 'colonial fascism' integrates the dependent country's economy, dominated by foreign capital, into the international capital economy.[13]

Whatever its validity, such an approach lies within an established tradition – not necessarily Marxist but often using Marxist insights – which exercises a wide influence throughout Latin American academic circles. It takes as its starting point the peripheral and dependent position of Latin America in the global economy and sets out to explain why, after 150 years of political independence, most Latin American countries remain primary producers, have monoproductive economies, and are still dependent on the advanced industrial powers, especially the United States, economically, politically, and culturally. This 'dependency theory', a variant of general theories of imperialism, has been formulated mainly by Latin American scholars and marks an intellectual break-through, a decolonizing of the academic mind, as it looks at Latin American problems from a Latin American perspective.[14] Economists and sociologists have been in the forefront of this development with the United Nations Economic Commission for Latin America as its original forcing house. Historians have lagged behind for reasons related to inaccessibility of sources, the slower pace of historical research and, perhaps, through the conservative outlook of academic historians. Many of the hypotheses which have been formulated by social scientists are therefore often based on slender historical evidence although analysis of the 1930s and 1940s tends to be crucial to their arguments as one of the key problems is exactly why the industrialization process which accelerated from the early 1930s failed to break the pattern of dependence.

Problems of modernization, development and the impact of Western-based technologies, and the peasant responses to them have encouraged some historians to follow political scientists and sociologists into the field of comparative studies. Although the most ambitious of these, Barrington Moore's *The social origins of dictatorship and democracy* (New York, 1966) does not touch on Latin America, his model of fascism as a political system by which modernization is achieved without changing the social structure and his application of it to Japan has suggestive possibilities. From this viewpoint, Vargas's Estado Novo and Perón's Justicialismo could be classified as fascist. However, there is one element which is crucial to Moore's thesis which is absent in the Latin American case, and that concerns the peasantry. With the exception of sinarquismo, peasants do not become key figures in the elaboration of radical right ideologies, as was the case with the Nazis. The stress which Moore places on the role of peasants and the reasons why labour-repressive systems provide an important part of the institutional complex leading to fascism, contrasts markedly with the Latin American situation where peasants for the most part lack economic independence and became enmeshed in clientilist arrangements with conservative or populist politicians and are not available for mobilization by the radical right, and indeed, proved difficult to organize even by the Castroite left which, unlike the radical right, had an interest in doing so.

Nor, in Latin America, was there the same anti-modern utopian strain which, it has been argued, was one key to the understanding of German Nazism (although not perhaps of Italian fascism). Industrialization was too desirable a goal as a means of achieving genuine independence to be rejected in favour of a peasant symbol of agrarian innocence. In any case, peasants who were often Indian, mestizo, black, or mulatto could not become carriers for an ideology of racial purity – at least on the right.[15]

It may be questioned whether the wide range of variables involved in cross-cultural analyses will produce fruitful results (except in the sense that comparative study can always pose new questions and open up new perspectives). Much more work needs to be done in comparative historical studies before convincing generalizations can be formulated. The difficulty – for historians at least – is that in trying to explain everything, one finishes by explaining nothing.

Historians may seem to have little to contribute to the continuing debate so long as many sociologists and political scientists are reluctant to give more weight to historical conditioning factors and reject the concept of political culture, but whatever advantages there may be in the fragmentation and specialization of disciplines in advanced industrial countries, these divisions constitute a major barrier to understanding developing areas. One field of study where this has been recognized and where the cross-fertilization of disciplines may throw new light on Latin American political processes is in the reviving interest in corporatism.

What might be regarded as the manifesto of this trend is the special edition of *The Review of Politics* vol. 36, no. 1 (January 1974) entitled 'The New Corporatism: Social and Political Structures in the Iberian World' and the book version published by Notre Dame University Press, 1974, edited by F. B. Pike. A further volume edited by H. Wiarda, *Politics and Social Change in Latin America: the Distinct Tradition* (1974), collects previously published articles including a major contribution by Richard M. Morse, the gadfly among United States Latin Americanists who has long been arguing for the recognition of the Thomistic roots of Latin American political behaviour and thought.

In *The New Corporatism* collection, J. Malloy explores corporatism as exemplified in the reformist military régime in contemporary Peru and argues that corporatism constitutes an empirically useful group theory of politics, at present reflected in three levels of analysis of Latin American politics: in the analysis of the institutional and cultural principles derived from the Hispanic tradition; in the analysis of group formation and interest articulation, which are inadequately grasped by liberal and Marxist group theories of politics; and in the analysis of how a political system has been organized and integrated, as in Mexico since 1917 and in contemporary Peru. Schmitter's seminal article suggests an operational definition of corporatism in terms of a distinctive modern system of interest representation, but he is concerned with wider implications and ramifications than the political culture arguments favoured by Wiarda's and Newton's articles which are confined to the Iberian world.

Ronald Newton, whose article 'On "Functional Groups", "Fragmentation" and "Pluralism" in Spanish American Political Society', in *Hispanic American Historical Review* vol. 50, no. 1 (1970) was an important and stylish first salvo in the current debate, presents the case for what he calls 'natural corporatism'. In contrast to corporatism in Europe between the wars which was adopted as an ideology and organizing principle once in power, 'natural corporatism' in Latin America 'has evolved slowly, unacknowledged, within or parallel to the conventional and more or less constitutional processes of electoral civic paralysis, *golpes*. . . . Where European-derived corporatism has figured at all in the doctrinal writings and programmes of political activists, it has been the property of isolated sects and sectarians of the extreme right with few prospects of immediate access to power.' (p. 39). Newton refers to natural corporatism as 'an organizing hypothesis' used by scholars to explain socio-political phenomena which have not been elucidated in terms of the categories of conventional liberal-developmental scholarship in Latin America. Corporate ways of articulating group interests lie at the core of Hispanic politics, and both leftist and rightist régimes must take cognizance of this tradition if they wish to flourish. Corporate representation is not the monopoly of the left or right, but can be deployed both by populist régimes as a means of achieving participation and mobilization and by the authoritarian régimes which succeeded them, as a means of depoliticization and demobilization.

Wiarda's article amplifies an argument he had earlier presented in 'Towards a Framework for the Study of Political Change in the Ibero-Latin Tradition', *World Politics*, vol. 25, no. 2 (January 1973) for the recognition of a distinctive Ibero-American political tradition embedded in corporatism 'about the only one of the great "isms" that correspond to her historic and political culture'. He also distinguishes between corporatist régimes of the 1930s and 1940s, where corporatism was a system of authority, stressing functional representation and the integration of labour and capital into a hierarchically ordered system, and a historical tradition embedded in Ibero-Latin American history, embodying a dominant form of socio-political organization that is hierarchical, élitist, authoritarian, bureaucratic, Catholic patrimonialist, and corporatist. While the discredited forms of corporatism associated with fascism were submerged and re-baptized under different names, the old corporatist tradition remained intact. Underneath democratic façades, the historic political culture of corporatist values was present all the time. Wiarda is a rare example of a political scientist taking historical influences seriously but one is bound to wonder if he is not doing his own cause and that of historians a disservice by overkill.

He also perhaps overestimates the influence of the United States in Latin America when he argues that because corporatist and integralist experiments had been discredited by European fascism the United States compelled Latin Americans to choose between false alternatives of communism and democracy by ruling out a middle way. The application of unilinear, ethnocentric development models deflected Latin Americans away from its real traditions and it is only now with the decline of United States cultural, economic, and political influence, and the discrediting of United States models, that Latin America, as in the 1930s, is searching for indigenous solutions.

The chapter by F. B. Pike (whose earlier book *Hispanismo, 1898–1936: Spanish Conservatives and Liberals and their relations with Spanish America* [Notre Dame, 1971] was a long overdue examination of mutual influences between Spain and Spanish America) suggests that in attempting to carry out a bourgeois revolution from above the Latin American technocratic élite have chosen methods, including developmental nationalism and paternalistic corporatism, designed to keep the lower classes in a dependent position and that corporatism now serves the security interests of the United States. Whatever criticisms may be brought against the corporate thesis generally or the various essays individually, this collection opens up a whole vista of possible approaches to the study of Latin American political and social movements.

Finally, Wiarda insists that corporatism is not to be equated with fascism or nazism – parallels are only superficial: Ibero-Latin tradition is a distinct and separate type, fundamentally different from popular stereotypes. Authoritarian yes but fascist no. 'Fascism,' he concludes, 'and fascist can hardly be applied in an Ibero-Latin context with any accuracy. As an adequate analytic term fascism may have outlived its usefulness.'

It would be a relief to believe that the semantic hair-splitting to which definitional studies of fascism invariably descend is a thing of the past and that as far as Latin America is concerned we can forget such irrelevant criteria but with capitalism in the Western world in crisis, and with the example of Brazil and Chile and other Latin American states before us, optimism may be premature. Fascism is a blunt instrument for political science analysis but for the victims of authoritarian rule the fine distinctions of academics will seem irrelevant.

Notes

1. For German efforts, see A. Frye, *Nazi Germany and the American Hemisphere, 1933–41* (New Haven, 1967) with extensive bibliography and *Der Deutsche Faschismus in Lateinamerika 1933–1943* (Berlin, 1966). Hispanidad is discussed in B. W. Diffie, 'The ideology of Hispanidad', in *Hispanic-American Historical Review*, no. 22 (August 1943).

2. The one exception is the Chaco war between Bolivia and Paraguay in the 1930s which in the former gave an impetus to fascist ideas but in the latter strengthened old-style caudillo rule. The siege mentality in Cuba since 1959 has produced results similar to those produced by actual warfare. The case of the Mexican civil war between 1913 and 1917 is not comparable as this created internal divisions.

3. The distrust is clear in the case of Germany and Spain but less clear in the case of Italy. See G. Rochat, *L'esercito italiano da Vittorio Veneto a Mussolini (1919–25)* (Bari, 1967). In Latin America scholars have virtually ignored police forces. It is a major research need and nowhere more than in Chile where the para-military *carabineros* held one of the keys to Allende's success or failure.

4. In a British context one has only to think of the shock impact of Powell's 'rivers of blood' speech.

5. The distinction between fascism and traditionalism in Spain is clearly

made in R. M. Blinkhorn, *Carlism and Crisis in Spain, 1931–39* (Cambridge, 1975).

6. 'Concientização' became one of the key concepts of the 1960s, associated with the Brazilian educator Paolo Freire but after 1964 in Brazil it became discredited because of its political implications.

7. The key intellectual influence in Spain was Ramiro de Maeztu, a half-English, Anglophile liberal who believed before the Great War that Spain could be regenerated by liberal capitalism. Experience as a reporter on the Western Front cured him of illusions about the 'defence of civilization', and with the publication of *La Crisis del Humanismo* in 1916 he began a new career as spokesman for Hispanic values culminating in *Defensa de la Hispanidad* in 1934, the key text for Hispanic right-wing movements.

8. Self-definition should be taken seriously in any analysis of fascist movements. Obviously structural factors are crucial in any definition but if people consistently reject the title, it is worth exploring the reasons why they do so.

9. They returned to active politics in 1950 and 1955 when Salgado polled 8% of the presidential vote.

10. We lack scholarly studies of anti-Semitism in Latin America. For Argentina there are two chapters in D. Eisenberg, *The Re-emergence of Fascism* (London, 1967). A useful discussion of the position of Jews in Latin America is the conference report, *Latin America and the future of its Jewish communities* (London, 1973).

11. The personalist element in Brazilian populism is well illustrated by its domestication of political leaders by using their Christian names – thus Getulio, Juscelino, Jangio etc., for Vargas, Kubitschek, Quadros – a contrast to the faceless military presidents after 1964. In Argentina the style was different. Perón distanced himself from the crowd and Eva's role was to act as intercessor. The Führerprinzip of nazism or Il Duce of fascism, or even El caudillo por la gracia de Dios of Franco is far removed from the Latin American populist style.

12. Ramiro de Maeztu had been Spanish ambassador in Buenos Aires in the late 1920s and had formed links with the Nueva República group. Another important Spanish influence justifying élite rule was Ortega y Gasset's *Rebelión de las Masas*, first published in 1926 but with very different underlying presuppositions to Maeztu.

13. In Parker's typology Italy, 1922–43 and Spain, 1940–49 are classic but stagnant fascisms: Germany, 1933–45 is classic but dynamic and Spain, 1960–75 and Brazil, 1967–? are colonial fascist and dynamic.

14. A useful short analysis of dependence theory is P. O'Brien, *A critique of Latin American theories of dependency*, Glasgow University Institute of Latin American Studies, Occasional Papers, no. 12. A. G. Frank, *Capitalism and underdevelopment in Latin America* (New York, 1969), is a key text whilst the writings of Paul A. Baran were an important early influence.

15. There have been instances of attempts to formulate ideologies of racial purity – such as proving Mexicans were Aryans – but more usual have been

ideologies of racial fusion: on this Integralists and Nazis clashed in Brazil. The Integralists' fanciful Indianism – their greeting was the Indian Tupi word *anauê* – was never taken seriously and they did not single out blacks for special consideration at a time when attempts were being made to organize them in the Frente Negra Brasileira. In 1933 Gilberto Freyre's *Masters and Slaves* was published which reversed the racial pessimism of Euclides da Cunha and those in the 1890s who were influenced by Gobineau and Gumplowicz. The influence of Freyre, who made a virtue out of racial necessity, was very great.

8 Fascism in Western Europe

Fascist and national socialist movements achieved comparatively little importance in western and northern Europe, with the single exception of Spain. Until recently they have drawn little historiographic attention. In the one case where there are major phenomena to study, the long duration of the Franco régime has inhibited scholarly investigation by Spaniards of its own origin and the inception of national syndicalism. Given the paucity of monographic works, the absence of broader analytical study is perhaps not surprising. There has thus been no real inquiry into whether there was such a thing as a unique 'west European' variant of fascism. The common assumption seems to be that the term *fascist* refers to all violent, authoritarian radical nationalist movements and that their differences are either unimportant or merely the inevitable result of national differences in nationalist movements.

The point of inception for fascistic ideas in the West has been a matter of debate. Miguel de Unamuno once said that the Spanish Carlists were the first fascists, but so simplistic a comparison cannot withstand analysis. Reactionary neo-traditionalist monarchism of the nineteenth century in both Spain and France lacked the distinctive characteristics and components of fascism, whether in terms of vitalistic, irrationalist culture, the development of a new state and system to cope with mass society and economics, or mass mobilization. This becomes clear from general works that deal in whole or in part with the monarchist ultra-right, such as Román Oyarzun's *Historia del carlismo* (Madrid, 1940, 1965), and René Rémond, *The Right Wing in France from 1815 to de Gaulle* (Philadelphia, 1969).

Though a major fascist movement at no time emerged in France, many of the specific ingredients of fascism appeared earlier there than anywhere else. This, of course, was also true of the notion of totalitarian democracy, communist ideas, and the modern revolutionary leftist dictatorship, simply because there was an earlier convergence of both the problems of modernization and the various aspects of modern development in France than in any other large country. Probably the first point at which specific pre-fascist ingredients can be identified is in the agitation of Paul Déroulède's 'League of Patriots' and the Boulangist movement in the 1880s. One of the classic motivations of fascism – status deprivation – weighed upon France rather than on Germany or Italy after 1871, and the French left, still at that point ultra-nationalist, felt defrauded by the character of the Third Republic just as did the nationalist left in central European countries a generation or more later. In Boulangism there was expressed a new kind of nationalism that was at the same time authoritarian, contemptuous of representative liberal democracy, and directed towards the masses. It sought to harmonize the interests of diverse classes and appealed especially towards small shopkeepers and the lower middle class. The central motif was national vengeance, requiring a doctrine of neo-militarism and a mystique of discipline and death rooted in the national soil and the popular culture.[1] Boulangism remained, however, rather more leftist than rightist in inspiration, and could not exploit any genuine social crisis, which was non-existent. In general European terms, it was premature, but when the so-called fascist era later dawned in central Europe, French society was too stable and mature for fascism.

The search for the roots of a French fascism has recently centered on the figure of Maurice Barrès, which has been studied by Robert Soucy, *Fascism in France: The Case of Maurice Barrès* (Berkeley, Los Angeles, London, 1972), and Z. Sternhell, *Maurice Barrès et le nationalisme français* (Paris, 1972), the latter, the richer work. Barrès was one of the first to attempt to formulate the idea of a national socialism, and his mystique of *la terre et les morts* anticipated much of the mythos of the new radical nationalism of the twentieth century. Sternhell and Soucy show that Barrès combined the search for energy and vitalism with an emphasis on national rootedness and a sort of Darwinian racism.

He also propounded hero worship and charismatic leadership, but remained in many ways basically conservative and failed in his efforts at broader mobilization.[2] Barrès later relapsed into traditionalism and a kind of fatalism that differed considerably from the subsequent fascist cult of will.

The core of the modern French right was formed by the Action Française movement of Charles Maurras. Ernst Nolte has judged it one of the three fundamental 'faces of fascism',[3] not in the sense of a fully developed fascism but rather as a seed-bearer of ideas and tendencies more fully developed in Italy and Germany. Yet even this seems to stretch the point, for the Action Française altogether failed to meet the criteria of Nolte's own 'fascist minimum' that he advanced in a later work.[4] Its reactionary qualities were not so radical as to oppose all practical conservatism, and it did not espouse the last principles included in Nolte's 'fascist minimum' – a 'party-army' and the goal of totalitarianism. Cultural neo-classicism clashed with vitalism and irrationalism, and the tactic of radical mobilization of the masses for violent or pseudo-revolutionary activity was lacking. The Action Française was in fact the most sophisticated and modern movement of the élitist, semi-traditionalist right. Eugen Weber's *Action Française: Royalism and Reaction in Twentieth-Century France* (Stanford, 1962) is a masterful and comprehensive account that narrates the entire history of the movement while analysing its ideology and cultural influence, as well as its effect on the royalist right in other lands. Edward Tannenbaum's *Action Française* (New York, 1962) is inferior in terms either of perspective or comprehensiveness.

Between the 1920s and early 1940s France generated more small fascist, semi-fascist, or pseudo-fascist movements of radical nationalism than any other country, yet none assumed truly major proportions and most failed to approximate the full model of the Italian movement. The largest of the organized 'leagues', as they were called in the 1930s, was the Croix de Feu of Colonel de la Rocque, which at one point claimed, no doubt with exaggeration, to have more than 700,000 members. Yet the Croix de Feu remained an amorphous veterans' association without clearcut ideology or goals. Rather than a French National Socialist party it was more nearly the French version of the Stahlhelm. There is a fairly extensive if partisan account by Philippe Rudaux, *Les Croix de Feu et le P.S.F.* (Paris, 1967).

The first of the new radical groups was the Faisceau band organized by Georges Valois and a few other dissidents from Action Française in 1925.[5] The source of its ideological inspiration was obvious, though the party dwindled away to nothing in the stable and prosperous France of the 1920s. The only other French group to employ the term *fascist* semi-officially – at least on occasion – was the Francistes of Marcel Bucard,[6] who also drew a subsidy from the Italian government[7] but were scarcely more successful than the Faisceau. The nearest thing to a serious fascist-type movement in France was the Parti Populaire Français of Jacques Doriot, organized by nationalistic ex-communists in 1936 and afterwards along lines that increasingly paralleled the earlier phases of the Italian model. But even Doriot and the PPF long protested their non-fascist character.

Study of these groups has become extensive but rarely thorough. The first attempt at a general treatment was J. Plumyene and R. Lasierra, *Les Fascismes français 1923-63* (Paris, 1963), which served as an introduction but lacked depth of true comprehensiveness. There are two general catalogues of fascist-type and collaborationist organizations in France. Henry Coston, ed., *Partis, journaux et hommes politiques d'hier et d'aujourdhui* (Paris, 1960), is the more extensive, a special number of *Lectures Françaises* edited by a sometime collaborationist. The second survey, also of general utility, is given in David Littlejohn's *The Patriotic Traitors* (London, 1972), pp. 185–290. The writers and aesthetes associated with the French fascistic groups, especially the PPF, were the most able of their persuasion in Western Europe and have been the subject of books by Paul Sérant, Tarmo Kunnas, and Jacqueline Morand.[8] Important articles on French fascism have been written by Eugen Weber,[9] Raoul Girardet,[10] and Robert Soucy,[11] and a brief summary has also been given by Nolte in his *Krise des liberalen Systems und die faschistischen Bewegungen.* Monographs on individual groups and parties are much rarer, one exception being Philippe Bourdrel's able study of the secret terrorist organization *La Cagoule* (Paris, 1970).

The major monographic study of French fascist movements is Dieter Wolf, *Die Doriot-Bewegung* (Stuttgart, 1967), an excellent account of Jacques Doriot and the Parti Populaire Français. It supersedes several unpublished dissertations[12] as well as all briefer accounts. An excellent piece of research, Wolf's book devotes considerable attention to Doriot's early communist years and his transition from revolutionary communism to semi-revolutionary national socialism. The analysis of the political background of the party's founders reveals that it was largely a convergence of elements of the extreme (communist) left and extreme right. Though there is no doubt that the PPF became the largest of hard-core fascist-type parties in France, Wolf reduces the membership figure of 295,000 officially claimed in January 1938 to a more realistic approximation of 50,000–60,000 regular members. The nationalization of social radicalism and the revolutionary power lust proceeded through a series of stages, and *fascist* remained a dirty word for many members of the PPF. Only in the collaborationist phase after German occupation was the transition to full fascism completed, and the wartime quality of the PPF then more closely approximated German national socialism than south-west European fascism.

Distinctions of phase and of quality have to be drawn between the more or less spontaneous, native French fascistic movements of the 1930s, however much inspired by foreign models, and the collaborationist period from 1940 to 1944. Serious students have long appreciated that the Pétainist régime itself cannot be considered intrinsically fascist, but rather one of a large number of syncratic, conservative authoritarian régimes that proliferated mainly in the southern half of Europe and to some extent in Latin America from the 1920s on. The recent symposium on *Le Gouvernement de Vichy 1940–1942* (Paris, 1972) tends to stress elements of continuity in the policies of the Vichy régime. The best synthetic study of Vichy is Robert O. Paxton's *Vichy France* (New York, 1972), which supersedes Robert Aron's *Histoire de Vichy* (Paris, 1954) (trans. as *The Vichy Régime*). It analyses the entire range of forces involved in Vichy, from reactionaries to moderate liberal modernizers, and finds that the genuine fascist elements had but minor roles in most sectors. Hard-line fascist and Nazi groups prospered much more in the German occupation zone of the north, but even then generated little independent strength. A complete catalogue of all collaborationist and fascistoid organizations in France under German occupation may be found in Littlejohn's book. J. Delperrie de Bayac, *Histoire de la Milice, 1918–1945* (Paris, 1969), is particularly useful with regard to Nazi influences.

Despite a broad variety of ideas, groups and personalities, French fascism added up to very little. This is not difficult to explain in view of the fact that almost none of the theoretical components advanced to account for the rise of fascism and nazism elsewhere were present in France. The country had not been defeated and was not suffering national status deprivation, at least prior to 1940, and after that date fascism remained identified with foreign oppressors. The French middle classes were severely buffeted by the depression but were not subjected to a genuine social crisis. However much criticized, the parliamentary system continued to sustain itself. The French left did not constitute a true revolutionary threat and there were no masses of unemployed veterans to mobilize. There was no crisis of modernization but rather a static equilibrium of moderate but not unreasonable development. Serious ethnic rivalry or concern was non-existent.

Thus when Maurice Bardèche looked back a generation later in his effort to re-define fascism, *Qu'est-ce que le fascisme?* (Paris, 1961), he found it hard to be specific. Rejecting either nazism on the one hand or the existing Franco régime on the other as synonymous with true fascism, he identified it instead as a spirit or an attitude – *la rêve fasciste* – the cultural mood of a time that sought physical and moral regeneration and the reconciliation of individualism and collective nationalism.

The situation in neighbouring Belgium was somewhat different, mainly because of the tensions resulting from the cleavage between Flemings and Walloons. The combined votes of the two chief Fleming and Walloon fascistic groups reached nearly 19 per cent in 1936, far and away the largest in western or northern Europe. The most important fascist party in the Low Countries was Rex, whose leader Léon Degrelle was probably the most flamboyant fascist chief in all of Western Europe. Rex began as a

Catholic youth movement that emphasized radical national regeneration. It was based primarily on the middle classes of the
Walloon provinces and only moved into a clearly fascist position
after 1936. There is a careful study of the early Rexist movement
by Jean-Michel Etienne, *Le Mouvement rexiste jusqu'en 1940*
(Paris, 1968), and further work is now in progress. Degrelle himself is unique among major fascist leaders in that he survived the
war – including many months of front-line combat on the eastern
front – and has been loquacious in self-justification.[13] There are
several chapters and articles that briefly summarize the world of
Belgian fascism, dealing both with Rex and the Flemish-based
Verdinaso and VNV parties,[14] and a recent booklet summarizes
the several minor post-war expressions of the ultra-right and neo-
fascism.[15]

Whereas Belgium harboured three different fascist movements
of note, the only one of any consequence in Holland was Anton
Mussert's Nationaal-Socialistische Beweging, which garnered 4 per
cent of the Dutch vote in the 1937 elections. Aside from a few
notes in general accounts,[16] it may best be approached through a
brief treatment in Werner Warmbrunn's *The Dutch under German
Occupation 1940–1945* (Stanford, 1963).

Adequate comparative study is lacking with regard to either the
several varieties of French fascism or the various groups in the
Low Countries. The only adequate monograph to treat a single
party completely is that by Wolf. More thorough comparative
study is required to sort out whatever differences may have
existed in bases of recruitment and specific types of doctrine or
ideological appeal. For example, some difference might be noted
between the more conservative and corporatist fascist-type parties
in the Low Countries (Verdinaso, the early Rexist movement and
Mussert's NSB, originally not anti-Semitic) and the more radical,
increasingly anti-Semitic Nazi-type groups (the VNV and the tiny
National Socialist Dutch Workers Party, the latter a carbon copy
of the NSDAP). While a healthy scepticism may be maintained
about the validity of any very rigid categorization of fascistic
groups, some degree of further sorting out is obviously in order.
It might be added that German occupation and satellite status

largely completed the nazification of nearly all these little groups, just as satellite status to some extent changed the direction of Italian fascism itself.

The minuscule fascist parties of Scandinavia were even weaker than those of France and Holland, with the temporary exception of the Lapua movement of Finland. The two would-be Swedish Nazi parties garnered 1.6 per cent of the popular vote in the 1936 elections, while their Norwegian counterparts of Vidkun Quisling's Nasjonal Samling (National Unification) group drew 2.16 per cent in 1933 and dropped to 1.84 per cent in 1936. The most important thing about Quisling has in a sense been the name, which became the symbol for political collaboration with Nazi occupation. The only reliable book on Quisling and his group in English is Paul M. Hayes, *Quisling* (London, 1971), accompanied by brief articles by Hayes[17] and T. K. Derry.[18] Ralph Hewings unsuccessfully attempted a revisionist biography entitled *Quisling: Prophet without Honour* (London, 1965), which is incomplete and poorly documented but nonetheless contains some interesting dissenting information. Hans-Dietrich Loock's *Quisling, Rosenberg und Terboven. Zur Vorgeschichte und Geschichte der nationalsozialistischen Revolution in Norwegen* (Stuttgart, 1970) is a solid account of occupation policy that also includes considerable material on Quisling's political background. Discussion of the pre-conditions for a Norwegian nazism may be found in A. S. Milward's *The Fascist Economy in Norway* (Oxford, 1972), and there is further extensive literature in Norwegian.[19]

There is no systematic effort at studying the Scandinavian fascist or nazi parties as a whole or comparatively. The principal compilation is in Littlejohn, pp. 1–82, and there is a brief review by Nolte.[20] Serious treatment of the nazi-type movements in Sweden and Denmark is confined to several works in the languages of those countries.[21]

If the weakness of fascism and nazism in most of Scandinavia would seem to require little explanation, the case of Finland was somewhat different. A small country but recently escaped from Russian domination, it had survived a revolutionary civil war that reversed for Finland the result obtaining in Russia. Nevertheless, the fear of Russian domination and hence of potential revolution remained. These might have provided powerful stimuli for fascism had it not been for the relatively stable structure of middle-class society in Finland and the influence of constitutional tradition. Despite genuine temptations that were much greater than in most of northern and western Europe, Finland did not succumb to fascism, and the decline of the fascist brand of anti-communism was in part responsible for Finland's ability to sustain its independence after 1945.

There is no adequate account of the Lapua movement and the temporary drift towards fascistic politics in Finland during the early 1930s. The most direct account in English is Marvin Rintala's *Three Generations: The Extreme Right in Finnish Politics* (Bloomington, Ind., 1962), but it is not altogether a well-balanced treatment. There are general articles by Rintala[22] and A. F. Upton,[23] and also a discussion of fascist tendencies and sympathies in Finland in C. Leonard Lundin's *Finland in the Second World War* (Bloomington, Ind., 1957). In Finnish there is more extensive treatment of individual aspects of radical nationalist and para-fascist politics,[24] but no complete and integrated study.

There would seem to be one categorical difference between the movements in Scandinavia and those in south-western Europe (Spain, France, Portugal, Belgium and, even to some extent, Holland). Those in Scandinavia tended to follow the Nazi model in their racism and mysticism, and often in their very choice of names. The Finnish Lapua movement placed emphasis on military expansion. By contrast, the south-western movements were much more similar to the Italian fascist pattern in terms of their absence of racism and their frequent connection to Catholicism, their lack of equivalent emphasis on neo-militarism and their rather conservative-functional orientation to corporatism. The similarity in origin of the major French fascist group to that of the Italian prototype is striking. The idea-world and emulative pattern of National Socialism was extended primarily to east-central Europe, Scandinavia, and Holland, where German cultural influence was stronger. The Italian model exerted greater influence over south-western Europe – and western Europe as a whole exclusive of Scandinavia – with some secondary influence in Austria, Hungary, and the Balkans. Only under the force of German occupation did Nazi influence and the desire to emulate Nazi practice become largely predominant.

All the factors that discouraged the growth of a strong and direct fascism in France were redoubled, as in Scandinavia, in the case of England, which produced only one significant group. Oswald Mosley's British Union of Fascists, founded in 1932, was indeed a clear-cut fascist group that did not shrink – like so many in western Europe – from the use of the label. It was partly modelled on Italian fascism, and followed the Mussolinian pattern insofar as its leader had only a year or two earlier been one of the most dominant younger leaders of the Labour party before becoming discouraged with personal and public prospects under the liberal democratic system. Anti-Semitism and Nazi influence soon became increasingly important, but the BUF was distinguished primarily by its impotence and could in no way be compared with some of the larger fascistic groups even in other liberal democracies such as France, Belgium or Finland. Indeed, one of the best accounts of the group, Colin Cross's *The Fascists in Britain* (London, 1961), tends possibly to exaggerate what importance it did have at its highwater mark around 1935–6. A later study by Robert Benewick, *Political Violence and Public Order. A Study of British Fascism* (London, 1969), is more solidly buttressed with a systematic scholarly apparatus and shows more concern to place the phenomenon in the broader setting of the British polity.[25] W. F. Mandle, *Anti-Semitism and the British Union of Fascists* (London, 1968), provides a short, balanced treatment of anti-Semitism.

Skeletal groups of British fascists have lingered long beyond the war years. A recent psychological study of communists and fascists in Britain has made an interesting analytic comparison and differentiation of the two types. Both communists and fascists were found to be more rigid, authoritarian, tough-minded, emphatic, and intolerant of ambiguity than the control group with which they were compared. Communists proved to be more overtly dominant and covertly aggressive, fascists more overtly aggressive and covertly dominant. Communists were the least ethnocentric group studied, fascists the most, and in general more conservative than communists.[26] These differences between small groups of British communists and fascists around 1970 were probably representative of counterpart elements in European radical politics as a whole during the inter-war generation.

If British fascism was extremely weak, the only group usually identified as an Irish fascist party, the National Guard or Blueshirt movement of Eoin O'Duffy, really was never a fascist organization at all. This is the conclusion of the only serious study, Maurice Manning's *The Blueshirts* (Dublin, 1970), which narrates the entire history of the group in convincing style and demonstrates that the patriotic conservatism and militia antics of the Blueshirts, coupled with a vague doctrinal interest in corporatism, amounted to no more than a kind of Celtic Croix de Feu. O'Duffy was not the stuff of which Duces and Caudillos are made, and resigned the leadership of his movement in 1934. His subsequent National Corporate Party scarcely got off the ground.

A different problem is presented by the case of Portugal, which lived under a right-wing authoritarian system from 1926 to 1974. Despite or perhaps because of this there has been virtually no genuine fascism in Portugal. The New State of Dr António de Oliveira Salazar was a conservative corporatist régime that shunned every kind of radicalism, including fascism. It lacked a genuine party or mobilized movement, for the National Union of the régime was merely an official front, not an autonomous movement of mass mobilization. The Salazar system rested on the military and bureaucracy, had no drastic new modern ambitions, and maintained rural Portuguese society as little changed as possible. The only genuine fascist movement under Salazar was the National Syndicalist group organized by Rolão Preto in 1932. It propounded a kind of fascist syndicalism under radical, modernizing dictatorship, and with considerable exaggeration soon claimed to have 50,000 members. After an abortive revolt in 1934 the movement was dissolved by the government. Salazar denounced it as having been 'inspired by certain foreign models' and singled out the National Syndicalist 'exaltation of youth, and the cult of force through direct action, the principle of the superiority of state political power in social life, [and] the propensity for organizing masses behind a single leader'[27] as fundamental differences between fascism and the conservative Catholic corporatism of the New State.

The most serious brief effort at analysing the structure of Portuguese authoritarianism is an article by Herminio Martins,[28] but it fails to apply any rigorous definition of fascism and lumps the entire Salazar régime under that category. An historical grasp of the Portuguese system may best be obtained through A. H. de Oliveira Marques, *History of Portugal* (New York, 1972), vol. 2. The best biography of Salazar himself is Hugh Kay, *Salazar and Modern Portugal* (London, 1970), which strives for a degree of objectivity, while the most useful of the many laudatory accounts by rightists is Jacques Ploncard d'Assac, *Salazar* (Paris, 1967). On the Integralist movement of the monarchist right – the Portuguese equivalent of Action Française, whence it drew much inspiration – see Carlos Ferrão, *O Integralismo e a República*, 2 vols. (Lisbon, 1964–5), and Rivera Martins de Carvalho, *O Pensamento integralista perante o Estado Novo* (Lisbon, 1971). The legal structure of the Portuguese corporative system has been studied in the dissertation of Manuel de Lucena, 'L'Evolution du système corporatif portugais à travers des lois (1933–1971)' (Institut des Sciences Sociales du Travail, 1971).

The most important case among Western countries is that of Franquist Spain, whose political system, when all is said and done, has more nearly resembled that of fascist Italy than any other country. The analytical problem has been complicated by the need to define and interpret the significance of the fascist state party – in this case, Falange Española Tradicionalista – within the Spanish system. Once it was found in the 1950s that the Falange had no independence and virtually no autonomous significance within the Spanish system, it was judged by more and more observers that the Franquist system as a whole was not really fascist, and this conclusion was by any strict definition doubtless correct.

However, the existence of a strong, autonomous mass party cannot be made an independent variable in a strict definition of fascism, for after the late 1920s the Italian fascist party itself became largely a bureaucratic appendage of the state, deprived of any very significant element of autonomy. The fact that the Franquist system has gone through a series of distinct, sometimes almost contradictory, phases merely parallels the Italian experience, in which one may distinguish, for example, between (a) the radical fascist movement of 1919–22; (b) the Mussolini coalition régime of 1922–5; (c) the establishment of the pseudo-totalitarian fascist state system in 1925–8; (d) the conservative, pluralistic authoritarian régime of 1929–34; and (e) the imperialistic, increasingly radical, Nazi-influenced and emulatory policy of 1935–43. In the Spanish case, the Falange went through the first phase of radical but impotent fringe movement from 1931 to 1936, the Franco régime passed through the coalition phase, such as it was, in three months of civil war during 1936 rather than three years, and the régime then was increasingly influenced by the radical Nazi-fascist tide between late 1936 and early 1942. The weakness and marginality of Spain helped to save it from military involvement, and after the passing of the radical Nazi-fascist era in 1943–5, the Spanish régime finally settled into a 'normal', peacetime structure of conservative, pluralistic authoritarianism and semi-corporative economics, in many ways similar to Italian fascism during its middle phase of relative normalcy. Two main differences are that Franco as absolute leader enjoyed the powers of head of state as well as head of government – something that Mussolini never possessed – and after 1945 the party bureaucracy of the régime had to be downgraded as a political entity considerably more than in the Italian experience. The post-fascist phase of the régime was finally made official in 1958 when the original Twenty-Six Points of fascistic Falangist ideology were quietly dropped, to be replaced by a set of anodyne 'Principles of the Movement' that merely exhorted to patriotism, unity, morality, and national well-being.

Spanish fascism proper thus refers essentially to the Falange, and more precisely to the Falangist movement in its historical and ideological heyday, from 1931 to 1937, and more tenuously to 1942. When all is said and done, Spanish fascism as an independent political manifestation was remarkably weak, as weak as fascistic movements in other western and northern European countries. In the climactic elections of 1936 – the last parliamentary contest in Franco's lifetime – the Falange failed to elect a single candidate and garnered only 0.44 per cent of the vote. This performance was rivalled only by Mosley's group, was surpassed by Swedish and Norwegian Nazis (as well as Mussert's more equivocal Dutch group), and was greatly exceeded by the Belgian and French fascist organizations. Falangism completely failed to mobilize support so long as Spain retained anything resembling a functional parliamentary political system. It only gained affiliates as the polity began to enter a phase of direct collapse in the spring of 1936, and finally achieved mass expansion under the impact of revolutionary civil war. Those very conditions, however, deprived it of independent organization and personality, since the counter-revolutionary forces were completely under the command of the military. Mass Falangism was thus immediately taken over and subordinated by a reorganized Spanish right. The situation was in that sense more similar to Horthy's Hungary and Antonescu's Romania than to Italy and Germany.

The weakness of fascism in the regular Spanish polity was due above all to the remarkable absence of a militant, modern Spanish nationalism, which Falangism could not of itself incite. To this must be added the lagging secularization of the middle classes, which permitted the Catholic right virtually to monopolize the position of a new anti-left alternative on the one hand, and the vigour of the revolutionary left in Spain, on the other hand, which deprived radical Falangists of any hope of attracting non-rightists to an 'alternative revolution'.

Falangism and fascism in Spain should thus be studied in the broader context of the modern Spanish right, whose varied components participated in the creation of the semi-pluralist structure of the Franquist system. No broad over-arching study of the modern Spanish right exists. I have presented brief introductions in earlier articles,[29] and a survey of some of the preliminary ideological schema may be found in the sections on the Catholic right in Fredrick B. Pike, *Hispanismo, 1898–1936* (Notre Dame, 1971). The predecessor of Franquism was the Primo de Rivera dictatorship, but there is no adequate account of that, either. Dillwyn F. Ratcliff's *Prelude to Franco* (New York, 1957) is only the merest beginning. Equally useful is the semi-official apologium by Julián

Pemartín, *Los valores históricos de la Dictadura* (Madrid, 1929). Juan Velarde Fuertes, *Política económica de la Dictadura* (Madrid, 1968), is an able study of economic policy.

The fullest account of the Spanish right under the second Republic, whence issued the forces that later made up the Franco régime, will be found in Richard A. H. Robinson, *The Origins of Franco's Spain* (London, 1970), which may be supplemented with articles on Carlism by Martin Blinkhorn[30] and on Alfonsine right monarchism by Paul Preston.[31]

Ernesto Giménez Caballero, the first exponent of fascist ideas in Spain, has recently been the subject of a dissertation by Douglas Foard, 'Ernesto Giménez Caballero and the Revolt of the Esthetes' (Ph.D. diss., George Washington University, 1972). Tomás Borrás has published a lengthy apologetic biography of Spain's leading fascist intellectual of the thirties and the organizer of the first genuine fascist group, *Ramiro Ledesma Ramos* (Madrid, 1971), and Ledesma's own memoir-history of the early years of Falangism and pre-Falangism, *Fascismo en España?*, has been re-issued (Barcelona, 1970). It is a key source. A recent study of the thought of José Antonio Primo de Rivera, principal leader of the Falange – Adolfo Muñoz Alonso's *Un pensador para un pueblo* (Madrid, 1969) – discounts the fascistic values with which its subject was never at ease and emphasizes the individualist and humanist aspects of his thought. David Jato, *La rebelión de los estudiantes* (Madrid, 1967), deals with Falangism as student revolt. There are numerous memoir accounts in the form of regional histories or sketches of the pre-Civil War Falange, and new volumes continue to appear from time to time.

The first critical history of the Falange itself was my *Falange: A History of Spanish Fascism* (Stanford, 1961), which concentrated on the Falange as an independent political entity from 1931 to 1937, but also treated its later evolution to 1942, and closed with a brief account of the effort to revive the party as a strong political force in 1956. This was followed by another dissertation, Bernd Nellessen's *Die verbotene Revolution* (Hamburg, 1963), which is mainly restricted to the Republican period and concentrates on the ideology of the movement. The best brief account of early Falangism and its counterparts is the section on 'Los fascismos españoles', in Ricardo de la Cierva's *Historia de la Guerra Civil española*, vol. I, pp. 507–75 (Madrid, 1969).

The appearance of my book provoked a desire for self-justification on the part of the last independent national chief of the Falange, Manuel Hedilla, who had been ousted by Franco in 1937. Hedilla, grown wealthy in his later years, hired the Falangist journalist and historian Maximiano García Venero to prepare a political biography of Hedilla and give the *hedillista* version of the climactic phase of independent Falangist politics in 1936–7. García Venero collected a valuable and extensive series of depositions, interviews, and memoranda from old-guard Falangists and prepared a lengthy volume, but when it was finished Hedilla submitted to pressure from the Spanish government and refused permission to publish the work.

Undeterred, García Venero made arrangements with the emigré Spanish left-wing press, Ruedo Ibérico, to publish the book through the latter's facilities in Paris, insisting that the rights to the manuscript pertained to him exclusively. The publication of a quasi-fascist apologia by an organ that declared itself of the revolutionary left posed a problem that was nominally resolved with the participation of the emigré leftist North American bibliographer and polemicist, Herbert R. Southworth. An apparently vague agreement was reached by which the publication of the book would be accompanied by bibliographical and critical notes prepared by Southworth. Ruedo Ibérico then brought out García Venero's full account of *La Falange en la guerra de España: la Unificación y Hedilla* (Paris, 1967), an extensive hedillista apologia that nonetheless contained important new information and documentation. It was accompanied simultaneously by a volume of Southworth's entitled *Antifalange: Estudio crítico de ' Falange en la Guerra de España' de M. García Venero*, which subjected the preceding book to intense and hostile page-by-page criticism, as well as trying to elaborate a general theory of fascism based on the concept 'imperialism'. This situation infuriated both García Venero and Hedilla, the latter in the meantime having instituted a suit against the former, claiming that the manuscript was his property, not García Venero's, and trying to suppress publication in France.

Caught in a crossfire of acrimony between the hedillistas and the left, García Venero then tried to rectify his previous apologia by publishing in Spain a more critical account of the events of 1936–7 under the title *Historia de la unificación* (*Falange y Requeté en 1937*) (Madrid, 1970). Hedilla died that same year, and his heirs, holding Spanish title to the original manuscript, eventually published most of it in Spain, together with other justificatory material, as the *Testamento político de Manuel Hedilla* (Barcelona, 1972).

The best reconstruction of the climactic events of April 1937, when the Falange was taken over by Franco and transformed into a broader and more syncretic state party, has been made by Ricardo de la Cierva, 'La Trayectoria de la Falange hasta la unificación de 1937', in *Aproximación histórica a la guerra española* (*1936–1939*), pp. 205–40 (Madrid, 1970), and, in brief and general terms, in his *Historia ilustrada de la guerra civil española*, 2 vols (Barcelona, 1971). There is an excellent account of the evolution of the Falangist organization from fascist party to subordinate state bureaucracy by Juan J. Linz, 'From Falange to Movimiento-Organización: The Spanish Single Party and the Franco Régime, 1936–1968', in S. P. Huntington and C. H. Moore, eds., *Authoritarian Politics in Modern Society*, pp. 128–203 (New York, 1970).

Only three Falangist leaders have published noteworthy memoirs or collections of writings. Franco's brother-in-law, Ramón Serrano Súñer, who managed much of domestic politics during the first years of the régime before serving briefly as foreign minister during the central phase of the Second World War, soon afterwards wrote an account of his political career from 1937 to 1942 entitled *Entre Hendaya y Gibraltar* (Madrid, 1947). Though totally apologetic, it is nonetheless a significant source. Serrano's close personal friend, Dionisio Ridruejo, was one of the régime's first propaganda chiefs. His post, his fervour, and his dark hair and short stature all combined to earn him the nickname of the 'Spanish Goebbels'. Years later he became the 'Spanish Djilas' after renouncing Franquism in favour of Western-style social democracy and drawing a brief prison term from the régime. His personal memoir, *Escrito en España* (Buenos Aires, 1962), is a key work, the only frank and searching memoir by anyone who has held important office within the Franco régime. Finally, the Falange's principal leader after the Serrano years, José Luis de Arrese, has issued a collection of his principal writings, *Treinta años de política* (Madrid, 1966), and announces plans for the publication of his political memoirs.

Several works may be recommended for the study of the evolution of the Franco régime. The classic political definition of the régime itself is Juan J. Linz's article, 'An Authoritarian Régime: Spain', in E. Allardt and Y. Littunen, eds., *Cleavages, Ideologies and Party Systems*, pp. 251–83 (Helsinki, 1964). The non-fascist source of Franco's main political inspiration has been analysed by Richard A. H. Robinson, 'Genealogy and function of the Monarchist Myth of the Franco Régime', *Iberian Studies*, pp. 18–26 (Spring 1973). The best biography of Franco is J. W. D. Trythall's *El Caudillo* (New York, 1971). A milestone among apologetic biographies was reached, however, with the publication of the first volume of Ricardo de la Cierva's *Francisco Franco: Un siglo de España* (Madrid, 1973), which manages to be both laudatory and intellectually serious and contains much new information. Among contemporary analyses of the Franquist system, the best is Jacques Georgel, *Le Franquisme* (Paris, 1971). The transition from semi-fascist autarchy to neo-liberalism in Spanish economic policy has been studied by Charles Anderson, *The Political Economy of Modern Spain* (Madison, Wisc., 1970).

The thinking of part of the minority of remaining neo-Falangist activists in the 1970s may be gauged by a recent collection of their responses to a political questionnaire by Miguel Veyrat and J. L. Navas-Migueloa, *Falange, hoy* (Madrid, 1972). The full history of Falangism and Franquism is, however, still to be written.

To summarize some of the consequences that may be drawn from the historiography of fascism and Nazism in Western Europe, considerably more study remains to be done in at least four areas. Though monographic investigation has accelerated in the past ten years, thorough individual case studies remain to be done in most instances. Only the Doriot and Mosley movements have been adequately investigated.

Second, systematic and comparative analysis of the social basis of the various movements and parties needs to be greatly expanded in order to gain a clear and complete picture of their places in West European political society.

Third, the notion that fascists had little or no coherent ideology needs to be corrected – or perhaps corroborated – by a careful and systematic analysis of differences and similarities in doctrinal content and precise goals of these groups.

Fourth, more attention is warranted to the question of sequences or phases in the evolution or metamorphosis of the fascistic parties. This will help to determine the extent to which different emphases were elicited prior to and during the several phases of the German diplomatic and military hegemony.

Such a programme of research would then facilitate the filling of what has already been called the principal interpretive vacuum – a comparative analysis and categorization of West European fascist groups, and a more appropriate answer to the question whether or not there really was a distinctive western or northern European brand of fascism.

Notes

1. See Zeev Sternhell, 'Paul Déroulède and the Origins of Modern French Nationalism', *Journal of Contemporary History* (October 1971), pp. 46–71.

2. For the early effort in France to mobilize a radical nationalist syndicalism, see George L. Mosse, 'The French Right and the Working Classes: Les Jaunes', *Journal of Contemporary History* (July-October 1972), pp. 185–208.

3. Ernst Nolte, *Three Faces of Fascism* (New York, 1966), pp. 29–141.

4. Nolte, *Die Krise des liberalen Systems und die faschistischen Bewegungen* (Munich, 1968).

5. See Yves Guchet, 'Georges Valois ou l'illusion fasciste', *Revue Française de Science Politique* (December 1965).

6. Later, under German occupation, the party broadsided its own brief *Sommaire du Francisme* (Paris, 1941) that read very much like a transcription of the Italian system but scarcely mentioned the term fascism.

7. This aspect of Italian fascism has been studied by Michael Ledeen, *Universal Fascism* (New York, 1972).

8. Paul Sérant, *Le Romantisme fasciste* (Paris, 1959); Tarmo Kunnas,

Drieu La Rochelle, Céline, Brasillach et la Tentation fasciste (Paris, 1972); Jacqueline Morand, *Les Idées politiques de Louis-Ferdinand Céline* (Paris, 1972). Of the first two, Sérant's book is somewhat broader ranging, that of Kunnas more technical and systematic. A book of parallel usefulness is J.-L. Loubet del Bayle, *Les Non-conformistes des années 30* (Paris, 1969). Though it does not deal directly with fascism, it illuminates the mentality of restless young intellectuals seeking new alternatives.

9. Weber, *Varieties of Fascism* (New York, 1964), pp. 130–39, and H. Rogger and E. Weber, eds, *The European Right* (Berkeley and Los Angeles, 1965), pp. 71–127.

10. Girardet, 'Notes sur l'esprit d'un fascisme français, 1934–1939', *Revue Française de Science Politique* (1955), pp. 529–46.

11. Soucy, 'The Nature of Fascism in France', *Journal of Contemporary History* (1966), pp. 27–55; and 'French Fascism as Class Conciliation and Moral Regeneration', *Societas* (Autumn 1971), pp. 287–98.

12. The principal is G. D. Allardyce, 'The Political Transition of Jacques Doriot, 1926–1936' (Ph.D. diss., University of Iowa, 1966), of which a précis under the same title was published in the first number of the *Journal of Contemporary History*. Two other noteworthy dissertations on the movement towards national conciliation and corporatism among sectors of the French left are Stanley Grossman, 'Neo-Socialism: A Study in Political Metamorphosis' (Ph.D. diss., University of Wisconsin, 1969), and Martin Fine, 'Toward Corporatism: The Movement for Capital-Labor Collaboration in France, 1914–1936' (Ph.D. diss., University of Wisconsin, 1971).

13. Degrelle's two principal publications are *Die verlorene Legion* (Stuttgart, 1952), and *Hitler pour 1000 ans* (Paris, 1969), but see also Louise Narváez, *Degrelle m'a dit* (Paris, 1961).

14. Jean Stengers, 'Belgium', in Rogger and Weber, op. cit., pp. 128–67; Nolte, *Die Krise*, pp. 272–6; Littlejohn, *The Patriotic Traitors*, pp. 131–84; and F. L. Carsten, *The Rise of Fascism* (Berkeley and Los Angeles, 1967), pp. 204–18. R. Pfeiffer and J. Ladrière, *L'Aventure rexiste* (Brussels, 1966), is more of a denunciation than a study.

15. Michel Géoris-Reitshof, *Extrème droite et néo-fascisme en Belgique* (Brussels, 1962).

16. Littlejohn, op. cit., pp. 83–130, and Nolte, *Die Krise*, op. cit., pp. 276–9.

17. Hayes, 'Quisling's Political Ideas', *Journal of Contemporary History* (Autumn 1966), pp. 145–57.

18. T. K. Derry, 'Norway', in S. J. Woolf, ed., *European Fascism* (London, 1968), pp. 217–30.

19. There is an account of the early years of the Nasjonal Samling by Hans Olof Brevig, *NS fra parti til sekt, 1933–1937* (Oslo, 1970); a general work by Hans Fredrik Dahl, *Hva er fascisme? Et essay om fascismens historie og sosiologie* (Oslo, 1972), that pays special attention to Norway; and a controversial psychohistorical study of Quisling by Sverre Hartman, *Forvarsminister Quisling – hans bagrunn og vei inn i norsk politikk* (Oslo, 1970).

(For these and succeeding references to works in Scandinavian languages I am indebted to my colleague Professor Pekka Hämäläinen.)

20. Nolte, *Die Krise*, op. cit., pp. 268–72.

21. The historian of Swedish Nazism is Eric Wärenstam, whose basic work is *Fascismen och nazismen i Sverige 1920–1940* (Stockholm, 1970). A subsequent somewhat popularized version, *Fascismen och nazismen i Sverige* (Stockholm, 1972), includes a chapter on the war years. An earlier study deals with radical right elements in the Swedish conservative youth movement, *Sveriges nationella ungdomsforbund och högern 1928–1934* (Stockholm, 1965). Some information on the influence of fascist and Nazi ideas on conservative and peasant groups in Sweden may be found in Rolf Torstendahl, *Mellan nykonservatismoch liberalism* (Uppsala, 1969). M. D. Shepard has written a dissertation on the leading figure of the non-Nazi radical right in Sweden, 'Adrian Molin, Study of a Swedish Right-wing Radical' (Ph.D. diss., Northwestern University, 1969).

Accounts of the Danish Nazis concentrate on the German occupation period, the only time in which they were of the slightest importance. The main work is Henning Poulsen, *Besaettelsesmagten og de danske nazister. Det politiske forhold mellem tyske myndigheder og nazistisken kredse i Danmark 1940–43* (Copenhagen, 1970), but there is also information in Erich Thomsen, *Deutsche Besatzungspolitik in Dänemark, 1940–1945* (Düsseldorf, 1971). Peter Gordy is currently completing a dissertation on Danish nazism at the University of Wisconsin.

22. Rintala, 'Finland', in Rogger and Weber, *The European Right*, pp. 408–22.

23. A. F. Upton, 'Finland', in Woolf, op. cit., pp. 184–216.

24. To cite only the book-length studies: A three-volume work by N. V. Hersalo and Hannes Raikkala, *Suojeluskuntain Historia* (Vassa, 1962–6), deals with the Civic Guards, a rightist paramilitary force sympathetic to fascistic ideas; P. K. Hämäläinen, *Nationalitetskampen och sprakstriden i Finland 1917–1939* (Helsinki, 1969), deals with the language controversy and includes information on fascistic influences on both of Finland's linguistic groups; Lauri Hyvämäki, *Sinistä ja mustaa. Tutkielmia Suomen oikeistoridikalismista* (Helsinki, 1971), contains several articles on Lapua and the extreme right; and Risto Alapuro, *Akateeminen Karjala-Seura* (Helsinki, 1973), is a sociological study of the Academic Karelia Society, the radical nationalist student organization which developed strong fascistic sympathies.

25. Mention might also be made of James S. Barnes, *The Universal Aspects of Fascism* (London, 1928), probably the major English eulogy of Italian fascism, as an idealized expression of what English admirers thought worthy of emulation.

26. H. J. Eysenck and T. T. Coulter, 'The Personality and Attitudes of Working-Class British Communists and Fascists', *Journal of Social Psychology* (June 1972), pp. 59–73.

27. Jacques Ploncard d'Assac, *Salazar* (Paris, 1967), p. 107.

28. Martins, 'Portugal', in Woolf, op. cit., pp. 302–36.

29. 'Spain', in Rogger and Weber, *The European Right*, pp. 168–207, and, on the problem of nationalism, 'Spanish Nationalism in the Twentieth Century', *Review of Politics* (July 1964), pp. 403–22.

30. 'Carlism and the Spanish Crisis of the 1930s', *Journal of Contemporary History* (July-October 1972), pp. 65–88. Blinkhorn is the author of a dissertation on the politics of Carlism, 1931–6, which is currently in press.

31. 'Alfonsist Monarchism and the Spanish Civil War', *Journal of Contemporary History* (July-October 1972), pp. 89–114.

Part IV

ZEEV STERNHELL

9 Fascist Ideology

While in our political vocabulary there are not many terms that have enjoyed such a considerable vogue as the word *fascism*, there are equally not many concepts in contemporary political terminology so notoriously blurred and imprecise in outline.

It would seem, in fact, that the study of fascism is still in its infancy, and that there are too few scholars anxious to avail themselves of a thorough understanding of this phenomenon. Such researches as are made are hampered, too, by the way fascism, which was supremely nationalistic and therefore above all exclusive, flourished in markedly different backgrounds – in the great industrial centres of Western Europe, as in the under-developed countries of Eastern Europe – and from its very beginnings appealed as much to the intellectual élite of the day as to unread peasants. Fascism has no sound and obvious footing in any particular social class, and its intellectual origins are in themselves confusing. In its most restricted sense the word *fascism* applies simply to the political régime in Italy in the period between the two world wars; at the other end of the scale, the 'fascist' epithet is used, and particularly by left wingers of various hue, as *the* term of abuse par excellence, conclusive and unanswerable.

The emotional content of this word has for a long time contributed to obscuring a political concept that was never in the first place very clear. When Mussolini and Léon Blum, Franklin D. Roosevelt, Franco and José Antonio, Codreanu, Pilsudski, Henri de Man, Joseph McCarthy, and Charles de Gaulle have each and all in their turn been labelled fascists, what then could fascism signify? And for as long as socialists were known as social fascists to the communists, while the Prussian Junkers, the Italian Conservatives, or the French Croix-de-Feu movement were designated as fascist by the very people whom Togliatti, Thorez, and

Thälmann denounced as fascists, how could it be possible, even
for the majority of politically sophisticated people, to discern
what fascism really meant?

Though the 1960s[1] have seen a break-through, in that the first
overall investigations of the subject have enabled us to block out
the shape of fascism in a way which only a few years ago would
not have been possible, yet it is clear that it is still no easy matter
to pinpoint fascism precisely, and that there still exists no definition of fascism acceptable to all, or recognized as universally
valid. We may with some justice feel more optimistic than Professor Hugh Seton-Watson, whose opinion it is that scientific precision is not at present obtainable and one may doubt whether it
ever will be,[2] but we cannot for that reason overlook the difficulties.

We should remember, however, that it is no easier to define
democracy: the concepts are too broad for the words. It is highly
probable that no single historical example can meet the exacting
requirement of a carefully constructed 'model' of fascism or of
democracy. That is what Professor N. Kogan may have had in
mind when, after having carefully constructed a six-point model
of fascism, and after drawing many of his examples of fascist
thought and practice from the Italian régime, he concludes rather
surprisingly that in actual practice 'Italy under fascism was not a
fascist state.'[3] This is indeed true, if Kogan is suggesting that Italy
under fascism was not an *ideal* fascist state, and the identical
demonstration could be applied to democracy or to communism:
what is the ideal model of democracy or of communism, what,
exactly, are its component parts, and where is it put into practice?

The task becomes more complex still when we narrow the field
of inquiry to the ideology of fascism. For many years, after all, it
was common form to see fascism either as completely wanting in
concepts or as having gotten itself up for the sake of the cause in a
few rags of doctrine, which therefore need not be taken seriously,
nor allowed even the minimal importance that is attached as a
rule to the ideas professed by a political movement. This attitude
was almost certainly bound up with a fundamental refusal to
view fascism as anything other than a horrid *lapsus* in European

history: in conceding to fascism a theoretical dimension one might have granted it a place and a significance in the history of our times, which many people, both of the right and of the left, and often for reasons that are at one and the same time similar and conflicting, were reluctant to do.

Furthermore, the official Marxist interpretation of fascism, which conceives of it as the creature of monopoly or finance capitalism and its ideology – a crude rationalization of capitalist interests – has also helped to keep the study of fascist ideology at a standstill. There was a long period when the very suggestion that fascism could be a mass movement, sustained by an ideology well suited to the necessities of modern politics and of mass society, ran *contra bona mores*, and throughout the war years the man who took this line was suspected – sometimes with good reason – if not of collaborating with fascism or nazism, then at least of evincing towards them a favourable attitude.

There were other interpretations of fascism which chose to argue, not that fascism or national socialism were lacking an ideology, but that the ideology was purely incidental and unimportant. They held that Mussolini and Hitler had come to power without stressing the nature of their doctrine, or once in power had not put doctrine into practice, and could therefore be characterized as nothing more than adventurers and opportunists with neither creed nor principle. It bears saying that this kind of reasoning is not often brought into play in the analysis of communism; and yet no one could pretend to discern in the October Revolution or in the seizure of power by other communist parties a meticulous putting into practice of the ideas propounded by Marx or Lenin, or any one of their disciples. It would be hard indeed to claim that the proceedings of the Soviet state are governed by an unfailing concern to see that policy conforms to the requirements of Marxist philosophy. Who would be capable, for that matter, of determining from day to day what those requirements were? And who would be recognized as competent to do so?

And yet, communist ideology is widely studied in order to obtain insights into communist behaviour; it is generally considered essential to our understanding of communism as a general system of social and political organization. There is no reason why an identical method should not be applied to fascism. Moreover, as Professor Eugen Weber has pointed out, even when fascist or national-socialist manifestoes were not really carried out, or even if they had not been carried out at all, we could still learn a good deal by examining them, especially if we compare them to similar programmes or doctrines evolved in other countries, and perhaps in other circumstances. Politicians as well as political scientists know very well that platforms and ideologies are significant, part-, ly because they do tell us something about what the candidate and his party think (would like to think, or would like the public to think they think), and partly because they reflect a public: the issues this public is likely to be affected by, to vote for, or in some way to support.[4]

This paper deals with fascism: it is confined to fascism and it deliberately omits nazism for reasons of space and division of labour between contributors, as well as for reasons of substance. A discussion of nazism would have widened its scope far beyond what can reasonably be contained within the framework of this volume, for nazism cannot, as I see it, be treated as a mere variant of fascism: its emphasis on biological determinism rules out all efforts to deal with it as such. The question is already a highil complicated one, and an examination of the specific characteristics of nazism, over and above what it has in common with fascism, would require not so much a study of fascism as a comparative analysis of fascism and nazism. This holds true even if one regards nazism as an exacerbated form of fascism: the exacerbation of a political phenomenon being in itself a new and different phenomenon. This is not to say that in certain strains of fascism there was no racialist factor: there was a school of fascism in France, for example, which in this respect resembled nazism more closely than it did Italian fascism. All in all, however, the evidence obliges us to concede that there comes a point when the degree of extremism in a political movement radically alters the very nature of that movement.

Furthermore, this article will confine itself to the study of fascist ideology. The term *ideology*, as Professor Martin Seliger has put it, is used to refer to a conceptual frame of reference which provides criteria for choice and decision by virtue of which the major activities of an organized community are governed. Therefore, the sets of ideas by which men explain and justify the ends and means of organized social action, with the aim of preserving or reconstructing a given reality, are ideologies. Two dimensions of ideological argumentation, however, can be observed in day-to-day politics. All action-oriented thought, from political philosophy down to party ideology, contains pragmatic considerations from the outset. For a party or movement holding power or engaged in the contest for power, the need inevitably arises for a more or less frank restatement of immediate goals. In shaping specific policies to deal with prevailing circumstances, no party has ever been able to avoid committing itself to lines of action which are irreconcilable with, or at least doubtfully related to, the basic principles and goals set out in its ideology. A conflict results not simply between ideology and action, but within ideology itself. The problem of preserving the movement's doctrinal purity exists in the parties of all political systems, and its existence attests to the fact of two-dimensional argumentation.[5]

Therefore the first crucial distinction in a discussion of fascist ideology is that between fascism in power and fascism in opposition, between movements and régimes, between origins and maturity. Fascism in power was something to which fascist parties made remarkably different contributions, depending on the country concerned. Every country where there was a fascist party had peculiarities duly reflected in its local political organizations; nevertheless, where a so-called fascist régime came into being, these national features usually became even more exaggerated. Thus movements have much more in common than régimes. They have indeed a great deal in common, and it is from this that a clear notion of what fascist ideology amounted to can be derived.[6]

Mussolini and the other fascist leaders were quite correct in arguing that the basic doctrinal postulates of fascist régimes had something of a universal character; but until the mid-sixties, strangely enough, the universalistic aspect of fascist doctrine was almost completely overlooked. And yet fascist ideologues never tired of announcing that fascism was, in the words of Sir Oswald Mosley, 'a worldwide creed. Each of the great political faiths in its turn has been a universal movement: conservatism, Liberalism and Socialism are common to nearly every country . . . In this respect, fascism occupies precisely the same position.'[7] Mussolini had already argued that 'Fascism as an idea, a doctrine, a realisation, is universal,' because 'never before have the peoples thirsted for authority, direction, order, as they do now. If each age has its doctrine, the innumerable symptoms indicate that the doctrine of our age is the Fascist one.'[8]

The second distinction to be borne in mind is between what, like Seliger, we may call the fundamental and the operative dimensions of ideology: the fundamental principles determining the final goals, and the operative ideology whose purpose it is to justify the policies actually devised or executed by a party. Deviations from the fundamentals are a universal phenomenon:[9] fascist movements and fascist régimes cannot be considered more unprincipled than any other movement or régime, especially where these are revolutionary. Writing on this issue in *The Communist Party of the Soviet Union* (London, 1960), Leonard Shapiro points out that he has 'as yet not discovered a single instance in which the party was prepared to risk its own survival in power for considerations of doctrine.' This does not mean that the clash between theory and practice never caused serious difficulties, of the same kind indeed as occurred in Italy and Germany, or within any one of the other fascist parties. Much of fascist opportunism, its practice of legitimizing intermediate goals no matter how much they conflicted with fundamental principles, is inherent in the nature of every ideology called upon to shape a new society. There is no denying though that as the gap widens between the final objectives and the initial blueprint for the remodelling of society, the discrepancy between ideology and practice becomes more important and thus encourages the tendency to accuse the régime of opportunism, or to disregard completely the ideology on which it claims to rely.

The adaptation of ideologies to changing conditions, be it falsely evaluated facts or unforeseen consequences of the realization of principles, is as general a phenomenon as the fact that no major piece of organization remains for long without ideological cover, even supposing it can come into existence without it in the first place.

In this respect therefore fascist ideology, far from being exceptional, rather proved the rule. Yet it is also true that here was an ideology which in fact aimed to be pragmatic as well as revolutionary and keep a firm grasp on everyday realities. Mussolini made it a political principle that fascist ideology be adaptable to the necessities of real life: ideology 'must not be a shirt of Nessus clinging to us for all eternity, for tomorrow is something mysterious and unforeseen.' Equally he was well aware that ideological argumentation existed on two different levels. Writing forty years ago, Mussolini anticipated some of the latest achievements of modern political science, and made a clear-cut division between 'the modest tables of our laws and programmes – the theoretical and practical guidance of fascism' and 'the fundamentals of doctrine', commenting that the former 'should be revised, corrected, enlarged, developed, because already in places they have suffered injury at the hand of time.'[10]

In promulgating an ideology that would be closely linked to action, both by inspiring action and by reflecting it,[11] and in developing the theory of the unity of thought and action, Mussolini clearly enunciated, and took to himself, a principle which other ideologies might cry down, but which they yet were obliged to put into practice on their own account. The difference between fascists and socialists or communists came down to this: for the latter, as stern guardians of an unalterable doctrine, were compelled to endless rigmaroles and pretexts and a myriad of explanations to justify the process of development, which for the fascists was in the nature of things political, since they insisted not only on the continual adaptation of ideologies to meet practical necessities, and the constant evolution of ideology insofar as the realities changed, but also on the importance of supplying ideological cover to such sectors of political reality as were lacking in it.

Fascism in its various forms was confined in the main to the role of a political movement: only in two countries did it go on to the actual seizure of power – and in Germany, at that, in a particularly exacerbated form – so that the fascist era may be said to have been an era of political movements rather than of régimes. In any case where the history of ideas is concerned, it is the political movement which is of greater interest. It can be traced with advantage back to its origins, to the source which, being more pure, illustrates an outline as yet unmuddied. Fascist ideology in all its essentials is best perceived in its origins, and fascist movements can be seen for what they really are before they have acceded to power and been transformed by compromise and pressure into yet another governmental party. The true nature of doctrines, and the differences between them, are always more clearly seen in the shape of their aspirations than when put into practice.

The intellectual crisis of the 1890s

In February 1936 the French review *Combat*, which was sympathetic to the fascists, published an article entitled *Fascisme 1913*,[12] by Pierre Andreu, one of the most faithful and authentic of Georges Sorel's disciples, in which he remarked on the curious synthesis of syndicalists and nationalists centered around the author of *Reflections on Violence*, and in nationalist circles connected with Action Française, immediately before the outbreak of the First World War. At about the same time, a similar comment came from Pierre Drieu La Rochelle, who a few months later – and in company with Bertrand de Jouvenel, a young economist of the left – became one of the leading intellectuals in the PPF, the largest of the French fascist parties. He observed that, 'looking back on that period, we can see how by 1913 certain elements of the fascist atmosphere had already come together in France, before they did in other countries. There were young men from all classes of society, fired by a love of heroism and violence, who dreamed of fighting what they termed the evil on two fronts – capitalism and parliamentary socialism – while culling from each what to them seemed good. Already the marriage between nationalism and socialism was on the cards.'[13]

The self-same formula had already been used in 1925 by Georges Valois, the founder of the first non-Italian fascist movement, Le Faisceau, to define the idea in which the substance of the phenomenon was contained: 'Nationalism + socialism = fascism.'[14] Some ten years later Sir Oswald Mosley picked it up in his turn: 'If you love our country you are national, and if you love our people you are socialist.'[15] It was a powerfully clear and simple idea, possessing immense attraction, and by the time the former Labour minister came to found the British Union of Fascists it was already shared by all the European fascist movements.

The shock of the war and its immediate consequences no doubt precipitated the birth of fascism as a political movement, but its ideological roots in fact go back to the years 1880–90, when an alliance sprang up between theories deriving from one or another type of socialism – whether non-Marxist, anti-Marxist, or indeed post-Marxist – and from nationalism. Those were the incubation years of fascism, as is attested to by Valois or Drieu, and equally by Gentile or by Mussolini. For on the eve of the First World War the essentials of fascist ideology were already well defined. The word did not exist yet, but the phenomenon it would eventually designate had its own autonomous existence, and thenceforward awaited only a favourable combination of circumstances in which to hatch into a political force. Fascist ideology is seen therefore as the immediate product of a crisis that had overtaken democracy and liberalism, and bourgeois society in all its fundamental values: the break-away was so disruptive as to take on the dimensions of a crisis in civilization itself.

Fascism was not a reflection of Marxism, nor did it come into existence simply as a reaction to organized Marxism; it had the same degree of autonomy that Marxism had, in that both were products of bourgeois society and reacted against that society, compared to which they each presented a radical alternative; both were agreed in that they put forward a new pattern of civilization. The growth of fascism therefore cannot be understood, or fully explained, unless it is seen in the intellectual, moral, and cultural context which prevailed in Europe at the end of the nineteenth century.

The changes that took place at this time, within the space of a single generation, were so profound that it would be no exaggeration to speak of them as constituting an intellectual revolution,[16] which in its themes and style was to pave the way for the mass politics of our own century. For the vast movement of thought of the 1890s was above all a movement of revolt: revolt against the world of matter and reason, against materialism and positivism, against the mediocrity of bourgeois society, and against the muddle of liberal democracy. To the *fin-de-siècle* mind, civilization was in crisis, and if a solution were possible it would have to be a total one.

The generation of 1890 – which included among others, d'Annunzio and Corradini in Italy, Barrès, Drumont, and Sorel in France, Paul de Lagarde, Julius Langbehn and Arthur Moeller van den Bruck in Germany – took as its point of departure not the individual, who as such had no importance in himself, but the social and political collectivity, which, moreover, was not to be thought of as the numerical sum of the individuals under its aegis. The 'new' intellectuals therefore inveighed violently against the rationalistic individualism of liberal society and against the dissolution of social links in bourgeois society. In identical terms sometimes, they one and all deplored the mediocrity and materialism of modern society, its instability and corruption. They decried the life of the great cities, which was dominated by routine with no room for heroism, and to the claims of the individual's powers of reason they preferred the merits of instinct, sometimes even of animality. Such is the soil to which Giovanni Gentile traces the root-origins of fascism, which he defines as a 'revolt against positivism'[17] and against the way of life fostered by industrial society, which revolt broke out at a time when the intellectual atmosphere was saturated with Darwinian biology and Wagnerian aesthetics, Gobineau's racialism, Le Bon's psychology, as well as the black prophecies of Nietzsche and Dostoevsky, and, later, the philosophy of Bergson.

Of course neither Bergson's philosophy nor Nietzsche's are to be confused with the use to which they have been put at the hands of the 'dread simplificators' and other exponents, any more than we attribute to Darwin the social Darwinism touted by the generation that came after him. And yet, though philosophers and scientists cannot be held responsible for the uses made of their teachings, for the way they are interpreted and the meaning read into their thoughts, it was nevertheless their teachings which, when put into the hands of a thousand minor intellectuals who frequently had little aptitude for careful philosophical reasoning, shaped a new intellectual climate. In the aftermath of the dreadful shock of the war, the Soviet revolution, and the economic crisis, that intellectual climate allowed fascism to burgeon and grow into a powerful mass movement. For the masses were by then well conditioned to accept a new interpretation of the world and of human realities, and even a new morality, as the foundations of a new order.

The contributions made by scientists and pseudo-scientists to this new vision of the world were in point of fact legion. As the notion of social Darwinism gained widespread acceptance, it stripped the human personality of its sacramental dignity. It made no distinction between the physical life and the social life, and conceived of the human condition in terms of an unceasing struggle, whose natural outcome was the survival of the fittest. Positivism also felt the impact of social Darwinism, and underwent a profound change. In the latter half of the century its emphasis on deliberate and rational choice as the determining factor in human behaviour gave way to new notions of heredity, race, and environment.[18] Thus, social Darwinism played a large part in the evolution of nationalism and the growth of modern racialism. So too its influence is clearly to be seen in the interest taken by the generation of 1890 in the study of psychology and the discovery of the unconscious. For the new theories of social and political psychology rejected out of hand the traditional mechanistic concept of man, which asserted that human behaviour is governed by rational choice. Opinion now dictated that sentiment and feeling count for more in political questions than reasoning, and fostered contempt for democracy and its institutions and workings.

Throughout Europe the same fears and the same passions began to find expression at the same moment, and men from very different backgrounds, engaged in fields of study that were often quite unrelated to one another, each played their part in the formulation of the new ideology. The onslaught on bourgeois society went hand-in-hand with the wholesale condemnation of liberal democracy and parliamentary government, for one of the ideological tenets common to this whole vast protest movement was the reforming of all institutions in the authoritarian mould. The call for a leader, a saviour embodying all the virtues of the race, was to be heard throughout Europe, at the turn of the century. When the march of events gainsaid these theories, the setback was invariably blamed on a plot, and the instigators, also invariably, identified as Jews and Freemasons hand-in-glove with the international financiers. The men who at the turn of the century revolted against positivism, and also against liberalism and socialism which they regarded as a vague form of positivism to be treated in a similar manner, joined forces not merely to attack certain social structures or the nature of political institutions, but also to impeach Western civilization itself, which in their eyes was fundamentally corrupt.

It must be stressed too that these rebels were not men relegated to the fringes of contemporary opinion. Whatever the verdict of the historian of ideas on the intrinsic worth of their individual writings, it must be said that it is not the historians who fashion the sensibilities of a bygone generation. The men who put together the ingredients of fascist ideology, as it was on the eve of the Great War, were well-known interpreters, rendering into common language the work accomplished by the giants of their own or of the previous generation. They brought within reach of the general reader a system of ideas which was not easily understood, and which they themselves from time to time deformed or oversimplified. Such are the writers who in point of fact inform the everyday reader of newspapers and popular novels, the average university and high school student, and the people who in the counties and country towns make up a social élite, and who in their day enjoyed a tremendous success. Julius Langbehn was renowned from the year 1890, when he published *Rembrandt als Erzieher*, the book in which he denounced the intellectual and scientific bent of German civilization, and sang instead the praises of irrationalism. The two ensuing decades saw Arthur Moeller van den Bruck steadfastly renewing the attack on liberalism and democracy, until he came to fame in 1922 with *Das Dritte Reich*.[19] The same is true of the Italian and French writers: d'Annunzio, Barrès, and Maurras ranked among the most important intellectuals of their generation, while Drumont's works went into more reprints than any other publication of the last century. Their thinking took root throughout the Latin- and French-oriented regions of Europe: they had an immense influence not only in Italy and France but in Spain, Switzerland, Belgium, and Eastern Europe, particularly in Romania. There was a professor at the Sorbonne, by the name of Jules Soury, who in 1902 published a book called *Campagne Nationaliste* – along the same lines as *Mein Kampf* – and was acclaimed as the equal of Bergson, while Gustave Le Bon was quoted at some length by the father of psychoanalysis and was sometimes seen as another Freud. Given the number of men writing on the subject, one may wonder if their prolific output does not account in some measure for the inattentive reception accorded to Hitler; for the author of *Mein Kampf* had nothing to say which had not already been said, and not by men of the lunatic fringe, but rather by the ranking intellectuals of the day.

In the years preceding the First World War Europe experienced an extraordinary revival of nationalism. Well before 1914 *Völkisch* ideology, the set of ideas which are crucial to the understanding of nazism, had found a widespread acceptance in German society, notwithstanding a remarkable flowering of the intellectual disciplines in that country, reminiscent of the classical period around 1800, over which Völkisch ideology nevertheless gained the upper hand. It must not be forgotten that, as Professor George Mosse has pointed out, the Nazis found their greatest support among respectable and educated people. Their ideas were eminently respectable in Germany after the First World War, and indeed had been current among large segments of the population even before the war. The essential element here is the linking of the human soul with its natural surroundings, with the 'essence' of nature, that the real and important truths are to be found beneath surface appearances. According to many Völkisch theorists, the nature of the soul of a Volk is determined by the nature of the landscape. Thus, the Jews, being a desert people, are regarded as shallow and dry people, devoid of profundity and totally lacking in creativity. Because of the barrenness of the desert landscape, the Jews are a spiritually barren people.[20]

The self-same themes are to be met in the nationalist ideology of France: the Frenchman, nurtured by his soil and his dead, cannot escape the destiny shaped for him by past generations, by the landscapes of his childhood, the blood of his forebears. The nation is a living organism, and nationalism is therefore an ethic, comprising all the criteria of behaviour which the common interest calls for, and on which the will of the individual has no bearing. The duty both of the individual and of society is to find out what this ethic may be, yet only those can succeed who have a share in the 'national consciousness', shaped over the course of the centuries: the Jews, as a foreign race, cannot enter upon this quest.[21]

In Italy, d'Annunzio and Corradini were the best-known spokesmen for a nationalist movement which reached far and deep, feeding on external defeat, as it had done in France in the aftermath of 1870. It was this movement indeed which by 1915 had brought Italy into the war, looking to war for glory. In France the young men of the coming generation were fired by patriotism, by a zeal for order, authority, and discipline, and were morally at the ready for war, many years before August 1914.

This resurgence of nationalism accounts, at least in part, for the failure of international socialism, and explains why the working class set off for war on a wave of patriotism, regardless of their long-standing tradition of anti-militarism and of countless resolutions adopted at each and every Socialist Congress. Throughout the years separating the two wars, the workers' movement did not recover, morally speaking, from this defeat, and it would weigh heavily in the balance when the fascist movements began to come to a head, and particularly, of course, in Italy.

Nationalism, socialism, and anti-liberalism

During the nineteenth century, nationalism and liberalism had combined to become a force for liberation and emancipation; nationalism was deeply imbued with democratic and universalist values, and inherited from the French Revolution and from the philosophy of natural rights. But then when it came under pressure from new economic conditions and from the bitter competition these conditions provoked on the world market – as this competition pointed up the divergent interests of the great European powers; as it was seen how unity in Italy and Germany was born of fire and blood; and as the impact of social Darwinism, and then of Marxist and internationalist socialism, made itself felt – nationalism gradually changed its character.

In the shape it had acquired by the beginning of this century the nationalist movement, in France as in Italy, bore little resemblance to the nationalist aspirations of Michelet or of Mazzini; the nationalist spirit abroad in 1848 died out, for the French after Sedan, for the Italians after Adowa. The collapse of the Ethiopian campaign in 1896 was seen by Enrico Corradini, the spiritual and political leader of the Italian nationalists, as the collapse of the Italian democratic movement and its supporters on the extreme left. The French nationalists – Déroulède, Barrès, Maurras – opined that the defeat of 1870 had been inflicted on a country already undermined by a revolutionary ideology, by rationalism and individualism. The Republic's inability to avenge the country's humiliation and restore to France her lost provinces, or even simply to prepare for war, stemmed from the fundamental weakness of liberal democracy, its impotence and incoherence. So it was that the new European nationalism became first and foremost a movement of revolt against democracy and a violent critique of the régime in all its weakness, incoherence and impersonal character: it was a party to the general revolt against the values inherited from the French Revolution and the Enlightenment.

At the same time the new nationalism produced diatribes against the rich and against economic injustices; it denounced liberal democracy both as a pattern of government and as a socioeconomic system, it demanded that the State take up authoritarian attitudes, and it attacked social injustices in the name of group solidarity. The nationalist movements sought to mobilize the most disadvantaged of the social classes, the people who were threatened by new techniques of industrial production and new forms of commercialization. This was the background that promoted the growth of a new variant of socialism – in France during the 1890s, in Italy or in Austria during the first decade of the twentieth century – which was not Marxist and not internationalist, but emphatically national. It was then that French nationalists first saw the possibilities of a synthesis of a certain type of socialism and of the nationalists' political authoritarianism, which went on to find acceptance in the Italian nationalist circles led by Corradini, and then among followers of Sorel and Mussolini, and finally gave birth to a fully structured fascist ideology.

Indeed in May 1898, during the period of violent unrest stirred up by the Dreyfus Affair, it was Maurice Barrès, while standing as the nationalist candidate for Nancy, who first coined the term 'Socialist Nationalism',[22] which owes its origins to the idea that national cohesion would come about through the solution of the social question. Twenty years later, Enrico Corradini announced at the Nationalist Convention, 'First and foremost, since it is by definition national in politics, nationalism cannot be anything other than national in economics also, since the latter is the basis of the former.'[23] As for Maurras, he declared that there was a 'form of socialism which, when stripped of its democratic and cosmopolitan accretions, would fit in with nationalism just as a well-made glove fits a beautiful hand',[24] and at his instigation Action Française made a considerable play for the support of the workers, from the moment it was realized how powerful was the disaffection of the proletariat from the liberal State.

A further experiment, which was nothing less than a trial run for fascism was the founding in 1903 of a National Socialist party, by a former socialist, Pierre Biétry. It was succeeded a year later by the Fédération Nationale des Jaunes de France. Yellow socialism – as opposed to Red socialism – preached national solidarity in lieu of the class struggle, and advocated the accession to property rather than expropriation, as well as workers' participation in company profits and a form of trade unionism in which workers' unions and management unions would exist side by side, which structure would be topped by a strong State, with an assembly of national and regional representatives sponsored by the trades and corporations. It goes without saying that the Yellow Movement was violently opposed to Marxism, while at the same time promoting the personality cult of the leader, who was in effect its mini-dictator; it was equally anti-Semitic. The Fédération des Jaunes de France, which has been described as 'obsessed with the idea of wresting the working class out of its socialist rut', was undoubtedly the first to try out the whole apparatus of fascist ideas in practical terms.[25] The French movement played the role of model for the Swiss and German yellow organizations with which it was closely connected. At the same time Austria produced the DAP (the German Workers' Party), founded the very year Biétry was launching his PSN.

National socialism was anti-Semitic, for anti-Semitism – social as well as racial – was the perfect tool for the integration of the proletariat within the national community and had the advantage of rallying the petty bourgeoisie in danger of proletarianization. Anti-Semitism gave the new radical right popular foundations and provided it with an instrument with which to appeal to the working classes and to arouse the masses: the anti-Jewish riots of the closing years of the century[26] bear a curious resemblance, by their violence and their scale, to the riots of the Nazis. The psychological determinism of someone like Jules Soury was no less influential than the racialism propagated by Houston Stewart Chamberlain or Alfred Rosenberg.[27] What early National-Socialism lacked was the social backdrop which would transform it into a political force: there were as yet no huge numbers of unemployed and frightened petty bourgeois, and no impoverished middle classes; it was fully possessed, however, of a framework of ideas no less developed than those of any other contemporary political movement.

Where all the European currents of nationalism were agreed of course was in their anti-parliamentarism. By the end of the 1880s nationalism and anti-parliamentarism had already coalesced in France. The synthesis of the two, when for the first time translated into political terms, evolved into *boulangisme*, the movement that launched on liberal democracy the first of the attacks to which henceforth it would be subjected. By the end of the decade a pattern of events had been established which thereafter became the classic gearing-in to fascism – namely, the shift from far left to far right of people with radical views on social problems and deeply opposed to liberal democracy. It had also become apparent how easily great sections of the working people could give their support to a party that took its social values from the left and its political values from the right, if by so doing they could make clear their dislike for liberal democracy or bourgeois society. This was where *boulangisme* broke new ground and opened the way to fascism.

Within two decades a very similar pattern of events took place in Italy: Italian nationalism was profoundly averse to the democratic movement backed by the extreme left, and here too the nationalist movement turned to the workers and peasants. Enrico Corradini began to elaborate on topics that foreshadowed corporatism, complemented by an unambiguous preference for protectionism and other measures designed to appeal to the nation as a whole, such as the expansion of Italian industry and commerce abroad, and a colonial solution to the problems of population and emigration. A political programme relying on colonialism and protectionism and corporatism might perhaps have the right solution and seemed to hold out hope and the prospect of betterment to a whole bloc of society, while at the same time taking great pains not to exacerbate the class struggle.[28]

Corradini was vehemently anti-Marxist and yet considered his nationalist doctrine to be socialist: in December 1910, some twelve years after Barrès, he read a paper to the First Congress of Nationalists, held in Florence, in which he spoke of 'our national socialism'. Already, however, he gave the phrase a wider meaning, reflecting the latest ideas of the Italian school of political sociology: 'This is to say that just as socialism taught the proletariat the value of the class struggle, we must teach Italy the value of the international struggle.'[29] Italy was, in the material as in the moral sense, a proletarian nation[30] and could only survive by taking to heart a lesson already well known to the working classes, and putting into practice the doctrine of unremitting struggle. Corradini expressed a fulsome admiration for the results achieved by the proletariat of Europe, and the way in which the doctrine of class struggle had been put into practical operation to the benefit of the workers. It was on this very point that nationalism identified most closely with socialism and at the same time found itself in violent opposition to socialism. It identified with socialism insofar as 'the basic belief of our essentially dynamic doctrine is struggle, international struggle, even struggle at home, has produced similar effects'.[31] Socialism and nationalism both insisted on the heroic virtues and the warrior spirit, as they both despised democracy and abominated liberalism.[32] On the other hand, socialism sought to impugn the concept of the nation, and in its place preached internationalism: in this and this only it erred. The nationalist movement, however, by integrating the proletariat into the national community, and thereby wiping out the identification effected by democracy of the nation with its bourgeoisie, would restore to the national community its authenticity and integrity and wholeness. Socialism was transcended in National-Socialism.

It is important too to realize that nationalists such as Corradini or Barrès saw the troubles of their respective countries almost exclusively in political terms: if poverty and social injustice prevailed, if Italy suffered defeat in her colonies or showed signs of weakness on the international scene, it could all be laid at the door of a weak and ineffective government and a political philosophy which envisaged the State as an agent for private and sectarian interests, putting itself at the service of pressure groups and social groups that were inimical to one another. The country's ailments derived from the State's inability to recognize the nation's interests, and having indeed lost all national feeling. The reforming of the State along authoritarian lines was therefore an essential preliminary to any attempt at rehabilitating the economy or reforming society. The first enemy to be destroyed therefore was the liberal and bourgeois State, just as it was essential to eradicate the philosophy of natural rights.

It was in Italy that anti-parliamentarism acquired a solidly structured and systematic character, relying on an analysis which in its day was the last word in social sciences. As early as the 1880s, it had been thoroughly formulated in the works of Mosca and Pareto. It was rooted in an intensely élitist and anti-democratic view of society, which according to Pareto is made up of a minority of very gifted individuals and a huge majority of mediocrities, and which is therefore always organized in the shape of a great pyramid, with a governing élite at the top, supported by a passive majority at its base: the State merely embodied the organized control of the majority by the minority.[33] Pareto's élitism bears all the marks of the powerful influence of social Darwinism: he does not scruple to compare the social organism with a living organism nor to make out a parallel between natural selection as it takes place in nature, and what he claims is a process of natural selection occurring in human society.[34] His theory of the circular movement of élites, and of constant warfare between sundry aristocracies, by virtue of which they continually succeeded one another, is a clear pointer to the origins of his sociology, the more so when, in his *Systèmes Socialistes*, he refers explicitly to Ammon and Vacher de Lapouge while discussing the anthropological characteristics of these élites, stressing that history is made by the conflict between one aristocracy and another, and not, as is so often thought, by the struggle of the lower classes against the aristocracy: 'So far as these lower classes themselves are unarmed, they are incapable of ruling; ochlocracy has never resulted in anything save disaster.'[35]

It should be emphasized that this élitist sociology did not confine itself to an analysis of an actual state of affairs, but went on to postulate a universal law, which had governed human society from its beginnings and should therefore be recognized as a norm of behaviour, rooted in the natural order. Not only did this analysis of the structure of society and power play a very influential part in the formation of fascist ideology but also contributed heavily to the aura of respectability and seriousness and trustworthiness which anti-democratic and anti-liberal ideas so very quickly acquired.[36] From the years that had led up to the French Revolution until at least the middle of the nineteenth century, the ideology of egalitarianism had appeared to be based on science – on the natural sciences as well as on the humanities. It was in the name of science and reason that people had battered at the ancient ramparts of privilege and run up the flag of liberty. By the beginning of the twentieth century things were indeed changed, for now it was the new humanities themselves that challenged all the assumptions on which liberal democracy was based. An intellectual climate was thus created that undermined the self-confidence of democracy and did much to boost the ascendancy of fascism.

If anti-parliamentarism, in the form it assumed under the influence of Italian political sociology, was allied to nationalism and furnished it with new weapons, it also gave nurture to certain forms of socialism, and particularly to revolutionary syndicalism. For inasmuch as they were opposed to liberal democracy and to bourgeois society, syndicalists and nationalists were of one mind; they evaluated the mechanisms of bourgeois society in much the same terms, and both conceived of society as being dominated by a powerful minority, with the apparatus of State serving their will. When material conditions were no longer propitious to one particular minority, then another élite rose to the top, in accordance with a process of continuous rotation of élite groups, each of which stirred up the masses to its own purpose. Each minority advanced a sustaining myth, to act as a goad to rebellion during times of transition from the rule of an established élite to the rule of a contending élite, and as a legitimizing fiction once the contending élite had established its dominance. Behind the façade of representative institutions and parliamentary procedures, the bourgeois government was just such an established élite.[37]

This analysis of power made by modern political sociologists had a familiar ring for any Marxist, which explains how a revolutionary socialist, such as Roberto Michels, took it up and used it to show that the existence of a dominating social group is absolutely essential to political and social life.[38] At the beginning of the century this theory found increasing favour in the militant circles of socialism, among those who most violently denounced parliamentary and democratic socialism and advocated direct action. Over against the school of socialists who preached the conquest of power by means of universal suffrage and who thereby relegated the revolution to the unforeseeable future – to the year 3000, their enemies said – the radical wing of the movement insisted on the theory of the avant-garde of the workers who, as a conscious and activist minority, would lead the proletariat into revolution. Traditional socialism had allowed itself to be tamed and assimilated into the bourgeois order; it had been lured into ministerial drawing-rooms and had come to recognize the passwords and play to the rules established by liberal democracy: to all this, syndicalism preferred the revolutionary violence of a proletarian élite. Roberto Michels showed how élitist doctrine, which saw in the masses a source of energy who yet had no will to shape social evolution, in no way conflicted with the materialist interpretation of history or the concept of class struggle.[39] Michels belonged to the revolutionary wing of the German socialists, which came very close to the syndicalism of the French and Italians, and he was bitterly critical of the German Social-Democratic Party: it was passive and lacked the spirit of combat, it had a predilection for parliamentary practices, and it was possessed of a bureaucratic and hierarchical organization which kept it in a state of paralysis and 'directed it out of the paths of manly striving, away from all acts of heroism.'[40] These were the words he used at a conference held in Paris in April 1907, on the subject of the relations between socialism and syndicalism, which he attended as the representative of the revolutionary wing among the German socialists, who most closely approximated the Italian and French syndicalists. Eventually Roberto Michels became a fascist.

At this same colloquy, Italy was represented by the great syndicalist leader Arturo Labriola, who stigmatized socialism as having become 'nothing more than a piece of parliamentary machinery, putting itself at the service of a handful of politicians'. He repeatedly castigated the official socialist movement for having accepted the rules of the game, for having become democratic and, in place of the class struggle, for preferring collaboration between the classes.[41] Some years later Labriola would discover the idea of the national entity, and end up by going over to militant nationalism.

France was represented by Hubert Lagardelle, the editor of *Le Mouvement Socialiste*, which was the doctrinal organ of orthodox Marxism in all its anti-parliamentary and anti-democratic aspects, fighting against all compromise and any deviation from the doctrine of class struggle. At socialist conferences Lagardelle was the very embodiment of doctrinal purity. In April 1907 he acclaimed 'the French workers' disaffection for the Republican State' as 'the culminating event in the history of these last years'.[42] The struggle against liberal democracy was the first and most important objective of socialism in the eyes of Hubert Lagardelle, who went on to become Marshal Pétain's Minister of Labour.

The leader of the CGT at this time was Victor Greffuelhes, and he, when debating the prospects for universal suffrage, concluded that, 'It seems clear to me that it should be relegated to the accessories shop,'[43] and proposed instead to implement the syndicalists' plans for direct action. According to yet another high-ranking syndicalist, Emile Pouget, direct action 'might proceed at a gentle and peaceable pace or, equally, by force and extreme violence'. Syndicalism and 'democratism' were irreconcilable principally because 'the latter, by means of universal suffrage, gives control into the hands of the ignorant and the *tardigrades* . . . and stifles the minorities who are the flag-bearers of the future'.[44] In this fashion, the extreme leftists in the socialist movement instilled in their sympathizers a contempt for democracy and parliamentarianism combined with the ardent desire for violent rebellion led by the minority of informed activists. Both France and Italy saw the same development of ideas among the far left syndicalists. In 1909 these exact sentiments were being voiced by Angelo Olivetti and the Italian revolutionary syndicalists; socialism would come into its own only in consequence of action on the part of the working-class élite.[45]

Hence the strenuous efforts that were made to prise the working class away from parliamentary democracy, and thus undo the work of the Dreyfus Affair, which had had an extremely important effect on the workers' movement throughout Europe. For during the Dreyfus Affair the French socialists had decided to come to the defence of the bourgeois Republic, and put their strength and organization at the disposal of liberal democracy, which was then threatened by a coalition of every possible party of the right, and by so doing they had set a precedent and a norm for every socialist party operating within a system of parliamentary government. This decision, instigated by Jaurès, no doubt saved the Republic but also had the immediate effect of dampening down the revolutionary zeal of the proletariat, which thereafter came to stand surety for the supremacy of the bourgeoisie. By giving support to government ministers and sharing in their counsels, the French socialists struck a heavy blow at the international solidarity of socialist parties. European socialists of the extreme left felt it in consequence essential to teach the proletariat to despise anything that smacked of bourgeois or liberal values, to hold in contempt bourgeois virtues and morals, and the bourgeois' respect for the law, for legal forms, for democratic government. The theorists of the syndicalist movement praised rather the warrior virtues, and violence, which begets morality, and the refining processes of social warfare; and in the writings of Georges Sorel syndicalism further discovered a rich seam of anti-intellectual and irrationalist argument.

Georges Sorel's work is well known today, and yet when in 1908 he published his *Reflections on Violence*, he was not saying anything that sounded unusual in syndicalists' ears. His books were quite simply a systematic reworking of the writings of socialist and syndicalist leaders far better known than Sorel himself. This was in fact how he acquired his importance and came to play such a large role, in Italy especially, in the conversion of certain syndicalist groups to the right. For Sorel and his associates contrived the synthesis of all the ideas and contemporary trends of thought which had in common the advocacy of revolt against a bourgeois society and all its moral and political values, revolt against the doctrine of natural rights, and revolt against liberalism and democracy. Revolutionary syndicalists and nationalists, as well as anti-democrats and anti-liberals of every colour, had now found common ground; the shift from revolutionary syndicalism to nationalism, or vice versa, had never in theory been beyond the bounds of possibility, and by the time the First World War loomed on the horizon it had taken on the appearance of inevitability.

In 1911–12, Sorel – the revolutionary syndicalist – put out a review called *L'Indépendance*, which was nationalist and anti-Semitic, at about the same time as two other publications were launched that rank among the more interesting and significant harbingers of fascism: *Les Cahiers du Cercle Proudhon* in France, and *La Lupa* in Italy. The Cercle Proudhon was founded in December 1911 and was presided over by Charles Maurras, with Georges Sorel as its moving spirit. It embraced both syndicalists and nationalists belonging to Action Française. A month later the first edition of *Les Cahiers du Cercle Proudhon* was published, and among its promoters two names stand out that are symbolic of the nature of the enterprise: Georges Valois, who belonged with the left wing of Action Française, who was the author of *La Monarchie et la Classe Ouvrière*, and who went on to found the Faisceau in 1925; and Edouard Berth, a disciple of Sorel's who in the 1920s shifted from the radical right to the extreme left. Nationalists and syndicalists alike were in agreement that 'democracy was the greatest mistake of the last century', that it had allowed the most appalling exploitation of the workers, and had set up and then substituted 'the law of gold for the law of blood' within the capitalist system. It followed that 'if we wish to conserve and increase the moral, intellectual and material capital of civilization, it is absolutely imperative to destroy the institutions of democracy'.[46]

The convergence of revolutionary syndicalism and nationalism is best illustrated by the symptomatic development of Sergio Pannunzio, who later went on to expound the theories that shaped the institutional reforms implemented by the fascists. As a young man, Pannunzio was a syndicalist, but a syndicalist who from the first found himself in agreement with Mosca, and said as much; he combined Italian national themes with ideas borrowed from Sorel. He not only insisted that it was time to leave the outworn traditional liberal State behind but also favoured an assumption which other syndicalists had made before him, that the longstanding hostility between two antagonistic social sectors – bourgeoisie and proletariat – was in fact 'schematic'. He maintained that there existed rather two blocs, one of which was reactionary and conservative, and the other revolutionary. To the second, only militant syndicalists and anarchists belonged, and thus the new concept of anarcho-syndicalism, of conflict between the conservative bloc and the revolutionary bloc, began to gain the upper hand over the socialist concept of class struggle. Pannunzio ended up by advocating 'the politics of energy', leading up to 'the decisive act' and the 'supreme daring' of Revolt – Revolt, and not Revolution, as Santarelli acutely remarks.[47]

As crisis succeeded crisis, first over Libya and then over interventionism, a number of syndicalist groups took up new stances which made a proven appeal to the nation and the people. More and more they leaned towards nationalism, and eventually infiltrated certain circles of traditional social-democracy. This regrouping of syndicalists and nationalists, which already amounted to fascism – though it as yet lacked the name – took place under the banner of *La Lupa*, a journal which first appeared the year before the Tripoli expedition. It was published in Florence and edited by Paolo Orano, a typical representative of the Italian school of syndicalists, whose goal it was to reconcile economic syndicalism and political nationalism. Among its contributors, *La Lupa* numbered Enrico Corradini, Arturo Labriola, and Roberto Michels, and could count on some help, albeit limited and not very concrete, from Sorel. The founder of modern Italian nationalism concentrated his endeavours on demonstrating that nationalism and socialism were well and truly identified with one another insofar as they both shared in the same specific 'virtuous substance'. 'For syndicalism the only moral imperative is to struggle. For nationalism the only moral imperative is . . . to wage war.'[48] They had a common adversary – the bourgeoisie.

In 1913 a new review was launched under the title *Lacerba*, by Giovanni Papini, who in 1904 had published *A Nationalist Programme*. *Lacerba* brought together Papini, Ardengo Soffici, and the Futurists, led by Marinetti. In a 1913 article, Papini called for 'a bloodbath': he saw war as the means for bringing about the internal regeneration of Italy and for destroying the false values of democracy. He and his colleagues combined nationalism with the subversion of established cultural and moral values.[49] In this we already see the influence of Marinetti and the Futurists: as early as 1909 the Futurists' Manifesto had set out the essentials of what subsequently became the moral ideals of fascism, to which the twenties and thirties made no new contribution:

1. We want to sing the love of danger, the habit of energy and rashness.

2. The essential elements of our poetry will be courage, audacity and revolt.

3. . . . we want to exalt movements of aggression, feverish sleeplessness, the forced march, the perilous leap, the slap and the blow with the fist. . . .

9. We want to glorify war – the only cure for the world – and militarism, patriotism, the destructive gesture of the anarchists, the beautiful ideas which kill, and contempt for women.

10. We want to demolish museums and libraries, fight morality, feminism and all opportunist and utilitarian cowardice.[50]

Marinetti remained faithful to fascism to the very end, and became an enthusiastic supporter of Salò Republic.

The shadow of war weighed more and more heavily over Europe, and against that backdrop the consciousness of each and every nation became gradually more susceptible to the influence of new trends. In the syndicalist and nationalist camp too, the wind of change was felt and shows particularly, for instance, in Roberto Michels's analysis of Italian neo-imperialism in terms of 'an imperialism of the poor', in which he enlarged on ideas put forward by Corradini. The world was divided into wealthy nations and proletarian nations, nations which already had a place in the sun and nations whom it behoved to win such a place; and this concept too would become one of the basic tenets of fascism. It entailed the transference of the indispensable struggle from the theatre of the interior to the exterior, and the elimination, in theory, of the problem of the proletariat, which would be absorbed into the sphere of the war waged by the entire nation: the future would be shaped by struggle, not between the proletarian and capitalist classes, but between the proletarian and plutocratic nations. Instead of a class, it was the nation now that was going to set the course of history, as the agent of progress and civilization; and this was the change of ideas which made the shift from left to right so easy, for on every other point the far left, composed of syndicalists and revolutionary socialists, and the radicals and nationalists of the new right, had already met and agreed. Anti-liberalism, anti-parliamentarism, anti-Semitism (except in Italy); the cult of the élite, of youth, of force and violence; the revolt against the rationalism of the Enlightenment; the advocacy of political authoritarianism – every one of the elements which went to make up fascism was by now in existence, and not merely in the shape of raw materials for they already had been elaborated into a relatively coherent system. By the time the old world crumbled away in August 1914 fascist ideology had a past history going back to the 1880s. A few years later, with the numbers of unemployed and terrified peasants and petty bourgeois growing to immense proportions, the trauma of war and the permanent state of insecurity induced by the Versailles treaty, the shock of defeat for some, of victory for others, that resolved none of their difficulties, the success of the Soviet revolution which had an effect – among others – of making people believe that anything was possible – all combined to create the conditions which allowed that ideology to become a true political force.

The collapse of the Socialist International on the eve of the war and the inability of the working classes to prevent the clash, the haste and near unanimity with which they ranged themselves, physically and morally, behind the established order, and at one blow shattered the solidarity of the proletariat, were tangible proof that the concept of class carried less weight, as a factor of solidarity, than the concept of nation. Confronted by the fervour which the idea of the nation aroused, the idea of class was shown up in all its artificiality: the nation was a reality, which the International could never aspire to be. In the course of the war the socialists were a legion who reached this same conclusion, particularly if they belonged among the syndicalists and revolutionaries of the far left. Among the latter there figured Gustave Hervé, one of the most popular and most vehemently anti-militarist and anti-patriotic spokesmen for European socialism, who altered the name of his newspaper from *La Guerre Sociale* to *La Victoire* and who, having spent a lifetime preaching hatred of anything that smacked, however faintly, of nationalism or of collaboration with the bourgeois state, after the war turned fascist.

The most famous of these converts, however, is of course Mussolini. In 1910 he was a young socialist editing a publication called *La Lotta di Classe*, but by 1914 he was putting out a daily newspaper called *Il Popolo d'Italia*. Mussolini's change of tack cannot be said to be unique or particularly extreme, nor was he motivated by political opportunism. He could well have taken on such a role as was played by Léon Blum, Emile Vandervelde, Otto Bauer, or Ramsay MacDonald, had he so wished. But for Mussolini it was not possible, since the socialism he professed was revolutionary and adhered strictly to the Marxist analysis of liberal democracy, its morals and laws, categorizing these as the outward signs of the supremacy and self-interest of the bourgeoisie, and not as universal values. Like many others, however, Mussolini saw the notion of class disintegrate under the impact of war, and immediately became aware of the immense reservoir of energy contained in the idea of the nation: after half a century of socialism, national feeling emerged as the moving force of history, and the nation was found to embody the fundamental values of society. As soon as this change was seen to have working possibilities, while the fine flame of socialism was all but extinguished, the equation between revolution and socialism was left with its first term only, and reduced to the will to destroy democracy and liberalism and in their place set up a new order. So it was that nationalism became the functional myth of fascism, and from that moment the battle was engaged with Marxism.

Mussolini was far from being the only person to take this path. A quarter of a century later the same assessment of events was reworked by a number of men who were among the most dynamic figures in the European socialist movement, and who all had a long record of opposition to Mussolini's system. The most brilliant of these men was undoubtedly Sir Oswald Mosley, the youngest minister in MacDonald's cabinet, followed by Marcel Déat, who was one of the few people still contributing to the theory of socialism in Europe in the period between the two wars, and a socialist minister in a government which had smoothed the way for the Front Populaire. Likewise, there was Jacques Doriot, a candidate to the General Secretariat of the French Communist party, who made the mistake of being in the right in advance of the times, and Henri de Man, the president of the Belgian Workers' party, and one of the most original socialist philosophers of the twentieth century, who in July 1940 welcomed 'the débâcle of the parliamentary régime and the capitalist plutocracy in the so-called democracies' as the advent of a new era: 'For the working-classes and for socialism, this collapse of a decrepit world, far from being a disaster, is a deliverance.' For, 'the Socialist Order will be thereby realized, not at all as the thing of one class or of one party, but as the good of all, in the name of a national solidarity that will soon be continental, if not world-wide.'[51]

In September of the same year Marcel Déat summed up the essentials of fascism: 'All things considered, I think it comes down to this one observation: the driving force of Revolution has ceased to be class interest, and has become instead the general interest; we have moved on from the notion of class to that of the nation.' He then added a comment which is utterly characteristic of fascist thinking: 'I shall not try to weigh in the scales the parts played in this undertaking by what is national and by what is social, nor to discover whether it was a question of socializing the nation or of nationalizing socialism. What I do know is that . . . this mixture is, in the best sense of the word, explosive: rich enough to set all the engine-forces of history backfiring.'[52]

A new civilization

In the period immediately after the First World War, as in the years preceding the second, the fascists clearly felt they were proclaiming the dawn of a new era, a 'fascist century' (Mussolini),[53] a 'new civilization' (Oswald Mosley).[54] And indeed, from its earliest beginnings, fascism presented itself as being nothing less than a counter-civilization, defining itself as a revolution of man, a 'total revolution', a 'spiritual revolution',[55] a 'revolution of morals',[56] a 'revolution of souls'.[57] For its ideologists, fascism – to use Valois's expression – was fundamentally a conception of life, a total conception of national, political, economic and social life.[58] 'Total' was a word of which all fascist writers were extremely fond, and it was one of the key terms in their vocabulary: fascism was to be the first political system to call itself totalitarian precisely because it encompassed the whole range of human activity. It was totalitarian because it represented a way of life, because it would penetrate every sector of social and intellectual activity, because it meant to create at once a new type of society and a new type of man.

A movement of revolt, fascism drew its dynamism from its 'disruptive power',[59] its total rejection of bourgeois society with its political and social structures and moral values. None of the elements that went to make up fascist ideology were new in themselves. What was new was the synthesis of these elements, a synthesis that only became possible in the aftermath of the war, and, of course, after the success of the Soviet revolution. In this sense, there is no doubt that fascism was the child of the post-war crisis: it was a politics of fear and crisis, inseparably bound up with the new difficulties liberal democracy was encountering.[60] But at the level of ideology, in its maturity, and even when, as in Italy and elsewhere, it had accumulated some years of experience, fascism still displayed essentially the same features that characterized the movement of revolt of the early years of the century.

In the minds of Gentile and Mussolini, Marcel Déat and Drieu La Rochelle, José Antonio and Codreanu, fascist ideology constituted a comprehensive alternative to liberal bourgeois civilization, its rationalism and individualism. After the nineteenth century, 'the century of the individual', the fascist twentieth century would be the 'collective century, and therefore the century of the State'.[61] Everything sprang from this fundamental principle. Fascist ideology saw itself as a reaction against the 'materialistic positivism of the nineteenth century',[62] which it sought to replace by a 'religious and idealistic manner of looking at life'.[63] It refused, in the words of José Antonio, 'to accept the materialistic interpretation of history',[64] or, as Mussolini thought, 'the materialistic conception of happiness . . . This means that fascism denies the equation: well-being = happiness, which sees in men mere animals, content when they can feed and fatten, thus reducing them to a vegetative existence pure and simple.'[65]

But it was a professional sociologist, Marcel Déat, who put his finger on a more specific cause of the malady: 'economic liberalism, which is bourgeois materialism, and its counterpart the working-class materialism of Marxism, both of which are incontestably the daughters of rationalism', that 'straitjacketed and calamity-stricken' rationalism which was a 'denial of all aristo- cratism, a negation of hierarchy, a negation of the person, a nega- tion of the State as an instrument of the community'.[66] This is the 'old eighteenth-century rationalism', 'a philosophy now two hundred years past its prime',[67] which still forms the basis of official liberal ideology today, and it was against this world of natural rights, individualism, matter, and reason, a world threatened by anarchy that fascism rebelled. 'We stand for a new principle in the world, we stand for sheer categorical definitive antithesis to the world of democracy, plutocracy, free-masonry, to the world which still abides by the fundamental principles laid down in 1789,' Mussolini said.[68]

In the minds of its leaders, fascism was very much a revolt of the younger generation: 'the present *Weltanschauung* of fascism may be summed up in one word – youth,' the English fascist James Barnes wrote.[69] The same sentiment was shared by Cod- reanu, José Antonio, Drieu La Rochelle, Oswald Mosley, and Georges Valois. For Léon Degrelle, the embodiment of the fascist revolt was a younger generation which 'would rather have blown everything up than start out on life following filthy paths, without even the smallest patch of clear sky in view.'[70] For Oswald Mos- ley 'the real political division of the past decade has not been one of parties, but a division of generations.'[71] And Adrien Marquet (a comrade of Déat's), the day neo-socialism was born, flabber- gasted Léon Blum with his shout: 'No one gives their lives for thirty seats in the Chamber.'[72]

Fascism, young, new, and modern, was also a revolt against decadence, and here, too, it was echoing one of the main themes of the movement of revolt of the latter years of the nineteenth century. The thought of Drieu La Rochelle and Léon Degrelle, like that of Barrès before them, was the reaction of a younger generation to a Europe whose 'morals are in decay, whose faith is debased, and which is sick to the teeth of individualism, fanati- cism and arrogance',[73] a Europe 'slowly going to rack and ruin', and expiring of manifold ills: country areas depopulated by the war, alcoholism, syphilis, the great industrial centres; towns full of 'cinemas and cafés, brothels, newspapers, stock exchanges, political parties and barracks'; a Paris that had become 'a centre of bohemian intellectuals, fast livers and homosexuals; drugs, music-halls, Catholic writers, Jews, Picasso's paintings . . .'[74] The fascists plumbed the depths of the sickness. *Gilles*, a novel which takes decomposition as its theme and is surely the most important work of fascist literature, abounds with images of death, annihilation and putrefaction. This world incapable of a virile and involuntary reaction, this rakish, self-satisfied world of heirs and descendants was, of course, the world of old bourgeois Europe, and the fascist rebelled against it. He would dig the grave of all the bourgeois virtues and of all the evils bourgeois power had spawned; he would be the herald of a new morality: 'To the financier, the oil-man and the pig-farmer who consider themselves the masters of the world and who want to run it according to the law of money, the needs of the automobile and the philosophy of pigs, and bend the peoples to the politics of the dividend,' George Valois said, fascism's answer was to 'raise the sword'. To the bourgeois 'brandishing his contracts and statistics:

– Two plus three makes . . .
– Nought, the Barbarian replies, smashing his head in.'[75]

The Barbarian, the fascist, thus saw himself as liberating the world from the bourgeois spirit and awakening a desire for reaction and regeneration that were simultaneously spiritual and physical, moral, social, and political. Fascism, for its ideologists, was a revolution of both the body and the mind, since for them the two were inseparable. This was where in the fascists' own view the originality of their movement lay: as an alternative to the economic man of liberal and Marxist materialism, they offered a brand of neo-idealism that put the spiritual above the material; in place of the liberal and pacific bourgeois and the city shopkeeper they offered the barbarian and the knight of the Middle Ages; as an alternative to the product of European rationalism they offered the cult of feeling, emotion, and violence; and in place of the degenerate man of a stay-at-home civilization to which physical effort had become repugnant, they offered the cult of the body, health, and the outdoor life.

The fascist rebellion thus took on the appeal of a new human adventure, for, in the words of Léon Degrelle, 'the great revolutions are not political or economic, . . . the true revolution . . . [is] the one that overhauls not the engine of the State, but the secret life of each soul.'[76] Fascism was a 'poetic movement' for José Antonio;[77] a 'state of mind', 'something spiritual and mystical' for the Belgian Rexist José Streel.[78] For the fascist-type life, to quote Gentile, was a mission, and the militant was a crusader who had to be prepared to make any sacrifice.[79]

Within fascism, therefore, we find the cult of duty, sacrifice, and the heroic virtues. Mussolini, required to sum up fascism in a few words, said, 'We are against the easy life.' For the fascist, life meant 'duty, elevation, conquest', it was 'serious, austere, religious'.[80] In the midst of the indescribable mediocrity that to-day surrounds us,' Degrelle wrote, 'we represent fearlessness, initiative, self-sacrifice and discipline . . .'[81] Life for the fascist 'is a continuous, ceaseless fight', and his creed is 'a doctrine which is not merely political: it is evidence of a fighting spirit which accepts all risks.'[82] This is why the new type of human being, the fascist man, would be a man who 'liked taking risks, [had] self-confidence, group-sense and a taste for collective enthusiasm'; 'the politics of ink, saliva and ideology he will counter with the politics of soil, flesh and blood.'[83] Fascism meant strength, willingness to serve, obedience, authority, self-denial, and for Henri de Man, as much as for the killer Joseph Darnand, it meant a new world which would be built by 'an élite preferring a lively and dangerous life to a torpid and easy one'.[84] For the head of the Milice, the French version of the Gestapo, 'the bourgeois way of life is over'. Fascism meant 'living dangerously';[85] it was, in Oswald Mosley's phrase, 'a great and hazardous adventure'.[86] This fascist adventure, adventure for adventure's sake, would produce the type of man who was always willing to 'try his luck', who liked to go for 'all or nothing',[87] and it did in fact ultimately produce the Mussolinian killer whose notorious motto, 'me ne frego', epitomizes the spirit of fascism.[88]

Fascist ideology thus offered 'a new, vigorous, brutal explanation of the world, of the kind men have always needed and will always need'.[89] Incorporated in it was the cult of physical strength – Oswald Mosley wanted men 'to live like athletes' – and of life, health, and blood, combined with an obsession with virility and a contempt for intellectuals. None of these various manifestations of what amounted to an apologia of the instincts were original contributions on the part of the fascists and, in fact, apart from the experience of the war, it would be difficult to find in their thought a single idea not already developed by Barrès, Marinetti, d'Annunzio, Corradini, or Langbehn. What fascism represented was the full flowering of the movement of revolt of the end of the nineteenth century. The generation that had lived through the trenches brought only a further dimension to the nostalgia for the front and for danger: war was where men were put to the test, it brought out men's primal virtues and basic instincts. 'War is my fatherland,'[90] Gilles said, his words an echo not only of the 'glorification of war'[91] of the Futurist Manifesto, written at the turn of the century, but also of Jules Soury's claim that war was 'the source of all superior life, the cause of all progress'.[92]

The corollaries of the cult of war and physical danger were the cult of brutality, strength, and sexuality and, of course, contempt for anyone who believed in reasoned argument and the validity of statistics. In this connection, Drieu La Rochelle, attempting to define what divided the fascist from the traditionalist, established a distinction which is vital to a proper understanding of the deeper nature of fascism: 'A monarchist is never a true fascist . . . because a monarchist is never a modern: he has none of the brutality or the barbaric simplism of the modern.'[93] Here we have the essence of fascism, and Drieu's words also reveal what makes of fascism a true counter-civilization: rejecting the sophisticated rationalist humanism of Old Europe, fascism sets up as its ideal the primitive instincts and primal emotions of the barbarian. Had not Marinetti, in 1909, said his response to the high culture of Europe was to 'destroy the museums, libraries and all the academies' and 'free this country of the fetid gangrene of its professors, archaeologists, cicerones and antiquaries'?[94]

Fascism was intent on changing man, but that was not all. Revolting against the big city and the great centres of industry, it wanted to alter man's environment and create for him a setting where he could lead a new life. The fascist revolution saw itself as a counter-revolution against an industrial revolution which had uprooted man from the open country and cooped him up in the city, and it proclaimed the superiority of the twentieth century, the country and the sports stadium over the nineteenth century, the urban hovel and the pub. In its desire to reconcile man with nature, save him from a lingering death and physical decrepitude and safeguard his primitive virtues and his natural environment fascism was possibly the first environmentalist ideology of this century, combining the pursuit of technical progress and industrial growth with the protection of nature as the environment in which a civilization of leisure and sport could flourish.[95]

The 'great moral revolution' which was what Robert Brasillach understood by fascism, that revolution of the senses directed against the prevailing political philosophy, was to be a revolution of the body and of sexuality. Fascism would create a 'new life' of 'camping, sport, dancing, travel and communal hikes' which would sweep away the fusty world of 'aperitifs, smoky rooms, congresses and [bad] digestions'.[96] This world would be a virile world, and it is worth remembering in this context what a preference fascist satirists showed for sexual imagery and vocabulary. It was the virility of the fascist, his healthiness and bounding energy which finally distinguished him from the impotent bourgeois, liberals, and socialists.[97]

But for all that fascism advocated a return to nature and the soil, it was not anti-modern. The fascist always showed a predilection for new industries and technical innovations, for aeroplanes and cars: d'Annunzio, Mussolini, and Hitler are familiar examples. 'We are the party of speed,' Drieu said.[98] Power, speed, vigour, toughness, solidity, and effectiveness are the essential fascist qualities, and they are also those of the modern motor, the car engine and sophisticated machinery. This taste extended to vocabulary. To convey the activist spirit of the fascist movement, Mussolini chose the phrase: 'Fascism is a dynamo.'

This movement which saw itself as one of new men was undoubtedly one of young men – those who had little vested interest in the established order, who felt strongly about the discrepancy between principles and practice, to whom rebellion came more naturally than to the rest of the population, and for whom ideology was something to be taken seriously. Belgian and Romanian fascisms both originated in student movements, and in France,

Spain, Italy, and England, the young – the oldest of them had just returned from the trenches – predominated.

Both at the level of ideology and for purposes of recruitment, the fascists were able to use the fact that their movement was associated with the younger generation to present their ideology as the only twentieth century system of thought. Were not liberalism, socialism, communism, and nationalism all products of the preceding century? And had they not all aged very badly? This youthfulness of a movement whose leaders were still in their twenties and thirties when they achieved notoriety or came to power goes some way towards explaining its dynamic, activist and, ultimately, revolutionary character.

Since they regarded their ideology as an ideology of life and movement, all the various fascisms chose to describe themselves as 'movements' rather than 'parties'. They all considered themselves 'anti-parties', because they challenged the inertia and dogmatism of the traditional political structures, declined to work out programmes or political manifestoes – refused, in other words, to play the game of traditional politics or accept its conventions.[99] They had, by contrast, an immense thirst for action, and not just action aimed at overthrowing the established order, but action for action's sake, since, in Mussolini's phrase, 'inactivity is death'.[100] The action the fascists glorified was not so much action with a specific end in view as action for its own sake: to act with blind passion, to think in terms of fist-fights and bursts of machine-gun fire was to rediscover the very principle of life itself. 'No man goes very far who knows where he is going'[101] was the principle Mosley adopted for himself, and Mussolini expressed the same sentiment in these terms. 'I am all for motion. I am one who marches on . . .'[102] And for José Streel, 'you must come on board, let yourself be carried by the torrent; in other words, you must act. The rest will take care of itself.'[103]

The war, in which the great proportion of fascists had had direct experience, furnished them with a criterion of behaviour: the Bergsonian '*élan vital*', reduced to the simple *élan* of the battlefield, was reinterpreted in terms of activism at home. Ex-servicemen played an extremely important part in the maturing of fascism. As depositories of the national heritage and guardians of the nation's greatness, they considered themselves the bearers of a special mission – to see that their own sufferings and the sacrifice of their comrades had not been in vain, and to refashion society as a fighting unit, inculcating in it the fighting soldier's heroic virtues of discipline, sacrifice, self-denial, and brotherhood. The ex-servicemen wanted to convey their unique experience to society as a whole and reshape and transform it in the light of that experience; they had a profound sense of being 'outside and above preceding generations'[104] and placed themselves 'above party and class [as we were] during the war'.[105] Society, however, being a class society, and politics being party politics, a politics of factions and interest-groups, it is not difficult to see how the ex-serviceman became the enemy of the established order, of political pluralism and pacifist and humanitarian values. Since he wanted the salvation of his country and wished to regenerate the state and refashion the world in his own heroic image, the ex-serviceman 'wants the government of the country'[106] but was not prepared to work his way up in the traditional way through the committees and antechambers of democracy. Consequently, he became a rebel.

The ex-serviceman thus came to occupy a position alongside a multiplicity of maladjusted and dissatisfied elements who would see in fascism a promise of solutions that the traditional right and left were unable to offer. Fascist ideology was without doubt that best qualified to attract the malcontents who found no place in the world as it was, despised the conformism of left and right, and yet felt much closer to their enemies the communists – as the communists did to the rebels – than to the bourgeoisie which, however, at the critical moment, and under the pressure of events, was to become their ally.[107]

With their thirst for action for action's sake and struggle for struggle's sake, the fascists appeared to be the only authentically revolutionary political organizations, the only movements unconditionally opposed to the established order, the only people whose revolutionary credibility – unlike that of the parties of the left, including the communist parties – had not been damaged by compromise. After its accession to power, Italian fascism should certainly be regarded as a régime, and that it formed a régime makes it a special case, but it, too, goes to prove the rule: the generation of fascists of 1935 went into opposition against the régime, dreaming of a fascist utopia, a fascism purged, authenticated, renewed. However puerile this revolt may have been – and of its futility there can be no doubt – it nonetheless represented a rebellion against the compromises, betrayals, and abandoned ideals of an ageing régime.[108] We may well wonder whether, had there been no war, similar difficulties would not have arisen in Germany. Certainly, in the cases of General Franco, Marshal Pétain, and Admiral Horthy, no sooner had they come to power at the head of what were fundamentally reactionary régimes, than they set about disbanding, muzzling, or neutralizing the fascist movements. Fascism did not take kindly to reaction.

The fascist élite, those for whom life was sacrifice, devotion, and self-denial, liked to imagine themselves as a kind of religious order, as *Croisés*, 'the handful of heroes and saints who will undertake the Reconquest'.[109] Drieu rhapsodized about the age of epics, cathedrals, and crusades,[110] and Marcel Déat proclaimed that 'Nietzsche's idea of the selection of "good Europeans" is now being realized on the battlefield, by the LFV and the Waffen SS. An aristocracy, a knighthood is being created by the war which will be the hard, pure nucleus of the Europe of the future.'[111] But it was Léon Degrelle, himself an SS officer back from the front, whose language best conveys the character of that new man that the fascist revolution would produce:

The true élites are formed at the front, a chivalry is created there, young leaders are born. That is where you find the true élite of tomorrow . . . and there between us a complete fraternity grows up, for since the war everything has changed. When we look to our own country and see some fat, stupefied bourgeois, we do not feel this man to be a member of our race; but when we see a young revolutionary, from Germany or elsewhere, we feel that he is one of ours, for we are one with revolution and youth. We are political soldiers, the badge of the SS shows Europe where political and social truth are to be found . . . we prepare the political cadres of the postwar world. Tomorrow, Europe will have élites such as it has never known. An army of young apostles, of young mystics, carried by a faith that nothing can check, will emerge one day from the great seminary of the front.[112]

The individual and the community

Fascist ideology was born of a political tradition that considered the individual a function of group life. The various currents of which fascism was the confluence – nationalism, revolutionary syndicalism, anti-parliamentarism, and anti-liberalism of every hue – all shared a view of man as a social animal. Even the nationalists of the latter years of the nineteenth century had seen man as nothing more than the vehicle of forces generated by the community, and their ethic was both unconditionally anti-individualist and violently antagonistic to the theory of natural rights and the rights of man. Fascist ideology thus appropriated to itself a view of man which in its most recent form was already a good fifty years old, and which in its earliest form was as old as the fundamental ideas of anti-revolutionary thought themselves. Such, then, is the genealogy of fascism's rejection of the 'individualistic' or 'atomistic' conception of man central to the world view of classical liberalism: the 'human individual is not an atom. Immanent in the concept of an individual is the concept of society . . . Man is, in an absolute sense, a political animal,' wrote Gentile.[113] According to him, the notion that man exists in perfect freedom anterior or exterior to society is simply a fiction. However much fascist thinkers may have differed on other questions, on this point they were all agreed. From José Streel, who asserted that 'the individual does not exist in the pure state'[114] to José Antonio in his polemic against Rousseau,[115] it was the 'mechanistic' view of society as nothing more than an aggregate of individuals that was attacked.

This view of man as an integral part of an organic whole is the basis of fascism's political philosophy. Fascism developed a conception of society which accorded moral privilege to the collectivity, its traditions, and particularly its juridical embodiment in the state, as against the empirical and transient individuals which constituted its membership at any particular time. According to Gregor, this was founded on the idea – most fully elaborated by

Gentile – that, insofar as man is outside the organization of society with its system of reciprocal rules and obligations, he has no significant freedom. Outside of society, man would be the subject of nature, not its master. He would be the enemy of all and friend of none. He would be threatened by persons and things alike. He would be in a state of abject dependence. There would be no freedom, no security, for each man would be exposed to the open wrongs of every enemy. There would be no assurance of life, much less of liberty. The freedom that man is supposed to barter away in part on entering society, in order to secure the remainder, has no real existence. It is, according to Gentile, an imaginary possession which then, by an imaginary transfer, is conveyed to society.

Man as a spiritual agent is an essentially social animal who finds freedom only in a rule-governed association with other men.[116] Ultimately, for Gentile, man has existence only insofar as he is sustained and determined by the community: 'for at the root of the "I" there is a "we".'[117] The Italian philosopher was here restating an argument that had been relatively common at the end of the nineteenth century, the main contention of which had been that the individual had no autonomy and only achieved the status of human being as a member of a community. In Mussolini's words: 'In the fascist conception of history, man is only man by virtue of the spiritual process to which he contributes as a member of the family, the social group, the nation, and in function of history to which all nations bring their contributions. Hence, the great value of tradition in records, in language, in customs, in the rules of social life. Outside history, man is a nonentity. Fascism is therefore opposed to all individualistic abstractions based on eighteenth century materialism.'[118]

In this sense, Mussolini, Gentile, and all the other fascist thinkers were traditionalist and conservative: man commences his rational and moral life as the denizen of a specific historical community. He rejects aspects of that community's prescriptions and proscriptions only when armed with sufficient reason. Man in the mythical state of nature, devoid of the rule-system governing human association, is a man devoid of human contacts, devoid of language, thought, and morality, devoid of humanity itself.[119]

Fascist thought did not stop there, however, but went on to develop a conception of liberty and an ideal of an organic society that went far beyond anything postulated by the first counter-revolution. Liberty, in Mussolini's terminology, was 'the liberty of the State and of the individual within the State'. This definition of liberty, which 'is to be the attribute of living men and not of abstract dummies invented by individualistic liberalism,' derived from one axiomatic tenet: 'the fascist view of life stresses the importance of the State and accepts the individual only insofar as his interests coincide with those of the State, which stands for the conscience and the universal will of man as an historic entity ... Liberalism denied the State in the name of the individual, fascism reasserts the rights of the State as expressing the real essence of the individual.'[120] Mussolini's assertion is of fundamental importance for the understanding of fascism: this identification of the individual with the collective will was the very cornerstone of fascist social and political thought.

The individual was only seen in terms of the social function he fulfilled and his place in the community. For Gentile 'the only individual who can ever be found' is 'the individual who exists as a specialized productive force',[121] and for Oswald Mosley 'real freedom' was 'economic freedom'. The English fascist leader defined freedom in language that is not unreminiscent of the language of a certain brand of popular Marxism: 'Real freedom means good wages, short hours, security in employment, good houses, opportunity for leisure and recreation with family and friends.' From this it followed that 'economic freedom cannot come until economic chaos ends; and it cannot end until a Government has power to act,'[122] until, in José Antonio's words, man's freedom was given 'a framework of authority, hierarchy and order'.[123]

In the fascist view, democracy, whose function was to guarantee and preserve the rights of the individual and which saw the individual as the supreme end of society, was to be replaced by a 'people acting organically on both the social and political planes',[124] for nations and societies were living organic totalities which were an end in themselves and which possessed their own hierarchy and articulation. 'These totalities,' wrote Marcel Déat, 'both came before, and transcended, their parts – individuals and secondary groups.' This conception of nation and society of course went directly against the French rationalist view, according to which these totalities either came into being under the pressure of circumstances or were created through the artifice of a contract. It was from this fascist view of the individual and the society that the highly romantic notion of the *Volksgeist* arose.[125]

It was, then, in subordinating himself to the group that the individual found his *raison d'être*, and in integrating himself into the community that he found fulfilment. In the words of Mussolini's Minister of Justice: 'Instead of the liberal-democratic formula "society for the individual" we have "individuals for society" ... For fascism, society is the end, individuals the means, and its whole life consists in using individuals as instruments for its social ends ... Individual rights are only recognized insofar as they are implied in the rights of the State.'[126] It was in this way, Gentile claimed, that fascism had resolved the famous 'paradox of liberty and authority. The authority of the State is absolute' and 'freedom can only exist within the State, and the State means authority.'[127] In the same vein, José Antonio maintained that 'to be really free is to be part of a strong and free nation.'[128]

In thus championing the state and the nation, 'this community of communities',[129] fascism extolled the values of the group, of the collectivity, of the national community, producing a 'new conception of a living community, where abstract brotherhood is replaced by a relationship of the blood',[130] and also providing a solution to alienation, to 'the frightening isolation of modern man, who, in the factory, the office and at home finds himself reduced to an orphan'.[131]

It was by way of such arguments that fascism arrived at that new man and new society so admirably characterized by Marcel Déat: 'the total man in the total society, with no clashes, no prostration, no anarchy'.[132] There can be no doubt that fascism's successes were in part due to man's longing to be merged with the collective soul and his exaltation at feeling, living, and acting in harmony with the whole. Fascism was a vision of a coherent and reunited people, and it was for this reason that it placed such great emphasis on march-pasts, parades, and uniforms – on a whole communal liturgy, in fact – and that it waged an implacable war against anything tending to divide or differentiate, or which stood for diversity or pluralism: liberalism, democracy, parliamentarism, multi-party system. This unity finds its most perfect expression in the quasi-sacred figure of the leader. The cult of a leader who embodied the spirit, will, and virtues of the people, and who was identified with the nation, was the keystone of the fascist liturgy.

For this romantic and mystic conception of life, fascism is a great adventure, an adventure one lives with all his being, a 'fever', Robert Brasillach used to say. But long before him, d'Annunzio had written about the heightening of the meaning of life attained through sacred objects, the symbols of a secular religion: instruments of a cult around which human thought and imagination revolve, and which lift these to idealistic heights.[133] This new religion was a product of the change in the nature of politics which had taken place at the end of the nineteenth century.

Both fascist ideology and fascism's political style were obvious products of the new mass society: fascist politics were a reflection of the enormous difficulties which political structures that had been inherited from the nineteenth century would have to overcome if they were to survive into the twentieth. Eugen Weber has pointed out that the liberal politics of the nineteenth century were representative and parliamentary. But the representative system of which parliament is the symbol functioned adequately only in a deferential society, where distinction of achievement and wealth had replaced distinction of birth, but where the concept of distinction as such survived and the elector, who respected his representative, trusted him to serve his interests. The parliamentary representative system had been worked out by and for an élitist society not much more inclusive than the aristocratic society it replaced. In the mass society that took over at the end of the nineteenth century, with its democratic structure and its egalitarian ideology, parliament either did not, or was no longer felt to, work properly. Its shortcomings stood out, the bargains of everyday give-and-take became evidence of corruption, and compromise acquired a pejorative meaning, for mass society spoke in high-flown generalities and could not allow anything less than integral fulfilment.

The mass electorate might have been more tolerant had it felt better represented. But the petite bourgeoisie on the one hand, the newly significant industrial workers on the other, did not recognize either the pattern or the language of parliamentary politics as their own. The latter reflected the psychology of nineteenth-century élitist politics, which had been rationalistic and utilitarian: liberalism and Marxism both argued that, in the end, men will understand their interests and act in consequence. But the psychology of a mass electorate, as John Stuart Mill discovered before Gustave Le Bon, is irrationalistic, and politicians learned to appeal not to mind, but to emotion, seeking less to persuade than to manipulate.[134]

'Man is not only a rational being,' José Streel said, 'to make a people happy, it is not sufficient to bequeath it perfect laws: it also requires a climate.'[135] For Mussolini, who was frequently criticized by his peers for what they considered to be excessive rationalism, and even for Gentile, feeling 'was prior to thought and the basis of it.'[136] These appeals to feeling as opposed to the dry and grey argumentation of liberal politics were an essential part of great campaigns to conquer souls and hold them. Power had to be attained, national unity forged, the collective will asserted, by all available means. Essentially democratic, in its propaganda if not in its essence, fascism addressed itself to sentiments, deeply rooted prejudices, and intuitions – not to intellect. Rational appeals are accessible to few; they are also subject to criticism. Reasoning invites examination, speculation and disagreement. Feelings can be shared, arguments seldom, and then by few:[137] intellectual argument is by definition an agent of division, destruction, and moral death.

Fascism was clearly the spiritual heir to that nationalism of rebellion and adventure which since the end of the nineteenth century had been advocating the rejection of industrial society and liberal and bourgeois values. The malaise that led the generation of 1890 to rebel against the status quo reappears in near identical form with fascism, at least at the level of ideology. The violence of the earlier rebellion was modified to suit the changed conditions of an age of mass movements, and fascism was to be a mass ideology par excellence, belonging as it did to that current of thought which since the turn of the century had sought to replace the tentative and uncertain analytical procedures of the intellect by the infallible instinct of the masses. It propagated the cult of impulsive feeling and glorified both impatient instinct and emotion, which it considered superior to reason. In isolation, reason was doomed to sterility; too cultivated an inclination towards intellectual analysis debilitated the will, blunted vitality and stifled the voice of one's ancestors. Moreover, it enfeebled the individual's instinctive self-confidence and could lead him to doubt the truths of the nation. Intellectualism bred individualism, and frustrated man's primal impulses.[138]

Fascist ideology thus took on the character of an anti-intellectual reaction which pitted the powers of feeling and emotion, and irrational forces of every kind, against the rationality of democracy. It was the rediscovery of instinct, the cult of physical strength, violence, and brutality. This is, of course, what explains the attention paid to scenarios, the care lavished on décor, the great ceremonies, the parades – taken together, they made up a new liturgy where deliberation and discussion were supplanted by song, torches, and march-pasts. Viewed in this way, fascism appears as the direct descendant of the neo-romanticism of the 1880s and 1890s, only now the revolt had taken on dimensions commensurate with a mass society whose advent the fin-de-siècle generation had scarcely even foreseen.

This mystical, romantic, anti-rationalist fascism was as much a moral and aesthetic system as a political philosophy: it constituted a complete vision of man and the community. Usurping the place occupied by revealed religion, its aims were to create a world of fixed criteria, a world freed from doubt and purged of all foreign accretions; to give back their authenticity to man and the community; and re-establish the compromised unity of the nation. Once all this had been achieved, all the members of the national community, being of one body with it and existing through it alone, would react as one man and respond identically to the problems confronting it; and once this unanimity had been forged, political and social problems would be reduced to matters of detail. Moreover, the proletariat would now be an integral part of a nation which had become a community governed by a unified system of values, a purified and disciplined unit sufficiently well armed to compete with hostile communities in the struggle for existence. The nation's decline into decadence would be halted, action and heroism would become the respected virtues, and in consequence the vitality of the nation, which would now have a foundation of organic solidarity, would be free to flourish. In this sense, fascism represented a desire to transcend the banality of the bourgeois world, the materialism of industrial society, and the platitude of liberal democracy; behind it lay the desire to give life a new meaning. This is why, in the final analysis, fascism bore the character of a new religion which was complete with its own mysticism and which rejected in its totality the world as it was.

A new 'socialism'

This mystical and irrational aspect of fascism, with its romanticism and emotionalism, was, however, only one side of the coin. The other was the fascism of 'planning'[139] – technocratic and managerial fascism, one might call it. Essentially socialist in origin, this fascism rejected Marxism, on the one hand, in the name of a modernized, national, and authoritarian socialism, and liberal democracy and bourgeois society on the other, in the first place in the name of social justice, but above all in the name of efficiency and technical and economic progress, which were the two aims that had to be given priority if the community was to survive the crisis that had come upon the world. For their realization these aims required first and foremost a powerful decision-making apparatus, in other words, a State free of the inherent weaknesses of the parliamentary system.

In this respect, this second fascism owes its origin far more directly to the great economic crisis of the twenties and the inability of traditional structure to adapt to new problems and new needs than does the other, romantic fascism. It was the defective functioning of the democratic institutions and the clumsy and futile efforts that were made to adjust institutions and doctrines created by and for the nineteenth century to quite different circumstances and situations which stimulated ideas about 'planning'. The failure of the Social Democratic and Labour Parties, and indeed of Marxist thought in general, in the period between the two wars, was a factor that greatly influenced the rise of fascism: the fascists' search for answers to the new problems and the solutions they recommended must be said to be an essential aspect of fascist thought. This form of fascism was, then, the result of a revision of Marxism and an expression of the attempt to adapt socialism to modern conditions on both the ideological and tactical planes. That this tendency should have manifested itself most clearly in the three industrial countries of Western Europe, and at a time when their respective working-class movements were either just reaching or had already passed the pinnacle of their power, was certainly no accident. There is clearly a close connection between Oswald Mosley's actions as a young Labour Minister and those of Henri de Man and Marcel Déat, and his thinking was the result of the same ideological shift and the same political analysis as theirs. Their development into fascists differed according to local circumstances: whereas Mosley was the first to burn his bridges and openly launch a fascist movement, claiming his kinship with Hitler and Mussolini as he did so, de Man and Déat would not identify themselves with the fascist revolution until the débâcle of 1940. Nevertheless, from the middle thirties onwards, the new socialism they were promulgating bore the essential characteristics of fascism, although it must be added that this fact did not prevent them from exercising ministerial powers on behalf of socialist parties, nor hinder the one from becoming president of the Belgian Workers party or the other the leader of the Parti Socialiste de France when it was a member of the Front Populaire government. For at that time there were no clear ideological boundaries, since the phenomenon was a new one and nobody knew how to diagnose it.

The criticisms the 'planners' and neo-socialists levelled at Marxism revolved around two fundamental questions: the problems of the class struggle, and the recognition of *le fait national*, that is to say, the acknowledgement of the legitimacy of the national framework and the necessity of taking action within it. 'I believe, to sum up,' de Man wrote, 'that the socialism of the generation to come will be, under penalty of total collapse, as different from that of our fathers as [that] was from the socialism that preceded the communist manifesto.'[140]

According to Dodge, this new socialism took as its starting point, 'the entirely changed significance of the class struggle in the contemporary world'. Indeed, with regard to class structure, not only did it now appear that the proletariat would never constitute even the majority of the society, but social identification could not be predicted on the basis of an interest-analysis alone. Thus there was an ineluctable distinction between two social groups, the proletariat and the new middle classes, both of which shared essentially the same relationship – the exclusion from ownership – to the means of production.[141] Drawing his own conclusions from this, de Man proposed the formation of a 'Labour Front' which would include all those elements which found themselves at the mercy of finance capitalism. When, after 1930, Marcel Déat began suggesting that the socialists should head a vast 'anti-capitalist' alliance, he was in effect putting forward the very same idea, and one which, incidentally, implied the extinction of socialist specificity.[142] *Planisme* was consonant with, and an expression of, the more general socialist ideology developed by de Man, notably in that this ideology explicitly maintained that the removal of a given enterprise from the private sector of the economy was a decision to be taken on pragmatic grounds and not a question of doctrine. In the same way, de Man pointed out how unrealistic were the Marxist propositions on agriculture in countries where the small farmer flourished, and he also argued that direct socialization should only be applied to those sectors of the economy where the processes of manufacture had in themselves already in fact been collectivized, that is, large-scale industry.[143]

The Plan was a product of the crisis, an answer to the crisis, and, finally, a bid to rescue the middle classes, the stratum of society which the crisis had hit hardest. In the long term, the Plan was a substitute for the abandoned socialist aim of restructuring society: since the structures of the national economy remained untouched, it became in the event the life-belt of capitalism.

The true significance of the Plan and of Henri de Man's thought can be perceived most clearly in their political corollaries: the author of *Au-delà du Marxisme* was in fact advocating a far-reaching reform of the system. Dodge tells us that he spoke of the necessity of establishing a strong state capable of withstanding the attacks of the money powers: the classical division of powers would have to be reapportioned in favour of a division of functions by which the Legislative would be reduced to a supervisory role; and under beneficent guidance the mixed economy of the nation would be organized to as large a degree as possible under corporatist inspiration. In a series of articles in *Le Peuple* entitled 'Corporatisme et Socialisme', de Man undertook to demonstrate that it would be a mistake to let the Fascists monopolize the appeal of corporatism, which he defined as '. . . autonomous grouping and action in virtue of interests which derive from the practice of a trade or profession'. On the contrary, such a principle of organization was exactly what was necessary if socialism were to avoid those evils of bureaucratization and centralization with which its opponents charged it . . . A systematic corporatist organization of society would allow the peaceful resolution of conflict.[144]

In spite of the provocation his proposals represented and the opposition to him that had arisen within the Belgian Workers' Party, on the death of Emil Vandervelde, Henri de Man became its President. It was in his capacity as leader of Belgian socialism that in June 1940 he announced the dissolution of his party as a gesture of welcome to the new world the Nazi victory had brought. In his view, the collapse of the parliamentary parties had cleared the way for the construction of a true and authoritarian socialism which, in its essential aspects, would be based on the Nazi model.[145]

The necessity of 'taking nationalism into account' and of rooting 'the national economy in the nation's soil'[146] constitute – along with the defence of the middle classes – one of the two pillars of neo-socialist ideology, which rapidly developed into a true fascist ideology. By moving 'onto the plane of a national reality', by 'falling back into their national framework', the peoples had abruptly created a totally new situation: 'they have forced us,' Marquet said, 'to follow them.'[147] In other words, just as they were on the point of leaving the SFIO to set up the Parti Socialiste de France, the neo-socialists arrived at conclusions which not only recapitulated those reached by Michels, Sorel, and Mussolini fifteen or twenty years earlier, but were, moreover, essentially the same as those reached by Barrès at the end of the preceding century, to wit: the allegiance of the masses could only be mobilized in the name of a more urgent and compelling reality – the nation. The concept of the *nation* would be the key concept of political organization in the twentieth century.[148]

In essence what Déat and his companions were saying was that the traditional Marxist conception of class had lost its relevance: 'Marxism is the socialist answer to the capitalism of 1850.'[149] The middle classes were as gravely affected by the economic crisis as anyone, and since they were harder hit than the proletariat and were threatened with proletarianization, they had come out in revolt against the capitalist system and the liberal state. It was up to socialism to harness the revolutionary dynamism of this social stratum that had been crushed by the development of capitalism. It was up to socialism to harness the rebellion of the 'middle classes' who 'in their attempt to liberate themselves' were calling for 'the restoration of the State and the protection of the nation'.[150] Léon Blum was correct in speaking of a fascist contagion: in their efforts to combat fascism, his former companions were adopting fascist methods; as Blum realized, the primacy of the idea of the nation, the denial of the proletariat's special status and the denial of its revolutionary capability in a world in crisis could not but result in the denial of the very idea of class in the Marxist sense of the term.

This line of reasoning made it possible for Drieu La Rochelle to speak of 'bourgeois workers', whom the 'Third Party' – the fascists – did not want to see destroyed but classed with the peasantry and the proletariat.[151] Mosley, José Antonio, and Belgian Rexism assessed the situation in very similar terms: the oppo-

sition was no longer between the proletariat and the bourgeoisie
but between the 'workers of all classes' and 'banking capitalism,
or hypercapitalism'.[152] This approach enabled economic parasit-
ism and social exploitation to be eliminated without prejudicing
the unity of the nation, which was compromised by the idea of the
class struggle, and allowed the preservation of the realities of nation, family, and profession, which the artificial concept of class
had threatened.[153] Twenty years earlier, it had been the abandonment of the idea of the class struggle, the pillar of his socialist doctrine, which had made Mussolini swing to fascism: with the
socialist ministers de Man, Déat, and Mosley; with the communist leaders Doriot and Marion; and with the thousands of socialist and communist militants who committed themselves to
fascism, we see the same process taking place. Thus this desire to
bring socialism up to date and adapt it to the modern world ultimately resulted in fascism.

The national socialism of the end of the preceding century had
taken the same path, its objective having been to unite the social
and the national, incorporate both nationalism and socialism
within one movement, and merge the right and the left. This
legacy was inherited by that form of fascism that wished to be
neither 'of the right nor of the left; because basically the right
stands for the maintenance of an economic structure, albeit an
unjust one, while the left stands for the attempt to subvert that
economic structure, even though the subversion thereof would
entail the destruction of much that was worthwhile ... Our movement will on no account tether its destiny to the vested interests of
groups or classes which underlie the superficial division into right
and left.'[154] This idea returns time and again, with only slight
variation, in the writings of all fascist thinkers. Mussolini, for instance, six months after the Fasci di Combattimento was formed,
indicated that it was 'a little difficult to define fascists. They are
not republicans, socialists, democrats, conservatives, nor nationalists. They represent a synthesis of all the negations and all the
affirmations ... While they renounce all the parties, they are their
fulfilment.' In the minds of its promoters, fascism, being highly
nationalistic and socially concerned, thus achieved a harmonious
synthesis between the forces of the past and the demands of the

future, between the weight of tradition on the one hand and revolutionary enthusiasm on the other. It borrowed from both the right and the left. In practice, of course, fascism's insistence on the cooperation of all social classes and their reconciliation within the corporative régime threw it irrevocably to the right.

Nationalism and socialism work to mutual advantage. Nationalism is to some extent fed from the social concern, and the social concern gains considerable impetus from the enhanced value acquired by all citizens in conditions of community euphoria. The desire to be a party above and far superior to all others is invariably there; very often much of the motive force behind it derives from a profound conviction that the society needs remaking from top to bottom. The nation must be renewed through idealistic energy largely generated from national solidarity.[155] Fascist ideology is part of attempts to cut out new political avenues, to forge doctrines fitted to the changing realities. The old right and the old left were not equal to the task because, according to Mosley, 'both are instruments for preventing things being done, and the first requisite of the modern age is that things should be done.'[156] 'We must dismantle the unwieldy machine of capitalism, which leads to social revolution, to Russian-style dictatorship,' José Antonio said; 'we must dismantle it, but with what will we replace it?'[157]

What was to take the place of the dictatorship of money, what middle road could be taken between 'hypercapitalism and state socialism'?[158] The answer was a controlled economy and corporative organization topped by a strong State, a powerful decision-making apparatus. It was a pragmatic system which did not set out to impose one property régime or another: however, it seemed to those fascist economists who came from the left that, as economic organization progressed, the active economic function of private capital would diminish until, its social utility extinguished, the significance and power of capital would disappear. De Man's Plan du Travail, which became the official policy of the Belgian Workers' party, envisaged a mixed economy in which

political power would be used to create the economic conditions in which the country's productive and consumption capacities would be adapted to each other. This objective implies a double change in the doctrine of socialization: in the first place, the carrying into effect of a plan on the national plane is no longer subject to the international plane but takes precedence, which means that nationalization must be the present state of socialism; in the second place, the crux of nationalization is not the transfer of property but the transfer of authority – which means that the problem of management takes precedence over that of ownership.[159]

These views were endorsed by official socialist bodies: by the Belgian Socialist party and by the French CGT. And it is not by accident that British fascism was born of well-founded reformist impatience among bona fide socialists: nevertheless, in their majority, European socialists did understand that these views came dangerously close to those expressed by corporatist economists, and which Italy and Germany were beginning to put into practice.

It was the Great Depression of 1929 that led socialists like Mosley, de Man, and Déat to take a public stand in favour of protectionism and national exclusivism. The economic crisis turned the socialists' gaze inwards towards the nation and towards the idea of a strong, powerful state, efficient and authoritarian, which would be capable of ensuring order and reconciling the divergent interests within the community; which would be 'the master of its money and capable of controlling the economy and finance'; and which would also, in the words of the neo-socialists themselves, be able to 'impose certain rules of conduct on the large capitalists' and 'prepare the ground for the controlled economy that is in the logic of things.' The present crisis, 'a crisis of democracy in general', was a crisis of 'a State that is too weak'.[160] In de Man's case, the need to modernize the policy-making structures led to the idea of 'authoritarian democracy'[161] as a replacement for the old parliamentary democracy. For José Antonio, the new world would be one of authority, hierarchy, and order;[162] order, authority, and decision, according to Sir Oswald;[163] and order, authority, and the nation for the French neo-socialists.[164] Thus all three formulations contain the terms order and authority; the third varies in accordance with particular local circumstances.

The reform of the relations of power and its structures, as we can see from these concerns, was the cornerstone of the fascist revolution.

Totalitarianism

'Ours will be a totalitarian state in the service of the fatherland's integrity,' said José Antonio, 'all Spaniards will play a part therein through the membership of families, municipalities and trade unions. None shall play a part therein through a political party. The system of political parties will be resolutely abolished, together with all its corollaries: inorganic suffrage, representation by conflicting factions and the Cortes as we know it.'[165]

Innumerable passages in an identical vein are to be found throughout fascist literature. Totalitarianism is the very essence of fascism, and fascism is without question the purest example of a totalitarian ideology. Setting out as it did to create a new civilization, a new type of human being and a totally new way of life, fascism could not conceive of any sphere of human activity remaining immune from intervention by the State. 'We are, in other words, a state which controls all forces acting in nature. We control political forces, we control moral forces, we control economic forces . . .' Mussolini wrote, 'everything in the State, nothing against the State, nothing outside the State.'[166] For him, the fascist state was not only a living being, an organism, but a spiritual and moral entity: 'The fascist state is wide awake and has a will of its own. For this reason, it can be described as "ethical".'[167] Not only does the existence of the State imply the denial of the individual's rights – 'the individual exists only insofar as he is within the State and subjected to the requirements of the State' – but the State asserts the right to be 'a State which necessarily transforms the people even in their physical aspect'.[168] Outside the State, 'no human or spiritual values can exist, much less have value': 'no individuals or groups (political parties, cultural associations, economic unions, social classes) outside the State'.[169] The concrete consequences of such a conception of political power and the physical and moral repression it would engender are not hard to imagine. Here again we see how the communist and fascist totalitarianisms differ: whereas the Stalinist dictatorship could never be described as an application of the Marxist theory of the State, fascist terror was doctrine put into practice in the most methodical way. In fascism we have the perfect realization of the unity of thought and action.

Italian fascism took its glorification of the State so far as to identify it with the nation. For Gentile, the State – and the nation – was not 'a datum of nature' but a creation of the mind; for Mussolini 'it is not the nation which generates the State; that is an antiquated naturalistic concept which afforded a basis for nineteenth-century publicity in favour of national governments. Rather it is the State which creates the nation, conferring volition and therefore real life on a people made aware of their moral unity.'[170] This view of the State is a perfect illustration of the difference between the Italian – one is tempted to say Western – version of fascism and nazism, which saw the State as the emanation of the Volk and the servant of the community and the race. It also explains why racialism was originally alien to Italian fascism: 'Racism or the principle of racial self-determination as it has been called in recent years,' the English fascist Barnes wrote in a résumé of Mussolinian ideology, 'is a materialistic illusion, contrary to natural law and destructive of civilization. It is the *reductio ad absurdum* of Nationalism; any truly logical application of it is farcical and impracticable.'[171] Only in Central and Eastern Europe did racialism form an integral part of fascist ideology; in Western Europe, it was very often a foreign import, as the various fascisms developed in the late thirties under the shadow of nazism and rapidly organized themselves on its lines. Although the keystone of Nazi doctrine, biological racialism cannot therefore automatically be considered integral to fascism at all times and in all places.

The fascist state, creator of all political and social life and of all spiritual values, would of course be the undisputed master of the economy and social relations. Political power was regarded as an instrument for reconciling and harmonizing the conflicting interests that existed within the community. The State would, therefore, take control of the levers of the economy, without however being obliged by this to mount an attack on private property. Fascist supporters of left-wing persuasions saw this as the weakness of the fascist case, since the retention of traditional economic structures seemed scarcely compatible with the establishment of a new social and human order. In the view of fascist thinkers, however, the primacy of the State and the subordination of economics to politics would be sufficient guarantee against the return of the old order of things: the novelty and originality of the system consisted in its making capitalism serve the community. Fascism, while doing away with the most sordid aspects of capitalism, would simultaneously benefit from its technical achievements and from the deep-rooted psychological motivations that underlay it. The pursuit of profit remained the moving force behind economic activity, and on this point there was nothing to distinguish fascism from liberalism; what did distinguish it, radically, from both liberalism and socialism was its assertion of the primacy of politics. For Oswald Mosley, 'capitalism is the system by which capital uses the nation for its own purposes. Fascism is the system by which the nation uses capital for its own purposes. Private enterprise is permitted and encouraged so long as it coincides with the national interests. Private enterprise is not permitted when it conflicts with national interests.'[172] And in Sir Oswald's view, 'This implies that every interest, whether right or left, industrial, financial, trade union banking, or banking system is subordinated to the welfare of the community as a whole, and to the overriding authority of the organized State. No state within the State can be admitted. "All within the state, none outside the state, none against the state."'[173] Hence it was capitalism, not private property, that the fascists attacked, and a clear distinction was drawn between the two: 'property is the direct projection of the individual on matter, it is a basic human attribute,' whilst capitalism, which 'has gradually replaced this property of the individual with the property of capital ... ultimately ... reduces bosses and workers, employees and employers, to the self-same state of anxiety, to the same sub-human condition of the man deprived of all his attributes, whose life is stripped of all meaning.'[174]

Just as the corporative system worked to the advantage not of the proletariat, but of the employers, so the capitalist system was not destroyed but rather perpetuated and, finally, saved by fascism. Even so, it cannot be denied that at the ideological level, the level of desiderata, fascism did aim to eliminate exploitation by bringing economic interests to heel. If an organic society is by nature inimical to political pluralism, it is no less antagonistic to the most flagrant forms of social injustice, and indeed this had to be so if the proletariat was to be integrated into the community and if social relations were to be fundamentally changed. For Mussolini, the very word 'corporation' was to be understood in its etymological sense of 'fashioning into a body', a 'fashioning' which was the essential function of the State and the one that would insure its unity and its continued existence. If the community is an organic whole, deviation is corrupting and cannot be tolerated. All must act as one, shunning dissension as intrinsically harmful and seeking that unity which alone can save in the providential person of one man. It was this unitary life, the life of the nation, which led fascists to speak of an identity of interest uniting workers and employers. This organic view of the nation led naturally towards collectivism and to an emphasis on the most neglected and the most productive sections of the national community. Herein lay the socialism of national-socialism, the inspiration behind its anti-bourgeois and anti-capitalist orientation. If we remember the *embourgeoisement* and governmentalization of contemporary socialists during the twenties and thirties, it is easier to understand why fascists attacked them not only for dividing the nation but also for forgetting their revolutionary spirit.[175]

To be sure, once in power the fascists themselves proved singularly modest in their reformist ambitions; there was little of their revolutionary zeal to be seen in the way of structural reform. Admittedly, the only fascism not to come to power in war-time was the Italian, but in its case, too, the fascist revolution found itself caught up in a process to which those parties of the left which joined capitalist régimes fell victim: like the French and Belgian socialists, like the British Labour party, the fascists proved content to do no more than manage capitalism. It is also true that the fascists were to a large extent neutralized by the forces of reaction, whom they could not afford to ignore. But had Léon Blum's

Front Populaire not come up against exactly the same problems? If fascism rejected Marxism and Bolshevism, it also rejected conservatism and the 'reactionary' label, and adopted a revolutionary ideology. On this all fascists were agreed: for some, fascism was the successor of the Jacobin dictatorship; for others, it had, in Italy, carried through a revolution as far-reaching as any, barring the French.[176] But if we leave aside for a moment its revolutionary aspirations, fascism is seen as representing a movement whose cardinal aim was to re-create that unity of the nation which had been ruptured by liberalism and individualism, and reintegrate into the nation the class most profoundly alienated from it – the proletariat. As the successor of national, anti-Marxist socialism, fascism constituted an extremely violent attempt to return to the social body its unity, integrity, and totality. And here we find the great internal contradiction which fascism was never able to escape: it wanted to be a movement of reunification, yet it became an agent of civil war. But, we may well ask, is that not the fate of any revolutionary movement?

Finally, thrown to the right by their hatred of class politics, which their organic nationalism rejected, the fascists found themselves, as a logical consequence of the conflicts with the left, driven into opportunist alliances which distorted their image, diluted their radicalism, and reinforced their anti-Marxism to the detriment of their nationalist collectivism. The revolutionary potential of the fascist movements was thus largely nullified by the workings of the left-right dichotomy in which they were trapped: at the critical moments, the only alliances open to them were with conservative and reactionary elements; ultimately, the fascists' greatest enemy was the left. Yet these alliances came about only where a left actually existed. As Eugen Weber has shown, in countries where there was no left, fascism was the revolutionary movement par excellence.[177]

Unlike those historians whose judgement seems rather to have been impaired than improved by 'detachment' and 'perspective', the fascists and revolutionaries of Bucharest and London, Oslo and Madrid knew full well what divided them from the reactionary right, and they were not taken in by propagandist attempts to tar them with the same brush. Admiral Horthy, General Antonescu, Colonel Count de La Rocque, Marshal Pétain, General Franco, King Victor Emmanuel, and the Belgian and British Conservatives were well aware that it was only pressure of circumstances that had brought them into favour with the movements of Szálasi, Codreanu, Déat and Doriot, José Antonio and Mussolini, Degrelle and Oswald Mosley, and they discarded them as soon as they could.

The European conservatives, whether dictators or liberals – including reactionaries like Maurras – felt little sympathy with a movement which was essentially national socialist, in the fullest sense of that term, and which, while it attacked Marxism, itself wanted to put social relations on an entirely new footing and considered the established order the relic of an outdated world. In this sense, fascist ideology was a revolutionary ideology, since its principles represented a distinct threat to the old order of things. Dynamic, activist, and imbued with a spirit of rebellion that was visibly repugnant to the partisans of the established order, fascism practised a populist élitism which felt nothing but abhorrence for the old European aristocracy. Fascism promoted the cult of youth, brutality, and violence, and aimed to create both a new type of man and a new civilization in which a modern knighthood would have supremacy over the liberal bourgeois and the decadent, conservative aristocrat. Crowning all would be the totalitarian State, which in the hands of the leader would become the most perfect instrument ever conceived for the creation of a new order. These objectives were not ones to which the classic right could subscribe, nor indeed could such objectives, in the long term, serve its own interests.

It was where the right was too weak to hold its own ground that fascism achieved its most marked successes. In times of acute crisis, the right turned to the new revolutionary movement – the only one capable of confronting communism – for assistance, but never treated it with anything less than the deepest suspicion. By contrast, where the right was sufficiently confident to face the Marxist left itself, where its positions were not unduly threatened and it had a solid social base, it did everything in its power to prevent the fascist phenomenon getting out of hand. It concentrated above all on manipulating fascist troops and spending money to safeguard its own interests. Western Europe, Spain included, is a good case in point. It was not the strength of the right but its relative weakness, its fears, and its fits of panic, which created one of the essential conditions of fascist success.

Bibliography

This short bibliographical study does not, of course, claim to exhaust its subject. The books and articles discussed are ones that have a direct bearing on the specific questions dealt with in this paper.

Paradoxical as it may seem, until about ten years ago there were scarcely any scholarly studies of fascist ideology available. It was not until the beginning of the sixties that works of a general nature, comparative studies which tried to go beyond specifically national frameworks, began to appear. The first were Ernst Nolte, *Three Faces of Fascism: Action Française, Italian Fascism, National Socialism* (London, 1965) (the English translation of *Der Faschismus in Seiner Epoche* [Munich, 1963]) and Eugen Weber, *Varieties of Fascism* (New York, 1964). These were rapidly followed by Hans Rogger and Eugen Weber, eds, *The European Right: A Historical Profile* (Berkeley and Los Angeles, 1966), Walter Laqueur and George L. Mosse, eds, 'International Fascism 1920–1945', *Journal of Contemporary History*, vol. I, no. 1 (1966), Francis L. Carsten, *The Rise of Fascism* (London, 1967), John Weiss, *The Fascist Tradition* (New York, 1967), S. J. Woolf, ed., *European Fascism* (London, 1968), and *The Nature of Fascism* (London, 1968) and, finally, A. James Gregor, *The Ideology of Fascism: The Rationale of Totalitarianism* (New York, 1969). Most recently, we have Paul Hayes, *Fascism* (London, 1973), and Adrian Lyttelton's brilliant *Seizure of Power: Fascism in Italy 1919–1929* (London, 1973).

The sixties also saw the appearance of works which traced the immediate intellectual origins of fascism, thus enabling us to turn away at last from the search for possible 'ancestors' of fascism, from Plato to Fichte, and concentrate on the contemporary intellectual climate and cultural environment. In 1961 Fritz Stern's *The Politics of Cultural Despair: A Study in the Rise of the Ger-*

manic Ideology (Berkeley and Los Angeles), appeared, and was an immediate success. This study of Paul Lagarde, Julius Langbehn, and Arthur Moeller van den Bruck is 'a study in the pathology of cultural criticism' (p. XI): it brings out clearly the nature of the revolt which rumbled beneath the surface of Germany from 1850 onwards: 'Their despair over the condition of Germany reflected and heightened the despair of their countrymen, and through these men we see the current of disaffection rising until it merged with the nihilistic tide of national-socialism. Above all, these men loathed liberalism . . . they attacked liberalism because it seemed to them the principal premise of modern society; everything they dreaded seemed to spring from it: the bourgeois life, Manchester-ism, materialism, parliament and the parties, the lack of political leadership' (p. XII).

Professor Stern uses the term *conservative revolution* to denote the ideological attack on modernity, on the complex of ideas and institutions that characterize liberal, secular, industrial civiliza-tion: 'our liberal and industrial society leaves many people dis-satisfied – spiritually and materially. The spiritually alienated have often turned to the ideology of the conservative revolution' (p. XVI).

Fritz Stern's work should be read together with George L. Mosse's *Crisis of German Ideology: Intellectual Origins of the Third Reich* (New York, 1964). Mosse shows how deeply the Nazi ideas were embedded in German history. They were current – in-deed, eminently respectable – among several generations of Ger-mans prior to Hitler's rise. Professor Mosse provides evidence of how these ideas became institutionalized in schools, youth move-ments, veterans' groups, and political parties. His work reveals the uniqueness of German fascism. Mosse is making a point of vital importance for the study and interpretation of fascism when he demonstrates that though fascism spread throughout Europe, the German variety came to be unique. 'It was unique not only in the way it managed to displace the revolutionary impetus, but also in the primacy of the ideology of the Volk, nature, and race. The revolutionary impetus produced an ideological reaction through-out the continent, but the German crisis was *sui generis*, besides being more deeply rooted in the national fabric. Nowhere else was the ideology planted so deep or for such a long time. Nowhere else was the fascist dynamic embedded in such an effective ideology. Deeply rooted as it was in a specific German heritage, it could hardly serve as an aid to the fascist movement in other countries' (p. 315).

The same subject is studied from a different angle in Walter Z. Laqueur's *Young Germany – A History of the German Youth Movement* (London, 1962). Laqueur gives a clear picture of the strength, vitality, and depth of völkisch ideology, which was based on the overriding importance of the idea of race as opposed to those of nation or State. Laqueur provides further evidence of the uniqueness of the German experience. Nazism's biological racialism makes it a case apart, and that it does so forces us to the conclusion that, however much an ideology may retain elements that link it to a wider family of ideas, its degree of extremism will give it the status of a separate phenomenon. Such a conclusion would not seem to conflict with that reached by Eugen Weber at the end of a work which still remains the best introduction to a comparative study of fascism: 'Fascism is pragmatically activist, National-Socialism theoretically motivated, or at least expressed' (*Varieties of Fascism*, p. 143). Although his whole book takes the form of a rigorous comparative analysis, Weber cautions his reader at the very outset against falling into a trap which nowadays is carefully avoided by students of socialism and communism. Which caution, however, does not prevent the author of the most recent of the works of synthesis (Paul Hayes, *Fascism*) from declaring at a very early stage in his book that 'the concept of racial superiority was a constituent part of fascist ideology' (p. 20).

The success of nazism very often obscures the specific characters of the various fascisms. Even as shrewd an observer as H. R. Trevor-Roper has written '"International fascism" is unthinkable without Germany' ('The Phenomenon of Fascism', in S. J. Woolf, ed., *European Fascism*, p. 37). Trevor-Roper's over-emphasis on the Nazi experience is a direct consequence of his fundamental conception of fascism. For him, 'the public appearance of fascism as a dominant force in Europe is the phenomenon of a few years only. It can be precisely dated. It began in 1922–23

... it came of age in the 1930s and it ended in 1945' ('Phenomenon of Fascism', p. 18). Trevor-Roper is a representative of that school of modern scholarship which sees fascism as a phenomenon extremely limited in both time and place, and as the product of one unique historical situation. Ernst Nolte's monumental *Three Faces of Fascism* also inclines towards this school of thought. For Trevor-Roper, the precursors of fascism are no more than 'parochial figures' who 'in the public history of that time [before 1922] had no place and a historian writing in 1920 would probably not even have noticed them' (p. 18). Is not Trevor-Roper yet one more illustrious victim of that much vaunted 'historical perspective'? Not only does the view of contemporaries frequently differ from ours; it may often be more accurate. Contemporaries knew perfectly well who were fascism's precursors, and they were quite able to identify pre-fascism. Here is what Julien Benda, writing in 1927, said in *La Trahison des Clercs* (Neuchatel, 1956), p. 234: 'About 1890, the men of letters, especially in France and Italy, realized with astonishing astuteness that the doctrines of arbitrary authority, discipline, tradition, contempt for the spirit of liberty, assertion of the morality of war and slavery, were opportunities for haughty and rigid poses infinitely more likely to strike the imagination of simple souls than the sentimentalities of liberalism and humanitarianism.' His entire book is nothing more nor less than an indictment, written after the First World War, of the fascist thinking that preceded political fascism by several decades. It is no accident that it has been the scholars who do not see fascism as a phenomenon limited to the period between the two wars who have paid the greatest attention to pre-fascism.

Weber's *Varieties of Fascism* is illuminating in this connection, since it shows how far fascist ideology had its roots in the European intellectual climate of the end of the nineteenth century; this is also the approach adopted by George L. Mosse, the last chapter of whose *Crisis of German Ideology* already anticipates the first of *International Fascism 1920–1945*. This short essay, in which Mosse depicts fascism not just in terms of a revolt but also in terms of the taming of that revolt, offers some important insights into the nature of fascism and pre-fascism. The same can be said of his study of d'Annunzio, *The Poet and the Exercise of Political Power* (Yearbook of Comparative and General Literature), no. 22 (1973), which is a study in the emergence of the fascist political style, the new political style which worked within the framework of myth, symbol, and public festivals. As a result of the rise of nationalism accompanied by the growth of a secular religion of the nation in the nineteenth century, and the changed nature of politics, politics became a drama, expressed through secular liturgical rites and symbols closely linked to concepts of beauty in which poetry felt at home (pp. 32–3). D'Annunzio excelled in this domain, and he did indeed create an entirely new political style. The romantic and mystical element represented by d'Annunzio was also present in futurism and its violent revolt, and in his *Intellectuals in Politics* (New York, 1960), James Joll gives an intellectual biography of Marinetti which is essential for an understanding of the intellectual climate from which fascism emerged. In two countries, Italy and France, a true literary avant-garde was involved in the development of fascist and pre-fascist ideology: besides d'Annunzio and Marinetti, there was Barrès, to whom two recent books have been devoted, Robert Soucy's *Fascism in France: the Case of Maurice Barrès* (Berkeley, Los Angeles, London, 1972) and my *Maurice Barrès et le Nationalisme Français* (Paris, 1972). In this context George Mosse's latest book will be extremely useful: *The Nationalization of the Masses: Political Symbolism and Mass Movements in Germany from the Napoleonic Wars through the Third Reich* (New York, 1975).

Studies of the socialist-national aspect of pre-fascism are rather restricted in number. The first to tackle the subject were Robert F. Byrnes, 'Morès the first national-socialist', *The Review of Politics*, no. XII (July 1950), and Eugen Weber, 'Nationalism, Socialism and National-Socialism', *French Historical Studies* (Spring 1962). Three recent articles deal with the same subject: Enzo Santarelli, 'Le Socialisme national en Italie: Précédents et Origines', *Le Mouvement Social* (janviers-mars 1965), my 'National-Socialism and Anti-Semitism: The Case of Maurice Barrès', *Journal of Contemporary History*, vol. 8, no. 4 (1973), and George L. Mosse, 'The French Right and the Working-

Classes: *Les Jaunes*', *Journal of Contemporary History*, vol. 7, no. 3–4 (July-October 1972). For Austro-Hungary, one would do well to consult Andrew Whiteside, *Austrian National-Socialism before 1918* (The Hague, 1962). Pre-fascist ideology appears in these studies as a genuine mass ideology and the movements it inspired as mass movements. The fascist explosion is thus examined in depth, and it is explained as the result of a very profound wave of opinion.

A work of the same orientation is the highly controversial book by A. James Gregor, which in my view is the most thorough, lucid, and erudite study of Italian proto-fascism. As a parallel study of Italian syndicalism and the Italian school of political sociology on the one hand, and of the evolution of Mussolini's political thought on the other, it is, in my opinion, absolutely necessary.

Of the numerous studies of anti-Semitism at the end of the nineteenth century and the beginning of the twentieth, I consider the following to be indispensable: Robert F. Byrnes, *Anti-Semitism in Modern France* (New Brunswick, N.J., 1950); Michael R. Marrus, *The Politics of Assimilation: A Study of the French Jewish Community at the Time of the Dreyfus Affair* (Oxford, 1971); Norman Cohn, *Warrant for Genocide: The Myth of the Jewish World Conspiracy and the Protocols of the Elders of Zion* (London, 1967); Peter G. J. Pulzer is excellent on *The Rise of Political Anti-Semitism in Germany and Austria* (New York, 1964). The subject is also discussed in Hannah Arendt's famous book *The Origins of Totalitarianism*, where it is examined within the context of an analysis of the concept of totalitarianism. The intellectual origins of fascism and some basic trends in European history which made fascism possible are masterly examined by J. L. Talmon, *The Unique and the Universal* (London, 1965) and 'The Legacy of Georges Sorel', *Encounter* (February 1970), pp. 117–60. Indeed, the true dimensions of fascism can only be understood in the context of the intellectual revolution that took place at the end of the nineteenth century, and in this field the best works to consult are James Joll's brilliant *Europe Since 1870* (London, 1973), the most recent work to date; Peter Viereck, *Metapolitics: From the Romantics to Hitler* (New York, 1941);

H. Stuart Hughes, *Consciousness and Society* (1961); John Weiss, ed., *The Origins of Modern Consciousness* (1965); Gerhard Masur, *Prophets of Yesterday* (1961), and W. Warren Wagar, ed., *European Intellectual History since Darwin and Marx* (1966). But to be properly understood, fascism must also be seen in its relation to the right, and here we come up against a crucial problem of interpretation: was fascism a phenomenon of the right, essentially reactionary in character, or was it a far more complex phenomenon, as the fascists themselves believed? To obtain an impression of the ideological context of fascism and of its position vis-à-vis the right, one would do well to refer to *The European Right: A Historical Profile*. The value of this collection of essays lies in its attempt, taking the latter decades of the nineteenth century as its starting-point, to establish a distinction between the old and the new right. Admittedly, the contributors disagree about what kinds of groups are to be labelled 'right' – old or new. Also, they come up against objective difficulties inherent in comparative studies, which apply especially to a comparative study that ranges over eleven countries, from Finland to England and has as its subject movements of the extreme right, since these have none of the social homogeneity or doctrinal clarity of the extreme left, and variations from region to region are far more pronounced. It is, however, in the very fact that the book undertakes such a study, and shows what possibilities it holds, that its importance lies. The distinction between the traditionalist and modern 'rights', between classical conservatism and 'right-wing radicalism' is, it must be said, not always made clear, and the standard of the contributions varies. Nevertheless, thanks in great part to the masterly General Introduction by Eugen Weber, which gives the whole work its meaning, and his two chapters on France and Romania, the book succeeds in throwing light on how the radicalism of the new right prepared the way for fascism, and thus provides a basis for establishing a clearer distinction between fascism and conservatism, fascism and reaction. From the viewpoint of the history of ideas, however, this volume has one serious defect: little attention is paid to the function of ideology in social agitation and politics.

A number of other works need to be consulted to help clarify the problem of distinguishing fascism from the 'right' and the factors that specifically characterize the fascist movements. *The Rise of Fascism*, by F. L. Carsten, is a very useful synthesis, and serves as a good introduction to a difficult subject. *The Nature of Fascism*, edited by S. J. Woolf, is quite different in character. It is the outcome of a conference held at the University of Reading in the spring of 1967, the purpose of which was to analyse fascism from the different standpoints of the historian and the social scientist. This comparative study is of considerable interest to the historian of ideas, even though the book contains only three papers on the problem of fascist ideology: N. Kogan's 'Fascism as a Political System', and two contributions on 'Fascism and the Intellectuals' from George L. Mosse and P. Vita-Finzi. This multi-disciplinary undertaking follows an earlier collective volume edited by Stuart Woolf, also prepared at the University of Reading, *European Fascism* (1968), in the introductory chapter of which Professor Woolf offers some remarkable insights into what specific attributes distinguish fascism from the right.

This problem, of major importance to the study of fascism, and crucial to a thorough understanding of the fascist phenomenon, is further elucidated in a number of studies devoted to more specific subjects. Eugen Weber's *Action Française* (1962), which is in fact an analysis of the whole of the French right, is indispensable for a deeper understanding of the general European thrust to the right. If we take Eugen Weber's book together with René Rémond's *The Right Wing in France from 1815 to De Gaulle*, expanded and revised in 1966, and Robert J. Soucy's 'The Nature of Fascism in France', in *International Fascism*, we have three works which contain observations whose relevance transcends French politics. Stanley Hoffman's works on Vichy, 'Aspects du Régime de Vichy', *Revue Française de Science Politique*, vol. 1, no. 1 (janvier-mars 1956), and 'Collaborationism in France during World War II', *Journal of Modern History*, vol. 40, no. 3 (September 1968), are illuminating on what divides fascism from the right, and the observations, insights, and theoretical reflections contained in these articles make one look forward with impatience to the appearance of the forthcoming *Vichy 1940–1944:*

La Dernière Contre-Révolution Française. The work done by
Weber, Hoffman, and Rémond, to which should be added Raoul
Girardet's 'Notes sur l'Esprit d'un Fascisme Français', in *Revue
Française de Science Politique*, vol. V, no. 3 (1955), demonstrates
clearly how misleading it is to identify fascism with the right.
Further evidence for this is provided in a number of works de-
voted to other countries: Stanley Payne's *Falange: A History of
Spanish Fascism* and Hugh Thomas's Introduction to José Antonio's *Selected Writings* for Spain; Weber's 'The Men of the
Archangel', in *International Fascism* and his chapter on Romania
in *The European Right*; for Italy, Adrian Lyttelton's 'Fascism in
Italy: The Second Wave', in *International Fascism* and the chapters on Ideology and Culture in his *Seizure of Power*. Lyttelton's
book, the most recent to be published on Italian fascism, is the
best book on the subject, and is absolutely essential for any serious
study of fascism.

In 'The Men of the Archangel', in many respects a pioneering
work, Weber strongly challenges the view that fascism was
necessarily a reactionary middle-class movement. His argument
constitutes the beginning of a comparative study of fascist
sociology and fascist appeal, and at the same time takes issue
with the view that fascism was the ideology of a declining bourgeois society. Weber draws our attention not only to the differences between Western and Eastern Europe – something Mosse
and Woolf also do – but also to the general problem of under-
developed countries, the role of fascism in non-Western societies
where significant movements of the revolutionary left did not
exist, where the working classes were not organized, where the
socialists were inaudible and the communists invisible. Here,
fascism faced no radical competition, and the fascists' own radicalism was able to develop free of the need either to defend itself
on the left or compromise too much with the forces of moderation
(pp. 104–5).

Weber's conception of the nature of fascism is challenged in
John Weiss's *Fascist Tradition* (1967), which is written in support
of the view that fascism can unambiguously be classified as a
right-wing conservative movement. John Weiss charges Eugen

Weber with being too ready to take fascists' ideological statements at their face value. According to Weiss, Eugen Weber
takes their 'leftism' far more seriously than he should (p. 136).

To give such short shrift to a work as solidly documented as
Weber's would require a book more solid, less hurried, and considerably more convincing than this. Moreover – though Weiss
could not have known this – Max H. Kele, in his *Nazis and
Workers* (1972), has implicitly confirmed what Weber said about
fascist recruitment and fascism's appeal to workers. The book is
a study of nazism, but has more general implications, since it
throws serious doubt on the famous view of fascism as an 'extremism of the centre' which we find developed in Martin Seymour Lipset's *Political Man* (1960).

The criticisms that Weiss makes of Weber are also those Dante
Germino makes of A. James Gregor. Germino, himself the author
of a well-known work, *The Italian Fascist Party in Power*, and an
important article, 'Italian Fascism in the History of Political
Thought', *Midwest Journal of Political Science*, vol. VIII, no. 2
(May 1964), criticizes the author of *Ideology of Fascism* for taking
literally some patently ridiculous and self-serving statements made
by fascist propagandists, and for drawing a portrait of fascism
which is unrecognizable because of the deep scars that have been
omitted (*American Political Science Review*, no. 64 [June 1970],
p. 165). The arguments put forward carry some weight: it is indeed difficult to subscribe to a definition of fascism as a 'humanism of labour', or to agree that the fascist idea of the community
should be defined in terms of the 'Kantian kingdom of ends'
(pp. 20–21 of Gregor's work). Gregor's pursuit of scientific objectivity and intellectual detachment has led him a little too far.
Nevertheless, his book cannot be fairly dismissed on the strength
of this kind of shortcoming, since Gregor's scholarship is exemplary. His study of proto-fascism and of Mussolini's and Gentile's
thought, and his analysis of Sorel, Pareto, Mosca, Michels and,
of course, Gumplowicz, who is a veritable discovery on Gregor's
part, are of an exceptionally high standard. Gregor gives a clear
account of the genesis and maturation of fascist ideology, and his
work is also invaluable in shedding light on the contribution of
some minor intellectuals whom one can, if one wishes, treat as

propagandists, but whose role in fascist Italy was considerable. Gregor deserves great credit for stressing that a Gini or a Papini are no less significant for an understanding of fascist ideology than a Gentile. These views, of course, place him in a totally opposed camp to such scholars as Ernst Nolte, for whom fascism can be summed up as Maurras, Mussolini, and Hitler, and yet it is the minor intellectuals who are read, and it is their thought that is most widely disseminated.

But Gregor's work is not solely a study of fascist ideology in Italy. It is the work of a social scientist who wishes not only to 'provide an historically accurate and objective account of the ideology of Mussolini's fascism', but also 'to suggest a general typology of revolutionary mass movements that reflects contemporary thinking with respect to the description and analysis of totalitarian movements' (p. IX). This leads the author to consider fascism as 'a developmental dictatorship appropriate to partially developed or underdeveloped, and consequently status-deprived, national communities in a period of intense international competition for place and status' (p. XIII). What this approach finally leads to is not entirely unforeseeable: Leninism, Stalinism, the African socialisms, and Maoism are so many fascisms that are either unaware of, or do not acknowledge, their true names. The concluding part of the book should certainly be read with great circumspection, although the concept of 'developmental dictatorship' as a definition of fascism offers wide scope for future research. Nevertheless, it seems odd that Gregor should have thought an analysis of one model – the Italian – sufficient to justify the elaboration of such vast theories: surely, before tackling the underdeveloped countries and/or before presenting conclusions intended to be universal in their application, the author should have cast a brief glance in the direction of the other European fascisms. All in all, however, this highly controversial book, although written in a language at times far from transparent, is extremely stimulating and original and should be required reading for every student of fascism.

But it is Ernst Nolte who has set himself the most ambitious task. *Three Faces of Fascism* is an attempt to give a comprehensive explanation of fascism. The book is based on the most meticulous scholarship, the command of the material is impressive, and the methodological rigour is admirable. The work has been translated into English and French, and was acclaimed an immediate success. In reviews by, among others, Klaus Epstein, Hajo Holborn, James Joll, Walter Laqueur, George Mosse, Wolfgang Sauer, Fritz Stern, and Eugen Weber, this masterly work was hailed as a very great book.

Professor Nolte's work contains such a wealth of observations, information, insight, and throwaway ideas that are well worth keeping that inevitably one takes issue with some. First, his method. A philosopher by training, and of the school of Heidegger, Nolte is writing history within a philosophical framework. Thus it is that, having rejected the historical and typological approaches, he opts for the phenomenological approach, which he conceives as an attempt to return to Hegel's integration of philosophy and history (pp. 539–40). It is this method that permits Nolte to consider it legitimate to claim universal validity for his conclusions in spite of the fact that he limits his study to an analysis of the political ideas of three leaders – Maurras, Mussolini, and Hitler – and disregards not only their own movements and all the other European fascist movements, but also the socioeconomic dimension of fascism. Nolte's analysis belongs strictly to the history of ideas, an approach perfectly legitimate in itself providing one is aware of the limitations and providing one reminds oneself that such broad generalizations as are found here cannot be put forward on the basis of such a narrow approach. Nolte is clearly floundering in problems of methodology, which explains how Action Française is elevated to the status of a fascism equivalent to nazism. The importance for Nolte of Action Française is clear: it provides him with the link he needs between the French and Soviet revolutions, testifies to the continuity of counter-revolutionary thought, and offers proof-positive of the very general character of that wave of revolt which swept nazism to power. In some ways, Ernst Nolte's approach recalls that of Gerhard Ritter and Friedrich Meinecke: Thomas More, for Ritter, Machiavelli, for Meinecke, and now Maurras, for Nolte, are so many proofs of the universality of evil, so many proofs that it was almost by accident, by a mere conjunction of political circumstances, that the Nazis arose in Germany.

This impression is considerably reinforced by the overriding importance Nolte attributes to the leaders of the movements, and by an observation he makes in this context which George Mosse, reviewing *Three Faces of Fascism* (*Journal of the History of Ideas*, no. 27 [1966], p. 624) has not failed to draw attention to. After the Führer's death, the Nazi leadership is said to have snapped back to its 'original position', becoming once more 'a body of well-meaning and cultured Europeans'. This sort of statement casts doubt on Nolte's understanding of Nazi ideology as well as on his analysis of bourgeois society. Moreover, nazism is by implication reduced to something very minor: it arrives in this world, and disappears from it, with the Führer, and the concentration camp commandant quietly returns home to become again what he has never really ceased to be – an exemplary citizen and a lover of high culture. But if this is true, is nazism, as Nolte thinks, really dead? Surely it cannot be, if all it needs is the reappearance of a Hitler to turn a good, cultivated, and law-abiding European into a Nazi?

Nolte's definition of fascism has a dual aspect: fascism, in his view, is to be seen as a revolt against the universal process of secularization, democratization, and international integration in the modern era; in its final stage, fascism takes on the form of a resistance to 'transcendence'. 'That Maurras' whole thought represents a resistance to transcendence and unconditional defence of the autarkic-sovereign, martial, aristocratic state of the *ancien régime* as a paradigm for France for all time, can hardly be doubted' (p. 530; all quotations from the 1969 Mentor edition). A page earlier, the argument reaches its conclusion:

The power of 'antinature' fills Hitler with dread: it is this 'going beyond' in human nature which is capable of transforming the essence of human order and relations – transcendence. What Hitler – and not only Hitler – feels to be threatened are certain basic structures of social existence. He too – like Maurras – is afraid *of* man *for* man. But he did not only think, he acted. And in his actions, he carried his principle to its irrevocable end. Hence it is possible to define Hitler's radical fascism, which called itself 'National Socialism', as follows: NATIONAL SOCIALISM WAS THE DEATH THROES OF THE SOVEREIGN, MARTIAL, INWARDLY ANTAGONISTIC GROUP. IT WAS THE PRACTICAL AND VIOLENT RESISTANCE TO TRANSCENDENCE (p. 529).

What Nolte does not tell us, as Wolfgang Sauer has already pointed out, is why this revolt was most radical in Germany? If the modernization process was universal, was fascist revolt also universal? If it was, why does Nolte deal only with France, Italy, and Germany? If it was not, why did the fascist revolt occur only in these (and some other) countries? (Wolfgang Sauer, 'National Socialism: Totalitarianism or Fascism', *American Historical Review*, vol. LXXIII, no. 2 [December 1967], p. 413). Anyone familiar with the fascist movements will find a large number of questions left unanswered, although it is true that these questions are easier to ask than to answer. Nevertheless, it is impossible, when one has come to the end of this exceptional work, not to be left with a feeling of unreality and to wonder whether nazism has not been reduced to the level of an abstraction, an intellectual exercise.

This feeling is not dispelled by the second aspect of Nolte's definition of fascism, which he presents in terms of anti-Marxism: 'FASCISM IS ANTI-MARXISM WHICH SEEKS TO DESTROY THE ENEMY BY THE EVOLVEMENT OF A RADICALLY OPPOSED AND YET RELATED IDEOLOGY AND BY THE USE OF ALMOST IDENTICAL, AND YET TYPICALLY MODIFIED, METHODS, ALWAYS, HOWEVER, WITHIN THE UNYIELDING FRAMEWORK OF NATIONAL SELF-ASSERTION AND AUTONOMY.' This definition implies that without Marxism, there is no fascism, that fascism is at the same time closer to and further from communism than is liberal anti-communism . . . (p. 40). This reads very much like something from the good old totalitarian analysis, which is itself not very new but dates back to the twenties and thirties: the Italian and French fascists both spoke at length of the points of similarity between communism and fascism. For Drieu La Rochelle, Stalinism was 'a red fascism' – which, by the way, would not surprise Professor Gregor. Here again we have an example of a contemporary arriving at an analysis which modern scientific research hails as a revolutionary achievement.

Yet even those fascists who recognized the common ground between themselves and the Marxists, while simultaneously fighting them to the death – and this goes for Degrelle and d'Annunzio, Doriot and Valois – always considered their real, natural enemy to be liberalism. This is particularly true as regards the origins of fascist thought. Nor does it seem to be anti-Marxism that lies at the root of Hitler's thought: is it not rather racialism and anti-Semitism? Was the enemy not the Jew, rather than the Marxist? Is this not a point of dissimilarity between nazism and fascism that simply cannot be ignored? Fascism was not, then, as Nolte would have us believe, simply a shadow of Marxism. It was an entirely separate phenomenon and had a reality of its own which Nolte, transported into other realms by the phenomenological method, does not always perceive.

In sum, however, even when one cannot agree with Nolte on every point, indeed, even when one is unable to agree with him on the essential points, it is obvious that this book will serve as a landmark to scholars for many years to come.

Notes

I am deeply indebted to the Warden and Fellows of St Antony's College, Oxford, for having elected me to a Wolfson Visiting Fellowship for the 1973–4 academic year. It was here, in this true home of scholarship, that I was able to prepare this study, after the Yom Kippur War.

1. See the bibliographical part of this essay. As far as possible, the quotations refer to the English translations of the primary sources.

2. Hugh Seton-Watson, 'Fascism, Right and Left', in *Journal of Contemporary History*, vol. I, no. 1 (1966), p. 188.

3. N. Kogan, 'Fascism as a Political System', in S. J. Woolf, ed., *The Nature of Fascism* (London, 1968), p. 16.

4. Eugen Weber, *Varieties of Fascism* (New York, 1964), pp. 10–11.

5. Cf. ibid., pp. 9–10; Martin Seliger, 'Fundamental and Operative Ideology: The Two Principal Dimensions of Political Argumentation', *Policy Sciences*, vol. I (1970), pp. 325–7.

6. Cf. S. J. Woolf's Introduction in *European Fascism* (London, 1968), p. 9, and Michael Hurst, 'What is Fascism', in *The Historical Journal*, vol. XI, no. 1 (1968) pp. 166 and 183.

7. Oswald Mosley, *The Greater Britain* (London, 1932), p. 14.

8. Benito Mussolini, 'Political and Social Doctrine', in *Fascism: Doctrine and Institutions* (Rome, 1935), pp. 31, 34, n. 2. Among other basic texts of

fascist thought and legislation, this volume contains 'Fundamental Ideas' written for Mussolini by Gentile.

9. Seliger, op. cit., pp. 327–8.

10. Mussolini, 'Political and Social Doctrine', p. 33.

11. ibid., p. 26: 'All doctrines aim at directing the activities of men towards a given objective; but these activities in their turn react on the doctrine, modifying and adjusting it to new needs, or outstripping it.'

12. *Combat*, no. 2 (February 1936).

13. Quoted in Michel Winock, 'Une parabole fasciste: Gilles de Drieu La Rochelle', *Le Mouvement Social*, no. 80 (July 1972), p. 29.

14. Georges Valois, *Le Fascisme* (Paris 1927), p. 21.

15. Oswald Mosley, *Tomorrow we live* (London, 1938), p. 57.

16. Cf. the recent studies by H. Stuart Hughes, *Consciousness and Society: the Reorientation of European Social Thought 1890–1930* (New York, 1961); Gerhard Masur, *Prophets of Yesterday: Studies in European Culture 1890–1914* (New York, 1966); W. Warren Wagar, ed., *European Intellectual History since Darwin and Marx* [*Selected Essays*] (New York, 1966); John Weiss, ed., *The Origins of Modern Consciousness* (Detroit, 1965).

17. Giovanni Gentile, 'The Philosophic Basis of Fascism', *Foreign Affairs*, no. VI (1927–8), pp. 295–6.

18. H. Stuart Hughes, op. cit., pp. 38–9. Cf. in particular Carlton J. H. Hayes, *A Generation of Materialism 1871–1900* (New York, 1963) and Jacques Barzun, *Race, a Study in Superstition* (New York, 1965), p. 162.

19. Fritz Stern's *The Politics of Cultural Despair* is the best treatment of Langbehn, Lagarde, and Moeller van den Bruck.

20. George L. Mosse, *The Crisis of German Ideology: Intellectual Origins of the Third Reich* (New York, 1964), pp. 4–5.

21. Zeev Sternhell, *Maurice Barrès et le nationalisme français* (Paris, 1972), pp. 263–73.

22. Maurice Barrès, 'Que faut-il faire?', *Le Courier de l'Est* (2ème série) (12 May 1898); ibid., *Mes Cahiers*, 14 vols. (1929–57), vol. II, no. 197; idem., 'Socialisme et Nationalisme', *La Patrie* (27 February 1903).

23. Enrico Corradini, 'Nationalism and the Syndicates', speech made at the Nationalist Convention, Rome, 16 March 1919, in Adrian Lyttelton's excellent anthology *Italian Fascisms from Pareto to Gentile* (London, 1973), p. 159.

24. Cf. the important article by Thierry Maulnier, 'Charles Maurras et le Socialisme', *La Revue Universelle*, vol. LXVIII, no. 19 (January 1937), p. 169. Maulnier is quoting from Maurras's *Dictionnaire Politique et Critique*.

25. Pierre Biétry, *Le Socialisme et les Jaunes* (Paris, 1906), and more particularly p. 99 and passim.

26. Cf. Stephen Wilson, 'The Antisemitic Riots of 1898 in France', *The Historical Journal*, vol. XVI, no. 4 (1973), pp. 789–806.

27. Jules Soury, *Le Système Nerveux Central* (Paris, 1899), p. 1778; *Campagne Nationaliste (1894–1901)* (Paris, 1902), p. 65.

28. Enzo Santarelli, 'Le Socialisme National en Italie: Précédents et origines', *Le Mouvement Social*, no. 50 (January-March 1965).

29. Corradini, 'The Principles of Nationalism', in A. Lyttelton, op. cit., p. 147.

30. Cf. Corradini's 'The Proletarian Nations and Nationalism' (1911), in A. Lyttelton, op. cit., pp. 149–51.

31. Corradini, 'Nationalism and Democracy' (political speech 1913), in A. Lyttelton, op. cit., p. 152.

32. Corradini, 'The Cult of the Warrior Morality' (December 1913), in A. Lyttelton, op. cit., pp. 155–8.

33. A. James Gregor, *The Ideology of Fascism: the Rationale of Totalitarianism* (New York, 1969), pp. 37–9.

34. Vilfredo Pareto, from *Les Systèmes Socialistes*, in A. Lyttelton, op. cit., pp. 72–5.

35. ibid., p. 78.

36. Gregor, op. cit., pp. 78–80.

37. ibid., p. 52.

38. Roberto Michels, *Political Parties* (London, n.d.), p. 395.

39. ibid., p. 407. The whole of Chapter II of Part VI of this work is of considerable interest.

40. 'Le Syndicalisme et le Socialisme en Allemagne', in *Syndicalisme et Socialisme* (Paris, 1908), p. 25. Speeches made at the conference held in Paris on 3 April 1907.

41. Arturo Labriola, 'Le Syndicalisme et le Socialisme en Italie', in ibid., pp. 11 and 9–13.

42. Hubert Lagardelle ,'Le Syndicalisme et le Socialisme en France', in ibid., p. 36.

43. Victor Griffuelhes, *L'Action Syndicaliste* (Paris, 1908), p. 37.

44. Emile Pouget, *La Confédération Générale du Travail* (Paris, 1909), pp. 35–6.

45. Michels, op. cit., p. 369.

46. 'Déclaration', in *Cahiers du Cercle Proudhon*, no. I (January 1912), p. 1.

47. Santarelli, op. cit., p. 50.

48. ibid., pp. 52–3.

49. Lyttelton, op. cit., p. 98.

50. ibid., pp. 211–12.

51. Hendrik de Man, Manifesto to the Members of the POB, quoted in Peter Dodge, *Beyond Marxism: The Faith and Works of Hendrik de Man* (The Hague, 1966), p. 197.

52. Marcel Déat, 'L'Evolution du Socialisme', in *L'Effort* (25 September 1940).

53. Mussolini, 'Political and Social Doctrine', p. 26.

54. Mosley, *Fascism: 100 Questions asked and answered* (London. 1936), Question 2.

55. 'What a Legionary believes', Romanian Fascist Catechism, in Weber, op. cit., p. 169.

56. Paul Marion, *Programme du Parti Populaire Français* (Paris, 1938), p. 83.

57. Léon Degrelle, *Révolution des âmes* (Paris, 1938). The term counter-civilization is used in very much the same sense as Annie Kriegel uses the term counter-society in her well-known works on French communism; cf. particularly *Les Communistes Français: essais d'ethnographie politique* (Paris, 1970).

58. Georges Valois, *Fascisme* (Paris, 1927), pp. 15–16.

59. Thierry Maulnier, *Mythes Socialistes* (Paris, 1936), pp. 169–70.

60. Michael Hurst, 'What is Fascism', p. 184. For the English fascist James Strachey Barnes, fascism was a result of the failure of 'liberal statecraft' (Barnes, *The Universal Aspects of Fascism* [London, 1928], p. 63).

61. Mussolini, 'Political and Social Doctrine', p. 26.

62. Mussolini, 'Fundamental Ideas', p. 8.

63. Gentile, 'The Philosophic Basis of Fascism', p. 293.

64. José Antonio Primo de Rivera, *Selected Writings*, ed. and intro. Hugh Thomas (London, 1972), p. 65.

65. Mussolini, 'Political and Social Doctrine', p. 21.

66. Marcel Déat, *Pensée allemande et pensée française* (Paris, 1944), pp. 63 and 99.

67. Pierre Drieu La Rochelle, *Chronique Politique 1934–1942* (Paris, 1943), p. 161. Twenty-five years earlier, in 1912, Barrès had said, 'The eighteenth century, which would like to go on living, is in its last throes. We have done with asking its advice on how to run our lives.' (Speeches in the Chamber, June 1912.)

68. Mussolini, *Fascism*, Appendix, p. 40 (speech before the New National Directory of the Party, 7 April 1926).

69. James Strachey Barnes, *The Universal Aspects of Fascism* (London, 1928), p. 164.

70. Degrelle, op. cit., p. 145.

71. Mosley, *The Greater Britain*, op. cit., p. 152.

72. Déat, Marquet, Montagnon, *Néo-Socialisme, Ordre, Autorité*, Nation (Paris, 1933), p. 43.

73. Degrelle, op. cit., p. 151.

74. Drieu La Rochelle, *Gilles*, pp. 179, 340–42, 384, 455.

75. Georges Valois, *Révolution Nationale* (Paris, 1924), pp. 97 and 151.

76. Degrelle, op. cit., pp. 153–4.

77. Primo de Rivera, op. cit., p. 57.

78. José Streel, *Ce qu'il faut penser de Rex* (Brussels, n.d.), pp. 106–8.

79. Gentile, 'The Philosophic Basis of Fascism', pp. 291–2.

80. Mussolini, *Fascism*, Appendix, pp. 9, 19, 36. Cf. Primo de Rivera, op. cit., p. 137: 'Life is a militia and must be lived in a spirit purified by service and sacrifice.' Cf. also Degrelle, op. cit., p. 6: 'The easy life is the death of idealism. Nothing revives it better than the lash of the hard life.'

81. Degrelle, op. cit., pp. 2–3.

82. Mussolini, *Fascism*, Appendix, pp. 19 and 36.

83. Marion, op. cit., pp. 99 and 104.

84. Hendrik de Man, 'Manifesto to the Members of the POB, July 1940', in Dodge, op. cit., p. 197.

85. Quoted in Michèle Cotta, *La Collaboration 1940–1944* (Paris, 1964), p. 128.

86. Mosley, *The Greater Britain*, op. cit., p. 159.

87. Degrelle, op. cit., pp. 3–4.

88. Mussolini, 'Political and Social Doctrine', p. 19.

89. Drieu La Rochelle, *Chronique Politique*, p. 69.

90. Drieu La Rochelle, quoted in Winock, op. cit., p. 44.

91. 'The Futurist Manifesto', in *Le Figaro*, February 1909.

92. Soury, *Campagne Nationaliste*, p. 185.

93. Drieu La Rochelle, 'Verra-t-on un Parti national et socialiste?', *La Lutte des Jeunes*, no. 2 (4 March 1934).

94. 'The Futurist Manifesto'.

95. Cf. Marion, op. cit., pp. 85–95.

96. ibid., pp. 91–4.

97. Drieu La Rochelle, *Chronique Politique*, p. 69.

98. Drieu La Rochelle, *Avec Doriot* (Paris, 1937), p. 12.

99. Cf. for instance Primo de Rivera, op. cit., pp. 52–4: 'We would be just another party if we were to formulate a programme of concrete solutions'; or Streel, op. cit., p. 105.

100. Mussolini, 'Fundamental Ideas', in *Fascism*, p. 13.

101. Mosley, *The Greater Britain*, op. cit., p. 159.

102. Mussolini, *Fascism*, Appendix, p. 38.

103. Streel, op. cit., p. 105.

104. Drieu La Rochelle, *Chronique Politique*, pp. 15–16.

105. Valois, *Révolution Nationale*, p. 13.

106. ibid.

107. Drieu's 'Gilles' never ceased to dream of a union of the 'valiant', of all the rebels, of young bourgeois and young workers who together would overthrow the 'freemason dictatorship' (*Gilles*, p. 422). For Paul Marion, this alliance would be one of 'all those who have had enough, all those who want a change' (*Programme of the PPF*, p. 110).

108. Cf. Ruggero Zangrandi, *Le long voyage à travers le fascisme* (French trans. Paris, 1963). Cf. also George L. Mosse, 'The Genesis of Fascism', in *Journal of Contemporary History*, vol. I, no. 1 (1966), p. 17.

109. Degrelle, *Révolution des âmes*, op. cit., p. 146.

110. Cf. Winock, op. cit., p 40.

111. Déat, *Pensée allemande et pensée française*, pp. 97–8.

112. Quoted in Weber, op. cit., pp. 41–2.

113. Quoted in Gregor, op. cit., p. 213.

114. Streel, op. cit.

115. Primo de Rivera, op. cit., p. 49.

116. Gregor, op. cit., pp. 212–13.

117. ibid., p. 214.

118. Mussolini, 'Fundamental Ideas', pp. 9–10; cf. Marion, op. cit., p. 98: 'A man is not just a certain number of pounds of organic matter. He is someone who has a long ancestry, a long history, comes from a particular region, has a particular job.'

119. Gregor, op. cit., p. 220.

120. Mussolini, 'Fundamental Ideas', pp. 10–11, cf. also p. 39.

121. Gentile, 'The Philosophic Basis of Fascism', p. 303.

122. Mosley, *Fascism: 100 Questions*, op. cit., p. 9 and *The Greater Britain*, op. cit., p. 22.

123. Primo de Rivera, op. cit., p. 55.

124. Streel, op. cit., p. 113.

125. Déat, *Pensée allemande et pensée française*, pp. 84–5.

126. A. Rocco, 'The Political Doctrine of Fascism', in C. Cohen, ed., *Communism, Fascism and Democracy* (New York, 1964), pp. 341–2; cf. also Mussolini, 'Political and Social Doctrine', pp. 22–3.

127. Gentile, 'Philosophic Basis of Fascism', pp. 303–4.

128. Primo de Rivera, op. cit., p. 133.

129. Marion, op. cit., p. 94.

130. Déat, *Pensée allemande et pensée française*, p. 110.

131. Marion, op. cit., pp. 93–4.

132. Déat, *Pensée allemande et pensée française*, p. 110. Cf. also René Rémond, *Introduction à l'histoire de notre temps: le XXème siècle de 1914 à nos jours* (Paris, 1974), pp. 126–7.

133. George L. Mosse, 'The Poet and the Exercise of Political Power: Gabriele d'Annunzio', *Yearbook of Comparative and General Literature*, no. 22 (1973), pp. 32–3.

134. Eugen Weber, in Introduction to Hans Rogger and Eugen Weber, *The European Right: A Historical Profile* (Berkeley and Los Angeles, 1966), pp. 17–18.

135. Streel, op. cit., p. 106.

136. Quoted in Gregor, op. cit., p. 225.

137. Cf. Weber, *Varieties of Fascism*, pp. 37–8.

138. Cf. J. L. Talmon, *Destin d'Israel: l'Unique et l'Universel* (Paris, 1967), pp. 75–81.

139. In 1933, Hendrick de Man's 'Plan du Travail' was adopted, on his recommendation, by an overwhelming majority of the Belgian Workers Party. The 'Planning' movement subsequently developed rapidly throughout Western Europe.

140. Hendrick de Man, 'Clarification', in *Le Peuple*, 24 September 1933, quoted in Dodge, op. cit., p. 143.

141. Dodge, op. cit., p. 178.

142. Marcel Déat, *Perspectives Socialistes* (Paris, 1930) especially pp. 43–85. Déat himself quotes Hendrick de Man, *Au-delà du Marxisme*, pp. 45, 63.

143. Dodge, op. cit., p. 144.

144. ibid., p. 160.

145. Cf. the address at Charleroi on May Day 1941 which served as the prototype of the speeches that he subsequently gave to various gatherings within the Labour Movement, *Travaille*, 6 May 1941, in Dodge, op. cit., p. 202.

146. Déat, *Néo-Socialisme*, p. 90.

147. Adrien Marquet, *Néo-Socialisme*, pp. 57, 60. It was at this point in Marquet's speech, 'Are not the nations in the process of moving onto the plane of a new reality?' that Blum made his famous remark 'I can tell you, I am appalled.'

148. Gregor, op. cit., p. 89.

149. Déat, reply to an inquiry by the weekly *Monde*, 1 February 1930, p. 10.

150. Déat, *Néo-Socialisme*, p. 76, cf. pp. 25–6 and 74 (Montagnon).

151. Drieu La Rochelle, 'Sous Doumergue', in *La Lutte des Jeunes* (7 May 1934).

152. Streel, op. cit., p. 143.

153. Cf. Primo de Rivera, op. cit., pp. 55, 62; Mosley, *Fascism: 100 Questions*, Question 8; Denis, *Principes Rexistes*, p. 17.

154. Primo de Rivera, op. cit., pp. 53–64. At the same moment, at the other end of Europe, Codreanu was offering a doctrine which neither clashed with the nationalistic prejudices of workers and peasants nor aroused their suspicion of city slickers out to use and discard them (Eugen Weber, 'The Men of Archangel', in *Journal of Contemporary History*, vol. I, no. 1 [1966], pp. 118–19).

155. Michael Hurst, 'What is Fascism', pp. 168–9.

156. Mosley, *The Greater Britain*, pp. 18–19.

157. Primo de Rivera, op. cit., p. 180.

158. Denis, *Principes Rexistes*, op. cit., p. 28.

159. Weber, *Varieties of Fascism*, pp. 50–51.

160. Déat-Marquet-Montagnon, *Néo-Socialisme*, pp. 23–4, 32–3, 53–4, 74, 95–8.

161. Dodge, op. cit., p. 180; cf. also pp. 182–92.

162. Primo de Rivera, op. cit., p. 65.

163. Mosley, *The Greater Britain*, op. cit., p. 20.

164. The title of *Néo-Socialisme: Ordre, Autorité, Nation.*

165. Primo de Rivera, op. cit., p. 133.

166. Mussolini, *Fascism*, Appendix, p. 40.

167. Mussolini, 'Political and Social Doctrine', p. 27.

168. Mussolini, *Fascism*, Appendix, pp. 38–9.

169. Mussolini, 'Fundamental Ideas', p. 11.

170. ibid., p. 12; Gentile, 'The Philosophic Basis of Fascism', p. 302.

171. Barnes, op. cit., pp. 59–60.

172. Mosley, *Fascism: 100 Questions*, op. cit., Question 35.

173. Mosley, *The Greater Britain*, op. cit., p. 27.

174. Primo de Rivera, op. cit., p. 178.

175. Weber, 'The Men of the Archangel', p. 104.

176. Barnes, op. cit., pp. 14–15; cf. also a characteristic passage by Robert Brasillach: '. . . We do not have much in common, in spite of appearances, Mr Conservative. We are defending a few truths in the way we think they ought to be defended, that is violently, passionately, disrespectfully, with our lives. At times, this has been of some value to us, Mr Conservative. It may be to you, one day. At moments when you think you can do without those compromising bodyguards, you prefer to talk of other things and look at them from a long way away. They are running their own risks, aren't they? That is their affair, not yours. It was you that said it, Mr Conservative. Their own risks. Not yours. We are not mercenaries. We are not the shock-troops of the *bien-pensants*. We are not the SA of conservatism.' (To a conservative, *Je suis partout*, 23 February 1940).

177. Eugen Weber, 'The Men of Archangel', pp. 124–5.

Part V

ALAN S. MILWARD

10 Fascism and the Economy

Attempts to formulate an accepted definition of fascism have never been wholly successful but there remains a measure of agreement that it is an apt, just, and convenient label for a particular set of political attitudes. There is less agreement about the question whether fascism constituted a set of political beliefs forming a separate political system, although it now seems quite usual to write of 'the fascist powers' in the inter-war period, emphasizing the essential similarities of the political systems of Italy and Germany. Did this similarity extend beyond the purely political sphere? Was there also a specific set of economic attitudes and policies which may equally aptly be labelled 'fascist'?

The confusion over whether fascism was a right-wing or a left-wing movement has in fact been largely due to the inability to fit the *economic* policies of fascism into these convenient mental pigeon-holes. The governments of Hitler and Mussolini ran the economy in each case through a battery of economic controls to which left-wing governments, outside the Soviet Union, could still only aspire, but the beneficiaries of their economic policies have usually been depicted as belonging to those social groups which would have usually supported more right-wing parties. If there were any consistent principles of economic thought and of economic action in fascism, how far did they represent the economic interests of those groups who supported fascist parties and governments? As soon as the feeble idea that fascism was solely a new label for personal and political opportunism is abandoned, the problem must be faced as to what forms of social discontent the movement fed on and what demands for social change it represented. For even if neither the political nor the economic ideas of fascism are accepted as constituting a consistent ideological view of the world, and even if both fascist economic and political programmes for action are interpreted as deliberate efforts to harness all discontents, however impossible to reconcile, it must still be accepted that support for fascist policies in German society was at least as strong as for any other policies and that this may also have been true of some periods in Italy. What did fascist movements see as the future of human society? Was there a distinct political economy of fascism? And how did it differ from that of other political groupings?

The more research that is published the less do existing theories of the political economy of fascism carry conviction. They are rapidly sinking to the status of arguments cited only because they can be conveniently contradicted. There does not now seem any reason to linger over them here and they will be described only briefly. Such brevity cannot do proper justice to the complexity of some of these ideas, but the intention of the essay is to suggest the conclusions to which current research is pointing rather than to analyse or criticize these theoretical concepts. After some of the existing theories have been reviewed, therefore, the extent to which the results of recent research amplify and modify them will be considered. The essay concludes with some suggestions which might help to formulate a more acceptable theory of the political economy of fascism.

The existing hypotheses

When the experience of fascism in power was still confined to Italy, the economic policy of fascism was often construed as an attempt to modernize and develop the economy. This was the standpoint of what is still one of the few works to try to deal in a comprehensive way with fascist economic policy (W. G. Welk, *The Fascist Economic Policy* [Cambridge, Mass., 1938]). Welk saw the main motive of fascist economic policy as the achievement of Italian national aspirations which had been long thwarted. In this respect the popular movement for intervention in the First World War, he argued, had shattered the old political framework and had produced a coalition of political and economic interests which was able to force through a strongly nationalistic economic programme. The normal workings of government were suspended and concentrated in a more centralized and powerful state. The modernization of the economy was one aspect of the modernization of the state, but this modernization necessarily was an intensely nationalistic one in which such goals as self-sufficiency and rearmament received the highest economic priority. Rapid industrialization and a high rate of investment in social overhead capital were an integral part of the fascist experience.

The idea that rapid economic development might require a greater degree of coercive power from the central government is frequently expressed. But the German experience shows that this is a very insufficient interpretation of fascism. Indeed any interpretation which depends on showing that the Italian economy in the 1920s and the German economy in the 1930s were in similar stages of development is not worth considering. Whereas Italy in the 1920s was still in the throes of a rapid industrialization which had begun in the decade before the First World War, Germany's economic problems were those of a highly developed economy in which the comparable period of rapid industrialization had been three quarters of a century earlier. The proportional contribution to the GNP made by the industrial sector of the Italian economy at the time of the March on Rome had already been reached in Germany in the 1870s. In 1921 in Italy 24 per cent of the economically active population was employed in the industrial sector; in Germany in 1925 the proportion was 42.2 per cent.

But the idea that particular types of government may be related to particular stages of economic development is a most persistent one. There have been several attempts to define the precise point of economic and social development at which fascism may occur in societies. Of these one of the more complex is that of Clemenz who, using the term on a wider front than here, suggests various points in political evolution, at stages of economic development certainly as widely apart as those of Italy in 1922 and Germany in 1933, at which a fascist 'counter-revolution' may emerge. Fascism, he argues, is inherent in capitalist society (M. Clemenz, *Gesellschaftliche Ursprünge des Faschismus* [Frankfurt a.M., 1972]).

In fact it was the German experience after 1933 which brought to the forefront this interpretation of fascism which had until then received less consideration. It laid the emphasis less on the nationalistic elements of fascist economic policy than on its anti-socialist and anti-communist aspects. The extreme form of this interpretation is the theory that the fascist state was the political tool of the major capital interests ('big business'). Once incorporated into Lenin's theory of imperialism, this view appeared as the statement that fascism was the last stage of imperialism. As profits declined 'monopoly capital' brought into power a government of despotic terror and brutality whose ultimate purpose was to unleash a war of conquest and thereby preserve imperialism and with it capitalism. This view is still maintained in publications in the Soviet Union and the German Democratic Republic. It is the theoretical basis of the work of Eichholtz where it is expressed in its most scholarly form backed by considerable research. 'The fascist state,' writes Eichholtz, 'was a state of monopolies, its policy the concentrated pressure of their economic relationships, that is to say of the conditions and needs of the ruling monopolies. The war was not an outburst of some kind of "demonic" power in and around Hitler; it was a war of monopolies for the control of Europe and the world. The fascist régime was entrusted with the function of preparing and carrying out such a war' (D. Eichholtz, *Geschichte der deutschen Kriegswirtschaft 1939–1945*, I, 1939–1941 [Berlin, 1969], p. 6).

The precise relationship between big business and fascism is perhaps the single aspect of the political economy of fascism which has come in for more attention than all others. The drive towards economic self-sufficiency and the high priority given to rearmament, together with the savage repression of socialist parties and labour movements, lent support to the idea that the fascist state was, in the economic sphere, a tool of 'business interests'. Without accepting the theoretical basis of the views of a writer like Eichholtz in their full rigour, many authors have proposed schematic explanations of fascism which link it closely to the pursuit of the economic interests of manufacturers and businessmen in general or to those of some particular section of the business community. The public divergences of interest between different industrial groups in Germany and Italy always suggested that any theory presupposing that the major capital interests were a monolithic bloc with a set of common goals would be some way from the truth. That there were different shades of support amongst different industries for fascist régimes is frequently suggested even by some who subscribe absolutely to the concept of fascism as the last stage of monopoly capitalism.

Kuczynski suggested that the business interests supporting fascism in Germany were those who benefited most precisely from the pursuit of economic self-sufficiency whereas manufacturers of consumer goods or those who depended heavily on exports for their profits were altogether less enthusiastic (J. Kuczynski, *Darstellung der Lage der Arbeiter in Deutschland von 1933 bis 1945*, sect. 6, vol. 1 of *Die Geschichte der Lage der Arbeiter unter dem Kapitalismus* [Berlin, 1964]). There have been several attempts to break down the real interests of big business in Germany along similar lines. Gossweiler attributes the birth of the fascist state to an internecine struggle among major capital interests which ultimately saw the victory of that group supporting nationalist 'German' policies over a similar group whose interests were more international (K. Gossweiler, *Grossbanken, Industriemonopole, Staat. Ökonomie und Politik des staatsmonopolistischen Kapitalismus in Deutschland, 1914–1932* [Berlin, 1971]). In a more sophisticated analysis Czichon divides the business world into those who wished to reinvigorate the economy after the crash of 1929 by orthodox Keynesian policies of reflation and those who preferred to effect the same thing by rearmament expenditure and who therefore gave their support to the NSDAP. An eventual split between the Keynesians over a policy of economic expansion in collaboration with the trade union movement shifted the decisive advantage to the Nazi side. (E. Czichon, *Wer verhalf Hitler zur Macht?* [Cologne, 1967]). These are all theories which relate specifically to the events in Germany but their starting point is to be found in earlier theoretical interpretations of the rise to power of the fascist party in Italy (E. Nolte, 'Zeitgenössische Theorien über den Faschismus', in *Vierteljahrshefte für Zeitgeschichte*, no. 15 [1967]). The position that fascism was the final stage of the imperialism of monopoly capital was laid down by the Third International in 1935 and this basic framework has since been used to incorporate a wide variety of more complicated explanations of the relationship between major capital interests and fascism without altering the underlying assumptions. The capacity of this interpretation to absorb and turn to purpose the results of historical research may be seen by tracing the evolution of the simpler ideas of 1935 into more complicated positions as indisputable evidence about the more popular origins of fascism has been published. The two editions of Guérin's work reveal this development most neatly (D. Guérin, *Sur le fascisme; fascisme et grand capital* [Paris, 1936, 1965]).

The common ground between such interpretations is that they suggest a positive *intention* on the part of major capital interests to bring to power a despotic government pursuing economic policies advantageous to them. Kühnl, however, has proposed a different scenario in which major capital interests, suspicious of the revolutionary postures of fascism and cautious of the support for fascism from other sections of the community, turned to its support only when it was the last available means of preserving the capitalist system. As the National Socialist Party took over the votes and influence of right and centre-right parties in Germany after 1929, business interests gradually came to see it as their only defence against an even worse fate, he argues, and tried to manipulate it as best they could in their own interests. He suggests that in certain complex historical circumstances the inherent instability of liberal capitalism may give rise to the fascist state as the last possible defender of the capitalist order. More than that, fascist movements only came to power with the collusion of the very authorities whose duty it was to protect liberal democracy (R. Kühnl, *Formen bürgerlicher Herrschaft; Liberalismus, Faschismus* [Reinbek bei Hamburg, 1971]). Although this thesis seems better to fit the facts that are so far known about the relationship between social forces and the NSDAP, it seems in one area to be on weak ground. Just how likely was the threat of a 'collapse of the capitalist system' in Germany in 1933 or in Italy in 1922?

One big stumbling block in making any theoretical connections along such lines between the fascist state and major capital interests is the anticapitalist rhetoric of much fascist propaganda. There is also the fact that early fascist manifestoes everywhere, including Germany and Italy, proposed radical changes in taxation and landholding and controls on the use of capital. An avowedly 'anti-capitalist' element existed in fascist parties. By using the division of capital into different economic categories according to the schema of Max Weber, Schweitzer tried to come to grips with these troublesome facts (A. Schweitzer, *Big Business in the Third Reich* [Bloomington, Ind., 1964]). The attitude towards capitalism of many whose businesses would be better described as 'small' or 'medium', he argued, was quite different from that of big business which they regarded more as enemy than ally. The apparent collapse of the capitalist economy in 1929 revived the strong anti-capitalist feeling among many lower-middle-class groups, and it was precisely in this area that the ideology of the NSDAP gained ground. Studies of voting behaviour have gone some way in confirming this generalization. Thus what Schweitzer calls 'an economic programme of counter-revolutionary anti-capitalism' evolved side by side with the 'cherished goal of big business of employing the power of the state for the invigoration of capitalist institutions that had suffered during the Great Depression' (p. 4). What emerged was a period of 'partial fascism' in which a far from monolithic state pursued these contradictory economic goals. It lasted until 1936, the beginning of the second Four Year Plan. The plan meant the victory of the Weberian category of 'political capitalism' over that of 'industrial capitalism' and the triumph of 'big business' over small, giving rise ultimately to what Schweitzer calls an 'organized capitalism', in which major capital and military interests shaped the economic and foreign policies of the government. But in Schweitzer's exposition the stage of 'partial fascism' is a necessary one on the road to 'total fascism', and a temporary and confused pursuit of anti-capitalist policies an essential prelude to the ultimate creation of a fascist capitalism. He does not seek to extend this interpretation to Italy but, superficially, it would not be hard to identify a period ending in 1926 or afterwards when the fascist state, in the economic sense, could be said to be 'partial' there.

Schweitzer's thesis marks the boundary between those interpretations which insist on the ultimate importance of the links between big business and fascism and a set of absolutely opposing interpretations which insist on the essentially anti-capitalist nature of fascism. Simplified greatly, the general standpoint of these is that fascism was a movement of those social groups threatened by the apparently inexorable trend of the capitalist economy towards increasing industrialization and concentration of capital. It drew its support from handicraft workers, shopkeepers, white-collar workers, and workers in the agricultural sector. This new political alliance demanded an economic programme aimed at stability rather than growth, at preserving economic inefficiencies in the interests of social harmony rather than at an intensification of economic development. Just as it contradicted all the political tenets of liberalism so, it is argued, did fascism also overturn the liberal concept of 'economic man'. Rejecting the concept of man as a rational being, fascism rejected also the rational constructs of economics. The world of irrationality which it sought to create was essentially antagonistic to the aims of capitalist society. It sought an irrational and perhaps unobtainable social and economic harmony of interest, a world of military heroes, of a secure and stable bourgeoisie, and of a sturdy and equally stable peasantry, a return to an imaginary pre-capitalist Golden Age.

This particular range of interpretation naturally enough attributes a very low priority to the economic aspects of the fascist state. Indeed its exponents seldom venture into the economic field at all. They are, however, concerned to draw an important distinction between conservatism, or the 'traditional right' and fascism, which they regard as a radical and revolutionary (or counter-revolutionary) force. This distinction made in the field of political theory is so profound as to constitute also a powerful inference as to the political economy of fascism. The economic tendencies of fascist states within this interpretation would be more correctly described as anti-capitalist than as capitalist. They were an attempt to arrest the dynamic of economic development and the social changes which that dynamic brought with it, or to value other priorities so much higher as to make that dynamic irrelevant (E. Weber, *Varieties of Fascism* [New York, 1964]).

The social basis of fascism

The existing theories on the political economy of fascism cover virtually the full spectrum of possibilities, yet not one of them is entirely convincing. Some of the other essays published in this book show that historians, political scientists, and sociologists have, very belatedly, begun to find out something real rather than merely hypothetical about the membership of and support for fascist movements. Much of what is known about the answers to these vital questions have been published in the *Proceedings of the Bergen Conference on International Fascism* by Norwegian Universities Press (1978). Some further information is published in this book in the essay by Professor Juan Linz. Unfortunately there is one huge gap in this research – Italy. In formulating any hypothesis on the political economy of fascism the first considerations must be to discover which socio-economic groups joined, supported, and paid fascist movements, and then to decide which groups benefited from fascist government. It is now possible to provide reasonably accurate answers for Germany and most other countries. But most arguments about Italy are still only inferential, and there remains the possibility that inferences made about the nature of Italian fascism on the basis of our knowledge of other fascisms will not be correct. In the economic sphere this is a consideration of great weight, not just because of the different levels of economic development of the Italian and German economies, but because there are many easily observable differences of economic policy between the two countries. It will suffice to mention one: whereas the pursuit of the economic aims of the German central government led very quickly to an economy insulated as far as possible from the influence of the international economy, the Italian economy remained relatively open to such influences for most of the period of fascist government. We may not therefore come to any firm economic conclusions on the basis of the pragmatic research so far done. But what does this research suggest about the social and economic bases of fascist movements?

Fascism ought not to be analysed by too crudely a materialist technique, however much it may have ultimately depended on real social and economic interests. It may be argued that the propensity to join a fascist party was determined more by psychological considerations than by social class. And certainly it would appear likely that people of a certain psychological predisposition were readier to accept a politics of violent action, of conversion, and of total rejection of much of the political past. In part this accounts for the fact that in some countries fascist movements mobilized groups which had taken virtually no part in previous political life and that a certain portion of the fascist vote can often be identified as new voters rather than voters won from other political parties. Studies of the membership of some fascist movements have shown a comparative over-representation of those with criminal records. In the case of the Arrow Cross party in Hungary the high proportion of convicted criminals is particularly noticeable, even when all those whose convictions were for 'political' offences including street fighting and assault on the police are discounted (M. Lackó, *Arrow-Cross Men, National Socialists, 1935–1944* [Budapest, 1969]). Out of a substantial sample of office-holders and party activists, 16 per cent had previous convictions for theft and over 7 per cent each for fraud and embezzlement. A further 16.7 per cent had convictions for a wide range of other non-political crimes.

It is probable that the mentality of fascist recruits was basically different from that of those who had taken an active part in earlier political movements. The political élites of the previous hundred years had moved in a world of rational and logical argument and had placed a low value on merely instinctual or emotional response. Insofar as there had been an appeal to groups outside the governing circles, it had been one of persuasion and education, not one of emotional conversion and manipulation. How little Quisling or Szálasi cared for what they thought of as these outmoded methods of political appeal may be seen from the incoherent nature of their final speeches in their own defence, when on trial for their lives. Fascist movements reached below the thin crust of rationality of liberal democratic politics to contact those who had only accepted the premises of a rational political world because they thought no alternative was respectable or because the only alternative had been some form of repressive absolutism.

And in doing so they aroused a wealth of personal feelings which had had to be repressed because they had been for the most part resolutely ignored by the political establishment.

Nevertheless, certain social groups and political parties were very resistant to the psychological appeal of fascist movements whereas others proved very susceptible. Once the special psychological appeal of fascism is accepted the problem remains that, in spite of the insistence in fascist propaganda on the movement as a force for national unity, support for fascist parties did not come equally from all sections of the population. Although industrial workers were prominent in the foundation of fascist groups, if those groups developed from small sects to genuine mass movements they attracted very little further support on the way from organized labour. Socialist and communist parties, together with purely Roman Catholic parties like the German Zentrum, held on to their voters much better than other parties in the face of a mounting fascist vote.

In fact the most complicated problem for all fascist parties was to effect the transition from a small revolutionary (or counter-revolutionary) sect, with ideas fundamentally different from the society in which they existed, to becoming a mass political movement living in a real political world and mobilizing a wide range of support in that world. The extraordinary difference between what could be thought and said in a small sect, such as the NSDAP until 1928, and the heavy responsibility attaching to every position taken up after that date is glaring. And nowhere did this apply with greater force than to economic questions. Because of the early connections of fascist thought with anarcho-syndicalism, both the membership and the social and economic ideas of fascist movements tended to be quite different in the stage of sect and in the stage of mass movement. So difficult was the transition between these stages and so great the differences made by it that there are two separate political economies of fascism to consider: (1) the political economy of the fascist sect, and (2) the political economy of the fascist movement.

For obvious reasons the first, although very interesting, is not very important. In fact in most European countries fascist sects remained sects, even in Norway where Nasjonal Samling by a series of political accidents was set up as a pseudo-government. The revolutionary anarcho-syndicalism of these sects appealed to organized workers as much as to any other group in society, as well it might, for its programme of political action depended on the existence of their organizations. The revolutionary syndicalists also provided the ideological basis of the Italian and German fascist parties and afterwards occupied important organizing positions in the mass movements. But the dream of a working-class fascist revolution remained a dream. Even in the first elections in both countries in which fascism scored significant successes, it was relatively less successful in those areas where the proportion of industrial workers in the electorate was highest. The first manifestoes of the fascist party in Italy and the NSDAP in Germany represent the economic programme of fascism as a sect; they had little relevance in meeting the precise economic demands of those who subsequently supported fascist mass movements.

It is now clear that in all the societies of which we have an accurate enough knowledge significant fascist mass movements had two main social foundations. The first was urban, and either middle class or with middle-class attributes, shopkeepers, and shop-workers, minor bureaucrats and officials, professional people, students, unemployed personnel from the armed forces, and handicraft workers. The other was rural, peasant landowners, sharecroppers and occasionally larger landowners. The actual mixture in each case differed with precise political circumstances; public officials for instance were often forbidden to join. But it was from an alliance of these groups that the fascist vote and much of the active support came, and these were the groups over-represented in fascist parties by comparison with their representation in other political parties.[1] That the urban middle-class group was moved towards fascism by socio-economic motives has been most cogently argued by H. A. Winkler in *Mittelstand, Demokratie und Nationalsozialismus* (Cologne, 1972).

One of the predominating reasons for the penetration of the NSDAP into these middle-class groups was their fear of economic evolution which seemed to leave them trapped and diminishing in political power between the two mighty and growing forces

of 'big business' and organized labour. There were almost three
million small enterprises, employing less than five people regular-
ly, in the industrial and service sector of the economy. The opposition to many aspects of rapid economic development of opinion-
forming circles, such as the Kathedersozialisten, in the second
half of the nineteenth century had, by championing the cause of
these independent middle-class groups, formed within them an
attitude very different from the ferociously competitive individualism with which they are supposed to have behaved in countries
which had industrialized earlier in periods when technology was
less massive. Interpreting each cyclical crisis of the economy as
evidence that they did not have the capital, the command over
other resources, and the political power to compete, they increasingly pressed for an economic programme of protection, of
restrictions on labour, on large firms, on department stores, and
on cooperative movements. From this consciousness of a common conservative economic interest came also their consciousness of themselves as a limited group, the *Mittelstand*. Their predisposition to support a fascist party was turned decisively into
commitment by the hyperinflation and then by the economic
crash of 1929.

The economic motives of rural fascist voters have not been so
well analysed. Heberle's study of Schleswig-Holstein shows how
the long fall of agricultural prices and the feeling that all other
parties had proved in their turn to offer no defence against this
trend turned an agricultural region with a preponderance of small
family farms into a pillar of the fascist movement (R. Heberle,
Landbevölkerung und Nationalsozialismus [Stuttgart, 1963]). This
electoral landslide, which happened to a lesser degree in two
other areas where the structure of landholding was similar, Hesse
and Baden, was not achieved without a conscious effort by the
party to formulate an agricultural programme to win support of
voters there, and to penetrate the social and economic organizations of the countryside. (H. Gies, 'NSDAP und landwirtschaftliche Organisationen in der Endphase der Weimarer Republik',
in *Vierteljahrshefte für Zeitgeschichte*, no. XV [1967]). 'The ideal-
typical Nazi voter in 1932,' according to Seymour Lipset, 'was a
middle-class self-employed Protestant who lived either on a farm

or in a small community, and who had previously voted for a centrist or regionalist political party strongly opposed to the power and influence of big business and big labour' (S. Lipset, ed., *Political Man* [Berkeley and Los Angeles, 1963], p. 149). In 1930 only 8.5 per cent of the membership of the NSDAP were workers employed in industry. Handicraft workers, shopworkers, officials, and the professionally employed, by contrast, were twice as numerous in relation to their proportion in the population as in other political parties. This political alliance lay also at the basis of the strong fascist movements in Austria, Hungary, and the Netherlands. There are seeming similarities with the socio-economic basis of Italian fascism where the headlong support of rural regions in northern and central Italy in 1921 affected the transition from sect to genuine political movement.

But what of 'big business'? Its importance for fascist parties has to be judged by counting neither heads nor votes but cash. Mussolini, but not the *fasci*, was receiving financial support from some Milan industrialists in 1919 and similar sources paid at that time for the publication of his newspaper *Il Popolo*. Important industrialists were prominent in the national list of the fascist party at its first contested elections and the businessmen's associations, Confindustria and the Associazione fra le Società per Azioni levied their members to finance the fascist party at the election. But we do not know what proportion of the party's funds this accounted for. Neither is it known how much support was subsequently given and in what circumstances. These questions have recently been illuminated for Germany for the period before 1933 (H. A. Turner, Jr, *Faschismus und Kapitalismus in Deutschland* [Göttingen, 1972]). Most of the representatives of German manufacturing industry gave their main support to the Brüning and afterwards to the Von Papen governments and only in December 1932 began to edge towards Hitler. Even then their motives were chiefly a distrust of Von Schleicher's interest in recovery in co-operation with the trade unions, and of the heavy public works expenditure. Most important industrialists still looked with deep suspicion on what they saw as Hitler's 'reactionary utopianism'. They thought only in terms of getting what immediate and contingent benefits they could out of a party which, while it might offer certain advantages, was also full of distant menace. Some of those, like Flick, who have long been known to have paid substantial sums to the NSDAP are now known to have paid even bigger sums to other non-socialist parties. And in other cases money was made available to leading figures of the NSDAP only to enable them to oppose the more anti-capitalist figures in their own party. This applied for example to the support from the firm which was subsequently to benefit most, I. G. Farben. It was limited, late, and mostly confined to the 'moderate' Funk.

None of this, however, seriously damages hypotheses such as those of Kühnl or Clemenz about the relationship of business and fascism, whatever it does to older and more rigid views. The question is still by no means completely answered as to what the relationship was between 'big business' and fascist parties, *once those parties were in power*. The brutally repressive policy towards organized labour meant that industrialists could forget entirely about interference from their work force. Interference from the government was another matter. In both Italy and Germany the objective of the industrialists' associations was to try to control their new masters and to effect the most favourable compromises possible with a party whose bedrock support did not seem particularly to favour pro-business policies. The ambiguities of the economic programme of the fascist movements in Germany and Italy contrasted with the clear and simple perceptions of the major industrialists of their own self-interest. In both countries the major capital interests were also well organized as pressure groups and in a good position to bring strong influence to bear on a new and insecure government. The subsequent evolution of this distrustful relationship is better considered in the wider framework of fascist economic policy in general.

It hardly seems likely that future research will change this picture of fascism as a broadly-based social movement drawing its support from disparate urban middle-class groups threatened by the process of economic change, and from small landowners and peasant farmers threatened by the same forces. Economically, its supporters had conflicting and very general aims such as guaranteed employment, safety from the pressures of organized labour and organized business, higher agricultural prices, security of land tenure, and a protection against inflation. From their stage as a revolutionary sect, however, fascist parties also inherited a revolutionary syndicalist anti-capitalist ideology and a small segment of 'working-class' support. On all this was superimposed the attempt by the business community to harness fascism to its own interests. What economic policies could possibly keep such an alliance together?

Common elements in the economic policies of the fascist states

Had economic considerations been as overriding in fascist propaganda as in that of the democratic parties, this new political alliance would have been more difficult to forge. But the fascist appeal to the people laid at least as much emphasis on the spiritual and emotional nature of man as on his material ambitions. Furthermore, the priority above all other matters of the political destiny of the nation and the *Volk* was a constantly emphasized theme. The transcendental nature of this theme was considered to lift it far above such issues as the distribution of economic rewards within society or the increase of material wealth. But National Socialism in spite of its exalted propaganda could no more emancipate itself *entirely* from the economic and social realities of society than the democratic parties. The low estimation which fascism accorded to the economic aspects of human existence did not eliminate the need for the formulation of an acceptable economic policy. In fact it was precisely in this area that the low esteem in which economics was held brought its own retribution. The pressure of the interests which supported the Nazi government was cushioned, not eliminated, by the autocracy of the régime. The supporters expected a different economic world, and the leaders themselves dreamed of a different and 'juster' system, a reactionary utopia. The movement never abandoned its erratic struggle towards the creation of a different society. The final justification of both the ideology and the revolution could only be the replacement of 'liberal man', greedy, selfish, and isolated, with 'fascist man', free from material desires, heroic, noble, and comradely. The other and more immediate political aims of the régimes did not exist to themselves alone, they were also judged against their value in the creation of that new society. Not only was the political upsurge of fascism based on vague but powerful demands for particular immediate economic and social changes but the ideology of the movement had helped it to a political break-through in some areas by expressing a most radical rejection of the social consequences of modern economic development. How far did fascist economic policy reflect the social composition of fascist movements? And how far did it try to implement the philosophical assumptions of the fascist ideology?

There is one obviously consistent aspect of fascist economic policy, so obvious that it need occupy little space here. For Germany, it has been most thoroughly analysed by T. Mason, *Arbeiterklasse und Volksgemeinschaft* (Cologne, 1975). Given the origins of the political support for the movement, such a policy involved little or no internal argument and no hesitations. This was the ruthless suppression of independent labour organizations and their supersession by organs of state control. It was easier for fascist governments to carry out policies hostile to the interests of industrial workers because they also initially gave a high priority to the reduction of unemployment. Registered unemployment in Italy fell from 541,700 at the end of 1921 to 122,200 four years later. The conquest of unemployment in Germany after 1933 absorbed enormous sums of public money. The effect of this in Germany was to initiate an increase in real earnings which was sustained until 1941. The upward movement of real wages, however, was relatively slight, partly because of agricultural protection and high food prices but also because the usual methods of political pressure on which workers had relied to increase wages no longer existed. The Reichs Labour Front was primarily an instrument of labour control and cultural propaganda. It did contribute to a certain improvement in working conditions as did its Italian counterpart, Dopolavoro. But the relentless pressure to hold down wages, even though it was repeatedly thwarted by the evasions of employers seeking labour, can be gauged from the fact that real weekly wages rose at an annual average of 2.8 per cent, for a longer working week, over the period 1933 through 1939 while the national income was increasing at an annual average rate of 8.2 per cent. In spite of an increase in net social product of 28 per cent between 1928–9 and 1937, the consumption of an average wage earner, as far as it can be calculated, seems to have improved very little over the same period. Less is known about the movement of real wages in Italy. The indications are that real wages and real earnings both moved downwards after 1926 during the attempt to stabilize the lira and as unemployment again increased. During the worst period of the depression, between 1929 and 1934, however, real wages in industry, for the employed, seem to have moved upwards once more whereas in the agricultural sector they began to fall. The steady upward pressure on prices after 1934 seems to have reversed this trend. Real wages may have fallen by as much as one-fifth by 1939, when they were well below their level in 1923. Were there any systematic comparative study of the question, it would probably show that those in regular employment, both in Germany and Italy, gained less in terms of material prosperity than their fellow workers in the liberal democracies, and that the distribution of income during the fascist period shifted in both countries significantly against the lower income groups. As a proportion of national income, in Germany wages fell from 57 per cent in 1929 to 52 per cent in 1938–9. Between 1933 and 1939 the proportional increase in the average income of the self-employed was almost one and a half times that of the average wage earner.

The attacks on unemployment by means of public investment in the provision of social overhead capital were not primarily motivated by considerations of welfare but by considerations of national strength. It was a common cliché of fascism that whereas all other political parties concentrated on the issue of the ownership of capital, fascism concerned itself only with whether capital was put to a socially productive use, regarding its ownership as a less important matter. Unemployed resources were seen simply as waste; there was no place in such an attitude for the hesitations which surrounded public relief schemes in liberal states. Petzina fairly describes the programmes of public investment in Germany as 'pre-liberal and mercantilistic' (D. Petzina, 'Grundriss der deutschen Wirtschaftsgeschichte 1918 bis 1945', in Institut für Zeitgeschichte, *Deutsche Geschichte seit dem Ersten Weltkrieg* [Stuttgart, 1973], vol. II, p. 757). The same terms describe the

Italian government's direction of investment into hydro-electric schemes, railway improvement, construction of express highways, and land reclamation. Such programmes were not new. In Italy there was already a long history of investment of this type in the south and in Sicily and, since unification, there had been sporadic attempts to direct investment into land reclamation. In Germany the NSDAP, with no clear idea how to fulfil their promise to end unemployment, at first reaped the benefits of the employment-creation programme initiated by the Von Schleicher government. The 'Reinhardt Plan' for building express motor roads was inherited in its basic ideas from plans developed during the Weimar administration. The difference was not in the originality of fascist policy but in the much greater sums of public money made available for this type of investment. The total expenditure on land reclamation in Italy from 1870 to 1921–2 had amounted to 307 million 1927 gold lira; in the period 1921–2 to July 1936 it was 8,697 million. The Von Schleicher government had initiated the 'employment-creation' programme in Germany with an allocation of 600 million Reichsmarks; in the first financial year of the Nazi régime actual expenditure on employment-creation was ten times that of the previous financial year and the total sum allocated for this purpose between the *Machtübernahme* and the start of 1935 amounted to 3,800 million Reichsmarks. The ideology of the fascist state freed it from constraints which in the depressions of the inter-war period were not very useful ones. Nevertheless, the enormous public expenditure on such investment projects was one aspect of a financial profligacy which called for increasingly drastic controls on wages, prices, and profits and which widened the rift between the fascist economies and their main trading partners in the international economy.

Insofar as the unemployed benefited from these projects, they did so inasmuch as their re-employment was an aspect of restoring national self-respect. In other areas of economic policy the relationship between the distribution of economic benefits and support for the movement was a much closer one. This was especially so in the agricultural sector. The main props of agricultural policy were a high protective tariff, an attempt to approach national self-sufficiency in food supply, which automatically brought a level of food prices well above prevailing prices on international markets, and an attempt to stabilize the land tenures and improve the conditions of the smaller farmers and tenants. The drive towards self-sufficiency also fitted in with the desire to be independent of strategic imports in a future war. Indeed it was not ultimately an achievable aim without a great expansion of the frontiers. But within the limitations of what was possible, the increase in national food production was consistently pursued. The 'battle of grain' in Italy concentrated on increasing wheat output. The average annual wheat harvest was increased to the point where after 1932, except in a bad harvest year like 1937, annual imports of wheat were about one-quarter their level over the period from 1925 to 1928. And this was not achieved merely by the expansion of the sown area but by a marked improvement in yields. The extension of agricultural education, the prizes and honours for efficient farmers, the subsidies for improved seed and for new equipment, all testified to the priority which the government gave to agriculture in a period of rapid industrialization. In Germany the pursuit of self-sufficiency in food was carried out on a wider front. In spite of the tendency under bilateral trading agreements to pay higher guaranteed prices for foodstuffs, the net value of all food products imported into Germany in the period 1935 through 1938 was only one-third that of the period 1925 through 1928.

As in Italy, a high priority was given to improving the standard of agriculture and the budget of the Ministry of Agriculture rose, until the end of 1939, at a rate exceeded only by those of the Ministries of War, Aviation, Interior, and Justice. Eventually agriculture was included in the Four Year Plan as a strategic industry and state credits made available for machines, housing, and land rationalization. But this expenditure brought less reward in Germany. Increases in output were only spasmodic and temporary. It has also of course to be remembered that the rise in per capita national income was not accompanied by a correspondingly large increase in food consumption. The steep increase in food prices served as one method of restraining the general level of consumption. This was the reality behind the statistical calculation that by 1938–9 83 per cent of Germany's food was domestically produced against 68 per cent in 1928. Yields of most crops did improve, but by comparison with most other West European countries they remained very low. Agricultural policy, highly favourable to the farming community, was in fact riddled with economic inconsistencies, which stemmed both from the electoral support of small farmers and the nature of the fascist ideology.

The material benefits to the farming community were great. They were rescued from the effects of the fall in world prices and their change of political allegiance after 1929 was rewarded also by the high esteem in which they were represented by NSDAP propaganda. Income from agricultural sales shrank less as a proportion of national income than wages, and the increase in self-employed farmers' earnings between 1933 and 1938 was over three times that of the increase in weekly wage rates. But the attempts at implementing fascist social ideas militated against the efficiency of farming methods. The attempt to create a secure hereditary class of yeomen farmers was summed up in the legislation to create the *Reichserbhöfe*, a new category of inalienable farm units. The size of these farms was set between 7.5 and 10 hectares, defined as 'that area of land necessary to support a family and maintain itself as a productive unit independent of the market and the general economic situation'. (D. Schoenbaum, *Hitler's Social Revolution: Class and Status in Nazi Germany 1933–1939* [New York, 1966], p. 157). That the new class of yeomen would be the source of an 'Aryan' regeneration of the population justified the revealing phrase 'independent of the market', even of the guaranteed sellers' market created by the *Reichsnährstand*. In Italy fascism did not attempt to alter the structure of landholding but the number of cultivators, not all of whom were landowners, increased between 1918 and 1933 by 500,000 and continued to mount after that date. The annual mean percentage rate of growth of capital in the agricultural sector seems to have been higher over the period from 1920 to 1939 than at any time before the First World War or in the decade after 1945.

As the industrial recovery got under way in both countries,

legislation was devised to keep the population on the land. In 1938 in Germany marriage loans were made available to farm labourers which could be written off if the labourer stayed put. New farm housing was exempt from taxation. In Italy legislation was designed specifically to prevent migration from the land to the towns in 1928 and 1929. These laws were a complete failure in both countries. Indeed in Italy this legislation was immediately followed by a widening of the gap between industrial and agricultural wages. The vision of a wholesome and stable rurality existed only in ideology and propaganda. It was strong enough, however, to prevent any reform of the severe structural problems which had bedevilled German agriculture in the 1920s. If any progress was made towards mending these structural weaknesses it came through the inexorable working of those economic forces which fascist legislation was struggling against. The percentage of labour employed in the agricultural sector in Germany fell from 28.8 per cent in 1933 to 25.9 per cent in 1939, whereas in the 1920s it had scarcely declined. The gap between rural and industrial wages was not narrowed. Rearmament in Germany and industrialization in Italy accelerated the decline of the very 'rurality' which fascist policy exalted. The number of new *Erbhöfe* created each year by the Reich fell, whereas the number of new farms created by the Weimar governments had grown every year. And the loss of labour from the land was in inverse proportion to the size of the farm because larger landowners were able, by manipulating tax benefits and subsidies, to retain their labour more successfully. The only apparent effect of these attempts to build a fascist society was to lower the efficiency of the agricultural sector.

Fascism's other main prop of support was a group with more conflicting and vaguer interests. The expansion of economic controls brought an expansion of public employment in the bureaucracy. The growth of employment in the tertiary sector of the economy in Germany in the 1930s was mainly in the public service area whereas in the preceding and succeeding periods of growth it was mainly in trade and commerce. There can be no doubting the social and psychological rewards and the importance of the new status accruing to officialdom in Germany. These have been excellently described by Schoenbaum (op. cit.) and by H. Mommsen, in *Beamtentum im Dritten Reich* (Stuttgart, 1966). But there is no equivalent of the clear material improvement which accrued to the rural supporters. And the attempts to shelter handicraft workers and small businesses from the winds of economic change were no more successful than those to create a yeoman class or to retain labour on the land. Early legislation favoured the Mittelstand and specifically protected individual businesses. But recovery and rearmament alike favoured the bigger firms. The number of small firms fell faster than in the 1920s and handicraft workers shared in the decline.

The conflict between the defence of the Mittelstand and the régime's final economic purposes was an insoluble one. The Four Year Plan determined the strategic priorities for public investment – synthetic fuels, aluminium, synthetic rubber, explosives, basic chemicals, steel, and non-ferrous metals. There was little room here for small firms and the Nazi government became closely associated with a circle of large firms whose production formed the manufacturing base of the war economy. Within the space of eight years the construction of a large air force combined with the government direction of investment to turn Germany into the world's largest manufacturer of aluminium. Inevitably, companies in the non-ferrous metals industry like Vereinigte Aluminiumwerke saw their directors intimately involved in government high finance and planning. Of the big steel corporations much the same could be said. But the closest association was with the giant chemicals trust, I. G. Farben. The main weight of investment in the Four Year Plan was in the chemical sector which was virtually the preserve of this one trust and the higher echelons of its personnel became in many cases the responsible civil servants for deciding further investment priorities in the sector (D. Petzina, *Autarkiepolitik im Dritten Reich* [Stuttgart, 1968]).

A similar tendency could be observed in Italy. The state corporations formed to increase and direct industrial investment seem to have bailed out the bigger rather than the smaller firms, although a good study of their activities still does not exist. The Istituto Mobiliare Italiano, created in November 1931, was chiefly an attempt to protect firms against the effects of the depression by providing capital against negotiable collateral. The Società Finanziaria Italiana was an intermediary institution to prevent bank collapses in the same period. But the activities of the Istituto per la Riconstruzione Industriale (IRI) were wider and it was seen by some industrialists as a government threat to their independence of action. It did shore up the position of the banks by taking quantities of depreciated industrial stocks off their hands. But this left it in some cases in control of the firms. By the end of 1937 it operated a large shipping trust made up of several of the biggest private shipping companies, whose finances had never recovered from the 1929–33 slump, and also a substantial steel-manufacturing trust. To this were then added important armaments, engineering, and shipbuilding firms. IRI itself issued shares which were subscribed to by the public. The Italian government had a controlling interest through IRI in firms whose assets were equivalent to 17.8 per cent of the capital investment in the country. These firms were often of special technological importance, and the access which they thus acquired to government sources of capital appears to have made capital much harder to acquire for smaller firms outside the magic circle. Exactly the same situation was produced in Germany by less direct methods. The Ministry of Economics had been empowered to declare vetoes on certain investments in 1933 and from the start of 1937 every large investment project needed government approval. The volume of private capital issues had by that time shrunk to one-fifth its level of 1928. When the capital market was re-opened to a wider range of private transactions after 1937, it now served only as a supplemental source of supply to those firms to whom government capital was streaming out under the Four Year Plan. After March 1936 bank loans in Italy were restricted to short-term commercial credit.

Although we are still quite ignorant about Italy in the 1930s, the evidence does point to the fact that there, even more than in Germany, fascism did eventually produce a very different set of relationships between government and private capital. The fears of businessmen that fascist governments would intervene in a field in which they would for the most part have preferred a complete liberty of action seem to prove ultimately fully justified, although to what extent their control over business and industry was restricted will probably always remain a matter of interpretation. Guarneri's opinion, that in Italy the limits of government intervention were 'suggesting a few names for the various boards of directors' cannot be accepted because of the much greater control over every aspect of the economy which the fascist government exercised (F. Guarneri, *Battaglie economiche tra le due grandi guerre* [Milan, 1953], vol. I, p. 317). Nor on the other hand has subsequent evidence borne out Rossi's argument that there were intimate connections between Italian manufacturing interests and the fascist government (E. Rossi, *Padroni del vapore e fascismo*, rev. ed. [Bari, 1966]). Fascist policy in Italy did in fact result in genuine limitations on the independence of action of industrialists but those limitations did not seriously endanger the things they most prized.

The formerly private associations of businessmen lost their independence by their integration into the administrative machinery of 'the corporate state'. Both in Italy and Germany they were transformed into instruments of economic control. But whereas in both countries the functions as well as the titles of these organizations changed, the personnel at the head of them usually did not. The threat to the independence of manufacturing interests came from the pressures which changed these businessmen into instruments of the state bureaucracy imposing a system of controls on their fellow businessmen. The line between government and business was blurred because the personnel became in many cases one and the same. The example of I. G. Farben had many parallels in Italy (L. Rosenstock Franck, *Les étapes de l'économie fasciste italienne; du corporatisme à l'économie de guerre* [Paris, 1939]). The first steps in this process were in fact taken in the period of exchange control and in Germany they went further than in Italy because the network of business committees subordinated to the party became the administrative channel through which permissible import quantities were assessed and import restrictions imposed. Even at this stage the manufacturers could easily thwart the more extreme policies of the Ministry of Economics since they were still basically assessing their own demand (J. S. Geer, *Der Markt der geschlossenen Nachfrage* [Berlin, 1961]). But the pressures of war were bound to weight the scales of power in favour of the government. The Italian invasion of Ethiopia and the League of Nations sanctions which it produced brought about a rapid deterioration in Italy's already dangerous foreign trading situation and produced the first serious clashes between the government and the business world which did not result in a compromise (R. Sarti, *Fascism and the Industrial Leadership in Italy, 1919–1940* [Berkeley, Los Angeles, London, 1971]). At this point the business world was coming into collision with the more fundamental principles of fascism. In Germany, with the advent after 1941 of more severe raw material shortages and with the extreme concentration of economic priorities which the war brought about, the Ministry of Armaments did eventually transform these committees into full-time organs of state administration.

One of the few major industrialists to commit himself whole-heartedly to the NSDAP before it came to power, the steel manufacturer Fritz Thyssen, was eventually driven into exile through his opposition to the government's determination to place the main weight of investment in the steel industry in a completely new works to use low-grade German iron ore at uneconomical prices. The Salzgitter works was in fact paid for almost entirely from the treasury and the opposition to it of the steel manufacturers meant that its management was closely controlled by party circles. Nothing could have more clearly demonstrated that, however sympathetic to the business world and however dependent on it, the Nazi government had its own interests which it was prepared to pursue. It was on the exact nature of these interests that the fears of the business world were chiefly concentrated. The assiduous and consistent pursuit of an aggressive foreign policy, and in Germany the callous racial exterminations brought a world of destruction and extermination which, well before May 1945, had nothing left in common with the advantages which the business world had hoped it might obtain from a fascist government. The decisive moment came in January 1944 when the Führer supported Sauckel's impossible plans to deport a further million workers from France during that year against the advice of

Speer and the Ministry of War Production to organize more war production in the occupied territories. From that moment the position of the Ministry of War Production and of the businessmen who ran it became increasingly weaker than that of the more radically fascist parts of the administration. The business circles which had sought to control the movement in 1933 now had their most pessimistic fears fulfilled; they had themselves become the plaything of a political revolution (A. S. Milward, *The New Order and the French Economy* [Oxford, 1970]). The last act of the Italian fascist party during the war was the Republic of Salò whose economic policy reverted to the radicalism of the manifesto of 1919. The movement had returned to being only a sect.

Until that time, however, cases like that of Thyssen were exceptional. The new governments did not, contrary to Kühnl's hypothesis, 'preserve the capitalist system'. They changed the rules of the game so that a new system was emerging. But until the fascist régimes began to founder in defeat major capital interests were able to accommodate themselves to the new rules almost as comfortably as to the old. How far the 'system' was modified is a question still waiting for an answer, but it is unlikely, in the vocabulary of contemporary controversy (which fascist theorists would have regarded as meaningless), that 'fascism' will be shown to have made many dents in 'capitalism'. In Germany the undistributed profits of limited liability companies rose fourfold over the period 1928 to 1939. Alterations of the tax structure and income distribution did favour the Mittelstand but there was no alteration of basic economic structures in favour of the particular social groups which supported fascism. Nor were the more philosophical denunciations by fascist theorists of materialism and liberal greed, nor their insistence on a stable social order, translated into government action other than in minor and ineffectual ways. In Germany the fascist period was a period of rapid economic growth and social instability and change. The annual rate of growth of national income in Germany of 8.2 per cent in the period 1933–9 was higher than in the period 1890–1913 and as high as in the so-called economic miracle of the post-war years. One aspect of this rapid growth was the 'rural exodus' from low-productivity agricultural employment to high-productivity industrial employment, so much lamented by fascist theorists. Italy's experience was a more mixed one: a rapid burst of growth over the period 1921–5, slowing down in the crisis associated with the revaluation of the currency, a steadier growth until 1929, a deep depression until 1934, and then once more a resumption of rapid growth. In spite of the pause in the middle of the period, national income per capita at current prices in the period 1936–40 was 16.5 per cent higher than in 1921–5. Although as in Germany this represented a massive growth of public expenditure on armaments, it also reflected the continued industrialization of the country. Agriculture contributed 34 per cent of GNP at constant prices in 1921 and 27 per cent in 1938; the comparable figures for industry are 24 per cent and 31 per cent. Economic growth was associated more with the fascist régimes in the inter-war period than with their liberal opponents.

Although economic growth satisfied some of the economic demands of those social groups which supported fascism, it threatened at the same time the very stability and freedom from the effects of economic evolution which they sought. It stemmed from and it furthered the nationalist aspirations of fascism. There was no necessary or implicit correspondence in the fascist state between growth and welfare. The growth of GNP was associated with quite different economic purposes – the exaltation of the nation and the ability to pursue an independent policy even to the extent of waging war. Given the promises of fascist ideology, war had an educative and re-integrative purpose in the fascist state and preparation for war was an important priority of fascist economic policy, in Germany after 1936 the first priority. 'Fascism,' wrote Mussolini, 'the more it considers and observes the future and the development of humanity quite apart from political considerations of the moment, believes neither in the possibility nor the utility of perpetual peace' (quoted by Welk, op. cit., 190). In both countries economic growth was partly a by-blow of an economic policy designed to promote territorial expansion.

This, although the most fundamental, was by no means the only contradiction to fascist economic policy. The tensions which arose came also from the contradictions between the radical-revolutionary view of the economic world expressed in the original fascist manifestoes and the retreat from this view which was imposed by having to satisfy the more conventional socio-economic demands of most fascist supporters. Not only was the fascist state committed at the same time to policies of reflation and stability, its further commitment to external aggression produced a volume of economic growth and social change which made the other goals of social and economic policy virtually unattainable. All these conflicting aims were the inescapable economic inheritance of fascist governments and all had to be pursued in the most unpromising international economic environment.

Indeed Mason has recently argued that the irreconcilable contradictions of economic policy in Germany were the cause of the war, which he sees as an escape into an irrational future, and also the chief determinant of the timing of the invasion of Poland (T. W. Mason, 'Innere Krise und Angriffskrieg 1938–1939', in F. Forstmeier, ed., *Wirtschaft und Rüstung am Vorabend des zweiten Weltkrieges* [Düsseldorf, 1975]).

A profligate financial policy was no longer in autumn 1939 able to achieve a satisfactory division of the national product between the conflicting claims of military and civil purposes. Increases in consumer purchasing power, acute shortages of labour, conflicting demands for materials, meant that the goal of war could no longer be pursued without a reversal of domestic economic policy. In these circumstances, he argues, the only political way out was to launch the war, because a war of annexation and looting was one solution to this impasse in economic policy. The war would permit effective restrictions on wages and consumer expenditure which would be otherwise politically impossible, and a ruthless policy of looting would ease the shortages. It is, however, rather a subjective judgement to suggest that the German economy was in a deeper crisis of policy in 1939 than at any time in the period 1936–44. Throughout all those years it pursued the same conflicting aims with the same vigour, and the staggering burden of public debt at the end dwarfed that of 1939.

The fascist economy and Europe

There was, of course, nothing in the fascist state to dissuade it from war. But how implicit was the Second World War in the political economy of fascism? Might it not be argued with equal cogency that the war was not merely, as Mason suggests, a short-term way out of a difficult situation, but also a necessary means to achieving the ultimate economic goals of the fascist state? In the act of war the inherent contradictions of fascist economic policy were less irreconcilable and preparation for war, no longer an additional contradiction in economic policy, might then become a vehicle for bringing nearer the completed fascist society. And since the completion of that society was more difficult within the frontiers of one or two countries, might not a war of territorial expansion have been an overriding objective both in Italy and Germany in creating a viable fascist society? Was the war in fact an attempt to create a fascist Europe and implicit from the outset in the fascist revolutions?

The magnitude of German plans, the consistency with which they were pursued, the extent to which they were central to the political ideology of the government, are all still much disputed. Two aspects of German policy, however, have always suggested that the Nazi government's economic aims were not just national ones but envisaged a socio-economic reconstruction of the whole continent. First, the theory of the economy of large areas (*Grossraumwirtschaft*) used to justify German trading policy after 1933 and economic policy during the occupations implied a specialization of economic function over an area roughly corresponding to that of the continent of Europe. Second, the diligently pursued 'racial reconstruction' of the continent was justified as being a necessary aspect of this much greater degree of specialization of economic function. Certain races had become in Nazi theory incapable of any but the most menial of these economic functions. How much light can be shed on those important questions by a consideration of the external economic policies of the German and Italian governments?

The origins of controls over foreign trade and exchanges in Germany and Italy were not expressive of fascist ideology; they were a pragmatic and unavoidable response to the collapse of international trade and to the actions of other powers. It was the Brüning government which introduced exchange controls in Germany to stop the outflow of capital and to control imports. As German trade continued to share in the decline of world trade over the next two years, the NSDAP never appears to have understood that the implementation of its own economic programme would certainly mean that trade and exchange controls would have to be retained at least until full employment was achieved. In fact it was the public works programme of the Von Schleicher government and the subsequent Reinhardt plan which first suggested that the exchange controls might not, as everywhere else, prove to be designed to meet a temporary emergency which was worse in Germany because of the devaluation of the pound sterling. When the expenditure on the *Autobahnen* was added to the cost of rearmament, of agricultural protection, and of the agricultural support programmes, it became clear that the government had given a higher priority to domestic recovery and the achievement of its longer term national aims than to reintegrating Germany into a reconstructed network of international trade and payments.

This was recognized by the 'New Plan' in 1934 which now gave the government the administrative capacity to regulate imports according to their political and economic desirability rather than merely to restrict their quantity. It was intended to reduce the import of manufactured goods over time and to alter the geographical pattern of German trade so that imports from developed countries would be replaced by imports of raw materials from the underdeveloped south-eastern European countries. In their turn German exports of manufactures would be diverted to underdeveloped countries. The mechanism chosen for this had already come into existence before the *Machtübernahme*, the bilateral trading treaty specifying the quantity and value of goods to be exchanged and an arbitrary exchange rate for the period of its validity. As the treaties proliferated all currency clearings were handled by a central clearing bank in Berlin. Germany thus developed a separate trading bloc in which she was the dominant power both politically and economically and which accounted for an increasing proportion of her international trade. National Socialist economists and publicists gave this bloc a specific fascist gloss in the theory of the economics of large areas. Germany was seen as the natural industrial heartland of Europe, the developed manufacturing core of the continent, while the peripheral states were seen as suppliers of foodstuffs and raw materials. This was a theory which had been popular in nationalist circles in the late nineteenth century, but it was transmuted into an overtly fascist concept by racial theorists in the NSDAP. It is possible in fact to identify two concepts of Grossraumwirtschaft in Nazi Germany. One is the specifically 'fascist' interpretation which saw German trading policy after 1934 as the first step in a reconstruction of Europe both racial and economic (for these two things were inseparable). The other is the older and vaguer idea of a politico-economic domination over eastern and south-eastern Europe.

The second and older concept had an obvious appeal to those German firms with specific plans and business interests in central and south-eastern Europe. In a period of very low international prices for food and raw materials, Germany was offering extraordinarily favourable terms to such exporters of primary produce as Bulgaria or Turkey. She was breaking her own policy of high agricultural protection to admit at high German prices guaranteed quantities of produce virtually unsaleable on the world market. In the situation of 1934 the underdeveloped European countries were being offered the only possibility open to them of economic development, guaranteed access to an increasingly prosperous market. The price for this was domination by the mark through the Berlin clearing, by German exports and by German business interests. In 1939 65.5 per cent of Bulgarian imports originated in Germany and the equivalent figure for Turkey was 51 per cent, for Hungary 48.4 per cent, for Yugoslavia 47.6 per cent and for Romania 39.2 per cent. The penetration of German capital and business interests into the economies of these countries proceeded so rapidly that before the first invasion and occupation of some of them certain German business groups, such as I. G. Farben and Karl Zeiss, had already submitted to the government detailed plans for furthering and extending their interests there after any occupation. Eichholtz has published some of this evidence in support of his hypothesis on the political economy of fascism (D. Eichholtz, op. cit.; D. Eichholtz and W. Schumann, *Anatomie des Krieges: neue Dokumente über die Rolle des deutschen Monopolkapitals bei der Vorbereitung und Durchführung des zweiten Weltkrieges* [Berlin, 1969]).

There can be no doubt that German trading policy was highly favourable to certain German business and industrial interests in this particular part of Europe. But the importance of the German trading bloc for German trade was still a limited one. Even by 1939 the six countries whose trade was most dominated by Germany took only 18.3 per cent of all German exports and supplied 18.5 per cent of all imports. It is sometimes argued that these imports were particularly important because of their strategic value, that Germany had an uninterrupted control over vital quantities of strategic raw materials. But this was not so at all. They were strategically important only in two areas, foodstuffs and bauxite. The success of German policy could be measured by the extent to which it encouraged alterations in the agriculture of these countries such that they did develop a genuine economic symbiosis with the German economy as exporters of those foodstuffs which were in genuine demand in Germany and which would be even more essential in the likely event of a European war and a British blockade of German food supply. This happened on only the most limited scale. In reality the construction of a German trading bloc was more a response to shortages of hard currencies than to long-term planning for a Grossraumwirtschaft. Any future Grossraum of the Nazi state would certainly include Poland and the Ukraine, but for political reasons German trade with Poland and the Soviet Union declined in the Nazi period. The Soviet Union had been one of the major trading partners of the Weimar state but between 1935 and 1940 German-Russian trade was quite insignificant. The Reichsmark trading bloc existed as an economic unit independently of wider political intentions and its existence did not foreshadow these intentions. It was not the result of an alliance between major capital interests and the fascist régime but one device among many which enabled that régime to pursue its own domestic economic priorities.

The price of pursuing these priorities was isolated from the international economy and, from the point of view of many German business interests, the advantages of this closed trading system were a poor substitute for what it had replaced. Over the last century the growth of exports from developed economies has been mainly due to access to markets in other developed economies. The capacity of central and south-eastern Europe to absorb imports of German manufacture had definite limits. Unless, therefore, the purpose of a reconstructed Europe was stability rather than growth the German trading bloc offered no satisfactory future. The percentage of German exports going to the United States, Britain, and France fell from 24 per cent in 1929 to 11.6 per cent in 1939, yet in the long run these were the markets on which the growth of German manufacturing capacity depended.

It is possible of course to resolve this paradox by arguing that the trading arrangements after 1934 were not thought of as permanent because the ultimate intention was to conquer Russia and to create an economic unit so large that there would ultimately be no need for any reintegration with the international economy. Within such far-flung frontiers and endowed with absolute command over so many resources, the difficulties attendant on pursuing the domestic economic priorities of fascism would be much less. Theoretically, the possibility always existed of an internal deflation and a devaluation of the Reichsmark. In reality the last date by which such a policy could have been adopted was 1936, but government expenditure continued to grow beyond that date. Expenditure on the armed forces rose from 18 per cent of total public expenditure in 1934 to 50 per cent in 1938. Between 1933 and the outbreak of war only about 80 per cent of this government expenditure was covered by normal treasury income, and the devices used to finance rearmament and the Four Year Plan increasingly shifted the burden onto the public debt. Even before the war, the need to make wage, price, and exchange controls more effective had already produced a completely separate price structure in Germany, and left no alternative to perseverance with exchange controls and bilateral trade. The increasing costs of rearmament might in fact be recouped from the proceeds of conquest. If this was the calculation it was no will o' the wisp; the financial payments alone from France to Germany in one year of the occupation were far greater than any possible calculation of the expenditure involved in conquering the country. The total contribution from the French economy to the German amounted to one-third of French national income in 1942, and almost one half in 1943 (A. S. Milward, *The New Order and the French Economy* [Oxford, 1970]). But the German public debt in its various forms continued to increase throughout the war leaving the Reich by 1944 in a situation where only the most draconian controls prevented a catastrophic inflation. And the continued existence of the Reich economy as a separate and insulated unit prevented any realization of the widely discussed schemes for a 'New Economic Order' based on a wider customs union in Europe or a closer integration of the national economies.

German external economic policy before 1939 had little, therefore, in common with the theoretical justifications provided for it in the concept of Grossraumwirtschaft. Nor does it foreshadow any pan-European plans. But once the war was launched and territory occupied did not these theories become translatable into real economic terms and did not the New Economic Order become possible? It was in fact only at the height of success of the campaign in Russia in 1941 that there was space and time for discussion of what the New Economic Order might be. Once the blitzkrieg strategy failed in Russia in January 1942 and German domestic economic policy was forced to concentrate on mobilizing all Germany's resources for war production, it was inevitable that the occupied territories should also come to be seen as part of 'the European war economy', as Reichsminister Speer called it. But in the interval when most of Europe was conquered and the German domestic economy no more committed to military output than it had been at the end of 1938, there were clear indications that external economic policy was not concerned merely with short-term exploitation to assuage domestic economic difficulties but did have also long-term pan-continental objectives.

After the occupation of Norway, the German administration there embarked on an expensive programme of capital investment designed permanently to change the economic orientation of the Norwegian economy from its reliance on a wide network of international trade to a close integration with Germany. A long-term investment project was begun to utilize the cheap electric current in Norway for the production of aluminium, which would be wholly exported to German aircraft factories. Aluminium production was to be increased more than six times which would eventually have left Norway with a manufacturing capacity 60 per cent above that of the United States in 1939! In order to diminish the dependence on food imports, enormous projects for using the extensive Norwegian moorlands for sheep rearing and cattle farming were begun as well as smaller plans for extending market gardening. A start was made in providing capital for the fishing industry, especially in the form of freezing and canning plant, so that the value and quality of fish exports to Germany could be increased. Onto these expensive projects Hitler grafted his personal plans for main roads and railways to link Berlin to Trondheim in the first case and the Norwegian arctic in the second (A. S. Milward, *The Fascist Economy in Norway* [Oxford, 1972]). Such long-term planning was not limited to Norway nor entirely to the period before the first defeats in Russia. The plans for the Norwegian aluminium industry were based on a permanent control over the allocation of bauxite supplies from Hungary, Croatia, and France. Even in 1943 the plans for producing more consumer goods in France for Germany were based on a general agreement, not subsequently properly fulfilled, to undertake joint planning of distribution of raw materials within the German and French economies. The purpose of the war was neither just to avoid economic collapse at home nor just to loot the occupied territories. But until more is known about economic policy in the occupied eastern territories it is not possible to say exactly what weight these longer-term plans had in the direction of the German economy. It is as yet still only possible to guess at the extent to which German economic policy did entail a reorganization of the continent, and therefore, also, at the economic goals of the war.

The Italian experience makes these matters no clearer. The concept of an Italian Grossraumwirtschaft and, after Germany's conquests, the concept of a joint Italo-German trade domination of the continent were both discussed in Italy. And during the worst period of the depression, and the Ethiopian war which followed afterwards, Italian trade controls seem to have aimed at creating a smaller version of the German trading bloc which would remove the pressure of external economic movements on Italian domestic economic policy. But how could such an ambition appear meaningful or realizable in the context of an economy like that of Italy? That it was even tried shows the inherent tendency of fascist economics towards the creation of an isolated economic system and the necessity of such isolation if the precarious balance of domestic economic policy was to be maintained. The recurrent deficits on commodity trade were the weakest point in the Italian economy in the inter-war period. After 1929 the weakness of the balance of payments was accentuated by the drop in remittances from emigrants. Not only was Italy's export capacity too low to emulate German policy but any attempt at creating a separate Italian trading bloc could only lead to a direct clash with German economic interests in the same area.

In fact, until 1928 the Italian economy remained relatively open, but as domestic economic policy struggled against the contrary international tides of falling output and mounting unemployment, trade and import controls increased until in April 1934 they were for the first time completely effective. From July 1935 the rearmament for the attack on Ethiopia could only be carried out by complete government control of the import of 'strategic' raw materials, including coal. The war itself brought economic sanctions imposed by the League of Nations and a system of rigid exchange controls in reply. No matter how unpromising the outcome, there seemed no alternative to abandoning the policy of the régime other than the creation of an Italian trading bloc controlled by a set of bilateral treaties on the German model. Persistence in a high level of public expenditure between 1930 and 1933 when normal treasury income was declining had already created a level of internal prices which made adherence to the trading methods of the 1920s even more difficult. The acceptance, indeed the usefulness and rightness, of war in the fascist state decided the issue. With the change in trading policy came also the attempt, as in Germany, to promote a higher degree of self-sufficiency, by developing high cost synthetic fuel and synthetic fibre industries. Mussolini spoke of such developments as the only way to preserve political autonomy (F. Guarneri, *Autarkie und Aussenhandel* [Jena, 1941]).

The outcome was chastening. The only two significant European primary exporters for whom Italy was a major market were Hungary and Yugoslavia. In both countries German trade gained ground precisely at the expense of that of Italy, aided by the rigour with which Yugoslavia enforced the League of Nations sanctions. Only Albania was left as an Italian economic preserve. The failure and its dangers were soon apparent. When the gold bloc countries devalued in October 1936, the gold content of the lira was reduced to bring it back into parity with the standard of the most open of the world's trading systems. But the drive towards war by Germany and the growing strength of the political ties with that country made Germany itself the indispensable source of strategic imports. More than that, as Italian exports of primary produce to Germany increased in order to pay for the mounting imports, Italy itself became merely another subordinate member state of the German trading bloc. The weakness of the Italian economy compared with the German meant that the Italian government was in reality only able to pursue its own fascist economic policies *in exchange for* political autonomy.

Because of the circumstances outlined above, there is little point in trying to assess from Italian external policy what the ultimate implications of the fascist economic system were for the continent as a whole. Nor does the Italian experience do much to clarify the ambiguities of German economic policy. It was not possible in either country to pursue the economic policies which the political bases of the fascist movement demanded and to ally these policies to the original fascist ideology and at the same time to adhere to the multilateral trading system which had been so potent a factor in European economic growth. But to what degree was the external economic policy of fascist states an attempt to create a trading system designed to cater to priorities other than economic growth? To what extent were such far-reaching policies, involving countries which had not experienced a fascist take-over, inherently necessary to preserve the fascist system in Germany and Italy? Was a war of expansion a necessary consequence of the political economy of fascism? These are questions which historians and economists must still answer.

Towards a more valid hypothesis

The argument presented above has travelled a long way from the hypotheses which were considered at the beginning of this paper. Not only are the initial assumptions all simplifications of history but in varying degrees they are inaccurate and misleading simplifications. The word *fascism*, however, will not go away. How meaningful an economic label is it? The historical evidence suggests that fascism emerged from a new combination of social and political forces and that this combination was responsible for an identifiably different set of economic attitudes and policies. It is not my intention here to present yet another comprehensive theory of the nature of this new combination of forces but, by extrapolating the present trend in research, to indicate certain aspects of fascism that may well prove essential to any future and more valid hypothesis of its political economy.

First, the revolutionary (or counter-revolutionary) ideology of fascist sects was not entirely submerged in the economic policies of fascist movements. It survived to play an economic role and has to be incorporated in any useful hypothesis on the political economy of fascism. In this ideology the Enlightenment, the French Revolution, and the evolution of the 'materialist' economic creeds of socialism and communism represented not progress but a deep and growing wound on human society. The assumptions underlying most economic theory were therefore seen as incorrect, vicious, and corrupting. The healing process could begin only with a small surviving unpolluted racial élite, uncorrupted by these assumptions. Mankind was to be re-created and the fascist élite was the germ of the new society. In Germany the SS saw itself as that new society coming to birth amongst the debris of the old. Its economic empire was the only one to escape the growing embrace of the Ministry of War Production after

1942 because it was a permanent thing for the future whereas war production was but temporary. As support dropped away from fascist movements over the last eighteen months of the war, they shrank once again to the original sect, a hard core of ideologists no longer needing to compromise nor to exist in a real political world. The Republic of Salò tried to implement the original fascist manifesto of 1919. And in the final unreality of the Berlin bunker the first priority became the survival into the future of the unpolluted Aryan élite in whose blood the instincts of fascism would still survive.

Second, this fascist ideology depended on the concept of an appeal to the people; fascism was an élitist politics for a mass age. It offered to the 'people' the vain hope of an element of personal economic independence in the face of apparently massive and impersonal economic forces. It extended the delusion that the unorganized might yet defend themselves against the inexorable economic pressures which they feared – 'big business', 'organized labour', inflation, and unemployment. Because of this and its original anti-capitalist rhetoric, it penetrated into the popular revolutionary socialist movements by way of anarchism and syndicalism. In Spain Ledesma actually chose the title 'national syndicalism' for this fascist movement. Fascist movements retained these revolutionary anti-capitalist ambitions and they were also not without influence on its economic policy. They formed, for instance, the intellectual background of Roberto Farinacci who rose to be Minister of Popular Culture in the Italian government and Fritz Sauckel who became Plenipotentiary General for Labour in Germany in 1942. Even at the height of his brutal labour 'recruitment' drives in Europe, Sauckel was still occupied, sometimes successfully, in trying to force 'the plutocrats' to improve working and living conditions.

Third, these early characteristics of fascism survived only as a guiding thread through the later experience of the movement. Fascism was mainly formed and shaped in the process of coming to power in Italy and Germany. In the course of acquiring in these two countries its essential mass support, it was quite transformed from its beginnings. It was in these two countries alone that fascism emerged from a small and violent sect to take power as the most important political movement. In the explanation of how this could occur the main roots of fascist economic policy may also be seen and understood.

The elements of a common national historical experience in these two countries must be stressed. They were the only two historically dominant nations in Europe to achieve their modern national unity late, in the face of opposition from the other European powers, and not to achieve it completely. It was this which encouraged an intellectual marriage between the deeply held traditional conservative sentiment of nationalism and the more rarefied and revolutionary ideas of fascism. Every political party had to account for its ideas against a nationalist alternative. The concept of a 'national socialism' came to the forefront in Italy during the First World War when the socialist party split on the question of whether to intervene in the war to pursue nationalist and democratic aims at the same time. In fact the nationalist party had already made inroads into the socialist party before 1914 and before Mussolini opted for intervention and formally split the party (K. Priester, *Der italienische Faschismus, ökonomische und ideologische Grundlagen* [Cologne, 1972]). The theoretical Marxist basis of Italian (and Mussolini's) socialism was not very rigorous. In a country with a very small class of industrial workers the rural origins of some of the leaders and supporters of the party had favoured a socialism which was already heavily imbued with anarchist and syndicalist ideas. The offspring of this marriage of nationalism and socialism was a nationalism with a much deeper popular appeal and a socialism far distant from that of Marx. The great importance of national power and national development in the fascist economy was already established.

But Italy's situation in the First World War was unique; a popular politics overturned the alliance of the liberal élite with Germany and forced intervention on the democratic side. In Germany conditions were far less propitious. Even after the Versailles Treaty, most political support still went to the established parties whose opposition to the treaty was just as strong, although less violently expressed, than that of the fascist groups. The common elements in the national historical experience of the two countries are by no means enough to explain the transition from sect to movement in Germany.

All historians have rightly insisted on the importance of the collapse of the international economic order with which the Weimar republic was so closely integrated in putting a new and more vigorous wind into the sails of German fascism. There is no need to rehearse those events here. But there was a third force tending to promote a mass fascist movement in Germany which had been lacking, indeed had not been needed, in Italy. The marriage of syndicalism and traditional nationalism had supplanted older conceptions of nationalism by a new and virulent conception of racial purity. The fascist élite was not only an intellectual élite but an élite of the blood. The re-creation of European society depended on a mystical brotherhood of true blood, because it was in the blood and not the brain that ideas were born. The worst threat to the healing of society came from the polluting presence of people of an alien race within the national frontiers. The commonly accepted idea that Italian fascism was not 'racial' and that these ideas constitute a fundamental difference between German national socialism and Italian fascism does not as yet rest on any profound examination of racial attitudes in the Italian fascist party. The question of purity of the blood, central to Nazi ideology, may have had very little use or relevance within Italy because it could drum up little support. The British Union of Fascists, who believed firmly in this set of racial ideas, also deliberately eschewed the use of them on the electoral platform at first because they were of no use as vote winners. Only in the decline of the party did they openly adopt, as a last desperate measure, an overtly anti-Jewish platform (W. F. Mandle, *Anti-Semitism and the British Union of Fascists* [London, 1968]). Nasjonal Samling had to turn its anti-Jewish electoral stance into an attack on 'international Jews' because it was useless in a country with so homogeneous a population as Norway. In Italy, as in Britain and Norway, the conditions were unpropitious for the acceptance of the racial ideology of the fascist sect by the fascist movement. In Germany, however, they were such as to permit the NSDAP to turn its *Weltanschauung* into an electoral opportunity. The First

World War and the rapid social change which followed had promoted a more virulent anti-Semitism, turning it from a defensive set of beliefs for defining 'Germandom' into an aggressive stance. For all nationalist parties to be against Weimar was also to be against 'Jews'; and the National Socialist Party was able to play on these important changes in attitude (W. E. Mosse, ed., *Deutsches Judentum im Krieg und Revolution, 1916–1923* [Tübingen, 1971]). The Jewish population was prominent in precisely those 'capitalist' occupations which the original ideology denounced, and it had also for obvious reasons supported 'liberal' causes. In these circumstances the fact of 'political anti-Semitism' was added to the racial fires. Those purifying fires were integral to economic policy. Auschwitz and German economic policy in Poland were as much the inescapable historical inheritance of Nazi economic policy as were the blast furnaces of Salzgitter. The campaign against the Jews of eastern Europe started at the same time as, and was an integral part of, the invasion of the Soviet Union. When in 1944 Germany faced extinction and labour had become a scarce economic factor, the concentration camps were allowed to use labour at risibly low levels of productivity while valuable resources were *increasingly* allocated to the slaughter of all who were deemed of the wrong race (J. Billig, *Les camps de concentration dans l'économie du troisième Reich* [Paris, 1973]).

But all electoral studies also show that this threefold explanation of the rise to power of fascism in two countries only is still incomplete. Something else was necessary – a period of extreme social mobility. The middle-class and rural support for fascism came from those who felt their economic and social status to be seriously threatened. In Italy this threat came from the onset of industrialization after 1900, accelerated by the demands of the war. Social groups changed status with great rapidity in what had long been a static society. The concern of fascist economic policy with such concepts as 'stability' and 'rurality' reflects the preoccupations of its threatened supporters. In Germany this social mobility was provided by the hyper-inflation, still lingering as a fearful memory to the middle classes when the depression of 1929 threw six million out of work in three years. Brought to power by social shocks of such magnitude, fascism sought inevitably to

avoid further similar catastrophes, blamed on 'international plutocracy'. Beneath the massive government expenditure lurked, as
Klein has shown, a constant fear of inflation which demanded
ever stronger economic controls and an increased isolation of the
German economy (B. H. Klein, *Germany's Economic Preparations for War* [Cambridge, Mass., 1959]).

The circumstances, therefore, in which fascist movements attained political power were such as to saddle them with a cum-
bersome revolutionary ideology which flew in the face of the
realities of modern economic development, an intense economic
nationalism, an inherent racialism which had overriding economic
aspects, and a widespread sentiment in favour of economic and
social stability. All these elements have to be taken into account
in formulating a hypothesis of the political economy of fascism.
In this light even the most consistent of the hypotheses, those
which equate fascism to a stage in capitalism or to the defensive
reactions of major capital interests, are inadequate. There was in
fact no way in which such disparate and contradictory elements
could be fitted together into a logical and coherent economic
whole, the more so as the acceptance of war as a necessary vehicle
for the assertion of national power greatly strengthened the role
of the major manufacturing interests in the state. The differences
in priority given to these various elements account for many
divergences between Italian and German economic policies in the
fascist period and it may well be that these differences will be seen
as more important and more interesting than the similarities. But
most economic historians have so far adopted the convention of
treating 'the fascist economies' as an entity in the inter-war
period. The historical evidence partly justifies this convention.
The new combination of social and political forces provided, at
the least, the opportunity for a different range of economic
policies; at the most it led to a revolutionary attempt at a socio-
economic reconstruction of the continent. Which of these two
views is nearer to the truth still remains to be decided, and that
can only be done by further research.

Note

1. Of particular relevance here are: W. S. Allen, *The Nazi Seizure of Power: The Experience of a Single Town* (Chicago, 1965); G. Botz, *Gewalt in der Politik* (Munich, 1976); H. S. Brevig, *NS – fra sekt til parti* (Oslo, 1970); A. A. de Jonge, *Het nationaalsocialisme in Nederland* (The Hague, 1968); G. A. Kooy, *Het echec van een 'volkse' Beweging* (Assen, 1964); J. Noakes, *The Nazi Party in Lower Saxony 1921–1933* (Oxford, 1973); K. O'Lessker, 'Who voted for Hitler?' in *American Journal of Sociology*, no. 74 (1968); N. Schäfer, *NSDAP: Entwicklung und Struktur der Staatspartei im dritten Reich* (Marburg, 1957); A. Szymanski, 'Fascism, Industrialism and Socialism: the Case of Italy', in *Comparative Studies in Society and History*, vol. XV, no. 4 (1973).

Part VI
Interpretations

11 Interpretations of Fascism

Twelve years ago George L. Mosse, in the first issue of the *Journal of Contemporary History*, boldly stated: 'In our century, two revolutionary movements have made their mark upon Europe: that originally springing from Marxism, and fascist revolution ... but fascism has been a neglected movement,' while many historians and political scientists had occupied themselves with the left-wing parties and revolutions.[1] Today fascism can no longer be called a neglected subject. Indeed, there is a large volume of books and articles, not only dealing with the fascist movements of individual countries but also many comparative studies, trying to establish the differences as well as the similarities between the various movements which have been called 'fascist'. This is partly due to the industry and devotion of Professor Ernst Nolte who in 1963 published one of the fundamental studies of the problem, a comparison of the Action Française, Italian fascism, and German National Socialism;[2] he has since then written several more books on the fascist movements[3] and has edited a volume of source material, assembling theories put forward by a large variety of writers on the subject of fascism during the past half-century.[4] His example has inspired many others, and the development of the New Left has provided another impetus to the study of fascism. No doubt some of the interest in the subject is purely political and polemical; but even on a more scholarly level the volume of recent publications seems to justify a survey of the theories, old and new, and a preliminary answer to the question to what extent they are new or merely restating older views, and what may be the most fruitful approaches to a further study of the problem. This paper does not pretend to be exhaustive but hopes to stimulate further discussion, by historians, political scientists, sociologists, and social psychologists, for the study of fascism invites a cooperative effort of several academic disciplines: a cooperative effort which is not always easy to achieve. This survey will largely neglect publications devoted to one country and concentrate above all on comparative and more general contributions to the subject.

One of the problems which from the outset occupied the attention of political analysts – and indeed remains one of the central issues of any analysis of fascism – was: where did the mass following of the fascist parties come from, and which social groups tended to support them? Clearly, it was not the industrial working class, which by and large followed the Marxist parties, nor was it the bourgeoisie proper which even numerically could not have provided a mass following. Hence the answer given by Italian critics of fascism as early as the early 1920s was that this mass support came from the *piccola borghesia*, the lower middle classes in town and country. Thus Giovanni Zibordi wrote in 1922 that Italy was 'a country which has a surplus of the lower middle classes, and it is they who, under the influence of special circumstances and favoured by them, have made as it were their own revolution, combining it with a counter-revolution of the bourgeoisie.' Zibordi observed at the same time that, among the followers of the fascists, 'those declassed by the war are particularly numerous: the youngsters who went to the front before they were twenty years old and came back at the age of 23 or 24, being neither able nor willing to return to their studies or their places of work in a regular fashion; the petty bourgeois from a very modest and inferior background who during the war became officers or NCOs . . . and who today cannot get reconciled to go back to their modest occupations.'[5] Zibordi's opinion was echoed in 1923 by Luigi Salvatorelli who stated 'that the petit-bourgeois element not only predominates numerically, but in addition is the characteristic and directing element . . . Thus fascism represents the class struggle of the lower middle class which exists between capitalism and proletariat as the third [group] between two combatants.' But he added that the lower middle class was not 'a true social class with its own strength and functions, but a conglomerate living at the margin of the capitalist process of production'.[6]

These views have since been echoed by numerous writers, Italian as well as non-Italian. Thus Palmiro Togliatti, leader of the Italian Communist party, wrote in 1928: 'The social basis of fascism consists of certain strata of the petty bourgeoisie in town and country . . . In the towns too fascism leans above all on the lower middle classes: partly workmen (artisans), specialists and traders, partly elements displaced on account of the war (former officials, cripples, 'arditi', volunteers).'[7] Another prominent Italian left-winger, Angelo Tasca, stated a few years later: 'This petty and middle bourgeoisie . . . formed the backbone of fascism in Italy and everywhere else. But the expression "middle class" must be given a wider meaning, to include the son of a family waiting for a job or for his inheritance to *déclassés* of all kinds, temporary or permanent, from the half-pay officer to the *Lumpenproletarier*, from the strike-breaker to the jobless intellectual.'[8] Similarly social psychologists like Erich Fromm and Wilhelm Reich wrote during the Second World War: 'Nazi ideology was enthusiastically welcomed by the lower sections of the *Mittelstand*, small shopkeepers, artisans, white collar workers and *Lumpenproletarier*'[9] and: 'The *Mittelstand* began to move and, in the form of fascism, became a social force.'[10] More recently a well-known American sociologist, Seymour Lipset, maintained: 'The thesis that fascism is basically a middle-class movement representing a protest against both capitalism *and* socialism, big business *and* big unions, is far from original . . . Data from a number of countries demonstrate that classic fascism is a movement of the propertied middle classes, who for the most part normally support liberalism.'[11]

At a conference in Reading some years ago, several speakers held that the lower middle classes were particularly prone to the fascist appeal. Thus Professor Kogan said: 'The lower-middle class, rejecting proletarian egalitarianism as socially degrading, while not having a secure position itself, would be most vulnerable to the fascist appeal.' And Dr Solé-Tura: 'Fascist movements came about as an expression of discontent in the lower middle classes of both town and country.'[12] Professor Nolte, on the other hand, has tried to define more precisely what sections of the lower middle class belonged to the original fascists: 'the cadres of its shock-troops were not formed from "the" petty bourgeoisie, but from certain fringe sections of the petty bourgeoisie, the "mercenaries" and the academic youth with its irrational inclinations.'[13] A more recent German study of the origins of fascism emphasizes that it was above all the economic and social threat to the existence of the Mittelstand which made it susceptible to fascist propaganda; 'a precondition of fascism is the economic threat to one or several groups of the Mittelstand and the capitalist bourgeoisie. If capitalism were "harmonious", "free from crises" . . . there would be no need of fascism.'[14] Thus the view that certain sections of the middle classes – whether propertied or threatened, lower-middle or middle, urban or rural – provided the first cadres and the mass following of fascism is widely held to the present day. It seems only a variant of this view if a well-known German historian, Martin Broszat, emphasizes that 'the fascist movements in all these countries (Germany, Italy, Hungary, and Rumania) discovered and used the national and political potential of the small peasants and agricultural labourers . . . Often the small peasants above all voted for the fascists because the latter were the first national party whose propagandists came into the villages and identified themselves with the interests and the feelings of the peasants.'[15] Yet fascism practically everywhere was a movement that started in the towns and was later carried from the towns into the villages; that is true even of eastern Europe where the rural character of the fascist movements was more pronounced than in the more western countries, and where the neglect of the peasantry by the traditional political parties was proverbial.[16]

Apart from the peasants, who indeed were particularly prone to listen to fascist propaganda, two other social groups were extremely prominent among the earliest followers of fascist parties, and indeed provided them with their first semi-military squads or storm troops (and both were very largely of lower middle-class origin): former officers and soldiers, especially ex-servicemen of the First World War, and university students and young graduates; during the first years after 1918 these two groups overlapped. Again Zibordi was one of the first to make this point.[17] It has been repeated more recently by Stuart Woolf, who, discussing the effects of the First World War, has pointed out that it 'created vast masses of ex-combatants who were to form the most fertile seedbeds of nascent nationalistic and fascist movements.'[18] And on the other side of the Atlantic, Professor Sauer has found: 'It may even be said that a distinct interest group was formed within the fascist mixture by what might be called the military desperadoes, veterans of the First World War and the postwar struggles, who had not been reintegrated into either the civilian society or the armed forces.'[19] Similarly a German historian has recently stated: 'It was no accident that ex-servicemen who had not been socially reintegrated formed the nucleus of the fascist movements.'[20]

Perhaps the enthusiastic participation of university students in the fascist movements, above all in central and eastern Europe, has been stressed less often. Especially the Iron Guard started as an organization of Romanian students, and in Germany and Austria the universities became strongholds of National Socialism many years before the so-called 'seizure of power'. Here it was in the first instance bitter economic distress and the dismal prospects of ever obtaining a post, but even more so the fervent nationalism and anti-bolshevism of the post-war years that drove many thousands of students into the Free Corps and the paramilitary formations of the right, and then into the fascist camp. From Finland to Spain, from Flanders to Italy, students were among the most ardent and convinced fighters in the fascist cause. Indeed, at least one recent writer has gone further and finds in 'the mass rush into the fascist movements above all the signs of an aggressive and violent revolt of the young'.[21] This seems to be too wide and too vague a formulation, for we would still like to know from what sections of the population these youngsters came; and it takes too little account of the many older men among the leaders as well as among the followers of the fascist movements.

All the writers quoted so far seek the social basis of the fascist parties in the middle class or certain sections of it. Quite different is the interpretation of those who believe that these parties were able to attract followers from *all* sections of society, but especially the uprooted and declassed elements. Again this interpretation was formulated as early as the early 1920s and has been frequently restated since. Curiously enough, it apparently was first put forward by a well-known communist, Clara Zetkin – an interpretation which differs considerably from later communist pronouncements on the subject. 'The carrier of fascism,' she stated in 1923, 'is not a small caste, but broad social groups, large masses which reach far into the proletariat . . . Masses of many thousands flocked to fascism. It became a refuge for those without a political home, for the socially uprooted, for those without an existence and the disappointed.'[22] And some years later a dissident communist theorist, August Thalheimer, wrote: 'Parasitic elements of all classes which are uprooted economically and socially, excluded from the direct process of production, are the natural elements, the natural tools of the "executive power which has made itself independent"' – a definition which he applied to Bonapartism as well as to fascism.[23] This definition was then taken up and developed further by another Marxist writer with a similar intellectual background, Paul Sering (Richard Löwenthal), who found

that this [fascist] party recruits itself from members of all classes, while within it certain groups are prevalent and form its nucleus, groups which have been called 'middle groups' in a confusing terminology. The bourgeoisie is represented, but only the bourgeoisie which is in debt and needs support; the working class is represented, but only the workers who are chronically unemployed and unable to fight, living in distressed areas; the urban lower middle classes join, but only the ruined lower middle classes, the rentiers are included, but only the rentiers expropriated by the inflation; officers and intellectuals lead, but only ex-officers and bankrupt intellectuals. These groups form the nucleus of the movement – it has the character of a true community of bankruptcy – and this allows the movement to expand beyond its nucleus into all social classes parallel with the crisis because it is socially interlinked with all of them.[24]

These views have been echoed more recently by several historians. Thus a German-American historian has stated: 'Historical evidence shows that support of fascism may not be confined to the classical elements of the lower middle class . . . but may extend to a wide variety of groups in the large field between the workers on the one hand and big business, the aristocracy, and the top levels of the bureaucracy on the other.'[25] Another American professor agrees: 'The component sectors of both fascism and nazism could not be reduced to lower middle classes and Lumpenproletariat; an assorted variety of social categories took an active part in fascist movements: war veterans, unemployed, young people, peasants. A common trait was recognized in all groups – their uprootedness.'[26] And a British survey concurs: 'Fascist parties, then, had a fairly uniform doctrine, but extremely varying social composition. From whatever class the support came, it was invariably made up of the chronically discontented . . . Poor aristocrats and gentry, ex-service or junior officers, unemployed or under-employed university graduates and students, ambitious small businessmen and aspiring youths from the lower middle and working classes, all became prominent as the élite of the élitists.'[27] There can be little doubt that this analysis is basically correct, that the term 'lower middle class' is too general and too vague to explain the wide differences in social background of the fascist leaders and followers (and the participation of large numbers of the working class). The element of uprootedness, of social insecurity, of a position threatened and assailed, of loss of status, is of vital importance for the problem; and in this century the greatest uprooter, the greatest destroyer of security was the First World War with its aftermath of revolution and civil war. This would also explain why no mass fascist movement arose in the aftermath of the Second World War, which was not followed by revolutions, civil war, and vast economic crises but by a great effort of economic reconstruction.

If violent opposition to socialist or proletarian revolution was one of the primary causes of the growth of fascism, it is also true that the fascist movements only developed *after* these revolutionary forces had been decisively defeated, when the threat had already disappeared.[28] In Italy the occupation of the factories by the workers ended in their evacuation and a signal defeat of the left, which was badly split and disunited. In Germany the left-wing risings of the early 1920s were defeated by the Free Corps and the army, and in the vast slump of the early 1930s the working-class movement was thrown onto the defensive and totally unable to act. In Hungary and Finland the fascist movements grew after the end of the civil war and decisive defeats of the local communists from which they were unable to recover. Again, the first to point this out, as far as Italy was concerned, was Zibordi who wrote in 1922: 'Fascism is . . . the instrument of a counter-revolution against a proletarian revolution which did exist only in the form of a programme and a threat.'[29] And, after the Nazi victory in Germany, Otto Bauer pointed out: 'But in reality fascism did not triumph at the moment when the bourgeoisie was threatened by the proletarian revolution: it triumphed when the proletariat had long been weakened and forced onto the defensive, when the revolutionary flood had abated. The capitalists and the large landowners did not entrust the fascist hordes with the power of the state so as to protect themselves against a threatening proletarian revolution, but so as to depress the wages, to destroy the social gains of the working class, to eradicate the trade unions and the positions of power gained by the working class.'[30] Recently a young German left-wing analyst has once more emphasized this point: 'Fascism is preceded by an attempt at proletarian revolution which largely ended in failure or by revolution-like risings of the proletariat (as in Italy). These revolutionary attempts of the proletariat were supported by sections of the lower middle class and semi-proletarian groups.' Preconditions similar to these, he continues, also existed in Austria, Hungary, and Spain before the establishment of conservative dictatorships.[31]

Was the threat then purely imaginary, the fear of proletarian revolution unjustified – or to put it more crudely, was it deliberately exaggerated by an unscrupulous propaganda? This, on the whole, is not the opinion of the modern historians. Thus Professor Trevor-Roper has stated: 'For fascism, as an effective movement, was born of fear. It might have independent intellectual roots; it might owe its form, here and there, to independent national or personal freaks; but its force, its dynamism, sprang from the fear of a new, and this time "proletarian" revolution.'[32] And Renzo de Felice has spoken of a double fear: 'The winning fascist faction accepted a compromise with the existing order, because of the fear of revolution that haunted the ruling classes in Italy. But the basic motivation of this faction was also fear of revolution, a fear of the left-wing fascists mobilizing and taking power.'[33] A younger German writer of the New Left has made this point in much more general terms: 'The fact that capitalist industrial society cannot be overlooked and the experience of being without any power, of being the prisoner of anonymous forces produce a fear which then seeks a firm support . . . In fascism there assembled above all the sections of the bourgeois middle classes which were declassed or immediately threatened with becoming déclassés. By their votes for fascism they protested against this threat.'[34] Yet relatively few historians have ventured into this field which they may feel belongs more properly to the social psychologists.

Indeed, social psychologists, social scientists, as well as historians, have stressed much more the loss of prestige and of social security which affected the masses after the First World War. This point was made in its classical form by Erich Fromm in 1942 and has been repeated often ever since:

The authority of the monarchy had been uncontested and, by leaning on it and identifying themselves with it, the members of the lower middle classes gained a feeling of security and of self-admiring, narcissistic pride . . . There was the lost war and the overthrow of the monarchy. The state and the princes had been secure rocks on which – seen psychologically – the petit bourgeois had built his existence; their downfall and the defeat shook the foundation of his existence . . . Not only the economic situation of the lower middle classes, but their social prestige too declined rapidly after the war. Before the war they could believe that they were something better than the worker. After the war the social prestige of the working class rose, and that of the lower middle class sank correspondingly. There was no one any longer on whom they could look down, a privilege which had always been one of the strongest positive factors in the life of the philistine.[35]

This interpretation has been restated by political scientists and others. Thus Professor Germani has told us: 'It is widely recognized that "disequilibration" had caused loss of status (in terms of prestige as well as in terms of power and wealth) for the urban middle class. Such loss had taken place both in relative and in absolute terms: decreasing distance because of the advance of the working class, absolute downward mobility in terms of unemployment, inflation, decreasing income, and decreasing political influence . . . The advance of the working class was resented as an "invasion" or "usurpation" of status.'[36] And a German writer has spoken emphatically of the 'fear of decadence' and added: 'Blind fear of decline has been one of the most powerful roots of fascist tendencies, and not only in Germany.'[37] There can be no doubt that these fears were not imaginary but largely justified, that the middle and the lower middle classes, the 'little man', had lost their stable place in society, their security and prosperity, that they felt helpless in the new order of things after the war, the victims of forces which they could not understand.

The social psychologists have pointed to other traits in the fascist make-up which had an important influence in attracting the masses. Thus Erich Fromm has enumerated the 'veneration of the strong' and the 'hatred of the weak', 'the longing to submit, and the lust for power';[38] and Wilhelm Reich wrote at the same time: 'The fascist mentality is the mentality of the "little man", suppressed, longing for authority and at the same time rebellious . . . The fascist is the sergeant in the vast army of our deeply ill civilization, the civilization of big industry.'[39] Reich also emphasized that the fascists strongly identified themselves with their Leader: 'every National Socialist felt himself, in spite of his dependence, like a "little Hitler".'[40] Fromm equally stressed another form of identification which worked strongly after the Nazi seizure of power:

A further impetus to loyalty towards the Nazi régime became operative after Hitler had come into power: for many millions, the majority of the population, Hitler's government was identical with 'Germany'. As soon as he had formed the government, 'to oppose him' meant no less than to exclude oneself from the community of the Germans . . . Apparently nothing is more difficult for the average person to bear but the feeling not to be at one with a larger group. Even if German burghers were strongly opposed to the Nazi principles, as soon as they had to choose between standing alone and belonging to Germany the large majority chose the latter.[41]

Such ideas have been fruitful in stimulating modern historians to accept terms and views imported from a different discipline. Thus Professor Mosse found: 'In under-developed countries, the stress upon the end to alienation, the belief in the organic community, brought dividends – for the exclusion of the workers and peasants from society had been so total that purely economic considerations could take second place.'[42] And the sociologist Dr Barbu stated:

One of the most fruitful approaches was to conceive of the party as a type of primary community, a corporate morality, which tried to reinforce the feeling of belonging to something, the primary emotional involvement of the individual . . . In an industrializing society it might appeal to the lower middle class, in a transitional society to the people who became available through a primary mobilization process, the peasants who left the villages to come to the towns. But the problem remained the same all the time: the fascist movement appealed to people who needed strong bonds . . . The fascist party offered a type of solidarity; it appealed to people who suffered from the disintegration of traditional or any kind of social solidarity.[43]

A young German historian wrote more recently of the 'salvation [found] in the submission to a strong authority. This can express itself in the identification either with a powerful collective – the state, the nation, the enterprise – or with the personality of the Leader: the "authoritarian-masochistic character" projects its ego-ideal onto a Leader figure with which he identifies himself unconditionally.'[44] Indeed, there seems no reason why such a process should only be at work 'in under-developed countries', for in modern industrial societies too the alienated might join a party with which they can totally identify themselves, all the readier if that party stands in total opposition to society and state and seeks to destroy them. This, of course, need not be a fascist party, but under certain political and social conditions, and as far as certain social groups are concerned, it would be a fascist party and Leader with whom the masses could identify most easily, to whose promise of reintegration they would most readily listen. The 'people's community' (*Volksgemeinschaft*) promised by the leaders of the Third Reich did not materialize, but millions were longing for it.

In the early stages of the rise of fascist movements, a very similar mechanism was operative on the local level. As Dr Adrian Lyttelton has found for Italy,

The origins of many squads are to be found in a loose, informal relationship between a group of adolescents, somewhat resembling that of a youth gang ... Primary ties of kinship or friendship were important in creating a feeling of camaraderie among the *squadristi*. The existence of this 'small group solidarity' served to protect the Fascist from the feelings of impotence and ennui common among those in the grip of large, impersonal bureaucratic organizations; they seemed to allow the individual to achieve both integration and independence. At the same time, of course, the violence which was the essence of *squadrismo* allowed an outlet for aggression.[45]

Exactly the same could be said of the 'gangs' of local storm-troopers, or indeed of their predecessors, the Free Corps and uniformed paramilitary associations in Germany.

There was another psychological factor, important for both Germany and Italy (but not for some of the other countries where fascist movements grew): the feeling of national shame which affected millions on account of defeat and, what was in their eyes, an ignominious peace settlement. This is most obvious for the countries defeated in 1918, Germany and Hungary; but it is also true of Italy, where the crushing defeat of Caporetto caused the same sense of shame, where the ultimate victory over the Austrians was 'mutilated' by the peace settlement, and where 'the war was won but the peace lost'.[46] This feeling directly inspired the first fascist enterprises and above all Gabriele d' Annunzio's expedition to Fiume, the dress rehearsal for the march on Rome. Recently a younger German historian has drawn our attention to 'the groups of enemies against which fascism directs the wrath of the masses'; he believes that 'those social groups are especially suited as objects of aggression which are distinguished from the large majority by their looks or their behaviour and which therefore can easily be recognized. Racial, national or religious minorities ... thus function only too often as objects of aggression. They have the additional advantage that they are rather defenceless so that the mob can discharge its aggressions without risk and punishment. Violence and murder ... committed against members of the minorities are looked upon not only as permitted but even as an honourable national service.'[47] Admittedly, all these factors cannot be measured by statistics and defy a more precise definition, but they seem important in any assessment of the roots of fascism, and helpful in any attempt to answer the question why fascist movements were able to attract vast crowds and to perpetrate deeds which any normal society would classify as criminal. Here again the primary catalyst would seem to be the First World War which accustomed millions to the use of violence and elevated it to the rank of a patriotic duty.

This once more is not a new perception but it was recognized as early as 1928 by the Italian socialist Filippo Turati (who had been a pacifist during the war): 'The war ... accustomed the youngsters as well as the grown ups to the daily use of usual and unusual weapons ... it praised individual and collective murder, blackmail, arrest, the macabre joke, the torturing of prisoners, the "punitive expeditions", the summary executions ... it created in general the atmosphere in which alone the fascist bacillus could grow and spread.'[48] Turati also thought that this spirit in particular affected the youngsters who, because of their age, had been unable to participate in the war but were all the more eager to win military laurels, especially in a situation where their lives were no longer at stake.[49] Because the Italian (and German) governments were notoriously weak and unable to cope with the ever-worsening economic crisis, there was 'a growing longing for a strong government', a 'yearning for peace and order', for 'a strong hand at the helm'.[50] The willingness of large masses to accept a Leader, who would overcome misery and strife and lead them to a glorious future, can partly be explained by the social and economic distress of the post-war period. As Professor Vierhaus has pointed out, 'sections of the population which politically and socially were without any orientation had a need of strong authority; they acclaimed the leaders in whom the masses not seldom put semi-religious hopes of salvation, to which the leaders and their propaganda replied with the vague but all the more effective promise of a general improvement, a better, proud national future.'[51] Indeed, fascist rallies often had the atmosphere of a revivalist assembly, and the masses shouted: 'The Leader is always right!'

Several historians have stated that – in contrast with all other parties and political movements – the Leader of a fascist party needed charisma, but very little effort has been made to define this charisma, or the social and psychological conditions under which it became effective. Thus Professor Seton-Watson has written: 'An obviously important feature of fascism which often gets left out . . . is the charismatic leader. Mussolini, Degrelle, and José Antonio Primo de Rivera were clearly men of outstanding abilities. Szálasi and Codreanu were complex personalities combining ruthlessness with strange flashes of nobility of character. Hitler still defies analysis.'[52] Yet it was Hitler before whom battle-hardened generals trembled, who was able to arouse the masses to a fever pitch, whose decisions were unquestioningly accepted by his enthusiastic followers. In a more general form Professor Vierhaus maintains: 'The Leader taking his stand on the basis of the plebiscite can only legitimize himself by his charisma, i.e. the fact that he stands above the ordinary and commonplace, by his personal authority. This has to rely on proving itself every day by deed and success; hence the ever-repeated public appearances of the Leader with a ceremonial which is cunningly adapted to different situations.'[53]

It has often been said that without Hitler there would have been no National Socialism, or that at least National Socialism would have been very different without him. This again seems a field where the historian or the political scientist might have to rely on the help of the social psychologist. A well-known psychologist has recently defined Hitler 'as the quintessential embodiment of Germany's and Austria's many defeat-shattered, uprooted "little men", craving for the security of belonging, for the restoration of power and glory, and for vengeance.' He gave expression 'to a state of mind existing in millions of people, not only in Germany'.[54] This is true, but it does not get us much further.

If the psychological factors which conditioned fascism are difficult to define and have to a large extent defied a more precise analysis, the same need not apply to the social preconditions of its growth. More than fifty years ago, in 1923, Luigi Salvatorelli, who understood fascism as a movement of the lower middle classes, thought that fascism developed in Italy because Italy was economically backward and thus had a particularly numerous petty bourgeoisie.[55] Ten years later the sociologist Franz Borkenau, who understood fascism in the same sense, added that its victory in Italy was due to 'the absence of a politically and economically adequate industrial bourgeoisie'. As fascism destroyed those sections of the working-class movements which were willing to reach a compromise with the bourgeoisie, 'the bourgeoisie of the most developed capitalist countries cannot afford such a policy. In countries where up to 75 per cent of the population belong to the proletariat in the proper sense of the term, democracy, reformism and free trade unions are virtually indispensable factors for the preservation of the status quo. To do without them is only feasible in countries where the proletariat is still weak enough simply to be suppressed . . . In more developed conditions this is not a question of advantages and disadvantages, but the destruction of the modern working-class movement is a total impossibility.'[56] When these lines were published Hitler had already been appointed chancellor of Germany.

Some years later Otto Bauer attempted another analysis of fascism from a Marxist point of view, which in his opinion rested on a social equilibrium:

The fascist dictatorship comes into being as the result of a peculiar equilibrium of the social classes. On one side there is the bourgeoisie which controls the means of production and circulation and the power of the state . . . On the other side stands the working class which is led by reformist socialists and the trade unions. Reformism and trade unions have become stronger than the bourgeoisie is willing to accept . . . Exactly as the absolutism of the early capitalist epoch . . . developed on the basis of the equilibrium of the forces of the feudal nobility and the bourgeoisie . . . so the new fascist absolutism is the result of a temporary equilibrium when the bourgeoisie could not force the proletariat to accept its will by the old legal methods, and the proletariat was unable to liberate itself from the rule of the bourgeoisie; and thus both classes fell under the dictatorship of the violent mob which the capitalists used against the proletariat until they themselves had to submit to the dictatorship.[57]

Bauer's opinion has more recently been restated by Dr Solé-Tura: 'Fascism is the solution found for the contradictions caused by the development of capitalism at a characteristic point of fundamental class equilibrium.'[58] Yet Bauer's comparison with the period of absolutism can hardly be maintained: the seventeenth century was a period when the feudal economy had long disintegrated, when the power of the nobility was no longer as strong as it had once been, when a new economic order based on the towns and the urban middle classes was developing: hence there could be a time of equilibrium when the princes were able to play off one group against the other. But it would be vastly overestimating the strength of social democracy and the trade unions to say that it balanced that of the bourgeoisie; the very ease with which social democracy was destroyed in Central Europe proves that this strength was more imaginary than real.

There is, however, another theory which may be more helpful in explaining why certain countries have been more prone to produce fascist mass movements than others. Professor Nolte has suggested a geographical classification combined with an approach based on social structure, 'the path of growing industrialization and a declining share of the agrarian population, which in Albania and Yugoslavia around 1930 comprised around 80 per cent of the total but in England counted for hardly more than 10 per cent. It could obviously be held that in the former group the social preconditions of fascism did not yet exist, while in the last group they existed no longer, that only in the centre of Central Europe fascism found the preconditions for a full development.' Although Nolte then proceeds to point to the obvious difficulties in accepting this interpretation, he concludes that 'the view which sees the primary cause of fascist movements in a certain mixture of social forces remains noteworthy and important.'[59] Indeed, it seems that societies undergoing a rapid social and economic transformation from a pre-industrial to an industrial society proved a favourite breeding ground of the fascist movements, that members of certain social groups found it particularly difficult to adjust themselves to social change, to accept a lower social status or the rise of a new social force, that the period of quick transition was the most difficult one: when the process of industrialization was more or less complete a new equilibrium was established, and with it greater social security, for the individual as well as for the group as a whole. Yet this theory, while it seems worth exploring in greater detail, still does not answer why the fascist movements developed in the 1920s and 1930s, and why they became mass movements in certain countries but not in others. Other factors to be considered here obviously are the stability or instability of political institutions, the strength or weakness of democratic and liberal traditions, the popularity or unpopularity of parliament and the political parties, the marked differences in the political and social structures of the European countries. Perhaps little headway can be made in this field until many more detailed studies have become available.

Another, much more tangible, precondition for the *success* of the fascists was their alliance with certain ruling circles and with the political right, and there does not seem to be any disagreement among the historians on this issue, irrespective of their political views. Thus more than ten years ago Nolte stated unequivocally: 'Hardly less than Hitler's oratorical gifts and passion, the German army, the connections of Dietrich Eckart and the protection offered by the director of [the Munich] police Pöhner contributed to make the National Socialist Party into what it was in 1923 . . . The collaboration of the state and of leading circles in society became at least as important for the development of National Socialism as for that of fascism' in Italy.[60] More recently another German historian has written: 'In reality National Socialism like other fascist movements could only reach power in alliance with the traditional Right, and it received its support because its attacks were to a very large extent directed against the political Left.'[61] From the political left a younger German writer agrees with this thesis: 'The system of rule established by Italian fascism too can be defined as an alliance between the fascist movement and the social upper strata. Yet the balance was different from the German form. Already during the period before the seizure of power Italian fascism had been unable to gain such a strong mass basis as German fascism. The result was that there the fascist movement, even after its "seizure of power", did not obtain the same position of strength in its coalition with the social upper classes as it did in Germany.'[62] Similar is the statement of an American historian: 'The general conclusion one can make from the rise to power of Mussolini and Hitler seems to be this: The radical Right had its best chance in societies where older but still powerful élites see their values and interests eroded by rapid and modernizing social change, change which generates a massive liberal and left threat to "old ways". When this happens conservatives, ultra-conservatives and reactionaries of differing ideologies and classes tend to unite and strike back "by any means necessary".'[63]

Indeed, one can go further and say: if a fascist party disregards the forging of a firm alliance with the forces of the old order and of the state and tries to seize power relying entirely on its own strength, the attempt is doomed to failure. This is the lesson which Hitler drew from his Munich putsch of 1923 when he aimed at drawing the Bavarian government and army onto his side but ultimately failed to achieve this end; when he came to power in 1933 he was appointed chancellor by the ancient fieldmarshal, he had the support of the army and of the bureaucracy, and he formed a coalition government with the right-wing German Nationalist party. When Horia Sima, the leader of the powerful Iron Guard, tried to sieze power in Bucharest at the beginning of 1941 he failed because the government of Marshal Antonescu and the Romanian army turned against him. Szálasi, the leader of the Arrow Cross movement, was unable to form a firm alliance with the traditional right in Hungary and the government of the Regent Horthy, hence he was excluded from power until he was raised to the position of a puppet leader by the Germans at the end of the war. Here a striking difference exists between the seizure of power by a fascist party and by a movement of the extreme left.

In spite of these facts, political commentators, historians, and political scientists seem to be agreed in using the term 'fascist revolution', while they are also aware that the fascist movements contained counter-revolutionary elements. Thus Zibordi wrote as early as 1922: 'It seems to me that fascism is at the same time the following: a counter-revolution of the true middle class against a "red" revolution . . . a revolution, or rather a convulsion of petty bourgeois, declassed and discontented sections, and a military revolution.'[64] The German former National Socialist Hermann Rauschning in 1938 coined the slogan of 'The Revolution of Nihilism' and declared: 'National Socialism has not only eliminated the positions of power held by the working class, which could justify the verdict that it is a counter-revolutionary movement, but it has equally destroyed the middle class, the political and social positions of the middle class, and of the old, leading social strata . . . The German revolution therefore is at least both: a social revolution and a counter-revolution.'[65] And from the German left it was stated at about the same time: 'The fascist revolution is thus a genuine revolution insofar as it presents an important scissure in the development of bourgeois society which necessarily is taking place in revolutionary forms and is caused by economic developments. Its typical results are: 1. a new higher form of the organization of the state; 2. a new reactionary form of social organization; 3. a growing check to economic development by reactionary forces which have usurped the power of the state.'[66]

Most modern historians concur that the fascist movements were revolutionary. Thus Professor Mosse speaks of the 'two revolutionary movements' of the twentieth century, of the 'fascist revolution', which in his opinion in the West 'was primarily a bourgeois revolution'.[67] Professor Sauer has stated in the *American Historical Review:* 'There is virtual agreement among scholars that fascist movements contained, contrary to the Marxist thesis, a true revolutionary potential.'[68] And Professor Bracher has written: 'An interpretation which sees in fascism and National Socialism only the final stage of a reactionary counter-revolution and denies it any revolutionary character amounts to an incorrect simplification of complicated processes. All four basic currents which have contributed to the ideologies of fascism and of National Socialism are simultaneously determined by revolutionary and by reactionary forces.'[69] But there are a few dissentient voices. Thus the American editor of an anthology on fascism maintains: 'Fascism cannot be understood if it is viewed as a revolution. It was a counter-revolution. Its purpose was to prevent the liberalization and radicalization of Italy and Germany. Property and income distribution and the traditional class structure remained roughly the same under fascist rule. What changes there were favoured the old élites or certain segments of the party membership.'[70] A similar view is held by a German left-wing analyst: 'As the beginning of a fascist dictatorship one must see the transfer of power to, or the taking over of power by the most reactionary forces existing which aim at the establishment of a rule of unlimited violence so as to secure the interests of the native, or maybe a foreign, monopoly capitalism. This need not necessarily be fascist parties, but could be the military, or leaders of conservative reactionary parties, or representatives of the higher clergy.'[71]

The issue seems to be confused by the fact that fascist parties – in Germany and in Italy – only came into power through an alliance with conservative and reactionary forces, but an alliance that did not last. Also, in both countries, the opposition of more radical, 'revolutionary' fascist groups had to be overcome before the dictatorship was securely established. Yet it would be silly to deny that there were genuine revolutionary elements in the fascist movements, especially so in central and south-eastern Europe, and that important changes in the existing social structure were introduced by the German – but less so by the Italian – dictatorship. As there were only these two fascist régimes, any generalization becomes very difficult. Perhaps the cautious statement by Professor Bracher that revolutionary as well as reactionary elements were present in the fascist ideologies might be extended to the fascist movements as such, and the proportions naturally varied from country to country. Wherever social conditions were particularly antediluvian and radical social reform was urgently necessary, for example in Hungary and Romania, the revolutionary elements would be stronger, and vice versa.

As the basic elements of fascist ideology, Professor Bracher has identified four currents: national imperialism, étatism, populist socialism, and racialism.[72] To these might be added two more: a kind of national romanticism, glorifying the agrarian and pre-industrial past and military virtues,[73] and corporativism,[74] which had little influence in Germany, but a much stronger one in Italy, Austria, and Spain. Whatever other elements we might add to this list, it seems clear that most of these components were traditional or reactionary, and that only very few could qualify as 'revolutionary'. There were no doubt 'populist' traits in the fascist movements, as several historians have recently emphasized, but the comparison with the *Narodniki* of tsarist Russia seems far-fetched and untenable – precisely because the *Narodniki* were a genuine revolutionary group inspired by a revolutionary creed.[75] In any case, very few historians and political scientists would today accept, without any qualification, Richard Crossman's assertion of 1939: 'In Central Europe, where the economic interpretation of history was the myth of the working-class movement, Racialism became the revolutionary philosophy of a discontented German middle class.'[76] The roots of German racialism went back far into the nineteenth century, and racialist ideas formed part of the traditional armoury of the right.

Discarded too has been the view which so intelligent an historian as Arthur Rosenberg held in 1934 that fascism is 'the counter-revolutionary capitalist, the born foe of the class-conscious working class. Fascism is nothing but a modern, popularly masked form of the bourgeois-capitalist counter-revolution.'[77] This view corresponded to that propounded at the same time by the Communist International that 'fascism is the open and terrorist dictatorship of the most reactionary, chauvinist and imperialist elements of the finance capital.'[78] It has been restated since in exactly the same form in Germany: 'The basic trait of fascism is – in the summarizing and still valid definition of Dimitrov – "the open and terroristic dictatorship of the most reactionary, most chauvinist and most imperialist elements of the finance capital."'[79] But the mere repetition of an old cliché does not make it any more correct or fitting a very complex reality. A critic of this view from the New Left was completely justified when he pointed out: 'Not the direct support by big capitalism caused the rise of fascism, but the economic crisis immanent in the capitalist system drove the frightened masses, above all the lower middle classes threatened by proletarianization, into the fascist camp . . . Only when fascism had become a mass movement support by big capitalists began to a larger extent.'[80] Indeed, large numbers of finance and other big capitalists and many members of the old aristocracies were frightened by the semi-proletarian and pseudo-revolutionary character of the fascist movements – and not without reason.

There can be little doubt that, under the fascist régime, the old ruling circles were partly replaced by 'a new political class',[81] drawn above all from the leaders of the fascist party whose origins were considerably lower down on the social scale than those of the older groups. This again was the case much more in Germany than in Italy where the old bureaucracy continued to rule almost unchallenged. And even in Germany those party leaders who entered the bureaucracy seem to have taken on its traditional attitudes and to have adopted its standards to a surprising degree.[82] But so far little research has been done in this field, and any more general conclusion must await further investigation. As Professor Schapiro has pointed out, Hitler engaged in bitter and prolonged conflicts with the bureaucracy (from which he often emerged victorious), while 'so far as Mussolini was concerned, he did not succeed in making very serious inroads into the state.'[83] It seems that there is a need here of more comparative studies. It may be the case that National Socialism against its will carried through a modernization of the administrative structure which the Weimar Republic had failed to obtain, while this was not achieved in Italy. It may well turn out, in any case, that the similarities between the two fascist régimes were as pronounced as the differences between them.

What are the conclusions of this brief survey? It seems that no fundamentally new interpretations of fascism have been put forward by the modern historians and political scientists, but that they have taken up and discussed – in one form or the other – the old interpretations of the twenties and thirties. Especially the views and ideas of Italian writers from the early 1920s, formulated from a close observation of the Italian scene, have to a large extent been confirmed by later research. But, in spite of the large volume of modern research and the many dozens of monographs and Ph.D. theses on the subject, a great deal of work remains to be done and in particular there is still a great shortage of good comparative studies. As we have seen, many modern historians are prepared to accept ideas from, and to cooperate with, social psychologists and sociologists, and this may produce more valuable results in the future. If this survey has not produced anything startlingly new, it hopes at least to stimulate further cooperation and research; for fascism remains one of the fundamental issues of the twentieth century and deserves the attention of all concerned about the fundamental traits in the development of our society. Today it is fashionable to call every dictatorship from Greece to Latin America 'fascist': a clear definition of what fascism was and what constituted a fascist movement would eliminate much confused talk and clarify the minds of many students. To equate the terms 'reactionary' and 'fascist', or to identify military dictatorship with fascism, is to misunderstand the nature of fascism.

Postscript

This essay was written more than five years ago. It stated at the beginning that, in more recent years, numerous books and articles on fascist movements in individual countries as well as many comparative studies had been published, that fascism was no longer 'a neglected movement'. The intervening years have brought a new flood of such studies, and it therefore seems appropriate to mention at least some of the more important ones, especially those which offer new conclusions or indicate new approaches to further research. This flood of new studies is proof of the vitality of a subject which is important not only for our understanding of recent history but seems relevant to certain problems of our present society.

Many of the recent studies discuss the social basis of different fascist movements, and there a certain consensus seems to have been reached. In Germany as well as in Italy some social groups were more inclined to follow the fascist appeal than others; this applied in particular to the old and the new Mittelstand, the self-employed, white-collar workers, lower-grade officials, as well as to students and members of some of the professions, such as teachers and doctors. It also applied, at least in certain areas, to peasants and landowners, although their support of fascism was less certain than that of the urban middle groups. The upper and the working classes, on the other hand, were considerably less inclined to accept fascist propaganda. These conclusions were reached by several German historians who contributed papers to the thirtieth congress of German historians held in October 1974 and now available in book form: Wolfgang Schieder (ed.), *Faschismus als soziale Bewegung – Deutschland und Italien im Vergleich*, which contains three essays on Italian fascism and three on National Socialism.[84] In spite of its title, the book does not make any comparisons between Germany and Italy, but apparently the reader is left to draw his own inferences from the details supplied. Similar conclusions with regard to the social basis of National Socialism are reached by Professor Childers in a contribution to the tenth anniversary issue of the *Journal of Contemporary History*, based on an analysis of voting patterns in the late 1920s and early 1930s.[85] But his conclusion that the 'old' middle class was more receptive to National Socialist propaganda than the 'new' seems somewhat doubtful and would need more detailed confirmation.

A certain amount of agreement seems also to have been reached on the issue of the relationship of the traditional upper classes and the fascists. Professor Henry A. Turner's detailed researches into the connections of German capitalists with National Socialism have cleared the air with regard to a topic obfuscated by partisanship and political bias.[86] A younger German historian has recently emphasized that the relationship between the upper classes and fascism was not necessarily a positive one. Especially in Hungary and in Romania the upper classes did not conclude an alliance with the fascists because this seemed too dangerous to them and because they did not want to disturb the social peace.[87] The result was that in Romania the Iron Guard was defeated by the army; and in Hungary the Arrow Cross only came into power at the end of the Second World War thanks to German support. In Italy and in Germany, however, the fascist 'seizure of power' was only made possible by the alliance with the established upper classes, with the army and the higher bureaucracy. Wherever a revolutionary 'seizure of power' was attempted and met with firm resistance by the army and the state authorities, it failed, be that in Germany or in Romania.

A question much discussed in recent contributions to the subject of fascism is whether it was an expression of anti-modernism, whether the fascist leaders were in reality modernizers, and whether fascism in the two countries where it achieved power resulted in a modernization of state and society. Again it was Professor Turner who opened the discussion in an essay on 'Fascism and Modernization' in which he posed these questions without attempting a definite answer.[88] A Canadian historian, Alan Cassels, has distinguished 'two prototypes of fascism': one in advanced industrial societies which was 'nihilistic and backward-looking', the other in under-industrialized societies which was forward-looking and modernizing and used corporative ideas to achieve this end.[89] In Germany, Dr Wippermann has pointed to the example of Romanian and Hungarian fascism which both tried to promote the modernization of an antiquated social structure and aimed at the consolidation and integration of the nation through the elimination of the Jews and other foreign elements.[90] Yet it seems impossible to construct two different types of fascism by the use of this model, for all fascist movements contained elements of a protest against modernization and urbanization as well as tendencies towards a restructuring of society in a more modern sense. The mixture may have differed according to the relative backwardness and development of the country in question, but the tendency towards modernization was present even in the most developed countries. For Germany, this has long been shown by Ralf Dahrendorf[91] and David Schoenbaum,[92] whatever Hitler's intentions may have been. If National Socialist ideology was backward-looking and tried to revive medieval ideas and social relations, Mussolini's quest for a new Roman Empire and a return to the soil was not precisely forward-looking either. But the relationship between these different and often contradictory elements clearly requires more detailed research. So does the relationship between fascist ideology and social reality on which little work seems to have been done in recent years.

In general, the emphasis of much recent research has been on the differences, rather than on the similarities, between different fascist parties and régimes. A point made by several historians is that the relationship between the bureaucracy and the ruling party was dissimilar in Italy and in Germany. In Italy, Mussolini's well known circular to the prefects of 5 January 1927 assigned to them control over the party and made even the party's federal secretaries subordinate to the prefects who were empowered to remove 'undesirable elements' from the fascist organizations.[93] There is no parallel to this from Germany, and during the war the tendency there was in the opposite direction. On the other hand, if the fascist party in Italy in the 1930s no longer had any political functions and became a mass organization of careerists and public functionaries,[94] its later role in Germany was perhaps not all that different. Although the opposite has been asserted recently, there seems to be no evidence that fascism in Italy – or for that matter in Germany – 'involved them [the masses] . . . in the day to day functioning of the system.'[95]

Another point that has emerged from the recent studies of fascism is that there is no generally accepted theory of fascism which could apply to the many countries in which fascist movements developed in the 1920s and 1930s. Indeed, several historians have stated that fascism cannot be explained by one simple formula,[96] that National Socialism was 'qualitatively different in its substance from Italian fascism',[97] that 'it seems unwise to continue with studies of fascism that start with the assumption that there must have been such a generic phenomenon.'[98] In short, the present trend among the historians is towards more detailed studies of single fascist parties or movements, and away from any generalization. If this leads us to new research and new monographs on individual countries this trend is very welcome; if it should lead to the neglect of comparisons and more general interpretations, this writer at least would regret it. Whether we study 'fascism' or 'fascisms' a comparison, bringing out the differences as well as the similarities, remains of vital importance, not only to the professional historian.

Notes

1. George L. Mosse, 'The Genesis of Fascism', *Journal of Contemporary History*, vol. I, no. 1 (1966), p. 14.

2. Ernst Nolte, *Der Faschismus in seiner Epoche* (Munich, 1963).

3. Above all, *Die faschistischen Bewegungen* (Munich, 1966), and *Die Krise des liberalen Systems und die faschistischen Bewegungen* (Munich, 1968).

4. *Theorien über den Faschismus* (Cologne and Berlin, 1967).

5. Giovanni Zibordi, *Critica socialista del fascismo* (Bologna, 1922), quoted by Nolte, *Theorien über den Faschismus*, pp. 80, 85.

6. Luigi Salvatorelli, *Nationalfascismo* (Turin, 1923), quoted ibid., pp. 130, 131, 135.

7. P. Togliatti, *A proposito del fascismo* (1928), quoted by Renzo de Felice, *Le interpretazioni del fascismo* (Bari, 1969), p. 181. The 'arditi' were Italian shock troops of the First World War.

8. A. Rossi (Angelo Tasca), *The Rise of Italian Fascism*, 2nd ed. (New York, 1966), p. 340 (first published in 1938).

9. Erich Fromm, *Die Furcht vor der Freiheit* (Frankfurt, 1966), p. 206 (written in 1942).

10. Wilhelm Reich, *Die Massenpsychologie des Faschismus* (Cologne, 1971), p. 68 (written in 1942).

11. Seymour Martin Lipset, *Political Man – The Social Bases of Politics* (New York, 1960), pp. 134, 174.

12. N. Kogan and J. Solé-Tura, in S. J. Woolf (ed.), *The Nature of Fascism* (London, 1968), pp. 13, 43.

13. Ernst Nolte, *Die faschistischen Bewegungen* (Munich, 1966), p. 65.

14. Manfred Clemenz, *Gesellschaftliche Ursprünge des Faschismus* (Frankfurt, 1972), pp. 147, 228. Compare another more simplified German view which has been put forward recently: 'their [the intellectuals'] arguments would never have brought fascism to power. This was achieved by the support of a whole social class, the lower middle class and the so-called new middle class. The lower middle class, above all the small "independent" shopkeeper, the enemy of the big concerns, was backward-looking, and was ultimately disappointed with fascism': Otto-Ernst Schüddekopf, *Fascism* (London, 1973), p. 132.

15. Martin Broszat, 'Soziale und psychologische Grundlagen des Nationalsozialismus', in E. J. Feuchtwanger, ed., *Deutschland – Wandel und Bestand* (Munich, 1973), p. 166 (English trans. [London, 1973], p. 138).

16. See especially Eugen Weber, 'The Men of the Archangel', *Journal of Contemporary History*, vol. I, no. 1 (December 1965), pp. 111, 114, 117.

17. See the quotation in n. 5.

18. S. J. Woolf, introduction to *European Fascism* (London, 1968), p. 4.

19. Wolfgang Sauer, 'National Socialism: Totalitarianism or Fascism?', *American Historical Review*, vol. LXXIII (1967), p. 411.

20. Heinrich August Winkler, 'Extremismus der Mitte?', *Vierteljahrshefte für Zeitgeschichte*, vol. XX (1972), p. 187. The article is above all a criticism of the fascism interpretation by Seymour Lipset.

21. Martin Broszat, in *Deutschland – Wandel und Bestand* (Munich, 1973), p. 170. (I am unable to find this quotation in the English translation, *Upheaval and Continuity – A Century of German History*, ed. E. J. Feuchtwanger [London, 1973], p. 134 ff.)

22. Clara Zetkin, 'Der Kampf gegen den Faschismus', protocol of the Enlarged Executive of the Communist International (12–13 June 1923), quoted by Nolte, *Theorien über den Faschismus*, pp. 89, 92.

23. August Thalheimer, 'Über den Faschismus' (1930), in Wolfgang Abendroth, ed., *Otto Bauer, Herbert Marcuse, Arthur Rosenberg u.a. – Faschismus und Kapitalismus* (Frankfurt and Vienna, 1967), p. 22.

24. Paul Sering, 'Der Faschismus', *Zeitschrift für Sozialismus*, pp. 24–5 (September–October 1935), p. 781. This analysis, published in the theoretical journal of the exiled SPD, was the first serious attempt at a Marxist analysis of the problem after Hitler's seizure of power.

25. Wolfgang Sauer, in *American Historical Review*, vol. LXXIII (1967), p. 410.

26. G. Germani, 'Fascism and Class', in S. J. Woolf, ed., *The Nature of Fascism* (London, 1968), p. 72.

27. Michael Hurst, 'What is Fascism?', *Historical Journal*, vol. XI (1968), p. 179.

28. This has been emphasized by Nolte, *Der Faschismus in seiner Epoche* (Munich, 1963), p. 397.

29. Giovanni Zibordi, *Critica socialista del fascismo*, quoted by Nolte, *Theorien über den Faschismus*, p. 80.

30. Otto Bauer, *Zwischen zwei Weltkriegen? Die Krise der Weltwirtschaft, der Demokratie und des Sozialismus* (1936), in Wolfgang Abendroth, ed., *Otto Bauer, Herbert Marcuse, Arthur Rosenberg u.a. – Faschismus und Kapitalismus*, pp. 153–4.

31. Manfred Clemenz, *Gesellschaftliche Ursprünge des Faschismus* (Frankfurt, 1972), pp. 213–14.

32. H. R. Trevor-Roper, 'The Phenomenon of Fascism', in S. J. Woolf, ed., *European Fascism* (London, 1968), pp. 23–4.

33. R. de Felice, in S. J. Woolf, ed., *The Nature of Fascism* (London, 1968), p. 250.

34. Reinhard Kühnl, *Formen bürgerlicher Herrschaft – Liberalismus-Faschismus* (Reinbek bei Hamburg, 1971), pp. 89–90.

35. Erich Fromm, *Die Furcht vor der Freiheit*, pp. 208–10.

36. G. Germani, 'Fascism and Class', op. cit., p. 89.

37. Wilhelm Alff, *Der Begriff Faschismus und andere Aufsätze zur Zeitgeschichte* (Frankfurt, 1971), pp. 124 ff., 141.

38. Fromm, op. cit., pp. 207–8.

39. Wilhelm Reich, *Die Massenpsychologie des Faschismus* (Cologne, 1971), p. 17.

40. ibid., p. 100.

41. Fromm, op. cit., pp. 205–6.

42. George L. Mosse, 'The Genesis of Fascism', *Journal of Contemporary History*, vol. I, no. 1 (1966), p. 21, with special reference to the Iron Guard and the Hungarian Arrow Cross.

43. Z. Barbu, in S. J. Woolf, ed., *The Nature of Fascism* (London, 1968), pp. 111–12.

44. Kühnl, op. cit., p. 89.

45. Adrian Lyttelton, *The Seizure of Power – Fascism in Italy 1919–1929* (London, 1973), p. 244.

46. These points have above all been made by Adrian Lyttelton, especially during a recent panel discussion at Oxford on 'fascism'. Cf. ibid., pp. 28, 30.

47. Kühnl, op. cit., p. 94.

48. Filippo Turati, *Fascismo, Socialismo e Democrazia* (1928), quoted by Nolte, *Theorien über den Faschismus*, p. 144.

49. ibid.

50. ibid., p. 149; L. Villari, *The Fascist Experiment*, p. 41, quoted by Paul Hayes, *Fascism* (London, 1973), p. 148.

51. Rudolf Vierhaus, 'Faschistisches Führertum', *Historische Zeitschrift*, vol. 198, no. 3 (June 1964), p. 629.

52. Hugh Seton-Watson, 'Fascism, Right and Left', *Journal of Contemporary History*, vol. I, no. 1 (1966), p. 194.

53. Vierhaus, op. cit., p. 629.

54. Henry V. Dicks, 'Deadly Fantasies', *New Statesman*, 16 February 1973, p. 235.

55. Luigi Salvatorelli, *Nationalfascismo* (1923), quoted by Nolte, *Theorien über den Faschismus*, pp. 135–6.

56. Franz Borkenau, 'Zur Soziologie des Faschismus', *Archiv für Sozialwissenschaft und Sozialpolitik*, vol. LXVIII (February 1933), pp. 513–47; quoted ibid., pp. 165, 170–71. The argument is further developed ibid., pp. 179–80.

57. Otto Bauer, *Zwischen zwei Weltkriegen? Die Krise der Weltwirtschaft, der Demokratie und des Sozialismus*, pp. 155–6.

58. J. Solé-Tura, 'The Political "Instrumentality" of Fascism', in S. J. Woolf, ed., *The Nature of Fascism* (London, 1968), p. 49.

59. Nolte, *Die faschistischen Bewegungen*, pp. 189–90. Cf. the geographical subdivision made by Wolfgang Sauer, in the *American Historical Review*, vol. LXXIII (1967), p. 421.

60. Nolte, *Der Faschismus in seiner Epoche* (Munich, 1963), p. 397. See also Lyttelton, *The Seizure of Power*, pp. 40, 118.

61. Heinrich August Winkler, in *Vierteljahrshefte für Zeitgeschichte*, vol. XX (1972), p. 190; very similarly the same, *Mittelstand, Demokratie und Nationalsozialismus* (Cologne, 1972), p. 180.

62. Reinhard Kühnl, *Formen bürgerlicher Herrschaft – Liberalismus-Faschismus*, p. 138.

63. John Weiss, *Nazis and Fascists in Europe* (Chicago, 1969), pp. 15–16.

64. Zibordi, *Critica socialista del fascismo* (1922), quoted by Nolte, *Theorien über den Faschismus*, pp. 83–4.

65. Hermann Rauschning, *Die Revolution des Nihilismus* (Zurich, 1938), quoted ibid., p. 343.

66. Paul Sering (Richard Löwenthal), 'Der Faschismus', *Zeitschrift für Sozialismus*, nos 24–5 (September–October 1935), p. 787.

67. George L. Mosse, in *Journal of Contemporary History*, vol. I, no. 1 (1966), pp. 14, 22.

68. Wolfgang Sauer, in *American Historical Review*, vol. LXXIII (December 1967), p. 412.

69. Karl Dietrich Bracher, *Die deutsche Diktatur* (Cologne-Berlin, 1969), p. 9.

70. John Weiss, *Nazis and Fascists in Europe*, p. 21.

71. Kurt Gossweiler, in Kurt Gossweiler, Reinhard Kühnl and Reinhard Opitz, *Entstehung und Verhinderung – Materialien zur Faschismus-Diskussion* (Frankfurt, 1972), p. 35.

72. Bracher, *Die deutsche Diktatur*, p. 9.

73. Kühnl, *Formen bürgerlicher Herrschaft – Liberalismus – Faschismus*, p. 122.

74. J. Solé-Tura, in S. J. Woolf, ed., *The Nature of Fascism*, p. 57: 'Corporativism, the fascist ideology *par excellence*, was not a modern, but a traditional ideology in Spain.'

75. The opposite has been maintained by Martin Broszat, 'Soziale und psychologische Grundlagen des Nationalsozialismus', in E. J. Feuchtwanger, ed., *Deutschland – Wandel und Bestand* (Munich, 1973), pp. 166–7.

76. R. H. S. Crossman, *Government and the Governed* (London, 1939), p. 276.

77. Historikus (Arthur Rosenberg), *Der Faschismus als Massenbewegung* (Karlsbad, 1934), p. 7.

78. Thus the 13th Plenum of the Executive Committee of the Comintern in December 1933, quoted by Nolte, 'Zur Phänomenologie des Faschismus', *Vierteljahrshefte für Zeitgeschichte*, vol. X, no. 20 (1962), p. 384.

79. Reinhard Opitz, 'Wie bekämpft man den Faschismus?', in Gossweiler, Kühnl and Opitz, *Entstehung und Verhinderung – Materialien zur Faschismus-Diskussion*, p. 46.

80. Kühnl, ibid., p. 41. For financial support of Italian fascism, see Lyttelton, op. cit., pp. 142, 208–11.

81. This is the formulation of S. J. Woolf, in the Introduction to his *European Fascism*, p. 12. Professor Vierhaus uses the term 'a new "ruling class" '; ibid., p. 627.

82. This emerges very clearly from an important thesis which, however, does not make any comparison with Italy: A. J. Caplan, 'The Civil Servant in the Third Reich' (Ph.D. diss., Oxford University, 1973).

83. Leonard Schapiro, *Totalitarianism* (London, 1972), pp. 66–7. Cf. N. Kogan, in S. J. Woolf, ed., *The Nature of Fascism*, p. 16: 'I have serious doubts whether the Fascist Party was ever a ruling party as such. Mussolini ruled as *Capo del Governo* . . . rather than as *Duce del Fascismo*'; and Lyttelton, op. cit., pp. 158–66, 200–201, 293.

84. *Historische Perspektiven* no. 3 (Hamburg, 1976). I am referring in particular to the essays by Michael H. Kater, 'Sozialer Wandel in der NSDAP im Zuge der nationalsozialistischen Machtergreifung', pp. 25–67; Hans Mommsen, 'Zur Verschränkung traditioneller und faschistischer Führungsgruppen in Deutschland beim Übergang von der Bewegungs- zur System-

phase', pp. 157–81; and Wolfgang Schieder, 'Der Strukturwandel der faschistischen Partei Italiens in der Phase der Herrschaftsstabilisierung', pp. 69–96.

85. Thomas Childers, 'The Social Bases of the National Socialist Vote', *Journal of Contemporary History*, vol. X, no. 4 (1976), pp. 17–42.

86. Henry Ashby Turner, Jr, *Faschismus und Kapitalismus in Deutschland – Studien zum Verhältnis zwischen Nationalsozialismus und Wirtschaft* (Göttingen, 1972).

87. Wolfgang Wippermann, *Faschismustheorien – Zum Stand der gegenwärtigen Forschung*, 2nd ed. (Darmstadt, 1975), p. 176.

88. 'These questions remain unresolved'; the essay was originally published in *World Politics*, vol. XXIV, no. 4 (July 1972), pp. 547–64; reprinted in Henry A. Turner (ed.), *Reappraisals of Fascism* (New York, 1975), pp. 117–39: see especially p. 125.

89. Alan Cassels, 'Janus: The Two Faces of Fascism', ibid., pp. 69–92; the quotation on p. 78. Similarly, Alan Cassels, *Fascism* (New York, 1975), p. 347. Cf. the distinction made by Otto-Ernst Schüddekopf, *Fascism* (London, 1973), p. 132.

90. Wippermann, op. cit., pp. 90–91.

91. Ralf Dahrendorf, *Gesellschaft und Demokratie in Deutschland* (Munich, 1965).

92. David Schoenbaum, *Hitler's Social Revolution – Class and Status in Germany, 1933–1939* (New York, 1966).

93. Piero Melograni, 'The Cult of the Duce in Mussolini's Italy', *Journal of Contemporary History*, vol. XI, no. 4 (October 1976), pp. 221–2; Schieder, op. cit., p. 87.

94. Schieder, op. cit., pp. 87, 90.

95. The assertion was made by Michael Ledeen, in *The Times Literary Supplement*, 9 January 1976, p. 36.

96. Thus Wippermann, op. cit., p. 136.

97. Thus Jost Dülffer, 'Bonapartism, Fascism and National Socialism', *Journal of Contemporary History*, vol. XI, no. 4 (October 1976), p. 123.

98. Thus Turner, 'Fascism and Modernization', op. cit., p. 133. In a recent paper which this writer was privileged to attend, Professor Klaus Hildebrand of the University of Frankfurt in general opposed the use of the term 'fascism', and suggested that for Germany the term 'Hitlerism' should be used.

EUGEN WEBER

12 Revolution? Counter-revolution? What Revolution?

Almost any discussion of fascism is bound to involve consideration, explicit or not, of its revolutionary or counter-revolutionary
nature. Fascists claimed to engage in a revolution. Their opponents denounced them as counter-revolutionaries. Most students
divide unevenly about this: many consider the fascists' counter-
revolutionary role self-evident, a few prefer to begin by taking the
fascists at their word, some still judge the charges unproven.

At any rate, the debate suggests the high symbolic, hence pas-
sional and practical, value of terms like revolution and counter-
revolution, increasingly loaded, in intellectual and political
intercourse, with an ethical burden that even the mass media perceive. The revolutions of the 18th century stood over the cradle of
the modern world; the modern world remembers. It is a long
stretch from the fall of the Bastille to the launching of a revolutionary new detergent, but it is worth the trip. As Sellar and
Yeatman would have said, revolution is a good thing. One never
hears of a counter-revolution in automobile design, though one
might be in order. Better accentuate the positive. As a result, the
struggle for political advantage involves minor but important
skirmishes for semantic advantage. Like the hero in a Western
movie, the movement that comes in riding on revolution can, as a
rule, expect our sympathy.

I shall suggest that, as of today at least, the issue is wrongly
joined. Like 'Left' and 'Right', Revolution and Counter-revolution have become anachronistic stereotypes, real because installed in vocabulary and minds, but confusing as categories for
understanding and scholarly analysis. Misleading, above all, because for a long time now the notion of revolution has been interpreted in one sense only, implying automatically that movements
directed to other ends (opposite, or simply different) could not be

described as revolutionary, and might well be counter-revolutionary, whether they wanted to be or not.

The very word, revolution, suggests the great modern prototypes: French and Russian. These more than suggest, they impose, a model of what revolution should be because it once was, of expectable actions and stages to which revolutionary developments should conform: the last throes of the dominant classes, the first phase of a bourgeois revolution overtaken by more popular challengers, duly put down in a Thermidor easily leading to Brumaire. Moderate change, radical advance, repression, and their dialectic, always open to further challenges. Interpretation provides the recipes of expectation. Sometimes of action too. History is born of history. From Marx's reference to *The Eighteenth Brumaire of Louis Bonaparte*, to Trotsky's description of the Soviet Thermidor when Stalin takes power, through Crane Brinton's *Anatomy of Revolution*, patterns are formulated and roles are prescribed where coming players (or reporters) learn their parts.

A French academic historian, writing about the student revolt of 1968, refers to barricades, red flags, 'the Faculty buildings resembling the Smolny Palace (*sic*) in Petrograd, the lecture halls [resembling] Soviets'.[1] And André Malraux, writing in 1972, resumes the twentieth century in one image: that of a truck bristling with guns. Obviously, the Russian revolution again, and one of the most familiar images of it.

Some responsibility for this lies in organized history and the generalization of historical knowledge, making available that pattern of revolution to which revolutionaries will henceforth conform. Those that fail to conform are not revolutionaries. 'The revolutionary knows his revolution as the wretched knows his want,' writes André Découflé, author of a recent work generally regarded as one of the more sensible treatments of a touchy subject.[2] But the wretched knows his want, precisely because he lives in it, the revolutionary seldom does more than imagine his revolution. And those revolutionaries who, today, in the perspective of history, still claim to know their revolution – in its unfolding beyond means to ends – must be naive indeed.

But history, storehouse of images and recipes that it is, does not exhaust the revolutionary's resources. Gracchus Babeuf could tell his readers, and later his judges, that the Republic was worthless: 'But it is not the real Republic. The real Republic is something we have not yet tried.'[3] The point, frequently made since Babeuf, proceeds from hypothesis to fact, and even against fact. Thus in Découflé: 'The hypothesis of the revolutionary project excludes the destruction of man, since it is [aimed at] his regeneration; and, in fact, it does not destroy him, despite the horrible enterprises of some of its managers. Beyond all the propagandas, the present chronicle of the Soviet Union bears abundant witness to this.'[4]

I like Découflé's reference to the managers of revolution, a handy and expressive term and a revealing one. But it is odd to find, in a book published in 1968, the reaffirmation of an ideal which remains entire though some of its managers betray it, the deliberate denial of historical experience by affirmation of its contrary, and all on the basis of an original hypothesis stronger than any observed fact. The Revolution survives all revolutions.

Far from fearing facts, the hypothesis consumes them, that is it assimilates them to its needs. Boris Porchnev turns the peasant rebellions of the seventeenth century into evidence of class struggles in the early modern period. Découflé hails Eric Hobsbawm's *Primitive Rebels* as a work on *revolutionary* phenomena, despite its French title: *Les primitifs de la révolte*. Even social rebellion of a primitive kind must be mobilized for revolution.[5] Such topical imperialism, perfectly dispensable in Marxist terms, conceals the difference between revolution and rebellion (a difference Hobsbawm himself in no wise ignores!) and deprives the critic of a category he could find useful in refining his terms.

Découflé does distinguish between insurrection, which finds its end in itself, and revolution which is *transhistorical*, 'situated in the realm of duration, temporal site of immanence'; and this permits the keen observer to distinguish between an insurrection, however long-drawn-out, and a revolution, however brief. Thus, the 'revolution' of 1830 was actually an insurrection that lasted eighteen years, while the Paris Commune of 1871, though only a few weeks long, can be identified as an authentic revolution, just like ... the Crusades![6]

It is Découflé's modest claim that such a conception helps to avoid a lot of shopworn debates and endows 'the category of rev-

olutions with an unusual extension and strictness [of definition]'.
To the uninitiated, the extensibility of the category and its flexibility appear more striking than its strictness of definition. Events
are promoted, excluded, or denied. The Crusades, of course, are
there in honour of Alphonse Dupront who (re)invented them.
Unless it is to fill the gap left when strict construction eliminated
the Agricultural and the Industrial revolutions. But what about
the revolution of 1830, demoted to a mere insurrection, yet very
much a revolution to its contemporaries: change of régime, of the
symbols of state, of the flag, of political personnel – isn't all that
enough, until next time?

Clearly, no. Political revolution is not real revolution, not the
transhistorical sort. The social aspect is missing when all we get
is a change of guard (and of uniforms) among the privileged
élites. The wretched continue in their wretchedness. They continue to be exploited: by their exploiters in their time; by intellectuals who have discovered the plus-value of poverty, in ours.

Old-style revolutions ignored the poor.[7] Aristocratic and oligarchic societies made aristocratic and oligarchic revolutions. The
poor were enlisted as cannon fodder. Their occasional uses did not
entitle them to higher ideological rank. War is waged by soldiers,
of course. It is not *about* soldiers, or for them.

Then, from objects of the revolution the poor became its subjects – and its energetic force. The French Revolution said it was
about the people. It was not; or only in a special sense. But it did
involve mobilizing the masses in a new and, now, doctrinally
necessary sense that could not exist before 'the people' had become the subject of politics. And Gracchus Babeuf, more
memorably than many, identified 'the people' with the poor
people, and the poor people with the majority of the people,[8] a
view that contemporary circumstances largely warranted. This
new doctrine, due like others to survive the conditions it reflected
when it was formulated, would soon coincide with economic and
social changes that suggested yet further appeals and further
mobilizations.

So, revolution, which had been about political power for
people who were far from poor, came to be said to be about the
poor, about the poor ceasing to be poor and, even though its

efficacy as a means to this end remained dubious, the myth took shape. The poor as energizing agents of real revolution turned into the poor as dynamizing ideal of prospective revolution. They had been other ranks in the armies of the revolution; now they became its flag.

Not everything, of course, went as one might wish. Thus, the revolution that had been supposed to precipitate the participation of excluded social groups (Third Estate, etc.) in the body politic, actually operated by the violent exclusion of other social groups (aristocrats and to some extent, although unplanned, the clergy). This pattern would be repeated on subsequent occasions. Fraternity henceforth would be affirmed by exclusion (of bourgeois, aliens, Jews); just as Justice became the act of taking from the old haves and giving to your supporters. Not, perhaps, the most desirable way of ensuring upward mobility or the redistribution of wealth, but effective enough up to a point.

In any case, the masses that cheered and hooted, stormed and stared, were a necessary stimulant and fuel of action. Revolution came to them less as a promise of better things, though it was that too, than as a gigantic holiday and adventure. For many, its goings-on were the first spectacle they enjoyed. And one of the greatest luxuries revolution afforded was the opportunity to see their 'betters' humbled. Like the peasants of Languedoc who welcome late-summer rains, good for their corn, bad for their landlords' wheat, with 'il pleut des insolences', the people welcomed the chance to be insolent in its turn, to see its 'betters' cut down to size, not excluding its revolutionary emancipators whom revolution carted through hooting streets that cheered them days before.

So, after all, the people could be wrong.[9] At the very least, its instincts could not be trusted. Not untaught. For Saint-Just, 'the people is an eternal child'; and Robespierre said as much. Lenin would build or rebuild a doctrine on this conviction. And a party. His *What Is To Be Done?* (1902) shows how the spontaneous development of the workers' movement had simply led to its domination by bourgeois ideology. This had to be remedied, a different ideology had to be provided. In due course, in places, it was.

But was this other ideology – creation of rebellious bourgeois and intellectuals – necessarily more revolutionary? I suppose so. More popular? Hardly, since it denied the possibility of government of the people by the people, and did this more deliberately, with a clearer view of the matter, than Saint-Just would or could have done. This is an issue we need not stir again, except to point out that the superior revolutionary capacity of a movement has little to do with its popular character or representativeness. Quite the contrary: the Leninist argument since 1902 has been that the more popular the movement, the less revolutionary it is likely to be, hence the less objectively representative of true popular interests. A form of élitism no less élitist for coming from the conventional left.

So the people, the poor people, already dubbed *proletariat* by Rousseauist and revolutionary antiquarianism, could continue to enjoy its heroic role, but (a big but) only the role that had been written for it. This is worth bearing in mind, but the point I wish to stress is different: the role in question, sketched at the end of the eighteenth century, written and rewritten through the nineteenth century, falls far short of changed realities in the twentieth-century West. When a neo-Marxist declares in 1973: 'The proletariat, producer and not consumer, is the absolute and inalienable ethical order . . .'[10] he is not only talking nonsense, but anachronistic nonsense. I doubt whether any human group, now or at any time, has been specifically invested with the mission of political liberation and social salvation for mankind. Many such groups have claimed and still claim the daunting responsibility. But that is no excuse for those trained to critical thinking to abandon the thoughtful examination of such claims. Clearly, political messianism and other cargo cults of the West are no monopoly of what we call the Right.[11]

A moment always comes however when revolutionary revelry must give way to discipline, the joys of insolence, the privileges of disorder, to the order of new privileges. The generous, self-indulgent revolution becomes a stern disciplinarian, sterner than the tyrant it displaced. By January 1794, unexpectedly early, the Committee of Public Safety advises its representative in the Calvados to moderate his zeal: 'Today we are less concerned to revolutionize than to set up the revolutionary government.' The fateful words are out. The revolution is made, or can be suspended. It is time to turn it into a régime: the managers of revolution into managers of the state.

This is where the rot sets in. Joseph de Maistre was right. In the end, all governments are monarchies, no matter what you call them, all governments are aristocracies. The young Chateaubriand had said as much in his reactionary essay on revolutions: 'What do I care if it be the King or the Law that drags me to the guillotine? . . . the greatest misfortune of men is to have laws and a government.'[12] Chateaubriand, writing in exile, had little sympathy for revolution. But many nineteenth-century revolutionaries faced that same quandary and failed to solve it: the state is always counter-revolutionary, yet without the state how can a revolution be carried through? Can anything be built except on the ruins – not of the enemy's camp so much as of one's own? Revolutionaries set out to make or remake history. Their opponents say that history is already made, or in the making, and waiting to advance on existing lines. The revolution succeeds, affirms precisely what its opponents used to say, and sets up a government to make sure it is done. That government, like every modern state, will seek the monopoly of violence, conforming not only to Max Weber's thesis on that score but to the more grandiose rule Joseph de Maistre decreed: 'all greatness, all power, all subordination, rest on the executioner: horror and bond of human association.' Remove the executioner and order disintegrates, powers collapse, society disappears. But society must be rebuilt, so it must be the revolution that disappears. A twist of the wrist, then, and the revolution has been juggled away. A great deal has been done. A great deal has been changed. The power of new rulers and freer trade in one case; the power of new rulers and the expansion of productivity in another. Electrification without soviets.

One other novelty: a reversal in the classic relations between state and revolution.[13] Where once upon a time making a revolution meant overthrowing the state, in the new situation it is the state that makes the revolution, becomes identified with it, so that opposition to the state is opposition to revolution. A revolutionary state is a contradiction in terms. But even a socialist state, or one so called, very soon disappears behind administration, institutions, police machinery, bureaucracy – or, rather, it becomes simply the flag that flies over the towering office building of the state.

At this point, presumably, the revolution institutionalized is ready for the challenge of another revolution that will break the frozen flow and set the great glacier of history on the move again. In this respect, a succession of revolutions is but part of the same vast forward movement (necessarily forward, in whatever direction it may face). This may have been what Proudhon had in mind in his toast to the revolution of 1848: 'properly speaking, there haven't been several revolutions, there has been only one and the same revolution.' The revolutionary wheel turns, but each revolution of the wheel propels it farther, each halt only a pause, each apparent failure a spur to further advance. Ce n'est qu'un début, nous continuerons le combat! As Babeuf affirmed, the revolution, the republic, may be worthless, but the true Revolution is still to come, the Common Weal remains to be achieved. Even a 'revolutionary' state, controlled by revolutionary leaders, can further the interests of this immanent force. The Revolution is a constant of history.

Perhaps. But all this begs a question: what revolution? La révolution, says Proudhon, est en permanence dans l'histoire. Not revolution in general, not any particular revolution, but *the* Revolution, identified, vaguely perhaps but enough for all to know, as Babeuf knew it, as Découflé's revolutionaries know it. Reference to revolution, says Proudhon, is necessarily reference to progress. But where does progress go? What is 'forward'? Towards what does the revolution advance?

Towards the Left, of course. It is no good to say that this has become, more than it ever was, an uncertain point of reference. The wretched are still on the earth. Their emancipation can be the pole star of revolutionary progress. If history tells us anything, it is that 'revolutions and revolutionaries are leftist.'[14] There can be debate as to whether the revolution belongs to gradualists, organized revolutionaries, radical leftists. There can be no revolution from other quarters. Any such suggestion is counter-revolutionary by definition.

The term counter-revolution itself evokes, as Joseph de Maistre noticed, violent action in an *opposite* and hence related sense to that of *the* revolution: 'a revolution [the OED tells us] opposed to a previous revolution or reversing its results'. The counter-revolution is condemned to a reflected identity only. It exists in terms of the revolution it opposes, and seeks to reverse. Revolution is the positive term; without it, no counter-revolution.

De Maistre, who understood how awkward such a definition can be if you are saddled with it, sought to escape it. The monarchy re-established, he insisted, though it is called counter-revolution, ne sera point une révolution contraire, mais le contraire d'une révolution: not an opposite revolution, but the opposite of a revolution. He seems to have been right. If a revolution is more than the violence that it involves, a project for radical change, an attempt at precipitate movement, then the monarchy restored, which conceived no such course, was not revolutionary even in a counter-revolutionary sense. The Restoration was not a revolution against the previous revolution(s), but an attempt to restore the state of things and the rate of evolution, the speed of movement, that had preceded revolution. It wanted to be the opposite of a revolution. That is what, insofar as it could be, it was.[15]

If the Restoration, while anti-revolutionary, was not counter-revolutionary, other régimes and movements in later years did adopt revolutionary methods to counter-revolutionary ends – that is, deliberately directed to opposing or reversing a particular revolution. Louis-Napoleon's government appears a case in point, typically adopting not only revolutionary methods but also some of the measures extolled by the revolutionaries with whom it competed. The Action Française was counter-revolutionary: explicitly so. Hungary after 1918 was revealingly torn between anti-revolutionaries (Horthy, Bethlen) eager to maintain a régime the very opposite of revolutionary, and counter-revolutionaries (Gömbös, Imrédy) ready to adopt the revolutionary panoply the better to fight what had become a *révolution introuvable*. Franco's insurrection fits the same bill: beginning on the pattern of classic nineteenth-century Spanish revolutions against the 'revolution' of the Popular Front régime, cannibalizing the would-be revolutionaries of the right, and adopting their most visible symbols (as King Carol II of Romania was to do) as a façade for the longest-lasting of anti-revolutionary counter-revolutions in captivity.

Can we ever untangle this skein? Many actions described as counter-revolutionary turn out to be simply repressive, though no less odious for that. Charles Maurras said that revolutions are made before they break out. That was the rationale for their preliminary repression. But such repressions did not, as a rule, involve revolutionary means. The *Cagoule* was scotched in France by fairly straightforward police methods. The Iron Guard in Romania was gutted by police and army terror only slightly beyond the country's past experience. The monopoly of violence was reasserted before it slipped away. In some places (Soviet Russia) even before it could be challenged. Both revolutionary and counter-revolutionary régimes rest foursquare on de Maistre's *bourreau*. But is this pre-emptive counter-revolution, as it has been called? Hardly. It is self-preservation of a conventional sort and, of course, an occasional excuse for the equally conventional elimination of political opponents. And the constant confusion of simple opposition with revolutionary, anti-revolutionary or counter-revolutionary action, a confusion that has its roots in fact, fantasy, theory and reality, allows whoever wills to give a dog a bad name before attempting to eliminate it. As Saint-Just explained to Robespierre in December 1793, measures of public safety are justified by the existence of counter-revolutionaries. No more counter-revolutionaries, no more need for public safety or for the dictatorship that is its instrument, *provided* human weakness does not lead people – the people? – into 'that maze in which the revolution and the counter-revolution march pell-mell'.

An illustration, here, not only of the ease with which the image of counter-revolution can justify pre-emptive repression, but of the difficulty of disentangling revolutionary from counter-revolutionary strands. Only the initiated can tell them apart. But the voice of revelation that addresses the few must, by others, be accepted on faith. No wonder that almost any action, movement, or régime can be interpreted as one wills and that Girondists and Enragés, Proudhonians, Trotskyists and Kronstadt sailors have been made to bear the brand of counter-revolution. In Bolivia, for example, where revolutionary activity is very much the order of the day, Trotskyist leader Guillermo Lora denounces the leftists whose radicalism leads only to counter-revolution, while a top figure of the pro-Soviet communist party dismisses Lora's POR as the best ally of reactionary forces.[16] Nor need we be surprised to read that 'the most accomplished contemporary form of the counter-revolutionary project' is North American-style democracy.[17] One does not have to claim a close approach to integral democracy for North American régimes to recognize the prejudice of such a phrase, that can pass unexamined (and often does) only in minds where the case has been pre-judged.

Even denunciation of neo-capitalism does not preserve one from the counter-revolutionary snare (increasingly reminiscent of those children's stories where one character after another tumbles down a trap). The pastures of objective perdition are broader than those of the Lord. Marcuse and the Freudo-Marxists have in their turn been denounced as counter-revolutionaries whose cultural terrorism finally leads to neo-fascism.[18]

In the last resort, counter-revolution does not even deserve rational interpretation. For Découflé, it 'seems to come less under the jurisdiction of sociology than of psychoanalysis: it borrows the modes of revolution and does its best to create its reflected image, determined as it is to take up the contrary position on every score.' A few lines later, Découflé refers very sensibly to Jung's remark that the most dangerous of revolutionaries is the one we carry in ourselves. But this is a predicament attributed to counter-revolutionaries alone. He insists rightly on the anxiety that drives them to extremes, but never on the anxiety that haunts successful (?) revolutionaries, once set in the seats of power.[19] And nary a word about *ideological* divergencies that may set revolutionaries and counter-revolutionaries apart. For the latter alone, doctrinal persuasions must be the rationalizations of inadmissible drives.

Analyses so one-sided are unsatisfactory even in their own terms. Equally important, placing the interpretation of counter-revolution on the psychoanalytic plane minimizes other factors (social, economic, etc.) and denies existence of ideologies or doctrines deserving rational examination: for themselves, and concerning their evolution or corruption, just as with revolutionary ideologies. One side is human and rational, the other is human only in its travesties: a sickness. Thus, one both begs the question and avoids it.

Let us fall back on a more serious work. In 1971, Arno J. Mayer's *Dynamics of Counter-revolution in Europe* sets out to examine the concept and to fit it into an analytic framework. My first and chief criticism of the work is that it accepts unquestioningly the Marxist stereotype of *one* revolution in our time, in terms of which counter-revolution must necessarily be defined. In other words, while Professor Mayer's Marxism is explicit, his definition of revolution is implicit. It thus avoids any suggestion that counter-revolution is not alone in need of definition, but revolution too. Mayer's general thesis, with which I disagree, is thoughtful, honest, and forcefully argued. It is therefore with the most sensible exponent of the dominant stereotypes that I take issue.

Mayer distinguishes between conservatives, reactionaries, and counter-revolutionaries. Reactionaries scorn the present for a lost, regretted, past. Conservatives, like Metternich, believe that stability need not mean immobility. Counter-revolutionaries are pretty much what we designate as fascists or radicals of the right: egalitarian, dynamic, adept at mass politics, often similar to 'the hated revolutionary rival', yet only pseudo-revolutionary at best, intending 'to create the impression that they seek fundamental changes in government, society and community',[20] but actually anchored in established order, values, and aspirations. Counter-revolutionaries pretend to represent an alternative revolution; they are, in effect, only an alternative to revolution. 'In style, method and appearance, their break with the politics of compromise and mutual concession is very radical indeed. But in all other major respects the counter-revolutionary project is in the nature of a stabilizing and rescue operation disguised as a millenarian crusade of heroic vitalism.'[21] True, conservative or reactionary anti-revolutionaries (so often the most visible of counter-revolutionaries in everyday politics and parlance) may turn against Mayer's revolutionary counter-revolutionaries, as King Carol of Romania turned against Codreanu. But this does not affect the ultimate kinship of all three categories in one objectively counter-revolutionary camp. Thus, having begun by brushing aside the threadbare confusions of the past, Mayer arrives at a more refined version of the same.[22]

We shall meet some of his arguments shortly. But, first, a crucial statement – crucial not only to Mayer's thesis but because it represents a widespread point of view: 'Counter-revolution is essentially a praxis. Its political doctrine is in the nature of a rationalization and justification of prior actions. It is a pseudo-doctrine.'[23] If counter-revolution is only the mirror image of revolution, this makes perfect sense. It is the violent start of reaction to the revolutionary challenge. Doctrine comes later and, dominated by this same challenge, it can only become a distorting echo of its original reactions: anger and fear.

So far, so good. But only for that counter-revolution, for those counter-revolutionaries, whose 'project is in the nature of a stabilizing and rescue operation' for the established order. And that, unless we fall back on 'objective' interpretations which should then include all those denounced for diversionist and counter-revolutionary strategies, lets out a number of fascist movements, not least National Socialism, much of whose history was but the acting out of some fantastic doctrines.

But these are pseudo-doctrines, 'inconsistent' (what political ideology is not so in practice?) and instrumental. This last suggestion, of ideology as an instrument of manipulation, confuses the concern of most modern politicians to find the most effective formula for selling their case and themselves, with the ideological constructs embodying their vision. Hitler was possessed. Obsessed. His obsessions were not 'calculated and instrumental'. It turned out that they worked that way. But Hitler's doctrine was the instrument of his dreams. The doctrine, the movement, then the people he ruled, became the means of their realization. The threat of communist revolution was only one aspect of the national deterioration he sought to stem and to reverse. To deal with this he planned a revolution that was not opposed to, but other than, the model most current at that time. Since another revolutionary project already held the field, his was an alternative revolution, not a counter-one. Codreanu also postulated a fundamental change. He encountered no revolution in his way, only the established disorder. As for Mussolini, I incline to think that the revolutionary threat, scotched or at least defeated by Giolitti's fabian tactics, seemed less a foil than a convenient pretext. For none of these was counter-revolution, in the sense of the term, the main concern.

Another example and one less debatable may clarify my case. Professor Mayer appears to place the origins of counter-revolutionary ideology in a reaction to socialist challenges.[24] Wherever this may have been so, it was not so in France. There is no evidence that Boulanger, Barrès, Maurras, were particularly concerned with fighting socialism.[25] Boulanger made the most of the Jacobin tradition that inspired both socialists and radicals of his day. Barrès was a socialist fellow-traveller between 1889 and 1896, Maurras's chief quarries were elsewhere. All addressed themselves first and foremost to what they saw as problems of public morality, vitality, and unity. They may have been deluded. They were not insincere.[26]

It is too easy to dismiss their old-fashioned patriotism, their new-fangled nationalism, as convenient derivatives for pressures they (or cleverer men) discerned but could not meet. What they (and cleverer men) thought they discerned was a flabby, deteriorating society. They worried about it. Divisive 'revolutionary' movements that preached class struggle were one aspect of this social decay, but hardly their dominant concern. And social justice, which socialists called for, was also a concern of theirs, because they thought it necessary to the renovation, revivification, unification that they sought. Much of what they said now has an irrelevant ring. We have discerned, we think, other more crucial seams and strains in the fabric of society. My only point, right here, is that their doctrines were not 'calculated and instrumental'. Not counter-revolutionary either, in intent, except (but I do not think that was Arno Mayer's meaning) in the case of Maurras who, of course, rejected everything that had happened since 1789.

This illustrates the need to be specific, placing events in their context which alone can show what was revolution, counter-revolution, some other kind of revolution, or no revolution at all. If, as Professor Mayer thinks, the reactionary and conservative coordinates of counter-revolution are central to its identification, then we must discriminate between counter-revolutions that may adopt a revolutionary façade, and alternative revolutions that have been found to adopt a conservative façade. Perhaps a reference to the old-fashioned categories of Movement and Resistance (out of July Revolution by André Siegfried) could help in this. Because it can suggest that Movement may direct itself against (post-)revolutionary régimes, and that the latter may find themselves resisting Movement. Only one thing is sure: there is no *juste milieu*, the very notion of it is eccentric. The more so as politics operate less in concentric ripples than in disorderly swings – towards extremes. And the motions of extremism matter more than its directions.

Fascist revolution in Italy, Nazi revolution in Germany, were carried out – like their forerunners in France and Russia – against the flabbiness and the failures of the existing régimes. Horthy and Franco led actions opposed to 'red revolution' in one case,[27] and to a Popular Front régime in another. They are thus properly counter-revolutionary. Rex, in Belgium, was neither revolutionary nor counter-revolutionary: political adventurism dressed up in currently-modish fancy clothes which happened to be fascist by historical coincidence.[28] And Salazar established his power, like Antonescu, in traditional terms.[29] It is worth repeating that repressive authoritarian régimes may borrow the rhetoric and methods of the class revolution, as others borrow the rhetoric and techniques of the alternative revolution, in order to cloak their inertia or their uncertainties. In both cases the revolutionaries will be eliminated, or put out of the way, by Franco, Antonescu, or Stalin.

The confusion becomes patent when all such action against revolutionaries or revolutionary forces is treated as one single phenomenon. In effect, most anti-revolutionary action, especially of the pre-emptive sort, is taken by conservative forces worried by threats against their order or their systematic disorder. Police repression, military action, or coup d'état, may be carried out against national revolutionaries as against Marxist ones. Nor, given the tug of war for possession of the revolutionary label, is it always clear, let alone admitted, which side in the conflict is counter-revolutionary.

Which side is revolutionary and which counter-revolutionary in Berlin 1953, Poznan 1956, Budapest 1956, Prague 1968? Or when Moscow and Belgrade, Belgrade and Tirana, Moscow and Peking, accuse each other of counter-revolutionism? History will tell if we cannot. But the 'direction' of history and, hence, its reading can change. In 1939 or 1940 many could fear with reason that it would confirm the racist dogma of triumphant nazism. Genetics and biology rather than sociology would have framed the mythology of the new age. Who can believe that they would have failed to do so very competently? Revolution, we are told, is the recognition of historical necessity, dyked up by inertia, confronted by counter-revolution. But history is what happens and, as such, invested with value only by those who perceive it as good or bad. Like plague or drought, a revolutionary movement is history because it is in history. So are its rivals, its opponents, its victims and its beneficiaries. The Spring of Prague proved abortive; the armies that crushed it got their way. Who stood for revolution? Who represented history?

Is revolution, then, like beauty, only in the eye of the beholder? Who is to say which is the real revolution and which the sham? Mayer shows no doubts, but he does not address the question when he explains that 'revolution is more productive of human growth, betterment and dignity than counter-revolution',[30] because this only holds for some revolutions, or some parts of some revolutions. We can attempt a list: 1789–92, but not the Terror; 1848 (but which?), but not 1830; the early days in Cuba, but not the repression that followed them. Every man his own historian. And even if the revolution is one block, as the famous phrase insists, the doctrinaire will make sure just what is cemented in it. Which brings us back to the subjective selectivity that we denounced to start with.

We should abandon the notion of one revolution, identified with only one direction or theme; replace the question: 'what is revolution?' by the question: 'what kind of revolution is it?'

In a war we do not say of one side that it wages counter-war.

Yet use of the term counter-revolution[31] suggests an authorized version which, misleading as to the motives and ends of movements that do not conform to an approved pattern, implies (though seldom explicitly) the superiority of, the virtue vested in, one kind of revolution only. We remember it as great, so many believe that it was good. Since revolution = good, counter-revolution = bad. Hence the importance of dubbing what we consider bad counter-revolutionary, a description as illuminating as the label 'fascist' freely applied to conservatives, liberals, and portions of the left. When, in the end, fascism and counter-revolution are treated as one, as if identity was self-evident, confusion is complete. Yet evidence at hand, far from justifying confident affirmations, seems to suggest we should proceed with caution – our strongest weapon, doubt.

What are modern revolutions about? The classic formula tells us: Liberty, Equality, Fraternity, or Death. But, as Saint-Just realized as early as 1791, liberty once conquered is easily corrupted into its opposite. Equality is either equality of opportunity, rightly criticized as basic inequality, or it entails injustice and constraint. Fraternity is the vaguest and also the most delusive of the terms. It may reflect the relieved elation of the original release from the constraints of order, but I doubt it. Is it there to compensate for its too-evident absence, or to replace a missing father-figure with a more accessible brother? Latecomer to the original revolutionary duo, fraternity is an invocation, as if for rain at the height of drought; but also a logical outgrowth of the egalitarian ideal: authority is no longer the father, but the brother – a wiser, more experienced, elder brother, standing shoulder to shoulder with you in the struggle, before he is metamorphosed into Big Brother. The figure of authority, thrown out by the door, climbs back through the window. Finally, Death: sole of the revolution's promises that it is certain to make good, whatever its orientation. Bystanders remembered that when, at the feast of the Supreme Being, on 20 Prairial, year II of the Revolution, the symbolic figures of Atheism, Discord, Ambition, and False Simplicity were consumed on a symbolic pyre, the statue of Wisdom that the flames revealed was black with soot.

We might note in passing that, for Marx and Engels, liberty, equality, and fraternity are fine, but hardly serious, since Marx and Engels rejected moral and ethical values, ideas like morality, truth and justice. Marxism, like its contemporary, phrenology, is a science, not an ethic. The revolution it talks about is part of a historical mechanism: hence, purged of values. We have just seen how seriously to take such claims.

Revolution and counter-revolution today both stem from the democratic doctrines of the eighteenth and nineteenth centuries, and from the breakdown of their political outgrowths. While true counter-revolution is the offspring of revolution, revolution is the creature of the régime against which it rises – even to the pettiest things. 'I went to the Convention,' notes Chateaubriand, 'and saw M. Marat; on his lips there floated the banal smile that the Old Régime has placed on everybody's lips.' Marat's smile, like Marat's ideas, had been acquired before the Revolution. It was the old régime that taught Robespierre his self-possession, Saint-Just his strict demeanour and his romanticism, so many deputies their courtesy and manners, Girondists and Jacobins their composure in the face of death. Superficial? Perhaps. But suggestive of more important carry-overs.

When Mayer sees the mainsprings of communism and fascism as 'drastically different, possibly opposite',[32] he is wrong. The great revolutionary creeds of the twentieth century were (among other things) all inspired by Social Darwinism. Nationalism, fascism, communism, all reflect belief in the survival of the fittest; in terms of nation (or of race, itself a confused notion of the nineteenth century), or in terms of class. This is why, at least one reason why, the distinction between fascism and communism is relative rather than absolute, dynamic rather than fundamental. Both are originally urban ideologies, devised and carried by middle-class intellectuals seeking to appeal to underprivileged and badly integrated sections of society. Both react against liberalism, its injustices, its inefficiencies, its decay; and both are its offspring.[33] Neither represents a revolt of the masses, though both seek to incite one. As the studies published by Lasswell and Lerner indicate, Nazi and Communist élites show striking similarities in recruitment and in evolution. The revolutions they make are, in both cases, 'operated by frustrated segments of the middle classes who . . . organized violent action to gain what they had been denied'.[34] The fascists benefit from 'the interested collaboration of the old cadres'.[35] Have Communists not done so? Who officered the Red army, or the French revolutionary armies for that matter? How far do the administrative, technological and intellectual establishments of Popular Democracies, so-called, depend on the old cadres and on their scions? And those who do not stem from them become a 'new class' much like the one that they displaced.[36] This is not what André Malraux had in mind when he declared that every communism that fails calls up its fascism, every fascism that fails calls up its communism;[37] but it is in these terms that the phrase makes good sense.

Mayer is right when he suggests key differences, structural and other, between communism and fascism. They can all be revolutionary, though different.[38] Both preach monistic solutions, establish orthodoxies, define heresies, march on specific ideologies – in Karl Mannheim's terms: 'systems of representations that pretend to offer complete explanation of social phenomena and permit discovery and advancement of solutions required by problems of social change'. They do not only start from a similar gnostic base. They also end in a would-be total system: legally unrestrained government, mass party, rigid ideology, pseudo-elections, systematic terror, state monopoly of mass communications, and a centrally-directed industrial economy. Isn't this fundamental similarity between totalitarian creeds and systems at least as important as their differences of view?

I do not seek to labour points that have long been made, though familiarity is no excuse for indifference to them; and I am not aware of convincing arguments raised against those who find the fundamental similarities of communism and fascism to be highly significant. My purpose here is not to estimate the moral worth of either, even by implication, but to discern their relation to revolution and counter-revolution, and see if the question itself makes sense.

The fact that both communisms and fascisms are violent and monistic in no way proves that they are the same. Merchants of absolutes can hawk different wares. One can choose between them. The question then comes up: is the direction of choice more relevant than the fact of choosing? The answer depends on the importance attributed to the choice. Is it on the level of a new car to buy, or on that of Salvation? In this case, right choice, viewed as a matter of life or death in the struggle for life and for history, is crucial. Both communism and fascism regard as intolerable and intolerably decadent the society which, having created values, tires of them, detaches from them, examines them, organizes uncertainty and tolerates doubt. Both communism and fascism are there to affirm and structure belief. Even their denials are affirmations in reverse. There is no qualitative difference between affirmation and denial, which means that one can shift quite naturally from one to the other, and explains the counter-revolutionary aspects to be found in the propaganda of both.[39]

Not in the propaganda alone: racism, torture, mass murder of genocidal proportions, ideological contortionism, is there much need to insist on similarities that some continue to deny and others to argue that they are superficial? The interest of such characteristic coincidences is not to mark them, but to see why and how they happen, what in the nature of a movement or a situation leads to this blemish and not to another. It isn't so much the state terrorism of modern revolutions that bears witness against them, as their inability to invent ends different from those of the régimes they claim to fight. The similarity of their means may be superficial. Yet it is precisely at the level of means that we place the difference between revolutionary and non-revolutionary creeds. We cannot escape our methods, and methods are often imposed by the situation, by the demands of the project. The revolutionary project, the revolutionary situation, have their corruption built in. One may well feel the justification of the project, the exaltation of the action. But it is well to note their implications too. We have failed to draw the conclusions of our findings for far too long.

And yet they differ, we are told, because they appeal to (and benefit) different social groups. This is far from proven. I have argued the contrary case in a number of publications;[40] data concerning leadership of the rival movements appears to support my interpretation; and I suspect that there has been even more hypocritical dissembling about the attitude of German workers towards nazism than there has been about the resistance of the middle classes. Finally, the argument itself is based on the unproved assumption that true revolution can only stem from a chosen class – or else represent it, an even more dubious view. Even if this were true, doctrinally speaking, just what is the difference between a national socialist revolution partly based on peasants, and a national communist revolution largely based on peasants? When Mao and Castro find room in the Marxist Hall of Fame, why exclude Strasser, or Hitler? The answer is obvious? Not in these terms. In all cases, tactics take precedence not over strategy only, but over ideology too. Tactics are the locomotive of revolutionary history. What really matters is making the revolution. The revolutionary knows or thinks he knows what will come of it. The doctrine is there to tell him. Or he doesn't care. But what comes of the revolution matters less than the event, the making of revolution. Belief in revolution for its own sake is one more thing radical Left and Right seem to have in common.[41]

But: they opposed each other. This cannot be denied. It need not be. Fascist revolutions were in effect directed against Communists – not exclusively, but also. In this sense, which has been treated as decisive and which is almost accidental, fascisms were counter-revolutionary: revolutions against a rival revolution. They did not seek, as the Enragés or Babeuf had done, to carry one revolution beyond a given stage; but to carry another revolution in a different direction, to define its aims (often similar to the other's) in terms of other principles, to define its foes (often similar too) in terms of different values. The coincidences so many have noted[42] were denounced by communists and their friends as camouflage; they were to be stressed by the communists' enemies to smear the communists. No one thought to remark that it is possible to react to similar problems in different ways – even on the immoderate plane. Revolution had been pre-empted: like the Frigidaire. Ironic, when one remembers that the Jacobins were nationalists. Convenient, in terms of the way the rival revolutionary movements oriented their appeal.

By doctrine and deliberate choice, communism focused its appeal with narrow intensity. This was (and it is oddly ignored) the basic doctrinal difference between it and fascism which, convinced that the social reality was a national one, accused Marxists of splitting the nation and, thus, weakening it. The fascist net was cast more widely. This has been cited as proof of reactionary opportunism. I incline to see it as a more appropriate response to modern conditions.[43] The debate remains open. But I note that, having at long last read the statistics of thirty years ago, Communist parties have now extended the working class well into what is still denounced as the bourgeoisie; and that doctrinaire internationalism has taken second place to the hard realities of national (and nationalistic) sentiment.[44] It is the tribute that virtue must pay to vice.

Digressions are hard to avoid. But every digression contributes to my case that fascism, too easily described as counter-revolutionary, is not a counter-revolution but a rival revolution: rival of that which claimed to be the only one entitled to the label, and which is still accepted as such. As Jules Monnerot has written, and he is in a good position to know: 'for the fascists, communism is not subversion attacking the established order, it is *a competitor for the foundation of power*.'[45]

If fascism was a rival revolution, what was revolutionary about it, what was it revolutionary about? As far as I can tell, revolutionary projects differed. I have tried to outline that of Codreanu in Romania.[46] In Italy, the Fascist leadership conducted its own Thermidor, and revolutionary élan seeped off between the seats of power. In Germany, however, National Socialism proposed and embarked upon a *sui generis* revolution, and one that was recognized as such by men as different as Hermann Rauschning, Denis de Rougemont and Jacques Ellul.[47]

It is still objected that National Socialism was not a revolution because it did not destroy capitalist economic structures and change the relations of production. But, on the one hand, it showed that control was as effective as formal nationalization. On the other hand, communist experience suggests that a total change in the relations of production finally leads to results that differ little as regards the relation between producers and the industrial machine. Decisions are still made in one place and executed in another. It would be a help if available facts could be discussed outside models constructed over a hundred years ago.

Finally, the objection illustrates my earlier point: inscription in the category 'revolution' is only possible within limited terms. Certainly destruction of capitalist economic structures is a revolutionary achievement. It does not prove that other lines of action, not entailing this, cannot be revolutionary too.

How would the German situation look, as presented in Nazi perspective? Here was Europe's 'proletarian nation', encircled by enemies, ruined, powerless, despoiled of its past glories, rebelling against defeat, against the world that caused it, against the forces to which it attributed its straits. The Nazi revolution would build a causeway through the ambient corruption, the loss of confidence and self-respect, the collapse of public (and private) morality, the decadent culture that wore the Germans down and made them flabby, weary and weak. It would reshape man. Manual and intellectual labour would be linked, personality reforged more through service than through schooling, art would become militant and committed to an ideal rather than to negative incoherence. The virtues would be revived: self-denial must replace self-indulgence, self-sacrifice would displace bourgeois selfishness, public spirit would rise where individualism flourished, school and work would contribute to moral, social and political indoctrination. Inspired by communism, perhaps, like the concentration camps with their pious slogans: *Arbeit macht frei*. But also by the practice of successive French Republics, by nationalist tradition, and containing all the themes of more recent cultural revolutions energized by violence and youth, led by a hero leader, inspired by the certainty that if you could first (re)create man, social and economic changes will necessarily follow.[48]

This is an attitude that has often been described as typical of fascism. It seems to belong in other revolutionary traditions. Malraux has spoken of Saint-Just as one who passionately hoped to change man by constraining him to participate in a transfiguring epic. The basic 'fascist' theme, including epic project, theatrical transfiguration, and constraint, appears in the French Revolution as naturally as in China or Cuba today. So does the theme of death and transfiguration: in the Commune of 1871, in the novels of Malraux, in the proclamations of Ché Guevara, or in Régis Debray's likening of Ché's passion to that of Christ.[49]

The 'action for action's sake' aspect of fascist movements re-appears in leftist movements of the 1960s. The student movements that cluster around the year 1968 appear inspired by the thought that first comes action, then an idea of what to do with it. In Latin America, some revolutionary groups develop a mystique of violence for its own sake, comparable to that of the declining Iron Guard. In Colombia one such organization calls itself *La Violencia*.

Incapable of solving, sometimes even of comprehending, the problems that they face, such covenants have recourse to what Ellul has called (in another context) *le terrorisme simplificateur*. Revolutionary war, says Régis Debray, is a sort of destiny for men who have chosen it in order to endow their lives with meaning. Should we attribute such adventurism to social origins and objective counter-revolutionism (remembering that Lenin dismissed leftists as petty bourgeois overwhelmed by the horrors of capitalism), or attribute it to despair – the kind of pessimism often ascribed to fascism? 'Pessimistic as to the issue of the struggle we undertook,' writes Debray of Guevara, 'disillusioned by the way the revolutionary cause evolved in Latin America', his revolt was a *mystical* revolt, a Christ-like self-sacrifice. Reminiscent of Albert Béguin's description of the classic road to fascism: 'the way of the revolutionary who has remained revolutionary, but who, by experience of failure or innate propensity, has come to despair of men'.

To despair of them, perhaps, but also to bring them a kind of hope that seems inaccessible otherwise. And so, around Valle Grande, in Bolivia, where Ché Guevara's body was brought after he had been shot to death, thousands of photographs of the Ché have joined the other pious images on local peasants' walls, and tales of miracles wrought by him are heard throughout the countryside.[50] Evidently, despair and redemptive action – even without hope – are not the preserve of fascists alone, but of other revolutionaries too.[51] Nor are they necessary characteristics of revolutionism of any sort, which readily admits dissatisfaction with men and things as they are, the more forcefully to assert the possibility of changing them.

True, the Nazi revolution was oriented not only against the

order of Weimar, which it denounced as disorder (a self-fulfilling prophecy to which Nazis contributed a great deal) and which went bankrupt through its own devices. It was also against modern society itself, or what it denounced as such: the devaluation of values, the destructuring of structures, the liquefaction of familiar references, 'a state of anomie unknown until that time'.[52] Nazi criticism did not limit itself to liberal society and economy, collapsing all around and which, when it worked, worked to demean mankind. It reached out to their concrete incarnations: industrialism, bureaucracy, the mechanization of life, the bourgeois spirit denounced as incarnation of meanness, mediocrity and moderation. Familiar themes today, more difficult perhaps to denounce as purely reactionary than they were at the time.[53]

At any rate, whether we like it or not, whether we trust it or not, the revolutionary project here is clear enough. The more evident in its revivification of the *fête révolutionnaire*, the exhilaration of the great ceremonies and displays that the first revolution inaugurated, the elation of living a vaguely defined but emphatic adventure: dawns when it is a joy to be alive.[54] Sacrilege? It may seem so to us, scarcely to the participants. If revolution is about the people, this was as close to a revolution as Western Europe has known in the past century. And most Germans seem to have perceived it as such at the time.

What were they being promised? The Nazi revolution held out the ultimate revolutionary promise: *changer la vie*, an absurd project unless associated with *changer l'homme*, Nietzsche's *noch nicht festgestellte Tier*. Professor Mayer warns us[55] that this too is typical of counter-revolutionary leaders who 'place greater stress on profound changes in attitude, spirit and outlook than on economic and social structures.' He may be prepared to apply this judgement to men like Régis Debray and Ché Guevara too, for whom the true end of communism is the creation of a new man; and to Découflé who seems to adopt Rimbaud's famous words as his slogan. And if he did, Mayer might be right. He would at least be consistent. At any rate, the project that aims to change life and man implies constraint. It did so for the idealists who sat on the Committee of Public Safety. It has done so since. Theories about the revolution are one thing. The practice of revolution is another. Revolution in practice is still another. These are platitudes we sometimes forget.

The Nazi revolution, like other revolutionary projects, proved self-defeating. We have not dismissed other revolutions for that. Babeuf did not do so. Découflé does not do so. Perhaps all revolutions are false: they lead elsewhere than they pretend to do. Why should one revolution be more false than others? In any case, how far does even the best-reasoned revolutionary project reflect the revolutionary perception of the masses? Especially the best-reasoned! Our understanding of this remains on the most impressionistic level. Which may be why we fall back on sociological or theoretical analyses which, in their different ways, provide something we think we can get our teeth into: the security of apparent fact or logical structure. When all that we do, too often, is treat assumptions as solid points of reference: wax fruit for working models of the real.

I do not think it has been often said (although the evidence is not exactly lacking) that most popular perceptions of revolution tend to be reactionary. We have not given enough attention to the nostalgic side of revolution which, when encountered, tends to be dismissed as an irrelevant primitivism similar to the coccyx. Yet a nostalgia for things past informs most visions of the future, if only because imagination has to build with blocks made of past experience, personal or vicarious. We enter the future backwards. The French Revolution itself was conservative, reactionary, aiming not to abolish but to restore (see Tocqueville), and only inadvertently revolutionary (see Hannah Arendt). It executed Louis XVI because Charles I had been executed. It looked back wistfully to the ancient world, and pushed its antiquarianism so far as to revive the notion of the *proletarian*, which Rousseau had fished out of the depths of Roman history. Much nineteenth-century revolutionism was consoled or sparked by nostalgic fantasies and yearnings, which survived in fin-de-siècle socialism as they did in explicitly reactionary movements. About the socialist and syndicalist workers he had known before 1914 (and we should remember just how few they were), an old French working man recalls: '. . . their confused dream carried them less towards the founding of a new world than to a return to forms of life they had known or heard tell about; and, the years and distance blurring the bad aspects, made the past appear a new Icaria.'[56]

In a way, all revolution is reaction. Not only in the original sense of the term: an action reacting against other actions or against a state of things; but in the sense that it draws so many references from the past. Is it so clear, when we look again, that reactionaries demolish in the name of the past (tradition), while revolutionaries demolish in the name of the future (progress)? Is the reality quite so simple? And, if it were, what matters more in the end: the demolition, or the ideals in whose name it is carried out?

Is not, after all, revolution simply the realization of *revolt*, that is of revolt or reaction against conditions or acts that are revolting, so that the only definition of revolution would be: the violent and successful embodiment of one sort of reaction which, in due course, becomes another sort of reaction. This is a question that becomes most pressing in our own time when, most of the traditional revolutions discredited, the torch of revolution seems to have passed to newer nations.

Professor Mayer has avoided discussing the independence and national liberation movements in the Third World.[57] Not surprisingly, since such discussion would reveal profound deviations and confusions in the Marxist doctrine of revolution. Yet, in the past score years, the movements and régimes of national liberation have been the chief representatives of revolution, the chief targets of counter-revolution, and any discussion of the two terms that avoids them begs far more questions than it faces.

Reference to the Third World is essential, because it places our question in perspective. Nowhere does the ambiguousness of the 'revolutionary' definition appear more evident. Nasser, surrounded by petty bourgeois or middle-class aides, many like himself once close to fascist-style ideas, adopts a 'socialist' position in 1961 and is recognized as such by the Russians who declare that backward countries, sparing themselves the dictatorship of the proletariat, can pass directly to socialism under the leadership of progressive national forces which include the anti-colonialist bourgeoisie. This novel interpretation meant, in effect, that Marxist doctrinaires could endorse 'national revolutions' being made to set up a national state on the nineteenth-century pattern, create a nation, institute all the most conventional characteristics of the society against which revolution is supposed to take place in the West. It meant endorsement of dictatorships and coups d'état that had little to do with Marxist theories, and also of millenarian revolutionary ideologies that had even less. It presented doctrinal quandaries (like that which François Bourricaud has outlined for Peru),[58] when in newly developing countries the industrial working class turned out to be a privileged class.

The notion of the privileged proletarian, launched by Frantz Fanon in *The Wretched of the Earth*, has often been applied in Latin America, whose writers seem to have coined the term 'proletarian aristocracy'. In such circumstances, revolution was forced to seek its partisans among the peasants and the urban sub-proletariat – the very social groups whose support was once supposed to prove the counter-revolutionary nature of fascism, and whose revolutionism tends towards nationalism anyway. All of which has led to the development of intricate and seemingly paradoxical patterns of opposition and of doctrinal heresy.

Inspired by Cuban example and by long native tradition, 'leftist' revolutionaries argue that a numerically weak working class, tending to reformism and 'aristocratized in fact by the relatively high salaries paid in large concerns', precludes adherence to the Marxist-Leninist model; and that, in any case, proletarian hegemony over predominantly peasant countries would be an aberration. 'The vanguard class in Latin America,' declares Debray, 'is the poor peasantry, united under the conscious direction expressed in student ranks.' More orthodox opponents of such 'petty bourgeois intellectuals' argue that politics cannot be treated as a simple arithmetical operation which holds majorities decisive; and that, faced with a peasantry that is 'backward and hardened in its ways', the proletariat remains 'the revolutionary class par excellence'. As for the Indian revolution, on behalf of the most oppressed majority of Latin Americans, this is no more than a racist notion designed to drive a wedge between exploited people whether in country or town.[59] In the end, the advocates of *foquis-*

mo and of a 'people's war' appear more like primitive rebel leaders of guerrilla bands, while their doctrinaire critics seem fated to revolutionary inactivity.

Such divisions are less interesting than the achievements and the fate of attempts at 'national revolutions' led by those 'national bourgeoisies' that the Russians have come to approve and the leftists to abhor. In Bolivia, for example, the MNR (National Revolutionary Movement), founded during the Second World War, has been denounced both as fascist and as communist. Its chequered career, which runs from revolutionism to collaboration with 'imperialism' and American business interests, shows it as a powerful force for change, unafraid of violence, and responsible for 'irreversible structural changes' in Bolivian economy, society, and politics. In its time, and to the extent possible at the time, admirers of Guevara tell us, the MNR 'carried the Bolivian people through the first stages of a revolution without precedent in Latin America.'[60] Yet, by the later 1950s, the MNR had decayed into corruption and opportunism. A more recent representative of revolutionary nationalism, General Juan José Torrès, supported by nationalists, socialists, and orthodox communists, harassed by Trotskyists, Maoists, and leftists who denounced him for refusing to arm the people, could not survive the tug of war between more and less radical revolutionary groups, all accusing each other of objective counter-revolutionism, and was to be swept out by a right-wing army coup in 1972.

Other examples could be cited. But perhaps the point has been made, *not* that would-be revolutionaries disagree among themselves, something that Lenin knew perfectly well, but that there are many ways of attempting a revolution, and even of making one. In conditions prevailing throughout most of the Third World, just as they did in Romania, for one, between the wars, the 'revolutionary patriotism' of Castroism, the 'revolutionary nationalism' of Bolivia or Peru, the 'struggle of national liberation' with its economic implications, can be very revolutionary indeed – especially where, as a Bolivian writer has put it, the nineteenth century is not yet over. This is why the debate between the National Left which places anti-imperialism first, and more orthodox doctrinaires who give priority to class war, is very revealing;[61] because the emphasis laid on anti-imperialist struggle, which is simply an aspect of nationalism, shows a perfectly logical direction to which revolution can turn. Just as the decay of the MNR's revolutionism indicates a very natural tendency, to be imputed not to bourgeois corruption but, as we have seen, to built-in factors that manifest themselves in all revolutions, whether they end in the contradictions of an Institutionalized Revolutionary Party as in Mexico, or those of a new class as in Eastern Europe.

Even when a successful revolutionary leader converts to the authorized version, as Pepin did to Rome and for similar reasons, the original revolution seems to harden into something else. Cuban peasants, in 1959, thought that the liberty the new revolution brought meant freedom from work, as well as from their old masters. They were fast enlightened. Their duty was to work even harder to build socialism. There were no more latifundia and no more sugar barons; but the peasants had to carry workbooks like every other worker: the infamous *livret de travail* that stained nineteenth-century capitalism and still survives in the Soviet Union. Absenteeism was punished; strikes were banned, salaries frozen, holidays diminished. The chief enterprise of modern states – propaganda – was massively increased, sometimes as education, a guise that can be traced back to the French Revolution and beyond but hardly confused with freedom. The distinction between the centre of decision and the executants persists. What we see in Cuba is a centralized, bureaucratic, police state, basically similar to other modern states, though more to some than to others. Does this go counter to Castro's revolutionary ideals? It does. Does it make the Cuban experience less revolutionary? It does not.

The same point can be made concerning Colonel Qadhafi, the Libyan leader. Qadhafi, who must be counted as revolutionary in the Libyan context, is clearly a reactionary in his ideology. He has, indeed, been denounced as a 'fascist dictator' by the Popular Front for the Liberation of Palestine (Paris *Herald-Tribune*, 20 August 1973). What are we to make of this?

Once abandoned the Marxist model of revolution stemming out of capitalism and industrialization, once adopted the abridged version of pre-capitalist societies hustling straight into socialism, revolution becomes not the resolution of a developed society's contradictions, but the accelerator of evolution towards development (and towards the contradictions development must bring). In this perspective, socialism is no longer a revolution creative of socio-economic progress of a special kind, but just a way to do more quickly what capitalism has done elsewhere, or has not done fast or well enough. The exploitation of man by state replaces the exploitation of man by man. The difference blurs between the developmental revolutions (Mexico, Bolivia, Cuba, Egypt, Algeria) cited by Edgar Morin,[62] and the developmental dictatorships of Borkenau and Nolte. Professor Mayer was right. Our findings, it would seem, do dilute his heuristic construct and blunt its cutting edge. But if a heuristic approach serves to apprehend some kind of truth or bring us nearer to it, perhaps that's just as well.

No wonder, then, that fascism is included in the category of developmental revolutions by qualified observers, together with the national revolutions of undeveloped or developing countries. We remain uncertain whether either kind or both should be labelled growing pains, revolution, or counter-revolution, unless it be pre-emptive revolution – a favourite for coups d'état from all quarters since the Ides of March. Only one conclusion seems clear. One cannot exclude fascists and Nazis from the revolutionary category of our times because of the equivocal nature of their rhetoric and their reformist hedging as they jockey for power, without applying the same standards to most 'national revolutions' of our day. So, either the latter are fascist – in which case the fascist model is shown to be actual and appropriate to present circumstances; or they are revolutionary, despite failure to measure up to Marxist definitions, and then the fascists are revolutionary too.

Who can gainsay that Qadhafi, Nasser, Castro, are (were) revolutionaries, their régimes radically different in essentials from preceding ones? The point is not that they have betrayed some ideal pattern of revolution but that, despite non-conformity to the dogmatic pattern, their particular role, action, effects, are very revolutionary.

There is no revolution to betray, because there is not one version of revolution only; and the contortions of Marxist theory reveal not its capacity to assimilate, or to adjust to, practice, but its anachronism.

It is not so much that the Marxist-inspired model of revolution involves us in time-consuming aberrations, as that it is beside the point.

Revolutions, revolts, rebellions, riots, risings, mutinies, insurrections, tumults, troubles, disturbances, coups d'état and civil wars figure in present history as in that of the past. The first rebels were angels. The first rebellion the Fall. We shall not be rid of the ilk in the foreseeable future. Perhaps we should not be. In any case, they exist, they demand our attention. Treating them in terms of one doctrine, relevant though it was in its time, suggestive though it remains in ours, lessens our grasp of the problem, limits our capacity for comprehension, increases the possibilities of confusion. Incantations hobble analysis. Even the restrictions imposed by terminological conformism pass into our thinking and hamper it. Political terminology becomes a political fact, intellectual terminology becomes a factor of intellectual activity. When we describe something as revolutionary or counter-revolutionary, half the interpretative process has been performed already, the other half will reflect what went – or, rather, what failed to go – before.

Yes, revolution is a continuing historical fact; but the context and objectives of revolutions change. Nineteenth-century revolutions, modelled on that of 1789, were supposed to be for freedom (constitutional, legal, of press, speech and economic enterprise), for the nation (patriotic and nationalist) and the state (a more efficient one, preferably a republic), against tyranny (and monarchy). Twentieth-century revolutions, on a model suggested by Marx and then revised by Lenin, are supposed to eliminate the bourgeoisie (not monarchy), to further the consciousness, unity and struggle of class (not nation), to take over the means of production (rather than free them for private exploitation). The relations that had to be changed in this, second, case lay in the sphere of economics (production), not of politics (the constitutional reflection of economic realities). There was a world of difference between the two revolutionary projects. And Marx, when he came along to say that the changed context of his time called for a changed revolutionary project, could appear as irrelevant in terms of the ruling ideology and terminology, and as counter-revolutionary to the tradition-directed revolutionaries of his time, as one who today denounces the Marxist project and its derivatives as anachronistic when they are applied in a context very different from that of their formulation.

The socialist revolutionary project spoke of and to an indus-trial society, dominated by the steam engine, by the conditions of life and labour this generated, and by their expression in liberal, individualistic doctrines and competitive economic organization. All this is gone or disappearing in the West. Which is not to say that want and war, injustice or exploitation, national rivalries and overweening states do not endure. But socialism has shown itself no more capable than other systems of solving such persistent problems. In any case, the point about Marxist analysis is not how correct it is in general terms, but how apt it can prove to pro-vide a dynamizing (revolutionary) interpretation and inspiration in specific historical circumstances. Highly appropriate to the needs of certain industrially developing societies, like those of late nineteenth-century Western Europe, its use in conditions like those that prevail in most Latin American or African countries seems restrictive or confusing, condemning would-be revolution-aries to ideological contortions and to awkwardness in practice. Meanwhile, and especially in developed countries that set the pace throughout the world, social mutations from the secondary to the tertiary sector, economic mutations from ownership to manage-ment, ideological mutations as the age-old rule of necessity wanes, have all wrought profound changes. New major problems take shape and call for new solutions: growth, the explosive pace of change, technology, automation, demography, mass media, in-formation and propaganda. Many progressive circles view pro-gress as the modern equivalent of the Fall. If only we could be left to die of our ills, they cry, not of our remedies! What has Marxism to propose about all this? The ideal of the nineteenth-century revolution: travail, famille, patrie, more industry, more productivity, eventually more goods to be enjoyed. On such grounds, less revolutionary systems can match and improve on it.

An anachronistic doctrine of revolution hampers its strategy, restricts its tactics and, finally, hamstrings its theory too. In the context of today, reference to socialist or communist theory increasingly suggests the absence of revolutionary theory. This is clear enough in those neo-Marxist variants, neither new nor Marxist, which substitute the poor for the proletariat, the struggle of poor against rich for the struggle between classes (specifically between industrial proletariat and bourgeoisie), the wars of nations for the wars of classes. If such revisionists ignore Marx's views on this score, it may be because reference to Marx would reveal their views as far from Marxist or, more simply, because they ignore Marx. At any rate, viewed in the light of such doctrinal decay, fascism is just one more recent avatar of revolutionary myth,[63] disputing this with ideological rivals with a prior hold upon it; the very assertion of its revolutionism a tribute to the evocative power of the notion.

A tribute, too, to the enduring power of millennarian dreams and to their actuality. For this is what survives in positive as well as negative stereotypes of fascism and communism. If fascism really was the ultimate spasm of capitalist society on its last legs, the need for it must be past today when capitalism, however uneasily, rules the world. The communist revolution, in its ideal form, has shown itself hardly more relevant or more possible. Both fascism and communism have failed, in their own terms, to achieve the fundamental revolutionary dream: *changer la vie*. Yet, at another level, that is beside the point, and the persistence of the issue proves the persistent relevance of revolution as a cause.

The very notion of changing life or man is an inheritance of 1789 and after, the apprehension, novel for mankind, that things can be different from what they have always been. *Belief* that change is possible, fundamental change, even more than the *fact* of change, is characteristic of the modern age. Revolutionary projects answer that belief, which constitutes the chief objective condition of their being. In this perspective, revolutions propose first to define, then to accelerate, what they say should happen and what, without their intervention, would not happen, or would happen otherwise. They express the general situation less in their content than in their form and, above all, in the crucial affirmation that radical change is possible and should take place. Fascists and communists may find themselves revolutionaries without a revolution (we haven't quite got there yet!), but the Revolution as part of the contemporary situation, of the modern view of life, is ready to adopt almost any guise that can express it.

This raises a different question: do revolutions really change, or do they transform, modifying institutional or ideological expressions of fundamentally similar structures? We know that revolutions wreak great changes, overthrow a régime, break with a given order or state of things. But does this represent a passage from one state to its contrary, or to another form, shape, avatar, of the same? This is not idle speculation or, even, simply an aid to theory. For it would seem as if most modern revolutions are made not to abolish the existing society and state of things but to seek integration in them.

The French and the Russian revolutions were made against societies and régimes incarnated by tangible groups: aristocrats, bourgeoisie. Whom are the new revolutionaries to eliminate? The bureaucrats? Who is their bourgeoisie? Only the workers know quite whom they should redefine as such from time to time, and they do so only because their avenging arm needs to point out some object for their wrath, some enemy in order to ensure their semblance of subsistence as a class. Sorel had sensed this vanishing trick when he tried to make workers fight to force the bourgeoisie to stay bourgeois, which was essential if the bourgeois were to continue to provide one of the two irreducible terms without which (*in ille tempore*) the dialectical evolution would have broken down. No class war, no clash, no synthetic issue into a new society: and that is just what happened. Over the years, the bourgeoisie, that Protean monster, far from eliminated by its successors-to-be, trained and indoctrinated them to assimilate the dominant culture and its values. Not counter-revolution but integration, appropriation, of the Revolution, of revolutions, of revolutionary ideas, mark the practice of the last hundred years.

In the long run, of course. In the short run, society reacts violently to challenges it cannot absorb. But brutal reactions become rarer as we go along. For revolutions are primitive, and primitive rebels are increasingly isolated, assimilated, or entertained to death. So, those who take the place of the 'bourgeoisie' take up only its succession. The new society is not the opposite of the old, but its prolongation and its heir. Undeveloped countries want to industrialize. Developed countries want more of what they have already for more people: immediate satisfactions, regular work, or less work, continuity, security, predictability, comfort, more efficient facilities, and fewer traffic jams. Pursuing the benefits of productivity, bowing to its demands, the parties of Movement and of Resistance both revolve among restricted options. What kind of revolution is there left to make when all revolutionaries propose in the end to establish similar values?

Some time before the March on Rome, Mussolini found occasion to remark, apparently with some surprise, that one could be both revolutionary and conservative. An incriminating remark? Certainly an actual one. As misery and exploitation grow less intense in the West, more complicated elsewhere, the revolutionary project becomes less concrete. In the wealthy West, revolution turns more towards intellectuals and dissatisfied members of the middle classes than to the underprivileged who are not revolutionary but reformist. But a less radical public demanding more costly public services (housing, education, health, social security) can prove more dangerous to the established order than the more vehement (ideological) radicalism of its predecessors. In Bourricaud's Peru, the dream of avenging revolution is replaced by the dream of development: industrial, educational, above all urban. In Lima or in Moscow ideals grow increasingly close: no more classes, only consumers. All revolutions now are oriented not to change existing standards but to enjoy them.

In the beginning was inequality, injustice, hunger, and want. Humanitarianism and political action remedied this (a bit), but only by relying on greatly increased productivity. Man in his numbers and in his way of life depends on technological efficacy and control, seeks to advance by increasing this dependence.

What revolution will change this? We are, as Jacques Ellul insists, the prisoners of our technology, the captives of our means. We may diversely estimate this predicament. It may not be a predicament at all, and I for one am far less moved by it than Ellul seems to be. But it is a fact. Consumer society has consumed the revolution. The advances of modernity – production, consumption – have changed the data a would-be revolutionary must consider. Since it is doubtful that revolution now can do much to alter relations of production, perhaps it will return to the more modest project of altering relations of authority.[64] But, judged according to current stereotypes, this would scarcely qualify as revolution at all.

Perhaps the sort of revolution that goes beyond the immediate event, the merely spectacular, is nowadays unlikely. At any rate, what is currently accepted as revolution is not of that sort. The would-be revolutionaries of today would do well to look away from their anachronistic models, which they have abandoned in practice anyway, and try to invent a revolutionary project appropriate to the contemporary context. That is not my concern. But history suggests that such a project must go beyond the spectacular aspects of life, unlock the gate that leads from the familiar to the unexpected, release history to move ahead to a new and unpredictable stage.[65] Marx understood this; and the revolutionary categories that he proposed corresponded to the society of 1850, as it had not yet learned to see itself. But it is not the structures of 1850 that revolutionaries should attack today. Such an attack could still make sense in the first half of the twentieth century, when nineteenth-century structures lingered on. That was when fascist and communist revolutionaries, rooted in nineteenth-century criticisms and ideals, attacked the surviving structures and their conservative, anti-revolutionary, or counter-revolutionary defenders. The offensive of the revolutionaries and the ensuing conflicts were part of the preparation of the changes we have lived. They grow less relevant as the modern mutation gains ground throughout the world.

We know too much nowadays to explain very much. We certainly know too little to explain anything thoroughly. But as long as our notions of historical change continue to turn on terms as imprecise as revolution and counter-revolution, they remain blocked, and focused on problems already left behind.

Notes

1. Max Gallo, *Gauchisme, réformisme et révolution* (1968), p. 133. Despite all this, he explains, May 1968 was not the revolution. (Unless otherwise indicated, all books quoted are published in Paris.)

2. André Découflé, *Sociologie des révolutions* (1968). There is no point in taking intellectual issue with the lunatic fringe. Découflé is used for reference because he represents the more respectable French students of the subject.

3. Quoted in John Anthony Scott, *The Defense of Gracchus Babeuf* (Amherst, 1967), p. 42.

4. Découflé, op. cit., p. 40.

5. ibid., p. 7, also pp. 11–12. One might ask in passing whether popular interest in or sympathy for social bandits and some of the other outlaws described by Professor Hobsbawm, who often prey more on their own kind than on the powerful and the rich, reflects even the most primitive form of social revolt. The solidarity of common folk against lawmen and tax collectors is rooted in human and local experience, not in social awareness, however dim. Take the case of smugglers, whom peasants took for granted, buying the salt or matches they sold, accepting their activities as part of the local economy, aiding them when they could. Though differently motivated, such attitudes no more reflect social revolt than our occasional sympathy for those who cheat the Customs or Internal Revenue.

6. ibid., pp. 13–14.

7. Thus, Cardinal de Retz, a seventeenth-century expert on the matter, in his *Mémoires*, concerning 'les émotions populaires': Les riches n'y viennent que par force; les mendiants y nuisent plus qu'ils n'y servent, parce que la crainte du pillage les fait appréhender. Ceux qui y peuvent le plus sont les gens qui sont assez pressés dans leurs affaires pour désirer du changement dans les publiques et dont la pauvreté ne passe toutefois pas jusques à la mendicité publique.

8. See Herbert Marcuse in J. A. Scott, op. cit., p. 103. Saint-Just had already declared: 'The miserable are the power of the earth.' (Speech of 8 Ventôse/March 1794).

9. Just how wrong can be seen from the remark a working man made to Ramon Fernandez, the literary critic, after the Sixth of February riots of 1934: 'Il nous faudrait des fusils et descendre vers les quartiers riches! ... Avec, à notre tête, un chef, un homme enfin: tenez, un type dans le genre de Gide!' Reported by Ramon Fernandez, 'Politique et littérature', *Nouvelle revue française* (1935), p. 286.

10. Michel Clouscard, *Néo-fascisme et idéologie du désir* (1973), p. 49.

11. Right and Left simply differ in the subject of their messianic fantasies:

nation or race for the one, proletarians or intellectuals for the other. Both can be fascinated by heroes. And both, recently, have turned their attention to youth, last brittle hope of those who have bet on so many other horses and lost. But youth (as ideology) is a product of adult society, as the industrial proletariat is a product of capitalist society, and seems as destined for assimilation as its predecessors. Even more so.

12. Chateaubriand, *Essai sur les révolutions* (1797), vol. II (Brussels, 1826), pp. 280–81.

13. See Jacques Ellul, *Métamorphose du bourgeois* (1967), p. 158. I have greatly benefited from the reading of this and others of his books. Ellul, with whom I do not always agree, is one of the few really original thinkers in France. The mass of those to whom the term is often applied are more liable to run in schools, like fish.

14. Gallo, op. cit., p. 107.

15. There was White Terror, of course. But the use of terror does not define a counter-revolutionary régime, any more than a revolutionary one. Both may use it and generally do. Yet violence and terror can be found in other régimes as well, with no particular ideological overtones. And let it be understood, once and for all, that the attempt to treat certain phenomena from a detached point of view, does not imply approval.

16. Lora, *Bolivie: de la naissance du POR à l'Assemblée populaire* (1971), p. 203; Ruben Vasquez Diaz, *La Bolivie à l'heure du Che* (1968), p. 99.

17. Découflé, op. cit., p. 18. Note the implication of deliberate policy ('project'), where the most one could assert might be an 'objective' role; and the objection that a counter-revolution must have a rival revolution to counter with a revolution of its own, suggesting (a) that the United States (and Canada?) represent a *sui generis* revolutionary cause, yet (b) that the only revolutions deserving the name are those that North Americans oppose.

18. Clouscard, op. cit., pp. 9–10, 72. Clouscard has excellent precedents. Much bandied about during the Terror, the term was even applied to Robespierre, in the Committee of Public Safety, after the vote of the law of 22 Prairial, year II. One danger of such confusionism was pointed out by Eugene Varga in this study of the economic crisis of the 1930's, *La Crise* (1935), pp. 264–5. Communists, he warned, have made the mistake of calling fascist dictatorship what was only 'the accentuated fascisation of bourgeois regimes'. This weakened the anti-fascist struggle, because workers said that, if that was fascism, then fascism is not as terrible as all that.

19. Découflé, op. cit., pp. 122–3.

20. Mayer, *Dynamics of Counterrevolution*, pp. 115, 116.

21. ibid., p. 78.

22. Compare Branco Lazitch, *Lénine et la 3e Internationale* (Neuchâtel, 1951), p. 211. In 1923 the KPD conference at Frankfurt would define fascism as 'a preventive counter-revolution in that it uses pseudo-radical slogans'.

23. Mayer, op. cit., p. 62. On p. 63 Mayer remarks that the counter-revolutionary project 'is far more militant in rhetoric, style and conduct,' where it can be likened to its revolutionary competitors, 'than in political, social

or economic substance', when in effect the political, economic and, in some ways, social substance of (say) the Nazi politics of the 1930s was more radical and innovative than that of most contemporary socialists.

24. Mayer, op. cit., p. 62: 'As of the 1870's it became increasingly clear that to be effective, the struggle against Socialism required a distinct popular ideology.'

25. In any case, how intense was the class struggle in France, when Georges Sorel had to initiate a hopeless though brilliant campaign attempting to revive it?

26. There is no vouching for Boulanger. He was certainly an opportunist, and hardly straightforward in his political dealings. But he was not intelligent enough to conceive a manipulative ideology, and hardly a typical revolutionary *or* counter-revolutionary leader.

27. A case where the encounter between straightforward (conservative) and camouflaged counter-revolutionaries is clear appears in Miklós Szinai and László Szúcz, eds, *The Confidential Papers of Admiral Horthy* (Budapest, 1965), pp. 112–18, reprinting a 14 January 1939 memorandum of Count Istvan Bethlen and the 'Rightist' opposition he represented. Bethlen criticizes the pro-Nazi Imrédy for being too sympathetic to the Germans and stirring up a hornets' nest with his anti-Semitic and land-reform proposals, liable to open the way to Arrow Cross overbidding. As for the revolutionary Arrow Cross itself, Horthy's lines of 14 October, 1940, addressed to the then prime minister, Pal Teleki, are revealing (pp. 150–51). Horthy says he has always been anti-Semitic, but he wants no precipitate measures that would only ruin the country. 'In addition, I consider for example the Arrow Cross men to be by far more dangerous and worthless for my country than I do the Jew. The latter is tied to this country from interest, and is more faithful to his adopted country than the Arrow Cross men, who, like the Iron Guard, with their muddled brains, want to play the country into the hands of the Germans.'

28. See Jean-Michel Etienne, *Le Mouvement rexiste jusqu'en 1940* (1968).

29. One can go further and ask if Pétain's National Revolution of 1940, overturning a Republic that all, including the Left, proclaimed was rotten, was less of a revolution than General de Gaulle's raping her faintly consenting successor in 1958, or Revlon's introducing a revolutionary shade of nail polish in 1973.

30. Mayer, op. cit., p. 2.

31. As when ibid., p. 66, Mayer speaks of the 'revolutionary opposites' of counter-revolutionary leaders.

32. ibid., p. 20.

33. Jacques Ellul, 'Le Fascisme, fils du libéralisme', *Esprit*, no. 53 (February 1937), pp. 762–3, defines fascism by its formal will to react against liberalism, and not as a true Reaction. But that applies to communism too, 'also formal negation of Liberalism and perhaps also its offspring'.

34. Daniel Lerner and Harold D. Lasswell, *World Revolutionary Elites* (Cambridge, 1966), pp. 230, 461, 463–4 and passim.

35. Mayer, op. cit., p. 89.

36. It was, of course, against this trend that Mao's cultural revolution was waged, and lost.

37. André Malraux, 'S.O.S.', *Marianne*, 11 October, 1933.

38. Was it the Fourth Congress of the Communist International (1922) which, while recognizing that fascists sought a mass base 'in the peasant class, in the petty bourgeoisie, and even in certain sections of the proletariat', insisted that the combat organizations they set up were counter-revolutionary, and thus arrogated to itself the coveted revolutionary label? Or was it fascist opportunism, and its incidental (as well as doctrinal) hostility to socialism and communism that gave the label up?

39. See Mayer's remark, op. cit., p. 66, that counter-revolutionaries favour the conspiratorial rather than the critical-analytic view of history. Is not this characteristic of many creeds addressed to masses? What about the Left's use of bankers, 'merchants of death' and, nowadays, multinational conglomerates?

40. Notably in 'The Men of the Archangel', *Journal of Contemporary History*, vol. I, no. 1 (December 1965). And Maurice Thorez, 'holding out his hand' in 1936 to the militants of fascist leagues, 'sons of the people' like the communists, seems to bear out my point.

41. See Malraux speaking in 1929 about the revolutionary characters of his novel, *Les Conquérants*, who were recognized as typical revolutionaries by experts like Trotsky. The revolutionary leader, says Malraux, '. . . doesn't have to define Revolution, but to make it.' Quoted in Jean Lacouture, *André Malraux* (1973), p. 136. Similarly, the Second Havana Declaration, quoted in Régis Debray, *Essais sur l'Amérique latine* (1967), p. 131: 'The duty of a revolutionary is to make the revolution.'

42. See, for example, Talcott Parsons' famous essay of 1942, 'Some Sociological Aspects of the Fascist Movements', in *Essays in Sociological Theory* (Glencoe, 1954).

43. Note that the question of private property, central both in Marxist doctrine and in categorizing fascism, was regarded as a secondary issue, incidental to major aims: productivity, employment, order, restructuring the society and the productive process. In this respect too, fascists in theory and National Socialists in practice showed themselves more flexible than their rivals.

44. Likewise, petty bourgeoisie and new middle classes, regarded by communists as the chief source of fascist support, are considered to play a positive role when they participate in the national revolutions of the Third World.

45. Jules Monnerot, *Sociologie de la Révolution* (1969), p. 553. His italics.

46. See above, n. 40, and Rogger and Weber, eds, *The European Right* (Berkeley and Los Angeles, 1965).

47. Ellul, *Autopsie de la révolution* (1969), p. 338.

48. Philippe Ardant, 'Le Héros maoïste', *Revue française de science politique* (1969). The hero is characterized by his abandonment of personal

selfishness. He is above all devoted to the collectivity, the fatherland, and Mao. As to how exciting it all seemed to the Germans, we can read about in witnesses like Nora Waln, *Reaching for the Stars* (Boston, 1939) or Emmanuel Mounier, *Esprit*, no. 49 (October 1936), p. 36: '. . . la fidélité dans la joie . . . le sourire du régime . . . Si vous voulez étonner un nazi, dites-lui qu'il vit sous une dictature.'

49. *Journal Officiel de la Commune*, quoted in Découflé, op. cit., p. 37: 'Paris a fait un pacte avec la mort.' Guevara, quoted in *Le Monde*, 27 April 1967, calls for two, three, several Vietnams, 'with their share of death and immense tragedies', for the sake of the blows they can deal to imperialism. As for death, 'let it be welcome provided that our warcry reaches a receptive ear, that another hand takes up our weapons, and that other men rise to strike up the funeral march and the crackling of machine guns and new cries of war and victory.' See also his *Créer deux, trois . . . de nombreux Vietnams, voilà le mot d'ordre* (1967), pp. 12, 13. Debray is quoted in Ellul, *De la révolution aux révoltes* (1972), p. 139.

50. Debray, op. cit.; Béguin, *Esprit* (October 1948), quoted in Lacouture, op. cit., p. 339; González and Sánchez Salazar, *Che Guevara en Bolivie* (1969), p. 237. The sympathetic Salazars entitle one of their chapters 'A Twentieth-century Don Quixote'. This is as revealing as the legend that has grown around another hero of the revolutionary left, the Colombian priest who died as a guerillero, Camillo Torres. A self-sacrificing and devoted Christian populist, Torres hardly seems a revolutionary leader of the classic pattern: rather, the idealistic chief of primitive rebel bands. See the book of his friend, Mgr Germán Guzmán-Campos, *Camillo Torres* (1968).

51. Raymond Aron, *Le Développement de la société industrielle et la stratification sociale* (1957), vol. I, p. 105, points out that in the nineteenth century optimism was on the liberal side: 'Le pessimisme était socialiste.' You could call a catastrophic pessimism (or optimism) the belief that things would have to get much worse before a vast explosion can open the door to betterment. This could, thanks to some confusion, provide a meeting ground for the socially pessimistic right and the doctrinally 'pessimistic' left.

There are less complicated ways of arguing this, by pointing to the frequent recognition that what one sought in one camp was more readily available in the other. Thus, in his *Chiens de paille*, written in the spring of 1943, re-read in April 1944, finally published in 1964, Drieu La Rochelle notes his disillusion with Hitlerism, too much of a *juste milieu*: 'Mon idéal d'autorité et d'aristocratie est au fond enfoui dans ce communisme que j'ai tant combattu' (p. 110). About that same time, Konstantin Roszevski, head of the emigré All Russian Fascist party, handed himself over to Soviet authorities and wrote to Stalin that Stalinism was exactly what he had erroneously called fascism, but purged of the exaggerations, errors and illusions of fascism. Rodzevski was to be condemned to death and executed in Moscow in 1946, but his opinion remains suggestive. See Erwin Oberlander, 'The All-Russian Fascist Party', *Journal of Contemporary History*, vol. I, no. 1 (1965).

52. Ellul, op. cit., p. 202.

53. I happen to disagree with them now, as I did then. But that is by the way.

54. The question has been raised how revolutionary such holidays really were. Not only Nuremberg but 1968 suggest equivocal answers. The recent documentary film, 'Français si vous saviez', shows newsreels of Pétain and de Gaulle being cheered by hundreds of thousands of enthusiastic Parisians at a few weeks' interval.

55. Mayer, op. cit., p. 65.

56. René Michaud, *J'avais vingt ans. Un jeune ouvrier au début du siècle* (1967), p. 14.

57. See his statement (Mayer, op. cit., pp. 6–7). To have done so 'would involve diluting the heuristic construct, leaving it with a blunted cutting edge.'

58. François Bourricaud, *Pouvoir et société dans le Pérou contemporain* (1967); Louis Constant, *Avec Douglas Bravo dans le maquis vénézuélien* (1968), p. 7; Carlos Romeo, *Sur les classes sociales en Amérique latine* (1968), p. 27 and passim.

59. Debray, op. cit., pp. 86, 202; Lora, op. cit., pp. 188, 203, 204.

60. Salazar, op. cit., p. 29. Even Trotskyists agree that 'the MNR is indisputably the greatest popular party Bolivia has known'. Lora, op. cit., p. 210.

61. Compare Lora, op. cit., pp. 185 ff.; Pablo Torres, *La Contre-insurrection et la guerre révolutionnaire* (1971), p. 39 and passim. Writing to Castro in 1965, Guevara equates revolution, 'the most sacred of tasks', with 'the struggle against imperialism of whatever kind'. Salazar, op. cit., p. 42, quotes the letter in full. In it we also meet, not for the first time, the Castroist slogan 'Revolution or Death' – another traditional revolutionary reference, hardly restricted to fascists.

62. Edgar Morin, *Introduction à une politique de l'homme* (1965), pp. 92–3. Half-failures all, Morin remarks, 'but isn't half-failure also a formula of life? Isn't that what we call success?'

63. I use the term in the Sorelian sense, to describe a combination of unifying images capable of instinctively evoking the feelings and ideas corresponding to a socio-political movement for the purpose of action.

64. Thus returning, *mutatis mutandis*, to Bossuet's description of an earlier situation: 'Les révolutions des empires . . . servent à humilier les Princes.' *Discours sur l'histoire universelle*, pt 3, ch. I.

65. I wonder whether the real revolutions of our time are not our wars. Burckhardt, speaking in 1868, noted that 'modern wars are but an element in modern crises; they do not carry in themselves and do not produce the effects of a true crisis; beside them, bourgeois life goes on its way.' Their short duration, Burckhardt explained, fails to mobilize the forces of despair from which alone could come 'the total renewal of life, the expiatory destruction of what was and its replacement by a new living reality'. The revolutionary projects of the time sought to remedy this. Yet Burckhardt's remark could now apply to their descendants, if we replaced the term 'bour-

geois life' with 'bourgeois values'. Meanwhile, the great wars of the twentieth century have proved effective midwives to the 'destruction of what was and its replacement by a new living reality', even without the help of deliberate revolutions. Perhaps Burckhardt's Basle colleague, Nietzsche, was right when he predicted our entry into 'the classic era of war', an era in which the functions that the nineteenth century attributed to revolution would be carried out by other means. See Jakob Burckhardt, *Considérations sur l'histoire du monde* (1938), ch. IV, especially pp. 159–60.

Index

Ibarra, Velasco, 289
Identity definition, 15
Ideology, 325 ff.
  critical bibliography, 385–99
  definition of term, 328–30
Imperial Rule Assistance
    Association, 21
Imrédy, Béla, 218, 234
Individualism, 364–71
Industrialization, 411
Industrialists
  link with fascism, 412 ff.
  role in Italy, 140 ff.
Insurrections, 490
Integralists, 61, 257 ff.
  see also Ação Integralista
    Brasileira
Intellectuals, 61–2
  despised by fascists, 359
  revolution, 333 ff.
International Symposium on
    Fascism and Europe (Prague,
    1969), 229, 238–9
Ireland, 310
Irigoyen, Hipólito, 270
Iron Guard, 28–9, 32, 49, 216 ff.,
    497
  documentation, 224–5
  persecution, 69
  populist character, 229
  western writings, 228–9
  see also Romania
Istituto Mobiliare Italiano, 431–2
Istituto per la Riconstruzione
    Industriale, 432
Italy, 19, 81 ff., 326
  agricultural community, 428–9
  anti-parliamentarism, 343
  becomes economic satellite of
    Germany, 446
  class struggle, 86–8
  conservative rebellion, 182
  economic deterioration, 434
  economic effect of attack on
    Ethiopia, 445
  economic policy, 410–11
  evolution of society, 95–6
  financial support, 100, 422–3
  foreign policy, 107–8
  foreign trade, 444–6
  growth following defeat of left,
    464
  influence on East European
    fascism, 215
  influx of recruits, 91
  loyalty to king, 97
  Ministry of Popular Culture,
    106
  nationalist movements, 342 ff.
  police discretionary powers, 94

political involvement of firms,
    431–2
post-Risorgimento, 40
Po Valley peasants, 41–2
progress of agrarian fascism,
    91–2
recruitment from lower middle
    class, 458–9
relationship with Church, 98–9
relations with Germany, 125–7
rise of *squadristi*, 468
see also Partito Nazionale
    Fascista; Partito Populare
    Italiano

Japan, 125, 293
Jews, 337–8
  Budapest massacres, 237
  in Mexico, 283
  persecution, 178–9
  policy of destruction in Germany,
    121
  Romanian 'solution', 226
  see also Anti-Semitism;
    Racialism; Zionism
Jodl, Alfred, 142
Juntas de Ofensiva Nacional
    Sindicalista, 26
Justo, General Agustin Pedro, 273

Kaas, Ludwig, 161
Karelia Society, 48
Keitel, Wilhelm, 142
Krauch, Carl, 135

Labriola, Arturo, 346, 350
Lacerba, 350
Lagarde, Paul de, 334
Lagardelle, Hubert, 346–7
Langbehn, Julius, 334, 336
Lapua movement, 48, 307–8
Latin America, 248 ff.
  absence of conditioning factors,
    250 ff.
  role of peasants, 293
  U.S. reformist aims, 291
Latvia, *see* Ugunkrust
Leadership, 56–8
  charismatic quality, 470
  identification of members, 466
Leadership principle, 37, 153–5
  validity, 197–8
League of Christian National
    Defence, 217
League of Patriots, 301
Ledesma Ramos, Ramiro, 26, 314,
    448
Legion of Archangel Michael, 217
  Sim's history, 226–7
  see also Iron Guard